Interaction Ritual Chains

PRINCETON STUDIES IN CULTURAL SOCIOLOGY

Editors

Paul J. DiMaggio
Michèle Lamont
Robert J. Wuthnow
Viviana A. Zelizer

A list of titles in this series appears at the back of the book.

Interaction Ritual Chains

Randall Collins

PRINCETON UNIVERSITY PRESS

PRINCETON AND OXFORD

Second printing, and first paperback printing, 2005
Paperback ISBN-13: 978-0-691-12389-9
Paperback ISBN-10: 0-691-12389-6

*The Library of Congress has cataloged the cloth edition
of this book as follows*

Collins, Randall, 1941–
Interaction ritual chains / Randall Collins.
p. cm. — (Princeton studies in cultural sociology)
Includes bibliographical references and index.
ISBN 0-691-09027-0 (alk. paper)
1. Social interaction. 2. Emotions—Sociological aspects. I. Title. II. Series.
HM1111 .C64 2004
302.22—dc21   2004041461

British Library Cataloging-in-Publication Data is available

This book has been composed in Palatino

Printed on acid-free paper. ∞

pup.princeton.edu

Printed in the United States of America

3 5 7 9 10 8 6 4

CONTENTS

Part II. *Applications*

FIGURES

PREFACE

THIS BOOK ARGUES for the continuity of a chief theoretical pathway from classic sociology to the present. Durkheim launched sociology on a high theoretical level by providing an explanation for some of the most central questions: what produces social membership, moral beliefs, and the ideas with which people communicate and think. The key is that these are linked together by the same mechanism: ideas are symbols of group membership, and thus culture is generated by the moral—which is to say emotional—patterns of social interaction. But whereas Durkheim is usually interpreted, and subjected to criticism, as a global theory of the moral integration of an entire society, I interpret the theory through the eyes of Erving Goffman and the microsociological movement; that is to say, in the spirit of symbolic interaction, ethnomethodology, social constructionism, and sociology of emotions. In their spirit, however, not the letter, since I put the ritual mechanism at the center and try to show how it makes maximal explanatory power out of the insights of these micro-sociological perspectives. Starting with a Durkheimian mechanism, we can see how variations in the intensity of rituals lead to variations in social membership patterns and the ideas that accompany them; all this takes place not on the global level of a "society" in the large sense but as memberships that are local, sometimes ephemeral, stratified, and conflictual.

I do not insist on the letter of Durkheim or Goffman either, but on the fruitfulness of what we can do with these ideas for theorizing a social world of flux and variation. Chapter 1 sketches the intellectual history of the social theory of ritual, with an eye to disencumbering what is most useful in the Durkheim tradition, from interpretations that have grown up around it like vines upon old trees in the jungle. Once having disentangled it, I amalgamate it with what is most useful in radical microsociology. Here Goffman is a pathbreaker, but I do some disentangling, too, to separate out what parts of Goffman are most useful for the current project.

Chapter 2 presents my formulation of the theoretical model, which I call by Goffman's term, interaction ritual (for short, IR). Since terminological accretions are hard to slough off, we are not necessarily confined to calling it by this term. We could call it, more generically, the mutual-focus / emotional-entrainment mechanism. It is a model of interactional situations varying along those two dimensions—how much mutual focus of attention occurs, and how much emotional entrainment builds up among the participants. Where mutual focus and entrainment become intense, self-reinforcing feedback processes generate moments of compelling emotional experience. These in turn become motivational magnets and moments of cultural significance, experiences where culture is created, denigrated, or reinforced. I illustrate the process of creating symbols by analyzing a first-hand video recording of the creation of new national symbols during the catastrophe of 9/11/2001. Rituals create symbols in first-order, face-to-face interaction, which constitutes the starting point in an array of further second- and third-order circuits in which symbols can be recirculated. Once infused with situational emotion, symbols can be circulated through networks of conversation, and internalized as thinking within the individual circuits of the mind. Ultimately the intensity of human concern with symbols, ranging from enthusiastic and obsessive to bored and alienated, depends upon periodic repetition of IRs; how meaningful these recirculated symbols are depends on what level of emotional intensity is reached in the first-order social encounters in which those symbols are used. Since we are often confronted with symbols apart from the interactional context that determines how alive they are, I offer some rules for unraveling symbols by tracing them back to the interactional situations in which they acquire what emotional significance they have, and then through their recycling in conversational networks and solitary experience.

Chapters 3 through 5 examine the implications of the IR mechanism. Chapter 3 presents an interactional theory of emotions. It emphasizes the differences among the specific emotions as conventionally recognized—anger, joy, fear, etc.—and the social emotion par excellence that I call emotional energy, or EE. Durkheim noted that a successful social ritual makes the individual participant feel strong, confident, full of impulses to take the initiative. Part of the collective effervescence of a highly focused, emotionally entrained interaction is apportioned to the individuals, who come away from the situation carrying the group-aroused emotion for a time in their bodies. Conversely, a weak or failed social ritual lowers the confidence and initiative of participants—it lowers their EE—as does being in the position of an outsider or victim who is emotionally battered by someone else's interaction ritual that does not allow one inside. An interaction ritual is an emotion transformer, taking some emotions as ingredients, and turning them into other emotions as outcomes. Short-term situational emotions carry across situations, in the form of emotional energy, with its hidden resonance of group membership, setting up chains of interaction rituals over time. Membership and its boundaries, solidarity, high and low emotional energy: these features work together. Hence the stratification of interaction—interacting with people who are higher or lower in power, and interacting from a position of status acceptance or rejection—gives each individual a jolt, upward or downward, to their level of EE. Social structure, viewed up close as a chain of interactional situations, is an ongoing process of stratifying individuals by their emotional energy.

Privilege and power is not simply a result of unequal material and cultural resources. It is a flow of emotional energy across situations that makes some individuals more impressive, more attractive or dominant; the same situational flow puts other persons in their shadow, narrowing their sources of EE to the alternatives of participating as followers or being relegated passively to the sidelines. Social dominance—whether it takes the form of leadership, popularity, intellectual innovativeness, or physical aggressiveness—is often acceded to by others who encounter such a person, because it occurs through emotional processes that pump some individuals up while depressing others.

Chapter 4 shows how IRs produce the flow of motivation from situation to situation. I widen IR theory so as to predict what will happen as individuals steer from one situation to another, by borrowing concepts from rational choice theory. Some social theorists may find the mixture uncomfortable or even heretical. On the face of it, the image of the calculating self-interested individual seems at odds with the Durkheimian micro-collectivity with its moral solidarity. My rationale is that rational choice theory is not really a model of situational interaction, but a meso-level theory of what individuals will do over the medium run of situations over a period of time. Choice implies working out alternatives, and in real life these present themselves gradually and through experience over a series of occasions. The anomalies of rational choice analysis arise because individuals in micro-situations do not calculate very well the range of alternatives hypothetically available to them; but calculation is not what is most useful in this model, but rather the propensity of individuals to drift, consciously or unconsciously, toward those situations where there is the greatest payoff of benefits over costs. Humans are not very good at calculating costs and benefits, but they feel their way toward goals because they can judge everything subconsciously by its contribution to a fundamental motive: seeking maximal emotional energy in interaction rituals.

The aggregate of situations can be regarded as a market for interaction rituals. The concept is not so startling if we recall the familiar sociological concept of a marriage market. Consider also its extension to the concept of sexual-preference markets (i.e. competitive matchups in a pool of available potential partners for short-term sexual and romantic relationships, subdivided by heterosexual and homosexual markets, and so on), and the notion of the market dynamics of friendship formation. Thus we may conceive of all IRs as a market. I do not mean this formulation to be offensive to people's humanistic sensibilities; people who seek romantic partners or make close friends are often genuinely committed to these relationships; they feel at home inside a common horizon of cultural experience; and they share positive emotions in an unselfconscious, noncalculating way. But these are micro-level contents of these interactions; the market aspect comes in at the meso-level, the aggregate of interactions among which individuals implicitly or explicitly choose. Not everyone can be lovers or close friends with everyone else, and the range of who is available and who has already commited themselves to someone else will have an inescapable effect on even the most romantic.

What I call IR chains is a model of motivation that pulls and pushes individuals from situation to situation, steered by the market-like patterns of how each participant's stock of social resources—their EE and their membership symbols (or cultural capital) accumulated in previous IRs—meshes with those of each person they encounter. The degree to which these elements mesh makes up the ingredients for what kind of IR will happen when these persons meet. The relative degree of emotional intensity that each IR reaches is implicitly compared with other IRs within those persons' social horizons, drawing individuals to social situations where they feel more emotionally involved, and away from other interactions that have a lower emotional magnetism or an emotional repulsion. The market for EE in IRs thus is an over-arching mechanism motivating individuals as they move through the IR chains that make up their lives.

What I have done here is to give a theory of individuals' motivation based on where they are located at any moment in time in the aggregate of IR chains that makes up their market of possible social relationships. We can also turn this picture around to see it from another angle. Instead of focusing on the individual, we can look at the structuring of an entire social arena or institution as a linkage of IR chains. The institution that I have in mind here is the economy in the narrow sense of the term: that is, markets for labor, goods, and financial instruments (for short, "material markets"). According to the well-known theory in economic sociology, material markets are embedded in relations of social trust and implicit rules of the game. I translate this into a situationally fluctuating pattern. What economic sociologists treat rather abstractly as "trust" is not a static element nor merely a background that sets up the arena for the economic game but upon which economic motives provide the dynamics of action. What we think of as "social embedding" is in fact in the center of economic action. Any successful IRs produce moral solidarity, which is another word for "trust"; but the IR chain produces more than trust, since the full-scale process of individual motivation is generated in IR chains. The mechanism is the same whether these chains are focused on material economic activities or on purely sociable relationships. EE-seeking is the master motive across all institutional arenas; and thus it is the IRs that generate differing levels of EE in economic life that set the motivation to work at a level of intensity ranging from enthusiastically to slackly; to engage in entrepreneurship or shy away from it; to join in a wave of investment or to pull one's money and one's emotional attention away from financial markets.

There is no sharp break between material markets and the market for emotional payoffs in IRs; these are all motivated by EE-seeking. Of course, participating in the material market is often less enthusiastic than constrained and perfunctory, making ends meet rather than positively seeking high emotional experiences. As hard-bitten realists would say, people work not for rituals but because they need material goods to survive. My counterargument is that social motivation determines even when people want to survive, as well as more normally what they want material goods for. Variations in intensity of economic action are determined from the side of variations in social motivation. The material market is motivated by demand for material goods because material resources are among the ingredients needed to produce intense IR experiences. There are feedback loops between the material economy and the economy of rituals; each is a necessary input into the other. In Max Weber's version, the intensity of motivation for a particular kind of religious experience drove the expansion of modern capitalism. In my generalization of this line of argument, the entire social-interactional marketplace for IRs is what drives the motivation to work, produce, invest, and consume in the material market. At the level of general theory, it is impossible to explain human behavior by separate spheres of motivation without a common denominator among them, since that would leave no way of choosing among them in concrete situations. The theoretical solution is to conceive of the market for high-intensity IRs and the market for material goods as unified, one flowing into the other. Although we cannot get from material motivations to deriving social motivations, we can unify these realms from the social rather than the material side.

Chapter 5 rounds out the applications of the basic IR mechanism with a theory of thinking. The central point is that IRs charge up ideas with varying degrees of membership significance by marking them with differing amounts of EE. Some ideas are therefore easier to think with than others—for particular individuals in a particular situation located in a chain of situations. Such ideas spring to the mind, or flow trippingly on the tongue, whereas other ideas are less attracted into the interaction, or even excluded from it by a tacit social barrier. Thinking is an internalized conversation—a theoretical point familiar from George Herbert Mead—and thus we can trace the inner linkages of ideas from external conversations through internal conversations and back out. This tracing is easiest to do empirically in the thinking of intellectuals, since we know more about their social networks with other intellectuals, and about the inner thinking that became externalized in their writing. From this entry point, the chapter moves on to forms of thinking that are only quasi-verbal, as well as verbal incantations and internal rituals that make inner selves so often different from outer selves. I offer examples, inspired by conversation analysis, of how to study internalized conversation empirically. The chapter draws considerably on the symbolic interactionist tradition, ranging from the classics to contemporary analyses by Jonathan Turner, Norbert Wiley, Thomas Scheff, and Jack Katz, among others. It concludes, nevertheless, that Mead's metaphors of the parts of the self (I, me, Generalized Other) can be replaced by a more processual model of the focus of attention and flow of energy in internalized interaction rituals.

Part II applies the general theory to specialized and historically located areas of social life. Chapter 6 is a theory of sexual interaction, treated micro-empirically: that is to say, what people actually do in erotic situations. It is not, first and foremost, a theory of what cultural meanings about sex exist in a culture, nor does it stay on the level of what statistical aggregate of sexual actions individuals perform with what degree of frequency; it is instead a theory of what kind of interaction actually happens when people have sex. What this is might seem obvious, but when examined sociologically large alternatives of interpretation open up. What people actually do, and what they find erotically stimulating, cannot be explained by individual motives of pleasure-seeking; what practices are considered sexual and what body zones become erotic targets are both historically and situationally variable. The erotic symbolism of the body is constructed by the focus and intensity of interaction rituals. The baseline form of erotic action—sexual intercourse—fits the IR model very closely. No wonder: sexual intercourse is an archetypal high point of mutual entrainment and collective effervesence, creating the most primitive form of solidarity and the most immediate standards of morality; the interlocking feelings of love and sexual possession are a ritually very tight membership in a group usually of size two.

On this baseline model, I show how nongenital sexual targets are constructed as they become the focus of attention in erotic IRs. Sexual ritual can also take forms that have relatively low solidarity among the participants—sex that is selfish, coerced, or otherwise not oriented toward membership with the partner of the moment. But these forms of sex do not escape social explanation: these are forms of sexual action in which the focus of attention is not so much local but in another arena, not on the relationship between the individual love-makers but on the larger scenes of erotic negotiation and display in which they seek membership and prestige. The micro-level of sexual interaction is shaped within a larger arena, a concatenation of IR chains. I illustrate this with the historical changes in the places where sexual negotiating and sexual carousing have taken place during the twentieth century, and in the array of practices that have thereby become eroticized. Among other things that can be explained in this way are the growth of distinctively modern forms of homosexuality.

Chapter 7 offers a micro-sociological view of stratification in the late twentieth and early twenty-first centuries. I describe stratification as seen from below, from the angle of the situations in which inequality actually is acted out. This micro-empirical view matches up, eventually, with the Weberian scheme of economic class, status group, and political power; but instead of taking these as macro-structures that can be grasped in their aggregate, statistical form, it shows how they can be recast in terms of the dynamics of everyday life. In our historical times, immediate social experience has come loose from the categorical identities of macro-stratification, giving greater weight to the dynamics of situational stratification. The changing distribution of resources for staging interaction rituals, and the changing conditions that once compelled people to be audiences for stratified rituals and now enable them to evade them, explain how this evaporation of deference rituals has come about.

Chapter 8 takes up a set of minor rituals that are carried out in private and in leisure situations, off duty from serious occasions. Such rituals have their historical ups and downs, which gives us an opportunity to look at the changing social ingredients that have gone into constructing these little rituals of privacy and sociability. Erving Goffman pioneered the study of such rituals, but as a pioneer he was too concerned with showing their general properties to pay attention to how they have changed historically. Ironically, he wrote just at the time that a massive shift in the rituals of everyday life was going on: the collapse of formally polite, overtly stratified boundary-marking rituals, which observers of the 1960s sometimes called the rise of the "counterculture" and which I prefer to call the "Goffmanian revolution." It is this revolution favoring standards of casualness over standards of formality that characterizes the situational stratification of the turn of the twenty-first century, where overt signs of class differences are hidden and formality is widely considered bad form. This is a recent instance of a shift in the prevailing rituals of everyday life, one of a series of such shifts that have taken place across the centuries.

Chapter 8 traces these micro-structural shifts in the ritualism of casual interaction by taking smoking rituals as a tracer element. The conditions that created various kinds of tobacco rituals since the sixteenth century, and fostered conflict over the legitimacy of such rituals throughout that time, cast light more generally on other kinds of substance ingestion. The same kind of analysis could have been performed by focusing on the social history of alcohol or drug use. These have been heavily studied by other researchers, although generally under other theoretical lenses; the analysis of tobacco ritual and anti-ritual may thus be fresh enough to bring out the analytical points more clearly.

The opportunity to change our perceptual gestalts, at least as sociologists, is all the greater because we are living in the midst of an under-analyzed phenomenon in everyday life: the success, after many centuries of failure, of an anti-smoking movement in the late twentieth century. The naïve explanation would be simply that medical evidence has now become available to show the dangers of tobacco, and that the movement to restrict and prohibit it has followed as a matter of normal public policy. Yet it would be theoretically strange if that were all there is to it. Our theories of social movements, of politics, of changes in lifestyles do not generally show much evidence that major social changes come about simply because scientists intervene to tell people what they must do for their material self-interest, whereupon they do it. This naïve explanation is generally unchallenged, within sociology as elsewhere in the academic world, perhaps because most sociologists are in the status group that is most committed to the anti-smoking movement; thus we do not see the triumph of the anti-smoking movement as a social phenomenon to be explained, because we view the issue through the categories promulgated by that movement. Ideological participants do not make good analysts of their own movement. By the same token, we are not very good analysts of the target of the movement, tobacco users in all their historical forms, as long as we see them only in the categories of addicts or dupes of media advertising in which they are conventionally discussed. By viewing the entire historical process with greater detachment, it is possible to contribute to a sociological, and not merely medical, understanding of addictive or persistently entraining forms of substance ingestion generally.

Rituals of bodily ingestion always have a physiological aspect, but that is not good theoretical grounds for handing over primacy to non-social scientists when we are explaining social behavior. Interaction rituals in general are processes that take place as human bodies come close enough to each other so that their nervous systems become mutually attuned in rhythms and anticipations of each other, and the physiological substratum that produces emotions in one individual's body becomes stimulated in feedback loops that run through the other person's body. Within that moment at least, the social interaction is driving the physiology. This is the normal baseline of human interaction, even without any ingestion of alcohol, tobacco, drugs, caffeine, or food; and when ingestion of these is added to the interaction ritual, their physiological effects are deeply entwined with and shaped by the social pattern. I am arguing for a strong form of social construction, not only of conscious mental processes, not only of emotions, but also of the experience of whatever is bodily ingested. The chemical character of whatever kind of substance is ingested also has some independent effect, and in some instances that effect may be overriding: strychnine will not act like sugar. But we would be entirely on the wrong footing to assume that all ingested substances are in the extreme categories like strychnine; most of the socially popular substances for bodily ingestion have had widely differing effects in different social contexts, and it is their social uses that have determined what people have made of them. Even in the instance of tobacco use in the late twentieth century, the overriding causal factors determining usage have been not in the physical effects per se but in those effects as socially experienced.

The aggregate effect of these chapters may be to provoke the question, doesn't all this sociologizing go too far? Doesn't it miss what escapes sociology, what makes us unique as individuals, and what constitutes our private inner experience? Is not the model of interaction rituals especially biased toward the image of the human being as the noisy extrovert, always seeking crowds, never alone, without an inner life? Chapter 9 meets these issues head on. Individualism itself is a social product. As Durkheim and his followers, notably Marcel Mauss, argued, social structures across the range of human history have produced a variety of individuals to just the extent that social structures are differentiated: the greater variety of social situations, the more unique each individual's experience, and the greater variety of individuals. Furthermore, it is not only a matter of society in some historical formations producing a greater or lesser variety of individuals; some societies—notably our own—produce an ideal or ideology of individualism. Social interactions produce both symbols and moralizing about them. Where the ritualism of social interactions celebrating the collective has dwindled, what has arisen in its place are situational rituals involving what Goffman pointed to as the cult of the individual.

Individuality comes in many different forms, many of which could be extroverted; so it remains to be shown how inwardly oriented personalities are socially created. I outline seven kinds of introversion together with the historical conditions that have produced them. Despite our image of introversion as a modern personality type, some of these types are rather common premodern personalities. Even in the modern world, there are several types of introverts, besides the hyper-reflexive or neurotic type, which some observers have seen in the image of Hamlet or a Freudian patient as emblematic of modern life. In fact, most types of introversion are not only socially produced, but have their patterns, when situations call for it, of extroverted social interaction as well. Even within the most extreme personalities, inward and outward play off of each other in an endless chain.

ACKNOWLEDGMENTS

SPECIAL THANKS are due to Michèle Lamont for her advice on the organization of the argument. For their comments, criticism, discussion, and information, I am indebted to Edward O. Laumann, Ira Reiss, Arthur Stinchcombe, Arlie Hochschild, Bryan Turner, Jonathan Turner, Tom Scheff, Rebecca Li, Bob Lien, Yvette Samson, Stephan Fuchs, David Gibson, Albert Bergesen, Mustapha Emirbayer, Mitch Dunier, Erika Summers-Effler, Regina Smardon, Deirdre Boden, Emanuel Schegloff, Paul Ekman, Theodore Kemper, Barry Barnes, Norbert Wiley, Gary Alan Fine, Arthur Frank, Hans Joas, James S. Coleman, Viviana Zelizer, Elijah Anderson, Geoff Ingham, James Jasper, Paul DiMaggio, Dan Chambliss, Darrin Weinberg, Susan Watkins, and Irma Elo.

Parts of chapter 3 appeared in Theodore D. Kemper, ed., *Research Agendas in the Sociology of Emotions* Albany: SUNY Press, 1990. A version of chapter 4 was published in *Rationality and Society* 5 (1993). A version of chapter 7 appeared in *Sociological Theory* 18 (2000). These are reprinted with permission of SUNY Press, University of Chicago Press, and the American Sociological Association.

PART ONE

Radical Microsociology

Chapter 1

THE PROGRAM OF INTERACTION RITUAL THEORY

A THEORY OF INTERACTION ritual is the key to microsociology, and microsociology is the key to much that is larger. The smallscale, the here-and-now of face-to-face interaction, is the scene of action and the site of social actors. If we are going to find the agency of social life, it will be here. Here reside the energy of movement and change, the glue of solidarity, and the conservatism of stasis. Here is where intentionality and consciousness find their places; here, too, is the site of the emotional and unconscious aspects of human interaction. In whatever idiom, here is the empirical / experiential location for our social psychology, our symbolic or strategic interaction, our existential phenomenology or ethnomethodology, our arena of bargaining, games, exchange, or rational choice. Such theoretical positions may already seem to be extremely micro, intimate, and small scale. Yet we shall see they are for the most part not micro enough; some are mere glosses over what happens on the micro-interactional level. If we develop a sufficiently powerful theory on the micro-level, it will unlock some secrets of large-scale macrosociological changes as well.

Let us begin with two orienting points. First, the center of microsociological explanation is not the individual but the situation. Second, the term "ritual" is used in a confusing variety of ways; I must show what I will mean by it and why this approach yields the desired explanatory results.

Situation rather than Individual as Starting Point

Selecting an analytical starting point is a matter of strategic choice on the part of the theorist. But it is not merely an unreasoning *de gustibus non disputandum est*. I will attempt to show why we get more by starting with the situation and developing the individual, than by starting with individuals; and we get emphatically more than by the usual route of skipping from the individual to the action or cognition that ostensibly belongs to him or her and bypassing the situation entirely.

A theory of interaction ritual (IR) and interaction ritual chains is above all a theory of situations. It is a theory of momentary encounters among human bodies charged up with emotions and consciousness because they have gone through chains of previous encounters. What

we mean by the social actor, the human individual, is a quasi-endur-
ing, quasi-transient flux in time and space. Although we valorize and
heroize this individual, we ought to recognize that this way of looking
at things, this keyhole through which we peer at the universe, is the
product of particular religious, political, and cultural trends of recent
centuries. It is an ideology of how we regard it proper to think about
ourselves and others, part of the folk idiom, not the most useful analytical starting point for microsociology.

This is not to say that the individual does not exist. But an individual
is not simply a body, even though a body is an ingredient that individuals get constructed out of. My analytical strategy (and that of the
founder of interaction ritual analysis, Erving Goffman), is to start with
the dynamics of situations; from this we can derive almost everything
that we want to know about individuals, as a moving precipitate
across situations.

Here we might pause for a counterargument. Do we not know that
the individual is unique, precisely because we can follow him or her
across situations, and precisely because he or she acts in a familiar, distinctively recognizable pattern even as circumstances change? Let us
disentangle what is valid from what is misleading in this statement.
The argument assumes a hypothetical fact, that individuals are constant
even as situations change; to what extent this is true remains to be
shown. We are prone to accept it, without further examination, as
"something everybody knows," because it is drummed into us as a
moral principle: everyone is unique, be yourself, don't give in to social
pressure, to your own self be true—these are slogans trumpeted by
every mouthpiece from preachers' homilies to advertising campaigns,
echoing everywhere from popular culture to the avant-garde marching-
orders of modernist and hypermodernist artists and intellectuals. As
sociologists, our task is not to go with the flow of taken-for-granted
belief—(although doing just this is what makes a successful popular
writer)—but to view it in a sociological light, to see what social circumstances created this moral belief and this hegemony of social categories
at this particular historical juncture. The problem, in Goffman's terms,
is to discover the social sources of the cult of the individual.

Having said this, I am going to agree that under contemporary social
conditions, very likely most individuals are unique. But this is not the
result of enduring individual essences. The uniqueness of the individual is something that we can derive from the theory of IR chains. Individuals are unique to just the extent that their pathways through interactional chains, their mix of situations across time, differ from other
persons' pathways. If we reify the individual, we have an ideology, a
secular version of the Christian doctrine of the eternal soul, but we

cut off the possibility of explaining how individual uniquenesses are molded in a chain of encounters across time.

In a strong sense, the individual is the interaction ritual chain. The individual is the precipitate of past interactional situations and an ingredient of each new situation. An ingredient, not the determinant, because a situation is an emergent property. A situation is not merely the result of the individual who comes into it, nor even of a combination of individuals (although it is that, too). Situations have laws or processes of their own; and that is what IR theory is about.

Goffman concluded: "not men and their moments, but moments and their men." In gender-neutral language: not individuals and their interactions, but interactions and their individuals; not persons and their passions, but passions and their persons. "Every dog will have its day" is more accurately "every day will have its dog." Incidents shape their incumbents, however momentary they may be; encounters make their encountees. It is games that make sports heroes, politics that makes politicians into charismatic leaders, although the entire weight of record-keeping, news-story-writing, award-giving, speech-making, and advertising hype goes against understanding how this comes about. To see the common realities of everyday life sociologically requires a gestalt shift, a reversal of perspectives. Breaking such deeply ingrained conventional frames is not easy to do; but the more we can discipline ourselves to think everything through the sociology of the situation, the more we will understand why we do what we do.

Let us advance to a more subtle source of confusion. Am I proclaiming, on the micro-level, the primacy of structure over agency? Is the structure of the interaction all-determining, bringing to naught the possibility of active agency? Not at all. The agency / structure rhetoric is a conceptual morass, entangling several distinctions and modes of rhetorical force. Agency / structure confuses the distinction of micro / macro, which is the local here-and-now vis-à-vis the interconnections among local situations into a larger swath of time and space, with the distinction between what is active and what is not. The latter distinction leads us to questions about energy and action; but energy and action are always local, always processes of real human beings doing something in a situation. It is also true that the action of one locality can spill over into another, that one situation can be carried over into other situations elsewhere. The extent of that spillover is part of what we mean by macro-patterns. It is acceptable, as a way of speaking, to refer to the action of a mass of investors in creating a run on the stock market, or of the breakdown of an army's logistics in setting off a revolutionary crisis, but this is a shorthand for the observable realities (i.e., what would be witnessed by a micro-sociologist on the spot). This way of speaking makes it seem as if there is agency on the macro-level, but that is inaccurate, because we are taken in by a figure of speech. Agency, if we are going to use that term, is always micro; structure concatenates it into macro.

But although the terms "micro" and "agency" can be lined up at one pole, they are not identical. There is structure at every level. Micro-situations are structures, that is to say, relationships among parts. Local encounters, micro-situations, have both agency and structure. The error to avoid is identifying agency with the individual, even on the micro-level. I have just argued that we will get much further if we avoid reifying the individual, that we should see individuals as transient fluxes charged up by situations. Agency, which I would prefer to describe as the energy appearing in human bodies and emotions and as the intensity and focus of human consciousness, arises in interactions in local, face-to-face situations, or as precipitates of chains of situations. Yes, human individuals also sometimes act when they are alone, although they generally do so because their minds and bodies are charged with results of past situational encounters, and their solitary action is social insofar as it aims at and comes from communicating with other persons and thus is situated by where it falls in an IR chain.

On the balance, I am not much in favor of the terminology of "agency" and "structure." "Micro" and "macro" are sufficient for us to chart the continuum from local to inter-local connections. The energizing and the relational aspects of interactions, however, are tightly connected. Perhaps the best we might say is that the local structure of interaction is what generates and shapes the energy of the situation. That energy can leave traces, carrying over to further situations because individuals bodily resonate with emotions, which trail off in time but may linger long enough to charge up a subsequent encounter, bringing yet further chains of consequences. Another drawback of the term "agency" is that it carries the rhetorical burden of connoting moral responsibility; it brings us back to the glorification (and condemnation) of the individual, just the moralizing gestalt that we need to break out from if we are to advance an explanatory microsociology. We need to see this from a different angle. Instead of agency, I will devote theoretical attention to emotions and emotional energy, as changing intensities heated up or cooled down by the pressure-cooker of interaction rituals. Instead of emphasizing structure, or taking the other tack of backgrounding it as merely a foil for agency, I will get on with the business of showing how IRs work.

Conflicting Terminologies

My second orienting point is the following. It might seem that encapsulating a comprehensive theory of micro-sociology is heavy duty to pin on the term "ritual." The term has been used in roughly the fashion that I will emphasize by some sociologists, notably Emile Durkheim and his most creative follower in micro-sociology, Erving Goffman: that is, ritual is a mechanism of mutually focused emotion and attention producing a momentarily shared reality, which thereby generates solidarity and symbols of group membership. But this theoretical heritage is not exact, and since Goffman, for example, wrote in a different intellectual era and had different theoretical alliances, I will have to defend my own particular usage by showing its fruitfulness for our problems. More troubling is the fact that "ritual" is a term in common parlance, where is it is used in a much more restricted sense (as equivalent to formality or ceremony)[1] than in this neo-Durkheimian family of sociological theories. Further confusions arise because there is a specialized body of anthropological work on ritual, and yet another body of "ritual studies" within the field of religious studies; and these usages tend to overlap in confusing ways, sometimes with the Durkheimian tradition, sometimes with the restricted sense of everyday usage. One of my preliminaries must be to display the overlaps and differences in theoretical connotation.

For orientation, let us note the principal divergence between anthropological and microsociological usage, while bearing in mind that neither is uniform. Anthropologists have tended to see ritual as part of the structure of society, its formal apparatus for maintaining order, or for manifesting its culture and its values. This is the reverse of the microsociological approach: instead of ritual as the chief form of microsituational action, ritual merely reflects macro-structure; ritual is a doorway to something larger, higher, and fundamentally static in contrast to the fluidity of IR chains. A long-standing anthropological theme is that ritual taking place in time reveals the timeless, the local manifests the total. In the varying terminologies of intellectual movements of the later twentieth century, this is the approach of structuralism, of symbolic anthropology, of semiotics and cultural codes. In general, the terminological usage of ritual in religious studies is closer to the doorway-to-the-transcendental approach of cultural anthropology than to the local source of action in radical microsociology. Where the microsociological approach takes the situation as the analytical starting point of explanation, the structuralist / culturological approach starts at the other end, with an overarching macro-structure of rules and meanings. The challenge for microsociology is to show how its starting point can explain that what often appears to be a fixed global culture is in fact a situationally generated flux of imputed rules and meanings.[2]

The problem is more than terminological. Durkheim provided sociologists with a mechanism for situational interaction that is still the most useful we have. He set this model up in the case of religious ritual in a way that enables us to see what social ingredients come together in a situation and make a ritual succeed or fail. Goffman broadened the application of ritual by showing how it is found in one degree or another throughout everyday life; in the secular realm as in the sacred and official worlds, ritual plays a key role in shaping both individual character and stratified group boundaries. The model holds potentially even more wide-ranging applications. The problem is that the intellectual history of the twentieth century weaves through and around Durkheimian themes but in a fashion that has often twisted them into quite different positions. Instead of a clearly formulated causal mechanism of situational ingredients producing variations in solidarity, emotion and belief, several intellectual movements have turned away the study of ritual toward an emphasis on reconstructing evolutionary history, on the functionality of social institutions, or the preeminence of culture.

I will begin, then, with a historical overview of the way in which ritual has been theorized, with an eye to bringing out the micro-causal shape of the Durkheimian model so that we can see it clearly amidst these other formulations. It is a matter of getting a theoretical program in focus and not confusing it with quite different programs that unfortunately use the same terminology.

My aim is not simply "back to Durkheim and Goffman." Like all intellectual figures, both lived in complex intellectual environments that are not our own. Their positions could be construed in a number of ways, because they were composed of several preexisting threads and got recombined with ongoing intellectual movements in the following generations. Such is the nature of intellectual life—building conflicting interpretations of canonized individuals for the sake of later intellectual maneuvers. Such a history is illuminating because it tells us where we are coming from and what intellectual ingredients we are working with—a map of the Sargasso Sea of ideas that makes up the turn-of-twenty-first century intellectual scene. To be sure, I am making my own intellectual construction out of Durkheim and Goffman, trying to forward my own intellectual project and its larger intellectual alliance. This is not a claim that there is only one objective way to construe Durkheim and Goffman, as if past intellectual politics were nothing but impurities upon a once-clear vision. But I will urge a strong pragmatic criterion: this way of building a Durkheim / Goffman model of situational causality takes us far in showing the conditions under which one kind of thing happens in social situations rather than another. Situations often repeat, but they also vary and change. Interaction ritual theory shows us how and why.

Traditions of Ritual Analysis

I will not try to review the entire history of writings on ritual; an excellent sketch is available in Bell (1992). Instead I will highlight the points that are most useful for situating theoretical problems.

Roughly speaking, theorizing has focused on subcognitive ritualism, functionalist ritualism, and the code-seeking program along with its critics; the latter strands are often lumped together in what is ambiguously called the "cultural turn." From the late nineteenth century to the late twentieth century, these have been partly successive, partly recurrent, and sometimes overlapping programs.

Subcognitive Ritualism

Analysis of ritual was very much in the air at the end of the nineteenth century. Anthropology and sociology were created to a considerable extent around discussions of the topic. These new disciplines emerged out of a variety of older ones. Historians like Numa Denis Fustel de Coulanges in the 1860s had searched out the sources of ancient Greek and Roman property, law, and politics, and found them in a succession of religious cults, participation in which marked the boundaries of household, clan, and political coalition. In the 1880s, religious scholars like William Robertson Smith had probed the ancient religion of the Semites, finding it in ongoing practices like the communal meals and sacrifices of Bedouin tribes. In the 1890s and following decades, classicists like Frazer sought to make sense of the host of minor deities and spirits who crowded the background of the Olympian gods elevated by Greek literary tradition, finding their meaning in practices at the shrines and sacred places of ancient everyday life. Working on convergent paths into this same material, Nietzsche already in the early 1870s seized upon the differences among the alabaster-statue Apollonian cults and the bawdy Dionysians, and pointed to the connection between the contrasting religious figures and the clash of social moralities. In the early years of the twentieth century, these lines of work crystalized in the Cambridge school of classicists around Jane Ellen Harrison, F. M. Cornford, and Gilbert Murray, who programatically interpreted all myths in terms of cult practices of their original adherents.

Another scholar of this tradition, R. R. Marrett (1914, 100) summed up epigramatically: "primitive religion was not so much thought out, but danced out."

The research program of these classicists and historical anthropologists was not very abstract or systematically theorized compared to what came later. Its guiding idea was to translate particular myths into conjectures about cult practices, and to correlate them with archeological remains of ancient cult sites. One popular intellectual movement (which has lasted down to current times, especially as revived by the popularistic wing of feminist thinkers) was to document a cult of the "Great Mother," a goddess-centered fertility rite that was regarded as preceding all other religions, until displaced by male-centered cults, perhaps deriving from migrations of conquering warriors. Another branch of analysis attempted to formulate the principles of "primitive mentality" and to show how these contrasted with later rational thought (a movement that has been roundly repudiated in the post-colonial period); related works traced the roots of early Greek philosophy to the development of religious concepts and mythology. All of these approaches used the evidence of ritual and myth for historical reconstruction; thus their theorizing tended to be rather concrete, looking for earlier historical stages, which were sometimes construed as universal evolutionary patterns. Freud's *Totem and Taboo* used anthropological descriptions on tribal rites as evidence of a remote period in which the sons really did rise up to kill their fathers, then instituted commemorative rites out of their feelings of guilt. Freud was operating with the theory derived from embroyological development that ontogeny recapitulates phylogeny, that is, the growth of the individual psyche parallels its collective history. Field anthropologists, who were often amateurs such as missionaries, medical doctors, or other travelers, concentrated on collecting curious ritual practices that could then be interpreted as survivals of a remoter period of human history.

Intellectual movements generally take place along an entire front of researchers who happen upon a body of new materials to study. The ideas with which they analyze their new-found data resemble each other because they formulate their intellectual tools by recombining the ideas of their predecessors. In the same way, as I have shown elsewhere, philosophers of each new generation operate within a lineup of existing intellectual factions, which gives a limited number of moves that can be made by recombining, negating, and abstracting existing ideas (Collins 1998). It is our own practice as members of the cult of intellectuals to elevate a few names as canonical writers and treat them as sole discoverers; and there is little harm in this as long as we take it merely as a convenient simplification and summary. As anthropology and sociology took shape as recognized disciplines, their treatment of ritual became more concerned with a theory of how society operates. Anthropological field-researchers shared in the movement to make sense of belief, especially belief that seems nonrational by modern standards, by grounding it in ritual practice. Van Gennep in 1909 brought much material together under the scheme of rites of passage from one social status to another.

I will take the Durkheimian formulation as emblematic of the intellectual achievements of the early classicists, ancient and religious historians, and field anthropologists. Durkheim, himself a pupil of Fustel de Coulanges, was the leader of a school of comparativists and synthesizers (Lukes 1973; Fournier 1994; Alexander 1982). His protégés Henri Hubert, Marcel Mauss, and others launched the "Durkheimian" program of interpreting rituals in relation to the social structures that they sustain, as in comparative analyses of the sacrifice (Hubert and Mauss 1899/1968) and of prayer (Mauss 1909/1968). The general statement was Durkheim's *Elementary Forms of the Religious Life* (1912), which remains the best source for summing up what this entire movement of researchers had achieved.

Why is it appropriate to call this movement subcognitive ritualism? Rationality, and more generally all belief, is the surface of human consciousness; it is what first meets us, usually in idealized form, like the beautiful myths of the Olympian gods or sermons from the pulpit drawing upon the Hebrew Old Testament. The program of ritual analysis goes beneath this surface. In an evolutionist generation, this procedure was often seen as stripping away modern rationality to find its irrational foundation or historical roots; if the image is reminiscent of Freud depicting ego emerging out of the passions of the id, it is appropriate to remember that Freud was working in the same generation as van Gennep and Durkheim, and was drawing upon some of the same sources of material.[3] The evolutionary postulate became outdated in later research programs, and remains a favorite whipping boy for intellectuals at the turn of the twenty-first century, and so it is important to emphasize that what I am calling the program of subcognitive ritualism does not stand or fall with social evolutionism.

Analytically, the point is that ideas and beliefs are not sufficiently explained in their own terms, whether one views them as Platonic essences or as products of individual minds; the subcognitive program is to understand how ideas arise from social practices. Durkheim formulated this sharply in 1912, first in a special case, then more generally. The special case is religious ideas, which Durkheim proposed can always be analyzed into the emblems of membership in the group that assembles to carry out rituals. The more general case comprises all the basic categories of the human understanding, the cosmological concepts and logical operations through which we think. These too, Durkheim argued, arise from the ritualism sustaining group membership. His evidence—and this marks the procedure of his research program—is comparative patterns that show how the structure of ideas varies with the structure of the group.

One other aspect of Durkheim's formulation generalized and expanded points adumbrated by Fustel, Nietzsche, and other forerunners. The subcognitive interpretation of rituals, as I have outlined it, explains cognitions by social practices, especially ritual practice. Durkheim's 1912 work explicitly adds that moral beliefs are also constituted by ritual practice. Again the thrust of the argument, and the logic of the evidence, is comparative: moralities vary with the organization of the group; change in group structure changes moralities. Nietzsche expressed this in a highly polemical way, in contrasting what he called the slave-morality of Christianity with the aristocratic hero-morality of the dominant Greeks. In fact, a whole range of moralities has emerged as different kinds of ritual practices have been discerned for different groups and historical periods. From his teacher Fustel, Durkheim learned that ritual participation sets the boundaries of groups, and hence the boundaries of moral obligation. His pupil Mauss was later to show how rituals could be used to set up temporary exchange across group boundaries, through such practices as ceremonial gift-exchange, thereby setting up still wider structures. Appropriately, this ceremonial gift-economy has subsequently been applied to the Homeric society of the Greeks (Finley, 1977). Both Fustel and Mauss showed that the ritual mechanism is not static but also creative, and also conflictual. New social connections can be established by extending rituals to new participants; and those excluded by rituals from group structures can fight their way into membership, as Fustel showed in sketching the history of ritual participation in the political coalitions of the ancient city states. The key point is that Durkheimian analysis provides not only a sociology of knowledge but a sociology of morals. This will lead us into the sociology of emotions capable of explaining the passions of righteousness, retribution, and rebellion, a sociology encompassing both anger and love.

The Durkheimian tradition has been continued and extended by a number of researchers up to the present: Lloyd Warner (1959), Kai Erikson (1966), Mary Douglas (1966, 1973), Basil Bernstein (1971–75), Albert Bergesen (1984), Thomas Scheff (1990), and others. The principles crystalized by the early generations of students of ritual are permanent additions to our stock of sociological knowledge, building blocks out of which more complex theories have been constructed.

Functionalist Ritualism

The generation of anthropologists and sociologists who studied rituals in the middle decades of the twentieth century may largely be called functionalist ritualists, to indicate a divergence in the Durkheimian school. The subcognitivist model was submerged in the functionalist program, but it is also detachable from it.

The aim of the functionalist movement was to show that all of the institutional practices of a society fit together and contribute to the maintainance of its structures as a whole. This approach has subsequently been dismissed as static. Indeed it has become so fashionable to dismiss functionalism that it is worth reconstructing the intellectual motives that once generated enthusiasm for this method of analysis (the best source for this is Goody 1995). As amateur anthropologists and text-oriented classicists gave way to a profession of field researchers, a group of Malinowski's followers began to emphasize that field work should study one whole society at a time, and analyze all of its practices as working institutions in relation to each other. This was carried out especially by Evans-Pritchard and Meyer Fortes, who examined each of several of African tribes with an eye to how its economy, political structure, kinship system, religion, and other institutions all functioned as part of a mutually supporting system. No institution could be understood in isolation: all were adapted to each other, and piecemeal changes in one component were not possible without either unraveling the whole or setting in motion countervailing changes that would bring the system back into equilibrium. This functionalist program opened up a promising set of tasks for field researchers, and also served as a polemical contrast to the methods of the older generation of amateur or library-based anthropologists. What the functionalists rejected were historicist interpretations that took a particular item out of context in its society as currently functioning, and interpreted it instead as a "survival" giving evidence of some earlier period of history. Functionalists turned their backs on history in order to reject speculative historical explanations (since isolated cultural items must have a contemporary function) and to get on with the business of showing structure in operation. The functionalists were consciously systematic, aiming at a general theory of how societies operate; a systematic theory of interconnected structures took priority over a theory of how structures changed, since the latter could be constructed scientifically only on the basis of the former.[4]

The functionalist program was easiest to apply in isolated tribal societies, or at least what appeared to be isolated and self-contained societies. Its guiding image was a set of structures functioning together as a unit, and thus distinct from other such functioning units outside its boundaries. Later critics would attack this point as well, arguing that the functionalists were too taken with the metaphor of society as a self-reproducing organism, or alternately that they modeled tribal societies on the ideology of the Western nation-state as a self-standing identity. Later it would be argued that tribes, too, have histories, and that they not only change over time but are to a considerable degree constituted by their "foreign relations" of trade, cultural prestige, military geopolitics, and kinship alliances (Chase-Dunn and Hall 1997). Such difficulties came especially to the fore after the functionalist program was generalized into a program for all sociological science, and applied to complex modern societies. The lead here was taken by Talcott Parsons and Robert Merton.[5] Functionalist theory became a systematic listing of the basic functions that any society needs to carry out; a model of change as the differentiation of structures specializing in those functions; and a study of the strains that occur when functions are not properly met, and of the responses that the system makes to restore equilibrium. Parsons added an emphasis upon a shared value system that orients each specific social system, together with sets of norms that provide blueprints implementing these values in actors' behavior. The functionalist program as grand theory became bogged down in debates from the 1940s through the 1960s over what is functional or dysfunctional, what determines which functional alternatives are implemented, as well as whether the functionalist outlook is conservative in that it casts stratification and inequality in a favorable light, while ignoring conflicting interests inside a society. Eventually the whole research program lost adherents. Some rejected it because of presumed ideological bias; others because it seemed impossible to make progress toward empirically demonstrable explanations of what actually happens under what conditions.

Functionalism is now generally so unfashionable that any theories once attached to it are likely to be dismissed out of hand. There is some tendency to dismiss Durkheim as a conservative evolutionist, and to see his concept of collective conscience as a reification on a par with (and indeed the source of) Parsons' overarching value sytem. I would argue, however, that the strength of the Durkheimian tradition has been its contribution to micro-sociology rather than as a theory of macro-level societal integration or social evolution. Especially in *The Elementary Forms*, Durkheim provides a model of how solidarity and shared symbolism are produced by interaction in small groups; thus it is an easy extension (although admittedly Durkheim did not make it, and might well have been hostile to it) to see these groups as local, ephemeral, or mutually conflicting, rather than integrated into one large society. "Collective conscience" can exist in little pockets rather than as one huge sky covering everybody in the society, and I have argued elsewhere (Collins 1975) that the Durkheimian mechanism provides a crucial component of a conflict theory that is quite the opposite of functionalism on the macro-level.

One frequent criticism of ritual analysis is that it is overgeneralized. Rituals are held to be omnipresent; but if everything is a ritual, what isn't? In that case, the concept is useless to discriminate among the different kinds of things that happen. The criticism holds up best against a notion of ritual as serving functionally to equilibrate society, operating as a pressure-valve to let off hostilities, or as a celebration of shared values, in either case acting to sustain and restore social order. When things go wrong there are rituals; when things go right there are rituals. Ritual analysis just seems to illustrate, on a micro-level, the conservative bias of functionalism: everything is interpreted as part of the tendency of society automatically to produce social integration. But the problem here is functionalism, not ritual analysis. If we take rituals out of the functionalist context, we still have a clear model of what social ingredients go into making a ritual, and what outcomes occur; and the strength of those ingredients are variables, which determines just how much solidarity occurs. Rituals can fail, or they can succeed at different degrees of intensity. We can predict and test just what should result from these variable conditions. Such ritual analysis is not a tautology.

In my own use of ritual theory, I am one of the worst of sinners, proposing to see rituals almost everywhere. But this does not reduce everything to one bland level, explaining nothing of interest. On the contrary, it provides us with a very generally applicable theory by which to show how much solidarity, how much commitment to shared symbolism and to other features of human action, will occur in a wide variety of situations. If it is any help in mitigating the prejudice against ritual theory, the theory can just as well be couched in terms (which I will explain later) of the causes and consequences of variations in mutual focus and emotional entrainment. I will claim that this theory can be universally applied; but that no more makes it vacuous than, for instance, Boyle's law relating volume, temperature, and pressure, which usefully applies to a wide range of circumstances.

Functionalist theory of ritualism had a more limited application than the functionalist program in general, and it made a number of important contributions to showing the mechanisms by which rituals operate. The functionalist ritualists are exemplified by Radcliffe-Brown (1922), who shows that a funeral operates to reintegrate a group after it has lost a member: beyond ostensible appearances, the ritual is for the living, not for the dead, and the greater the concern that the rite be carried out to bring the soul to rest, the greater the threat to the group and its need to reintegrate itself.[6] This is the sub-cognitive interpretation, but carried further in the direction of a program for understanding group structure and function. Radcliffe-Brown is still a micro-functionalist, but he gives us empirical materials to work upon that we can recast as ritual ingredients bringing about variable outcomes.

Goffman's Interaction Ritual

The most important of the contributions emerging from functionalist ritualism were made by Erving Goffman. Goffman was uninterested in questions of the institutional integration of society as a whole. He reserved the right to pick his own level of analysis, and his functionalism operated at a level that was distinctively his own: the functional requirements of the situation.

Goffman writes like a functionalist when he depicts ritual as following rules of conduct that affirm the moral order of society.[7] But Goffman's consistent emphasis is on the micro level of immediate interaction; and the "society" that is affirmed and that makes its demands felt is not some mysterious remote entity but embodies the demands of sociality in the here-and-now.[8] The situation itself has its requirements: it will not come off unless the actors do the work of properly enacting it. Social reality itself is being defined. What social institution people believe they are taking part in, the setting, the roles that are being presented—none of these exists in itself, but only as it is made real by being acted out. Goffman is a social constructionist, except that he sees individuals as having little or no leeway in what they must construct; the situation itself makes its demands that they feel impelled to follow.

Most famously, each individual's self is being enacted or constructed in the situation; here again, this is the construction of self under social constraint. The constraint is most palpable because it comes from one's stance vis-à-vis others; once the actor has taken a line as to what one's self is (and what the situation is), he or she is constrained to keep their line consistent. The recipient or audience of these constructions is constrained as well, under a palpable pressure to go along with the line the actor presents, to fall in with the spirit of the performance, and to overlook and excuse breaches that would threaten the definition of who people are and what they are jointly enacting. This is a functionalist analysis insofar as it starts with functional needs and goes on to show how they are met. But since Goffman operates on a level of micro-detail that was unprecedented at his time, he helps point the way toward seeing just how the pressure for ritual conformity is felt, and thus allows us to turn his micro-functionalism into a mechanism of the micro-production of solidarities and realities.

Goffman defines ritual as follows: "I use the term "ritual" because this activity, however informal and secular, represents a way in which the individual must guard and design the symbolic implications of his acts while in the immediate presence of an object that has a special value for him" (Goffman 1956/1967, 57). This parallels the definition that Durkheim set out in analyzing religious ritual; after arguing that the distinguishing feature of religion is a division of the world into the two realms, the profane and the sacred, he states, "[R]ites are the rules of conduct which prescribe how a man should comport himself in the presence of these sacred objects" (Durkheim 1912/1965, 56). This has a functionalist tone: society and its sacred objects exist, and these constrain the individual to act in a rule-following, symbolically laden fashion toward these objects. But these definitions are just the entry points for the analyses that Durkheim and Goffman carry out in detail; and these allow us to see not merely that rituals have to be produced, but also under what conditions they are produced and are effective, and under what conditions they are not produced or fail. Both Durkheim's and Goffman's definitions assume that the sacred objects are already constituted. Micro-empirically, this means that they have been carried out before, so that this instance is a repetition of what went before. This is not an isolated ritual but an interaction ritual chain. Putting Durkheim together with Goffman reminds us that rituals not only show respect for sacred objects, but also constitute objects as sacred; and if the ritual is not carried out for a time, the sacredness fades away.

Let us look more closely at the main types of rituals that Goffman finds in everyday life. There are the salutations, compliments, and stereotyped verbal interchanges that make up the polite or friendly routine of verbal interaction. These are on the surface meaningless. "How are you?" is not a request for information, and it is a violation of its spirit to reply as if the interlocuter wanted to know details about one's health. "Good night," "hello," and "goodbye" do not seem to convey any explicit content at all. But it is easy to see what these expressions do by comparing where they are used and not used, and what happens if they are not used when expected. They may be omitted without social consequence if the situation is highly impersonal, such as a brief commercial transaction at a ticket window. But if they are omitted when there is a personal relationship of friendly acquaintanceship, the feeling is a social snub; failure to greet someone one knows, or not to ceremonially mark their departure, conveys the sense that the personal relationship is being ignored or downgraded. (I shall have more to say on this subject in chapter 6, in discussing various kinds of kisses.)

Thus various kinds of minor conversational routines mark and enact various kinds of personal relationships. They are reminders of how persons stand toward each other, with what degree of friendship (i.e., solidarity), intimacy, or respect. They convey in fine detail, known tacitly to everyone, the differences between total strangers, persons in fleeting utilitarian contact, persons enacting certain organizational roles, persons who know each other's names and thus recognize each other as individuals rather than as roles, persons who have a friendly concern for each other's affairs, buddies, confidantes, family members, lovers, and so on. "Hello, Bob" has a different meaning than "Hello," and than "Hello, dear," or "Hello, Mr. Knight" or "Hello, Your Honor."[9] Introductions, whether by a third party or by oneself, are significant moves because they shift the entire level of interaction from one institutional sphere to another. Changing from one kind of greeting, small talk, or departure ceremony to another is the most palpable means of changing the character of a social relationship.

There is a fine-grained temporal aspect to the use of these verbal rituals. If we think of social life as taking place in a string of situations, that is, encounters when persons are physically copresent (or otherwise linked into an immediate focus of attention), then in order to get the situation focused, it is usually necessary to start it off with an act that explicitly notes the existence of such a situation and that defines what kind of situation it is. "Hello" and "goodbye" and their equivalents are used to open and close situations; they are transition rituals marking when a certain kind of encounter is starting and ending. This transition-marking aspect of verbal rituals is coordinated with the relationship-marking aspect. The friendly "Hello, Bob" (or whatever marker is chosen) says that we have had a friendly relationship of personal recognition beyond institutional roles before, and that we remember and resume that relationship, linking past situations with the present into a chain. (This is one specialized meaning of "interaction ritual chain.") The "goodbye" and its variants at the end says: we have shared a certain kind of situational reality for the time; it is now coming to an end; we leave on friendly (or respectful, or intimate, or distant, etc.) terms. Thus the ending ritual sets things up for the future, marking that the relationship is still there and will be resumed (Goffman 1971, 79). Parents kissing children goodnight, a ritual especially emphasized with small children, is a version affirming that, though one person is going off now into the altered reality of sleep, the other one is still there and will be there when the child awakes. The old bedtime prayer for children "Now I lay me down to sleep, I pray the Lord

my soul to keep. . ." does the same thing in a religious context, invoking larger communal realities, as the goodnight kiss does for a purely personal relationship.

I have elaborated Goffman's analysis in order to bring out the vast extensions possible of his rather condensed theoretical remarks on the topic. In his key early papers "The Nature of Deference and Demeanor" (1956/1967) and "On Face Work: An Analysis of Ritual Elements in Social Interaction" (1955/1967), Goffman gives a taxonomy of ritual elements. Politeness to others, including the salutations just discussed, is a form of deference. This subdivides into what Goffman calls "presentational rituals" (looking ahead to his book then in progress, *The Presentation of Self in Everyday Life* [1959]), by which an individual expresses regard for the value of others, and "avoidance rituals," which are taboos that the actor observes in order not to infringe upon the other person. Among the latter is respect for privacy, of which an important aspect is the ecology of everyday life, allowing other persons a backstage where they can do the things that do not make an optimal impression—ranging from bathrooms and bedrooms to private offices and kitchens where a situational performance is being prepared, and the alley behind the house where the garbage is collected. Here, too, Goffman is working up material that will become the frontstage / backstage model in his first book. Goffman explicitly connects these two kinds of everyday ritualism with Durkheim's classification of ritual into positive and negative rites (Goffman 1956/ 1967, 73).

Deference is what individuals do toward others; demeanor is the other side of the interaction, the construction of a social self. Here Goffman is invoking the symbolic interactionist concept of the "me" or self-concept; but he declares it simplistic to see this merely as viewing oneself from the role of the other. Demeanor is a form of action, the work that he calls "face work." It is not merely one-sided action, but reciprocal. The actor acquires a face or social self in each particular situation, to just the extent that the participants cooperate to carry off the ritual sustaining the definition of the situational reality and who its participants are. There is reciprocity between deference and demeanor.[10] This situational self is typically idealized, or at least staged to give a particular impression; it certainly does not convey a full picture of what the individual's self might be if one took all the moments of his / her life together. This idealization is inevitable. For Goffman, there is no privileged reality standing outside of situations, but only a chain of situations and preparation for (and aftermath of) situations.

Goffman's early fame came in large part from delving into the seamy side of everyday life. This gave an impression among many sociolo-

gists as well as the general public that he was a practitioner of exposé; the Durkheimian basis of his analysis was mostly ignored. But Goffman chose his materials analytically, designing his research to show how the normal rituals of everyday life are carried out, above all by contrasting them with situations in which they are strained or violated. Thus Goffman drew upon his fieldwork that was carried out incognito in the schizophrenic wards of a mental hospital (Goffman 1961; this research was also cited as the empirical basis for his description of ritual and face work in Goffman 1955 and 1956) to make the point that one becomes labeled as mentally ill because one persistently violates minor standards of ritual propriety. He went on to draw the irony that mental patients are deprived of backstage privacy, props for situational self-presentation, and most of the other resources by which people under ordinary conditions are allowed to show their well-demeaned selves and their ability to take part in the reciprocity of giving ritual deference to others. Goffman's research strategy is like Durkheim's investigation of suicide, not so much to show why people kill themselves but to reveal the normal conditions that keep up social solidarity and give meaning to life.

In the same vein, Goffman gave much attention throughout his research career to the troubles of carrying out rituals effectively. Bloops and blunders, moments of embarrassment, rendings of the presentational façade, frame breaks, all these were studied as ways of demonstrating that the ordinary reality of everyday life is not automatic, but is constructed by finely honed interactional work. Goffman was concerned with sophisticated deviants for the same reason. He studied confidence artists because these are professionals attuned to the vulnerabilities of situations, and their techniques point up the details of the structures of normalcy that they take advantage of in order to cheat their victims. He analyzed spies and counterespionage agents because these are specialists in contriving, and in seeing through, an impression of normalcy; the fine grain of normal appearances becomes plainer when one sees a secret agent tripped up by minor details (Goffman 1969). Goffman's topic here seems exotically adventurous, but his conclusion is about the crushing pressures of keeping up normal appearances, and the difficulty in contriving them; spies and counterspies often fail because of the difficulty in managing high levels of reflexive awareness or layers of self-consciousness in presenting their false cover, while being on guard against give-aways, all the while giving off an appearance of normalcy. Here again, the extreme instance highlights the mechanism that produces the normal. Life follows routine rituals for the most part because it is easiest to do so, and full of difficulties if one tries to do something else.

Goffman has a reputation for a Machiavellian view of life: individuals put on false fronts, which they manipulate to their advantage. Life is a theater, and actors use their backstages in order to plot how they will deceive and control others on the frontstage. True enough, especially in *The Presentation of Self*, Goffman gives considerable material from industrial and occupational sociology to just this effect: teams of salesmen who suck in a customer and trick him or her in order to extract a higher price; workers who put on a show of compliance in the presence of their managers but go back to working at their own pace in the absence of supervision; managers who pretend to be completely knowledgeable about what the workers are doing, and who hide behind the locked doors of executive bathrooms and lunchrooms in order not to be seen in a casual or vulnerable situation. This material makes Goffman compatible with a conflict theory of social life, and I have exploited the connection to show how Goffman provides micro-foundations for Dahrendorf's class conflict of order-givers and order-takers (Collins 1975).

How can we reconcile the apparent two sides of Goffman—the Machiavellian and the functionalist Durkheimian? For Goffman, the requirements of rituals are fundamental: any conflict, any individual maneuvering for advantage must build upon it. Self-interested action is successful only as it respects ritual constaints. Manipulation is possible precisely because ordinary life is an endless succession of situations that have to be acted out to be defined as social realities, and that constrain both actor and audience to take part in the work of keeping up the impression of reality. The everyday reality of class conflict on the factory floor—the supervisor trying to get the workers to work harder, the workers putting on a show of compliance during the moments when they are ceremonially confronted by the manager—is a kind of theatrical performance; both sides generally know what is real or unreal about the situation; both put up with it, as long as the show of respect is maintained.[11] The show of cooperation is the situational performance through which conflicting interests are tacitly managed.

Goffman makes this explicit in discussing the aggressive use of face work. It is possible for individuals to set out to dominate situations, insult others, have jokes at their expense, even drive them out of the situation and the group. But situational prestige goes to the person who does this by keeping to the normal forms of ritual interaction. A successful insult is one that is done within the expectable flow of conversational moves, inserting double meanings so that on one level it remains appropriate.[12] Put-downs and one-upmanship are successful when the onus for breaking the smooth playing out of the interaction goes to the recipient, who incurs dishonor either by being unable to shoot back a smooth and appropriate reply, or by breaking the frame entirely with an angry outburst. This is Goffman's model of conflict: individual advantage comes from manipulating the normal rituals of solidarity, deference, and situational propriety. And the individual, although self-interested, is nevertheless interested in what can be found only in social situations; individuality and egotism are oriented toward socially constructed goals.

The *Presentation of Self* model might be taken as an egocentric contriving of one's social demeanor: one puts on one's face, like putting on one's clothes, in order to make a certain impression; it is a model of impression management. A whole field of research has grown up around this interpretation. But Goffman's point is that demeanor is part of a reciprocity among participants who are all contributing to a situational reality. One pays attention to the style of one's clothes and grooming (which might in some circumstance be a fashionable déshabillé) not merely to make an exalted impression in the eyes of others; it is also a sign of respect to the person to whom one presents oneself, showing that one regards him or her as worthy of seeing one's best self; and it is a sign of respect to the situation. This logic remains in effect even when there are transformations in popular culture, so that rejecting traditional demeanor becomes a mark of belonging to a social movement, or an emblem for youth, or a vogue of casualness emulated by everyone; the degree of respect shown for situations of public gathering is conveyed by demeanor rituals, whatever the particular style demanded by the group. Thus in the compulsory casualness at the turn of the twenty-first century it is just as much a violation for a man to show up at a party wearing a necktie as it was for him to show up not wearing one in the 1930s.

Goffman's overall theoretical model is often hard to discern. Each of his publications was organized around a theoretical discussion, into which he wove his own, usually quite innovative, collection of microempirical materials. Often the substance of these materials was so striking that his theoretical concerns were lost from sight. Additionally, Goffman changed his terminology from one writing to the next, obscuring whatever cumulative refinement was taking place. His explicit references to Durkheimian ritual theory are in his earliest papers, and they drop out thereafter. Goffman appeared successively as analyst of ritual, of life as theater, of total institutions, of the ecology of everyday life, of games and strategies, of human ethology, of frames of reality construction, among other topics. Nevertheless, Goffman's Durkheimianism is one constant point of anchorage; everything he does remains consistent with this position, and indeed elaborates it, and throughout his career he rejected interpretations that stressed his supposed similarities to symbolic interaction, ethnomethodology, and Machiavellian conflict theory.[13] Let me summarize what Goffman gives us as materials for a refined model of interaction rituals, grouped into rubrics which I will shortly use in presenting that model:

1. Ritual takes place in a condition of *situational copresence*. Goffman is a pioneer in spelling out the various ways in which human bodies assembled in the same place can affect one another. Even when people are in what he calls unfocused interaction (Goffman 1963), there is tacit monitoring, to make sure nothing abnormal or threatening is in the offing; when this happens, it quickly attracts attention. Conversely, even when a person is alone in public, he or she feels obligated to disarm the reaction of others whenever he or she makes a sudden or unexpected move. Thus talking to oneself out loud when one forgets something and has to retrace one's steps is a tacit signal that bizarre-appearing behavior has a normal meaning (see "Response Cries," in Goffman 1981). Being oblivious to other persons takes tacit interactional work: there are minute adjustments of gaze, eye contact, and trajectory of pedestrian traffic that are finely attuned, ranging from "civil disattention," to friendly acknowledgement, to accosting attention, to aggressive control of public space. More complicated tacit relationships take place between little groups in each other's interactional range: a couple in public, for example, gives off tie-signs ranging from holding hands to bodily alignment that convey their unapproachability insofar as their relationship attention is already taken up (Goffman 1971).

2. Physical copresence becomes converted into a full-scale encounter by becoming a *focused interaction*. It now becomes a mutual focus of attention, again varying in intensity and obligation. A fairly high level of engrossment is illustrated by the mutual attention that participants in a conversation feel obligated to maintain: "Talk creates for the participant a world and a reality that has other participants in it. Joint spontaneous involvement is a *unio mystico*, a socialized trance. We must see that a conversation has a life of its own and makes demands on its own behalf. It is a little social system with its own boundary-maintaining tendencies" (Goffman 1967, 113). Participants become constrained to keep a topic afloat, and to move from it to another topic by smooth transitions. They are under pressure to take it seriously, that is, to accord it the status of a reality that is at least temporarily believed in. This is true even if the topic is explicitly framed as in some sense unreal—jokes are to be taken in a humorous frame; stories of one's own tribulations and other's atrocities are to be taken in an appropriately sympathetic and partisan vein; accomplishments in an admiring vein. There is situational pressure for agreement, and for allowing the

other to present a line, however patently fabricated, as long as it remains situationally consistent.

To be sure, the theatrical model is only a metaphor, as Goffman himself notes in his concluding statement of *The Presentation of Self in Everyday Life*. He goes on: "This report . . . is concerned with the structure of social encounters—the structure of those entities in social life that come into being whenever persons enter one another's immediate physical presence. The key factor in this structure is the maintenance of a single definition of the situation" (1959, 254). Goffman is echoing the symbolic interactionist watchword, the "definition of the situation"—that which makes a shared reality effectively real for its participants, as W. I. Thomas famously argued. What Goffman adds by his translation into the terms of micro-interactional ritual are the mechanisms by which this comes about, and the telling emphasis: a *single* definition of the situation, one reality at a time. And this definition needs to be upheld by active efforts, and defended against breakdowns and rival definitions. It is above all the single focus of attention that is the eye of the needle through which the power and the glory of interaction ritual must pass.

In Goffman's later work, especially *Frame Analysis* (1974) and *Forms of Talk* (1981), he describes quite complicated situational realities: frames around frames, rehearsals, recountings, debriefings, make-believes, lectures, broadcasting troubles, performer's self-revelations. These indicate the subtleties that make up the differences among formality and informality, relationships that take place on the frontstage and on various kinds of backstages. Although the terminology is different, Goffman is in effect adding complexities to the basic model: situations are rituals calling for cooperation in keeping up the momentary focus of attention and thus giving respect both to the persons who properly take part and to the situational reality as something worth a moment of being treated seriously. In keeping with his earlier work on the troubles and vulnerabilities of constructing situations, Goffman now shows even more complicated situations that have even more complicated requirements and vulnerabilities.

Ultimately, all these frames are ways in which attention is focused. This allows us to connect with the theatrical model. In its early, simpler version, there are frontstages and backstages. In effect the frontstage is the situation where attention is focused, incorporating some public who joins in the focusing; the backstage is where work is done to prepare so that the focusing can be effectively carried out. The frontstage is the performance of a ritual; the backstage, Goffman reminds us, is usually there because rituals—at least complicated ones—don't just come off by themselves but have to be worked up to. In his later writings, such as *Frame Analysis*, Goffman shows that there can be stages within stages.[14] Whenever there is a play within a play, there is opportunity to shift stances, so that actor and audience may quite rapidly move into a backstage for some frontstage, or vice versa.

3. There is pressure to keep up *social solidarity*. Rituals are entraining; they exert pressures toward conformity and thus show one is a member of society. Goffman discerns a variety of kinds of solidarity, for example, in that he suggests the various kinds of social relationships that are enacted by the different shades of deference rituals. These range in time and continuity from brief face engagements, to acquaintanceship anchored in past relations, to the obligations incurred by varying degrees of intimacy. There are boundaries among different kinds of social bonds, as well, and persons perform ritual work both to keep up an expected tie and to fend off intrusions that would shift it to a closer level (Goffman 1963, 151–90).

4. Rituals do honor to what is socially valued, what Durkheim called *sacred objects*. Goffman shows that these are transient and situational. In modern societies, the foremost of these is the individual self, treated as if it were a little god in the minor presentational and avoidance rituals of everyday life (Goffman 1956/1967, 232).

5. When ritual proprieties are broken, the persons who are present feel *moral uneasiness*, ranging from mild humorous scorn, to disgust, to, in extreme cases, labeling the violator mentally ill. Ritual equilibrium can be restored by apologies, which are part of the flow of deference rituals in conversation (Scott and Lyman 1968; Goffman 1971). This is an everyday version of Durkheim's analysis of the punishment of crime, which is carried out not for its effect in deterring or reforming the criminal (effects that may well be illusory), but as a ritual to restore the sense of social order (Durkheim 1895/1982). Whatever operates on the large scale, Goffman indicates, can also be found in the small.

The Code-Seeking Program

It remains to deal briefly with the branch of ritual analysis influenced by the French theoretical movement of structuralism and its offshoots, which has been prominent in interdisciplinary circles in the latter half of the twentieth century. This is not the place for a full-scale history of the larger topic of cultural theory during this period; I will treat only the way in that ritual theory turned into a version of cultural theory that left ritual behind. Toward the end of this period—which is the intellectual time that we are still living in—there are moves toward bringing the situation back in; and this is where the current program of IR theory fits into contemporary movements, but putting a radical emphasis on microsociology.

Durkheim had proposed that the structure of ideas varies with the structure of the group. In his early formulation in *The Division of Labor in Society* (1893/1964), Durkheim argued from broad historical comparisons of religion and law that a small society with uniform conditions produces a concrete, particularistic collective consciousness, whereas a society with a complex division of labor develops a more abstract consciousness to encompass variations in experience (275–91). In *Primitive Classification* (1903/1963), Durkheim and Mauss adduced ethnographic evidence for the classification systems and social structures of tribal societies. In *The Elementary Forms of Religious Life* (1912/1965), Durkheim argued that the categories of the understanding in the Kantian sense, the conceptual means by which persons think, are constructed socially: space is the geographical extension of the group; time is its patterns of periodic reassembly; causal force takes its prototype from *mana* or religious power, which is in effect the moral pressure of group emotion; category schemes that divide up the universe do so originally on the model of totemic emblems that mark membership in social groups and boundaries among them. (For detailed analysis of the implications of Durkheim's epistemology, see Anne Rawls 2003.)

But this correspondence between ideas and social structure might be taken to run in either direction. This ambiguity in Durkheim's formulation led to divergence of opposite research programs: a sociology of knowledge that stayed close to the original program of explaining variations in ideas by variations in group practices; and a structuralist program that viewed ideas as the codes or transcendental patterns according to which groups became structured.

In the light of Durkheim's model of rituals, we can take ritual as the missing link between group structure and group ideas. Rituals are the nodes of social structure, and it is in rituals that a group creates its symbols. But it is methodologically easier simply to correlate ideas with types of society, or, even further from the context of social action, to correlate ideas with each other; one no longer needs to do the micro-ethnography of ritual action. Ritual drops out, leaving the system of symbols as the object for analysis. This was the pathway trod by Lévi-Strauss.

At the height of his structuralist ambition, Lévi-Strauss proposed in *Structural Anthropology* (1958/1963) that the same structure underlies each social and cultural institution of any particular society: its kinship system, the layout of its campsite (for instance, clan moities divide the campsite into halves), its art style, language, mythology, and everything else. What was necessary to demonstrate this was the translation of each component into a formal code. Lévi-Strauss had made a start with a massive comparative analysis of kinship systems (*The Elementary Structures of Kinship*, 1949/1969), showing that various marriage rules, such as different forms of cross-cousin marriage, had distinctive structural consequences: kinship forms could be analyzed as the working out of choices for symmetrical or asymmetrical exchanges, which in turn implied short cycle and long cycle, restricted and generalized exchange. In a later terminology we could say that marriage rules generate network structures. Lévi-Strauss's analysis did not exhaust all types of kinship systems, but it gave confidence that it could be done, and it led to efforts to formulate these systems in mathematical terms.

Kinship codes were to be the entry point into codes that generate all aspects of culture and social organization. Troubles popped up, however, in this grand program from the beginning. It quickly became apparent that the variety of languages did not correspond to the variety of kinship systems, and that many other aspects of social institutions did not easily correspond with one another.[15] Lévi-Strauss at this point in his career had proposed an extremely ambitious version of the functionalist program to show not only how the various institutions of a particular society hang together and mutually support one another, but to demonstrate that they all were workings out of the same underlying code. As it became apparent that this project was unlikely to come off, Lévi-Strauss retreated to a narrower (although still very large) field in which code-seeking analysis could be carried out: the structural interpretation of myths.

Around this time, Lévi-Strauss came to hold that the grand unifying system is a set of elaborations from binary oppositions. The notion was taken from the structural linguistics of Saussure. His central argument was that the unit of meaning, the distinguishable sound-elements or phonemes, are structured by contrasts with other sound-elements. Each language builds upon an arbitrary set of sound-distinctions or differences. Together these make up a system, and it is only within the context of such a system that specific lexical items are meaningful.[16] Lévi-Strauss had already made a move toward seeing structure as a language in *The Elementary Structures of Kinship*, where he argued that the exchange of marriage partners is not only a rule-generated structure but a system of communications: women sent as wives from one family to another are messages, and their children, who circulate further through the system, are both replies and reminders of connections.

Lévi-Strauss (1962/1969) now proceeded with an attempt to decode myths across entire culture regions. His focus was no longer on distinct tribal units, abandoning the claim to show that each tribe had its own code. Instead Lévi-Strauss embarked on a search for the code of all codes. Formal parallels among the elements of myths, and their combinations and oppositions in particular narratives, can be interpreted as a code organized on binary dichotomies. Myths structure the world into categories of what goes together and what is opposed. A system of myths thereby lays down the frames for thinking, as well as marking boundaries of what is permissible and what is monstrous, and therefore implicitly who is a proper social member and who is not. These are still Durkheimian resonances, but the emphasis has shifted from social structure to symbolic structure. As Lévi-Strauss sought the fundamental code of the human mind, the message that he deciphered was about the transformations of earliest human history. The mythologies of South America tell us of the break between the raw and the cooked, emblematic of the separation of humans from animals, and of culture from nature; more particularly it is a history of the totemic emblems that constituted human social groups. Ironically, Lévi-Strauss's structural method had now returned to the historicist anthropology that the functionalists had critiqued; but here was Lévi-Strauss again taking cultural items out of the context of their functioning present-day society, and interpreting them as historical survivals. Instead of respecting the integrity of the living social system, Lévi-Strauss was assembling bits and pieces of symbolism from disparate cultures into a comparative system showing the workings of the primitive mind; his was a more formalized version of Frazer or Lévy-Bruhl, only repudiating their evolutionism and the notion that the primitive mind is less rational than the modern. Lévi-Strauss vacillated between presenting a model of the timeless human mind, a sort of eternal Durkheimian collective consciousness, and a historical reading of what that mind was thinking at the birth of human societies. Lévi-Strauss has been an admirably bold and adventurous thinker, but we need to penetrate the façade of the way he worked. This was to bring together one large body after another of empirical literature from the field records of anthropologists, while shifting from one structural interpretation to another as difficulties popped up, without ever explicitly admitting that a hypothesis had failed or that he had changed his mind (see Schneider [1993] for an analysis of Lévi-Strauss's inconsistencies).

Lévi-Strauss, of course, was not alone in the structuralist movement that became so prominent in the 1950s and early 1960s in France. A widened scope of application as well as refined analytical tools came from the Russian and Prague formalists in literary criticism and comparative folklore (Jameson 1972). Shklovsky, Bakhtin, Jacobson, and others singled out recurring or archetypal plot structures, especially the plot tensions and oppositions that create drama and narrative direction; following Saussure, it is the oppositions that create meaning. The formalist method acquired a dynamic or generative element, examining literary technique with an eye to how new systems of cultural meaning are created by metaphoric and metonymic transformations of prior texts and representational systems. Using these tools, the French structuralist movement ranged widely across all items of culture, seeking the code by which they are generated. Barthes (1967), for example, analyzed haute couture fashion as a system of oppositions and combinations, conveying structural relationships and implicitly placing persons in social hierarchies. Baudrillard (1968/1996) applied the method to modern, commercially distributed culture with its cycles of new products released seasonally or annually that target an array of market niches. The world of material consumption can be viewed as text-like; the tools for analyzing the structure of languages, myths, and literary works can be extended to the sets of oppositions and combinations that structure human interpretation of the entire material world. Derrida and others elaborated on the epistemological implications of structuralist analysis; the term "deconstruction" implies the activity of taking apart commonly accepted cultural items to show the structural ingredients from which their meanings were made.

At this point the structuralist or code-seeking program exploded, as its later followers, most famously Derrida and Foucault, turned against its central premise. The deconstructionist or postmodernist movement critiqued the notion that a single structural code exists. Lévi-Strauss proposed that cultures are built upon a binary code, but was never able to demonstrate it convincingly. Instead there may be multiple axes of differentiation; symbols can convey a number of contrasts; sign systems are polysemic, conveying multiple meanings. The importance of ambiguity and multiple penumbra of meaning-resonances had been stressed since mid-century by literary critics examining the effectiveness of literary style, especially in poetry (e.g., Empson 1930). The deconstructionists broadened the point, thundering out the argument (not unmixed with ideological animus) that cultural systems can be read quite differently by persons in different historical epochs, in different social locations, and indeed by the same person taking a succession of viewpoints.

The broader structuralist movement thus came up against much the same problems as did Lévi-Strauss: scholars are committed to a method for seeking codes, but we never securely arrive at a code that we can agree is fundamental to all the others. In effect, the later deconstructionists, without being aware of it, have come back to a more situated viewpoint: like microsociologists, they have had to return primacy to the particular location in which the construction of meaning takes place. But microsociology is barely known in the French intellectual scene and in the literary disciplines that take their direction from it; and the Durkheimian origins of the structuralist movement are generally forgotten.[17] In effect, the code-seeking program abolished ritual, or looked high over its head. Its emphasis on cognitive structures led to a search for codes, mentalities, or structures of the mind that transcend all situations; its location is somewhere outside any particular space-time location. Lacking a microsociology, postmodernists see the locatedness of meaning-construction as broadly historical, in the framework of overarching history of ideas (as in Foucault's writings on sexuality), or in the historical phase of capitalism or global economy or electronic communications networks (for those who retain a structural mechanism). These moves have the ironic consequence of returning to a single, overarching framework for the imposition of meaning, leaving no means of seeing how meanings are indeed situationally constructed.

The Cultural Turn

This entire set of developments has sometimes been labeled "the cultural turn." This omnibus term can be misleading because it lumps together what I have called the "code-seeking" program with its modifiers and critics. In its original structuralist version, the program takes all items of culture—indeed, all human institutions in the broadest sense—and treats them as a text to be decoded, seeking the underlying semiotic structures of which they are manifestations. By the late 1960s and 1970s, this program had given rise to its heretics, critics from within, who argued for the polysemic, ambiguous nature of codes. In the Anglophone intellectual world of the late twentieth century, many have been followers or importers of these French intellectual movements. In contrast to the rather uncritical enthusiasm for structuralism and poststructuralism in anthropology and literary theory, the cultural turn in sociology has been more ambivalent. Anglophone sociologists generally regarded the French structuralist movement with skepticism and from a distance, but they pursued their own version of a "cultural turn" in a movement that self-consciously emphasized to culture. This movement was split between those doing research on how the production of culture (typically, specialized high culture) operates, and those who argued for the autonomy of culture from reductive explanations.

A prominent version of the "cultural turn" occurred within the thriving intellectual field of social movements. By the 1970s, this field had made important explanatory advances by formulating resource mobilization theory, demonstrating how material conditions for mobilizing and sustaining a movement—including its organization, financing, and networks—affect its growth and fate, quite apart from the extent of its grievances. Any successful paradigm tends to spin off rivals looking for new research territories to open, and thus the next phase of social movement theory took a cultural turn toward examining movement frames, or group traditions and identities, and the flow of these cultural resources from one social movement to another. Mobilizing material and organization resources, and using cultural resources are not incompatible in social movements, and indeed the two aspects tend to go together; but the contentious character of intellectual life often made it seem as if there were a war between rival positions, operating either without culture or by putting culture first.

By the 1980s and 1990s, cultural sociologists were attempting to loosen the restrictions inherent in the paradigm of culture as an autonomous, and therefore an ultimate explanatory, device. Sociologists have given greater emphasis to the flexibility of culture in the flow of situational interaction. In Ann Swidler's (1986) well-known formulation, culture is a toolbox from which different pieces can be extracted for use according to the differing purposes and strategies of social action (see also Emirbayer and Mische 1998; Lamont 2000). Sociologists have thus attempted to overcome the implicitly static bias of cultural analysis and to show how new cultures can be created out of older ones.

In one respect, these developments have been remote from ritual theory. The code-seeking program, exemplified by Lévi-Strauss and Barthes, dropped Durkheim's ritual action entirely; and even anthropologists who specifically studied religious rituals saw them as performances determined by the code, if allowing some local flexibililty in how the rituals are carried out. Recent developments within the "cultural turn," especially by social movement theorists, have given more emphasis to micro-situational action; and sometimes this is even referred to as ritual. Yet these conceptions of ritual carry the heritage of terminological confusion that I have been reviewing. Ritual is seen as action, but action heavily constrained by past culture—something between a manifestation of what the underlying culture prescribes, and a device for generating new culture.

IR theory pushes this development to a clear conceptual break. In Durkheim's formulation, rituals create culture, and sometimes reproduce existing culture. In either case, culture is socially alive only when rituals are successful, that is, when the situational ingredients exist to make rituals emotionally intense and cognitively focused. IR theory gives a precise mechanism for showing when new cultural symbols are generated, and when old symbols retain social commitments or fade away as no longer meaningful. The emphasis in IR theory, obviously enough, is to put ritual interaction in the center of analysis, and to derive the ups and downs of cultural belief from it. We may, if we like, regard IR theory as a further twist within and beyond the cultural turn; IR theory radicalizes the trajectory of criticism of the code-seeking program. But it is also a return to an older Durkheimian formulation in which social morphology shapes social symbols. Current IR theory differs from the classic version mainly in giving a radically micro-situational slant, stressing that the social morphology that counts is the patterns of micro-sociological interaction in local situations.

What does IR theory add? First, it is a theory of situations themselves, showing how they have their own local structures and dynamics. Second, it puts emphasis on the situation, not as a cognitive construction but as a process by which shared emotions and intersubjective focus sweep individuals along by flooding their consciousness. It not so much a matter of knowledgeable agents choosing from repertoires, as it is a situational propensity toward certain cultural symbols. Third, ritual creates cultural symbols. This is in contrast to the thinking of many who have taken the cultural turn, for whom culture remains the trump card in the social deck, an ultimate category of explanation behind which it is impossible to go. IR theory provides an empirical mechanism for how and when symbols are created, as well when they dissipate, why they are sometimes full of magnetism for the persons who invoke them, and why sometimes they fade into disrespect or indifference. Interaction ritual theory provides a processual model for the construction of symbols; it has the further advantage of showing just when and to what extent those meanings are shared, reified, and imposed, when they are ephemeral—and all the gradations in between.

Classic Origins of IR Theory in Durkheim's Sociology of Religion

In the particular fields that study religion and related forms of ceremony, even during the heyday of the code-seeking program, some scholars have continued to study ritual. This analysis has generally been slanted by using the tools of the code-seeking program, notably among structuralist anthropologists and many scholars in the field of religious studies, including the now specialized field of ritual studies. Their predominant orientation is that the ritual is determined by the code.[18] But since the code is unknown and must be discovered, the researcher describes the pattern of the ritual, and uses it as evidence for how the code is structured; then the direction is reversed, and the code is now taken as an explanation of why the ritual is carried out in this manner. There is an underlying circularity in the method: positing a code that is then taken as explanation of the ritual behavior that is seen as evidence for the code.

Religious ritual is thus interpreted as a revelation of the divine, a doorway into the transcendental (e.g., Drewal 1992; Martos 1991). This is rather close to participants' own view of ritual, a form of going native. And insofar as scholars sympathetic to religious beliefs are already in some sense natives in religious commitment, this may be one reason why the structuralist approach to ritual appeals to many religious scholars. A modified version of this position is that religious ritual reveals the underlying religious code; it is a reading of a transcendent text, which becomes imminent in the ritual. In contrast, the analysis of interaction ritual as a set of processes that produce belief is an inherently secular viewpoint; it takes seriously what religious persons are doing, but interprets their action, as Durkheim did, in a secular manner.[19] At this point it is worth our while to return to Durkheim himself, and start out again from his model of social ritual.

Durkheim set forth most of the components of social rituals in his discussion of how religion is socially produced, using as his example the tribal gathering of Australian aborigines. He intended this analysis to have wide application, and he interspersed his account with examples drawn from modern political life, commenting frequently on the generality of these processes. These texts are perhaps the most worthy of close attention of all of classic sociology, and so I will quote from them extensively in building up a general model of interaction ritual.[20] With a little theoretical self-consciousness, of course, we can see that this very activity of respectful attention is a way of treating Durkheim's texts as sacred objects of a cult of sociologists. Fair enough; this activity not only affirms our identities as members of the sociological professiona stretching back to Durkheim's generation, but it will make us better and more acute sociologists, sharpening our consciousness of the tools by which we can see into the inner workings of social life in all its varieties.

Let us take this material in three stages: the ingredients that go into making rituals happen; the process by which a condition of collective effervescence or collective consciousness is built up; and the results or products of a ritual.

First, the ingredients. Here Durkheim places emphasis on the *physical assembly of the group*. The starting point is when human bodies come together in the same place:

The life of the Australian societies passes alternately through two distinct phases. Sometimes the population is broken up into little groups who wander about independently of one another.... Sometimes, on the contrary, the population concentrates and gathers at determined points for a length of time varying from several days to several months. This concentration takes place when a clan or a part of the tribe is summoned to the gathering, and on this occasion they celebrate a religious ceremony, or else hold what is called a corrobbori.... These two phases are contrasted with each other in the sharpest way. In the first, economic activity is the preponderating one, and it is generally of very mediocre intensity.... The very fact of concentration acts as an exceptionally powerful stimulant. (Durkheim 1912/1965, 245–47)

The sociology of ritual is thus a sociology of gatherings—of crowds, assemblies, congregations, audiences. Through Goffman's eyes, we can see that these gatherings can also be quite small scale: a couple of acquaintances stopping to talk, or merely nodding in passing, or even strangers avoiding each other's glance on the street; or, at the intermediate level, a small group eating and drinking around a table. The point is not merely the banal one that people interact best when they are together; there is the much stronger implication that society is above all an embodied activity.[21] When human bodies are together in the same place, there is a physical attunement: currents of feeling, a sense of wariness or interest, a palpable change in the atmosphere. The bodies are paying attention to each other, whether at first there is any great conscious awareness of it or not. This bodily inter-orientation is the starting point for what happens next.

Durkheim goes on to indicate that this bodily assembly varies in its frequency and intensity. When this happens, there are striking differences in behavior of both group and individual:

There are periods in history when, under the influence of some great collective shock, social interactions have become much more frequent and active. Men look for each other and assemble together more than ever. That general effervescence results which is characteristic of revolutionary or creative epochs.... Men see more now and differently than in normal times. Changes are not merely of shades and degrees; men become different.... This is what explains the Crusades, for example, or many of the scenes, either sublime or savage, of the French Revolution. Under the influence of the general exaltation, we see the most mediocre and inoffensive bourgeois becoming either a hero or a butcher. (Durkheim 1912/1965, 241–42)

Once the bodies are together, there may take place a process of intensification of shared experience, which Durkheim called collective effervescence, and the formation of collective conscience or collective consciousness. We might refer to it as a condition of heightened intersubjectivity. How does this come about? Durkheim indicates two interrelated and mutually reinforcing mechanisms:

1. *Shared action and awareness*: "[I]f left to themselves, individual consciousnesses are closed to each other; they can communicate only by means of signs which express their internal states. If the communication is established between them is to become a real communion, that is to say, a fusion of all particular sentiments into one common sentiment, the signs expressing them must themselves be fused in one single and unique resultant. It is the appearance of this that informs individuals that they are in harmony and makes them conscious of their moral unity. It is by uttering the same cry, pronouncing the same word, or performing the same gesture in regard to some object that they become and feel themselves to be in unison. . . . Individual minds cannot come in contact and communicate with each other except by coming out of themselves; they cannot do this except by movements. So it is the homogeneity of these movements that gives the group consciousness of itself. . . . When this homogeneity is once established and these movements have taken a stereotyped form, they serve to symbolize the corresponding representations. But they symbolize them only because they have aided in forming them" (Durkheim 1912/1965, 262–63).

2. *Shared emotion*: "When [the aborigines] are once come together, a sort of electricity is formed by their collecting which quickly transports them to an extraordinary degree of exaltation. Every sentiment expressed finds a place without resistance in all the minds, which are very open to outside impressions; each re-echoes the others, and is re-echoed by the others. The initial impulse thus proceeds, growing as it goes, as an avalanche grows in its advance. And as such active passions so free from all control could not fail to burst out, on every side one sees nothing but violent gestures, cries, veritable howls, and deafening noises of every sort, which aid in intensifying still more the state of mind which they manifest" (Durkheim 1912/1965, 247).

Movements carried out in common operate to focus attention, to make participants aware of each other as doing the same thing and thus thinking the same thing. Collective movements are signals by which intersubjectivity is created. Collective attention enhances the expression of shared emotion; and in turn the shared emotion acts further to intensify collective movements and the sense of intersubjectivity.

Now we come to the results of ritual. Collective effervescence is a momentary state, but it carries over into more prolonged effects when it becomes embodied in sentiments of group solidarity, symbols or sacred objects, and individual emotional energy.

The experience of heightened mutual awareness and emotional arousal gives rise to *group emblems, markers of group identity*:

> So it is in the midst of these effervescent social environments and out this effervescence itself that the religious ideas seems to be born. . . . We have shown how the clan, by the manner in which it acts upon its members, awakens within them the idea of external forces which dominate them and exalt them; but we must still demand how it happens that these forces are thought of under the form of totems, that is to say, in the shape of an animal or plant.
>
> It is because this animal or plant has given its name to the clan and serves as its emblem. . . . [T]he sentiments aroused in us by something spontaneously attach themselves to a symbol which represents them. . . . For we are unable to consider an abstract entity, which we can represent only laboriously and confusedly, the source of the strong sentiments which we feel. We cannot explain them to ourselves except by connecting them to some concrete object of whose reality we are vividly aware. . . . The soldier who dies for his flag, dies for his country; but as a matter of fact, in his own consciousness, it is the flag that has the first place. . . . Whether one isolated standard remains in the hands of the enemy or not does not determine the fate of the country, yet the soldier allows himself to be killed to regain it. He loses sight of the fact that the flag is only a sign, and that it has no value in itself, but only brings to mind the reality that it represents; it is treated as if it were the reality itself.
>
> Now the totem is the flag of the clan. It is therefore natural that the impressions aroused by the clan in individual minds—impressions of dependence and of increased vitality—should fix themselves to the idea of the totem rather than that of the clan: for the clan is too complex a reality to be represented clearly in all its complex unity. . . . [The tribesman] does not know that the coming together of a number of men associated in the same life results in disengaging new energies, which transform each of them. All that he knows is that he is raised above himself and that he sees a different life from the one he ordinarily leads. However, he must connect these sensations to some external object as their cause. Now what does he see about him? On every side those things which appeal to his senses and strike his imagination are the numerous

images of the totem. . . . Placed thus in the center of the scene, it becomes representative. The sentiments expressed everywhere fix themselves upon it, for it is the only concrete object upon which they can fix themselves. . . . During the ceremony, it is the center of all regards." (Durkheim 1912/1965, 250–52)

What is mutually focused upon becomes a symbol of the group. In actuality, the group is focusing on its own feeling of intersubjectivity, its own shared emotion; but it has no way of representing this fleeting feeling, except by representing it as embodied in an object. It reifies its experience, makes it thing-like, and thus an emblem, treated as having noun-like permanence. In fact, as Durkheim underlines, *sentiments can only be prolonged by symbols*:

> Moreover, without symbols, social sentiments could have only a precarious existence. Though very strong as long as men are together and influence each other reciprocally, they exist only in the form of recollections after the assembly has ended, and when left to themselves, these become feebler and feebler; for since the group is no longer present and active, individual temperaments easily regain the upper hand. . . . But if the movements by which these sentiments are expressed are connected with something that endures, the sentiments themselves become more durable. These other things are constantly bringing them to mind and arousing them; it is as though the cause which excited them in the first place continued to act. Thus these systems of emblems, which are necessary if society is to become conscious of itself, are no less indispensable for assuring the continuation of this consciousness. (Durkheim 1912/1965, 265)

Since Durkheim is often regarded as a static theorist of social organization, of structures fixed into a functionalist system by a value system, it is worth stressing how dynamic his conception is. Society becomes patterned by symbols, or more precisely by respect for symbols; but the symbols are respected only to the extent that they are charged up with sentiments by participation in rituals. Sentiments run down and fade away unless they are periodically renewed. Religion, the specific case under consideration here, is not simply a body of beliefs, but beliefs sustained by ritual practices. When the practices stop, the beliefs lose their emotional import, becoming mere memories, forms without substance, eventually dead and meaningless. By the same token, new symbols can be created; whenever the group assembles and focuses its attention around an object that comes to embody their emotion, a *new sacred object* is born:

Also, in the present day just as much as in the past, we see society constantly creating sacred things out of ordinary ones. If it happens to fall in love with a man and if it thinks it has found in him the principal aspirations that move it, as well as the means of satisfying them, this man will be raised above the others and, as it were, deified. Opinion will invest him with a majesty exactly analogous to that protecting the gods. . . . And the fact that it is society alone which is the author of these varieties of apotheosis, is evident since it frequently chances to consecrate men thus who have no right to it from their own merit. The simple deference inspired by men invested with high social functions is not different in nature from religious respect. It is expressed by the same movements: a man keeps at a distance from a high personage; he approaches him only with precautions; in conversing with him, he uses other gestures and language than those used with ordinary mortals. . . .

In addition to men, society also consecrates things, especially ideas. If a belief is unanimously shared by a people, then, for the reason which we previously pointed out, it is forbidden to touch it, to deny it or to contest it. Now the prohibition of criticism is an interdiction like the others and proves the presence of something sacred. Even today, however great may be the liberty which we accord to others, a man who should totally deny progress or ridicule the human ideal to which modern societies are attached, would produce the effect of sacrilege. (Durkheim 1912/1965, 243–44)

One chief result of rituals is to charge up symbolic objects with significance, or to recharge such objects with renewed sentiments of respect. Along with this, individual participants get their own reservoir of charge. The "sort of electricity" that Durkheim metaphorically ascribes to the group in its state of heightened excitement is stored in batteries: one component of which is the symbol, and the other pole of which is the individual. Participation in a ritual gives the individual a special kind of energy, which I will call *emotional energy*:

The man who has obeyed his god and who for this reason, believes the god is with him, approaches the world with confidence and with the feeling of increased energy . . . . since society cannot exist except in and through individual consciousness, this force must also penetrate us and organize itself within us; it thus becomes an integral part of our being and by that very fact this [our being] is elevated and magnified. (Durkheim 1912/1965, 242)

Elsewhere in the same work, Durkheim says,

> But it is not only in exceptional circumstances that this stimulating action of society makes itself felt; there is not, so to speak, a moment in our lives when some current of energy does not come to us from without. . . . Because he is in moral harmony with his comrades, he has more confidence, courage and boldness in action. . . . (178)
>
> There are occasions when this strengthening and vivifying action of society is especially apparent. In the midst of an assembly animated by common passion, we become susceptible of acts and sentiments of which we are incapable when reduced to our own forces; and when the assembly is dissolved and when, finding ourselves alone again, we fall back to our ordinary level, we are then able to measure the height to which we have been raised above ourselves. History abounds in examples of this sort. It is enough to think of the night of the Fourth of August, 1789, when an assembly was suddenly led to an act of sacrifice and abnegation which each of its members had refused the day before, and at which they were all surprised the day after [i.e., the abolition of feudalism by the assembly of nobles and commoners in the French Revolution]. That is why all parties, political, economic and confessional, are careful to have periodic reunions where their members may revivify their common faith by manifesting it in common. (241)

This socially derived emotional energy, as Durkheim says, is a feeling of confidence, courage to take action, boldness in taking initiative. It is a morally suffused energy; it makes the individual feel not only good, but exalted, with the sense of doing what is most important and most valuable. Durkheim goes on to note that groups hold periodic assemblies to revivify this feeling, drawing again on his point that sentiments fade out over a period of time if they are not resuscitated by another experience of collective effervescence. I would add that this feeling of emotional energy has a powerful motivating effect upon the individual; whoever has experienced this kind of moment wants to repeat it.

A final item in the list of ritual effects is *morality*. The individual feels moral when he or she is acting with the energy derived from the heightened experience of the group. And indeed, since Durkheim is building a theory of human institutions from the ground up, without assuming any preexisting beliefs or moral standards, he is also indicating that rituals are the source of the group's standards of morality. It is the heightened experience of intersubjectivity and emotional strength in group rituals tht generates the conception of what is good;

what is opposed to this is what is evil. Transferred to symbols and sacred objects, the concept of moral good is attached to beliefs in religious beings, and to their secular equivalents:

> [W]e cannot fail to feel that this [feeling of strength and social approval in having done one's duty] depends upon an external cause, but we do not perceive where this cause is nor what it is. So we ordinarily think of it under the form of a moral power, which though immanent in us, repesents within us something not ourselves: this is the moral conscience. . . . (1912/1965, 242)
>
> We say that an object, whether individual or collective, inspires respect when the representation expressing it in the mind is gifted with such force that it automatically causes or inhibits actions, *without regard for any consideration relative to their useful or injurious effects*. When we obey somebody because of the moral authority which we recognize in him, we follow out his opinions, not because they seem wise, but because a certain sort of physical energy is immanent in the idea that we form of this person, which conquers our will and inclines it in the indicated direction. Respect is the emotion we experience when we feel this interior and wholly spiritual pressure operating upon us. . . .
>
> The very violence with which society reacts, by way of blame or material suppression, against every attempted dissidence, contributes to strengthening its empire by manifesting the common conviction through this burst of ardour." (237–38; emphasis in the original)

For Durkheim, the touchstone of morality, and of the sacred, is that which is a value in itself, apart from its utilitarian value. Respect for sacred objects, and for the group sentiments behind them, is a higher value than the merely mundane, individual consideration of "useful or injurious effects." All merely mundane goods are sacrificed to the moral sentiments. Here Durkheim echoes his argument about precontractual solidarity in *The Division of Labor*: what holds society together is not self-interest, and it is only where utilitarian exchanges are embedded in ritual solidarity that any sustained cooperation on practical matters can take place.[22]

THE SIGNIFICANCE OF INTERACTION RITUAL FOR GENERAL SOCIOLOGICAL THEORY

The Durkheimian model addresses the central questions of social theory; and it has implications that extend to all corners of contemporary microsociology. It asks the basic question: What holds society together?

And it answers the question with a mechanism of social rituals. Furthermore, it answers it with a mechanism that varies in intensity: society is held together to just the extent that rituals are effectively carried out, and during those periods of time when the effects of those rituals are still fresh in people's minds and reverberating in their emotions. Society is held together more intensely at some moments than at others. And the "society" that is held together is no abstract unity of a social system, but is just those groups of people assembled in particular places who feel solidarity with each other through the effects of ritual participation and ritually charged symbolism. The total population of France, or the United States, or anywhere else one might consider, consists of pockets of solidarity of different degrees of intensity. A population can be washed by waves of national solidarity on occasion, but these are particular and rather special ritually based events, subject to the same processes of ritual mobilization as more local pockets of solidarity.

This means that the Durkheimian model is entirely compatible with a view of stratification and group conflict. Indeed, it provides key mechanisms for just how stratification and conflict operate. Rephrase the question as, What holds society together as a pattern of stratified and conflicting groups? The answer is social rituals, operating to create and sustain solidarity within those groups. We can elaborate a more complicated answer, and later chapters will do so. Among those complications are these: that some groups have more resources for carrying out their rituals than others, so that some groups have more solidarity and thus can lord it over those who have less; and that these ritually privileged groups have more impressive symbols and fill their members with more emotional energy. We may examine more fine-grained processes of stratification: looking inside the very group that is brought together by participating in a ritual, we can see that some individuals are more privileged than others, by being nearer to the center of the ritual than others. Rituals thus have a double stratifying effect: between ritual insiders and outsiders; and, inside the ritual, between ritual leaders and ritual followers. Rituals are thus key mechanisms, and we might say key weapons, in processes of conflict and domination.

Durkheim famously argued that the utilitarian, economic dimension of life is not basic, but depends upon precontractual solidarity; that rituals provide the basis for a situation of social trust and shared symbolic meanings through which economic exchanges can be carried out. Here I am making a similar argument with regard to social conflict: conflict is not the primordial condition of social life, a Hobbesian war of all against all, but is analytically derivative of social solidarity. That is to say, effective conflict is not really possible without the mechanisms of social ritual, which generate the alliances and the energies of the partisans, as well as their most effective weapons in dominating others. And the goals of conflict, the things that people fight over, are formed by these pattern of social rituals. The flashpoints of conflict, the incidents that set off overt struggle, almost always come from the precedence of symbols and the social sentiments they embody. All this is to say that social conflict, which I and many other theorists have argued is the major process structuring social life, especially on the macro-level of large-scale structures (Collins 1975; Mann 1986–93), requires for its explanation a Durkheimian microsociology of interaction rituals.

The central mechanism of interaction ritual theory is that occasions that combine a high degree of mutual focus of attention, that is, a high degree of intersubjectivity, together with a high degree of emotional entrainment—through bodily synchronization, mutual stimulation / arousal of participants' nervous systems—result in feelings of membership that are attached to cognitive symbols; and result also in the emotional energy of individual participants, giving them feelings of confidence, enthusiasm, and desire for action in what they consider a morally proper path. These moments of high degree of ritual intensity are high points of experience. They are high points of collective experience, the key moments of history, the times when significant things happen. These are moments that tear up old social structures or leave them behind, and shape new social structures. As Durkheim notes, these are moments like the French Revolution in the summer of 1789. We could add, they are moments like the key events of the Civil Rights movement in the 1960s; like the collapse of communist regimes in 1989 and 1991; and to a degree of significance that can be ascertained only in the future, as in the national mobilization in the United States following September 11, 2001. These examples are drawn from large-scale ritual mobilizations, and examples of a smaller scale could be drawn as we narrow our attention to smaller arenas of social action.

Interaction ritual theory is a theory of social dynamics, not merely of statics. Among social theorists there is a tendency to regard ritual analysis as conservative, a worship of traditions laid down in the past, a mechanism for reproducing social structure as it always existed. True enough, ritual analysis has often been used in this vein; and even theories like Bourdieu's, which combine Durkheim with Marx, see a mutually supporting interplay between the cultural or symbolic order and the order of economic power. For Bourdieu, ritual reproduces the cultural and therefore the economic fields.[23] But this is to miss the transformative power of ritual mobilization. Intense ritual experience creates new symbolic objects and generates energies that fuel the major social changes. Interactional ritual is a mechanism of change. As long as there are potential occasions for ritual mobilization, there is the possibility for sudden and abrupt periods of change. Ritual can be repetitive and conservatizing, but it also provides the occasions on which changes break through.

In this respect IR theory mediates between postmodernist and similar theories that posit ubiquitous situational flux of meanings and identities, and a culturalist view that fixed scripts or repertoires are repeatedly called upon. The contrast is articulated by Lamont (2000, 243–44, 271), who provides evidence that there are "cultural and structural conditions that lead individuals to use some criteria of evaluation rather than others." The argument is parallel to my use of IR theory, which pushes the argument at a more micro-situational level: that the operative structural conditions are those that make up the ingredients of interaction ritual; and that cultural repertoires are created in particular kind of IRs, and fade out in others. To show the conditions under which ritual operates in one direction or the other is a principal topic of this book.

Intense moments of interaction ritual are high points not only for groups but also for individual lives. These are the events that we remember, that give meaning to our personal biographies, and sometimes to obsessive attempts to repeat them: whether participating in some great collective event such as a big political demonstration; or as spectator at some storied moment of popular entertainment or sports; or a personal encounter ranging from a sexual experience, to a strongly bonding friendly exchange, to a humiliating insult; the social atmosphere of an alcohol binge, a drug high, or a gambling victory; a bitter argument or an occasion of violence. Where these moments have a high degree of focused awareness and a peak of shared emotion, these personal experiences, too, can be crystalized in personal symbols, and kept alive in symbolic replays for greater or lesser expanses of one's life. These are the significant formative experiences that shape individuals; if the patterns endure, we are apt to call them personalities; if we disapprove of them we call them addictions. But this usage too easily reifies what is an ongoing flow of situations. The movement of individuals from one situation to another in what I call interaction ritual chains is an up-and-down of variation in the intensity of interaction rituals; shifts in behavior, in feeling and thought occur just as the situations shift. To be a constant personality is to be on an even keel where the kinds of interaction rituals flow constantly from one situation to the next. Here again, IR theory points up the dynamics of human lives, their possibility for dramatic shifts in direction.

IR theory provides a theory of individual motivation from one situation to the next. Emotional energy is what individuals seek; situations are attractive or unattractive to them to the extent that the interaction ritual is successful in providing emotional energy. This gives us a dynamic microsociology, in which we trace situations and their pull or push for individuals who come into them. Note the emphasis: the analytical starting point is the situation, and how it shapes individuals; situations generate and regenerate the emotions and the symbolism that charge up individuals and send them from one situation to another.

Interaction ritual is a full-scale social psychology, not only of emotions and situational behavior, but of cognition. Rituals generate symbols; experience in rituals inculcates those symbols in individual minds and memories. IR provides an explanation of variations in beliefs. Beliefs are not necessarily constant, but situationally fluctuate, as a number of theorists have argued and as researchers have demonstrated (Swider 1986; Lamont 2000). What IR theory adds to contemporary cultural theory in this regard is that what people think they believe at a given moment is dependent upon the kind of interaction ritual taking place in that situation: people may genuinely and sincerely feel the beliefs they express at the moment they express them, especially when the conversational situation calls out a higher degree of emotional emphasis; but this does not mean that they act on these beliefs, or that they have a sincere feeling about them in other everday interactions where the ritual focus is different. IR theory gives the conditions under which beliefs become salient, by rising and falling in emotional loading. Everyday life is the experience of moving through a chain of interaction rituals, charging up some symbols with emotional significance and leaving others to fade. IR theory leads us into a theory of the momentary flow of internal mental life, an explanation of subjectivity as well as intersubjectivity.

Durkheim held that the individual consciousness is a portion of the collective consciousness. This is tantamount to saying that the individual is socialized from the outside, by social experience carried within. This is surely true, as most social scientists would agree, as far as early childhood socialization is concerned. The argument of IR theory carries this further: we are constantly being socialized by our interactional experiences throughout our lives. But not in a unidirectional and homogeneous way; it is intense interaction rituals that generate the most powerful emotional energy and the most vivid symbols, and it is these that are internalized. Contrary to an implication of Freudian theory and others that stress early childhood experience, socialization once laid down does not endure forever; emotional energies and symbolic meanings fade if they are not renewed. IR theory is not a model of a wind-up doll, programmed early in life, which ever after walks through the pattern once laid down. It is a theory of moment-to-moment motivation, situation by situation. Thus it has high theoretical ambitions: to explain what any individual will do, at any moment in time; what he or she will feel, think, and say.

Viewed in the abstract, this may seem like an impossibly high ambition. But consider: there are considerable theoretical resources available for this task. We have Durkheimian theory, which yields an explicit model of what produces sentiments of group membership; of symbols that formulate social values, and through which humans think; and of emotional energies that animate individuals. This theory is cast in terms of conditions of varying strength, so that we can tell which situations will generate higher or lower levels of solidarity, respect for symbols, and emotional energy. And this model is of wide applicability: it fits not only the great collective events of religion and politics, as Durkheim himself pointed out, but it can be brought to bear on the level of everyday life situation by Goffman's line of application. More and more details of how to apply the Durkheimian ritual theory to everyday life situations are becoming available, as I will attempt to show in later chapters, by drawing on such resources as Meadian symbolic interactionist theory of thinking as internalized conversation, along with contemporary research on conversation and on emotions, and on the ethnography of everyday life. The totality of social life is the totality of situations that people go through in their everyday lives; we have a powerful and wide-ranging model that explains what will happen in those situations. An offshoot of this situational microsociology is the internalization of social life in individuals' subjective experience: the sociology of thinking and feeling.

Why not follow this theoretical research program as far as it will go? Some intellectuals have philosophical commitments that hold them back from taking this path; we do not want a theory that explains everything, and we construct arguments to rule out the possibility of any such a theory succeeding. There are lines of metatheory, going back to Max Weber and to his Neo-Kantian precedessors, which hold that the territory of social science is the realm of human meanings and human freedom, *Geisteswissenschaft* as opposed to *Naturwissenschaft*, a realm in which deterministic explanations do not apply. But such arguments are hardly conclusive: they try to lay out in advance and by conceptual definition what we can and cannot find along particular lines of investigation. Social theory and research moves along pragmatically, in the real flow of intellectual history; philosophers and metatheorists cannot legislate what we will not be able to explain in the future.

The program of interaction ritual theory is to take the intellectual tools that we have, and to apply them: to all situations, all emotions, all symbols, all thinking, all subjectivity and intersubjectivity. Intellectual life is an exciting adventure when we try to push it as far as we can. There is surely more emotional energy in exploration than in conservatively standing pat and trying to avoid extending our understanding beyond the boundaries set up by intellectual taboos. IR theory, as an intellectual enterprise, is a set of symbolic representations riding on its surge of emotional energy; it is the intellectual version of effervescence that gave élan to Durkheim and his research group, to Goffman and his followers, and to today's sociologists of emotion and process in everyday life. What I attempt to show in this book is some vistas that open up as we ride this intellectual movement into the future.

Chapter 2

THE MUTUAL-FOCUS /
EMOTIONAL-ENTRAINMENT MODEL

AT THE CENTER OF AN INTERACTION RITUAL is the process in which participants develop a mutual focus of attention and become entrained in each other's bodily micro-rhythms and emotions. This chapter will present the details of this process in an explicit model of processes that take place in time: a fine-grained flow of micro-events that build up in patterns of split seconds and ebb away in longer periods of minutes, hours, and days. Rituals are constructed from a combination of ingredients that grow to differing levels of intensity, and result in the ritual outcomes of solidarity, symbolism, and individual emotional energy. This model enables us to examine carefully each part of the process. We will see what contingencies and variations can occur in each segment, and what effects these have on the outcomes. There are many different kinds of collective consciousness or intersubjectivity: different kinds of group membership, of symbolism, and of emotional tones of social experience. I will put forth a theory of how variations in interaction rituals generate the myriad varieties of human social life.

At a number of points, it is possible to bolster the theoretical model by empirical evidence from contemporary microsociology, notably studies of verbal conversation and studies in the sociology of emotions. As an illustration of what we can get from theoretical analysis of live video recordings of natural human interaction, I will present an analysis of a documentary film of firefighters and street crowds in the September 11, 2001 attack on New York City. This raw data brings out vividly how some IR conditions lead to merely momentary, others to long-term, effects.

RITUAL INGREDIENTS, PROCESSES, AND OUTCOMES

Figure 2.1 depicts interaction ritual as a set of processes with causal connections and feedback loops among them. Everything in the model is a variable.

Interaction ritual (IR) has four main ingredients or initiating conditions:

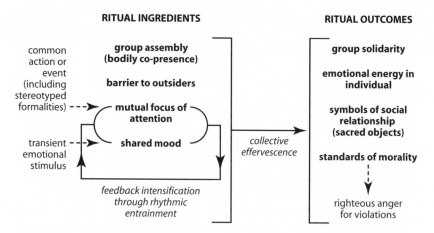

Figure 2.1 Interaction ritual.

1. Two or more people are physically assembled in the same place, so that they affect each other by their bodily presence, whether it is in the foreground of their conscious attention or not.

2. There are boundaries to outsiders so that participants have a sense of who is taking part and who is excluded.

3. People focus their attention upon a common object or activity, and by communicating this focus to each other become mutually aware of each other's focus of attention.

4. They share a common mood or emotional experience.

These ingredients feed back upon each other. Most importantly, number 3, the mutual focus of attention, and number 4, the common mood, reinforce each other. As the persons become more tightly focused on their common activity, more aware of what each other is doing and feeling, and more aware of each other's awareness, they experience their shared emotion more intensely, as it comes to dominate their awareness. Members of a cheering crowd become more enthusiastic, just as participants at a religious service become more respectful and solemn, or at a funeral become more sorrowful, than before they began. It is the same on the small-scale level of a conversation; as the interaction becomes more engrossing, participants get caught up in the rhythm and mood of the talk. We shall examine the micro-empirical evidence on this later. The key process is participants' mutual entrainment of emotion and attention, producing a shared emotional / cognitive experience. What Durkheim called collective consciousness is this micro-situational production of moments of intersubjectivity.

There are four main outcomes of interaction rituals. To the extent that the ingredients successfully combine and build up to high levels of mutually focused and emotionally shared attention, participants have the experience of

1. group solidarity, a feeling of membership;

2. emotional energy [EE] in the individual: a feeling of confidence, elation, strength, enthusiasm, and initiative in taking action;

3. symbols that represent the group: emblems or other representations (visual icons, words, gestures) that members feel are associated with themselves collectively; these are Durkheim's "sacred objects." Persons pumped up with feelings of group solidarity treat symbols with great respect and defend them against the disrespect of outsiders, and even more, of renegade insiders.

4. feelings of morality: the sense of rightness in adhering to the group, respecting its symbols, and defending both against transgressors. Along with this goes the sense of moral evil or impropriety in violating the group's solidarity and its symbolic representations.

These are the basic elements of the theory.[1] In the following sections I will examine the evidence on how each of these operates.

Formal Rituals and Natural Rituals

At first glance, what seems to be missing in this list are just those items that make up the usual definition of "ritual." In common parlance, a ritual is a formal ceremony, the going through of a set of stereotyped actions: reciting verbal formulas, singing, making traditional gestures, wearing traditional costumes. As we have seen from Durkheim's analysis of religious ritual, the formality and the stereotyped activity are not the crucial ingredients; they only contribute to the core process of intersubjectivity and shared emotion, which is to say to the experience of collective consciousness and collective effervescence, insofar as they contribute to a mutual focus of attention. This is indicated on the far left side of figure 2.1, where a dashed arrow flows from "common action or event (including stereotyped formalities)" to "mutual focus of attention." Stereotyped formulas can generate a socially successful ritual, if indeed the participants also experience a shared emotion, and if they go on to heighten their sense of mutual participation by becoming strongly aware of each other's consciousness. Without this, the ritual is merely "formal," an empty going through of the forms, even a dead ceremonialism.

Mutual focus of attention is a crucial ingredient for a ritual to work; but this focus may come about spontaneously and without explicit concern that this is happening. Goffman's examples of the little interaction rituals of everyday sociability are generally of this sort. Whether you call people by their first names or not is usually not a matter of conscious attention, but it is a small-scale ritual nevertheless; and as we shall see, the difference between high-solidarity conversations and low-solidarity conversations happens on the level of rhythmic features that have no formally recognized rules attached to them. Goffman's examples come from the small scale of momentary social encounters, but spontaneously enacted rituals occur also on a larger scale of public groups, as in the examples Durkheim gives of political and military situations parallel to religious rituals. The crowds gathered during the French Revolution were often improvising new rituals. These were highly effective, even at their first moment without the resources of stereotyped activities, because they had a high degree of mutual focus and shared emotion. Out of such situations, as Durkheim was fond of noting, new symbols are created.

We may refer to those interactions as "natural rituals" that build up mutual focus and emotional entrainment without formally stereotyped procedures; and to those that are initiated by a commonly recognized apparatus of ceremonial procedures as "formal rituals." From the point of view of what makes an interaction ritual work, the core ingredients, processes, and outcomes are the same. Both natural ritual and formal rituals can generate symbols and feelings of membership, and both can reach high degrees of intensity. Beyond this commonality, not all symbolic memberships are of the same kind, and the details of how rituals are put together will affect the kind of membership categories that result. As we shall see, rituals initiated by formal procedures have a stronger effect on broadcasting and affirming a rigid sense of group boundaries than do rituals that begin spontaneously by a naturally occurring focus of attention and shared emotion. The latter give a more fluid sense of membership, unless they become crystallized and prolonged in symbols, which thereby tend to make subsequent IRs more formal. (We will examine the evidence for this pattern in chapter 7, "Situational Stratification.")

Failed Rituals, Empty Rituals, Forced Rituals

Not all rituals are successful. Some fail dismally, even painfully; some mercifully fade away. Some are rebelled against as empty formalities, undergone under duress, gleefully discarded when possible. These variations are useful for refining our theory, and for testing the conditions that make rituals operate. Unsuccessful rituals are important substantively as well, for if every social encounter of everyday life from the most minor up to the major public gatherings is to be put in the scale and weighed against the standard of ritual intensity, we would not expect ritual intensity to be the same everywhere. Since I am going to argue that life is structured around the contrast between successful, socially magnetic ritual situations with their high degree of emotion, motivation, and symbolic charge, and situations of lesser ritualism, it is necessary to sharpen our eyes as to what makes the difference between rituals that are strong and those that are weak. Individuals are attracted to the most intense ritual charges they can get, indifferent to lesser rituals, and repelled by others; we see best what is doing the attracting if we look at what is causing the indifference and the repulsion.

Failed rituals are easiest to see in the case of formal rituals, since there is a public announcement and widespread understanding that a ritual is being attempted. Then we shall cast a glance at natural rituals that fail: political or other gatherings that don't click, demonstrations that don't come off; and at the little Goffmanian rituals of everyday life that don't work.

What is to be our criterion of ritual success or failure? In the case of formal rituals, we have terms that participants will use: "an empty ritual," "merely ceremonial," "fell flat." Figure 2.1 allows us to state a broader criterion that will work for natural as well as formal rituals: most immediately, there is a low level of collective effervescence, the lack of momentary buzz, no shared entrainment at all or disappointingly little. There are further signs of failure on the output side: little or no feeling of group solidarity; no sense of one's identity as affirmed or changed; no respect for the group's symbols; no heightened emotional energy—either a flat feeling unaffected by the ritual, or worse yet, a sense of a drag, the feeling of boredom and constraint, even depression, interaction fatigue, a desire to escape. These imply a continuum of just how badly rituals fail, from mildly missing the mark down through strong ritual abhorrence. These strongly negative states are as important as the highly positive ones. Think of historical events—such as the smashing of icons in the Reformation—as well as moments in personal chains of life experiences—such as a rebellion against a kind of formality that one wishes never to go through again.[2]

In this respect, natural rituals fail for much the same reasons that formal rituals can be empty: the political crowd that mills around aimlessly, its members' attention distracted to things happening outside the person making the speech or away from the enemy symbol to be confronted—individuals and little subgroups drifting away until those who are left are caught up in a deflationary emotion like rats leaving a sinking ship; the party that remains mired in little knots of perfunctory conversations and never builds up a collective effervescence. Here the missing ingredients are both a lack of shared attention—since duos are too fragmented from the larger group—and lack of a shared initial emotion that can be built up and transformed into a sense of collective participation. Low-intensity, perfunctory, or halting conversations exist in abundance, and in obvious contrast to those conversations that are engrossing. Although our normal form of attribution is to regard the conversations as indicators of the personalities one is encountering, these are situational outcomes that can be explained, as we shall later see in more detail, by the differing matchups of stocks of significant symbols to talk about, and by the level of synergy among the emotional energies of the parties to the conversational situation.

A nice contrast of successful and unsuccessful interaction rituals may be seen in the variety of New Year celebrations: some have a peak moment of genuine enthusiasm at the stroke of midnight (in this respect these celebrations are a mixture of traditional forms and natural, unscripted interactions)—while others consist in flat and prefunctory greetings for the new year. What makes the difference? My observation is that New Year celebrations that work are ones in which, in the hour or two before midnight, people in an assembled crowd start making noise—with the usual whistles, rattles, perhaps firecrackers—but above all making noises at each other, in their direction, better yet, in their face. This leads to entrainment; people start making noises and throwing streamers at each other, often breaking down barriers of acquaintanceship by drawing strangers into interaction. Notice that this interaction has no cognitive content; it is very much like small children running around and making noises at each other. In the context of the New Year celebration, this intruding noisily into someone else's personal space, sometimes even bodily in the mild and playful form of throwing streamers or confetti at them, is taken as friendly and not hostile or deviant. This mutual entrainment in noise-making builds up to a crescendo of noise as everyone is focused on counting down the seconds to midnight; when the anticipated focal point is reached, there is a burst of solidarity gestures, people hugging and kissing each other, even strangers. Compare the more staid New Year party: Individuals continue in normal conversations, saying intelligible things. This keeps them in distinctive little pockets of shared mentality, cutting them off from a larger intersubjectivity that might encompass the whole group. Interactions have not been reduced to the lowest common denominator, as in the mutual noise-making ties; shared emotion does not build up; and the climax of the stroke of midnight is given only perfunctory acknowledgment, immediately after which many participants say they are tired and want to go home. Successful rituals are exhilarating; failed rituals are energy draining.

An additional type may be called forced rituals. These occur when individuals are forced to put on a show of participating wholeheart-edly in interaction rituals. Forced rituals appear to be especially drain-ing when persons are impelled by their own motivation, rather than by external social pressure, to throw themselves enthusiastically into interaction rituals, taking the lead in attempting to make the rituals succeed. Such forced rituals may even succeed, in the sense that other people do become entrained into showing greater level of animated involvement. But they feel forced insofar as the level of collective effer-vescence is higher than it would be normally given the existing ingre-dients of shared attention and emotional stimulus; the mutual entrain-ment has an element of deliberation and self-consciousness rather than a natural flow. It can take considerable effort to be the convivial host or gracious hostess, the life of the party, the spark plug of the political rally. The energy-draining effects of forced rituals are widely known from the aftermath of job interviews, especially in the round of sociable visits accompanying academic job talks, where they are referred to col-loquially as "interaction fatigue." Where the individual's social posi-tion is such that they feel motivated to take the lead in a continuous round of interactional conviviality, the cumulative affects of energy drain can be considerable.[3]

Forced rituals are energy draining, not EE creating, and the experi-ence of going through many forced rituals will tend to make individu-als averse to those kinds of ritual situations, even creating what appear to be anti-sociable personalities. But forced rituals differ from success-ful IRs precisely by having an unnatural, overly self-conscious, mutual focus and emotional entrainment. Thus, instead of participants becom-ing naturally charged up by emotional entrainment, they have to put energy into giving the impression that they are charged up. Even those same individuals who are turned off by forced rituals, I suggest, gener-ally undergo some other kinds of ritual interaction that do succeed and that produce positive emotional energy. The difference between forced rituals (along with other kinds of failed rituals) and successful rituals is what steers individuals' IR chains away from the former and toward the latter.

Is Bodily Presence Necessary?

Ritual is essentially a bodily process. Human bodies moving into the same place starts off the ritual process. There is a buzz, an excitement, or at least a wariness when human bodies are near each other. Goffman (1981, 103) noted that even "when nothing eventful is occurring, persons in each other's presence are still nonetheless tracking one another and acting so as to make themselves trackable." From the point of view of evolutionary theory, humans as animals have evolved with nervous systems that pay attention to each other: there is always the possibility of fighting, or spreading an alarm; or, on the positive side, possible sexual contact and more generally sociable gestures.[4] On the whole, the latter kind of evolved orientation toward positive interactions appears more central, since it helps explain why human bodies are so sensitive to each other, and so readily caught up in the shared attention and emotional entrainment that generates interaction rituals.

Yet isn't it possible to carry out a ritual without bodily presence? In modern times we have long-distance communications: by telephone, by video representations such as television, by computer screen. Is it not possible to generate mutual focus and emotional entrainment through these media of communication? In principle, these are empirical matters that can be studied experimentally: we could compare the amount of shared attention and emotion generated by these various interactional media, and their outcomes in level of solidarity, respect for symbolism, and individual EE. In lieu of systematic evidence, I suggest the following patterns.

First, can formal rituals, such as a wedding ceremony or a funeral be conducted over the telephone? The very idea seems inappropriate, and it is unclear that this has been attempted except in the rarest instances. What would be missing? The lack of feedback, of seeing the others present and being seen by them, would surely diminish the sense that one is paying one's respects. Without bodily presence, it is hard to convey participation in the group and to confirm one's identity as member of the group. Especially lacking would be the micro-details of the experience. A funeral is less meaningful without immediate visual cues from the other participants: the uncomfortable body postures, seeing faces tearing up, all the contagious emotional behaviors that pull one one deeply into the mood and start the watering in one's own eyes. In some kinds of ritual occasions—mainly commemorative celebrations congratulating an individual—persons will phone in their greetings, which may even be broadcast to the assembled crowd. But this is a relatively small segment of interaction, and such an action should be expected to bring only a partial feeling of participating: it would seem highly inappropriate at a funeral or a wedding, where the assembly's role is to stand by and witness, or to engage in collective responses. As an experiment, one might rig up the ritual equivalent of a conference call, in which every participant has their apparatus for communicating with everyone else at a distance. My hypothesis is that a conference call ritual would feel quite unsatisfactory to everyone, because the deliberate vocal messages are only a small part of what generates the feelings of participation. Presumably the effect would be stronger if most the participants, although wired-up, were actually together carrying out the ritual, while the distant participant was wired to all the others and could eavesdrop on at least the sounds they make as they orient to each other—a stronger effect, but one that still does not provide the full sense of emotional participation.

Is the visual mode better? It is possible to watch a funeral or a wedding on television, usually that of a famous public figure. During the fall of 2001, for example, there were sometimes moving TV memorials for 9/11 victims. These long-distance rituals can give a sense of shared emotion, solidarity, and respect for symbolism. Examing this more carefully: what details give these effects? The main effect appears to come from camera close-ups of the faces of members of the crowd, rather than of the ceremonial formality itself. Television here approximates bodily feedback, in effect allowing members of the remote audience to see others like themselves, picked out in the moments when they are displaying the most emotion and the most engrossment in the ceremony. Conversely, we would expect that where the TV cameras focus on disaffected members of the audience, who are looking bored or away from the scene, the remote audience would feel greater distance, witnessing a failed ceremony.

Television is a combination of picture and sound, and these need to be teased apart. The reader may easily perform the experiment. Turn off the sound of the TV while watching a ritualistic event, such as an athletic contest. Alternatively, move away from sight of the screen, leaving the sound on. Palpably, the stronger sense of involvement, of being pulled into the action, is from the sound. A burst of cheering from the crowd, the mood of anticipation of upcoming celebration, will pull the absent viewer back to the screen. Compare the situation where one is watching the picture without the sound: if the action seems to heat up—the team is making its drive, the clock is running down, the baseball team has men on base—there is an irresistible tendency to turn the sound back on. What is missing is not primarily the verbal explanation of the meaning of what is happening, the voices of the announcers, since the experience of watching verbal captions on the screen is not a substitute for the sound; above all, one seeks the sound of the crowd, to share fully in the sense of excitement. This is essentially what the lure of the game-spectacle is all about: the pleasure of those moments of having one's own emotions raised by a noisy crowd expressing the same thing.

Two further observations confirm the preference for bodily participation within an assembled group. After a particularly exciting or up-

Figure 2.2 Celebrating victory by ritualized full-body contact. U.S. and Russian troops converge in Germany (April 1945).

lifting moment of vicarious participation, one wants to seek out someone else to tell about it. Thus, if one had been alone watching a game, a political election, or other engrossing public event, one wants to find someone else to share one's excitement with. If the excitement is strong enough, it isn't sufficient merely to tell the news, even in a loud, enthusiastic, repetitive voice. At peak moments of victory, or suspense followed by dramatic success, the excited viewer reaches out to touch, hug, or kiss someone. IR theory suggests testable details: the IR payoff should be highest in talking excitedly with someone who is also excited by the event; whereas viewers' own enthusiasm for their experienced drama ebbs away proportionately if the person they try to convey it to is less enthusiastic, passive, or remains uninvolved.

The same pattern is visible in sports celebrations and in other victory celebrations, as depicted in the famous photos of kissing and hugging on the street at the announcement of victory in World War II. Sports victory celebrations are events of predictable intensity, since there is a regular schedule leading up to championship games. At peak moments, built up emotionally in proportion to the amount of tension through the series of previous contests, there takes place an informal ritual in which the players touch each other repeatedly while repeating

Figure 2.3 Marking the end of World War II
(August 14, 1945).

a few simple words or cries of victory. The bigger the victory and the
more the suspense, the more body contact, and the more prolonged
contact: the range goes from slapping hands, to body hugs, to piling
onto a heap of bodies at the playing field.[5] This is a stratified ritual,
since the fans would also like to participate not only with their voices
but by getting bodily as near to the players as possible. They are usually prevented from approaching them, thus leaving the high degree
of bodily contact as a solidarity ritual reserved for the elite in the center
of the ceremony; the fans can only watch, vocally participate, and engage in some bodily contact with each other.

Another observation supporting the preference for bodily present
rituals is that attendance at sports events and other mass audience occasions has not declined with the availability of television. This is so
even though, for many sports, television provides a better view of the
action and the details of the athletes' performance. But people nevertheless prefer to go to the game, especially if it is a "big game"—that

Figure 2.4 A ritual victory pile-on: high school hockey championship (2002).

is, a game in which the consequences are considered important and hence one can confidently expect to be part of an excited crowd. Watching on television is a second best if one cannot get tickets; and in that case, the preferred spectator experience—again, related to how much emotional intensity the game is expected to generate among its spectators—is to assemble a group of fans, a mini-crowd that provides its own resonance for building up shared excitement. Even for games that are routine—without important implications in the league standings, or other such significance—a large part of the pleasures of attending consists in just the moments when the crowd collectively builds up a sense of anticipation and its shared enthusiasm over the flow of events.

Games are rituals, contrived to produce situations of dramatic tension and victory; the rules of scoring and moving into position to score have been tinkered with over the years in order to make it "a better game"—which is to say, to provide moments of collective emotion. It is perfectly in keeping with such developments that sports emblems become sacred objects, venerated and treated with respect. Sports celebrities are themselves sacred objects, in just the same manner that Durkheim (1912/1965, 243–44) describes a political leader becoming an emblem for the crowd of which he is a center of attention (see chapter 1). The overt intent of the game—to win victories by following certain rules of competition, or to display athletic skill—is merely the surface content. What motivates people to witness games is primarily the experience of being at a highly successful ritual: successful because it has been contrived so that the ritual ingredients will all be present to a very high degree, especially the occurrence of strong emotion in a setting where it can be amplified by bodily interaction within the crowd focusing attention on the action of the game. The leisure time of modern societies—since the mid-nineteenth century when a sufficiently large group of spectators became available, free from the constraints of household and work—has become dominated by this species of deliberately invented ritual, designed to provide moments of ritual solidarity that previously would have been provided by religion, warfare, or political ceremony.

Sports events do not have the same recognized status as other formal rituals, but are generally regarded as a form of play, of the non-serious part of the world. Nevertheless, they are eminently successful in providing high points of ritual experience, and for many people they are preferred to participating in religious rituals (as evident when games compete with church services on Sundays). Games are natural rituals insofar as they unconsciously or nondeliberately bring about the ingredients for a successful ritual. But they are scheduled, predictable, and contrived (using a ritual technology to generate what might be considered an artificial ritual experience), and they bring together a community that has no other coherence, and no other purpose, than the experience of the peaks of ritual emotion itself.

The mechanism operates in the case of other forms of entertainment. Attending a concert has little advantage over listening to recordings as far as hearing the music is concerned; generally one hears it best on recordings. It is the experience of belonging to a focused crowd that provides the lure of a popular entertainment group; all the more so if the entertainers already have the status of being a sacred object, giving fans the additional excitement of being close to them—even if it is hundreds of feet away in a big arena. The main experience of the pop concert is the mood of the other fans; this is a textbook case of mutual buildup of emotion through bodily feedback in all its modalities. The same applies to a classical music performance, although the mood is more sedate, in keeping with the difference in social-class tone and atmosphere. Here, too, it is the experience of being at a special event—the hush of attention before the orchestra starts, the collective focus on the musicians—that makes the experience at the opera or the symphony a more significant experience than listening to the same music privately at home. This is not simply a matter of being seen by other people at a high-culture event—since under contemporary conditions these crowds are typically anonymous, in contrast to the more enclosed high-status communities in previous centuries who recognized each other at the opera—but comes from the subjective feelings of the ritual experience. The hypothesis is that participants have a stronger identification as persons attached to high culture if the crowd has been enthusiastic in response to the performance, than when the collective response is weaker; and that the effect of ritual intensity is stronger than the effect of being recognized by other people.

Televised and radio-broadcast concerts have such effects only weakly. The same holds for political and religious gatherings. Politicians' campaign speeches, nominating conventions, and important official addresses are televised and can be experienced at a distance. Nevertheless, persons who are strong partisans want to be physically present, confirming a reciprocal relation between identity and physical presence. The hypothesis is that attending political events in person increases partisanship, to the extent that the speech is a "good one"— in other words, that it involves the interplay of speaker and crowd that builds up shared enthusiasm; and reciprocally, those persons who already have an identification with the political leader or faction have a stronger desire to take part. The running off of these repetitive relationships is a self-reinforcing IR chain.

Religious ceremonial, too, can be broadcast by radio and television, and ministers (primarily in the United States) have made their reputation as media evangelists (Hadden and Swann 1981). Nevertheless, broadcast religious services do not displace personal attendance, but reinforce and enhance it. The successful media evangelist broadcasts not just the preaching or the events at the altar, but a large crowd at the worship service: the cameras make an effort to portray the congregation into which the remote viewers and listeners can project themselves. Broadcast evangelists become media stars; this further enhances their draw as sacred objects that audiences want to be close to. There is a rush to attend the service in person, indeed precisely when it is being broadcast, as if this amplifies the halo of being in the center of religious action. The draw of close personal contact—as close as big crowds allow—operates for traditional as well as evangelical churches; tours of the pope draw enormous crowds.

Religious services, like other collective experience of ritual, vary in their intensity. Distance media can provide some of the sense of shared attention and emotion, which give a feeling of attraction, membership, and respect. The strongest effects are reserved, however, for full bodily assembly. Conversion experiences—coming forward to be born again, or otherwise committing oneself to a life of religious dedication—hap-

Figure 2.5 The preacher as a sacred object: Billy Graham and admirers (1962).

pen primarily at big evangelical meetings (Johnson 1971). Personal presence in a crowd, worked up collectively to a strong shared emotions, gives the impetus for reshaping one's identity. The downside of religious conversion confirms the pattern as well. A considerable proportion of persons who are born again drop out of religious participation within a year; many persons are born again numerous times (Bromley 1988; Richardson 1978). It is the big, intense religious gatherings that bring forth the emotion and the shift in membership attachment; as one settles back into the routine of smaller and less collectively emotional church services, and then drifts away from attending, the identification and the emotional energy also fade.

I have drawn these comparisons from large-scale, for the most part formal ceremonial gatherings, and conclude that remote communications give some sense of ritual participation—if at a lower level of intensity—especially through hearing the voices of the audience and through visuals that focus on audience members like the viewers themselves. Does this hold for small-scale natural rituals such as sociable gatherings? In principle, one could hold a party via a conference call, but I have never heard of anyone doing it. At most, I have suggested, a missing guest might phone in to a celebration that is taking place, to address those who are bodily present; but this confirms the sense that the one on the phone is the one who is missing, and indeed the content of the message generally mentions that voice contact is a poor substitute for being there in person. The same is true of appearing by remote visual, such as sending a video tape. When video conferencing becomes widely available, there will be opportunity to test the intensity that can be reached in social rituals carried out by a combination of remote voice and picture. My prediction is that parties and visits will not go away; that remote hookups however vivid will always be considered weak substitutes for the solidarity of actual bodily presence (Turner 2002 reaches similar conclusions). People will go on meeting for a drink or for coffee when they have something important to discuss, or want to establish or express a personal tie. One difference between remote communication and bodily presence is that the former does not usually involve taking refreshments; although there is no reason why persons could not have a drink vicariously, telling each other over the phone what they are drinking, even toasting each other. But this is almost never done; it seems a violation of the spirit of the drinking ritual not to be drinking together, touching glasses, raising them to one's mouth together.[6] The physical substance ingested—the alcohol, coffee, tea, soft drinks, the party cake, the shared dinner, or, in older times, a shared smoke—of course have some sensory character of their own. But they are not solitary pleasures, of the kind they would be if several persons tried to carry out a dinner party by telephone, with each eating their own meal while talking on the line. The ingestion of food and drink is part of the bodily coparticipation; these are ritual substances when they are consumed together in the atmosphere of a sociable occasion.[7] If, we should admit, some degree of intersubjectivity and shared mood can take place by phone, and perhaps by remote video (although the effect would be diminished by lack of reciprocal communication), this nevertheless seems pale compared to face-to-face, embodied encounters.

On the whole, it appears that large-scale, relatively formal rituals come off better by remote communication than do small-scale natural rituals. This seems to be so because large-scale rituals are working with established symbols, already build up through previous iteration of an IR chain. Relatively impersonal rituals convey membership in large groups, only part of which ever assembles in one place; and thus distance communication gives a sense of something large that one belongs to. But this is effective only if there is at least intermittent personal contact with some other members, worshipers of the same symbols. And the remote broadcast must convey the audience's participation, not merely its leaders or performers.

How then do we assess recent forms of communication, including email and the Internet? For the most part, these lack the flow of interaction in real time; even if electronic communications happen within minutes, this is not the rhythm of immediate vocal participation, which as we shall see, is honed to tenths of seconds. There is little or no buildup of focus of attention in reading an email, no paralinguistic background signals of mutual engrossment. A written message may attempt to describe an emotion, or to cause one; but it seems rare that email is used for this purpose. A hypothesis is that the closer the flow of emails is to real conversational exchange, the more possibility of a sense of collective entrainment, as in a rapid exchange of emails in a period of minutes or seconds. But even here it is dubious that strong feelings of solidarity can be built up, or the charging up of a symbol with collective significance.

My main hypothesis is to the contrary: the tendency to drop ceremonious forms in email—greetings, addressing the target by name, departing salutations—implies a lowering of solidarity. Email settles into bare utilitarian communication, degrading relations, precisely because it drops the ritual aspects.

The electronic revolution under way since the mass computerization of the 1980s and 1990s will no doubt bring further elaborations of distance communications. Nevertheless, the hypothesis of IR theory is that face-to-face communications will not disappear in the future; nor will people have any great desire to substitute electronic communication for bodily presence. People will still prefer to assemble for little social gatherings with intimates, for parties with friends; entertainment and sports events will still be considered most satisfying through attendance at live performance; political gatherings will generate more enthusiasm than their remote images. Occasions with a strong sense of sacredness will be those where people want to be there in the flesh in the presence of the spirit; weddings, funerals, high religious experiences will be attended in person or, if not, will be felt second rate.

Similarly for the inculcation of culture. Teaching by remote television hookup, already used for mass education, will be felt to be an inferior form to student-teacher contact in the same room, even if this is confined to the mutual flash of recognizing attention or inattention, and the adjusting of mood by speaker and audience.[8] For the same reason, electronic shopping, despite its convenience, is unlikely to make shops and shopping malls disappear. The experience of being in the store itself is an action on a stage, enhanced amidst the buzz of other people (Ritzer 1999; Miller 1998). Shopping in well-appointed settings is a combination of show, museum, and crowd experience, part of the "bright lights" and the action of urban experience. Buying something may be regarded as paying the price of admission to the experience, as much as or more than paying for the utiliarian value of the object purchased. For some people, and on some occasions, shopping is a utilitarian act; but the component of social ritual is a considerable part of its allure.

Not to say there may not be a great increase in the use of distance media, and that sheer economic and practical pressures may not squeeze out face contacts as inherently more troublesome and expensive. IR theory has a prediction here too: the more that human social activities are carried out by distance media, at low levels of IR intensity, the less solidarity people will feel; the less respect they will have for shared symbholic objects; and the less enthusiastic personal motivation they will have in the form of EE.

There is a special proviso. It is possible that electronic media of the future might be designed just so that they can target those aspects of human physiology that make IRs work. IRs build up high levels of focused attention and emotional entrainment; conceivably communications devices of the future could attempt to send, from nervous system to nervous system, just those signals that most enhance these shared experiences. There might well be something dangerous in such devices. For if high levels of IR intensity are the peak experience of human lives, electronic devices that send such signals would be tremendously appealing, especially if they could artificially raise such experiences to a high level on demand. IR-producing equipment might well create an extreme form of addiction. In another variant, if the devices could be manipulated by an external agent rather than by the receiver, they would be enormously powerful devices of social control. These possibilities, although perhaps still remote, are worth considering as implications of a mature IR theory. The advance of microsociology suggests dangers ahead; against these, theoretical understanding provides our best forewarning.

The main point of these comparisons is to show what bodily presence does for the intensity of IRs. Bodily presence makes it easier for human beings to monitor each other's signals and bodily expressions; to get into shared rhythm, caught up in each other's motions and emotions; and to signal and confirm a common focus of attention and thus a state of intersubjectivity. The key is that human nervous systems become mutually attuned; the comparison of various distance media shows the importance of the vocal modality, and that visual focus operates above all through monitoring other audience participants. If nervous systems could become directly entrained at long distance, the effects would be the same as bodily presence.

The Micro-Process of Collective
Entrainment in Natural Rituals

The IR model is not just a theoretical construct; it describes, with greater or lesser precision, what observably goes on in social encounters. Durkheim was, of course, laying out the initial concepts, and Goffman never stated very systematically just what were the processes of everyday interaction ritual, much less examined the causes and effects of their variations. I have attempted to do this, guided in part by the implicit logic of Durkheim's analysis, while suggesting refinements according to what subsequent micro-interactional research has turned up. Some of the most useful evidence has been gathered by microsociological researchers following the ethnomethodological program, by sociolinguists and linguistic anthropologists, and by psychologists. These research schools have their own theoretical agendas, and thus for my purposes it has been necessary to take their findings out of the theoretical context in which they were presented, and reinterpret them in the light of how they fit or modify (or possibly reject) IR theory. On the whole, the fit has been encouraging. Now there is also microsociological research carried out by Scheff and coworkers with an explicitly Durkheimian orientation; and micro-situational work in the sociology of emotions. I will argue for the coherence of many lines of work with a refined model of mutual focus and emotional entrainment.

A good micro-conversational example of the buildup of collective effervescence in natural rituals is shared laughter. The sounds of laughter are bodily produced by a rhythmic repetition of breaths caught and forcefully expelled; at the height of hilarity, this happens involuntarily. Most laughter (and its strongest intensity and pleasure) is collectively produced. Once laughter begins, it can feed upon itself.

Here is an example where one young woman is telling her sister about swimming in the nude (Jefferson 1973):

Olive: . . . . there's two places where the hot wahder comes in'nyih g'n get
        right up close to'm en ih yuz feels like yer [takin a *douche*]
Edna: [huh huh huh] ahh
        hah hah=
Olive: =[HUHH HUHH HUHHH HA HA uhh ha-uhh ha: : ha: :] huh
Edna: ...[hhh HUH HUH HAHH HA HA HA HA HUH HHHHEH!]

The brackets [indicate where both persons are vocalizing at the same time. Here Edna starts to giggle as Olive builds up to her punch line; the underlining of *douche* indicates vocal stress, but looking at this closely we see that Edna already anticipates something is coming. The equal sign = indicates precise turn-taking, with no gap between the utterances; Olive starts laughing just as Edna very briefly pauses in giggling. Now Olive has raised the volume (indicated by capitalization), and Edna, after a brief pause and one more light giggle, follows her. A few moments later Olive starts to quiet down and gradually decelerate (the colons : indicate that the syllable is drawn out); Edna is still laughing very hard in the normal gasping rhythm, but when Olive has decelerated almost all the way down, Edna brings her laugh to a halt abruptly.

Laughter may start with a humorous remark or incident, but can be prolonged thereafter by further remarks or gestures, which in themselves are not funny, but in the context of the rhythm contribute to further outbursts of collective breath expulsion.[9] One further example (from Jefferson 1985):

Joe: Yih'n heah comes the inspecta.
Carol: eh-huh-huh-huh-[huh HA HA HA HA] HA *HA HA HA*
          [ha ha ah!
Mike: [U h - I t ' s B i g D a d d y]
James: [*Oh* : : let's seh let's seh . . . .

Mike's remark "It's Big Daddy" comes in just on the beat when Carol is stepping up from giggling to loud laughter, and it has the effect of making her emphasize even more strongly the next series of *HA HA HA*. She quiets down when James intrudes a different kind of speech act (suggesting what they should do now), whereupon Carol abruptly forces her laugh to an end (the exclamation mark).

Laughter illustrates both the collective and rhythmically entraining aspect of micro-interactional ritual.[10] It also points up a central reason why people are attracted to high-intensity interaction rituals: perhaps the strongest human pleasures come from being fully and bodily absorbed in deeply synchronized social interaction (McClelland 1985). This is why shared laughter—otherwise merely an uncontrollable interruption of breathing patterns—is so pleasurable. It exemplifies the more general pattern of collective effervescence, and explains why people are attracted to high-intensitly interaction rituals, and why they generate feelings of solidarity. The symbols that represent these interactions hold deep connotations of pleasure for group members, and this helps make them sacred objects to defend, as well as reminders of group interactions that members would like to reestablish in future encounters.

Conversational Turn-Taking as Rhythmic Entrainment

Collective effervescence in natural rituals is not confined to momentary bursts like laughter. There is a longer process of building up a heightened mood, which can be seen through the methods of analyzing micro-details of conversation pioneered by ethnomethodologists. As we shall see, entrainment occurs especially through falling into shared rhythms—in fact shared rhythms at different periodicities in time, from the level of the speaker's turn, down to the level of fine-grained resonances that make up the paralinguistic pitch of the vocal tones.[11]

Ethnomethodology began as a theoretical program of radical micro-reductionism, emphasizing the local—which is to say, situational—production of the sense of social structure. Ethnomethodology fostered ultra-micro-empiricism, investigating social interaction in hitherto un-paralleled detail, especially by using the new portable recording devices that were just then becoming available in the 1960s and 1970s. The theoretical orientation for this research was to ferret out ethno-methods: that is, the devices by which actors sustain a sense of social structure, the tacit methods of commonsense reasoning. Thus ethno-methodology cuts at a rather different angle than the Durkheimian IR theory: the former is concerned with cognition and structure (even if structure is taken in some sense as an illusion, a mere collective belief), the latter with emotion and solidarity.[12] Nevertheless, it is easy to demonstrate that the most important research findings of ethnomethologi-cally inspired researchers display the central mechanisms of the rhythmic entrainment model.

The most common type of everyday interaction is the ordinary conversation. This has been studied since the 1970s with great precision by conversation analysists using tape-recordings. Here we find a very high degree of social coordination, indeed at the level of tenths of seconds. Sacks, Schegloff, and Jefferson (1974) specified a set of turn-taking "rules" by which conversation appears to be governed. These may be recast as a Durkheimian process once we note that the "rules" are not always followed, but that interactions break down in particular ways when particular patterns are violated.[13]

The key turn-taking rules are as follows: one person speaks at a time; when the turn is finished, another person speaks. The full force of this is not apparent until we see the minute coordination of tempos with which this is carried out. In a successful conversation, the gap between one person ending their turn and the next person starting is typically less than 0.1 second; alternatively there are very slight overlaps (ca. 0.1 sec.) between speakers.

As an example, consider the following (from Heritage 1984, 236):

E: = Oh *honey* that was a lovely *luncheon* I shoulda *ca*:lled you
      s:soo[:ner but *I:*] l:[lo:ved it. It w's just deli:ghtfu[:l.   ]
M: [((f))Oh:::] [(   )   [Well]=

```
M:   = I w's gla[d        you] (came)]
E:                [′nd yer f:]friends ] ′re so da:rli:ng,=
M:   = Oh:::[: it w′z:]
E:             [e-that P]a:t isn′she a do:[:/l?]
M:                                   [iYe]h isn't she pretty,
        (.)
E:    Oh: she's a beautiful girl.=
M:   = Yeh I think she's a pretty gir[l.
                             [En′ that Reinam′n::
        (.)
E:    She SCA:RES me.=
```

Two women have just left a luncheon party, chatting enthusiastically.
The reader might read the transcript out loud several times to get the
rhythm. The underlinings (Oh *ho*ney that was a lovely *lu*ncheon I
shoulda *ca*:lled you s:soo:ner) are emphases. The colons (:) mean that
the sound is prolonged. Parentheses that are empty ( ) or that contain
an unintelligible sound (f) indicate that the speaker's voice is too soft
to articulate anything. Parentheses containing a word (came) indicate
that the speaker is fading, usually when someone else is speaking at
the same time.

Evelyn (E) is in a rhythm, and Marge (M) is like a counterpoint in a
singing duet, following along with her. Nothing very important is
being said here, but a strong social meaning is conveyed. The rules of
turn-taking are being adhered to very closely. The equal sign (=) is
used to indicate that as soon as one person stops the other starts. Virtually every new utterance is right on the beat. The parenthesis with a
dot in it (.) indicates a gap of 1/10 second or less; these are the only
breaks in this conversation, and these are so small that they cannot
actually be noticed. In the conventions of conversation analysis, a parenthesis containing a number indicates the amount of silence between
utterances. For instance (1.0) means a 1-second gap. These are minis-
cule bits of time, but they are socially very significant. Humans can
perceive what happens in units down to about 0.2 seconds; below that
they blur together and are unconscious. That means that a gap of 1.0
seconds is actually about 5 beats of consciousness, bam-bam-bam-
bam-bam. If there is a gap in a conversation of 1.0 second, it tends to
feel like a deafening silence; and even a smaller gap feels like the
smooth flow is broken.[14]

A more sociological way to state the turn-taking rule is: successful
talk has no gaps and no overlaps; no embarrassing pauses between
speakers or within utterances, and a minimal amount of struggle over
who gets the floor to speak at any one moment. What we mean by

successful talk here is that it is socially successful, a conversational ritual generating solidarity among the speakers. The success of conversational turn-taking, like the degree of solidarity in IRs generally, is variable. Some conversations are awkward, lacking in solidarity because they are full of pauses, and other conversations are hostile and mutually at loggerheads because the participants keep interrupting one another and struggle to keep the other from speaking. The point that stands out is that successful conversational ritual is rhythmic: one speaker comes in at the end of the other's turn with split-second timing, coming in right on the beat as if keeping up a line of music.

We may characterize conversations that follow this pattern as high-solidarity conversations: friendly chatting or animated discussions among friends. But solidarity is a variable; not all conversations are of this sort, and in fact this variability is just what we want to explain. Some interactions are more solidary than others, thus producing the differentiated field of social encounters that make up real life. The turn-taking "rules" can be violated in two directions. Two (or more) persons could all speak at the same time. Or turn-taking can fail because one person stops talking and the other person does not pick up immediately. In fact, the gaps need not be very large in order to signal that there is a breakdown in solidarity; what is colloquially known as an "embarrassing pause" is often on the order of 1.5 seconds or less. The baseline of normal solidarity conversation is that turns are coordinated at tempos of tenths of seconds; anything as long as 0.5 second is already missing several beats, and longer periods are experienced subjectively as huge gaps.

For this kind of failure of solidarity, consider the following example (Heritage 1984, 248):

A: Is there something bothering you or not?
    (1.0)
A: Yes or no
    (1.5)
A: Eh?
B: No.

This is obviously a strained relationship. A and B could be a parent and child, or two spouses who are not getting along. What is striking here is that the gaps are, after all, not really very long. But in conversational time, 1.5 seconds seems like an eternity. Even a shorter break is noticed by conversationalists, because it seems like an "embarrassing pause." And embarrassment, as Goffman (1967) noted, is a sign that the social relationship is not working as expected.

The other way solidarity can break down is through a violation of "no gap, no overlap" in the other direction. This is the pattern that we find in angry arguments, when both participants try to talk at the same time, typically speaking louder and faster in an effort to override the other. "Having the floor" is a tacit agreement as to where the focus of attention will be; a conversation is an IR that moves the focus of attention, according to these agreed-upon "rules," from one speaker to another. Ritual solidarity breaks down when no one wants to talk; the focus of attention evaporates into thin air. It also breaks down when the participants want to maintain a focus of attention, but they dispute who is going to be in the focus, and thus whose words are going to be the symbolic object that will receive ritual attention and endorsement.[15]

Consider the following example (Schegloff 1992, 1335):

A: . . .we have a concern for South Vietnam's territorial integrity which is why we're the:re. But our primary concern regarding *our* personnel, *any* military commander has that primary *loyal*[ty.

B: [No? Are:n' we there because of U.N. uh—doctrine?

A: [No:::

B: [Aren't we there under the [the (   ) -

A: [*Where* didju ever get *that* cockeyed idea.

B: Whaddya *mea:n.*

A: *U.*N. doctrine.

B: We're there, representin' the U. *N.* No?

A: Wouldu- You go ask the U.N., and you'll get laughed out. *No..*

B: We're there because- of our interests.

A: [Yes.

B: [We're not there wavin the U.N. flag?

A: We're- There's no U.N. flag *there.* Thet's not a United Nations force. The United Nations has never taken a single action on this. ((pause))

A: [I-

B: [*No.* I think (this ti::me)- I think you're *wrong.*

A: *Sorry* sir, I'd suggest yuh check yer facts.

B: I think y- I uh [(   )

A: [I will refrain from telling you you don't know what cher talking abou[t,

B: [I [wish you *would.*

A: [I just suggest you [talk- you check yer facts.

B: [I wish you *would.*

B: Because this's what I read in- in the *news*papers.

[That we represent-

A: [Well, then you been reading some *pretty ba:d*
newspapers.

B: [We represent the U.N. there.

A: [F'give me, but I gotta go.

A: Sir, I would suggest thet if that's the case you switch newspapers.

B: Well I hope I c'n call you ba:ck an' *correct* you.

A: L'k *you* check it out. 'n call me.

B: I'll do [so.

A: [Okay?

B: I certainly *will*.

A: Mm *gu*'night.

As the argument builds up, the speakers interrupt each other, then talk over each other for extended periods. Even as they attempt to close off the discussion at the end and return to normal politeness, they can't refrain from additional digs and overlaps. The pattern of emphases throughout also conveys a series of vocal jabs.

This is not a full-scale treatise on sociolinguistics, so we will have to forego many complexities.[16] But let us note a few objections. "No gap, no overlap" may be culturally variable. That is, the generalization is based on tape-recordings made among native English speakers in the United States and Britain, and may not be valid everywhere. Thus there are tribal societies (according to comments made by participants at symposiums where this conversational model has been presented) where typically there are fairly long gaps between one speaker and another; indeed, speaking too quickly after another is regarded as a violation. This suggests a reformulation, but not necessarily a rejection of the model of conversation as solidarity-producing rhythmic coordi-nation.[17] The key process is to keep up the common rhythm, whatever it may be. Where this is done, the result is solidarity; where it is vio-lated, either by speaking too soon or too hesitantly, the result is felt as aggressive encroachment, or as alienation, respectively.[18]

An advantage in getting beyond the rule-following frame of refer-ence is to see how conversations have to be built up over time; thus they go through crucial passages where the conversation (and hence the social relationship) may or may not come off. Many conversations do not get off the ground; opening gambits are not taken, or do not hook into sufficient response to start building up the rhythmic coordi-nation. Once a conversation takes off, it builds a self-sustaining mo-mentum; as is clear from everyone's experience, this varies tremen-dously from one combination of interlocutors to another. Indeed, this is a principal way in which lines of social cleavage are enacted; one can say, as a crude approximation, that members of the same status group are those who are able to sustain highly entraining conversational rituals whereas members of different status groups are those who cannot. This captures part of the ingredients that make or break a conversational IR. But there are also instances in which the flow can go either way, given the same participants.

An example easy for academics to observe is the question period at the end of a lecture or conference presentation. Frequently this begins with a long pause; the subjective experience of members of the audience at that moment is that they can think of nothing to say. Yet if the pause is broken, usually by the highest-status member of the audience asking a question, the following question tends to come after a shorter pause; and by the third or fourth question, multiple hands go up. This shows that the audience was not lacking in symbolic capital, in things to talk about, but in emotional energy, the confidence to think and speak about these ideas; not that they had nothing to say, but that could not think of it until the group attention shifted toward interaction including the audience. Nor is this a matter of the speaker being uninteresting; often an especially successful speaker is the biggest show-stopper. This is best understood as a process of monopolizing the focus of attention; the speaker is elevated into too remote a realm, surrounded by too much of an aura of respect (Durkheimian sacredness) to be approached.[19] Once the approach has been made (high-status members of the audience are best positioned to do so because of their store of EE), and the focus of attention shifted to a back-and-forth exchange, the momentum flows another way, and questions seem to be pulled in as if by magnetism.

This flow of initiative from one speaker to another is the turn-taking process again. The classic conversation analysis model of Sacks et al. expressed this in a simplified way: the last speaker gets to determine the next speaker, either by addressing someone or by taking another turn him / herself. David Gibson (1999, 2001) provides a more refined model, based on examining the sequence of turn-taking in a large number of management meetings in a large corporation. Gibson shows that there are a few typical ways in which turns pass from one speaker to another, while other possible sequences of turns are extremely rare, and may be negatively sanctioned. Most typically, one person speaks, then another answers (in Gibson's representation AB:BA, A speaks to B, then B speaks to A). If this goes on at length, it constitutes a kind of conversational ping-pong game, in which two persons monopolize the conversation and everyone else is reduced to spectators. We can understand the situational force in this when we note that the spectators often chafe in the role but cannot find a way to break in once the pair has the momentum. Other typical patterns are for the speaker to address the whole group (or make an undirected remark into the air). Gibson gives this as AO:XA, indicating that the most typical next turn is for someone in the group to take the floor but direct a comment back to A. Even when there is an interruption (instead of AB:BA, there is AB:XA, where X is someone who wasn't addressed), typically the interrupter breaks into the ongoing conversation, usually speaking to the last speaker (AB:XA) or to the last person addressed (AB:XB), but not to someone completely new. I would say that a group conversation is like passing a ball around, where the ball consists of the focus of attention. This focus entrains everyone present to follow its progress around the room; when someone breaks in, it is done by latching onto someone who either immediately or very recently was in the focus. The metaphor of passing a ball isn't quite right; it is more like the image of a ball on a screen in time-lapse leaving a trail of electronic particles just behind it. Once again we see conversational IR as a flow of entrainment in a focus of attention; this remains so even when there is a struggle over getting into that focus. As Gibson emphasizes (2001), the structural constraints on getting the floor—getting into a temporally limited attention space—are a major determinant on how influence is situationally enacted, even in formal organizations.

A similar process operates in large public gatherings such as political rallies and debates. A rousing political speaker draws interruptions of applause; but the audience starts to build up its applause in the seconds preceding the speaker coming to his / her punch line; viewed on video tape, it looks as if the crowd is making the speaker say the words that they will greet with their peak of coordinated noise (Atkinson 1984; Clayman 1993). Examining the sequence in micro-detail, we see that both speaker and audience are caught up in a rhythm; the speaker's rhetorical utterances have a pattern of stresses and pauses, repetitions, and accretions (this is what gives public speaking a distinctive rhetorical tone), which let the audience know that something is coming, and at what moment they can join in with maximal effect. Similarly on the audience side: recordings of applauding or booing show that the audience builds up its noise in a distinctive rhythm; a few initial voices or handclaps unleash a rapid acceleration of noise as the full audience joins in; whereas abortive applause fails at a certain moment in this temporal sequence if this rapid acceleration has not taken off, tacitly signaling to others that if they join in they will be exposed in an isolated minority instead of joining triumphantly in a shared focus of attention. For similar reasons, booing is harder to bring to a critical mass of participation, and drops off in a shorter time than applauding. As is generally the case in micro-interaction, solidarity processes are easier to enact than conflict processes. As I will show elsewhere, the implication is that conflict is much easier to organize at a distance, against unseen groups, than in the immediate interactional situation.

In the following example (from Clayman 1993, 113), bbbbbbbb indicates sustained booing; xxxxxx indicates applause; zzzzzz indicates a buzz of uncoordinated audience sounds. Capitals (XXXXX; BBBBBB) indicate loud applause or booing; x-x-x-x-x-x and b-b-b-b-b-b indicate weak noises, and x x x x or b b b b are isolated single hand claps or boos:

DQ: . . .and if qualifications alo::ne (.) .h are going to *be*: the *is*sue in this campaign. (1.0) *George Bu*sh has more qualifications than Michael Dukakis and Lloyd Bentsen com*bi*ned.

        (0.6)
AUD: xxx-xxXXXXXXXXXXXXXXXXXXXXXXXXXXXXXXXXX[XXXXXXXXXX=
AUD: [b-b-b-b
AUD: XXXXX[XXXXXXXXXXXXXXXx[xxxxxxxxxx-x-x-x h x h x x x x (8.5)
AUD: [bbbbbbbbBBBBBBBBBBB[BBBBBBBBBbbb-b-b (2.9)
MOD: [Senator Bentsen-

Here the applause, after a scattered beginning, successfully accelerates, and continues for a typical rhythmic unit for applause consisting of about eight seconds (very strong applause responses go on for another one or even more such eight-second units). Halfway into the applause segment, there is a failed effort to get booing going; a second effort successfully builds up to loud booing toward the end of the applause segment, and even overtakes the applause at just the moment when the moderator attempts to return to the debaters. Even with this momentary triumph, the booing quickly subsides thereafter while the applause fades more slowly. As we see from the numbers in parentheses, the booing lasts for a much shorter time (2.9 vs. 8.5 seconds).

These processes of rhythmic coordination are almost always unconscious. The success or failure of a natural ritual is felt rather than thought, at least initially; although, of course, reflective persons could comment on it, to others or to themselves, thereby putting a verbal interpretation upon it. There is a repertoire of cultural symbols that make up the content of these conversations; and we shall examine later just where the significance of symbols arises and how it is propagated from one IR in the chain to another. Possession of a stock of shared symbols is one of the ingredients that goes into the success (and lack of such possession is a condition for the failure) of an IR to build up collective effervescence. What we are examining here, in analytical sep-aration, is the micro-mechanism by which situational solidarity occurs; this is what charges up the ongoing social significance of a stock of verbal symbols, or dissipates them into meaninglessness.

Experimental and Micro-Observational Evidence on Rhythmic Coordination and Emotional Entrainment

Besides turn-taking, other aspects of interaction become rhythmically coordinated, some to a very fine degree. Films of conversations show that speakers and listeners both tend to time their bodily movements to the rhythm of the words being spoken (Condon and Ogston 1971; Kendon 1970, 1980; Capella 1981). The body movements are rapid and subtle: nodding the head, blinking eyes, and other gestures. Often they are too rapid to be seen by the normal eye and become visible only when a film shot at 24 frames per second is played back frame by frame. Much of this research has centered on interactions between mothers and babies, the epitome of a high-solidarity situation. Neo-nates as young as a few weeks or months synchronize vocalizations and movements with those of adults (Condon and Sander 1974a, 1974b; Contole and Over 1981), long before they learn to talk. This sug-gests that rhythmic synchronization may be the basis of talking—an outgrowth of naturally occurring IRs. Infants in hospital nurseries often engage in contagious crying; they also match the pitch level of voices that they hear (Hatfield et al. 1994, 83). Electroencephalograph (EEG) recordings reveal that synchronization can occur between the rhythmic brain waves of adults who are conversing, as well as between infants and adults (Condon and Sander 1974a, 1974b). When EEG syn-chronization does not happen, there are typically group boundaries; it is less likely in conversations between black and white adults than among whites.

Besides the timing of gestures and brain waves, conversationalists synchronize various features of their voices: pitch register and range, loudness, tempo, accent, duration of syllables (clipped or drawled sounds) (Gregory 1983; Hatfield et al. 1994, 28). As a conversation goes on, partners tend to adapt their speech patterns and rhythms to one another (Gregory 1983; Jaffe and Feldstein 1970; Warner 1979; Warner et al. 1983). Erickson and Shultz (1982, 72) sum up: "Whereas there is no metronome playing while people talk, their talking itself serves as a metronome." In some conversations, synchronization comes and goes, building up and fading at different moments; but especially among couples engaged in lengthy conversations, synchrony built up and stayed high (Capella and Planalp 1981; Capella 1981).

Rhythmic synchronization is correlated with solidarity. Psychologists have shown this for several kinds of micro-behavior. On the vocal dimension, where conversations are closely coordinated in rhythm, the speakers like each other better (Hatfield et al. 1994, 29, 41–44). This is also true for bodily movements; among young couples, those who felt the most rapport were the ones whose videotaped movements had the greatest degree of mimicry and synchrony. The most striking synchrony is found among male / female couples in the process of moving from acquaintance to courtship, where the pair gradually turn more and more of their bodies toward each other, mirroring each other's gestures and touches, becoming absorbed in gazing at each other. Synchronization builds up from momentary and partial to full body synchronization, and new lovers can stay locked into this mode for hours (Perper 1985, 77–79).

Psychological experiments and detailed observations have shown that fine-honed mimicry and synchronization occur quite widely among humans. There is nevertheless a limitation on much of this research thus far. We know that synchronization and emotional contagion often happen, but there is less evidence on when it happens more, less, or not at all. Psychologists have tended to approach this issue by comparing individuals to find what character traits are related to being more susceptible or less susceptible to emotional contagion (Hatfield et al. 1994); what we miss is the dynamics that make some situations build up to high synchronization, while others fail. The experimental method fosters an orientation to individual traits, especially when research subjects are administered questionnaires asking them to describe their typical behavior and feelings, a method that abstracts away from the flow of situations. The radical microsociologist, on the other hand, is inclined to think that anyone can be molded into anything, given a strong enough situational process (or chain of such situations). In terms of figure 2.1, psychological experiments and micro-observational analysis alike have piled up evidence for shared mood, action in common, and, to some extent, rhythmic entrainment. What is largely missing is the mutual focus of attention. I suggest that this is what makes the difference between situations in which emotional contagion and all the other aspects of rhythmic entrainment build up to high levels, and those in which they reach only low levels or fail completely. This is above all what rituals do: by shaping assembly, boundaries to the outside, the physical arrangement of the place, by choreographing actions and directing attention to common targets, the ritual focuses everyone's attention on the same thing and makes each one aware that they are doing so. This is the mechanism that needs more fine-grained research.

A convenient instrument for gauging the degree of solidarity that exists in an interaction is provided by the sociologist Stanford Gregory: a device for analyzing tape recordings of the sounds people make during conversation. By applying instrumentation for Fast Fourier Transform analysis (FFT) to conversation recordings, Gregory and his colleagues (1993, 1994) show that acoustical voice frequencies become attuned as conversations become more engrossing. This is rhythmic synchronization at a level much more fine-grained than the 0.2-second segments of which humans can be consciously aware. The micro-frequencies of voice tones in high-solidarity conversations converge on a fundamental frequency in a region of the sound spectrum below the range in which cognitively meaningful information is carried. If the higher-pitched frequencies are electronically removed (the ones that carry the content of what is being said), the recording sounds like a low-pitched buzz; it is quite literally this humming sound that is the "sound of solidarity." This suggests a nonintrusive, nonverbal means of researching solidarity in situations.

Synchronization of bodily movements has been found in large groups mobilized for collective action. One study of a macro-ritual, a political demonstration, found that the micro-coordination of movements among the demonstrators was much higher than a comparison group of ordinary pedestrians, and greater even than a marching band (Wohlstein and McPhail 1979). This is what we would expect if the demonstrators had the highest degree of emotional arousal and solidarity of these social groupings, feeding back into their shared actions and mutual focus of attention.

On the extreme micro-level, this synchronization must be unconscious. Synchronized gestures occur within time segments as rapid as 21 milliseconds (0.02 seconds), but humans are capable of overtly reacting to a stimulus only in 0.4 or 0.5 seconds, with some athletes capable of responding in 0.250 ms. (Kendon 1980; Hatfield et al. 1994, 38). Only slow playback of film frames reveals these patterns; indeed, people in conversation can synchronize their gestures in half of a film frame (42 ms.). Other synchronized behaviors, such as brain waves, or voice pitch range (how narrowly or widely the micro tones vary) are not even noticeable without specialized instruments. How, then, are people able to synchronize? The implication is that they have fallen into the same rhythm, so that they can anticipate where the next "beat" will fall. Chapple (1981) has called this *rhythmic entrainment*. Individuals who get into the flow of an interaction have made a series of adjustments that bring their rhythms together; hence they can "keep the beat" with what their partner is doing by anticipation, rather than by reaction.

It is because of these shared rhythms that turn-taking can be so finely coordinated, so that in a high-solidarity conversation the gaps are less than 0.1 second, less than we can perceive without instruments. "I say: 'I'll talk to you *la*-ter,' and as I especially delineate the pacing of '*la*-ter,' with a precisely accented undulation, you tightly latch on to the pulsing of my moves and place your 'Goodbye' on the next down-beat to end the phone call" (Sudnow 1979, 114). In his book *Talk's Body* (1979), the ethnomethodologist David Sudnow compared the experience of learning to play jazz piano with the experience of producing a flow of words at a typewriter keyboard. Both, he noted, are bodily activities that become successful when it is no longer a matter of transcribing notes (either musical or verbal) but of throwing oneself into the rhythm of making musical phrases or sentences. Thus adults encourage small children in learning to talk, not by explaining what words mean, but by joining with them in a speech rhythm; initially this consists largely of nonsensical sounds or the same words playfully repeated over and over.

Emotional contagion is a socio-physiological fact. Sociophysiology (Barchas and Mendoza 1984) shows how an individual's physiological condition is affected by current and recent social experience. Face-to-face social interaction takes place among physiological systems, not merely among individuals as cognitive systems or bodily actors. From an evolutionary perspective, it is not surprising that human beings, like other animals, are neurologically wired to respond to each other; and that social situations that call forth these responses are experienced as highly rewarding.

Sociable conversation—talking just for the sake of keeping up friendly contact—is the most basic of all interaction rituals; and that solidarity is constructed and intensified within a ritual by rhythmic coordination. If the key process is to keep up the conversational flow, then what one says is chosen in order to keep up one's expected participation, not because one necessarily believes it, thinks it important, or has anything worthwhile to say. Conversation is thus doubly ritualistic: formally in the sense of following the patterns of the interaction ritual model; and substantively ritualistic (i.e., closer to the ordinary, pejorative use of the term) in the sense of going through the motions for the sake of the activity, rather than for its apparent content. The content of talk is chosen for the sake of the rhythms of interaction. In William Butler Yeats's phrase, these are "songs rewritten for the tune's sake."

Joint Attention as Key to Development of Shared Symbols

Rhythmic coordination and emotional entrainment are necessary ingredients of an IR; but it also requires a mutual focus of attention. This is what George Herbert Mead (1925, 1934) called taking the role of the other, and he proposed that it is the key to what makes human consciousness. The importance of mutual focus is demonstrated by a considerable body of research on cognitive development. Tomasello (1999) marshals evidence from experiments and observations on small children, chimpanzees and other primates, other mammals, as well as from comparisons with autistic children.

Human infants from soon after birth engage in turn-taking pseudo-conversations with adult caretakers; these interactions have the same finely modulated rhythmic back-and-forth flow of turns as high-solidarity talk. Infants also engage in affect attunement, matching and building up emotions. In our terminology, several components of the IR model are operative: bodily assembly, emotional entrainment, collective effervescence. We can also infer that one important outcome is present, a solidarity tie, at least in the form of attachment to a particular adult parent or caretaker. It seems also the case that infants are acquiring a level of emotional energy from these interactions. We can infer this from the negative case, where infants raised without much interaction with caretakers are deeply depressed (see research on WWII orphanages, and on monkeys fed by wire-dummy mothers rather than live mothers: Bowlby 1965; Harlow and Mears 1979). In terms of Mead's model of the "I," "me," and "Generalized Other," the infant engaging in this kind of rhythmic and emotional entrainment with an adult has none of these components of the self. There is an action component that Mead called the "I," but the baby's action is strongly entrained toward the adult, and thus consists largely in the emotional energy that is in the pattern of social solidarity. There is no cognitively independent "I."

Around nine to twelve months occurs a momentous change, which Tomasello refers to as "the nine-month revolution." Now the child is able to engage in joint attention with an adult, a scene in which both point to or carry out an action toward an object. This is a three-component interaction, involving two persons and the object to which they are jointly paying attention. The child now is showing not just an awareness of the object or of the other person, but an awareness that the other's focus is the same as his / her own focus. This is what IR theory calls the mutual focus of attention. The pointing or gesturing toward the object is often vocal—the act of naming and referring to the object; it is the beginning of language as a use of symbols that have shared meaning (Bruner 1983). These vocal gestures are genuine symbols, not just "signs." They embody practical procedures for getting things done that have become habitual through the experience of practicing with a particular other person; they are mental references. From this time onward, children begin to learn to talk in the shared adult language. In contrast, autistic children, who have difficulty learning to speak, also have great difficulty with joint attention, as well as in playing with other children.

Tomasello interprets the process of joint attention as emerging from the child ascribing a sense of intentions to the other person, a desire that precedes the action; not that this is a consciously represented notion of the child as having an intentional self, which is projected onto the adult—since there is as yet no symbolic apparatus in which a child could formulate such a representation—but a recognition by the child that the other is "like me."

The full-scale IR model is now complete: on the ingredient side, there is now mutual focus of attention, joining and enhancing the already existing emotional entrainment; on the outcome side, shared symbols are now being created. There is another change in the child's behavior at this point. After age 1, shyness starts to emerge, as well as coyness around others and in front of mirrors; the child is developing a self-image from the viewpoint of other people. In the terminology of G. H. Mead, the child's self now has a "me," going along with the capacity to take the role of the other.

For the IR model, the "nine-month revolution" via joint attention or mutual focus is the crucial turning point, launching the child into the full-fledged human world of shared symbols. There remain many different ways in which persons can orient toward symbols, so let us trace the child's development, using Tomasello's summary, one stage further. Around age 3 to 5, children come to see other persons not only as intentional agents but as mental agents; that is, not only do they recognize that other people have an intention behind their actions, but they recognize them as having mental processes that are not necessarily expressed in action. The child at the "nine-month revolution" carries out joint attention with an adult and perceives the verbal gesture not merely as a physical movement that the adult is making with his / her mouth (similar to a physical gesture with a finger) but as an intentional reference, an action of communicating. The child is entering into a world of shared symbolic gestures, taking completely to heart what meaning the adult is communicating. The child at the three-to-five-year transition is now perceiving that what other persons say is not necessarily what they actually believe or what they will actually do; the child's universe has expanded to include the possibility of false beliefs and lying. Put more positively, the child perceives that other people do not always see the world the same way they do, and that there are a variety of perspectives from which it can be seen.

The change is easiest to encompass in Mead's term, the "Generalized Other." This change makes the self's representation of the world more abstract; in addition to taking the perspective of particular other people and aligning oneself with them, the child now can take the perspective of other people in general, an intersection or resultant of all these perspectives. This changes the child's inner self as well. It is now possible both to internalize rules and increase the amount of self-direction under social influence, and simultaneously to have a stronger sense of self as an autonomous, self-reflective agent. These are the years that children become deliberately willful, the "terrible twos" and "terrible threes," when children show or flaunt increasing autonomy from parents' demands; this stage is a shift away from the very strong social embeddedness that follows directly from the joint attention consciousness in the "nine-month revolution."

And this is also the period when external talk begins to be internalized; children talking to themselves out loud, or to imaginery playmates, and then increasingly in subvocal self-talk, internal conversation. What is emerging is the additional level of reflexivity in Mead's theory of the self, in which the "I" can now deliberately manipulate symbolic representations, distancing itself from the here-and-now and from immediate social demands, to think of alternative pathways out of the situation. In this sense, Mead's conception of the "I" is an adult "I"; it emerges in this full reflexive sense as an independent agent only after the Generalized Other has crystallized.

Solidarity Prolonged and Stored in Symbols

High levels of emotional entrainment—collective effervescence—are ephemeral. How long will the solidarity and the emotional mood last? This depends on the transformation of short-term emotions into long-term emotions, which is to say, the extent to which they are stored in symbols that reinvoke them. Symbols, in turn, differ as to what kind of group solidarity they invoke, and thus what symbolic / emotional memories or meanings will do in affecting group interactions, and personal identities, in future situations.

Consider a range of situations where collective emotion is generated. At the lowest level are situations where a number of people are assembled, but with a very low focus of attention. Such would be people in a public waiting place like an airport departure lounge, or a queue lined up for tickets. Here there is little common mood, possibly even impatience and annoyance because the focus of different individuals and subclusters are at cross purposes. Nothing is prolonged from these situations except the fleeting desire to get it over with and get out of there.

At a higher intensity are situations with a buzz of excitement: being on a busy street in a city, in a crowded restaurant or bar. There is a palpable difference between being in an establishment where there are lots of people and one that is nearly empty. Unfocused crowds generate more tacit interaction than very sparse assemblies, and thus give a sense of social atmosphere. Even though there is no explicit interaction or focus of attention in such places, there is a form of social attraction to being there. Being in a crowd gives some sense of being "where the action is," even if you personally are not part of any well-defined action; the lure of the "bright lights of the city" is not so much the visual illumination but the minimal excitement of being within a mass of human bodies.[20] As Durkheim indicates, the first step toward building up the "electricity" of collective effervescence is the move from sparse to dense bodily assembly. But in this alone there is little sense of solidarity with a recognizable group, and nothing that can prolong a sense of identification. What is lacking are symbols by means of which one could identify who was there, and that could reinvoke a sense of membership upon seeing them at another occasion.

A somewhat higher level of solidarity becomes possible in crowds that are focused by acting as an audience. Here the momentary sense of solidarity may become quite strong, insofar as the crowd takes part in a collective action—clapping, cheering, booing. These momentarily shared events, as we have seen, involve considerable micro-temporal coordination, a condition of collective entrainment that has very strong boundaries, intensely palpable when they are violated: one feels embarrassed when clapping at the wrong time or booing when others do not join in. The sense of collective solidarity and identity is stronger to just the extent that the crowd goes beyond being passive observers to actively taking part. This is an experience not only of responding to other people in the crowd (and to those on the stage, the playing field, or the podium) but of affecting them, thus becoming more of a part of the mutual entrainment by throwing oneself into it more fully.[21] Thus applause is no mere passive response; the pleasure of the performance is to a considerable degree created in those moments when one has the opportunity to applaud, and from the audience's side the performer or the political speech-maker is being used to facilitate one's own feeling of collective action. Such effects are visible in a very high degree in collective experience where the crowd becomes very active, and especially in destructive or violent acts. Thus taking part in an ethnic riot

(Horowitz 2001) is not simply a way of acting out a preexisting ethnic identity, but a way of strengthening it, re-creating or even creating it. The greater the entrainment, the greater the solidarity and identity consequences; and entrainment reaches much higher levels by activity than passivity.[22]

Often these focused crowds acquire a symbol that can prolong the sense of the experience: usually this symbol is taken from whatever it was that the audience was consciously focused upon. For sports fans, this is the team itself, usually encapsulated in shorthand emblems; for entertainment fans, it is the performers, or possibly the music, play, or film itself that becomes the Durkheimian sacred object. But focused crowds nevertheless have rather weak long-term solidarity; their symbols, although charged up by the crowd's moment of collective effervescence, do not reinvoke the crowd itself, which on the whole is anonymous to most of its participants.[23] There is no way for members of the group to recognize each other or identify with each other, except via what they clapped for. Those who happened to be together at an exciting moment at a sports stadium do not have much of a tie afterward. They may share some collective symbols, such as wearing the same team emblem, but their solidarity is rather situationally specific, reserved for those occasions when they happen to be at another sporting event, or in some area of conversation around just those symbols. These are examples of secondary group identities: groups whose members do not know each other personally. Benedict Anderson (1991) famously called them "imagined communities," but this is not quite accurate. What they imagine—what they have an image of—is the symbol that they focus upon, and the "community" is a volatile and episodic experience that comes out just at moments of high ritual intensity.

Focused crowds develop their collective effervescence in those moments when they are active rather than passive spectators. But since their feeling of solidarity is prolonged by symbols that are for the most part presented to them from outside, they do not have much opportunity to use those symbols in their own lives, as ingredients for constructing similarly engrossing IRs. These are passively received symbols that must wait to be recharged when there next occurs a performance of the concert, the game, or the political assembly. At best, they can recirculate the symbols in a second-order, conversational ritual, a reflexive meta-ritual referring to these primary rituals.

In contrast to these situations where symbols are charged up by anonymous crowds, are situations that charge symbols with specific group membership. On the level of individualized encounters, personal ties are generated and enacted through IRs that produce a momentary level of intersubjectivity that is attractive enough to be repeated. I have already noted how the use of personal names is a ritual affirming the individual character of the relationship. Calling someone by their name during the course of an encounter is not just a demonstration that one knows that person's name; these rituals of personal address are typically carried out repeatedly, in virtually every encounter, even where it should be obvious from earlier encounters that the person's name is known. What is communicated is that one thinks of that person as an individual, and that this is a situation in which he or she is being treated as an individual, with a biography, a past history of relationships, in short, an IR chain. And the ritual of personal address is collective (at least in sociable situations), carrying the sense that it ought to be reciprocated, that each should call the other by his / her name; it is the enactment of a tie, individual person to individual person. An illuminating contrast is tribal societies where members of the same kinship group often do not know each other's personal names: they refer to each other, and address each other, by a title or relationship term—wife, sister's brother, second son.[24] There are corresponding situations in Western societies where individuals are referred to not by their names but by their title or position. These encounters are further down the continuum of relationships from the ritually marked meshing of individualized IR chains, but not all the way down to merely situationally anonymous coparticipation like members of a momentarily focused crowd; these are intermediate situations where there is recognition of where one fits in a group, but not of what distinguishes oneself as an individual within it.

Personal name-address rituals are a version of symbols that are used to prolong membership from one situation to the next. They also illustrate the point that the greater degree of symbolic memory and membership prolongation is connected to a greater degree of personal identification with those symbols. For a modern Western person, there is generally nothing more intensely personal than one's own name. But as our cross-societal comparisons show, there is nothing inherent or natural in identifying oneself and others as a unique individual; it is the ongoing flow of everyday name-addressing rituals that keep up these identities both as to our selves and as to others.

Contributing to a similar level of prolonged personal membership identities are the everyday conversational rituals of personal narratives. The contents of this talk are such things as what one did that day, or stories about one's experiences from the past. Much of the exchange of friendly relationships is the willingness for both sides in turn to act as a sympathetic audience to these stories, and also to take one's turn on the stage and offer some narratives of one's own. We may think of this as a circulation of particularistic cultural capital, in contrast to the generalized cultural capital that is widely available and known to larger groups, who do not necessarily know each other as personal identities. No doubt, much of the content of talk in these personal narrations is "filler," material to fill up the time spent together so that there is something to talk about. These personal narratives do not have to be true, they need mainly to be dramatic, to blow up the little mishaps of everyday life into adventures or comedies, minor adversities into martyrdoms and local scandals, in order to become good raw material for the dramatic performances on the conversational stage that make for a lively and engrossing conversation. What Goffman noted about staged performances in general holds here for conversational ritual in particular: the audience enters into the spirit of the performance by not questioning it but by taking it in a situational mood, whatever will build up the highest level of momentary collective effervescence. Successful conversations of this sort generate and cement social ties, which by the particularistic nature of their contents are ties into particular social relationships.

Sociable talk also typically involves talking about third persons, especially those known to the participants. These narratives expand the dramatic material that can be used for enhancing the success of the conversational ritual. They have a further effect, structurally very important for the prolongation of group membership: these third-person narrations, or gossip, circulate the identities of individuals within the network of those who talk to each other (Fuchs 1995). Both individual names and narratives about them are symbols, which get charged up with significance through the amount of momentary effervescence of the conversations in which they play a part.

Thus a person can become a symbol both by direct observation—the way a politician, a religious leader, or a sports figure can become an emblem for those who have seen this person in the focus of a collective ritual—and by indirect observation, by having stories and qualities attached to that person's name insofar as they are subjects for lively conversations. Whether they are positive or negative does not matter so much as the intensity with which the name figures in these conversational dramas. The accuracy of these accounts is a minor consideration in successful conversational ritual, and the further the network goes from the source, the less of a consideration it becomes at all.

This pattern applies not only to the famous, widespread reputations known among persons anonymous to each other, but also to persons whose reputations are merely local, confined to particular networks of persons who have personal links with the person being gossiped about. In the latter case, the circulation of reputation plays back into face-to-face encounters; when you meet someone of whom you have heard stories or descriptions, or who has heard about you, you are now participants in a conversation that has an additional layer of depth. It is not just the immediate symbol-repertoire that each person has to talk about with the other that determines what will be said and what kind of relationship will be enacted, but the halo or penumbra of reputation that each has in the mind of the other figures into what conversational moves will be made and how those moves are interpreted.

I have couched the analysis in terms of sociable conversations, in relationships that are friendly and casual. The same kinds of creation and prolongation of membership and identity goes on in more serious interactions, including the utilitarian encounters of business and professional life. Encounters in the world of work also have the structure of IRs, charging up cultural items with membership significance. These items include the communication that is part of the work itself, as well as work-related discussions that go on in backstage debriefing and strategizing, and that carry over into quasi-sociable shop talk. The cultural symbols thus given significance consist both in the occupational lore in a more general sense—the technical jargon that engineers use about their equipment, the financial shorthand of stockbrokers and investment bankers, the style of negotiating among business executives in a particular branch of industry—but also of the particular information that people in that network talk about. Entrée into and success within a particular occupational network is not only a matter of having the generalized cultural capital of that group—that which is known widely among persons who may not be acquainted with each other—but also of having particular knowledge of who did what, who has what track record, who has been connected to whom, "where the bodies are buried." The latter form of knowledge or particularized cultural capital or symbolic repertoire may well be the most important kind, especially for the dynamics of fluidly moving situations, such as business transactions where time is of the essence, or analogously for scientists or other intellectuals attempting to innovate on the cutting edge before someone else does so. Here too, as in the world of private sociability, symbolic reputations are amplified to higher levels in networks that have enough redundant social ties so that symbols circulate in at least some closed loops, reinforcing the significance of a symbol because it is heard from all sides, and probably exaggerated in the retelling.[25] What needs emphasizing is not simply that these are specialized languages or local knowledge, but that these are membership symbols that are effective to just the degree that they have an emotional loading. The concept of utilitarian communications at work might seem to rule out their having an emotional quality, but this is a mistake. It is precisely those business or professional encounters that have a special excitement, tension, or enthusiasm to them that turn those items of communication into charged symbols; they become "buzzwords" in the original, nonpejorative sense, items that carry a buzz of cutting-edge significance.

In sum, there are several distinctive ways in which symbols circulate and prolong group membership beyond ephemeral situations of emotional intensity. One is as objects that are in the focus of attention of emotionally entrained but otherwise anonymous crowds. The second is as symbols built up out of personal identities and narratives, in conversational rituals marking the tie between the conversationalists and the symbolic objects they are talking about.[26] These symbols generally operate in two quite different circuits of social relationships; typically, the symbols of audiences, fans, partisans, and followers circulate from one mass gathering to another, and tend to fade in the interim; the symbols of personal identities and reputations are the small change of social relationships (and of business relationships), generally of lesser momentary intensity than audience symbols but used so frequently and in self-reinforcing networks so as to permeate their participants' sense of reality.[27]

Both the generalized symbols of mass audiences and the particularized symbols of personal networks prolong the emotional loadings of IRs. They do so in differing time-patterns and subject to differing contingencies. Generalized mass-audience symbols are dependent upon the reassembling of big groups, and individual members of those groups usually have little initiative in whether the big assembly will come about or come off. And since these generalized symbols do not usually get a comparable recharging of their emotional level through the ordinary interactions of everyday life, they are prone to greater volatility. This is what characterizes political and religious movements; and insofar as there are generally shared economic symbols (a stock market index; the prestige of a particular hot-selling product), these too are subject to volatile swings in their collective significance, and hence in their social and economic value.[28] On the other hand, particularized symbols of individual identities and memberships in networks personally known to their participants have greater inertia. That does not mean they are fixed; identities and reputations are capable of changing, especially if the links among particular persons who make up a network change, and all the more so if the network shifts between more redundant and more sparsely linked forms. These changes in membership and reputation are especially important in the realm of professional and business relationships; indeed, it is just these shifts that make up a career.

The Creation of Solidarity Symbols in 9/11

The contrast between personal membership ties and impersonal symbols of anonymous crowds can be observed quite starkly in a single event: the destruction of the World Trade Center towers in the September 11, 2001 attacks. The case also shows the dynamic and emergent quality of symbols, the further layers in which they can be circulated, and the uses to which symbols can be put once they have been created. I base the analysis on "9/11," a documentary film consisting of live footage of firefighters and street crowds during the attack (Naudet and Naudet 2002).

Applying IR theory, it is apparent that for the anonymous crowds in and near the towers, the destroyed towers themselves did not become a symbol of group solidarity, but the firefighters became their symbol; whereas for the firefighters, the destroyed towers became their symbol. Let us see how this came about.

The video shows people in the streets in the moments after the first plane hit the towers and during their collapse. What was an unfocused crowd becomes a focused crowd, or set of crowds—not particularly dense, but comprising clusters of ten or twenty people visible at the same time in the film. The smoke draws their attention; they stare in the same direction, utter exclamations, align themselves more closely together. The early mood that they express is wonder, surprise, an increasing sense of shock. Aside from the shared focus, there is not much interaction or talk in the street crowds. From the lack of Goffmanian tie signs, it appears that the crowds are made up of strangers to each other, drawn together only by the shared event. At first, they are passive spectators. Later, as debris fills the air and the buildings begin to fall, they run away; their action spreads the crowds out even more; we see individuals here and there darting down the street. Many of those who are nearest to the towers, or who had come out of the buildings, display expressions of being stunned.

For the most part, the video does not show strongly expressed and socially communicated emotion. There are not even very frequent expressions of fear. There are some scenes of workers inside one of the towers coming down from the stairs above and passing through the upper lobby on their way outside; they appear quiet and orderly, not panicking, scrambling, or pushing. It appears here that the very orderliness of the crowd has set the contagious mood, and keeps down the experience of fear. (This would follow from William James's theory of emotions: running away makes one afraid; and a crowd running will make its members even more afraid.)

Figure 2.6 NY City firefighter in process of becoming hero symbol (September 14, 2001).

Figure 2.7 Street crowd running from World Trade Center area as first tower collapses (September 11, 2001).

The only expressions of fear visible on the film are occasionally by persons in the street crowd. Looking at these instances in detail we see that these are physically isolated individuals, not those who are close together and talking to each other, but bodily separated on the fringes or in sparser parts of the crowd on the street.

Compare the firefighters, whom we see during their prior routine in the firehouse, in vehicles on the way to the towers, inside the tower lobby, and finally upon returning to the firehouse afterward. The firefighters show no overt expression of fear on the film. Nor do they show any expression of "courage" as a special emotion; this is just an interpretation placed on their behavior after the fact. The firefighters follow the normal routine of doing their job. This is what enables them to be unafraid, since it gives them something to do other than to flee; and they are doing it collectively. It is also the case that they have no sense, at least at first, that anything unusually dangerous is happening; i.e., there is a special difficulty in that the fire is seventy stories high in a building in which the elevators are not working and so they have to climb stairs to get to the fire. But this is their normal job, to get to a fire and put it out. There is no indication at the command post (which is where most of the firefighters on the video are shown) that anyone thinks there is danger of the building collapsing, since the fire is far above. Even after lights go out, electricity is off, debris starts falling, and the commanders order firefighters to evacuate, the commanders still act calmly looking for exits, not hurrying, not panicking.

One might argue that the firefighters are trained, and experienced, at doing this sort of thing—confronting fires in big buildings; occasionally there must be danger of a building collapsing, but that seems to be a remote issue not much considered. There is presumably a routine concern over becoming burned or asphyxiated, but these are normal dangers, and the sheer size of the World Trade Center building does not add anything different to their subjective experience. But it should be emphasized that "training" per se does not guarantee performance in situations of stress; there is considerable evidence that police and army training does not prevent a large proportion of soldiers from freezing up in combat, or police officers from firing wildly and incompetently (Keegan 1977; Collins forthcoming).

"Training" is not simply a matter of learning; it is above all establishing identity with the group who carry out their skills collectively. Maintaining collective identity is an ongoing activity, an IR chain; and it is this that we see in the video of the firefighters. The "courage" that outsiders interpet the firefighters as having is a version of Chambliss's (1989) "mundanity of excellence"—the sense that members of an elite occupation have that their situation, for themselves if not for outsiders, is a routine one, where they can accomplish what others cannot, by focusing carefully on their skills and not being distracted by anything else. In this case, they are not being distracted by fear; their collective focus and their routine excludes it from the center of their experience. IR theory adds that the mundanity of excellence is based on group participation, collective focus and mood, keeping each other calm and focused on the routine task. Doing one's job collectively under stress is the result, and it feeds back into their group identity and solidarity.

The video shows considerable indications of solidarity among the firefighters both before and after the attack. Prior to going out to the towers, the filmmakers had filmed the group's routine for a month. They had concentrated on the induction of a new, probationary firefighter into the group, who goes through mild hazing rituals such as doing the scut-work of the fire station, and who is given encouragement by experienced firefighters as they look forward to his real initiation when he would take part in his first big building fire. The video also shows group solidarity at the end of the day, when firefighters come back to the station, hug each other, greeting each other warmly for having survived and returned. From subsequent footage we see that the firefighters treat the stationhouse as their home; this is where they prefer to gather after the disaster, rather than individually with their families.

The contrast between the firefighters and the street crowds shows a highly focused, high-solidarity group drawing emotional strength— not blatant enthusiasm, but a quiet form of EE—from going on together with a difficult task; while less focused, low-solidarity crowds show shock, and in the thinnest parts of the crowd, fear. The solidarity that the firefighters already have, and that they recycle and increase through their experience of working together in the disaster, is just what is lacking among the crowds in the streets; the latter have no prior identity, only the momentary focus on the building they see on fire, and later on, collapsing. They lack social strong support, and lack anything to do that has ongoing collective significance.

Nevertheless the crowd has many of the ingredients of a natural IR: bodily assembly, mutual focus of attention, shared mood. Why don't individuals in the crowd transform the shared shock and fear into solidarity? Rituals are emotion transformers, and can turn negative emotions into positive ones. The members of the crowd are all focused on the towers, which they see burning and collapsing; why don't the towers become a symbol of membership? The towers represent a very negative experience, but that in itself is not a bar to becoming a group symbol. The symbol of Christianity, the cross, is an emblem of an extremely negative event, a crucifixion; it is a symbol of undergoing suffering as a form of ritual consecration and emerging through it strengthened and triumphant. In fact something like this emerges from the 9/11 disaster, too, with the great upsurge of national solidarity in the following days and months. The image of the towers burning and collapsing is an ephemeral event in time, but it was recorded and repetitively displayed on television and in news photos during the subsequent hours and days. The image was available to become transformed into a symbol, but it was not—at least not for the crowd of witnesses, both those nearby and those further away who witnessed it through the mass media.

Structurally, the street crowds had no way to reassemble, to bring itself back together as a group. They had no identity as a group, except as those who were eyewitnesses to the disaster. But this itself was a group with vague boundaries, made up of those in the towers themselves, those nearby on the streets experiencing different degrees of awareness of what was going on, and shading into those who were watching or hearing about the events on the mass media or by hearsay as they unfolded. This group never crystallized an identity. What did crystallize was the dual identities of "New Yorkers"—an encompassing membership of everyone in the city, even though the vast majority were no more closely involved in the disaster than people outside the city; and "Americans," as the national unit who was the target of the attack. Thus during the coming days and weeks people began to display symbols combining those two identities: hats, shirts, and other emblems of New York, and American flags. Above all, what tied together these symbols, was the main emergent symbol of the event: the firefighters, as emblems of solidarity and courage.

The video shows, however, that the firefighters do not see themselves in the same light as the crowds of spectators, and later admirers. In the firefighters' self-perception, they have failed: they did not reach the fire, nor put it out, nor save anyone from the fire. They have renewed their solidarity through their greetings to each other when they arrived back at the station, but there is no feeling of triumph. The collapsed buildings are a strong focus of attention for them; a negative symbol that draws them back. They display a strong desire to go back to the site and start digging through rubble for survivors; a need to feel that they have accomplished something. They are affirming their identity as the group that worked through the disaster, in a symbolic way taking possession of the disaster.

The digging through the ruins is to a considerable extent a ritualistic action. Given the scope of the damage, it is extremely unlikely that anyone will be found alive, and no one is. Nevertheless it is an obsession to be there, and to go through the motions, the action itself keeping hope alive. The video shows their collective focus while digging in rubble, heightened at moments when they cry "quiet!" and pass along the cry; ostensibly this is in order to listen for possible victims, but it has the effect of focusing the attention of the group, giving themselves more collective energy. They pass the buckets of rubble rapidly at first, but in subsequent clips they are working more slowly. The initial emotion gradually wears off. Nevertheless, seven-and-a-half weeks later (New York Times, Nov. 3, 2001) when in a more realistic and utilitarian attitude, the mayor's office declares the site closed to any further spontaneous, voluntary action by the firefighters so that it can be cleared by heavy equipment, there are emotional fights that take place between firefighters and the police attempting to enforce the closure order. The firefighters treat the site as a sacred place that belongs to them, and react with outrage that they are being excluded from it.

Two kinds of ritualistic actions go on in the 9/11 event, and one plays into and becomes the symbolic material for the other. The firefighters already have ritual solidarity and group identity; but they have suffered losses to their ranks, and perhaps even more, to their sense of professional pride; hence they seize upon the demolished buildings as a symbolic place to affirm their collective participation.

Figure 2.8 NY firefighters struggle with police over access to WTC site. Fire-fighters wear full paraphernalia for symbolic effect, although salvage work had previously been done in casual work dress (November 2, 2001).

Their ritual is to go back to the demolition site and look for dead bodies; since the site implicitly belongs to them alone—they are the only ones who are allowed to be there—it strongly affirms their identity as exclusively at the core of the event, and at the center of its emotions.

The passive crowd of witnesses, nearby and more remote, have no strongly organized basis for identity; but their attention is drawn from the initial focus, the buildings, to the firefighters and their symbolic activity. In the hours and early days after the collapse, coming back from digging, the firefighters are greeted by crowds lining the streets waving American flags. These are the images picked up by the media and broadcast widely, adopted nation-wide as symbols. On the video, the firefighters say they don't feel like heroes—since they haven't done anything, haven't accomplished anything, in fact have failed to do their job. From the inside, in their subjective experience, they are not symbols for themselves; what they see as a symbol is something outside themselves, their collapsed towers.[29]

Occupying another layer of social reality is the experience of the spectators. In seizing on firefighters as heroes, the crowd is focusing on the persons with the most EE, confidence, and purpose; they make them emblems of their own collective solidarity in the face of the disaster; and they participate with them by cheering them. They also associate the several emblems together: American flags, New York City emblems,[30] and firefighters. These symbols are repeatedly brought together over the coming weeks and months, as large-scale ritual gatherings are enacted: at sporting events, music concerts, as well as political assemblies. At this point, the symbols are circulating in a chain of self-reinforcing IRs; the presence of symbols charged up with emotion, fresh in memory, motivates and facilitates creating these new ceremonial gatherings; and the renewal of emotion by the crowd's focus of attention at those ceremonies charges the symbols again, making them ready for the next round of use.

These video recordings, together with subsequent reporting of events, document the successive layers of short-term and long-term effects of IRs. There is the raw experience, which we have seen through two vantage-points, the perspective of the onlooking crowds and that of the firefighters called into action. Next comes the transformation of those experiences into symbols; here the different kinds of participants choose different aspects of what they witness to make into emblems of emotional remembrance and group solidarity. The first of these is momentary, situational intersubjectivity; the second is the prolongation and re-creation of experience on another order, as symbolically crystallized intersubjectivity. Yet more temporally remote, and more remote, too, in the kinds of social networks involved, is a second order of circulation of newly created symbols among persons who are far away from the initial experiences. Further out in time, the reflexive use of symbols becomes more contrived, more overlaid with the practical contingencies of staging ceremonies, increasingly entwined with the politics of self-display and factional advantage as the new symbols sediment onto the layer of old symbols already in normal social routine. In this larger context of use, the emotional intensity that the symbols had while fresh begins to cool, their life dependent, like all symbols, on the intensity of the gatherings in which they will again be invoked.

RULES FOR UNRAVELING SYMBOLS

The world is full of symbols. Some are our own, meaningful to ourselves in one degree or another. Some are markers of other groups, sharply visible where they mark boundaries against enemies or distrusted outsiders, or exclusions upward or downward in felt rank. Others are only episodically or dimly perceived. We are surrounded by a vast spectrum of symbols and group identities, some living, some dying or dead; some are living but their significances are invisible to us in our particular locations, since we are not close enough to feel what they convey.

It is a fallacy to take symbols at face value, as if we can read their meaning from what participants say they mean. It is as naïve as a child who thinks that "How are you?" means a request for information about their health; or an awkward teenager who treats "How are things going?" as calling for a simple reassurance instead of as a ploy to find a topic to chat about. We are in much the same position if we treat religious symbols as if they were a self-sufficient explanation of what people who invoke them do.

The tribes of the Baliem valley of highland New Guinea say they will not fight at night because spirits of the dead are out after dark, and so they must stay in their huts (Garner 1962). But this is hardly an adequate explanation in the context of the tribe's normal routine. The tribes, engaged in endless feuding with their neighbors in raids and set-piece battles at their frontier, limit the amount of fighting in many ways. They settle for one death or serious injury at a time, which suffices to end the battle and start off into a round of ceremonies in the villages. Even when no one is hurt, they take tacitly agreed upon rest breaks during a day of battle; they call off a battle when it starts to rain, in order not to spoil their war make-up; they do not attack during days when the enemy is carrying on a funeral or a victory celebration. The spirits of the dead that are invoked in explanation of why they do not fight at night are part of a larger routine of agreements and justifications that limit most of their fighting to particular times and places. The gatherings of the tribes to fight one another are the most intense and most important membership rituals of the group, and it is from and around this that other symbolic representations are formed and sustained. The spirits who are supposed to be out at night occupy a similar part of the symbolic universe, as does the spirit of the last dead person to be killed by the enemy, whose restlessness is regarded within the tribal culture as impelling the warriors to go back to the battlefield for revenge. More simply put: their battles are chained together as a series of rituals reaffirming membership through enmity; their religious symbols are reminders of the emotions felt during each battle, and especially in their high points where someone is killed, which operate to reinvoke the next ritual in the chain.

Contemporary evidence confirms the dependence of religious beliefs upon social interaction (Stark and Bainbridge 1985). Persons who join religious cults typically are not to any great extent acquainted with, nor committed to, the beliefs of the cult before they join it. They are initially attracted to the cult because they are brought by friends, relatives, and acquaintances. Their belief grows as they take part in the cult activities. In mainstream churches as well, those who have the strongest adherence to its doctrines are those who have the most personal friends who are also members; social ties brings ritual participation, and this brings belief. And those without close ties in a cult or church tend to drop out, and their belief fades away.

To invoke the content of an item of culture gives us a description of some cognitive aspects of a chain of social situations. The cultural framing or native justification of the action is at best an ad hoc explanation of it. Why do they do it? Because they say X; or because that is the way that people do things in X part of the world. This may be on the way to an explanation, but it is no final resting place for a sociological theory.

In support of a cultural approach, Garfinkel's (1967) statement is often quoted, that the person is not a "judgmental dope." If this is taken to mean that the person is not simply pushed around by shared cultural rules, that is accurate enough. But if it is set forth as a claim that persons are aware of the sources of their own behavior, or even their own thoughts and emotions, it is surely wrong. We operate through an emotional magnetism toward and repulsion from particular thoughts and situations in the flow of everyday life; we are seldom reflective about this, and are often grossly inaccurate in our assessments when we are reflective.

Social action has a very large unconscious component. It is unconscious precisely because by focusing our attention upon a collective object of action, or upon symbols derived from it, our attention is defocused from the social process in which we are entrained while doing so. To be sure, on special occasions we may move into the observer mode, and make an object of attention out of the very social action that we were once unreflectively embedded in. But this puts us into a different situation, that of the second-order observer, where we are no longer an actor.[31] Action itself always reduces reflexivity, and induces a belief in the symbols and symbolically framed objects that fill out attention at that moment.

Thus I conclude with some rules for unraveling symbols. Sociological research works best if we can start with interaction rituals and move forward, witnessing how the intensity and focus of the interaction generates symbols to be used in subsequent interactions. But there are times when we are confronted with the symbol already made. How are we to go about interpreting its social meaning?

To begin, judge how intensely symbolic the item is. Is it treated with respect, as a sacred object, as a realm apart from ordinary life? Is it given a spatially separate zone, a special physical location that is approached only with care? Are there special qualifications as to who can approach, and who is excluded? Is it emotionally and vehemently and self-righteously defended? Conversely, does it attract vehement attackers, also self-righteous in their attacks? Is it treated as an item of more than personal value, proclaimed as a value that is or ought to be widely shared? Is it regarded as incommensurate with merely utilitarian values? Such claims to far-reaching value are equally characteristic of positive and negative symbols; especially intensely charged are those symbols that are positive to some persons, negative to others.

Our analysis is usually attracted to those symbols most highly charged in these respects. But we may notice as well what appear to be bygone symbols, neglected sacred places, vestiges of once-frequented emblems now in decay, like monuments in public parks covered with pigeon droppings, or defaced with graffiti, an overlay of one emblem upon another.

Next, reconstruct as best as possible what IRs have surrounded that emblem. Who assembled, in what numbers, with what frequency or schedule? What emotions were expressed, what activities brought a focus of attention, what intensity of collective effervescence was generated? To what degree were individual participants charged with emotional energy; and what did it motivate them to do? What were the barriers to participation: who was divided by the ritual from whom? Who was thereby ranked over whom?

We attempt to put together a history of ritual participation around the symbols that we see surviving today, or sticking up in the distance from the sands of social interaction where we do not ordinarily tread. Sometimes this becomes an ideal for historical reconstruction; if need be, a conjectural history, since even a hypothetical scheme of who did what ritual action is a better guide to conceptualizing the meaning of symbols than taking those symbols as freestanding and unaffected by social process. For the most part, except when dealing with remote history, we are in a better situation as researchers, and the rules for unraveling symbols becomes a guide to a research program.

Further, our task does not end at reconstructing those primal moments when the ritual was in full blast, at its most intense. We are concerned too with tracing the secondary circulation of symbols. Who uses these emblems (including their verbal representations and other emblems-of-emblems) for other interactional situations beyond the actual gathering of the group of ritual participants? What are the range of situations in which these symbols circulate? Do they become topics for rounds of conversation with acquaintances; for injection into other public ceremonial; for debate with opponents of those ritual practices? We have, in short, a primary realm of living rituals and the symbols that they charge with significance; and a secondary realm where those symbols become circulated in the IRs that make up the surrounding social networks, whether taken as positive or negative emblems, or just treated reflexively as items of news, gossip, reputation. They become representations of groups who are somewhere else, at a distance.

Finally, there is a further, third order in which symbols circulate: what individuals do with them when they are alone, outside the presence of other people. Do they physically carry the symbols around with them, or access them alone, like a religious person carrying an emblem or visiting a shrine? The most intimate level of circulation is inside individuals' minds, in the inner conversations that make up thinking, in the fantasies that make up the inner self. This third order of symbolic circulation is even harder to get at than the second order; but we may as well list it here, since I am laying out a maximal program, an ideal for the sociology of rituals and symbolic life to aim at even if it may be largely unattainable for the present state of research. We might as well say that this is a sociology to dream about, and indeed, it encompasses a sociology of dreams. For if dreams take place in images, those images are internalized or synthesized out of pieces internalized from the circulation of symbols on the first and second orders of social interaction, and from the thinking that takes place in the waking mind. Let us go all the way in our ambitions: a complete sociology of the circulation of symbols would be a sociology of humans' inner lives as well as their external lives. The research task is to move forward, from what evidence we have of where charged up symbols exist publically, to fill in more and more of the histories of how they have been formed and circulated.

To end with a brief illustration: In late-twentieth-century America, guns in the hands of civilians became an object of widespread public attention. Many of their proponents treat guns in just the way that we would consider, under the above criteria, as symbolic objects—that is, as a gun cult. Their opponents too treat them as abnormally negative, as emblems of evil. From either side, guns are treated with special respect, given as special status. They occupy distinctive places: on gun racks in trucks, in display cases in homes. The very efforts of opponents to keep them locked up, fitted with trigger guards, kept apart from children, have the effect of further emphasizing their special character and the special status of those who have access to them. To be sure, these restrictions and the physical segregation of guns are often consciously motivated in utilitarian terms, as safety practices; but utilitarian justifications often overlay symbolic practices and reinforce rather than undermine them.

Considerable discourse is devoted to justifications of guns, and to critiques of those justifications. Guns are justified because it is the constitutional right of Americans to possess guns; because they are part of the American heritage of liberty, and represent a stand against the encroaching power of the government; because they are used for sport shooting and hunting; because they are weapons of defense against criminals, a bolster to the forces of good against the already well-armed forces of evil. The sociologist of rituals does not take these arguments at face value. Aside from various inconsistencies in the arguments and practices themselves,[32] it is not a sociological explanation of behavior to invoke the reasons given, especially on occasions of public justification and debate over already existing practices. Instead we should ask, Why do particular people come to believe in these reasons, or rather, in what circumstances do they invoke them? Did they have these beliefs first and as the result of so believing did they decide that they should acquire guns? Or did they acquire the guns first—if religious practices are any clue, because of induction from friends and acquaintances who already had guns—and then acquired the verbal justifications?

Then we must ask, What is it that possessors of guns do? Is their activity intensely ritualistic enough so that we might call them members of the gun cult (or indeed, of different kinds of gun cults)? Are guns put in the center of attention of group assemblies, surrounded with a shared mood? Here we may investigate the primary ritual that goes on at gun shows, firing ranges, gun dealers' shops. Examine the ritualistic aspects of hunting, with special traditions and procedures of the male outdoors-expedition. Intermediate on a continuum of group exclusiveness and identification would be gun theme parks, fantasy exercises with pseudo-weapons (such as paintball fighting ranges). Most intensely cultist of all are paramilitary groups and their war exercises.

We would want to study, too, the second-order circulation of gun symbols. On the most banal level: When do people talk about guns, and with whom?[33] Is there a sharp disjunction in the form of talk between those who possess guns (i.e., those who take part in primary gun rituals) and those who do not? Further out in the symbolic circulation are the ways in which emblematic representations of guns are publicized in the news, in statements of politicians, and, of course, in the mass media of entertainment.[34] All these can recirculate back into the immediate conversational circles of people who have guns, shaping or reinforcing their emotional resonances with their weapons. In general, we might expect that the existence of a vehement public discourse, the political controversy pro and con guns, will intensify the boundaries; outside opposition would encourage a stronger sense of membership inside the gun cult, perhaps making some old-fashioned hunters into more intensely ritualistic supporters of guns as symbolic emblems.[35]

Finally, there is the third level of circulation of symbols, their use by individuals privately, alone. Some of this is visible in ritualistic action, insofar as there are actual objects that can be manipulated: guns that people spend their time holding, taking apart, cleaning and reassembling, looking at and admiring. Many individuals who are intensely involved with guns spend much of their leisure time reloading ammunition; a large part of the display at gun shows are equipment and supplies for reloading spent shells with live charges. There is some utilitarian element in this, insofar as reloading one's own ammunition is cheaper than buying it fresh; but the long hours that gun cultists spend on reloading ammunition suggests that this is a ritualistic affirmation of their membership, something like a member of a religious cult engaging in private prayer, in actual physical contact with the sacred objects, like fingering the beads of a rosary.

On the most intimate level of symbolic circulation, we would like to know who thinks about guns, and in what kinds of inner conversations, or imaginery situations? In what chains of interactions are these thinking-occasions embedded? And what are the consequences of these inner thoughts and fantasy scenarios? For which people—for which kinds of IR chains—do gun thoughts remain inward and harmless; and for which chains of inner and outer interactions do gun symbols reemerge into action? An extreme instance would be the brooding of the teenager who takes the gun to school to avenge an insult, acting out the practices that he has gone through before on the firing range.

These are difficult questions to research, but from the perspective of IR theory, not impossible ones. Thoughts are internalized from the symbols of first-order and second-order rituals; and they are charged up with emotional energy from what happens at each moment of flow in that chain that makes up an individual personality. A sociology of thinking is just another component problem, if an especially difficult one, for a sociology of IR chains.

Much of the symbolic experience of everyday life is not so dramatic as the examples I have sketched here. But our aim throughout is the same: to keep the action of IRs in the center of analysis, whether we can observe it easily, or whether we must reconstruct it from any and all available clues. We will see how this is done in subsequent chapters, including the formation of sex symbols in chapter 6, and of tobacco symbols in chapter 8, where we can observe not only the creation of symbolic practices, but their rise and fall.

Chapter 3

EMOTIONAL ENERGY AND

THE TRANSIENT EMOTIONS

EMOTION IS A central ingredient and outcome of IRs. It is time now to examine emotions more closely. Among other benefits of doing so is to highlight the contribution that sociology of emotions makes to macro-sociological theory. And we shall see, via a circuitous route, the emotion-laden view of macro-sociological structure and hence of the place of individuals within it will give us some leads for a sociological theory of differences in personality.

Emotion implicitly occupies a crucial position in general sociological theory. As we attempt to make sociological concepts more precise and more empirically grounded, we find that many of the most important rest to a considerable extent upon emotional processes. Durkheim raised the central question of sociology: What holds society together? His answer is the mechanisms that produce moral solidarity; and these mechanisms, I have argued, do so by focusing, intensifying, and transforming emotions. Parsonian sociology, which took the most reified, agentless side of Durkheim, put the argument in equivalent terms: society is held together by values. But values, to the extent that they exist (and leaving open the issue of how far they are shared, and under what conditions), are cognitions infused with emotion. On the conflict side of sociological theory, Weber's central concepts also imply emotion: the legitimacy that underlies stable power, the status group ranking by which stratification permeates everyday life, the religious worldviews that motivated some crucial periods of economic action. When we attempt to translate any of these concepts into observables, it is apparent that we are dealing with particular kinds of emotions. Marx and Engels are perhaps furthest away from theorizing about emotional processes: in their analysis, everything is structural (even alienation, which for Marx is an ontological relationship, not a psychological one). But it is apparent that in Marxian analyses of class mobilization and class conflict, emotion must play a part—whether it is the mutual distrust within fragmented classes that keeps them from mobilizing, or the solidarity that dominant classes have and that oppressed classes acquire only in revolutionary situations. In these respects,

Marx and Engels's conflict theory comes close to a dynamic version of Durkheim's themes.

The sociology of emotions thus bears upon the central questions of sociology. What holds a society together—the "glue" of solidarity—and what mobilizes conflict—the energy of mobilized groups—are emotions; so is what operates to uphold stratification—hierarchical feelings, whether dominant, subservient, or resentful. If we can explain the conditions that cause people to feel these kinds of emotions, we will have a major part of a core sociological theory. There is, of course, a structural part of such a theory, and a cognitive part; but the emotional part gives us something essential for a realistic theory—its dynamics.[1]

These classic sociological theories implicitly concern emotions, but they do not usually refer to them explicitly. This is because our theories have a macro-primacy, or at least deal with social life at a level of considerable abstraction and aggregation. We are told of something called "legitimacy," and of "values," floating somewhere in a conceptual sky beyond the heads of real people in ordinary situations. If we attempt a micro-translation of sociology—not a micro-reduction, but a grounding of macro-concepts in real interactions across the macro-dimensions of time and space—we are led to see the importance of emotional processes. In other words, the micro-translation of macro-concepts yields emotion.

For the most part, this is not what most micro-theories have stressed. Mead and symbolic interactionism emphasize process, emergence, and cognition; Schutz and phenomenology emphasize routine and cognition; exchange theory emphasizes behaviors and payoffs; expectation states theory again stresses cognition. Emotion of course could be brought into these theories, but it is central to none of them.[2] On the other hand, there is a burgeoning field of sociology of emotions, but until recently it has been largely treated as a specialized enclave, cut off from general issues of sociology.[3] But several prominent versions of microsociology do not have to be pressed very far to yield the central micro-dynamics of emotion as a social process—a process that will serve to unpack the macro-sociological issues mentioned at the outset.

One of these is Garfinkel's ethnomethodology. At first sight, it seems to be pitched on a different level. With its concern for the construction of mundane reality, and its heavy use of phenomenological abstractions, it seems to be essentially a cognitive theory. Cicourel (1973) even called his own version "Cognitive Sociology." Nevertheless, I want to suggest that ethnomethodology reveals emotion at its core. Garfinkel's most important contribution is to show that humans have intrinsically limited cognitive capabilities, and that they construct mundane social order by consistently using practices to *avoid* recognizing how arbitrarily social order is actually put together. We keep up conventions, not because we believe in them, but because we studiously avoid questioning them. Garfinkel demonstrated this most dramatically in his breaching experiments, in which he forced people into situations that caused them to recognize indexicality (i.e., that they rely on tacit acceptance of what things mean contextually) and reflexivity (that there are infinite regresses of justifying one's interpretations). Interestingly enough, the reactions of his subjects were always intensely emotional. Usually it was an emotional outburst: becoming nervous and jittery, shaken, displaying anxiety and sometimes shock (Garfinkel 1967, 44, 221–26) Sometimes it was depression, bewilderment, or anger at having been put in a situation where they constructed a reality they later discovered to be false. In short, when people have to recognize that they are tacitly constructing their social worlds, and in an arbitrary and conventional way, rather than simply reacting to a world that is objectively there, they show intense negative emotions.

Garfinkel's breaching experiments reveal something very much like Durkheim's world. In this case, conventional social reality is a sacred object. Garfinkel's experiments, violating the sacred object, call forth the same effects as violating a ritual taboo would have for a tribal member, desecrating the Bible for a Christian, or defaming the flag for a patriot. In Durkheim's theory, moral sentiments attach to sacred objects. When they are violated, this positive sentiment of moral solidarity turns negative, into righteous anger directed against the culprit. Just so in Garfinkel's experiments: there is outrage against the violator of everyday cognitive conventions. Garfinkel's strategy parallels Durkheim's: to show the conditions that uphold a social fact by revealing the opposition that occurs when it is broken. Durkheim used suicide and crime as means of highlighting the social solidarity that is their opposite; Garfinkel extended the method to reality-construction as a whole.

Ethnomethodology's lack of explicit focus on emotions is misleading. One could well say that everyday life reality-construction is an emotional process, and that the emotions that uphold reality come forth in intense form when the social reality is broken. Furthermore, Garfinkel has shown that human cognition is limited; social order cannot be based on rational, conscious agreement. Durkheim (1893/1964) argued the same, but in the context of criticizing utilitarianism. If cognition does not hold society together, then, what does? Garfinkel tends to leave this on the level of cognitive practices (mostly borrowed from Schutz); but it is a peculiar form of cognition—cognitive practices for how to get by without too much cognition. Ethnomethodology seems to have a mysterious x-factor underlying social order, which the very notion of index-icality prohibits us from probing. But let us take the plunge: leave the cognitive plane, and recognize the x-factor as emotion.

Interaction ritual theory gives the most fine-grained picture of how emotions are transformed in the process of interaction: rituals begin with emotional ingredients (which may be emotions of all sorts); they intensify emotions into the shared excitement that Durkheim called "collective effervescence"; and they produce other sorts of emotions as outcomes (especially moral solidarity, but also sometimes aggressive emotions such as anger). This puts us in a position to use the flow of emotions across situations as the crucial item in the micro-to-micro linkage that concatenates into macro patterns. The most important of these patterns of IR chains is what from a macro viewpoint appears as stratification. Social order is produced on the micro level: that is to say, all over the map, in transient situations and local groups, which may well be stratified by class, race, gender, or otherwise divided against each other. Interaction ritual produces pockets of moral solidarity, but variably and discontinuously throughout a population. Now if we trace individual human bodies moving from one encounter to the next, we see that the history of their chains—what sociologists have conven-tionally referred to as their positions in the social structure—is carried along in emotions and emotion-laden cognitions that become the in-gredients for the upcoming encounter. And then as the IR does its work, it intensifies, transforms, or diminishes those emotional ingredi-ents so that those human bodies come out of the situation charged with emotional outcomes, which in turn set up what will happen in their next situations.[4] In what follows, I will show that research on stratifi-cation gives us clues as to how emotional ingredients and outcomes are shaped. Stratification theory contributes to a theory of the distribu-tion of varying emotions; and the microsociology of emotion contrib-utes to the patterns of stratification.

DISRUPTIVE AND LONG-TERM EMOTIONS, OR DRAMATIC EMOTIONS AND EMOTIONAL ENERGY

A necessary first step is to widen our conception of emotion. Ordinary usage refers to emotions as experiences that are, for the most part, sud-den and dramatic. "Don't be so emotional" is advice predicated on this conception. The famous emotions are the most dramatic ones: fear, ter-ror, anger, embarrassment, joy, and so forth. Some people and some cultures are regarded as too "unemotional" (as in the late-twentieth-century disparagement of "WASP" culture). But both Goffman and

Garfinkel force us to see that there are also emotions that are undramatic; they are long-lasting, underlying tones or moods that permeate social life. Garfinkel's mundane reality, for example, is characterized by the feeling—I stress that this is a feeling rather than an explicit cognition—that "nothing out of the ordinary is happening here." This is an uninteresting emotion, from the point of view of the actor; but if Garfinkel is right, considerable work went into producing that feeling of ordinariness, and, into keeping ourselves from seeing that work itself. Mundane reality is a members' accomplishment.

In Goffman and Durkheim, the ordinary-life, long-lasting feelings are more apparent. These theories stress solidarity, feelings of membership, and in Goffman's case, feelings about one's self. These are, if everything goes well, smoothly persistent sentiments; though in some important cases they may have an "up" feeling tone, or a "down," depressed tone. Solidarity feelings, moral sentiment, the enthusiasm of pitching oneself into a situation, or being carried along by it, and, at the other end, depression, alienation, embarrassment—these are recognizably longer-lasting kinds of emotions. Garfinkelian mundanity is merely a generic emotional quality at the middle of the plus-minus scale.

My aim is not to enter into terminological controversy. It would be useless for us to define emotions in such a way that we can talk only about the dramatic, disruptive emotions. Whatever we call them, we must also be able to talk about the long-term emotional tones, even the ones that are so calm and smooth as not to be noticed. In theoretical terms, it is the long-lasting ones (that I discuss as emotional energy, EE) that are of greatest importance. But I will also attempt to show that the dramatic, short-term emotions are best explained against the backdrop of the long-term emotions.

There are four emotions that virtually all researchers agree are found in all societies, and that may be considered the primary emotions (for a summary of research, see Turner 2002, 68–79). These four are anger, fear, happiness, and sadness / disappointment. Mammals share with humans the primary emotions of fear and anger / assertiveness. In humans, these emotions have their physiological base in the amygdala, an evolutionarily primitive part of the brain. Happiness, however, is not based in a particular part of the brain, but is spread out, not only in the primitive amygdala, but in the cortical and subcortical areas, which are evolutionarily later; that is to say, happiness is physiologically generalized, across the major regions of the brain including those involved in human symbolic functioning. Similarly for sadness, which has no distinctive brain location; it operates physiologically through the failure of neurotransmitters and in the flow of hormones in the endocrine system.

Happiness and sadness can be expressed in a number of terms: joy, elation, enthusiasm, effervescence—in contrast to disappointment, dreariness, and depression. These are related to the basic psycho-physiological pattern that I am calling high and low emotional energy. From the point of view of IR theory, it is not surprising that these two emotions lack a specific location in the brain. They are distinctively human blends of emotion and cognition, implicating the entire workings of the cognitive regions of the brain. High and low EE come from the entrainment of communicative gestures and emotional rhythms that are distinctive to human intersubjectivity; from an individual viewpoint, they are tightly woven together into the human self. Thus what from a narrower viewpoint may be considered an expression of joy—as a momentary emotional experience—is carried over as a long-term mood of emotional energy, of varying duration and degree of intensity. EE gives energy, not just for physical activity (such as the demonstrative outbursts at moments of acute joy), but above all for taking the initiative in social interaction, putting enthusiasm into it, taking the lead in setting the level of emotional entrainment. Similarly, sadness or depression is a motivational force when it is a long-term mood, reducing the level of activity, not only bringing physical listlessness and withdrawal (at its extreme, the avoidance of being awake), but making social interaction passive, foot-dragging, perfunctory.

Emotional energy, in IR theory, is carried across situations by symbols that have been charged up by emotional situations. Thus EE is a central part of the arousal of symbols that humans use to talk and to think with. Here again, the findings of physiological research bolster IR theory: "joy" in the narrower sense of short-run experience, high EE in the larger sense of long-term mood, is not a specific part of the brain firing but an overall activity of the brain's cognitive and emotional functioning. Similarly, "sadness," taken more broadly and in the long-term as low EE, is an overall decline in the functioning of the entire neuro-endocrinological system. To say that symbols are carried on EE is not merely a metaphor. The physiology buttresses the sociology.[5]

Interaction Ritual as Emotion Transformer

The basic model of ritual interaction (IR) is spelled out in chapter 2 as the mutual-focus / emotional-entrainment model. Let us review all the places that emotions occur in the model.

One initiating ingredient is that participants share a common mood. It is unessential which emotion is present at the outset. The feelings may be anger, friendliness, enthusiasm, fear, sorrow, or many others. This model posits an emotional contagion among the persons present:

because they are focusing attention on the same thing and are aware of each other's focus, they become caught up in each other's emotions. As a result, the emotional mood becomes stronger and more dominant; competing feelings are driven out by the main group feeling. On the ultra-micro level, this happens by the process of rhythmic entrainment physiologically. That is to say, activities and emotions have their own micro-rhythm, a pace at which they take place. As the focus of interaction becomes progressively more attuned, the participants anticipate each other's rhythms, and thus become caught up "in the swing of things." Participants feel sadder in the course of a funeral, more humorous as part of a responsive audience at a comedy show, more convivial during the buildup of a party, more engrossed in a conversation as its rhythms become established. All these are versions of "collective effervescence"—even if that has a connotation of happy excitement, the more general condition is a high degree of absorption in emotional entrainment, whatever the emotion may be.

The outcome of a successful buildup of emotional coordination within an interaction ritual is to produce feelings of solidarity. The emotions that are ingredients of the IR are transient; the outcome however is a long-term emotion, the feelings of attachment to the group that was assembled at that time. Thus in the funeral ritual the short-term emotion was sadness, but the main "ritual work" of the funeral was producing (or restoring) group solidarity. The emotional ingredients of a party may be friendliness or humor; the long-term result is the feeling of status group membership.

I refer to these long-term outcomes as "emotional energy" (EE). It is a continuum, ranging from a high end of confidence, enthusiasm, good self-feelings; down through a middle range of bland normalcy; and to a low end of depression, lack of initiative, and negative self-feelings. Emotional energy is like the psychological concept of "drive," but it has a specifically social orientation. High emotional energy is a feeling of confidence and enthusiasm for social interaction. It is the personal side of having a great deal of Durkheimian ritual solidarity with a group. One gets pumped up with emotional strength from participating in the group's interaction. This makes one not only an enthusiastic supporter of the group, but also a leading figure in it. One feels good with the group, and is able to be an energy-leader, a person who stirs up contagious feelings when the group is together.

At the low end of the emotional energy continuum, the opposite is the case. Low emotional energy is a lack of Durkheimian solidarity. One is not attracted to the group; one is drained or depressed by it; one wants to avoid it. One does not have a good self in the group. And one is not attached to the group's purposes and symbols, but alienated from them.

This is not the way the term "emotion" is commonly used, and commonsense categories have difficulty in grasping that EE is emotion at all. Folk-categories usually point at emotions only when they are dramatic shifts, disruptions of the normal flow of social energy. We are particularly likely to overlook middle levels of EE, in which the flow of energy toward social situations allows everything to proceed normally and hence is taken for granted. But without this emotional energy flow, social interactions could not take place.

There are more differentiated variants of emotional energy as well, besides this up / down, high / low in solidarity and enthusiasm. We will see that there are two major dimensions of stratification (power and status) that produce specific qualities of emotional energy. But while we are considering the main, generic level of emotional energy, I will mention one more Durkheimian feature. Emotional energy is not just something that pumps up some individuals and depresses others. It also has a controlling quality from the group side. Emotional energy is also what Durkheim (1912/1954) called "moral sentiment": it includes feelings of what is right and wrong, moral and immoral. Persons who are full of emotional energy feel like good persons; they feel righteous about what they are doing. Persons with low emotional energy feel bad; though they do not necessarily interpret this feeling as guilt or evil (that would depend on the religious or other cultural cognitions available for labeling their feelings),[6] at a minimum they lack the feeling of being morally good persons that comes from enthusiastic participation in group rituals.

Feelings of moral solidarity generate specific acts of altruism and love; but there is also a negative side. As Durkheim pointed out, group solidarity makes individuals feel a desire to defend and honor the group. This solidarity feeling is typically focused on symbols, sacred objects (like a tribal totemic emblem, a holy scripture, a flag, a wedding ring). One shows respect for the group by participating in rituals venerating these symbolic objects; conversely, failure to respect them is a quick test of nonmembership in the group. Members of the ritual group are under especially strong pressure to continue to respect its sacred symbols. If they do not, the loyal group members feel shock and outrage: their righteousness turns automatically into righteous anger. In this way, ritual violations lead to persecution of heretics, scapegoats, and other outcasts. Such events bring out clearly yet another transformation of emotion by rituals: from specific initiating emotions to their intensification in collective effervescence; from collective effervescence to emotional energy carried in individuals' attachment to symbols; and from symbol-respect to righteous anger.

Detailed microsociological evidence of such emotional transformations is provided in the work of Scheff and others (Scheff 1990; Scheff and Retzinger 1991; Samson 1997). Scheff's theoretical model builds also on Durkheim, but gives emphasis to the emotions experienced by individuals as touching their selves. For Scheff, intact social bonds (which, from the point of view of IR theory, are the result of carrying out a successful IR) give participants a feeling of pride; broken social bonds (an unsuccessful IR) results in a feeling of shame. Scheff and his collaborators examine social interactions in micro-detail by using video and audio recordings (largely from marriage counseling sessions, as well as from family interactions). Pride and shame are documented in the patterns of body alignment, eye gaze, speech hesitations or flow, loudness as well as overt expression of emotions. These data show the ups and downs of mutual focus and emotional entrainment on the second-to-second level.

Scheff goes on to point out that shame—the sense of broken social attunement—can either be immediately expressed and brought into the interaction as a topic; or it can be by-passed, repressed from conscious verbal attention. By-passed shame, he argues, is transformed into anger. This sets up a cycle of repeated failed interactions: for example, a married couple or parent and child may shame one another by breaking the attunement of interactions, but ignoring the shame; it thereby comes back in angry moves later in the same encounter, or in later encounters. Emotional dynamics recycle through the IR chain, since each episode of broken attunement generates more shame and more anger, which comes out in yet further patterns of interaction.

The negative effects of broken attunement can also be read in a comparative light, as a demonstration of the importance of attunement. Scheff shows that Durkheimian solidarity, operating on the micro-level of situational encounters, is highly attractive to individuals, and is experienced as pride, a favorable social self. The failure of solidarity, down to the minute aspects of coordinating mutual participation in a conversation, is felt as a deep uneasiness or affront, which Scheff refers to as a feeling of shame. In the Durkheimian model, violation of solidarity brings the reaction of righteous anger; this results in yet another highly ritualized interaction, a ritual of punishment. Durkheim's theory of crime (1895/1982) holds that punishment has the effect of reinforcing the group's commitment to its symbolic ideals, whether or not it is successful in deterring the violator from future transgressions. In Durkheim's view, punishing criminals is carried out not as a utilitarian act to manipulate the reinforcement schedule of the criminal, but as a ritual to maintain the group's solidarity. Scheff shows a similar dynamic operating through individual emotions: violation of solidarity brings anger; but the ritual expression of anger does not bring a return of solidarity in an alienated relationship, but rather leads to a further round of shame, anger, and ritual retaliation. Durkheim stops his analysis at the point where the punishment ritual takes place, and does not inquire what it does to the criminal's future behavior. Scheff extends the Durkheimian model into a chain, a vicious cycle.

But there is yet another way in which the emotions might be transformed. The failed interaction—the breakdown of solidarity that generates shame—can be followed by a different sequence. The failure itself can become the explicit focus of attention for an interaction in which the shamed or violated person gets to express his or her feeling of outrage directly to the perpetrator; if the latter acknowledges it, social solidarity is reestablished. This is the model of "restorative justice" implemented by the criminologist Braithwaite and others (Braithwaite 1989; Strang and Braithwaite 2000). Criminals are confronted at group meetings by their victims as well as other members of the social networks on both sides. These encounters have often been remarkably successful in reconciling the contending parties and in reducing repeated offenses. In terms of IR theory, these reconciliation circles work because they are high intensity IRs; all of the ingredients of figure 2.1 are present to a high degree. The mutual focus of attention is enforced, in part, because a police officer makes the offender pay attention to what the victim is expressing. The initiating emotional ingredient is high: the strong feelings of shame and anger; these feelings are shared and transformed, because all the persons in the circle get to express their opinions and feelings, and are swept into a common mood. The result is that the offender is shamed and ritually punished, but then is reintegrated into the group by participating in the group emotion of collective solidarity. Restorative justice groups are a striking example of how an IR can take any topic and any initiating emotion, and transform it into solidarity.

STRATIFIED INTERACTION RITUALS

The model of interaction rituals gives us the general process of interaction. IRs themselves are variable, insofar as rituals can be successful or unsuccessful, that is, in terms of how much focus and emotional contagion actually takes place, and hence how strongly the participants become attached to membership symbols. Because of these variations, interactions are stratified: some persons have the power to control others through rituals, while others are passive or resistant; some persons are in the center of attention, while others are marginalized or excluded. These are the two dimensions of power and status. As we shall see, just where people are located in such IRs is a major determinant of individual personalities.

Power Rituals

Power operates on the micro-interactional level by all those factors that bring together individuals who are unequal in their resources such that some give orders and others take orders, or more generally dominate the immediate interaction. This is an interaction ritual, insofar as it involves focusing attention on the same activity, and becoming aware of each other's involvement; and it has a shared emotional focus, which builds up as the ritual successfully proceeds. (As always, it is also possible that the ritual will not proceed successfully, that it will break down into avoidance or conflict; but let us deal with that variant separately.) The focus of a power ritual is the process of giving and taking orders itself. As many organizational studies show (especially the classic studies of informal work groups, many of which are used as an empirical base by Goffman [1959]), the order-takers do not necessarily carry out the bosses' orders; for that matter, the bosses do not always expect them to do so, or do not even know very clearly what they want done. But the crucial item of attention is showing respect for the order-giving process itself. Order-givers are in charge of a Goffmanian frontstage performance; they take the initiative in it, and if they are successful, they uphold the organizational chain of command. For this reason, the order-giving classes have a Goffmanian "frontstage personality"; they are attached to their frontstage roles. In Durkheimian terms, order-givers enhance or sustain their emotional energy by dominating during power rituals; and their ritual stance makes themselves loyal to the symbols of the organization. Their cognitions are of the "official" sort (see evidence summarized in Collins 1975, 62–87).[7]

People who are order-takers participate in these rituals in a different way. They are required to take part: whether by the raw coercion of military force (as in the army, a prison camp, or in feudal / aristocratic societies), or by the slightly more long-range coercion of a paycheck, fines and privileges, or chances of promotion wielded by bosses, teachers, and other persons in authority. The situation of taking orders, of being coerced, is in itself alienating. But persons subject to authority usually cannot evade it directly; their resistance usually occurs in situations when they are out of the direct surveillance of an order-giver—for example, in Goffmanian backstages where they criticize or ridicule their bosses, or in their normal work routine, in which they put in a perfunctory performance. In this sense, the order-taking classes have a "backstage personality."

Order-takers nevertheless are required to be present at order-giving rituals, and are required to give at least "ritualistic" assent at that moment. They and their boss mutually recognize each other's position, and who has the initiative in the ritual enactment. Power rituals thus are an asymmetrical variant on Durkheimian interaction rituals. There is a focus of attention, in this case, on the order-giving process. But the emotions that are invoked are constrained; there is a tone of respect, of going along with what the order-giver is demanding. The more coercive and extreme the power differential, the more emotional contagion there is. The medieval peasant, or the child who is being beaten, is forced to put him or herself into a state of compliance, of going along with what the master / parent / authority figure wants. It is a coerced focus of attention; the order-takers have to try hard to anticipate what the order-giver wants. Conversely, the order-giver uses coercion precisely to feel this mastery over the subordinates' minds, to "break their will."[8] Less coercive forms of order-giving have correspondingly less powerful ritual effects.

According to this theory, a successful order-giving ritual coerces a strong mutual focus of attention, and produces a situationally dominant emotional mood. But it is a heavily mixed emotion. Insofar as there is successful role-taking on both sides (and that is at the core of any successful ritual), the order-giver feels both his / her own sentiment of mastery, and the order-taker's feeling of weakness. On the other side, the order-taker has a mixture both of his / her own negative emotions—weakness/ depression, fear—and the mood of the dominator, which is strong emotional energy, dominance, anger. This explains why persons who are severely coerced (concentration camp inmates, marine corps recruits, beaten children) tend on one level to identify with the aggressor, and will enact the aggressor's role when possible in the future: they have an emotional complex of fear and anger, although situationally the fear side is dominant when they are taking orders. Conversely, order-givers who use extreme coercion acquire sado-masochistic personalities, because of the role-taking that goes on, thus blending anger / dominant feelings with a sense of the fear and passivity that they invoke in their subordinates. Thus the experience of momentary, situationally dominant emotions gives rise to long-term emotional styles, which is a large part of what is meant by the term "personality."

Power rituals produce complex emotions. Order-givers and order-takers share the dominance / anger / fear / passivity complex, but in very different proportions. Considered analytically, power rituals appear to be less effective than status rituals in generating large amounts of EE for dominant individuals; for subordinates, on the other hand, power rituals have serious emotional consequences. Exercising order-giving power increases one's EE insofar as it coincides with being in the center of attention of a situation of emotional entrainment rising to a palpable level of collective consciousness, which is what I call a status ritual: intense versions of this coincidence include military officers in combat, athletic coaches in the course of a contest, and somewhat less dramatic occasions in business and professional activities where there is a shared level of intensity among the participants. When the power ritual does not coincide with a status ritual, the person exercising power does not usually experience much EE gain, but at any rate it keeps the power holder from losing EE. Order-takers, however, generally lose EE, especially when the power ritual does not bring about a solidarity ritual.

Order-givers and order-takers also share an orientation toward dominant symbols, but again with a different blend of emotions. Order-givers identify themselves with the sacred objects of their organization; they respect these symbols as ideals, and are foremost in requiring other people to kowtow to them too. This is the conservatism of dominant classes, their self-appointed motivation as upholders of tradition, as restorers of law and order, and as righteous uprooters of heretics and deviants.

Order-takers, on the other hand, have an ambivalent attitude toward the dominant symbols. They are alienated from these symbols, and privately speak and think of them cynically, if they can get away with it.[9] Thus the modern working class is generally alienated from the business ideals of their bosses, and troops ridicule the rhetoric of their commanders. These symbols become, so to speak, negative sacred objects; when and if rebellion is possible, a suddenly liberated order-taking class wreaks vengeance on the symbols that they formerly had to bow to. (Kids without career chances in the academic system, who are forced order-takers in schools, thus tend toward acts of vandalism and other forms of "deviance" directed precisely at the "sacred objects" in whose name they are subordinated: see Cohen 1955.) It is also possible that order-takers hold the dominant symbols in a kind of superstitious respect; that is, if they are so tightly coerced that there is little opportunity for distancing themselves, no backstages into which they can retreat from their masters' surveillance, they are ritually forced to show respect for the sacred symbols at all times. Thus arises the "loyal retainer" mentality, found among long-time servants and peasants (and in a different context, among children who are strongly coerced by their parents, but also strongly controlled, and given no opportunities to rebel). The difference between these two kinds of order-takers' attitudes—alienated or subservient—depends primarily upon ecological structures: whether coercive control is continuous, or allows breaks into backstage privacy.

I have schematically outlined two polar types of participation in power rituals: order-giving and order-taking. But power rituals are a continuum. There are several kinds of positions in the middle between the extremes: persons who are order-transmitters, who take orders from someone above them and give orders to others below; these persons tend to blend the order-givers and order-takers culture into a narrow and rigid "bureaucratic personality."

There is another kind of midpoint between extremes: the person who neither gives nor takes orders, but who interacts with others in egalitarian exchanges. Analytically, this is a point within the power dimension where there is no power; hence the effects of order-giving and order-taking are both neutral. To explain what will happen at this neutral level of power, in "horizontal" relations among equals, we must turn to the status dimension.

Status Rituals

I am using the term "status" not as a general term for hierarchical differences of all kinds, but in a restricted sense of belonging or not belonging. At the micro-level of the encounter, status is the dimension of inclusion or exclusion. This, too, is a continuum; in everyday life, it appears as popularity versus unpopularity.

This dimension of membership versus nonmembership is analytical, in the sense that any individual (and any interaction) can be classified both as to where it stands in terms of status membership, and in terms of power inequality. That means that every interaction is producing both status membership effects and power effects, and every individual is subjected to both of these kinds of effects from one situation to the next. The power effects, however, might be zero, if there is no order-giving and order-taking in that situation; on the other hand, even extreme situations of order-giving also have a status dimension, insofar as the group is assembled and some membership feelings are being generated.

In what ways can individuals differ in their status group participation? Here we need to tease apart four aspects. Two of these are characteristics of the micro-situation itself and the individual's location within it. Two are meso-level characteristics of the IR chains: what happens over time as situations repeat.

First, on the micro-level, we must ask, How successful is the interaction ritual? In other words, does it build up to a high level of collective effervescence, a moderate level, or little emotional entrainment at all? The higher the ritual intensity, the more emotion is generated both in the immediate present and for long-term effects. *Ritual intensity* thus operates as a multiplier for the other three aspects of ritual effects.

Again, on the micro-level: Where is the individual located as the IR takes place? There is a continuum from persons who are on the fringes of the group, just barely members, barely participating; others nearer the core; at the center is the sociometric star, the person who is always most intensely involved in the ritual interaction. This person is the Durkheimian participant of the highest degree, and experiencing the strongest effects of ritual membership: emotional energy, moral solidarity, attachment to group symbols. At the other end, there is the Durkheimian nonmember, who receives no emotional energy, no moral solidarity, and no symbolic attachments. This is the dimension of *central / peripheral participation*.

Next, on the meso-level, as IRCs string situations together: What proportion of their time do people spend in each other's physical presence? This is the dimension of *social density*. At one end of the continuum individuals are always in other people's presence, under their eyesight and in their surveillance; this leads to a high degree of conformity, a feeling of social pressure on onself, but also a desire to make other people conform as well. At the other end of the continuum individuals have a great deal of privacy (social and physical spaces where others do not intrude; Goffmanian backstages) or of solitude (other people are simply not around). Here pressures for conformity are low. Social density is a quantitative matter, an aggregate of a chain of situations over time. An individual might occasionally be in other people's presence, perhaps even in very intense IRs, but their effect is quite different than if he or she were almost always in such situations. That is to say, a person with a high degree of privacy or solitude (low overall *social density*) might treat these occasional high *ritual intensity* episodes as sharp breaks from ordinary consciousness, either as wonderful and longed-for experiences, or as unwelcome intrusions and threats to his or her privacy. Which of these is the individual's response depends on additional features (his or her peripheral / central position and location in the power dimension).

Again on the meso-level: Who are the participants who come together in the aggregate of IR chains? Is is always the same persons, or a changing cast of characters? This is the dimension of *social diversity*, which might also be called the dimension of *localism / cosmopolitanism*. Specifying the argument of Durkheim's *Division of Labor in Society*, low diversity should produce local solidarity, strong attachment to reified symbols, literal-mindedness, and a strong barrier between insiders and outsiders. There is high conformity within the group, along with strong distrust of outsiders and alien symbols. At the other end of this subdimension, there is participation in a loose network consisting of many different kinds of groups and situations. Durkheimian theory predicts the result of cosmopolitan network structure is individualism, relativistic attitudes toward symbols, abstract rather than concrete thinking.

Stated in terms of emotions, this implies that persons in cosmopolitan networks have relatively weak feelings of conformity to group symbols; emotional coolness of tone; and generalized trust in a wide range of interactions. When symbols are violated or ritual procedures go badly, members of tight, localized groups respond with anger and fear (especially if rituals are backed up by coercion on the power dimension). Can there be ritual violations in loose cosmopolitan groups, where there is less intensity and conformity? Yes, because there can be violations of the appropriately casual and sociable tone of interaction.[10] Goffman (1959, 1967) concentrated most of his analysis on situations of cosmopolitan interactions, and depicted just such violations and their sanctions. Following Goffman, I would suggest that persons in these situations respond by amusement to minor ritual violations by others, and with embarrassment, contempt, and a desire to exclude perpetrators of more serious violations of the sociable order. The persons who commit these Goffmanian sacrileges feel anxiety and embarrassment.

Durkheim's (1893/1964) pioneering analysis did not pull apart these various dimensions built around the mechanism of ritual solidarity. His terminology conflates all four into an overall level of what he called "moral density." His most differentiated argument distinguished "mechanical" and "organic" solidarity, which was a move in the direction of seeing multiple causes. In effect, "mechanical solidarity" is the overlap of high *social density* and low *social diversity* (localism), with an implication that there is also high *ritual intensity*, and that most individuals experience relatively *central participation*—which also seems to assume that the group is lacking in *power* differences. To be sure, this overlap would constitute extremely high degrees of solidarity, conformity, and attachment to the group as the sole source of emotional energy. "Organic solidarity" is a situation of high *social diversity* (cosmopolitanism; i.e., the modern division of labor, as contrasted to undifferentiated small tribal or rural communities); but he left it unclear what variation there might be in the other dimensions. Durkheim seems to have envisioned relatively high ritual intensity, so that organic solidarity would provide sufficient solidarity, morality,

and conformity to keep modern society together. But he (and his followers and critics) were never satisfied with the organic solidarity theory. An underlying problem was the failure to distinguish enough subdimensions to recognize all the different combinations that might exist,
and that indeed are found all across the historical landscape.

This, then, is my set of hypotheses about how the various dimensions of interaction ritual affect emotions. By way of summary, let us
recapitulate the model, first in terms of the effects on long-term emotions (emotional energy), and then in their effects on short-term, transitory emotions.

Effects on Long-Term Emotions: Emotional Energy

The IR chain model proposes that individuals acquire or lose emotional energy in both power and status interactions. Order-givers
maintain and sometimes gain EE, order-takers lose it; being in the
focus of attention and thereby successfully enacting group membership raises EE, experiencing marginality or exclusion lowers it. Interaction rituals are connected in chains over time, with the results of the
last interaction (in emotions and symbols) becoming inputs for the
next interaction; thus EE tends to cumulate (either positively or negatively) over time.

Emotional energy is an overall level of being "up" or "down," ranging from enthusiasm to depression. Between interactions, EE is carried
in the individual's stock of symbols, in the cognitive part of the brain;
it is an emotional mapping of the various kinds of interactions that
those symbols can be used in, or that can be thought about through
symbols. Thus emotional energy is specific to particular kinds of situations; it is a readiness for action, that manifests itself in taking the initiative in particular sorts of social relationships or with particular persons.[11] Thus there is EE specific to power situations—expecting to
dominate, or be dominated—as well as an EE specific to status situations—expecting to be a central member, or a marginal one, or not to
be accepted at all. Furthermore, these emotional energies tend to be
specific to particular networks and groups, or to particular kinds of
them: some persons feel full of confidence and initiative in a gathering
of professional acquaintances, but not in a sexual situation; some feel
confidence in a business negotiation, but not a political one; persons
who dominate the center of attention in an intellectual gathering may
fade into shyness at a drinking party. It is in this sense that, as we will
see, sexual drive is a form of EE.

People move through the chain of encounters that make up their
daily lives on an up-and-down flow of EE. They are more attracted to

certain situations than others, and sometimes feel disinterest or repulsion. In each situation as it unfolds, their own emotional and symbolic resources, meshing or failing to mesh with those of the people they meet, determines to what extent the IR will be successful and unsuccessful. These outcomes, in turn, raise or lower EE. The end result is motivation to repeating those sorts of encounters with particular persons and to avoid them with others.

Emotional energy manifests itself both physically and psychologically; but its underlying basis—the form in which it is "stored," so to speak—is not as physical energy per se. EE has a cognitive component; it is an expectation of being able to dominate particular kinds of situations, or to enact membership in particular groups. The cognitive side of this is that symbols (particularized memories as well as generalized ideas or emblems) have emotional energy attached to them, in the sense that the symbols call forth a high or low degree of initiative in enacting social relationships using those symbols. But this is not ordinarily a process of conscious calculation, of the actor thinking "I will get a good feeling of power or status if I interact with so-and-so." Instead, certain symbols come to mind, or appear in the external environment, and spark off propensities (positive or negative) for social action. The "expectation" may work on a subconscious level. It is an anticipation of being able to coordinate with someone else's responses, of smoothly role-taking in the ongoing flow of the interaction, and thus anticipating the buildup of emotional force that goes on within a successful IR. The process of rhythmic entrainment of the ultra-micro aspects of interaction is the mechanism by which emotional contagion occurs within a successful interaction. Thus there is a very fine-grained, micro-anticipation that happens within the interaction itself (on a level down to fractions of a second), as well as a more long-term expectation of being able to enter into such micro-coordination with particular kinds of people. Emotional energy exists as a complex of these kinds of expectations, a priming for successful ritual interaction in particular settings.

The low end of EE is depression, manifested in withdrawal, both from expressiveness and activity. Depression appears to be a more complex process than high EE.[12] Experience at the low end of the power dimension brings depression: low energy, loss of motivation. But this may happen only when order-takers experience a strong degree of being under someone else's control. When their lack of control is only moderate, they may typically respond by anger—by a temporary increase in the output of EE, as vigorous reactance against the situation that is controlling them (Frijda 1986, 290). The middle level of negative interactional experience—in temporal terms, an episodic and atypical experience of being subordinated—thus has a distinctive emotional effect.

Negative experience on the status dimension has a similar contour: declining EE, with a flare-up of anger in the middle range and where the flow of emotional expectations from the IR chain is episodically dashed. Over the long run, I suggest that failure of membership in a group ritual brings a degree of depression commensurate with the degree of social exclusion. Kemper (1978), however, argues that low status brings anger as well as shame. Scheff (1990; Scheff and Retzinger 1991) present evidence that exclusion on the micro-level of the encounter, breaking attunement, brings shame, which may get into a spiral with anger. From the point of view of IR theory, shame is a form of low EE, with a distinctive cognitive component directed toward one's social image (i.e., social membership) in a particular group. Anger occurs when there is an abrupt negative change in expected social membership feelings. It is a short-term emotion due to the disruption of expectations; the long-term effect of membership loss is nevertheless depression. Hence there is no long-term increase in vigor of the sort that an angry reaction brings for moderate levels of put-down on the power dimension, that is, when there are structural opportunities for mobilizing rebellion.[13]

Scheff's model is a valuable complement to IR theory because it specifies emotions generated by both high and low levels of Durkheimian solidarity. Successful interactional attunement or an intact social bond generates pride; breaking the bond generates shame. In the terms of IR theory, pride is the emotion attached to a self energized by the group; shame is the emotion of a self depleted by group exclusion.[14] As we will see below, nonverbal and paralinguistic measures of pride and shame can be useful as measures of high and low EE. Pride is the social attunement emotion, the feeling that one's self fits naturally into the flow of interaction, indeed that one's personal sense epitomizes the leading mood of the group. High solidarity is smooth-flowing rhythmic coordination in the micro-rhythms of conversational interaction; it gives the feeling of confidence that what one is doing, the rewarding experience that one's freely expressed impulses are being followed, are resonated and amplified by the other people present. When Scheff speaks of shame as the broken social bond, I take this to mean that the rhythm is impaired, that one's spontaneous utterances are choked off—even for fractions of seconds—that there is a hesitancy about whether one is going to be understood, and hence about whether it is possible to formulate a clear or understandable utterance at all. The shared rhythm is what enables each person to anticipate what the other will do, not in specific contents, but in rhythmic form: a certain rhythm of talk is launched, characterized by a certain energy, a certain emotional flow. The conversational ritual generates high solidarity to just the extent that its participants pick up the same rhythm, molding their utterances to the rhythm that they have established in the past few moments, and riding its waves to anticipate just how their next set of utterances will flow one upon the other. By observing these rhythms, we can see emotional energy in the process of being manifested in the micro-situation.

The main long-term emotional energies resulting from stratified interaction, then, are: high levels of enthuasiasm, confidence, initiative, and pride, resulting from controlling the attunement of interaction in either a power or status situation; low levels of the same (i.e., depression, shame), resulting from being dominated in a power situation, or excluded from a status situation. There is one other long-term emotional disposition: the amount of trust or distrust of other people. At the trust end of the continuum, this simply manifests itself as high EE, willingness to take initiative toward certain social situations. At the distrust end, it comes out as fear of particular situations. Distrust / fear is attached to particular structural configurations, namely distrust of those who are outsiders to the local group; it is the result of the structural subdimension of status group interaction, in which there is tight local closure of group boundaries.

Emotion Contest and Conflict Situations

In power situations, gains of emotional energy by one person and EE loss by the other person are reciprocally related. This may also happen in sociable situations. Some persons act as energy drainers, bringing other persons down while dominating the situation. Consider the micro-mechanisms of an interaction ritual: the common focus of attention, the rhythmic coordination that intensifies emotions. Persons who control the situation can frustrate this process. They can break the micro-rhythm, by not responding to the signals the other person is putting out (by changing or reframing the topic, starting new activities, ignoring and overriding nonverbal contact cues). This is one way that order-givers establish their dominance, perhaps most likely when there are signs of challenge to their control. It also makes up the substance of aggressive status contests that happen in sociable conversations (i.e., what Goffman [1967, 24–25] calls face-work contests).

Such contests are an activity that breaks the focus of ritual microcoordination and prevents the circular buildup of anticipations on both sides. In smoothly running situations, one's own ability to use symbols in thinking and talking depends upon anticipating the other's reactions, and feeling the surge of symbolic group membership with each successful use of a commonly recognized symbol. Dominance contests break this down (whether by the deliberate intention of one person, or just inadvertent lack of interest in the other—i.e., the dominant or more attractive person's emotional energies are directed elsewhere). The result for the person who is unable to carry through their intentions and anticipations is that there is a blockage in the smooth flow of their own thoughts, words, and actions; they are unable to project a micro-future in this situation, and this is what it means to lose emotional energy.

If the failure of an interaction ritual to achieve coordination and emotional buildup debilitates one person, though, why shouldn't it bring down the other person emotionally too? According to the basic IR model, the emotional flow is a group process; what one side fails to get, the other side should fail to get also. But in some kinds of situations the result may be unequal. Consider larger group structures in which particular micro-interactions are embedded: the boss confronting a rebellious worker within an organization; or an athletic contest before a group of spectators. The person who dominates the micro-situation has the possibility (which may be overt or only subjectively felt) of gaining recognition in the larger group context. And conversely, this individual may bring along previously generated feelings of membership in the larger group structure, the emotional energy of being a dominant figure capable of mobilizing an enforcement coalition (in a formal organization), or of being a popular person (before an audience of fans).

Chambliss (1989) has studied this interaction in the case of athletic contests (competitive swimmers), and has found that there is a major difference in outlook between high-level performers (consistent winners) and lesser performers (losers). The difference is manifested in the details of behavior: winners are meticulous in performing their routines in ways that they have deliberately developed; they have built up their own rhythms and stick to them in the face of competitive opposition. The winners make themselves the focus of attention; they set the expectations around themselves. Losers, however, let the winners become the focus, and adapt their micro-behavior toward them. This implies that a winner (perhaps dominant persons generally, in dominance contests more widely as well as in athletics) has a sense of control throughout the situation: winners maintain and build up their own rhythmic coordination, their anticipation of what they will do, setting the micro-rhythmic pace. Losers (and persons who are subordinated in dominance contests) allow someone else to break their own flow of anticipation of what will happen in their own activities. These dominated persons can cope with the situation, can maintain some anticipa-

Figure 3.1 Winner focuses on the goal, loser focuses on the
winner. Final lap of relay race, which runner E is about to win.

tion about what will happen only by focusing on the other person as
the lead, rather than by projecting their own volitional future. In effect,
such a person can recoup some emotional energy from the situation
by becoming a follower, attaching themself to someone else's lead.[15]
The more they resist such attachment, the less emotional energy they
will have.

In terms of the IR model, one could also say that the dominant person makes oneself the focus of the interaction. He or she becomes, in some sense, a Durkheimian sacred object. Microsociologically, that is just what a "sacred object" means—it is the object upon which attention of the group is focused, and which becomes a symbolic repository of the group's emotional energies. When someone feels oneself in this position, they have a store of emotional energy for their own use; it makes that person "charismatic." For others, the person who is a "sacred object" compels attention. They become spectators to that person. Their attitudes as spectators can vary. If they throw themselves completely into acquiescence, they become compliant admirers, who want to attach themselves and draw some flow of the "sacred" emotional energy for themselves (like fans asking for an autograph).

At the other extreme, they may be resentful would-be or failed competitors. But even their resentment is a feeling based upon recognizing that the other person has a special status as "sacred object" that they do not have. Chambliss (1989) describes this difference as the "mundanity of excellence." Persons inside the social realm of winning / dominance experience a mere routine, in which they have smooth anticipated control of situations—that is, a great store of "emotional energy" available to them in contest situations. But persons on the outside looking in see a mystifying difference, a gulf to greatness that they feel they cannot cross. These differences are, of course, most exaggerated in highly publicized contest situations, like the Olympic athletes Chambliss studied. In lesser degrees, dominant persons are also little "sacred objects" at least in certain small local situations, while subordinated persons are left with the choice of being participating spectators of their dominant energy, or feeling the energy drain of opposing them.

There is fine-grained micro-situational evidence of this process in a study by Erickson and Schultz (1982) of video-taped interactions between junior college counselors and students. Typically, these dyads fell into the same rhythm of syllables by pitch and loudness, both in their own turns and in the turn-taking rhythm as they shifted from one speaker to the other; these beats were often synchronized on the microkinesic dimension with body movements. This pattern could be interpreted as a baseline of IR solidarity. At times, one person takes the lead in holding the rhythm, while the other person flounders for fractions of seconds (usually in small-scale upsets on the order of a few quarter-seconds) in an unrhythmic pattern, then follows the pattern maintained by the first. These recordings display situational dominance on the ultra-micro level of seconds. There are also instances where the tapes show the two persons' rhythms mutually interfering with each other; or where both go along in different rhythms, as if deliberately in opposition to one another. In follow-up interviews where the subjects were shown tapes of themselves and asked to describe what was going on, they tended to comment on the "uncomfortable moments" where the rhythmic coordination broke down, but not on the moments when their rhythms were in sync. It appears that the participants took solidarity for granted, and only noted its absence. For the most part, the subjects seem to experience the pattern of the interaction subliminally; it was only after repeated viewing of the tape recording, and repeated discussions with the experimenter about their reactions to "uncomfortable moments," that students began to become consciously angry about what they came to see as their dominated position in the interaction.[16]

Power derives from a variant on the basic IR model. In its Durkheimian formulation, successful rituals produce group solidarity. Teasing apart the mechanisms and fine-grained processes of an IR, we could say instead that successful IRs produce heightened mutual focus and bodily emotional entrainment. Power is an asymmetrical focus of attention upon such a situation, so that one side battens on the energy that all the participants have mutually produced. In a power ritual, the social battery is revved up, but the benefit goes largely to one side.[17]

Short-Term or Dramatic Emotions

Most research on emotion has focused on the short-term, dramatic emotions: the "phasic" rather than the "tonic," the outbursts that disrupt the ongoing flow of activity (Frijda 1986, 2, 4, 90). My argument is that the short-term emotions are derived from the baseline of emotional energy; that it is against the backdrop of an ongoing flow of emotional energy that particular disruptive expressions are shaped. Surprise, for example, is an abrupt reaction to something that rapidly and severely interrupts the flow of current activity and attention. This is also the general pattern of more important short-term emotions.

The positive emotions become intense largely because of a contagious buildup during an interaction ritual. This is the case with enthusiasm, joy, and humor: all of these build up in social situations as the result of a successful ritual. Psychological analysis tends to take these emotions from the individual viewpoint. For example, joy is explained as the result of the momentary expectation of success in some activity (Frijda 1986, 79). This is sometimes true; but joy and enthusiasm are particularly strong when an assembled group is collectively experiencing this expectation or achievement of success (e.g., fans at a game, political partisans at a meeting). Further, the group itself by a successful emotional contagion can generate its own enthusiasm (which is what the flow of conversation at a party does).

These kinds of positive emotional outbursts are relatively short and temporary in their effects. They happen upon a baseline of previous emotional energy: for a group to establish this kind of rapport, its members need to have previously charged up some symbols with positive attraction, so that these symbols can be used as ingredients in carrying out a successful ritual. A previous cumulation of emotional energy is thus one of the ingredients in making possible the situational buildup of positive emotion. Frequently, the positive emotions (joy, enthusiasm, humor) are generated by a group leader, an individual who takes the focus, who is able to propagate such a mood from his or her own stores of emotional energy. This individual thus serves very much like an electric battery for group emotional expressiveness. Persons who occupy this position in IR chains are what we think of as "charismatic." In general, "personality" traits are just these results of experiencing particular kinds of IR chains. (This is true at the negative end as well, resulting in persons who are depressed, angry, etc.)

The negative short-term emotions are even more clearly related to the baseline of emotional energy.

Anger is generated in several ways. Psychologically, anger is often regarded as the capacity to mobilize energy to overcome a barrier to one's ongoing efforts (Frijda 1986, 19, 77). This means that the amount of anger should be proportional to the amount of underlying effort; and that is the amount of emotional energy one has for that particular project. High emotional energy may also be called "aggressiveness," the strong taking of initiative. This can have the social effect of dominating other people, of lowering their emotional energy, of making them passive followers. This implies that there is a connection between the generic quality of high emotional energy—especially the EE generated in power situations—and the expression of the specific emotion of anger.

The disruptive form of anger, however, is more complicated. That is because anger in its intense forms is an explosive reaction against frustrations. Truly powerful persons do not become angry in this sense, because they do not need to; they get their way without it. To express anger is thus to some extent an expression of weakness. However, persons who are powerful can afford to become angry; their power-anger is an expression of the expectation that they will get their way against the obstacle. In the case of a social obstacle—the willful opposition of some other person—it is an expression of the powerful person's confidence that he or she will be able to mobilize an enforcement coalition to coerce the opposition into compliance, or to destroy the resistance.

Previous stores of EE thus determine when and how someone will express explosive anger.[18]

The most violent expression of anger occurs when one feels strong in overcoming a strong frustration. If the frustration itself is overwhelmingly strong, the feeling is fear, not anger. Persons who are weak do not manifest anger in the same way. It is only when they have enough resources to be able to mount some resistance (or at least some social privacy, a separate social circle in which they can utter symbolic threats) that weak persons, order-takers, have anger. This follows from the principle that the core of anger is the mobilization of energy to overcome an obstacle. It is only when there are enough social bases of support to generate EE that one can react to a frustration (in this case, being dominated) by mobilizing anger. Persons who are too weak (i.e., in their IR chains they lack resources or space in which to mobilize any other socially based EE), do not react angrily to domination but succumb to depression.

In between these two situations there are selective outbursts of anger. This is the targeted anger that individuals feel against particular other persons. It occurs because these individuals are structural rivals in the market of social relationships: for example, two women competing for the same man, or two intellectuals competing for the same audience. Here one does not feel angry against someone who is stronger than oneself (rebellious anger), nor against someone weaker (dominance anger); rather, this is a case of someone frustrating one's own projects. The anger here is not really "personal"; there is no role-taking (as in the dominance / subordination forms of anger), although the target is a person, and the underlying structure is a social one; it is only an accident that the obstacle to one's goals happens to be a person.

An especially Durkheimian form of short-term emotion is *righteous anger*. This is the emotional outburst, shared by a group (perhaps led by particular persons who act as its agents) against persons who violate its sacred symbols. It is group anger against a heretic or scapegoat. Such anger only happens when there is a previously constituted group. One can predict that righteous anger is proportional to the amount of emotional charge of membership feelings around particular symbols. The amount of such charge, in turn, is highest where the group has high social density and a local (rather than cosmopolitan) focus. Where the group networks are diffuse and cosmopolitan, on the other hand, the short-term emotion felt at disruption is embarrassment on behalf of the disrupter—resulting in status exclusion, unwillingness to associate with that person, rather than in a violent ritual punishment to restore symbolic order.[19]

Righteous anger has great importance in political sentiments as well as in the dynamics of local communities (scandals, witch-hunts, political hysterias). The theoretical difficulty is understanding just how this kind of anger relates to the power and status dimensions of group structure. In the Durkheimian model, it seems to be the group in general, and all its adherents, who are outraged at the violation of its symbols. But anger, and hence violence as a punishment (burning a witch or heretic at the stake, throwing drug dealers or gamblers or abortionists in jail) is related to the power dimension, since the use of violence is the ultimate sanction of power. To explain righteous anger, we need to observe the power and status dimensions in conjunction—in instances where the status group structure is dense enough and locally closed enough so that there is a strong sense of group membership, attached to reified symbols; and where this ritual community has a power hierarchy within it, which regularly exercises coercive threats to enforce obedience to orders. Under these circumstances ritual violations (violations of membership symbols on the status dimension) are taken as a threat to the power hierarchy as well.

Righteous anger is a particularly intense emotion because it is expressed with a strong sense of security: the individual feels that they have the community's support, and not merely in a loose sense. Righteous anger is an emotion that is an evocation of the organized network that has been previously established to use violence. Persons who feel righteous anger are evoking their feeling of membership in an enforcement coalition.

As evidence, I would point to the fact that the most violent punishments for ritual deviance (witch-burning, public tortures, and executions in medieval patrimonial states; violent atonement for taboo violations in tribal societies) occur where the political agents are both highly coercive in their ordinary operations, and are active in enforcing group cultures (Collins 1974; Douglas 1966). Heresy trials and violent ritual punishments have declined in keeping with the degree of the separation between church and state; it is where these spheres (the power hierarchy and the status community) are fused that righteous anger is most prevalent. In some degree, however, the political hierarchy still remains the focus of status rituals—through its claims to be a community as well as an organization for wielding power. This makes it possible to mobilize deviance-hunting as a form of status intrusion into the political sphere, even in relatively differentiated modern societies. And it is advocates of a return to the fusion of community with polity who are most strongly involved as "moral entrepreneurs" in modern deviance-hunting. Such advocates often come from the localized sectors of modern society, especially the remnants of traditional and rural communities. In addition, the attempt of socialist regimes to keep up a high level of collective solidarity helps to explain their concern for rituals of conformity.

Fear is another short-term negative emotion. The most intense and briefest forms of fear are those that most sharply disrupt activities; at the extreme, intense fear experience is next to a startle response. Crying is an expression of fear in a more complex sense: it is a social call for help in distress. Adults do not cry very much, because their horizon widens out. Instead of relatively short-term and simply physical threats or discomforts, the most important form of fear becomes fear of social consequences: fear of being coerced or fear of social exclusion, which are more long-term experiences. Furthermore, since the problem is itself the social situation, crying (which is a communication of help-lessness) is subordinated by more complex adjustments of EE. One cannot usually so readily call on others for sympathy, if one is being coerced or excluded.[20] Crying, as a form of emotional communication, is upstaged by a more direct emotional response in the form of fear and avoidance.

In social relationships, fear is generally a response to someone else's anger. It is an anticipatory emotion, the expectation of being hurt. Thus it is most directly related to long-term emotional energy deriving from subordination on the power dimension. It occurs in similar circum-stances to depression, but it has a more confrontational structure. Whereas depression is a withdrawal of EE (i.e., withdrawal of attention from particular activities), fear is a kind of social cringing before the consequences of expected actions. Depression is a sinking of EE level because of the bludgeoning effects of negative social situations;[21] fear is a negative anticipation of what will happen, which assumes enough EE to take some initiative, or at least remain alert to situations that carry social dangers. Hence one can experience fear of status loss (membership exclusion), as well as fear of power coercion. On the power dimension, fear is mobilized together with anger in cases where a person is able to mobilize anger, but has low confidence in being able to win positive results from its expression.

Transformations from Short-Term Emotions into Long-Term Emotional Energy

The results of various short-term emotional experience tend to flow back into the long-term emotional makeup that I have called "emo-tional energy." Emotional energy, though, does not have to depend upon the dramatic emotions; situations of uncontested domination or belonging add to one's store of confidence and sense of attraction to-

ward particular kinds of situations; undramatic feelings of subordination and unpopularity have similar negative effects. The dramatic
short-term emotions also spill over, though it is an unexamined question whether their very quality as dramatic makes them more important for long-term emotions, or brackets them as a sort of exception.
In the case of positive short-term emotions (joy, enthusiasm, sexual
passion), it seems likely that these experiences should build up the
store of EE, although perhaps in a very situation-specific way (i.e., one
becomes attached to repeating just those situations with particular
partners).

   In the case of negative emotions, there is a long-standing clinical tradition that sees traumatic situations as the major determinant of long-
term social and psychological functioning. Particular experiences of
intense anger, fear, or shame are regarded as controlling one's whole
subsequent functioning. This may well be true, to a degree; but it
should be seen against the background of the overall level of emotional
energy. A person who generally has favorable, if undramatic, experiences on the power and status dimensions of their everyday interactions, will likely get over an episode of extreme anger, fear, or shame.
It is only when the individual's overall "market position" of interactions is on the negative side that particularly intense dramatic experiences are stored up and carried over as "traumas," especially in highly
charged memories of the sort that Freudian therapy is designed to ven-
tilate. Max Weber's conception of stratification as inequality of life
chances in the market thus extends not only to material economic
chances but to the realm of emotional health.

   Scheff's model reformulates Freudian theory as a carryover of emotions through an interactional chain. There is a shame / rage cycle in
which an individual who experiences a shaming situation feels rage
against the perpetrator, which can lead to further conflicts; these typically have unsatisfactory outcomes, resulting in further shame and
rage. Rage at oneself can also become part of a self-reflective loop, intensifying this process. Scheff presents evidence that the traces of previous emotional arousals, especially anger, can remain at an unconscious, trace level; and that there are unconscious shame behaviors
that are manifested in the micro-details of interactions. The limitation
is that Scheff and Retzinger (1991) have chosen a sample of cases—
couples in marital counseling—in which these shame / rage cycles are
well established; but they have not considered the cases in which the
cycle does not occur or quickly terminates. That is to say: Scheff concentrates on conflictual social relationships among individuals who
are relatively equally matched, who are at the middle levels of dominance and popularity, such that they can continue long cycles of sham-

ing and raging at each other. More extreme differences in power would not allow a conflictual cycle to go on; and if persons are not confined to the same network of status interactions (i.e., their market possibilities are more open) they may cut short a shame cycle by leaving that interaction and finding another where the resource lineups may be different.

The Stratification of Emotional Energy

IR chains often have a circular, self-perpetuating form. Persons who dominate rituals gain EE, which they can use to dominate future IRs. Persons who are at the center of attention gain EE, which they can use to convene and energize still further gatherings, thereby making themselves yet again the center of attention. In this way, powerful persons re-create their power from situation to situation, while those whom they dominate re-create the low energy level that makes them followers and subordinates. Status group leaders re-create the energy that makes them popular; groupies, fringe members, and outcastes are carried along in their positions by the repeated flow of lower EE.

Changes, of course, are possible chiefly if and when the composition of the persons encountering one another shifts, since in a perfectly closed cycle there would no way of getting out of a low-EE situation, or of failing to confirm one's high EE. Thus even high-EE persons (like political leaders, or sociability leaders, or in specialized kinds of EE, sexual stars or intellectual dominants) move into an arena where they become overmatched by someone else with still greater EE (and hence become a medium fish in a bigger pond); and low-EE persons may find a different arena where they avoid old situational match-ups and find others that generate more solidarity (e.g., by graduating from high school). These are matters of how the entire array of IR chains, which makes up the population of a society, are arranged across time and space; and thus we widen out perspective to relatively more meso- rather than micro-analysis.

We may visualize the stratification of society, not as a matter of who owns what material resources, or occupies what abstract position in a social structure, but as an unequal distribution of emotional energy. Positions in a social structure are macro-level abstractions; we can see stratification in a more empirically realistic way, as well as keep ourselves focused on its processual dynamics, by looking closely at exactly what stratification is enacted in micro-situations. Material "resources" are often repetitively available from one interactional situation to another, but what makes them "resources" hinges upon the micro-inter-

actions that allow someone to appropriate them; and that is a question
of who takes the initiative to take them and use them, and who passively accepts that these material objects are so used. Material property,
as enacted in situations, is really the EE that particular persons have
in acting upon those objects.[22] Where the right to property is conceded,
the distribution of emotions is asymmetrical, in that someone's high
EE in appropriating those objects is matched by someone else's low EE
in allowing them to be appropriated or at least standing by watching
the other person display them. Similarly, Bourdieu's "cultural capital"
is too static a conception if it is taken merely as the counterpart in the
hierarchy of culture to a hierarchy of economic capital.[23] Another way
to say this is that the key to stratification is not material property, nor
cultural differences, but inequalities in emotional energy. It is the processual flow of EE that enables people to wield material and culture,
or lets others wield those over them.

The simplest version of stratification is an energized upper class,
lording it over a depressed lower class, with moderately energized
middle-class persons in between. Take this pattern as an ideal type; it
does yield a crucial point, that stratification generally works because
those who dominate have the energy to dominate situations in which
they encounter other persons. The winning generals are usually the
most energetic ones; so are the richest financiers; in the specialized
realm of intellectual domination, the stars of world science, philosophy, and literature generally are what I have called "energy stars" (for
evidence on generals, see Keegan 1987; on philosophers, Collins 1998).
To say this is not to make a moral judgment about any of these people:
first, because what they are doing may well be manipulative, destructive, or selfish; and second, because their energy is not their own, in
the sense that it arises interactively from chains of IRs, and thus from
the network positions that put them into a positively accumulating,
upward series of EE-enhancing encounters. My argument is far from
holding that the upper classes are uniquely energetic individuals; they
are products of processes that affect all of us, and in which all of us
(very likely) are pretty much interchangeable. About any such dominant energy star, it is possible to say, there but for the grace of God
(i.e., the luck of IR chain trajectories) go you or I. Dominant persons
are not intrinsically heroes, but it is socially significant that they often
appear as such. Persons with lower amounts of EE are impressed by
those who have accumulated a lot of it; such people have an EE-halo
that makes them easy to admire. They are persons who get things
done; they have an aura of success surrounding them. And since having high EE allows one to focus attention, one can get a certain amount
of rise in one's own EE by following them, becoming part of their en-

tourage, taking orders from them, or even viewing them from afar. Thus high EE gives dominant persons a kind of micro-situational legitimacy. This is not necessarily the same thing as the ideologies of legitimacy that Weber typologized (although it may undergird this formal legitimacy); I would hold that micro-situational legitimacy is by far the kind most worth having.

The stratification of EE thus makes the other aspects of stratification particularly solid and hard to dislodge. When the upper class has really high EE, no one even thinks of dislodging them, or even wanting to. That is, of course, an ideal type. A crucial point follows: A portion (perhaps a large portion) of what we conventionally call the "upper class" may consist of persons who have inherited their wealth, rest on their laurels from an earlier period of action, or otherwise not show very much EE. In such cases, the real distribution of EE differs from the formal, ideological conception of stratification. What we want to look for as sociologists is the real distribution of EE, and how it matches up against this surface appearance.

A perfectly self-reproducing stratification of EE is an ideal type. Patterns resembling this in degree have existed at various historical times. But these can break down in a variety of ways: some of these can shift very rapidly, since the mechanisms that generate EE are quite volatile, and conflict generates its own immediate patterns of EE. The mobilization of collective EE in social movements is a prime case of this. A stable hierarchy of EE can also break down in a different sense: not so much in the case of political action in which there are massive collective struggles, but in the case where energizing situations become fragmented. Instead of a hierarchy resembling the energized upper class, the depressed lower class, and a plodding middle class, we may get a purely local, episodically shifting situational stratification of EE in which almost any encounter is up for grabs. These topics will be taken up in later chapters.

Appendix: Measuring Emotional Energy and Its Antecedents

It is sometimes raised as a criticism against IR theory that emotional energy is merely a hypothetical construct, or even a tautology. In reply, I wish to underscore the point that EE is an empirical variable.

We must be careful to distinguish EE from other kinds of emotions that are displayed. First, EE is not simply a matter of showing a lot of excitement, agitation, loudness, or bodily movement. These are characteristics of the dramatic or disruptive emotions: shouting or lashing out in anger, squealing and gesturing with joy, shrieking or running around in fear. EE instead is a strong steady emotion, lasting over a period of time, not a short-term disruption of a situation. A general characteristic of EE is that it gives the ability to act with initiative and resolve, to set the direction of social situations rather than to be dominated by others in the micro-details of interaction. And it is an emotion that allows individuals to be self-directed when alone, following a smooth flow of thoughts, rather than a jerky or distracted inner conversation. (For more detail on the latter, see chapter 5.)

Second, EE is a long-term consequence of IRs that reach a high degree of focused emotional entrainment, which we can also call attunement, collective effervescence, or solidarity; but EE is not the attunement itself. In figure 2.1, the ingredients and processes on the left side and middle of the diagram happen earlier than the outcomes on the right side; EE is a consequence that carries over after the individual has left the situation. Thus we must be able to measure it apart from the collective arousal itself. But it is also important for us to be able to measure the degree of collective effervescence or solidary entrainment within a situation, since this is the causal condition that produces EE.

Thus we wish to measure (a) the level of collective attunement reached at the height of an interaction, and see if it predicts the level of (b) emotional energy carried away by individual participants. With good measures of (b), we can also examine how long EE lasts, and test Durkheim's proposition that EE fades away over a period of time unless a sufficiently intense ritual attunement is reenacted.

The following briefly overviews the different kinds of verbal and nonverbal phenomena that we can use as measures of EE, and as measures of the chief causal variable, situational attunement or solidarity. A clue is that attunement is a collective pattern, EE an individual one.

Self-report.   I have defined EE as the continuum from enthusiasm, confidence, and initiative at the high end, down to passivity and depression at the low end. EE exists empirically in one's flow of consciousness and in one's bodily sensations: it is the most important item in one's own everyday experience. It is not difficult to observe rises and falls in one's own EE in different situations; with close self-observation, one can notice it rise or fall in a matter of seconds within any particular situation. Patterns of EE could be systematically studied by having individuals give reports on their subjective experience in various kinds of situations.

EE can also be measured objectively, by outside observers. Here the best measures are for the most part unobtrusive, although they do call for close observation of micro-details.

Bodily postures and movements.   High EE is generally expressed in an erect posture, moving firmly and smoothly, and taking the initiative in relation to other persons. Low EE is indicated in postures and movements that are shrinking, passive, hesitating, or disjointed. Since high EE is social confidence, it is manifested in movements toward other people, especially movements that take the initiative and that lead to establishing a pattern of rhythmic coordination. Low EE, conversely, is found in movements and postures of withdrawal, and low initiative; low-EE persons in a social situation show a pattern of following others' nonverbal leads, or a freezing of movement. Conflict at moderate levels of EE may be indicated by a rapid or jerky alternation between orienting toward and away from the others. Scheff and Retzinger (1991) describe this pattern, which they interpret in terms of the self-oriented emotions of pride (turning toward the other person) and shame (turning away).

We need to be careful to distinguish bodily measures of EE from those bodily movements that represent the process of collective entrainment within a social situation, although the one can lead directly into the other. High or low EE is visible in body postures and movements when an individual is alone. When an individual enters an interaction, EE is visible in the moments leading up to the high point of entrainment (whatever level that may be). That is to say, the high-EE person takes the initiative in setting the tone of the interaction, and the low-EE person lags behind or follows passively. EE must be observed in the dynamics of how the individuals lead or lag in the interaction, apart from the observation of how much entrainment finally results. This peak level of entrainment is a measure of collective effervescence.

At peak moments the pattern tends to be jointly shared among all participants: in high solidarity moments, bodies touch, eyes are aligned in the same direction, movements are rhythmically synchronized (see Figures 2.2, 2.3, 2.4, 2.5, 8.6, and 8.7). At moments of failure of the interaction, bodies turn away from each other, heads turn downward or inward toward one's body, eyes look down or away. (For an example, see Scheff and Retzinger 1991, 54–56.)

Bodily measures also express the dramatic short-term emotions, which need to be distinguished from high and low EE more generally. On specific emotions, see Ekman (1984) and O'Sullivan et al. (1985), who also indicate the extent to which the body can be controlled so as to mask emotions, and which body movements tend to be involuntary and thus are genuinely unguarded expressions of emotion.

Eyes.   Solidarity is directly expressed in eye contact. As Scheff and Retzinger (1991) show, persons in a situation of high attunement look at each other. This occurs in a rhythmic pattern, viewing the other person's face, responding with micro-expressions, then periodically looking away (to avoid staring). In moments of intense solidarity (such as group triumph or erotic entrainment) the mutual gaze is longer and more steady. In a situation of low attunement, persons lower their eyes and turn away for prolonged periods. These are measures of high or low attunement or collective effervescence, and they tend to be symmetrical across participants. EE is seen in the eyes, as in the case of bodily postures and movements, as a temporal pattern for each individual as they approach the situation. Initiative or lack of initiative can be seen in establishing eye contact; high or low EE is manifested in dominating or avoiding mutual gaze (Mazur et al. 1980; Mazur 1986).

Voice. The amount of enthusiasm, confidence, and initiative (high EE) versus apathy, withdrawal, and depression (low EE) can be measured paralinguistically, that is, in the style rather than the content of talk. (See Scherer 1982, 1985, for studies of the emotional dimensions of recorded speech.) Since the flow of speech in an interaction is also a measure of the amount of attunement or collective solidarity, we must be careful to observe in micro-detail the patterns of the individuals as they approach the vocal interaction, as distinguished from the degree of attunement that is reached collectively.

A refined study that separates out these several aspects is Erickson and Shultz (1982: see especially 85–96, 103–117). This study demonstrates measures of voice rhythms charted at twenty-four frames per second, but typically visible at quarter-second intervals. These fall into five patterns: (i) a shared rhythm, with the beat falling at about one-second intervals; this may be interpreted as normal solidarity; (ii) "individual rhythmic instability," as one individual follows the previously set mutual rhythm while the other is momentarily disorganized: an indicator of dominance or interactional centrality on the part of one speaker in relation to the other; (iii) mutual rhythmic instability, as both speakers slow down or speed up the rhythm for a brief period before returning to the baseline rhythm: a temporary failure of the interaction ritual: a display of low solidarity; and (iv) mutual rhythmic interference and (v) mutual rhythmic opposition, which are two types of micro-interactional conflict: in (iv) the conflict is ongoing, whereas in (v) a dominance struggle is won by the speaker who overcomes the rhythm of the previous speaker and gets acquiescence to the new rhythm.

The characteristics of (iv) and (v) are worth quoting directly from the authors:

Mutual Rhythmic Interference [iv] A kind of mismatch between the behavior of one individual and the other, lasting a few moments, involving the persistence by each party in rhythmic patterns that are regular for each individual but different across individuals, for example individual A's behavior is patterned in a rhythmic interval of 1 second duration, while individual B's behavior over the same period of time is patterned in a rhythmic interval of .75 second duration.

Mutual Rhythmic Opposition [v] . . . . Momentary rhythmic disintegration between the behavior of one individual and the other, involving deviation of 4–5 twenty-fourths of a second from the previously established periodic interval. Coming in this much too soon or too late at turn exchange has the effect of "tugging" at the underlying rhythm. This tugging is seemingly competitive; at the very least it indicates a lack of cooperation or integration in the mutual behavior of speakers, since one speaker does not participate in the rhythm used by the previous speaker. After the momentary tug occurs, however, the previous speaker adapts to the new rhythmic interval, and so the lack of temporal integration between them involves momentary opposition rather than continuous interference (Erickson and Schultz 1982, 114–15).

The troubled moments (ii, iii, and v) also tended to coincide with shifts in body posture and proxemics, or, changes in body orientation between the speakers.

These voice rhythms thus show variations in solidarity, as well as fine-grained indications of who sets the rhythm and who follows it. For our purposes, (ii) and (v) indicate taking the initiative and setting the pattern, which are indicators of EE—high EE for the individual who sets the rhythmic pattern, low EE for the individual whose rhythm is determined by the other. Pattern (i) is an indicator of high solidarity; (iii) and (iv) are indicators of low solidarity.

Measures of interactional solidarity are also available from the ultra-micro analysis of the sound-wave frequencies at subliminal levels, using Gregory's (1994; Gregory et al. 1993) Fast Fourier Transform (FFT) analysis. FFT analysis finds rhythms of vocal coordination at a level below .5 KHz (KiloHertz, thousand cycles per second), a region in the sound spectrum that is heard only as a low-pitched hum. Although participants are not aware of the sounds they are making on this level, their voice rhythms converge in conversations that they subjectively rate as more satisfactory interactions with a higher level of rapport.

Comparing Gregory's measures at the level of thousands of cycles per second and Erickson and Schultz's measure at the level of quarter-seconds, it is apparent that several levels of rhythmic coordination overlay each other, at different orders of time-frequency. The relationships among these different time-orders are yet to be investigated, as well as their connection with IR ingredients and outcomes.

Other indicators of conversational attunement or solidarity have been displayed in chapter 2: a close pattern of turn-taking with minimal gap and overlap; rhythmic entrainment in shared laughter, applause, and other simultaneous vocalizations. Conversely, gaps between turns, and prolonged overlaps among speakers contesting the floor, indicate low solidarity.

Indicators of conversational solidarity are easier to tease out than indicators of EE, since the latter involves showing who takes initiative in establishing the pattern of the interaction. Some aspects of individual voices are probably not good measures: loudness of tone and speed of talking are too easily confounded with specific disruptive emotions such as anger. Better indicators of EE are fluidity, hesitation pauses, and false starts on the part of each particular individual. Ability to get the floor, versus incidence of contested speech turns, is another indicator; methods are demonstrated in Gibson (1999).

Hormone levels.   Mazur and Lamb (1980; see also Kemper 1991) have shown that the experience of dominating an interaction has continuing effects upon hormone levels (especially testosterone). These hormones may provide a physiological substrate for medium-run flows of EE across situations. It should be noted that testosterone is found in females as well as in males, although in lower amounts (Kemper 1991); hence the pattern could be operating for both sexes. The important comparison is for shifts in hormone levels within the same person across situations, not necessarily for relative hormone levels across different individuals. Studying hormone levels requires intrusive measures, which are especially intrusive when this is done by drawing blood samples, and thus such studies have been done largely by volunteers who are trained medical personnel; saliva measurements have also been used. It would be worth seeing how shifts in hormone levels relate to shifts in other measures of EE. It is not clear whether EE shifts are related to absolute or relative levels of testosterone, and of other physiologically active substances. In any case, whatever physiological substrate is involved must interact with the cognitive components by which EE is carried along as a propensity to respond positively or negatively toward particular kinds of interactional situations; and with the level of mutual focus and emotional entrainment that constitute the immediate process of social action.

Facial expression.   I do not place emphasis on facial expressions as indicators of EE. Ekman and Friesen's (1975/1984, 1978) manual shows the ways in which specific emotions are expressed in the several zones of the face, such as joy, anger, fear, sadness, and disgust. But these are indicators of the short-term, disruptive emotions. It is not clear that there are specific facial indicators for high and low EE. It is possible that facial measures of EE could be developed. High EE should be found in facial expressions of confidence and enthusiasm; low EE as expresssions of apathy and depression. These should be distinguished from facial indicators of momentary happiness and sadness, since high and low EE should be prolongations across situations.

Even if facial measures are not the best way to measure EE, I would urge microsociologists to study Ekman's facial indicators of emotions and make use of them in situational observations; they provide useful auxiliary information, and may show patterns of short-term emotional expression that are related in various ways with flows of EE across situations. Ekman's research (1984) is valuable also because it indicates which zones of the face are most easily controlled by deliberate efforts to mask emotions, while other zones tend to express spontaneous emotions.

It would be useful to study all or several of these measures simultaneously. Especially worthwhile would be to compare each of the objective measures—body posture and movement, eyes, voice, etc.—with self-reports of high or low confidence and initiative. Arriving at objective measures is desirable insofar as they are less intrusive, and thus easier to use in observational research. The result of such multi-measure studies should be to show which measures are redundant, and which are most highly correlated with long-term patterns (i.e., with the flow of EE across situations).

The two approaches to measuring EE—subjective self-observation and objective observation of other people—may also be used together. If subjective measures are pursued, persons can become better self-observers by training in objective measures, enabling them to attend to one's own bodily sensations, movements, and postures in detail, as well as to those around them.

What I would like to stress, in using either subjective or objective measures, is that these processes always happen in micro-interactional situations; the level of EE should always be studied in relation to the kind of situation that is occuring at the moment, and within the chain of situations from the immediate past. It is less useful, in using subjective measurements (such as questionnaires, interviews, or time-diaries), to ask for a global assessment: "how much enthusiasm, confidence, and energy (or depression, apathy) have you been experiencing in your life?" Such information gives an indication of the overall drift of situational outcomes, but it is more valuable to be able to show what the situational conditions are in which these observations take place.[24]

To study shifts of EE in real-life situations, it would be desirable to follow people's experiences across a chain of interactions. A medium-term design would be necessary. Possibly this could be constructed in a laboratory situation lasting several days. Observation in natural conditions would also be desirable, especially to estimate how long emotional effects of interactions may last. I suspect, however, that the time-decay of emotional energy, if it is not reinvested and reinforced by subsequent interactions, may be less than a few days.

Chapter 4

INTERACTION MARKETS AND MATERIAL MARKETS

INDIVIDUALS MOVE through their everyday lives encountering other people with whom they carry out some degree of interaction ritual, ranging from the barest utilitarian encounters and failed rituals to intensely engaging ritual solidarity. Who each person will interact with and at what degree of ritual intensity depends on who he or she has the opportunity to encounter and what they have to offer each other that would attract them into carrying out an interaction ritual. Not everyone is going to be attracted to everyone else, and these patterns thus take on the character of a market for interaction rituals. Sociologists have long made use of particular versions of interpersonal markets: the marriage market; the dating market; in recent history, the evolution of the latter into a market for various kinds of shorter or longer-term sexual liasons—or set of markets, subdivided for example into heterosexual, gay, bisexual, etc. (Waller 1937; Laumann et al. 1994; Ellingson and Schroeder 2000). By extension, we can conceive of a friendship market, which among other things accounts for the tendency for people to find their friends in the same social class and culture group (Allan 1979; McPherson and Smith-Lovin 1987). With a further generalization, we arrive at a view of the entire macro-distribution of social encounters across time and space as a market for interaction rituals of varying degrees of intensity.

The market for interaction rituals provides a way of conceptualizing the connection between micro and macro. As critics of radical microsociology have pointed out, situations do not stand alone: any particular situation is surrounded by other situations that the participants have already been in; they may look ahead to other situations in the future, some of which are alternatives to interacting with the person one happens to have in front of him or her at the moment, like people at a cocktail party looking over the shoulder of their boring conversation partner to see who else they might talk to. This is just what makes interactions market-like. It also explains the quality that situations have: a degree of emergence, where things can happen that have not happened before and that an individual could not anticipate from his or her own experience alone; but also a degree of constraint or even coercion, such as in the feeling of being trapped because there are only certain people available whom one can talk with (or be friends with, have sex with, marry, etc.) and only certain ways of carrying out the talk (the sex, etc.) that will work.

Because of such emergence, it is sometimes claimed that situations are entirely unpredictable. Anyone who has ever been to a reception at a professional meeting, or struck up an acquaintance while traveling, or attended a party or a job interview, knows that this is far from true, down to the details of what people are going to say. But these are situations in which the individuals involved have a relatively limited stock of similar social symbols and therefore things to talk about, and so that is what comes out of their mouths—what do you do, where are you from, what are the differences between east coast and west coast, do you know so-and-so. If the situations are more wide open, and you as a participant do not know in advance much about what kind of people are going to be there—that is, you know nothing about their previous IR chains—the possibilities for what might happen appear to be an immense blank horizon. That is only to say, situations are sometimes very unpredictable from a single participant's viewpoint. Situational action is predictable to a sociological observer who knows the individuals' IR chains, and hence what emotional energy and stock of membership symbols each has coming into the interaction. In a rough way, this is just what an old-fashioned dinner hostess did in deciding who to seat next to whom. With more analytical refinement, a sociologist can examine the ingredients for making rituals that individuals have accumulated, and thereby predict what their combination of ingredients will bring about.

The market for interaction rituals gives us several insights. It gives us a theoretical model of how individuals will be motivated, not just in a single situation, but in the longer-run trajectories of their lives; and it shows how cultural symbols are passed along in chains, sometimes acquiring greater emotional resonance, sometimes losing it. Interactional markets might appear to be something that operate in people's private, leisure lives, their times of sociability but not in the serious realm of work; sociological market models, after all, started out with marriage, dating, and sex. But a major extension is possible. In addition to interaction markets in the sense that we have been considering them, there are also material markets, by which I mean just those markets for goods and services that economists have traditionally studied. The two kinds of markets can be connected: we do this conceptually by seeing material markets as providing some of the conditions, the material underpinnings, that are among the ingredients for IRs to be initiated. Material conditions for interaction rituals are necessary but not sufficient, of course, since the main ingredients of IRs are emotions and symbols largely recycled from other IRs. But without the material conditions, even the most successful IRs must come to an end. Thus we can connect the two kinds of markets, for interactions per se and for material goods and services, as one flowing into the other; not only do material markets flow into the ingredients for IR markets, but IR markets also provide the crucial social components of material markets. As we shall see in more detail, there are several such components: the motivation to work and invest, and the so-called "human capital" of relationships and trust within which material markets are embedded.

I will start the analysis with the market for motivation, which is to say the market for emotional energy. This strategy of presenting the argument is useful because it points directly at a crucial aspect of the debate over the application of market models to sociology, and conversely at the underpinnings of mainstream economic analysis provided by economic sociology. I will begin by entering the terrain of rational choice theory, which is the most explicit attempt to apply economic models to social phenomena. Those familiar with the history of mid-twentieth-century sociology will remember that before this movement was called "rational choice" it existed indigeneously in sociology as "exchange theory," and it was developed by sociologists such as Willard Waller, analyzing marriage markets, George Homans studying solidarity in small groups, and Peter Blau researching bureaucratic employees trading advice and conversational ploys at cocktail parties.[1] My argument will be that market models of social interaction come up against some basic paradoxes, and that it is necessary to invoke the market for IRs in order to resolve them.

Problems of the Rational Cost-Benefit Model

The rational actor perspective has several appealing qualities for a sociological theory dedicated to building all explanations from micro-interaction. It begins with a motivated actor and avoids reifying macro-entitites such as culture or structure; these are valid concepts only to the extent that they can be derived from the action of individuals. And it has a general explanatory strategy: all social action is explainable in terms of individuals attempting to optimize their expected benefits relative to the costs of their actions.

There are also a number of difficulties. First, there are classes of behavior that seem to escape from cost / benefit analysis. These include emotional behavior, altruism, and morally or value-motivated behavior generally. Persons will override material interests when these non-material ends become salient. There is a related argument, going back to Durkheim's "precontractual solidarity," that exchanges based on ra-

tional self-interest cannot even take place unless there is a prior framework of values that established the rules within which such exchanges
occur. Thus rational action might seem to be only a portion of human
social action, indeed a subordinate part.

Second, there is no *common metric* that would make it possible for
actors to compare costs and benefits among different spheres of action.
Within the sphere of material goods and services, money can be used
as a standard of value. With some stretching, one can also attempt to
measure with money the value of personal health, safety, and life itself.
But although such equivalences are made after the fact in insurance
settlements and law suits, it is not clear that individuals themselves
typically plan their actions by comparing, for example, danger to life
and limb against a monetary equivalent. More widely, how do individuals choose between money, life, and honor? Is there a common metric
for comparing power with these other goods? How much status or
how much vengeance is equivalent to how much effort or physical risk
or leisure, and can one assume such equivalences are stable across all
times and all persons? To define all such goods as components of an
abstract utility function of goods and services that individuals maximize is to beg the question of how individuals actually make a decision to pursue one good rather than another. To posit a preference
schedule is merely ad hoc unless we can explain what forms it will
take. And if persons do not have a common denominator, they may be
rational in each sphere separately, but unpredictable in the way they
jump from one sphere of action to another.

Third, there is a good deal of evidence that individuals in natural
situations do very little calculating. The concept of "rational choice"
may be more of a metaphor than an actuality. Goffman's (1967) studies
of naturalistic interaction show persons engaging predominantly in ritualized behavior. Garfinkel (1967) and his school of micro-researchers
find that the most important "ethnomethods" are to avoid raising
questions as to the rationale for behavior, in order to stay out of infinite
regresses of contextual explanation. Garfinkel describes the usual procedures of social interaction as conservative with interactants assuming the normalcy of appearances, and engaging in ritual repairs to
paste over episodes where interaction breaks down. The ethnomethodological findings are broadly similar to the "bounded rationality"
school of organizational analysis, which ascribes to actors a limited
cognitive capacity in the face of complexity. March and Simon's (1958)
"satisficing" and "troubleshooting" behavior parallels on the organizational level the preference for assuming background normalcy, which
Garfinkel finds in everyday interactions—we might call this the
"Simon and Garfinkel principle." And finally, there is the evidence of
psychological experiments (Kahneman et al. 1982; Frey and Eichen-

berger 1989) that show that actors presented with problems of calculation are biased toward nonoptimizing heuristics.

Evidence that individuals do not calculate very much in micro-situations, or that they calculate badly, need not undermine the rational actor theory more generally. The theory's main proposition is that behavior moves toward those courses of action that give the greatest return of benefit over cost; individual's behavior should be "rational" in this sense in the medium run, but it is not necessarily given how they arrive at this line of behavior. It could occur by trial and error. It may occur by sheer pressure of costs, so that certain lines of behavior are not possible to sustain. Action may well take place unconsciously, without conscious calculation, and still be constrained by rewards and costs. Unconscious behavior could come out at the same place as consciously calculated behavior. This is not to say that behavior must always be unconscious; but if an unconscious mechanism exists that leads toward medium-run optimizing outcomes, then individuals who rise to the level of conscious calculation would tend to come to the same conclusions as those exhibiting the non-conscious behavior.

In what follows, I will argue that all three of these problems may be solved in the same way. First, emotional, symbolic, and value-oriented behavior is determined by the dynamics of interaction rituals (IRs). Emotional energy generated by experience of group solidarity is the primary good in social interaction, and all such value-oriented behaviors are rationally motivated toward optimizing this good. Since IRs vary in the amount of solidarity they provide, and in their costs of participating, there is a market for ritual participation that shapes the distribution of individual behavior.

Second, IRs generate a variable level of emotional energy (EE) in each individual over time, and that EE operates as the common denominator in terms of which choices are made among alternative courses of action and disparate arenas of behavior. The valuation of money and of work occurs because of the way in which these fit into the market for IRs. Individuals apportion their time to these various activities to maximize their overall flow of EE. The economy of participation in interaction rituals is an integral component of the economy of goods and services.

Third, I invoke the model of micro-situational cognition, such that individual thinking is determined by the emotional energy and the cognitive symbols generated by interaction rituals. This is congruent with micro-situational evidence of noncalculating behavior; while the aggregation of micro-situations (interaction ritual chains) is subject to interactional markets that bring about rational tendencies in the medium-run drift of behavior.

The Rationality of Participating in Interaction Rituals

Figure 2.1 presented the IR model in the form of a flowchart of ritual ingredients and ritual outcomes. Here I will put this model to use, showing how the emotional energy outcome (EE) is the key to individual long-term motivation. Let us look at the IR model again, now given in figure 4.1 with greater detail on feedback processes.

There are two kinds of feedbacks—short term and long term. The first we have already considered, as the intitiating ingredients (physical density and barriers to outside involvement) that feed into mutual focus and emotional entrainment, which in turn reciprocally builds up to the situational engrossment that Durkheim called collective effervescence.

Long-term feedbacks occur when the outcomes of one IR feed back into the conditions that make it possible to carry out a subsequent IR. Persons who have gone through an IR experience giving them a feeling of group solidarity want to do the ritual again, especially when they are feeling that the solidarity is beginning to dissipate. Hence the long feedback loop (the dotted line in figure 4.1) from *group solidarity* back to *reassembling the group. Emotional energy* also facilitates further IRs, in part because persons with high EE have the enthusiasm to set off a new *emotional stimulus* and pump up other people (an obvious example is the charismatic politician or evangelical religious leader; in the private sphere, an enthusiastic individual who initiates a conversation); in part because persons with high EE have the energy to make strong *efforts to reassemble the group*, or to collect a new group. And finally, when people have *membership symbols* pumped up with significance from past IRs, they possess cognitive devices for reminding themselves of past rituals, and also a repetoire of emblems and emblematic actions that they can use as a *visible focus of attention* or a *shared activity* to get an interaction focused again. This is how a single IR becomes an IR chain.[2]

Interaction rituals operating at high levels produce all of the values that are usually thought to evade explanation by rational choice theory. Religious commitment originates in ritual assemblies, and is intense to the degree that high levels of mutual entrainment are sustained by members of a group. Conflict situations produce dedication and willingness to sacrifice oneself when the experience of mobilization or combat is a high-density interaction ritual with the extremely salient initiating emotions of fear and anger, which are experienced collectively by a group and transformed into solidarity. Dedication to political ideals is anchored in rituals of large-scale group assembly. Similarly, there are small-scale, more personal interactions that produce altruistic behavior: friendship that reaches high degrees of solidarity from successful interaction rituals in relatively scarce, intimate conver-

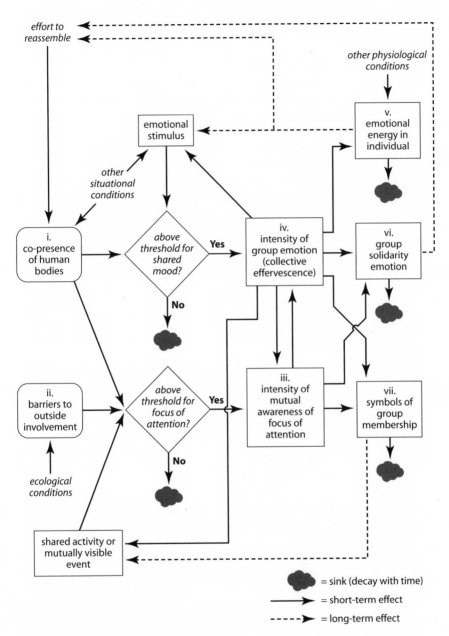

Figure 4.1 Flow chart of interaction ritual.

| | Person A | | |
	No	Short Time	Long Time
No	0, 0	0, 0	0, 0
Person B Short Time	0, 0	1, 1	1, 1
Long Time	0, 0	1, 1	3, 3

Figure 4.2 Payoffs for sustaining mutual focus.

sations; sexual love resulting from high-intensity erotic IRs; parent-child love deriving from the rhythmic cuddling and playing that parents do with infants and small children and that both sides find so delightful. All of these experiences are regarded by the individuals involved as extremely rewarding. Successful IRs, either in large or intimate groups, are regarded by most people as the most significant events of their lives.

How does one apply a rationality model to IR-based emotional solidarity? Solidarity is a good; and individuals are motivated to maximize the amount of solidarity they can receive, relative to costs of producing it. Solidarity, however, is a collective good; it can only be produced cooperatively. But it is a fairly simple type of collective structure. Interaction rituals are not subject to the free rider problem. A solidarity game has a structure like that in figure 4.2:

Both A and B get solidarity payoffs only if both contribute to maintaining a mutual focus of attention and allow themselves to be drawn into the common emotional buildup; and the higher levels of payoff depend upon each sustaining the focus to equal lengths. Given a taste for solidarity (or for its correlate, emotional energy), it is highly rational for individuals to join in an interaction ritual when they can.

Complexities could be added. Larger groups reduce dependence upon any particular individual. An individual who does not participate in the ritual carried out among other persons, but only passively observes it, reaps a much lower level of solidarity from it, and so the overall structure of incentives remains similar to the two-person group. Figure 4.2 includes no cost of participating in a ritual. In actuality there is at least some cost of effort; but since successful IRs generate emotional energy, individuals feel invigorated and feel that they have more than recouped the cost. An interaction ritual is costly only if one or a minority of participants put a great deal of effort into it unsuccessfully. Whether this happens depends on conditions outside a single ritual situation, especially the emotional motivation and the repertoire of emotionally charged symbols that the whole array of individuals bring to the situation, which in turn depend upon their opportunities in the ritual marketplace as a whole. I will introduce such cost conditions as we broaden the analysis from the single situation to an array of alternative situations.

The Market for Ritual Solidarity

If it is always rational within the immediate situation to take part in an interaction ritual, what limits an individual's participation? Why should high-intensity rituals ever end, and why should people spend any part of their lives doing anything else? In the short run, interaction rituals come to an end because of emotional satiation. There is a diminishing marginal utility, in that emotional arousal plateaus at some point; beyond this point solidarity remains high for some period but mutual emotional arousal fades. This is a physiological characteristic of emotions.[3] This short-run satiation, however, does not eliminate the tendency to medium-run repetition of these rewarding situations. We will examine this point in more detail. Successful IRs give individuals both emotional energy and membership symbols, which are resources easily reinvested in producing further IRs. The result, one can foresee, is that there will be an intermittent chain of IRs of the same kind, repeating as soon as the short-term satiation periods are over.[4]

This pattern of intermittent ritual assemblies is empirically realistic to a degree; people do develop a taste for church services, for parties with their friends, or for political rallies. But can we explain how such propensities wax and wane? What determines which IRs an individual will join rather than some other rituals, and why some individuals develop more of a taste for ritual solidarity than other persons? To answer this we will consider the positions of individuals in the overarching market for ritual interactions.

Reinvestment of Emotional Energy and Membership Symbols

Interaction rituals are cumulative not only in the short run but also in the medium run. That is, individuals who have taken part in successful IRs develop a taste for more ritual solidarity of the same sort, and are motivated to repeat the IR. This happens through the production of emotional energy (EE) in individuals, and the creation of symbols representing group membership.

The emotional energy of individuals goes up and down depending upon the intensity of the IRs in which they have taken part. EE is transitory. It is highest at the peak intensity of an interaction ritual itself, and leaves an energetic afterglow that gradually decreases over time. The time-decay of EE has not been measured; a reasonable approximation may be that it has a "half-life" between a few hours and a few days, although it may well be modified by experience in further IRs within that period. EE is not solely determined by IRs; we should not rule out the possibility that low EE (depression) is influenced by physiological conditions; similarly high EE can be pumped up at least briefly by alcohol, drugs, and other bodily inputs. This is indicated in figure 4.1 by the arrow from *other physiological conditions* to *emotional energy in individuals*. What I would insist upon, though, is that any such physiological inputs flow through the full set of IR processes, and thus are amplified or diminished by them (and vice versa).[5] Some IRs use these kinds of physiological pump-primers (e.g., alcohol at a party) as part of the technology of ritual production.

A person's fund of EE is one of the key resources that determines his or her ability to produce further interaction rituals. Individuals who have stored up a high level of EE can create a focus of attention around themselves, and stir up common emotions among others. Such high-EE persons are sociometric stars; at the extreme they are charismatic leaders. Lacking such unusually high levels of EE, the emotional energy generated in prior IRs facilitates subsequent IRs of moderate intensity. At the other extreme, individuals whose prior experience in IRs has given them little emotional energy, lack one of the key resources to become initiators of subsequent high-intensity interactions. Their depressed mood can even depress others, so that they are avoided in the market for interactional partners.

EE is one key resource in a market for IRs. Some individuals have more EE resources than others to invest in IRs; we can expect accordingly that some individuals will demand more return for their EE investment than others. And some individuals will have a greater range of opportunities to invest their EE successfully, whereas others will have few situations in which they can successfully be admitted as participants. Accordingly we expect that EE-rich individuals will be less committed to a particular region of the market, whereas others are tied to the only groups that will accept them.

The other key resource in the market of interactions is *membership symbols*, the items upon which a group has focused attention during an interaction ritual. All items of culture lie somewhere in this continuum of symbolic arousal; they are loaded in varying degrees with membership significance, ranging from low to high, in relation to particular groups. The possession of highly charged membership symbols facilitates subsequent IRs. When several individuals value the same collective symbol, it is easy for them to evoke it in an interaction and achieve a high degree of focus around it. It provides a content to talk about or a focus for action. Collective symbols tend to be used repeatedly in IRs of a well-established group, and hence to be recharged with feelings of solidarity; the symbols and the interactions are chained together over time.

Match-Ups of Symbols and Complementarity of Emotions

At any moment in time, a population of individuals have varying degrees of EE and varying stocks of collective symbols, charged up with membership commitments by their previous experience in IRs. Their behavior can be predicted through a market process. Individuals move toward those interaction that feel like the highest intensity interaction rituals currently available; that is to say, they move toward the highest EE payoffs that they can get, relative to their current resources. Since membership symbols are specific to particular groups, some forms of cultural capital do not match up well in some interactions: the interaction ritual does not reach a high level of intensity, and the EE payoff is low. Individuals are motivated to move away from such interactions. Where membership symbols of the participants match up well, IRs are successful, and the EE payoff attracts them toward such situations.

In the micro-situations of everyday life, the process of matching up symbols takes place largely as a conversational marketplace: who talks to whom, and at what length and with what degree of enthusiasm. Talking is determined by participants matching up things they have to talk about. The extent to which they are willing to talk to each other depends also on the comparisons each makes, implicitly or explicitly, to other conversations they could be having with other people in their network, who have varying stocks of symbols. Each conversationalist compares the topics possible in the match-ups offered according to how much they find them interesting, important, entertaining, or culturally prestigious. Each conversation takes place in the context of a market for possible conversations; choices are spread out in time, but sometimes the situation presents a visibly market-like character as in a cocktail party where there are many possible conversational match-ups and any conversation can be broken off to take up another.

Persons with more resources can demand more in exchange from those they interact with; the symbol-rich and the EE-rich more easily

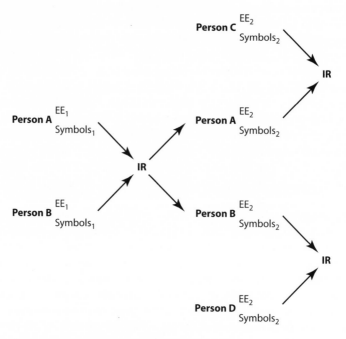

Figure 4.3 Interaction ritual chains.

get bored and dissatisfied with a conversation. There is a tendency for unequals in symbolic possessions to exchange little with each other and move on to find a more equal matchup. Whether this happens or not in a particular situation depends on additional conditions: whether there are opportunities to shift to someone else, and who is available—the interesting persons to talk to at the cocktail party may be already tied up, much like the belle of the ball who had her dance card fully filled (in an earlier era, to be sure, when there were such things as dance cards). The degree of constraint on staying with or moving away from the current conversation depends not only on the local match-up but also on the extent to which tight match-ups prevail in the surrounding conversational marketplace. Conversations between unequals are also affected by the relative EE levels of the participants, which can sometimes motivate one to defer to the other and the other to accept the deference rather than breaking off the conversation.

The chain of IRs over time is given schematically in figure 4.3. Person A and Person B encounter each other, each possessing a level of EE and stock of symbols as of time 1. The degree of success or failure of whatever IR takes place now transforms the EE and symbol stock for each; EE is increased, decreased, or recharged at the same level at which it came in. Symbols are charged with greater significance, or are drained of it by their failure in the IR, and, in addition, new stocks of symbols might be acquired. A and B now leave the encounter, primed with levels of EE and symbol stocks that they can use in their next encounter, which schematically might take place with C, D, or again with each other.

The stock of symbols an individual can use during an encounter comes to a considerable extent from their prior IR chain. New symbols can also be created, if the IR is at least moderately successful, and in two ways. This could happen unilaterally, as one person passes new symbols to the other; this could be regarded as symbolic learning during an encounter, the transfer of symbolic capital through a network, but with one proviso: this is not simply cognitive learning by filling one's memory banks, but acquiring symbols that have a membership significance and an EE charge. What an individual can "learn" from an encounter that is socially significant is what symbols mean for membership in a particular group; this might take place by experiencing the social use of some symbol that one already has some acquaintance with but up until now had not felt its significance. Acquiring symbols from other people is a process that builds up over time, as one comes to feel the membership resonances more deeply. To be naïve is not just to have never heard of something significant, but perhaps, more embarrassingly, to have heard of it but have no sense of what it means, and thus to refer or react to it inappropriately.

New symbols are also sometimes created collectively within a conversational interaction. This usually comes from a very successful IR, reaching a high level of mutual focus and emotional entrainment. Here the converation may generate new ideas and insights, or coin a new phrase and launch a buzzword, a witticism worth remembering, jokes worth recirculating. The events of the encounter itself may become symbolic resources as well, if the encounter creates a new level of reflection about other people or the participants' understanding of each other. It becomes memorable—and an object of further reflection and symbolic recirculation—when it brings a dramatic change in relationships, such as forging or breaking an alliance or setting off an antagonism between the participants. In this respect there is a parallel between love affairs and business or professional relationships: in the heightened excitement of the flirtation and negotiation period, the creation of emotionally loaded symbolic stocks is facilitated.

I have illustrated the process of matchups from the natural rituals of conversations. The pattern is similar with other kinds of natural rituals. These include collective participation in events such as games and entertainment. Some of these gatherings are commercial, and it might seem that one needs no prior cultural capital to gain entrée, but only the price of a ticket. But without some degree of symbolic stock, you are not likely to be a very deeply involved participant, capturing little of the emotional resonances of the entertainment ritual that give it the sense of a collective membership symbol. Typically you need to have acquired some of the symbols from one's prior experience in a network of encounters, or to be accompanied by someone who explains what is going on and inducts you into the proper frame of experiencing it. Such transfer of symbolic stocks is all the more necessary where entertainment is put on privately: traditionally in such social pastimes as music-making, singing, dancing, or card-playing; contemporarily in music listening or sports. The forms of leisure rituals historically change but their significance as membership symbols does not (even though during the late twentieth century sociable gatherings generally eliminated most participatory rituals except conversation and television-watching).

Such activities create palpable boundaries or rankings among those who are more accomplished than others. All these activities involve gradations of skill, which are typically remarked upon by those present and recycled afterward in converations and thus become part of individuals' social reputations; some persons are better dancers, better singers, better players at a game whether it be bridge, nineteenth-century English cricket, or twentieth-century American pickup basketball games. Skill in such activities is part of the stock of membership symbols, reminding us that symbols are not things or even merely cognitions, but ways of communicating membership. Talking is the process of using verbal symbols with greater or lesser effect on the focus of attention and emotional entrainment, and thus includes the style and rhythm of talk as much as the sheer abstract stock of symbols that persons remember. Dancing is a bodily symbol, an enactment of a degree of membership, whether it was done (in a prior historical era) by proper performance of a stately minuet or by inability to perform anything but a peasant dance, or by displaying no dancing skills at all (a nineteenth-century hostess would have said "having no social graces"). Transposed into a different time and arena, there are similar inclusions and exclusions in knowing or not knowing the manners of the mosh pit. These are bodily enacted symbols, directly performing membership with the persons danced with or played with in a game; and the same is true of the behavior of persons listening collectively to music and displaying or failing to display enjoyment at the appropriate moments through such rituals as applause. All such natural rituals, then, even without passing along conversational symbols, buildup from the ingredients of symbolic stocks that participants bring to the interaction, and at their conclusion leave those participants with a renewed or altered stock of membership symbols.

The process of reinvesting and recycling symbol stocks occurs by participation in formal rituals as well as informal ones. The individual needs to be in the flow of prior symbols, or opportunities to be introduced to them, to take part successfully in the ritual of an aristocratic court, in church ceremonial, in the formalities of political institutions. The sum of one's symbolic membership stock is made up of symbols used in conversational IRs, in other natural rituals, and in formal rituals; while the relative value of formal and informal rituals has changed historically, some such overall stocks of symbols remain crucial for negotiating the chain of situations that makes up everyone's lives.

The simplest version of IR markets are static and self-reproducing; this is the model that Bourdieu posits as omnipresent. Those who know formal rituals best go on carrying them out, keeping up a round of membership in these elite circles of public attention; those without symbolic knowledge remain excluded, and never have the opportunity to acquire the most prestigious membership symbols. Similarly in informal rituals of conversations, the popular stars of sociability go on reproducing their own conversational capital, and the symbol-poor and the unpopular remain excluded, and must be satisfied with their own low-intensity, low-prestige conversations.

This simple model of the reproduction of market dominance in IR markets, however, does not yet take account of the place that EE plays in the process of negotiating encounters. For a successful IR to take place, it is not simply a matter of person A and person B matching up their membership symbols, and similarly matching up their EE levels. Two high-EE persons do not necessarily get along with each other well. Each is used to being in the center of attention, taking the initiative, dominating the conversation, controlling the ritual. In politics, charismatic leaders are not close associates of each other but are usually quite separate; they might even be rivals, each surrounded by their distinct social circles.[6] And so it goes with popular hostesses, leaders of street gangs, ebullient jokers who are the life of the party. There is room in any gathering for only a limited amount of attention space, and for some to be in the center means others must be more passive or peripheral.

The theory of IR chains implies that persons who already have very high EE, and thus are good at charging up a gathering as its emotional leader, will choose gatherings in which they are most likely to be in the center of attention, and to avoid gatherings where they have to share the spotlight with others of equal emotional dominance. At the opposite end of the spectrum, very low-EE persons may be consigned to each other's company by the IR market, but that does not mean they will seek each other out. One generally observes that low-status, marginal persons at the fringe of a cocktail party do not create counter-circles with their own effervescence rivaling those at the center of the party, but remain relatively dispersed.

The typical pattern is for high-EE persons to interact with those of moderate EE.[7] Moderate levels of EE provide entrée into a potentially successful IR. A collection of such persons will have the energy to initiate a focused encounter, and if they also share symbols to generate a strong mutual focus, their mutual entrainment and buildup of effervescence will increase the EE level for everyone. Another pathway is that the person who is already an energy star, highly pumped up by the previous IR chain, acts as a unique catalyst, getting the encounter going focused around him or herself, with the result of further reinforcing his / her EE. Thus particular combinations of EE may result in shifts in the distribution of symbolic capital, and result in more dynamic patterns than a simple reproduction of stratification by the recycling of cultural capital.

Because individuals with high-EE levels do not generally want to match up with other similar individuals on the EE dimension—even though there is a tendency to match up on the symbolic dimension—there arise occasions for trade-offs. High-EE individuals generally have opportunities to accumulate a lot of symbolic capital; but if they interact with a group of followers, EE-poorer as well as symbol-poorer, some of the latter can acquire symbols that they did not already have. This is done by being willing to be subordinate, to give deference, to be part of the supporting cast and not vie for the center of attention. The willingness to do so is the result of emotional complementarities. Persons with high emotional energy are by definition full of confidence, and subjectively full of pride; they expect to dominate encounters, and expect their symbolic capital to be appreciated. An individual whose EE is very high compared to his or her relative symbolic resources in that situation (i.e., the person is used to dominating interactions but is currently overmatched by being unfamiliar with the local membership symbols being used) is unlikely to act humbly enough to learn the new symbols by paying deference to those who can impart them. High-EE persons thus tend to stay within their own orbits of cultural exchange; if the IR market moves away from them, they may have difficulty adjusting, becoming embittered and angry at the loss of their centrality. Very low-EE persons, at the other extreme, are not very good at acquiring new cultural stocks situationally either; they are too depressed to get into the group, too likely to repel others with their depression, or too likely to become the butt of their jokes and occasions for in-group entertainment by the more popular.

Between these extremes, persons in the shifting mid-range of EE may often find themselves in interactional matchups where they feel over-matched but not debilitatingly so. Their moderate level of EE leaves them emotionally willing to defer to others at least locally and situationally, and in return to get infusions of new symbolic capital from other persons whose previous IR chains have left them better stocked. In this way, changes in the distribution of symbolic resources can occur; the result is symbolic mobility, and as the enriched stock of symbols is successfully reinvested, EE mobility as well. The EE-rich and the symbol-rich can fall, and the EE-moderate (if not the EE-poor) and the symbol-deprived can rise. Thus there is volubility in IR markets.

In sum, the circulation of symbols takes place generally by matching up similar symbols among persons who are already primed to give them similar membership significance. EE also circulates and is reproduced, but via a pattern of complementarity rather than in direct matchups among persons of identical EE. Thus IR markets have a local stratification: circles with their EE leaders in the center of attention, surrounded by EE followers, with a penumbra of the EE-poor or EE-outcasts. But symbols can be composed of many different things, and collective focus on these different symbols sustains many different groups and many different kinds of gatherings or milieux: those focusing on specific realms of professional or business affairs, leisure-time specialists in carousing, followers of various arenas of entertainment, devotées of religious practices, political enthusiasts, intellectual circles.

This poses a theoretical problem: if individuals are EE-seekers, but there are many different arenas of interaction, and thus many different ways they could get EE, how do they choose among them? These are disparate realms of symbol circulation, which often stand in a "horizontal" relationship to one another; they are not a homogeneous currency of cultural capital marked along the single dimension of high and low.

The answer is that individual "choices" come about, not by comparing symbols along a scale of their objective value, but purely from the viewpoint of the individual actor in the flow of situations in which those symbols are used. Individuals feel their way toward those situations in which, through the local combination of ingredients for making an IR happen, the EE payoff is highest. EE operates as a common denominator for choosing among symbolic currencies. The world is symbolically heterogeneous, full of different pockets of meaning; individuals negotiate their paths through their world, simple or chaotic as it may be, on the flow of emotional energy. And that is to say, on the relative success or failure of IRs in producing EE for their participants, situation by situation.

Attraction toward or repulsion from particular situations often happens automatically, without much self-awareness, as individuals simply feel their energies pulled into certain interactions and away from others. Under certain circumstances, individuals may plan ahead, deliberately thinking through possible interactions. The key component of such "imaginative rehearsal" (in symbolic interactionist terminology) is the EE loading of the concepts with which they carry out the thinking; thus IR chains indirectly affect conscious reflection over courses of action.

From an economic point of view, there are numerous imperfections in the market for IRs. Many or most individuals are prevented from trying out a wide range of alternative interactions, by ecological or social barriers. There is no implication that IR markets produce a social optimum or a market-clearing price. The market for social interactions is best described as a series of local barter markets, shaped by the ecological conditions of the society. It remains the case that individuals, confronted with interactional situations, move toward those that give the highest payoff in emotional energy. Individuals' behavior in regard to interaction rituals is rational behavior.

Emotional Energy as the Common Denominator of Rational Choice

Emotional energy is the common denominator in terms of which individuals decide among alternative IRs. Whether one is most attracted to a church service, a political rally, or an intimate conversation is determined by each individual's expectations of the magnitude of EE flowing from that situation. Since EE is highest during an intense IR in progress, but decays with time after the IR is ended, recency is an important feature of which IR has the strongest emotional attraction at a given time.

But how do individuals decide between emotional payoffs from IRs and other kinds of goods? Does this model imply that individuals are social solidarity junkies, who will always choose in favor of a church ritual or a sociable encounter (whichever has highest EE), and against going to work or saving one's money? Let us broaden the analysis of the market for IRs. As figure 4.4 indicates, IRs have costs in addition to the reinvestment of emotional energy and of membership symbols, which we have just considered. Thus at the left side of the IR model there is the market for material goods and services (for short, "material market"), which flows into the IR market. The two markets can be analyzed as a single, unitary market *if* one is willing to begin with the *IR*

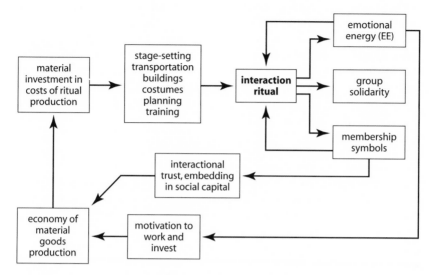

Figure 4.4 Interaction ritual and production of material resources.

market side as the ultimate determinant of valuation of goods in both markets. That is to say, the IR market producing emotional energy can be used to generate the valuation by individuals of material goods and services, but not vice versa: we cannot get a preference schedule for EE from the preference schedule for money or any other good within the material goods market.

I am not contending that individuals always value social solidarity more highly than material goods. What I will attempt to show, however, is that we can predict under what circumstances individuals spend relative amounts of effort in each particular sphere. I will attempt to show that EE operates as a common denominator facilitating choice.

There are three ways in which material production becomes part of a unitary process of motivational choice. (I) Material conditions are part of the resources necessary for carrying out IRs; hence to maximize EE, individuals will have to put some energy into producing these material conditions for IRs. As the market for IRs becomes both more expansive and expensive, it generates motivation for expanding material production as well. One may recognize here a twist on the Weberian theme that religion (more generally, IRs) motivates capitalism (material markets). (II) In addition, material production itself takes place in situations that generate their own levels of EE. There are naturally occuring IRs within people's work lives, which determines that some persons will get most of their EE from working. In this way we can

explain why some persons become "workaholics" and money fetish-
ists, persons who value these activities and goods more than would
be predicted merely from the material market alone. Both (I) and (II)
integrate the market for material production with the market for IRs.
We will also discuss a third pathway integrating the two kinds of markets: (III) how the social embedding that makes material markets possible is provided by the flow of IRs among market participants.

(I) Material Production Is Motivated by the Need for Resources for Producing IRs

If we grant that individuals pursue EE payoffs of participating in interaction rituals, it is also true that individuals need material goods and
that they will spend a certain amount of time and effort in working to
procure them. How then do they calculate whether to work or to seek
the best available payoff in EE? My suggestion is that people rarely
find it necessary to make such choices. The conditions for a successful
IR include assembling the group, focusing attention, excluding extraneous activities and nonparticipants. Where such conditions do not
occur naturally, by ecological or organizational accident, work must be
put into making them happen. Group members have to put effort into
assembling. Homes, church buildings or convention halls are important for staging an IR by setting boundaries and facilitating a focus
of attention; highly institutionalized rituals invest in special costumes
or props. There are costs of transportation, real property, and other material means for the production of rituals. The cost of entering a ritual
that has an ongoing history, is familiarity with the stock of symbols
that participants use as a medium of attention. To achieve ritual solidarity at a scientific convention requires the investment of many years
of education and experience; to get the solidarity payoff as popularity
leader in a round of parties requires another type of investment, in the
accoutrements, skills, and transient fads of sociability. Any kind of IR
typically has some level of material costs that went into producing the
current level of cultural capital of its participants.

As indicated in figure 4.4, the market for ritual participation is constrained by the material resources of would-be participants. If this is
the case, *the motivation of individuals for work is affected by the market for
ritual participation.* Suppose someone prefers to spend all of their time
in religious, political, or sociable rituals, and never do any work for
material rewards. Unless this individual has previously accumulated
sufficient property, she or he will eventually be unable to participate
in IRs for lack of material resources to attend or take part. At the extreme, this individual will be unable to feed or shelter him or herself,

and become physically incapable of any action at all. The market for materially nonproductive IRs is self-correcting in this respect. If individuals spend so much time in IRs that their material resources dry up, the rituals break down, and participants have to return to materially productive work until they have accumulated enough resources to stage another ritual.

This is empirically the case. High-intensity rituals (church services, political rallies, parties) are scheduled only intermittently, to make time for work. When conditions for IR mobilization are extremely high—such as a time of revolutionary upheaval, which generates very strong emotions and a collective focus of attention around the fight for political control—work grinds to a halt. Nevertheless, such high levels of mobilization dissipate over a matter of days or weeks because it becomes materially impossible to sustain mass participation without break.

Starting from the assumption that individuals care about nothing but maximizing their EE, we arrive at the conclusion that materially productive work will also take place, precisely to the degree that there are material expenses for taking part in IRs. The assumption of EE primacy may seem extreme, but nevertheless it is in keeping with major sociological themes: that humans find life meaningful only if they are integrated into a social group (Durkheim's analysis of suicide); that social definitions determine the value of objects and activities; that status-ranking within groups is a powerful motivational force. What the model of a market for IRs does is give a predictive mechanism for the variations in EE-seeking within a population; and it links this to the material costs of producing IRs.

The motivational links between the IR market and the material production market takes place at two points: motivation to invest in production, and motivation to take part in the market for consumer goods. The motivation to seek material goods can be manifested through investing either labor or capital; here IR market theory meshes with conventional economics, in that individuals' availability of these resources and their relative opportunities for returns affect the particular mix of investment. The theory of IR markets leaves intact much of existing economic analysis of the movement of prices, production, and finances. What IR theory adds is an empirically determinative mechanism for the flow of motivation to work and to invest, from the realm of social interactions into the realm of economic quantitites. EE-seeking affects not only production but consumption. IR market theory implies that the market for consumer goods is driven by the extent to which such goods are direct or indirect inputs into the IRs through which EE is distributed. IR market theory suggests the need for a range of empirical research on this point. The market for automobiles or other means of transportation, the market for clothing, the market for entertainment as well as for religious or political ceremonial, the market for homes and buildings as places of assembly and display: all of this can be charted historically in relation to the kind of IR markets that they sustain, and in relation to their pull upon economic production.

I have proposed that individuals' motivation to work, invest, and consume is predictable from their market opportunities and constraints in the sphere of IRs. The analysis that I have just given of the market for EE is a micro-economics, designed to show the rationality of the behavior of the individual in such a market. The macro-economics of such markets remains to be studied. One hypothesis is that we should not necessarily expect a negative correlation between high levels of IR participation and high degrees of effort put into materially productive work. On the contrary, where there are high IR payoffs for an increasing part of the population, and while the costs of rituals are also rising, many individuals are strongly motivated to work to be able to afford the requisite level of investment in IR participation. This has been suggested, for example, in the economics of tribal societies: Mauss (1925/1967) argued that tribes that periodically assemble for competitive potlatch ceremonies are highly productive during the remainder of the year in order to produce the goods necessary for an impressive potlatch. Sahlins (1972) shows that the ostentatious ceremonial of the tribal big-man structure acts as a collection point for material goods.

We have an opposing image of precapitalist societies as ones in which work motivation is kept to a minimum, merely covering subsistence, because most attention is devoted to the ceremonial aspects of life. This is in part a legacy of Weber's vision of medieval Catholic society draining off social energy into religious ceremonial; hence the Protestant Reformation, in abolishing monastic and clerical excesses, turned this energy into the secular economy. Weber's analysis is empirically wrong, although it contains the germ of a useful analytical point. Religious energy can indeed be turned into economic activity: what Weber overlooked was that there was an economic takeoff of the Catholic Middle Ages, which centered on the capital accumulation and investment by the monasteries themselves (Gimpel 1976; Southern 1970; Collins 1986, 45–76). Religious ceremonial is not the only kind of interaction ritual, although for a period it was the leading sector that organized the most energy and attracted the most material investment. The period of secularization in Europe that began with the Renaissance and Reformation was to a large extent the spilling over of the market for IRs into secular channels, at first through the courts of the nobility, later into a vast middle-class market for entertainment and status display. The analytical point is that IRs, whether religious or secular, can be the leading edge of expansion of economic production. I suggest a more precise formulation: it is the expansion of a market for IRs, rather than the static size of the IR sector, which shapes the flow of EE and brings about changes in the motivation of material production.

(II) Emotional Energy Is Generated by Work-Situation IRs

The foregoing has analyzed the condition in which work and leisure-time rituals are mutually exclusive, and has attempted to show that a high demand for leisure IRs will create a high demand for the material inputs for staging such rituals. In many instances, however, materially productive work and the production of emotional energy through IRs are not mutually exclusive. Every social situation exists somewhere on the continuum of conditions that make it a low, medium, or high-intensity IR. Conditions in the realm of work generate their own degrees of emotional energy and solidarity, ranging from zero up through very high intensities. At the high end of the spectrum, some work situations generate high levels of EE in their participants: the business executive at the center of a decision-making network, the busy professional, the skilled craftsperson surrounded by advice-seekers and apprentices, the salesman in a favorable marketplace. There is a type of charisma in the realm of work, produced by the same variables that operate in nonpractical IRs. Individuals whose work life consists of high levels of ritual interaction density will have high levels of EE, and find their work lives to be highly motivating for them, more so than sociable or other non-work interactions.[8] The slang term for such people is "workaholics."

For persons in such situations, there is no conflict between material rewards and EE incentives. The same structure typically gives them both high EE and high material payoffs. They are at the center of favorable market or authority networks, which simultaneously generate high ritual density and high income. Under these circumstances, there is no need for the individual to calculate the financial payoff of their time and effort. If they simply follow the flow of emotional energy, it will lead them into those work situations that bring them the greatest (or at least acceptably high) material payoff as well.

The IR model is also capable of predicting when individuals will be most consciously focused upon monetary calculations. High-intensity IR makes a sacred object, a membership symbol, out of whatever object is the focus of attention within the interactional situation.[9] Some work situations are explicitly focused upon money: above all, sales negotiations and financial dealings. Individuals who experience high IR intensity in such situations will be most strongly motivated to treat money, or the process of monetary calculation itself, as the highest good. Ironically, it is not because monetary calculation is intrinsically the highest good that they act this way; this becomes the attitude of individuals precisely to the extent that they are involved in IRs that focus them upon monetary calculation. They become money-making junkies. For such individuals, there is no diminishing marginal utility of money, even at very high levels. The IR model predicts that billionaires will continue to seek yet higher profits, precisely to the extent that their lives are organized around IRs of financial dealing, and that these IRs bring higher EE payoffs than the alternative ritual occasions available to them.[10]

A similar process operates at all levels throughout the labor force. Many individuals experience moderate or weak levels of IR intensity at their work. The IR model predicts that they are much less committed to their work, and to the material payoffs it brings.

Individuals who work alone constitute a special case. If no additional conditions are present, the IR model predicts that they have very weak EE incentives to put effort into their work. They will continue to work because they need material resources in order to live and to participate in nonwork IRs that offer them more EE. But how do we explain individuals who work alone but nevertheless show high levels of work motivation?

The strongest example of such individuals are persons in intellectual occupations, such as writers and scientists. A special application of IR theory explains their behavior: their work consists in organizing systems of symbols, which are in turn emblems of membership in particular groups within the intellectual world. Intellectual creativity consists in making mental coalitions among ideas, representing real coalitions that can be established among their corresponding intellectual groups. Evidence supports this model on several points. Creative scientists and other intellectuals have high emotional energy; this is indicated by their personality descriptions and by the fact that the most eminent intellectuals also tend to be the most prolific producers (Simonton 1984, 1988; Price 1986). And such creative individuals tend to have the closest network contacts with other highly active intellectuals; creativity clusters in social groups within the intellectual field (Collins 1998). Thus creative intellectuals are pumped up with the EE of being close to the center of ongoing intellectual action, at the intense center of intellectual IR chains.[11]

No doubt there are other sources of psychic benefit in work besides the EE that it generates from the surrounding social relationships. For instance, there is the pleasure in exercising a skill, and perhaps the aesthetic aspects of a work setting. The IR-market theory proposes, however, that EE-maximizing is by far the strongest of such motivations, and that the distribution of IRs at work gives a good approximation to the motivating effects of work situations.

If one had a survey of the IR intensity of all interaction situations, one could calculate the distribution of EE payoffs to all persons, both in their work and their nonwork experiences. From this it would be possible to describe an overall market dynamic as individuals attempt to maximize EE. Putting together (I) the motivation for material work, investment, and consumption driven by the distribution of leisure-time IRs, and (II) the distribution of EE produced indigenously by IR conditions in the social relations of work, we can arrive at an overall picture of the flow of EE into economic activities.

(III) Material Markets Are Embedded in an Ongoing Flow of IRs Generating Social Capital

It has often been pointed out that markets—which is to say, material markets—are embedded in social structures or cultures without which the markets would not be able to function, or to come into existence in the first place (Granovetter 1985; DiMaggio 2002). This so-called "social capital" has often been discussed, and I will make only the following points. There are two main aspects of embedding: shared trust among coparticipants in economic activities, and, more generally, a set of ground rules, customs, or procedures that define what the actors are doing and how they can expect each other to do it.

Shared trust, which is often what is meant by "social capital" in the narrow sense of the term, is generally attributed to network ties. Quite so; and what we mean by network ties, when viewed microsociologically as events in the flow of everyday life, consist in a certain kind of repeated social interaction. A casual encounter does not usually count as a "tie"; what is meant are interactions that take place repeatedly and that are picked out by the participants themselves as significant (e.g., network researchers usually start with a questionnaire asking to list "three best friends," "people you talk about business problems with," etc.) . Network ties are a particular kind of IR chain, those in which similar symbols and emotions are recycled and sometimes augmented—and to a higher degree than other interactions those persons have with other people. Thus the amount of "social capital" that individuals have is determined by the extent to which there is an ongoing flow of micro-situational ingredients for successful IRs—and IRs that are attractive enough compared to other possible interactions so that they are repeated instead of broken off.

Another way to say this is that positions in networks are created and sustained on the micro-level by the degree of success of IRs. Networks are not fixed, although it is convenient for us as network analysts to treat them as fixed and preexisting so that we can examine the effects of being in different network positions. Network ties become created by just the kind of matchups of membership symbols and emotional energies that I have been discussing. And network ties vary in their strength, precisely as the situational ingredients that go into them vary.[12]

"Social capital" or trusting relationships are determined by the market for interactions. Social capital facilitates the operation of material markets, not just in general as a structural embedding in a featherbed (or warm bath) of trust, but in a variable and distributed way across the population of people who take part in the economy. As many researchers have pointed out, some people are richer or poorer in social capital than others. High-intensity pockets of social trust contrasts with low-intensity regions, and even more pointedly with regions of intense social distrust—which are based on IRs with negative contents. Social capital is an individual good or resource; the fact that it is simultaneously a collective good, a feature of the embedding that makes markets operate more smoothly and effectively, means that social capital is inevitably stratified. And the overall level of social capital in the material economy shifts over time through variations in intensity of membership propagated via shared emotion; that is just what a business boom is: an increased intensity of trust that spreads out to include more people. Conversely, a business bust is a decline in the sense of trust that other people will also be buying and investing; a panic is a shared negative emotion, in which the collective feeling builds up a sense of certainty that business is going to fall.

Shared trust is Durkheimian social membership. The other form of embedding is shared cultural understandings; these, too, are products of IRs, Durkheimian collective symbols. Here again we can say that markets are embedded in cultures, and that to a considerable extent those cultures are generated in an ongoing fashion by the social interactions that take place among the actors in a material market. Here again the particular shape and extent of those shared symbols is variable and both regionalizing and stratifying. There are shared business cultures that build up in particular spheres: in production markets, networks and climates of investors, financial markets, and occupational milieux. Material markets are not simply sustained by an overarching culture of agreed-upon practices and beliefs, such as what constitutes an acceptable currency of exchange. As Zelizer (1994) shows, there are distinctive kinds of currency that in practice are confined within particular kinds or circuits of exchange. These currencies are quite straightforwardly Durkheimian sacred objects, like the shells that circulated in the famous South Sea kula ring (Mauss 1925); they exist to differentiate the levels of capitalist markets today, from financial instruments accessible only to the highest financial circles, down to the earmarked currencies of poor people's welfare payments.

The patterns of sharing symbols do not just constitute market capitalism in general but also give it its structure as particular production markets. As Harrison White (1981, 2002) has argued, what makes something a market is a recognized kind of product that is being produced by several competing producers.[13] Every business needs to know what business are you in. Which is to say, which competitors are you tracking and emulating, and also trying to avoid head-to-head competition with by finding a niche in the space of differences in quality and quantity produced. Producers need competitors, because it is by monitoring each other that they can tell what the consumers out there seem to be willing to buy, and thus to strategize about what else they may be willing to buy in the future. Consumer demand is not simply an exogenous quantity, but something that is constructed by what is being offered by producers. Hence there is no reliable way for producers to monitor the exchange directly; they need to look in the mirror of the market "in which producers see each other" (in White's famous phrase). The dynamics of change in producers' markets thus is driven by the ongoing monitoring of producers by each other, and a particular market may be characterized as a mutually monitoring producers' clique or network. Those who are far from the network center and hence are not good at monitoring it generally do not do well in finding favorable niches in that market. Conversely the successful innovators are generally those who know the market because they have already worked in it; successful new organizations tend to be spin-offs from well-established organizations.

The point I want to stress here is that every product market is constituted by the IR chains of these mutually monitoring producers. The personal computer market of the 1980s, the cell phone market of the 1990s, the automobile market of the early 1900s, are all social constructions in the sense that these products had to get defined as competing with each other over a particular group of consumers, and in the process to construct what sorts of things these products could be used for. Brand names acquire their cultural force and presence by their competition and contrast; Coca Cola and Pepsi mutually define each other and thus build up the social presence of the market they are both in. Cadillacs and Mercedes-Benz (at particular times in business history) held their distinctive images by contrast to other cars, those regarded as on the same level of quality and those viewed as on lower-quality levels.

There is an ongoing flow between two regions of social interaction rituals and hence of symbol circulation: the mutually monitoring producers' networks, which keep promoting their products vis-à-vis each other; and the buying public, which gets caught up in a buzz of enthusiasm for some products that it takes as specially prestigious or au courant, and that consumers display as part of their self-presentation in everyday life and as the content of some of their conversations. Producers and consumers are both realms of networks, and thus of IR chains; the producers' network is smaller and more concentrated, whereas the consumers constitute a concatenation of different networks, with greater or lesser focus. Movements of enthusiasm or disillusionment by consumers can shift the emotional resonance of material products as collective symbols, in effect shifting the amount of EE connected with those brand names. Such shifts in turn feed back into the considerations of the producers as they try to modify their existing product lines to find favorable niches. Thus the symbols that are given meaning by one network—producers or consumers—resonate further in the other network. The initiative, however, is generally from the producers' side; it is these smaller and more concentrated networks that make the earliest and most decisive moves that begin to pump up material objects into Durkheimian sacred objects, which will in turn generate the biggest profits. This is a dynamic and ongoing embedding of material markets in the symbols and emotions of interaction markets. Not just capitalism in general is being sustained by this embedding, but the very process of the struggle over capitalist innovation and profit.

• • •

We turn now to several remaining cases of allegedly anomalous behavior, in order to show that this behavior is rational in terms of maximizing EE.

Altruism

Altruism is a situation in which an individual gives away something of value to benefit someone else. Altruists are usually depicted as giving away material goods and sometimes as risking their lives. I suggest that all cases of altruism are cases of apparent conflict between interests in social solidarity and interests in material goods (including one's body, seen here as a material good). If the market for IRs is the prime determinant of EE, altruism is not irrational; it is even predictable.

The simplest form of altruism is the case where individuals sacrifice material goods for the group in which they are ritually mobilized. IR theory predicts that the higher the level of ritual intensity in collective activity, the more that individuals will sacrifice to the group. This practice is well known to fund-raisers who time their collections just after the emotional high point at rallies and meetings, and who attempt to build up a rhythmic crescendo of gift-giving or pledge-making within the group. Risk to one's life, which from the point of view of individual self-interest is the supreme sacrifice, occurs regularly when well-integrated groups are mobilized against collective danger or for intergroup combat. There is a good deal of evidence that the degree of ritual solidarity in combat military units directly determines the willingness of individual soldiers to risk their lives (Keegan 1977; Shils and Janowitz 1948).

More complex forms of altruism are those in which members of one group give gifts to nonmembers. Such situations always have the structure in which the charity-giving group has higher resources and power than the charity recipients. Such recipients are never a power threat; giving gifts focuses attention upon the donors' power superiority as a group, as well as on their material possessions themselves as superior to those of others. The focus of a charity-giving ritual is explicitly self-congratulatory, generating symbolic capital in the process of giving away material capital. It is notable that groups that assemble as privileged interest groups (e.g., business associations) or as upper-class sociable celebrations (ostentatious gatherings of "High Society") balance their ritual display of dominance by publicizing their gatherings as devoted to charitable activities. Charitable contributions are made in material goods, or in time and effort, whichever is in most abundant supply. Persons who make large charitable contributions typically do this in a situation of highly publicized ritual participation, so that the same investment serves both ends.

The question of altruism is almost never posed in terms of sacrificing power. It is typically regarded as a high degree of charitable contribution to take the lead in a charitable organization, or to be in the forefront of ritual assemblies that make charities a focus of attention. Far from being a sacrifice of power, there is a power payoff for charitable participation of this sort. In a premodern religious context, great physical abnegation by monks and ascetics made them the center of ritual attention, and extreme displays of self-sacrifice gave one the reputation of being a saint and often enabled one to become the head of a religious organization. Individual physical sacrifice of one's body is thus predictable whenever high levels of ritual mobilization takes place around such self-sacrificing individuals.[14]

Are there any power altruists, or in other words, those who give away power to others? Not apparently, among those whose power comes from their centrality in intense IRs. If anything, such altruists are also highly egotistical. A possible exception might be organizational executives who delegate authority. But this is typically power that derives from a chain of resources, based in low-intensity interactions; and the expressed motive for delegating authority is not usually to further an altruistic cause or demonstrate one's own altruism, but as an instrumental technique for making power more effective. Even here, it appears, powerful persons rarely give away power that will challenge their own.

Altruistic leaders are easy to explain: they get a great deal of EE not only from being in the center of admiring attention, but also from exercising power over their followers. Altruistic followers, especially at the humbler ranks, might seem harder to explain, especially since (as indicated in chapter 3) being subjected to someone else's power decreases one's EE. This is often a matter of what situational niches are available. There is only a limited amount of attention space for individuals to act as group leaders. Individuals who give away considerable power to others, such as joiners of charismatic movements, are presumably those who had little prospects of acquiring power for themselves in their own IR marketplace. They have little power-generated EE to sacrifice, and receive much higher EE payoffs from total commitment to ritual participation.[15]

Altruistic behavior is not an anomaly for rational action. It is predictable from the distribution of interactional situations from which individuals derive their EE.

When Are Individuals Most Materially Self-Interested?

The IR model does not propose that individuals are never concerned about their material self-interests. It says that individuals normally can attend to the ritual sources of EE, and this will determine most of their material goods earning and spending behavior as well. But note also that high-intensity rituals are a relatively small portion of all situations. Since situations vary all across the continuum of ritual intensity, the IR model straightforwardly predicts in which situations individuals will show the greatest concern for material self-interest. These are the situations in which individuals are most isolated from the presence of the group.

Thus individuals going shopping by themselves may experience no immediate ritual influences upon their emotional energy.[16] If the goods that they buy (e.g., staple foods and household necessities) have not been the focus of ritual situations, there will be little symbolic motivation to value certain products. Similarly, political choices may be made to some extent in isolation. The practice of voting in privacy is explicitly designed to remove citizens from group pressures that would occur if voting took place, for instance, by a collective show of hands, or worse yet, by collective raising of voices.

Such isolation may be only relative, insofar as individuals may have recently taken part in collective rituals such as political rallies that have charged up membership symbols in their minds and that now guide their private behavior. IR theory proposes that explicit calculation of material self-interest occurs to the degree that individuals have been insulated from collective rituals focused upon these choices. This is not to say that when collective participation does take place, it must always focus upon nonmaterial issues. A political rally may be explicitly concerned with taxes or property values. In such cases, one might say that material self-interest and the EE of collective participation are mutually reinforcing. But it might be more accurate to describe this as a situation in which the material interest itself becomes a collective symbol of group solidarity. Thus participants who are charged up with group enthusiasm may contribute more to an insurance-reduction campaign than what they can expect to gain from it in lower premiums. Financial and property interests can also become symbolic interests, driven by the dynamics of EE-producing rituals. Here we may have a departure from purely material rationality, in the direction of an overshooting commitment to particular material interests.

The Bottom Line: EE-Seeking Constrained by Material Resources

Since all social goods are experienced in interactional situations (or are offshoots, through symbolic memory or anticipation, of interactional situations), we may say that all the various kinds of social payoffs that appear to escape from self-interested maximization are means of gaining EE. Altruism, power, etc., are merely alternative forms of EE-producing social rituals, and the question of the rationality of seeking these kinds of goals reduces to showing why particular individuals would seek each particular route to an EE payoff. My answer is that there is a market for interaction rituals, such that individuals invest what social, material, and emotional resources they have at the time in relation to the opportunities available for attaining EE payoffs in particular kinds of situations. The market for IRs makes it rational for some individuals to act altruistically or to seek power, to be a lover or be the party clown. Emotional and nonmaterial-seeking behavior is rational behavior, once we take EE as the central payoff that persons are seeking. There is an advantage here from the sociological side in seeing such behavior as rational: it gives us an apparatus for predicting, in the contours of the market for IRs, which individuals under what circumstances will pursue these various social goals.

The difficulty raised at the outset of this chapter of finding a common denominator is solved in the same way. Emotional energy is the common denominator of all social comparisons and choices. Every alternative is assessed in terms of the amount of EE it carries, whether as a gain or a loss. Power, altruism, love, and every other social goal is measured by the same yardstick, the increment or decrement that the interactional process involved in it produces for one's emotional energy. Situations in which one gains (or loses) money or material goods are assessed in the same way; that is, working for material gain is first and foremost a situation in which emotional energy is gained or lost in the social interaction itself. Persons who are highly motivated to make money are in an interactional market in which their work interaction is the major source of EE in their lives; "workaholics" are obsessed with their work lives because it is the sole high-EE interaction available to them. The same may be said about spending money, or handling money (and other financial instruments) as in investment, entrepreneurship, organizational politics, gambling, or the like: these are first of all situations of social interaction, which carry their own EE weight. For some persons, being a consumer is the main form of everyday social interaction that produces an EE payoff; for other persons, their EE high points occur when they interact as an invester, or as a practitioner of leveraged buyouts. It is a complication, but not an insoluable difficulty, that some persons work alone, and that activities focusing on finances sometimes take place in solitude. I suggest that in these cases money has become a Durkheimian sacred object, an emblem of the EE with which it originally generated in interactional situations. The internalization of financial symbols parallels the internalization of intellectual symbols, which explains the high-intensity inner conversations of intellectual thinking. The business-obsessed invester seeking out the hum of the stock exchange, and the business enterpriser in a constant buzz of plans and telephone calls, are magnetized by high-energy niches in social networks.

By such considerations, we may analyze all material and monetary goals into their component everyday interactional situations as sources of EE. Thus there is a common denominator among the trade-offs of socializing with one's friends, working late at the office, playing the stockmarket, or giving money and time to a political campaign. If we start with money as the common denominator, we cannot incorporate nonmonetary, social goods into a common metric; if we start with EE as the metric, then material-monetary goals become measurable in terms of their direct social and indirect social-symbolic EE payoffs.

The previous sketch shows how the numerator of the benefits / costs ratio is put into a common metric. How, then, is this composite numerator compared to the denominator? For the costs of any choice or social pathway are not merely in EE but also in the material means of ritual production. To go to a church service or a political rally may produce a surge of EE, but it also costs real materials for transportation, for the church building, the microphones, prayer books, minister's salary, and so forth. If individuals are comparing costs and benefits, how do they put these real costs into a common metric with the emotional benefits (and with the emotional resources also invested on the cost side)? I suggest that individuals do not usually have to take costs directly and consciously into account; nevertheless material costs have an impact upon the choices that are made. That is because if the material resources are not available for carrying out an interaction ritual, the ritual will fail, and little or no EE will be produced. The group will not be assembled, attention cannot be focused, emotions cannot be amplified. *Pathways that do not lead toward production of material resources sufficient to sustain IRs will also fail to produce EE.* Thus individual behavior is motivated immediately and directly by EE-seeking; indirectly and implicitly individuals are driven to produce material goods, to just the degree that these resources are demanded by their favorite rituals. Production in the material economy is initiated and shaped by the market for IRs.

The formula:

$$\text{maximize ratio} \quad \frac{\text{benefits (EE)}}{\text{costs (EE + material)}}$$

becomes: seek maximal EE benefits among the array of IR opportunities. This array is restricted because some IR situations are closed off when material resources are not available for a successful EE-generating IR to be carried out.[17]

The rationality of material costs is indirect. People seek benefits directly in terms of their emotional common denominator, and become guided by material costs only in the long run, often contrary to their anticipation and beyond the realm of their attention. I am arguing that pursuing a business, giving a party, or fighting a war are all motivated in the same way; in each case, one seeks EE according to what is immediately attractive and what is emblematic of past EE payoffs. If, in fact, the enterprise sinks or sails according to the level of material resources available, the participants do not usually find that out until they are well into the swing of things. Costly, material-consuming enterprises like wars typically come to an end, not necessarily because the emotions are exhausted, but because ignored costs mount up to the point where the enterprise can no longer be sustained.

SOCIOLOGY OF EMOTIONS AS THE SOLUTION TO RATIONAL CHOICE ANOMALIES

Let us now take up the experimental anomalies noted at the outset of this chapter in the list of difficulties for rational choice theory (Kahneman et al. 1982; Frey and Eichenberger 1989). These anomalies fall into four main types:

1. Overestimating a single pathway of action and failing to examine alternatives. There is a strong tendency to overlook opportunity costs, the gains foregone from the paths not taken. In general, individuals are unwilling to search fully for information.[18]

2. Once a choice is made, persons tend to stick with it. Persons are generally unwilling to reconsider, to change a choice already made. They avoid changing their estimation of probabilities even after disconfirming experience; they are especially resistant to changing the categories through which they frame their problem. As in point (1), persons are rather averse to calculating, pure and simple. By the same token, they are apparently even more averse to recalculating, readjusting fundamental cognitive choices once they have been made. Here the evidence converges with naturalistic observations of the ethnomethodologists, and of conversation analysts, which show that persons resist changing their taken-for-granted routines.

3. When persons frame the situation (such as estimating the likelihood of a given event occurring), they prefer to focus upon cultural stereotypes rather than information of a statistical nature. If there is no cultural stereotype readily available, persons become fixated on the initial baseline from which their observations are made. In the absence of a preexisting stereotype, one arbitrarily creates a typical case and judges what happens subsequently in reference to it. Persons want their world of experience to be framed from the outset, and they very quickly establish a model of what is happening, then use it as a lens through which to view whatever comes next.

4. Another series of behaviors are more directly emotional. Persons are over-optimistic about the future payoffs of their chosen alternative. Once they have invested in a particular pathway, they tend to stick with it, investing further in it rather than spreading their risks; sunk costs or endowments create an emotional bias toward protecting and enhancing the pathway already entered. Once such an investment is made, when risks and costs become salient one tends to protect prior investments, seeking to avoid losses more than to make gains. In sizing up new possibilities, persons prefer the framing that defines the alternatives in terms of potential gains rather than as potential losses. And one avoids risky alternatives more if they are framed as applying to oneself, or to persons with whom one has a social bond, than if they are stated as impersonal or hypothetical possibilities.

This latter case is one of the few instances of rational choice anomalies that permits a comparison between choices in social and nonsocial contexts. Most anomalies research deals with a detached actor, either hypothetical or experimentally constructed by physical isolation and by strict control of what can go through channels of communication, and so the person is prohibited from using the normal modes of decision making, that is, drawing upon the emotional energies and symbols of the surrounding social situation. When a real-life actor is made the explicit focus of attention, she or he becomes the dominant frame in terms of which decision-relevant emotions are marshalled.[19]

Virtually all such research focuses strictly upon material gains and losses, leaving out the interactional situations in which such ends would actually be negotiated; hence we have no way of knowing what EE loading would actually exist in real-life choices. In effect, anomalies research constructs a situation in which the only possible object of emotion is the material gain or loss itself. If we take the experimental situation in itself as a form of interaction ritual, the object focused upon in that situation is the material good (the token or hypothetical money that the experimenter gives experimental subjects and that they are told to accumulate). The experimenters, who regard themselves as outside the experiment, are in fact constructing the social reality that they claim to be researching. The initial choice, or the initial endowment, becomes the sacred object for that interaction; protecting or enhancing one's sacred object becomes the value in terms of which one structures all subsequent action. The experimental research situation is an emotional vacuum; it is filled by the only object with any emotional charge at all, the material goal or sunk cost. This is not to say that such experimental results are entirely artificial; persons in real economic life may also act in this fashion, provided that they are making their business decisions in a social vacuum as well.

At this point we may as well recognize that most research and theorizing in the rational choice tradition is not really micro, in the sense that the term is used in this book. It appears to be micro because it is about individuals; but individuals are a larger unit of analysis than are situations; individuals are really abstractions from a long chain of situations. Rational choice research (also carried out under the label of exchange theory) gives a deceptive appearance of being micro for another reason: because its experiments are typically carried out in a few hours or less. But these are not naturally occurring situations, but have been structured so that there is a speeded-up flow of exchanges compressed into those minutes or hours. In real life, it could take weeks or even years to make so many bargaining exchanges with a number of partners. Rational choice is not a micro-theory, but a compressed meso-theory. Taken literally, "rational choice" is the wrong micro-mechanism of how situational thinking actually takes place. As noted at the beginning of this chapter, this does not necessarily undermine the usefulness of the theory as a model of human behavior in the medium run, provided we understand with what micro- and meso-mechanisms we are actually dealing.

The Microsociology of Material Considerations

If an individual is going to engage in thinking about future situations, what symbols will come most readily to mind? It will be those symbols that have the highest EE charge. Accordingly, if they are going to plan, or to compare alternatives, their mental search will begin with the most strongly charged ideas, and these will become most salient in their decisions. If one set of ideas, linked to a particular situational alternative, has an overwhelmingly high charge compared to other situation-linked ideas, the person will come to a rapid decision. One alternative appears overwhelmingly right, and it feels unnecessary to consider the others.

Consider now the rather narrow range of ideas that are focused on in experiments involving rational choice anomalies. Money, investments, material costs and gains: these are to some extent familiar conceptions from everyday interaction, although some persons focus upon these in their conversational interactions more than others do. The everyday mode of thinking and talking about money and material possessions come from their focus within conversational rituals concerned with social status. Perhaps the most common form of speech in which money plays a part in sociable conversation consists in bragging about one's wealth or possessions (often indirectly and surreptitiously by complaining about the high costs of things that one buys). This is frontstage talk about money; in the intimate sphere within the family, money is the primary topic of domestic quarrels.[20] The result of such conversational rituals is to give money a fairly simple emotional loading; it is something one has, as part of one's status identity.

Ordinary conversation about money and possessions does not usually focus upon calculating alternatives, considering opportunity costs, or the like; money-concepts acquire an emotional resonance as showing one's social membership in the group of persons who can sustain talk about money-affairs at a given level of stratification. Money may be real capital, but talk about money is a symbolic capital that directly determines social membership. If this is what money symbolizes emotionally for most persons, when we put them into an experimental situation and ask them to calculate potential costs and gains, it is no surprise that they tend to treat the monetary symbol in that context as an endowment to be protected; the emotional focus upon the money emblem keeps them from letting their attention range more widely toward assessing the framework of probabilities and assumptions within which their decisions are to be made.

To broaden this discussion, we may go in two directions: to consider choices that do not involve money; or to consider persons who are much more familiar in their daily social encounters with financial transactions. Let us take the latter first. Persons who are monetary professionals also have a propensity to rational choice anomalies, although for reasons opposite from those that bring about anomalies among persons concerned only in a casual manner with conversation about money. For ordinary persons, money is a symbolic category relatively little charged with situations of calculation; it is a relatively static emblem of social rank membership, or of power within the family. For monetary professionals, on the other hand, situations in which they deal with money are likely to be very highly charged emotionally; they take place in encounters of intense focus of social attention and a great deal of shared emotion. Thus the typical everyday life situation of a gambler or of a stockbroker comprises a high-intensity IR in which money is at the center of attention: for such professions, money becomes the sacred object par excellence (Abolafia 1996). Members of these occupations tend to be subject to rational choice anomalies (Slovic, Fischoff, and Lichtenstein 1977) precisely because they think in terms of symbols that are highly emotionally charged. The very intensity of their focus upon money (or upon their sunk costs, particular strategies chosen, financial-action frames adopted) narrows their attention to those symbols and causes them to ignore the larger range of calculations.

The other broadening of this discussion is to cases where the choices considered are nonmonetary, but involve general estimates of the prob-

abilities of various kinds of events and the payoffs of various courses
of action. Here the problem for most experimental subjects is generally
that none of the alternatives is framed by very strongly charged symbols. Hence persons fall back upon baseline assumptions or other initial framing devices; they create a temporary cognitive sacred object,
faute de mieux. If they have available a cognitive stereotype they will
use it to do their thinking with. To use a stereotype can be considered
"irrational" only from the point of view of another framework that
has the emotional value-symbol "rational" attached to it. In the course
of everyday thinking, however, one simply maximizes EE. In the
round of conversational interactions, some verbal symbols become relatively more highly charged with EE; one uses whatever such symbols
are available when an occasion for thinking arises. If everyone in a
community is bragging about how much money they have by describing the things they spend it on, the immediate EE payoff comes from
joining in with bragging of one's own. There is an economy of thinking
based on EE flows. One thinks efficiently and economically by ex-
pending as little EE as possible, relative to how much EE one gets back
from the process of doing the thinking; moreover, since in most situations there is an immediate emotional tone, it is not long-term EE payoffs that are determining, but the short-term, indeed immediately processual EE feedbacks that are overriding.

Thinking that involves a good deal of searching among little-known
alternatives (that is to say, symbolic concepts that have low-EE loadings) is unrewarding, an EE-drain; it is avoided whenver possible.[21]
The preferred alternative to thinking is to use symbolic categories that
are already highly EE-charged, that spring readily to mind; here thinking is easy and spontaneous. Thinking in available cultural stereotypes
is efficient thinking, in terms of an EE metric.

How, then, does any other conception of "rationality" ever arise?
Who makes the judgment that certain kinds of thinking is "anomalous"? Obviously, it is another social community, one that has charged
up a different set of categories as its sacred objects. Such are the communities of statisticians and mathematically oriented economists. For
them, numbers have become emblems of group membership, and
sources of solidarity and emotional energy; what ordinary persons (especially those with the common pattern of ritualized math-aversion)
tend to view and *feel* as a symbolic marker of an alien worldview and
an alien group, is for the statistician / economist a taken-for-granted
emblem of their own group membership.[22] As in the case of all social
groups with strong patterns of interactional enclosure and group solidarity, statisticians and those in similar professions take their own
symbols for granted; for these professionals, statistical ideas are

charged with higher emotional energy than other symbols; they jump easily to the mind and flow off into a series of mental statements leading to conclusions that seem obviously superior to all other modes of conceptualizing such topics. The very concept of "rationality," as identified with mathematical-statistical calculation, is itself a value-emblem, anchored in the emotional energy and the group solidarity of such a profession.

In everyday life, persons carry out their thinking by using the verbal concepts most charged with EE by their personal group interactions. I have argued that such behavior is broadly rational, not in the restricted sense of the cognitive sacred objects that belong to the communities of statisticians, mathematicians, and economists, but in the specific sense of maximization of benefits relative to costs, where the common denominator is EE. This does not mean that everything takes place in everyday thinking in a uniform manner. The variations, however, are predictable from the IR-EE model.

Let us consider two special cases. First, take the case where an individual's EE is low in regard to every situation and every symbol in his or her environment. No alternatives are emotionally very appealing; no thoughts spring to mind with great spontaneity. This would occur if that person's IR life is impoverished. One might think that this would be an ideal person to engage in rational calculation, dispassionately considering all the alternatives and deciding without sources of bias. But IR theory proposes that this person would be sunk in apathy, unable to decide. Emotional energy is necessary to get the thinking process going, as well as to supply alternatives and provide focus.

Then there is the case where a person faces a number of alternatives with approximately the same level of emotional loading. This person's IR market situation is very complicated; or there are many contingencies, which make it difficult to anticipate which alternative will bring stronger EE payoffs than others. In such situations, IR theory predicts that the person becomes genuinely stalled. His or her behavior is indecisive and vacillating. If this stalling occurs among alternatives that have relatively high emotional loadings, the indecisiveness becomes agonizing. The existence of such situations does not imply an imperfection in the IR model of cognition. On the contrary, it is one empirical alternative that it can account for.

Emotional energy is a common metric in terms of which individuals weigh alternatives. To speak less metaphorically, the EE loading of symbols determines which ideas spring most readily to mind, and which have the greatest appeal in one's thinking. What is the form of this EE scale? It is certainly ordinal; is it experienced in such a way that it has properties of an interval scale? It is doubtful that the human actor can directly observe the EE levels of various situations and symbols, to stand back and read off their values. Instead, one responds directly to whatever EE value is highest. There may very well exist zones of indeterminacy, in which is it impossible to tell which EE level is higher than another. This may lead to a stalled situation; since EEs are transitory, different situational alternatives may decay at different rates (depending on their recency and repetitiveness); what may be a stalled comparison at one moment can become resolved at a later time.

In this analysis, I have not distinguished among behavior under certainty (full knowledge of all outcomes), under risk (known probabilities of outcomes), and under uncertainty (in which neither of these hold). Within any immediate situation, an individual responds directly to the EE flow occuring in that group. This is equivalent to behavior under certainty. When we step back and consider this same individual in a longer timeframe, moving toward some parts of the market for IRs and away from others, we are in the realm of uncertainty.[23] Similarly, thinking by use of symbols loaded with EE from interactional experiences is likely to be thinking under uncertainty.

The distinction between certainty and uncertainty may have little effect on an EE-based model of behavior. If EE levels are high, individuals act as if outcomes are certain. EE gives them high confidence; this may be objectively misplaced (the often-found overestimation of future success), but it makes it unnecessary to complicate our model of the human cognitive agent. When EE levels are moderate, however, uncertainty may become more salient. A reasonable hypothesis is that when an individual's IR experiences generate only moderate levels of EE, one feels more uncertain; and that uncertainty itself makes it more difficult to clearly focus upon a given alternative. Symbolic IRs within one's mind become harder to construct; real IRs with other persons are less successful if they try to focus upon a particular source of uncertainty. Areas of uncertainty thus have low EE-loadings, and both individuals in their own thinking, and groups in their interacting, will tend to focus away from them. This aversion to areas of uncertainty fits the observed heuristics of most people's behavior.

Research on decision making or situational thinking converge on the theme that the human being has limited information-processing capacity, that she or he operates in a situation of bounded rationality. How then are decisions made? With a degree of arbitrariness; given a limited cognitive capacity, it makes sense to reduce alternatives and to avoid complex calculations.[24] But what gives an actor the tendency to treat one feature rather than another as arbitrary, or to use heuristics that make some particular item especially salient?

The answer is the emotional energy loading of various alternatives or their symbols. Features of the situation (or the range of possible situations about which decisions could be made) that have low-EE loadings are ignored. Decision making concentrates on whatever features evoke the highest EE. Grappling with alternatives is highest when there are several features that all evoke fairly high EE levels.

This is consistent with the various models of cognitive heuristics and anomalies. March and Simon's (1958) satisficing implies disattending routine areas, which would generate little emotional intensity in their social interactions, and focusing upon problem areas, which should be those with the greatest collective emotional arousal.[25] Garfinkel's (1967) ethnomethods similarly imply that ritual accounts will be offered when there is a breach in normal expectations, generating emotional arousal and mobilizing participants into focusing their attention on the trouble. Most anomalies of the Kahneman and Tversky sort hinge upon overestimating a single alternative and ignoring the full range of considerations (leaving aside opportunity costs, being over-optimistic about future payoffs for one's chosen alternative, focusing narrowly upon stereotypes, being unwilling to engage in full informational search, or to change one's categories). In all of these cases, one concept is overcharged relative to others. This is expectable if thinking is determined by a focus mechanism, and if the particular symbols focused upon are those that are most charged with EE by their occurence in recent social interactions.

Situational Decisions without Conscious Calculation

The fact that most empirical studies of individuals in micro-situations find them doing little conscious calculating need not impugn the rational action model of behavior, provided that it can be shown how individuals move toward optimizing their medium-run balance of benefits over costs. The two prongs of my argument have contributed to this goal by showing that behavior motivated by nonmaterial benefits is rational behavior; and that there is a common denominator that enables individuals to weigh the payoffs of disparate kinds of goods; they do this by moving toward the strongest available source of emotional energy.

If human beings are EE-seekers, it is not necessary that they should engage in conscious calculation. Where I have used the term "choice" or "decision" in the preceding descriptions, it should in most instances be taken as metaphorical. Human behavior may be characterized as emotional energy tropism. Social sources of EE directly energize behavior; the strongest energizing situation exerts the strongest pull. Subjectively, individuals do not experience such situations as controlling them; because they are being filled with energy, they feel that they control. They may well describe their behavior, if they are reflective about it, as a firm decision, a strong sense of volition. But they need not exercise any conscious calculation over the costs and benefits of various alternatives. When EE is strong, they see immediately what they want to do.

The notion that cognition is crucially entwined with emotion is the next step beyond recognition of cognitive heuristics. Advanced efforts in artificial intelligence (AI) to model the human actor have aimed to combine cognitive architecture with emotion (Carley and Newell 1990). A successful model would incorporate the social network of IRs that load symbols with EE, and a cognitive process driven by these emotional loadings. Ultimately, if social science is to be able to model real human thinking in an AI, it will have to incorporate an interactional basis for emotions that motivate the selection of cognitive symbols in the ongoing flow of situations. As I have argued elsewhere (Collins 1992), a truly human AI would have to be constructed with devices for tuning in the rhythms of human speech and producing them back to real human interlocutors; it would be a robot with emotional capacities that would learn the human use of symbols by interacting with people in the same way that a baby learns to talk.

I have attempted to broaden the realm of rationality, to show that nonmaterial, emotional and symbolic behavior may also be analyzed as the optimizing of benefits in relation to costs. This theoretical strategy may seem to have a very high intellectual cost, since it involves using emotional energy as central dynamic around which everything else, including material interests, revolve. But this strategy has the advantage of making the model of the actor congruent with the findings of noncalculating behavior on the micro-situational level. I believe that these advantages outweigh the costs of changing certain conceptual biases of the rational choice tradition.

What is jettisoned is primarily the tradition of taking money as an emblem of all rationally disposable goods. It also becomes unnecessary to postulate abstract utility conceptions. Emotional energy is an empirically based concept, and it is possible to measure it directly and to show the social conditions for its variations. The theoretical change I am proposing makes it necessary to jettison the notion of "calculation" or "choice" as a description of short-term situations, or rather to reconceptualize just what is going on when individuals steer their behavior among alternatives. The theory of maximization under material constraints becomes more powerful when applied to the emotional currency of social life and the structures of interaction that produce it.

Chapter 5

INTERNALIZED SYMBOLS AND

THE SOCIAL PROCESS OF THINKING

In IR theory, thinking is the third-order circulation of symbols. It follows upon the first-order creation of symbols in intense IRs, and their second-order recirculation in conversational networks. Thinking is yet another loop, now into imaginary internal conversations, which are themselves IRs taking place in the mind. Perform a gestalt switch: instead of starting with the individual engaged in thinking, start with the overall distribution of symbols among a population of people. Visualize what the pattern would look like if you could see it from the air, through a time-lapse photography in which symbols were marked in colors, so that we could trace where they flow, and follow their EE levels as intensities of brightness. We would see symbols circulating as streaks of light, from person to person, and then—our camera zooming in for a close-up—flowing in chains within a particular person's mind.

The effort here, as in previous chapters, is to dynamize Durkheim, to set his model in motion. Durkheim presented an abstract, static sociology of knowledge: the categories in which people think are collective representations determined by social morphology. My aim is to broaden and particularize the theory, to explain who will think what at particular times. Similarly with the other major sociological theory of thinking: Mead's theory of internal conversation among parts of the self, internalized from social interaction; thought as imaginative rehearsal through taking the role of the other. Again, we are presented with an abstract model, in this case, of the inner structure of the self; but not of what thinking occurs in particular situations.

Combining the two theories yields a radically microsociological theory of thinking. Conversation is interaction ritual, charging up symbols with membership significance; thought is internalized conversation, flowing on the EE charges that symbols have at a particular moment in time. In the conversational market an individual moves toward those conversations in which his or her stock of symbols and level of EE produces the highest IR effervescence, and avoids those conversations that reduce EE. The same happens in the internal conversations of the mind: thinking flows into those internal conversations that generate the most EE in the unfolding mental situation.

We shall have to confront an additional complication: whereas external conversations are constrained by the immediate situation of the persons matching up their stock of symbols and EE levels, an internal conversation presumably could go off in any direction whatever; after all, the person who is doing the thinking is imagining the other side of the conversation as well as his or her own side, and thus could supply any possible match-up. Nevertheless, as I will attempt to show, internal conversations are not unbounded or random but have a shape that resembles IR chains. Thinking always takes place in some situation in time, and thus is surrounded by overt IR chains, which both set the starting point for internal thinking, and supply its symbolic and emotional ingredients. Some kinds of thinking stay close to the external situation; these are the easiest case for sociology to deal with. Some kinds of thinking are very strongly shaped by internalizing a structured social network of communications; such is the case with intellectual thinking, which I will present as our best evidence so far for the sociological theory of thinking. There remains the kind of thinking that floats away from its starting point into chains of associations; this will be most difficult to handle sociologically, but even here, as we shall see, patterns can be found.

METHODS FOR GETTING INSIDE, OR BACK OUTSIDE

What methods can a sociologist use for studying thinking? I raise the question here, not out of a positivist belief that there is a single correct method that must always be applied, but out of the practical sense that theory advances best in tandem with empirical observations. This has been the case with Durkheim, Mead, Goffman, Weber, and virtually any other important sociological (or psychological) theorist that one might mention. By the same token, it is clear that one cannot lay down in advance what empirical research methods must be. This is particularly so among the leading microsociologists. Goffman, Garfinkel, Sacks, Schegloff, Scheff, Katz, and other key innovators have invented methods as they went along, and they would hardly have made their discoveries if they had followed a methods textbook, say, as published in the year 1950.

Methods involve confronting obstacles, looking consciously at the problems that arise. How can we get inside other people's heads? Are we confined to describing what is inside our own? Biases may arise because each of us is different from other people. And the bias may go deeper: even in examining one's own thought—or getting other people to report on theirs—there is the issue of how thought is changed by self-conscious reflection, and by interrupting it so as to report on it. There is also the problem of nonverbal thought, thought in images, physical actions, and emotions; and quasi-verbal thought, not formulated into the articulate speech in which we externalize it. Nevertheless, obstacles are not necessarily blockades, but can be stimulants to ingenuity and openings to further directions of theory and further devices for research. If the problem of the sociology of thinking were simply a matter of getting what is inside outside, some of these problems might be more severe. But we have good theoretical reasons to believe that what is inside began with ingredients, and is shaped by processes, which were internalized from social interaction. We are not in the position of the philosopher dealing with the problem of solipsism and trying to deduce the existence of an external world from the viewpoint of a hermetically sealed individual mind.[1] There is no rigid barrier between the interior or mental and the external or social; these are regions that are connected by processes, going both inward and outward. By studying these processes we can learn much about the sociology of thinking.

1. The obvious method of studying thought is introspection: observing one's own thoughts and reporting them. These thoughts could be the researcher's own; or other people's thoughts that have been reported for various reasons, either spontaneously or because a researcher has asked them to recall their thoughts. Another kind are thoughts as described by a novelist using the technique of stream of consciousness. Now consider the methodological problems: are these thought reports biased as idiosyncratic and unrepresentative? Such a verdict cannot be asserted in advance; we will know how representative or unrepresentative they are only by making comparisons. And comparisons always take place under a theoretical scheme. We are interested, as sociologists, in the form that thinking takes. There are often some details of content that are unique in each instance; although we should not overrate this, before looking at the amount of stereotyping of mental expressions that actually exists. But what we want to know is whether a theoretical model can account for the patterns and the variations. It is useless to consider empirical observations without some theoretical questions in mind. If we are only idly observing thoughts without any conception of what patterns they might flow in, it is glib to conclude that there is no pattern. In this case, I want to show that thinking is related to the external chain of social situations in which the thinking takes place, and we can hardly assess whether such patterns exist if we do not look for them. I further want to consider the internal chain of thoughts as a kind of IR chain; and that calls

for examining the patterns of all the instances of introspection against such a model.

Are our own introspections fatally biased, or are someone else's thought-reports? Is it better or worse to have the introspections generated by an explicit research scheme, or are they best taken when they are presented accidentally and without the interference of researchers? We have hardly advanced far enough in collecting and analyzing a great deal of introspections to answer these questions definitively.[2] But anticipating what I will present later, I suggest that problems of representativeness and bias do not loom large. Once we see that there are several types of thought, and that these arise in particular situations of external IR chains and follow particular patterns of internal flow, it appears that—as a crude initial generalization—there is no reason to rule out any particular kind of introspective data as invalid. Similarly with the alleged problem of distortions introduced by self-consciousness and self-interruption arising from the research process: for one thing, self-interruption is a form of thought that occurs naturally as well. In addition, introspective reports vary in terms of just where self-consciousness intrudes: often an observer (who might be oneself) remembers a considerable chain of thoughts before self-consciousness over the reportability of these thoughts breaks in; and the patterns of these chains before the self-conscious break are similar to introspections collected in other manners.

2. Another method is to catch thought on the way in, during the process of internalization. This is the classic data used by Cooley and Mead in formulating what became the symbolic interactionist theory of the self; parallel work was done in Russia by the school of Vygotsky (1934/1962) on the development of child's language. Here is one instance:

> Julia, a 30-month-old child, is in the kitchen alone while her mother is out of the room. There is a bowl of eggs on the table. When the mother reenters the kitchen, Julia is dropping the eggs on the floor, one after another, while saying to herself: *"NoNoNo. Mustn't dood it. NoNoNo. Mustn't dood it!"* (from Wiley 1994, 63)

Julia is speaking in her mother's voice, imaginatively taking the role of the other. Eventually the voice will become completely internal and silent, and develop into a form of self-control. In symbolic interactionist theory, the Generalized Other is being formed as a stance incorporating all outside interlocutors and their viewpoints. At the age of two-and-a-half years, the child is still carrying on a process of semi-external thinking, speaking the parts of the dialogue aloud; later during the period from three to five years, the dialogue becomes silent and internal, constituting thought in the form that makes up the adult mind.

This childhood material is evidence for the sociological model of thought as internalized from external conversations. It does not give us particular details for how this process continues to go on among adults; for the most part, it appears, adults do not have an intermediate phase during which they speak the other's part to themselves aloud before internalizing it. But this sometimes happens, especially when one learns a new word, or someone's name, that one is trying hard to remember; or when a particularly striking thing is said in a conversation or a public performance, so that the hearer wonderingly or admiringly repeats it aloud. The latter is an instance of an intensely focused, emotionally entraining interaction encapsulated in a symbolic expression; the heightened entrainment is visible in the overt repetition of the symbol. It is a testable hypothesis that speaking words aloud in this fashion makes them especially likely to be remembered, and to become a prominent part of one's internal conversation.

3. Conversely, there is internal thinking on its way to externalization, blurting out before its time, or before it takes the shape that conventional conversational rituals are supposed to have. Goffman (1981) broached the topic under the heading of "response cries." These include apparently involuntary exclamations, grunts, sounds of effort or pain, as well as mutterings to oneself in verbal form. Goffman's line of analysis is that the social situation is always something to be dealt with, even when the interaction is unfocused. Human beings in each other's physical presence, like animals warily grazing on the same landscape, have at least a back-channel consciousness of what each other is doing. For the most part they are concerned only with signs of normalcy, and against this background they become alerted to signs of abnormal shifts in others' action that might come to involve them. Hence an individual acts to make oneself accountable, engaging in a form of self-dramatization that broadcasts what he or she is doing, including occasions when the action has to be shown to concern only oneself. Grunts and mutterings are not designed to communicate, that is, to draw other people into a focused interaction. But they are social expressions, called forth by the presence of other people; as Goffman says, "they do not mark a flooding of emotion outward, but a flooding of relevance in" (Goffman 1981, 121).

Goffman is pursuing the Durkheimian program, making everything into a version of social interaction. How then can we deal with similar expressions, which are made in private, when there are no other people around? These must be internalizations of once-external situations; one can cry by oneself because one once cried for others; one makes overt sounds of grunting in moments of physical effort because one has previously displayed one's efforts to others in this way. This line of analysis would have to be checked empirically, and it may be doubtful whether it would cover all the instances of the inarticulate sounds people make when they are alone. What is more important is that we can pay sociological attention to a class of expressions that are a kind of thinking out loud, both when alone and in the presence of other people. This is where we catch thinking in transition, on the wing, without having to resort to introspective reports; and thus we can examine its form and its connection to social circumstances.

The most obvious, articulate version of such externalizing thought is rehearsals, where an individual prepares a speech that he or she intends to make to another person. Here the more interesting instance is not the speech for a formal gathering, which may well be written and then spoken aloud, but the speech for more informal, sociable interactions (but also for work interactions, such as asking the boss for a raise or telling an employee that he or she is being fired). As noted, upper-middle-class persons have more hesitation pauses in their speech than working-class persons, micro-moments during which the speaker is subvocally trying out alternative things to say (Labov 1972). This is evidence that differences in typical social class interaction produce differences in thinking, not just in form but in the amount of internal dialogue. Working-class speakers tend to use more formulaic utterances, which are reeled off without a hitch and thus without a pause for thinking. There is a social distribution of thought-rehearsals.

Thinking out loud, sometimes referred to as self-talk, is the most socially accessible version of thinking. Some of this can be made available for research only by self-reports, namely self-talk that takes place when one is alone. An important borderline form is cursing. This is sometimes actual communication to another person, but since that is dangerous, the most common form of cursing appears to be in situations of being alone or quasi-alone, as in Katz's (1999) study of drivers cursing in their cars at other drivers. Cursing is particularly revealing because it makes available for analysis the most highly ritualistic forms of thought, where the content matters much less than its action as a kind of magical incantation, and as a transformer of emotional energy.

4. Intellectuals' thinking is especially accessible, since intellectuals formulate their thoughts for publication. Since the audiences that will read or listen to an intellectual's productions are highly structured, it is easiest to show in this instance just how the internal and external structures correspond to each other. And since writers go through a

series of phases between reading and taking notes on others' publications and talks, formulating their own shorthands, outlines, drafts, and their final publications, we are in good position to see how points along the continuum from internal to external (and vice versa) differ from each other. We need not assume that internal thought simply mirrors external communication, but can investigate the conditions that make it vary.

5. There are different kinds and types of thought: differing among persons as personality styles; differing among moments for the same person. This variation provides no grounds for objection to the sociological approach; we can turn these differences to our analytical advantage, by using them for comparisons, and showing the conditions under which one or another type of thought takes place. Indeed, if thought were invariant in form, it might be harder to give a theoretical explanation of it, as we would not be able to use the method of comparisons to find what theoretical model best fits. Thought takes place in words, but in different degrees of conventional articulateness; it also takes place in pictures and other kinds of sensory imagery, and sometimes in motor schemes of bodily movement. Can we connect these differences in mode of thought with different situational circumstances, in external and internal chains?

One dimension of difference that yields good theoretical results is the speed at which thinking takes place. Some forms of thought are quick, indeed fleeting and hard to catch; other forms are plodding, even deliberately so; others occupy the middle ground between. We can document these speeds especially well in studying writing, in its various degrees of externalization. The speeds of thought correlate nicely with different situational contexts, and mesh with the IR model of rhythms and emotional energy.[3]

In what follows, I will draw on a variety of these methods. In some parts the argument is necessarily essayistic, given the stage of our research in this field. Since Mead developed his theory of the self engaging in internal dialogue, the principal sustained theoretical investgation along these lines has been Norbert Wiley's *The Semiotic Self* (1994). I will push the argument further away from Mead's emphasis on the inner structure of the self, and more in the direction of Goffmanian radical microsociology. Throughout these various methods of investigating thinking, let us keep an eye on the goal: a theory that tells us under what social conditions thinking takes one form rather than another.[4] In what situation will a particular individual think a particular thought, and what form will that thought take? These situations are places in IR chains, moments in time when symbols have been charged

up with a given social and emotional history, and when they are ready
for use in an anticipated situation just coming up on the horizon. I will
begin by reviewing what we know about intellectual thinking, the kind
about which we know the most.

INTELLECTUAL NETWORKS AND CREATIVE THINKING

In what follows, I draw upon my study of philosophers across world
history (Collins 1998). This provides evidence that symbols, and thus
the topics that intellectuals think about, are internalized from personal
interactions in networks. So too with the emotional energy that drives
individuals, in particular network locations, along their chains of
thought more enthusiastically, confidently, and obsessively than others. It shows us too how new ideas are created out of the distribution
of symbols already available at a moment in time, by being reshaped
for anticipated audiences.

Successful intellectuals have more network ties to other successful
intellectuals than less successful intellectuals do. I put it in these terms
to indicate that this is the judgment of history on the importance of
these thinkers' work: in ordinary terms, the great philosophers are
more closely connected to other great philosophers than are those in
any other rank of philosopher; secondary philosophers have somewhat fewer ties into the core of the intellectual community; minor philosophers have the fewest ties of all.[5]

Such ties are of several kinds, all of which are stratified in the same
way. The more important the philosopher, the more likely he or she is
to have been the pupil of one or more teachers of high rank. These
chains concatenate across the generations from teacher to pupil: the
highest ranked philosophers, the biggest stars among the major figures, tend to come from dense networks that have built up among a
series (indeed parallel and interacting series) of eminent thinkers.
Hence the more eminent the philosopher, the more indirect as well as
direct ties to eminent predecessors he or she has on the average. Secondary thinkers have fewer indirect as well as direct ties to important
thinkers, and minor thinkers have fewer still.[6]

These ties concatenate both upstream and downstream, across the
generations both backward and forward in time. Great philosophers
have more pupils and grandpupils who are relatively successful than
lesser philosophers do; intellectual success propagates forward but
also backward—having pupils who do important work is part of what
gets an individual a long-term historical reputation as having had very
important ideas. This last point seems counterintuitive; presumably

the future cannot cause the past; what happens after one's death cannot determine what a thinker will do while he or she is alive. Here again we need to make a gestalt switch. The individual is not determining what the network does, but rather vice versa; it is the action of the entire network across generations that determines how much attention is paid to the ideas that are formulated at any particular point in it. And given that ideas are always multi-sided symbols that are linked to other symbols both by chains of grammatical exposition and by connotation and nuance, ideas become reinterpreted in different contexts. Thus the "importance" of a particular thinker's formulations is not established until following generations of intellectuals have done their work on them. This is not an argument that canonical reputations are merely constructed, irrespective of what the merits of those ideas actually were; it is an argument that the merit of those ideas is not contained in themselves, in some platonic sphere outside of history, but is created by the entire network as it works with ideas that are constantly being decomposed and reintegrated in varying combinations. That image of a few lonely isolated minds, rising like mountain peaks above their mere worldly compatriots, is understandable enough as a Durkheimian emblem that the intellectual community makes out of those whom it puts in its focus of collective attention. As sociologists, we should be looking not through the lens of the myths, but at the larger structure that produced those myths, which is to say the formulation and long-term flow of ideas in networks.

In addition to the vertical concatenation of ties across generations, horizontal ties to important contemporaries are more common among successful than less successful thinkers. These ties are to both friends and foes. Eminent philosophers are especially likely to have had disputes, directly and reciprocally, as well as at greater distance, with other important philosophers. On the friendly side, we find that important thinkers tend to belong to groups of other thinkers as personal acquaintances. These groups tend to form early in their careers; these are not merely the clubbing together of persons who are already famous, but groups of would-be thinkers who have not yet done the work that will make them famous. Again we find a pattern that might tempt us to teleology, the future determining the past. Breaking the individualistic gestalt, we can say that the group makes its career together, their interaction promoting the intellectual creativity of all.

These network patterns are visible at long distance across the expanse of history. Shifting the resolution of the microscope, let us ask just how the network is affecting the thinking of individuals in these situations. What does one get from an eminent teacher that will make him or her creative? It cannot be simply passing along the teacher's own ideas, a transmission of cultural capital; to receive and repeat one's teacher's ideas makes one a follower, at best a minor thinker—and in general it is the lack of strong originality that distinguishes minor thinkers from more important ones. To be an important thinker in one's own right means to create new ideas. Often that means breaking with one's teacher. Such breaks have been interpreted as an Oedipal rebellion against the father-figure, but the Freudian model provides no explanation. They are far from universal, since minor figures do not break with their teachers, but occur only when structural conditions are present that open up space for new positions to be formulated.

If not ideas, then, what does the future-great pupil get from the great master? One pattern that is transmitted, even across breaks in ideas, is high EE. Eminent thinkers are energy stars. They are highly productive, turning out large amounts of published (and often unpublished work), only some small portion of which becomes famous. They work extremely long hours, seemingly obsessed with their work; their thinking is itself energizing for them, as if they are magnetically drawn along by their chains of thought. At the peak of momentum in these spells of thinking (which often takes the form of writing), ideas come into their heads—in some cases, they report, as if they are taking dictation. This pattern, found among those most magnetized by their work, gives some credence to the notion of "inspiration," as if the creative thinker is a genius, uniquely in touch with a creative flow from some higher region. The metaphor is misplaced, but it translates into a sociological truth: there are particular locations in intellectual networks where a few individuals become highly focused, highly energized, putting together streams of symbols in new ways; and those symbols do indeed come from outside, not from a mysterious realm of creative spirit, but from the dynamics of the intellectual community internalized in that person's mind and now on their way to being externalized again.

Not all creative individuals have the same flamboyance—and the same publicity focused upon their private behavior—but they all have relatively high degrees of emotional energy concentrated in their work. The eminent teacher is impressive because he or she transmits this attitude, this intense focus upon intellectual symbols as important above all else, and as magnetically enthralling and energizing for those who come into their orbit. The network ties that count in my evidence are personal contacts: the patterns described earlier occur by being physically in the presence of the other person, as well as (sometimes) corresponding with him or her. The network patterns that we summarize as eminence breed eminence; intellectual creativity is contagious, operating as a kind of tribal mana, transmitted by sound of voice and personal touch on pieces of paper from one to another. The pattern of network ties holds across all historical periods, from India, China, and Greece in the 500s BCE on through Europe of the 1940s;[7] that is to say, it holds across periods with vastly different forms of communication, both where most intellectual life occurred in direct debate, and where the mass production of texts has made them available almost everywhere. Across these changes, the importance of personal contact has not shifted. The Vienna Circle of the 1920s and '30s and the Paris existentialists of the 1930s and '40s have the same kinds of network patterns that can be found in the generations of Socrates or Mencius. Although modern intellectuals make their reputations as writers of texts, the social process that goes into making these individuals creative in this way is still structured around face-to-face interactions.

Contact with the impressive teacher is an IR at a high level of intensity. The lecture or other encounter focuses attention on words, concepts, and techniques of thinking that become sacred objects, indicating membership in the center of the intellectual community. These symbols become internalized in the minds of the listeners, a version of what I will refer to later as reverberated talk. Creativity takes place inside the individual mind as a recombination or development of these ideas and techniques. How this takes place we will see more fully after adding a few pieces to the puzzle.

Consider now what happens in a horizontal membership group. Here we find a different type of network structure. Where vertical master-pupil chains connect lineages and mediate remote links, the group of peers is a high redundancy network producing a strong sense of collective identity and of participation in a common project. Such a group assembles in coffee houses, student taverns, sometimes in roommates' bull sessions, sometimes in salons, in publishing houses, bookstores, or editorial offices. There are enacted repetitive chains of IRs, with a high focus of attention on intellectual topics, making these mental worlds more vivid than the external world of ordinary affairs. The intensity of the informal discussion, like the formal lecture, again makes sacred objects out of central ideas, topics, techniques of argument. The group can reinforce the status of teachers as sacred objects, giving them more reputation among initiates than among the general public. This increases the attention and repect given to teachers in lecture classes and makes these occasions more successful as rituals—indeed sometimes elevating a mediocre lecturer into a memorable figure by dint of the atmosphere of celebrity. The group also generates criticism of eminent figures of the previous generation, giving mutual support for breaking with them in new directions. This, for instance, is how Karl Marx was launched into his intellectual trajectory: in the Berlin coffee house group called "Die Freien," members competed among themselves to radicalize their critiques not only of Hegel but of those who had not broken with him far enough.

The group mobilizes EE collectively, and launches their careers collectively, moving up into the larger attention space. At this point, typically, the group breaks up, as its former members sharpen their differences to form separate positions. During the earlier phase, when the group was still intact, members may have engaged in plenty of arguments among themselves, providing much of the emotional effervescence that made the group a center of action. Now the friendly arguments of comrades-in-arms turn unfriendly, sometimes becoming bitterly hostile. Again Marx provides a good example, constructing his first notable works by attacking the rest of "Die Freien," while keeping alliance only with one intellectual compatriot of his youth, Engels.

We are trying to infer the micro-situations of individuals at central locations in intellectual networks. Zoom back out to capture another pattern visible in long-term networks across the generations: new positions appear together as rivals. Within a single generation, an active lifetime of intellectual work of about thirty-five years, there are typically three to six big names constituting rival positions in an intellectual field such as philosophy. This is also the number of intergenerational chains or schools of thought simultaneously perpetuated from teacher to student. I call this pattern the "law of small numbers." The number of important thinkers or schools occasionally goes below two, or above six, but these high and low configurations are inimical to creativity. When a single position dominates, there is no creativity: a single eminent teacher or teaching lineage dominates; there are no star pupils working creatively in new directions, only loyalists who break no new ground. Creativity occurs in a situation of rivalry. Rival intellectual chains depend tacitly upon each other, and structure each other's direction of thought.

Two positions is the rock-bottom minimum for creative development, but three is more typical. Two positions can easily give rise to a third, as a plague-on-both-houses. A chief mechanism of producing new ideas is to recombine pieces of past ideas in different selections and with different emphases. With the existence of prior intellectual networks, there are plenty of ingredients to recombine into new ideas. It is not dearth of ingredients that limits the formulation of new ideas. Creativity is also done with an eye toward the receptivity of audiences. Such recombinations of ideas can occur successfully up to about six positions. Beyond this upper limit, the history of networks shows that some of the lineages become cut off in the next generation, failing to recruit new students who carry on the impetus. Violating the upper limit can occur only for a short time, and is penalized by the breaking off of some lineages until the total falls to six or less. The structural limit is not usually consciously recognized by intellectuals during the generation when it is being violated, but it is felt in a sense of crisis of making one's way among a welter of positions, a sensation of being squeezed out by lack of recognition for the importance of one's work.

The law of small numbers fits two pieces into the puzzle. It shows how ideas are shaped, not only by combination and further development of ideas and techniques from prior networks. The most "creative," which is to say widely influential, ideas are shaped by oppositions, formulating a stance in controversies that attract the most attention. Opposing schools of thought carve up the attention space into niches, giving each other their identities and boundaries. Creative thinking is a process of making coalitions in the mind both positively and negatively. Ideas are symbols of membership and simultaneously of nonmembership, marking who is inside the thought-collective and who is beyond its boundaries. Intellectuals depend both on allies and even more on their rivals; the closer to the core of the network, the better they know the cutting points that carve up niches in the attention space.

Intellectuals at the core of networks have an intuitive, immediate sense of who lines up with and against whom on what issues. Their thinking covers ground swiftly; unlike for marginal intellectuals, there is no need to spell things out; they know what arguments follow from what concepts; ranging ahead, they have a sense of what arguments can be further constructed, what directions can be opened up, what applications made. The symbols that make up the content of their thinking are loaded with EE; they represent not just their object of reference, but the activity of thinking and talking that goes on in intellectual groups. Thus for the core intellectual in the vortex of creative thinking, the symbols flow rapidly together into new combinations and oppositions, as if by magnetic attraction and repulsion. The role of the thinker is to concentrate them in one focus of attention in his or her consciousness, and to set their flow in motion.

The law of small numbers shows another reason why network position is crucial in launching a star intellectual career. What one picks up from an eminent teacher, besides his or her EE and stock of symbols, is a demonstration of how to operate in the intellectual field of oppositions.[8] Star intellectuals are role models, to use that much-abused term, but in a fashion that cannot be picked up at a distance, and only by seeing them in action.

From the law of small numbers it follows that every individual's intellectual career passes through a structural crunch. Star teachers have many more pupils than three to six; and there are many more young discussion groups than can become creative and famous. Each person's career trajectory consists in coming to grips with the recognition of what one's opportunities are in the intellectual field. Each experiences in their own way an impersonal sorting process going on around them. Some decide to become followers of an existing position: retailers of some other theorist's ideas to a peripheral audience of students or textbook readers, or its representatives out in the intellectual provinces away from the hot center where the ideas were formulated, like followers of Parisian ideas in American literature departments. Another way to make a career as a follower is as a specialist, applying theories and techniques to particular problems, especially on the empirical side. These moves create smaller attention spaces, with their own jockeying for positions of leadership, governed by their own local law of small numbers.

Others stay the course of their youthful ambitions, modeled directly upon their star teachers and predecessors. Among these, careers pass through a tipping point. Cumulative advantage goes to those who find a vacant niche in the attention space, one of the slots available inside the law of small numbers. Their ideas receive attention from the field, giving them still more EE, more motivation and capacity for obsessive work, more speed in developing the possibilities for expanding their ideas at the forefront of current debate. On the other side of the tipping point are those intellectuals in the process of being squeezed out. Their work, although initially promising, meets little recognition, sinking their EE. They experience lessening confidence, less energy for performing sustained hard work; they become more alienated, less oriented toward the scene of current action. They become liable to extraneous problems, susceptible to being knocked off their career trajectory, "calamity Janes" to whom bad things just seem to happen, makers of excuses, embittered carpers. The micro-processes feeding back and forth between intellectual networks and an individual's thinking are cumulative, both in positive and negative directions. What kind of thinking one does depends on one's location in the network, both at the beginning of a career and as the career develops. There is a sociology of unsuccessful thinking, as well as of the kind that history extolls as creative.

Non-Intellectual Thinking

Intellectual thinking is only a small proportion of thinking. Consider now the thinking of nonintellectuals, and of intellectuals when they are "off duty," engaged in more ordinary types of thought.

The general theoretical aim is to see how thinking is predictable from the situation within an IR chain in which the person is situated.

Anticipated and Reverberated Talk

The simplest and most predictable form of thinking is that which is closest in time to the situation of action. Such thought consists in words on the verge of being spoken, or of words already spoken that have such emotional entrainment that they carry over into the individual's mind almost literally by reverberation. These forms of thinking, as noted, may pass through an intermediate phase between inside and outside as self-talk.

The following example is an office clerk talking to herself:

"I'd better get the DPOs for the new supplies. Oh no! We're not using those any more." (Wiley 1994, 61)

Here the self-talk conforms closely to the pragmatist model of George Herbert Mead. The clerk gives herself instructions for what to do next. The verbal thought creates a mental situation of thinking ahead; in this situation she finds the first plan of action is not going to work (the DPOs, Department Purchase Orders, are no longer being used), so she tells herself that, and begins to formulate a different plan of action.[9]

A great deal of ordinary thought is of this form. When engaged in practical action, one often engages in a kind of running commentary or thought-instruction on what is to be done; this happens as well in sociable rather than utilitarian situations—as in carrying out a conversation—as when one pauses briefly to consider which words to say next. Here another aspect of the pragmatist model is in evidence. According to Mead and his forebears (especially Dewey and James), actions proceed habitually, without conscious reflection, as long as things are going well; it is only where the action encounters an obstacle that conscious thinking intervenes. This formulation is somewhat exaggerated, since thinking about upcoming actions can take place considerably before an obstacle is encountered (and in addition, there is a form of thinking, which we consider later, that is free-floating and more of a form of sociable talk within the mind). Consonant with the pragmatist model, when an action is in full swing amd one is entrained fully in the physical rhythm, there is no need for verbal self-commentary. The thinking that anticipates an upcoming situation is often is tied to a feeling that special concentration needs to be put upon the action.

Anticipatory thinking to guide a practical action is also visible where an action is rehearsed immediately beforehand, in physical movements: the batter taking practice swings, the golfer's waggle of the club before a shot. These are truncated representations of what will happen when the planned action actually occurs; and thus are a form of thinking ahead: this is what I intend to do. But they are also ritualistic confidence builders. Some of these rituals have overtly stereotyped elements, such as crossing oneself, which draw on larger ritual solidarities (one professional basketball player during the 2002 season was viewed blowing a kiss toward the basket whenever he lined up for a free throw). Other preparatory rituals, although more idiosyncratic, are ways of getting into a rhythm set by oneself, rather than becoming entrained in the rhythm set by one's opponent. Verbal self-instruction can be ritualistic in the same fashion.

Some thought-instruction occurs a little further along the time line, not just monitoring but acting as a form of cheerleading during action: *okay, that's good . . . all right! got it! a little more now. . . .* Here we have another aspect of self-talk, even in what appear to be purely practical situations. The talk is not merely practical, but motivational. Athletes report such self-talk in moments of intense competition. A golfer:

> "Walking off 16, a lot of things went through my mind," he said. "I was like, *is this the way you want to lose another major? Is this the way you want to be remembered, screwing up an Open championship?*" (*San Diego Union*, July 22, 2002)

A tennis player:

> "My legs today were getting tired," Serena said. "I had to keep thinking, '*OK, Serena, five and one? Or four and two? Which do you want?*' That got me motivated just to keep running and to keep fighting." (*Los Angeles Times*, June 9, 2002)

Self-talk of this sort appears most frequently when the situation is an anxious one, or when the sense of momentum has not yet been established. It is often visible when a course of action is first being initiated, and especially when the speaker is moving from a position of inertia to one of action.

> *"All right, let's get going. What do I want? What do I need to do today?"*

This is self-talk while waking up in the morning; it has an undertone of writer's block, too, as the thinker (myself) is wrestling to get himself settled into a time-consuming task of carrying out a writing obligation. Such self-talk tends to be repetitive, using the same formulas over and over again; the repetition itself acts as a kind of incantation, a rhythmic entrainment in one's own words, which operates to focus one's attention, to "pull oneself together."

Thought Chains and Situational Chains

The more difficult case to explain sociologically is thinking that strays from the immediate situation into chains of association toward elements that may be quite remote. Here we have two leads: the thought chain begins in a particular situation, and it constitutes a chain of situations in the thought sequence itself. Such chains are more far-flung when the situation is one of "inner sociability," just thinking for the sake of entertaining oneself, much in the way that sociable conversationalists are talking for the sake of sociability. But the chain can also be seen when the starting point is utilitarian.

In the following example, a young waitress is hurrying to work:

> "Only eight minutes, takes five to change. I've got to book [hurry]." Imagery: a disgustingly filthy locker room. Visions of me running from table to kitchen table. Sounds. Forks and knives scraping plates, customers yelling over each other. "I have to make money. At least it's not as bad as last summer." Memory imagery: a tiny dumpy diner. Visions of me sweating. Sensations of being hot. Visions of thirty marines eating and drinking. Sounds: country music on a blaring juke box. "Miss, miss." "I'll be right there, just a minute please." Sensations of burning my arms in a pizza oven. Visions of dropping glasses. Sounds: glass breaking, manager yelling, marines cheering. "Oh God, get me out of here." Sensation: cringe, humiliation. "I hate waitressing. Can't wait to graduate and get a decent job." Visions of a paneled, brightly carpeted office with scenic pictures and healthy plants. Visions of me fifteen pounds thinner in a new skirt suit from Lord and Taylor. A great-looking co-worker pouring us coffee. Sounds of a clock chiming five o'clock. "Sure, I'd love to go out Friday night." (Wiley 1994, 64)

The thought-chain begins in a practical situation: the waitress is noting how much time she has and tells herself to hurry. Her thought now expands into a chain of memories and imagined situations, some real and some fantasy. The chain switches modalities: some parts are visual; some are imagined sounds (voices, music, glass breaking); some are physical sensations (being hot, sweaty, burning oneself); some are emotions and bodily sensations (cringing, humiliation—two aspects of the same experience, since humiliation is a sense of shrinking away bodily before the gaze and jeers of other people). This is not simply an internal dialogue in the sense of one voice answering another. The voices themselves speak in a variety of stances: her own statements in the internal dialogue ("I've got to book. . . . I have to make money. . . . I hate waitressing"); her own voice imagined in past dialogues ("I'll be right *there, just a minute please."*); other people's voices remembered from past dialogues (*"Miss, miss."*); her own voice remembered in past internal conversation (*"Oh God, get me out of here."*); her own voice in an imagined future dialogue (*"Sure, I'd love to go out Friday night."*).

This internal "conversation" is not carried out simply among voices representing parts of the self. Instead, the waitress's own voice, speaking in the present, is the central self who holds the thought process together and sets it on its course; this voice is "answered" typically by images of various sorts. She tells herself she has to hurry; she receives a visual answer, first of the locker room where she will change clothes, which is unpleasant enough. And then the unpleasantness theme is amplified by the next set of images of all the unpleasant aspects of her job. She then replies to the unspoken message by telling herself: *"I have to make money. At least it's not as bad as last summer."* These are two arguments; apparently she is not convinced by the first, so she goes on to the second one, comparing the present to last summer. Now the imagery replies again, building into a full-fledged replay of a humiliating situation. This was in fact an intense IR, the group of marines all focused on her, cheering together at her (to them, no doubt comic) debacle; the scene crystallized symbolically in her mind, in the very words she said to herself at that moment of emotional intensity: *"Oh God, get me out of here."* The words reverberate in her mind; the current situation with its degree of similarity—the unpleasant feelings of going to work at a job she detests—brings back the emblem of the old situation as if magnetically linked.

Nevertheless, in the ongoing inner thought sequence of the present, she pulls herself together in her own voice. First by reflexively distancing herself from the situation, objectifying it and commenting on it: *"I hate waitressing."* This is just the method that Blumer extolled by which one begins to get control of a situation by redefining it. She goes on to add further imaginative leverage over the immediate situation: *"Can't wait to graduate and get a decent job."* This statement is responded to by visual imagery again: the office scene that she would like to be in. And now the bandwagon is rolling in a positive direction. She embellishes the situation in favorable respects: losing fifteen pounds, having an expensive new suit; and—why not?—a new social circle and love life.

The thought sequence shifts across time away from the immediate upcoming situation; nevertheless it is held together by a common theme or mood. It starts as self-talk for a practical purpose, getting ready for work; but the problem of work is not just the utilitarian one of making sure the timing is right, but a motivational one, of getting up the energy to carry out a job she dislikes. Her own voice is the part of her self pushing toward a goal. The conversational "partner" is the imagery, remembered sounds, sensations, past voices, past thoughts, which respond to her. These images do not so easily go along with her goal-oriented, optimistic theme, and, in fact, tend to "argue" against her. But she—her own present voice—perseveres, and finally the imagery-as-conversation-partner falls into the positive mood, and even embellishes it. The present voice keeps more of an even keel; the imagery is more extreme, both negatively and postively. The whole thought episode is what we might call, in ordinary terminology, working up one's willpower. Wiley (1994, 67, 108–9, 121–24) describes this as a process of generating solidarity among the parts of the self, an internal interaction ritual that generates emotional energy.

In the following example the thought chain does not begin in a practical situation, but in a moment of idle thought, "down time" between tasks or social encounters. A professor (myself) is walking to his lecture:

> Music is going through my head, an aria from *Don Giovanni*, which I had seen the previous weekend with my wife. *"What scene is that from?"* Vague images of different scenes in the opera. I notice a woman, of professorial age and dress, ahead of me amidst the crowd of students on the walkway. *"Is that the egregious Elizabeth Dougherty?"* On closer approach, it is not the woman professor I am thinking of. *"Damn economists."* Vague imagery of economists on a university committee. *"Economists have bad values."* Feeling pleased with myself for the lapidary formulation.

Here again is an interplay of "conversational participants," in which imagery takes its turn and sets off further responses. Images, words, the music itself carry an emotional tone that weaves the associations together. First, the tune from *Don Giovanni* is quite strongly playing in my head, not in snatches but from beginning to end. The music is related to the act of walking: both are actions, with an ongoing rhythm; both, in this case, are filling a period of dead time. (I do not generally listen to recorded music, and thus when I hear live music it reverberates vividly in my mind during several days afterward.) The thought that follows is idle curiosity, a pleasant conversation with myself to name the tune.

Now I notice a woman who resembles my colleague, a professor who is superficially pleasant and smiling, but who almost always takes the opposite side of issues from me in committee meetings. The previous weekend, in gossipy conversation with my wife, after our pleasant night at the opera, I had complained about this woman. There is an associational link between this recent conversation with my wife, the opera *Don Giovanni* (which is also about love and deception), and this woman. In the immediate situation where I think I recognize her, there now intrudes the interactional problem: do I have to exchange polite pleasantries with her, if she is going the same direction I am?

That problem is quickly obviated because it is a misidentification. But the theme sticks in my mind. *"Damn economists.—Economists have bad values."* Elizabeth Dougherty is an economist, who happens to hold a position in the sociology department in which I am a member. The comment is echoing another theme that came up in a series of department meetings during the past months: another colleague had objected to hiring a new professor, not on the grounds that this person was not a good scholar, but because he was trained as an economist rather than a sociologist. I had not agreed with that argument when it first came up, but as my disagreements with the economist in the department had become more obvious to myself in recent weeks, I was somewhat rueful about having dismissed the argument so quickly. Imagery then comes into my mind of economists on another university committee, where I do not so much disagree with them but find their manner of assessing faculty promotions to be a bit ridiculous in their emphasis on a rigidly quantitative scheme of ranking professional publications. This committee (which was scheduled to meet that very morning just after my lecture, and thus was in my upcoming situational chain) shares a certain amount of intermittent humor in poking fun at economists' terminology in their letters of recommendation. Thus I feel pleased, at the end of this internal conversation, for summing things up with a phrase about economists, which although no doubt (objectively viewed) is unfair as a generalization, has a nice ring of bringing the matter to a conclusion. Successful ritualistic formulations generally sacrifice accuracy for pungency.

Overall, this thought-episode moves from solidarity to solidarity, with a challenge in the middle: it starts with the up-beat of the opera, and resonates with the solidarity of a weekend with my wife (who had traveled across the country to join me); it meets the challenge of having to deal with someone whom I pretend to get along with, and against whom I assemble an imaginary coalition that includes my departmental colleague who warned against economists; then, broadening the enemy coalition to other economists whom I don't like, the thought-sequence adds the solidarity of a larger group who also puts economists down.

IR chains are EE-tropic; we make our way from encounter to encounter, and within a conversation from topic to topic and utterance to utterance, picking up immediately past symbols and moving onward from them in search of the greater EE outcome. A similar pattern appears in the thought chains of inner conversation: one symbolic representation leads to another, not merely because of similarity but because

they have been charged up with similar kinds of membership significance, and because they are weighted emotionally by recent interactional usage, and by past interactions that were especially emotionally
intense. The inner thought chain is also an EE-tropism, magnetically
drawing in those images, verbal and otherwise, which put together the
strongest internal solidarity one can imagine out of presently available
ingredients. The thought chains of ordinary thinking in this respect resemble intellectual thinking, formulating coalitions in the mind.

The Metaphor of Dialogue among Parts of the Self

Consider now the theoretical framework in terms of which we conceptualize thought as a social process. The preeminent model comes from
Meadian symbolic interaction: "Thinking is simply the reasoning of the
individual, the carrying-on of a conversation between what I have
termed the 'I' and the 'me' " (Mead 1934, 335). "I talk to myself, and I
remember what I said and perhaps the emotional content that went
with it. The 'I' of this moment is present in the 'me' of the next moment. . . . I become a 'me' in so far as I remember what I said. . . . It is
what you were a second ago that is the 'I' of the 'me' " (Mead 1934,
174). Wiley elaborates the model with an alternative formulation from
Charles Sanders Peirce: "[A]ll thought is addressed to a second person
or to one's future self as to a second person" (quoted in Wiley 1994,
42). In this version, the internal conversation takes place between the
"I" and the "you," addressing yourself in the second person. This is a
form of self-address that is particularly noticeable in self-imperatives,
such as in the utilitarian situations noted earlier, and thus fits the pragmatist emphasis on practical action in the upcoming situation.

Nevertheless, there are forms of thinking that are not overtly in a
dialogue form. In the examples analyzed earlier, for the most part there
is no dialogue between speakers. (The chief exception is the office
clerk: "I'd better get the DPOs for the new supplies. Oh no! We're not using
those any more.") In the waitress's thought chain, she remembers a conversational sequence: "Miss, miss." "I'll be right there, just a minute
please." But this is not in her present voice; and it is the imagery that
keeps up the interlocutor's part of the conversation and carries along
the thought-sequence or internal interaction. The professor's thought
sequence begins, not with a statement by the "I" or any other voice,
but by the imagined sounds of music, which just "came into his head";
the professor did not consciously intend to start singing this music to
himself. He then makes various statements, but never replies to them
in words; what strings the sentences together into a coherent line of

thought is the intervening images and the memory connotations of past conversations.

Wiley (1994, 58) broadens the symbolic interactionist model of the internal conversation to include six kinds of participants: me, I, you, temporary visitors (particular imagined persons), permanent visitors (the Generalized Other), and the unconscious. This is an effort to deal with the complexity that thought sequences can display. But it is not yet complex enough, if we consider the role that imagery can play in keeping up a part in the "conversation"; and we also might say it introduces complexity where we need a different kind of simplification. In a sense, it doesn't matter whether a thinker addresses oneself as "you," "I," "me," or "we," or even leaves the hearer of the utterance unaddressed. Many of these utterances can be equivalent as speech acts, that is, as moves in the internal turn-taking that is the thought sequence.

Thus Mead's basic concepts, "I," "me," and "Generalized Other" are not so much roles that one plays in an inner conversation, as theorist's categories for designating the various kinds of structures, or better yet structured processes, which make up the human self. As we have seen in chapter 2 in reviewing evidence on the development of children's talk, it is possible to analyze the capacity for taking the role of the other, and we see the phases and social conditions through which it arises. It is important not to reify this concept, for the role-taking process varies not just developmentally but across situations; children generally expand their role-taking from particular other people to a Generalized Other, but not all others are equally generalized (this is implied in the data of chapter 3 on concrete and abstract modes of thinking), and even persons with quite widely Generalized Others can on occasion do their thinking in terms of a particular audience. Having an internalized standpoint of other people makes it possible to formulate a self-conception, which sociologists might want to designate as "me." In languages that differ greatly from English, the terminology becomes less appropriate, but people who use these languages nevertheless have self-conceptions, capacities for taking the role of the other, and actor viewpoints.[10]

The same kind of thing should be said about Mead's "I," which he formulated as an unsocialized self, an impulse to action. For Mead, the "I" has no content, since it is pure action; once it has taken action, or formulated a thought-statement, it now becomes visible for inspection as a "me," but has lost its spontaneous quality as the "I": "I cannot turn around quick enough to catch myself" (Mead 1934, 174). The "I," as Wiley says, is a reflexive blind spot, a standpoint that can be seen from but which cannot be seen except by turning it into something else. But this formulation of the "I" mixes two points: that the self is organized around a viewpoint in the ongoing present; and that there is a spontaneous impulse to action. That the self is an ongoing viewpoint of consciousness, and as such is analytically distinguishable from everything else, appears to be true. But this hardly means that the self, as impulse to action, is unamenable to further analysis. Impulses to action vary a great deal, in their energy, forcefulness, confidence, or in lethargy and timidity. From the point of view of IR theory, the "I" is emotional energy. Thus it is far from being an autonomous element irreducible to anything in the social situation: one's "I" is called forth in varying strengths by present interactions and past symbolic residues, magnetically attracted to some situations and repelled by others.[11] And this dynamic operates, as I have tried to suggest, in the inner chains of situations that make up sequences of thought.

The Meadian framework of "I," "me," and "Generalized Other" has been a useful step in the development of a sociological theory of the self; and the model of internal conversation among parts of the self has given us a model around which to accumulate many observations, especially in child development. But we should recognize that these are metaphors, a loose language for conveying something like what we want to say as sociological theorists. We need to improve on the metaphors, as we move into a more refined sociological theory of thinking.

Verbal Incantations

Consider now the class of mental expressions that operate not so much for the content as the form. These can be silent or vocal, part of inner dialogue, muttered "under one's breath" or in talking to oneself, pseudo-addresses to others who do not really hear, and even interjections into overt talk with other people. The most accessible example is cursing.

The most elaborate study is Jack Katz's "Pissed off in L.A." (in Katz 1999), in which he asked students to interview someone about the experience of getting angry while driving. Cursing arises in the specially structured situation of driving a car, which involves a combination of frustrations. You are liable to have other drivers obstruct the smooth flow of your driving by cutting you off, driving too slowly or too close, not allowing you to change lanes; and such frustration is amplified because there is generally a lack of communication with the driver who is frustrating you. Katz emphasizes that cursing and other angry responses result from the feeling that one is being ignored as a conscious agent. What an angry driver does is an attempt to get "in their face" in a situation that is not at all physically face to face, but pretty much all facing in the same direction, and generally face to tail pipe. An alternative interpretation is that drivers get angry because they feel endangered by the other driver's behavior. But this seems not to be the main component, since drivers react similarly at low speeds, as in traffic jams or parking lots; and on the highway, their response is generally to do something equally or more dangerous.

Cursing is not the only thing that frustrated drivers do. They also attempt to communicate their anger, and make known their presence, by cutting the other driver off in return, tail-gating him or her, or shining their bright lights in the other's mirror. The fact that typically the other driver either does not recognize these signals, or takes them as just bad driving behavior calling for further retaliation, makes the first driver still angrier. Angry behavior in driving is an attempt to establish normal communication in a situation where most conditions frustrate it and the messages sent are generally misread. The same actions that from the point of view of the angry driver are righteous forms of communication, to "teach the other guy a lesson" for bad driving, are from the point of view of the recipient just the kind of action that calls for righteously angry lesson-teaching.[12] Viewed from the angle of an ensemble of acts among a population of drivers, there is a cycle of bad driving behavior promoting more bad driving behavior, a kula-ring of negative Maussian gifts circulating on the highway.

Cursing, in Katz's view, is a "magical" act. It is not an overt behavior to communicate about or ostensibly rectify the situation, but is carried out in the privacy of one's own car, usually with little sense that the other driver knows that he or she is being cursed. Cursing has no practical effect, but it gives the air of setting things right, as if by magical pronouncement.[13]

What I wish to focus on here is not the driving situation per se, but the micro-dynamics of cursing. We may take Katz's formulation further: cursing is not only "magical" but ritualistic in the full sense. It is stereotyped, repetitive, and rhythmic; it strongly focuses attention, builds up emotional intensity, and establishes social membership boundaries, in this case by placing emphasis on the barrier of exclusion between inside and outside and in pronouncing those on the outside of the barrier as the essence of polluted and evil. Cursing, for all its bad moral reputation in "proper" social manners, is a moral act; it is carried out with a sense of self-righteousness, and a compulsory quality as if the curser is being pulled into the action by a larger force. As Katz shows in the case of drivers cursing (and otherwise retaliating against) what they consider to be bad drivers, the angry person feels that he or she is voicing the claims of the larger community of drivers, teaching the offender a lesson. Cursing is a kind of primitive justice, magical punishment in a special form adapted to the modern social environment of individual selves demanding ritual respect.

What does the individual get out of cursing, as a mental action taking place in the situational flow? Two elements: antinomian energy and rhythmic self-entrainment. Cursing is the expression of taboo words. The words have special emotional force precisely because they are taboo; they call for attention because they break a barrier against what is supposed to be improper to utter. To be sure, some forms of cursing become so popular that they lose some of their antinomian status; but they continue to be spoken with a special intonation or emphasis to indicate that they do stand out. The person who peppers his or her talk with "*shit*," "*fucking*," and other expressions that were once highly improper in polite society still invokes a counterpart social world somewhere in which these terms are still taboo; without this, the terms would lose all rhetorical significance.[14]

In the IR model, a central process is the transformation of an initiating emotion by intensification. Taboo words get their force from their connotation of being prohibited; they are products of IR chains, carrying along the emotional loading given by the persons who are shocked. Taboo words are reflexive products of prior rituals, encapsulating in imaginary form the emotion that goes with rupturing the skin of a primary, highly proper ritual, and building on this a secondary ritual of performing that rupturing. This is one thing that a person gets out of cursing: antinomian energy, the jolt of something different from normal. A curse focuses attention and energizes the situation. Seeking antinomian energy is a principal attraction for people to insert cursing in their thought-train.

The other thing that one gets from cursing is rhythmic self-entrainment. It is a way of enhancing the rhythmic aspect of one's own utterances, getting oneself into a flow. Cursing is a way of pulling oneself together, focusing one's attention, building emotional energy through a brief private ritual.

The mechanism becomes visible if we examine the details of the vocal action. Typically, when one starts cursing (e.g., triggered by some momentary frustration), one keeps on cursing until the full phrase has been said, even if the little problem has solved itself by that time. Consider "*Damn it to fuckin' hell, you stupid son of a bitch*," uttered at the maddening delays and irrelevant replies of a telephone automatic voice system: the positive aspect of the experience is the feeling of getting the body engaged, the bite of the mouth, the vigorous shaping of the words on the lips and tongue. Curses are a workout for the vocal muscles, and allow one to throw one's body into it. The above phrase can be parsed as a series of heavy beats: "*damn* it to *fuck*in' *hell*, you _stup_id _son_ of a _bitch_." These are institutionalized phrases, formulaic, negative talismans, ritualistic in a strict sense, as if they have to be said just that way or else they lose their efficacy. The experience is palpable: if you cut off a curse in mid-beat, or wind up uttering the rest of the formula without the proper intonation, you lose the energy of the utterance as it trails off at the end, a disagreeable sensation of not accomplishing what you set out to do—_cursus interruptus_. You have not ritually countered the negative situation, but just added a pallid ritual failure onto the primary negative. Imagine yourself saying, "_damn_ it to _fuck_in' _hell_, you _stup_id . . . oops, i beg your pardon, no problem. . . ."

Cursing provides some measure of emotional energy, mobilizing oneself to counter a frustration that momentarily stymies one's flow of action and train of consciousness. The energy comes from the rhythmic formula, and the self-entrainment built up by expressing it bodily. Cursing is an action of EE-seeking, not merely a displacement from frustration to aggression. As Katz noted, drivers generally become angry not because they are already in a bad mood, frustrated at some other event in their lives that they are displacing onto other drivers, but quite often in situations where they feel good because they are in a nice flow of driving on the open road. It is where that smooth flow, the expanded self-entrainment of driver in the motion of the car, becomes blocked by some other driver, that this special form of social frustration occurs, which is countered by ritual measures to restore the flow. The positive appeal of cursing is not explained by the Freudian repression model as a catharsis of bottled-up energy. Rather the curser builds up energy over the course of uttering the formula, getting self-entrained in its rhythm. It is a ritual of self-solidarity.

Cursing is not part of the deep self, but is called forth by the emotional dynamics of the situation. Katz noted that persons who curse will express whatever negative stereotype can be fitted to the situation. Racial slurs come out when the offending driver can be identified as a racial type; but the mechanism is opportunistic and unprincipled: old people, young people, women, men, rich people, poor people, all are categories for insult if there are cues for identifying the bad driver as such.[15] Cursing is formulaic and therefore stereotyped. It is repetitive, because the rhythm is a large part of its appeal; it is obsessive and trans-individual, pulling the individual out of him or herself into a collective act of imprecation. For all these reasons, cursing is impersonal, not really honed to the case at hand; and it is insincere. It does not express deep seated attitudes of racism, sexism, and all the other taboos of liberal tolerance. Instead, the taboo quality of these stereotypes is just what gives them a magnetic attractiveness to the ritualistic situation of cursing. This is part of what it means to describe cursing as "magical." Cursing is cobbled together for the sake of the ritual, providing a moment of remedial self-solidarity, but it has no practical effectiveness. It does not even have any real cognitive content; what one says in cursing cannot be taken literally, or even seriously. As Katz notes, moments later, after coming out of the magic spell, the person forgets what he or she said, or feels ashamed of it.

Let me now extend the argument, first to the range of situations in which cursing happens, and then to other forms of thinking that have a similar structure of incantation. We have examined cursing as a form of self-talk, unheard by the target of the curse, or by anyone else as intended recipient.[16] There is also:

1. Cursing at someone, a move in the escalation of conflict in a direct confrontation. As noted, here the ritual tends to entrain its recipient into the same kind of formulaic verbal expression.

2. Cursing at someone/something, a target not present, in the course of conversation. Here the curse is a collective stance (or at least an attempt to bring others in on one's side), expressing group shared hostility or mockery.

3. Cursing to punctuate one's remarks; not attacking anyone, but just showing generalized antinomianism. This style of talk is often benignly regarded as "salty," "colourful," among other euphemisms, which is to say that it is taken as entertaining, a mark that the extra rhythms and emotional emphases of interpolated taboo words come off as a stylistically successful performance.

This third type of cursing, denatured and inoffensive, leads us into the larger category of verbal incantations. As a borderline case, note the type of "swear words" that are not in themselves obscene or taboo in a negative sense. The exclamation *"Jesus Christ!"* or *"Oh God!"*—when uttered by a person who is not religious—is similar to expressions used to invoke antinomian energy; except in this case the words themselves are holy words, names of high respect. As Durkheim noted, the sacred is a realm of what is set apart from ordinary, mundane affairs; it must be approached with respect, and is dangerous even when regarded as beneficent. Taboos and positively valued sacred objects share the same dynamics. It is the invocation of special ritual status that brings the little shock of attention and jolt of emotional energy; there is a quasi-antinomian flavor in so far as a religious term is being used in a nonreligious and disrespectful way. Religious terms that have been turned into mere exclamations or incantations can be regarded as historical residues in an era of secularization; but their incantational use also keeps a sense of their sacred quality alive, without which the terms would no longer serve even to punctuate one's talk.

In the historical background of these formulaic expressions are oaths. An oath was originally a ritual, carried out publicly, in which someone bound him or herself to carry out an action, or otherwise to give special weight to one's words as in claiming to tell the truth. An oath, like a contemporary verbal incantation, is a form of pulling oneself together; self-entrainment in the rhythmic formula produces a little momentary rise in emotional energy. Under another terminology, EE is willpower; an oath, similarly, is a ritual of commitment, binding one's will, better yet, will-enhancing or even will-creating. Oaths still survive today in the narrow circumstances of public organizations at their most formal: oaths taken in court, in the ceremony of swearing in to public office, and, to a diminishing extent, in marriage ceremonies. The historical trend has been to replace formal public oaths with private and transiently situational exclamations and curses.

Historically, an oath invoked symbolic objects. One said not merely "*I swear*," but "*I swear by . . .*" a god or religious object, one's own honor, or some other object held in high regard. The vocabulary of today's exclamations carries over to some extent from historical oaths. The counterpart of the formal public oath, binding oneself in front of witnesses to a course of action, was, on the negative side, a formal cursing. This was a communal action, not merely an individual one.[17] When the pope excommunicated someone (typically a secular lord who claimed the right of making clerical appointments or collecting revenues on church property), the formula was to proclaim that the excommunicated was damned to hell. In a long chain of secondary and increasingly secular circulation, these symbolic emblems were formed into such expressions as "*Damn you!*," "*Oh hell*," and eventually the merely emphatic "*Hell, yes!*"

Among verbal incantations are exclamations. These may arise in situations of surprise or celebration, but they do not necessarily express an existing emotion so much as they create the emotion felt to be appropriate for the occasion. Just as body contact among participants is a way of carrying out a celebration, stereotyped vocal expressions are also called for, whether along the lines of "*Hooray!*" or "*Awright!*" or quasi-meaningful expressions such as "*Unbelievable!*" and other variants of hyperbolic comment on the extraordinary nature of the occasion. Celebratory rituals are EE-enhancers and EE-prolongers.

These kinds of verbal incantations are intrinsically social, entraining the group into a collective, heightened mood. They also have a place in the internalized and quasi-internal rituals of thought, exemplifying a range of favorite personal expressions that individuals use to keep up their flow of attention, and to keep oneself oriented in a direction of intended projects. One's silent thought stream is punctuated by private incantations: curses, exclamatory emphases, and expressions idiosyncratic to the individual, which one uses to keep oneself in rhythm, or to start up the rhythm when one feels stalled or sidetracked.

The stronger the entrainment felt (or sought for), the more the impulsion to utter the expression aloud. The extrusions of inner conversation into overt self-talk occur when the impulse to rhythmic self-entrainment is strong. Silent forming of the words is not as effective as the full physical expression with lungs and vocal apparatus, and for really strong statements, gestural accompaniment.[18] Similarly with cursing: there is relatively little forcefulness in cursing in inner conversation. The motor action of speech is central to feeling like you are expressing a true curse; and via the James-Lange principle of bodily action enhancing the emotion, the emotional resonances are felt more strongly when the cursing is aloud.

The pattern can be confirmed by comparison. Vocal self-talk occurs when there is a block in the flow of action, a need for an incantation to get oneself going or to get back into one's trajectory. Self-talk does not happen when there is a smooth flow of action, self-entrainment already going on either in a physical action or in a mental chain. In the midst of thinking about a project, or engaging in intellectual thought, there is little impulse to vocalize (which would tend to slow down the thought); it is only when something external happens to slow things down—for example, a momentary problem with the computer—that one is likely to lapse into vocal self-talk.

SPEEDS OF THOUGHT

There is great variety in kinds of thought, but these can be grouped in ways that make them amenable to sociological explanation. Grouped by topic or purpose, there is practical thinking, sociable thinking, and serious thinking: that is, there is a form of thinking that parallels each of the institutional arenas of external life. There is thinking that corresponds to the activities of political institutions, economic activities, religion, the intellectual world, family life, recreation, and so forth. Most of this thought is easy to chart from the outside in, since most of it stays close to the activities in which the individual engages in that sphere; it is typically anticipatory or reverberating talk from those chains of activities. Much thought is rather predictable because it is tied to institutionized interactions that are themselves routine. The main forms of thought that depart from being close extensions of these activities are intellectual thought (whose patterns we have already considered) and what we may call sociable thought.

The latter is thinking that takes the form of a sociable conversation with oneself—aimless, unconstrained, time-filling—much in the way that a sociable conversation with a friend meanders wherever it can get to while passing the time in an entertaining way. Nevertheless, as we have seen, external conversations are highly constrained by match-ups of stocks of symbols and complementarity of emotions, and are shaped by the dynamics of IRs, and these have counterparts in the inner chain of thought. Inner thought can be much looser than external conversations, however; why and how this is so is part of what we must now consider.

Kinds of thought differ also in their medium. Some thought occurs in words; some in visual or other sensory imagery; some in motor schemas. The last of these we can largely neglect in a sociological analysis. Thinking in motor schemas is the earliest form of representation in human development (Piaget called it "sensory-motor intelligence"; Bruner referred to it as "enactive" representation), and it continues to operate throughout adult life. Without it one could hardly walk, sit down, drive a car, or otherwise get around and feel at home in the physical environment; special forms of it are acquired when one learns how to release a bowling ball, swing a golf club, or play a piano. But for the most part, thinking in motor schemas happens close to the ac-tual physical action itself; there is sometimes a brief moment of prepa-ration, anticipating the overt action, but people hardly go off into long streams of thought in the form of motor schemas.[19] For the most part motoric "thinking" is closely analogous to verbal anticipatory talk, pre-dictable from the same conditions that explain the physical action itself.

Is thinking in imagery closely tied to the external situation, like motor schemas, or does it float off into remote chains of association, as verbal thinking sometimes does? Both; but under different circum-stances. Turner (2002) infers from evolutionary evidence that the human animal first developed visually dominant, with its larger brain wired more closely to visual input instead of the olfactory input im-portant for most animals, giving it the capability of spotting danger at a distance. In Turner's argument, verbal thinking is too slow for the practical exigencies of life; if the human animal hunting on the savan-nah had to rely on the plodding formation of sentences in an internal conversation to make decisions, we would have been killed off long ago. This argument seems to me not decisive, since alongside this ca-pacity for linking visual imagery to quick motor action humans have added the skills of fine-tuning verbal rhythms and picking up auditory nuances; thus some persons (and perhaps most modern persons) are verbally dominant in their thinking, even though on occasion they think in imagery.

When people think exclusively in imagery, I would suggest, the imagery is closely tied to the immediate or upcoming situation. This is the type of scenario envisioned by Turner (and in the examples that Mead gives of imagining prospective situations, with Mead's usual pragmatic emphasis on physical action): the human animal sees signs of a danger, visualizes the alternatives, and plunges into one of them. (It could equally well be signs of opportunity: the auto driver visualizing an alternative route around a traffic jam ahead; the erotically attuned glimpsing signs of receptivity from another person and imagining scenes to follow.) Here again, if the concern is to give a sociological explanation of the content of the thought, the situational dynamics will do the job, since the thought is closely connected to them.

Visual imagery goes further afield, for the most part, when it is part of a sequence of inner conversation. In an earlier section, both of the extended analyses of inner conversation (the waitress and the professor) involved sequences of inner talk and imagery responding to one another. The imagery was not simply free-floating: it acted as a conversation partner to the verbal voice, arguing against it or allying with it by bringing in supporting materials. The imagery, as it appears at a particular point in time, is a move in the interactional sequence of the self, part of the construction of the inner IR chain. Here imagery follows the same temporal rhythm as the inner voice;[20] it seems to be part of the same rhythm in which the self is entrained during that episode of the stream of consciousness. The imagery is being called out by the verbal thinking, and vice versa; but the rhythm (and generally speaking, the topic or issue) is set by the verbal voice. It is this voice that you identify with as yourself; it is the center of consciousness, your capacity to speak in an inner conversation. This suggests that if we can sociologically explain verbal thinking, we will explain a good deal of visual imagery-thinking along with it.[21]

A crucial dimension along which to array kinds of thought is their speed. We have seen, for instance, that incantational self-talk is relatively slow. The emphatic rhythm is central to its effectiveness; a strongly felt verbal incantation must be spoken aloud, which makes it slower than most inner thought. If one wants to carry out a verbal incantation silently, one must slow down one's verbal thinking, just in order to mark the rhythmic emphasis. (The reader may demonstrate this by thinking a curse or celebratory exclamation.) Silent thought, far down the continuum, flashes by, skipping much of the grammar of overt talk. When one is groping for a new idea, it often takes the form of a mere gestalt, an incipient speech-action, that one struggles to "put into words." This gestalt, however, is not usually a picture; it is an action-trajectory in the chain of verbal utterances, a sentence or set of sentences that one wants to say, that one has a sense that one will be able to say, but which is not yet formulated. Some of these incipient sentences are never formed: thought drifts off in other directions; the little bubbles do not float to the surface and coalesce into a big, publicly visible bubble. These are some of the inner depths of thought; we can put them into some sociological order by considering the entire continuum of speeds of thought.

To examine this continuum, look at the special case of writer's thought. This ranges along different degrees of externalization.

At one extreme is the writing of formalities, such as official documents, boilerplate wordage that can only be plodded through by a lawyer. It is written as if by a nonperson, as objectively as possible, cutting off any spark of human interest.

Next is writing intended for publication. This may have different rhythms, but they are generally all relatively slow to write. One feels this immediately when sitting down to turn one's notes into a publishable paper or book, or when writing up a spoken lecture. Publishable writing has a deliberate, relatively slow-paced rhythm; part of the difficulty of getting oneself to write it is pushing past this barrier, shifting from the mode and speed of thinking in the more informal media into writing for the imaginary audience implied by publication. It is, more than any other form of writing, for the Generalized Other.

Writing personal letters, by contrast, is writing for a particularized other; it can be breezier in tone, more rapid in flow, more casual in vocabulary. It is relatively more backstage, where publishable writing is frontstage, the construction of a formal ritual frozen in print.

Email as of the turn of the twenty-first century is still a new form, with not yet settled customs. Some writers treat it as a version of personal letter-writing, others as closer to casual conversation, or as rapidly dashed-off notes, without concern for punctuation or spelling, much less ritual greetings. Because of this variability in social interpretation, email is an ambiguous form of communication. Sometimes cryptic messages are perceived as hard to follow or viewed as insulting; it is prone not to be taken seriously by recipients, who regard it as a less significant call on their attention than other forms of written or spoken communication. From the writer's side, email is fast and casual, tempting one to think little but to send the thought on the fly. Lacking the nonverbal presence of face-to-face talk and the rhythmic entrainment of telephone talk, it is only loosely disciplined by the imagined audience.

Notes written to oneself, not intended for anyone else, are easy and quick to write. There is no pressure to make sense that can be read objectively; words and phrases, along with idiosyncratic diagrams, symbols, and shorthand, are shaped only to remind oneself of a train of thought. (Of course, one can make notes which are closer to the form of published writing; I am setting out the ideal types along the continuum.) Notes to oneself are similar to the most casual and unformed parts of inner thought: they represent trajectories, intentions, tension vectors for future thought-action. Eventually they may become transformed up the continuum, becoming notes to others, letters, drafts, publications. Or they may remain stuck at one of the lower stages, notes clogging old boxes in the offices of writers and would-be writers, just as most random thoughts remain nothing but random thoughts, never formed into overtly spoken sentences.

For the professional writer, there is another form of writing, intermediate between notes to oneself and the pathway toward publication: outlines that put notes into order, getting thought-topics and arguments into a sequence in which they can be turned into grammatical sentences and organized paragraphs, sections, and chapters. This activity is generally concerned with the meta-grammar, the overall architecture of the argument (or the fictional plot, the literary effect, etc.). In the process of making an outline, further thinking and creating is often done: arguments are developed by trying to fit the pieces together; difficulties are encountered that call for replies; concepts are found vague, ambiguous, multi-sided, contradictory, and these must be worked into into a coherent overall statement. The writer during this phase is moving outward from fragments of ideas, leading edges that have the feel of going somewhere, while the path to creating a meaningful statement for an audience remains vague. Working out those trajectories is a process of confronting the imaginary audience more concretely: one imagines what a reader will say, tries to meet objections, thinks of ways of appealing to the concerns and interests of the audience—easiest to do if it is a specialized intellectual audience and one knows its previous work and current concerns well.

Writing an outline is intermediate in degree of structuredness, between inward thought-like notes (or cryptic thoughts themselves) and the publishable text. Writing an outline sometimes moves quickly, sometimes slowly; quickly when one sees how it will hang together for some distance ahead, indeed sometimes so quickly that one cannot keep up with all the branches that open up as one visualizes the whole; slowly when one encounters obstacles, has too many fragments without sequence, too many pieces that have not yet been worked through in relation to each other, or too many parts of the overall argument that remain blank. Writing at this stage is often like laboriously piling up pieces, this way and that, until the mound is high enough, and the roller coaster plunges down hill. At some point the outline is done (at least for the time being), and writing goes into its next phase, transforming fast-moving insights into full grammatical sentences that flow at normal readable speed.

Consider now the differences among the thought processes at different points along the writer's continuum. Thought moves slower or faster, depending on several conditions. One is how much concern there is for grammar and form. Grammar is part of the public structure: the sequence among words, and the proper treatment of relationships among parts of speech, is a matter of making one's thoughts clear to persons who are distant, unacquainted with one's immediate personal context. It is also a following of rules that are customary in public and especially in published discourse, rules that are upheld by canonical authorities (academies, writers of grammar textbooks, school teachers). Following these rules is taken by readers as a sign of membership, and failure as a sign of nonmembership, in a community of literate persons. Grammar is ritualistic in just that sense.

Formal, grammatical writing (and hence turning one's thinking into that form) is generally slower and less fluid than informal and private thinking. There are subvariants, however, since one who has internalized the grammar, and is in full flow of writing momentum in the formal mode, may move along quite rapidly (although not as fast as the same person's informal thought); whereas someone who is not a comfortable member of that writing community, or who is struggling with a writing block at that moment, will think ponderously, slowly, and indeed even sometimes grind to a halt.

Grammar, the most public and constraining form of language, contrasts with other aspects of verbal thought. Writers' notes and outlines (judging from my own), consist largely of isolated phrases: most often nouns, sometimes adjectives; there are relatively few verbs, and those are typically in the form of gerunds ("writing"), infinitives ("to explain"), or imperatives ("check"—i.e., typically instructions to myself, meta-comments rather than part of the writing content itself). The grammatical and architectural structure of writing at this incipient stage is mostly left unformulated, indicated only by the ordering of phrases on the paper (often indicated by arrows or numbering), or by private short-hand (use of dashes, equal signs, directional arrows). Writers' thinking is thus only potentially, and as a vector of future action, oriented toward the full external community. One reason that intellectuals' published writing is often bad, is because it has not been fully transformed from self-oriented notes and drafts into fully grammatized writing; since the notes are heavy in nouns and weak in verbs, and those few verbs are rarely in a form in which they do the work of driving a sentence, much such writing is heavy, leaden, insufficiently dynamicized. This might lead one to infer that inner thought—at least among intellectuals—is heavy, undynamic, a mere file-cabinet of abstract nouns. That is not so, at least for creative thinkers, since their inner thinking is fluid, intuitive, putting together new combinations, moving blocks around; it is precisely because the thinker wants to move them around rapidly, try them out in new combinations, that he or she encrypts them into their most portable units, into nouns with a minimum of trailing grammar that would drag long expressions in their train. Inner conceptual thinking moves to its own rhythm and thus has to strip away the rhythm of fully spoken or written sentences.[22]

If verb inflections along with grammatical particles are the most public form of speech, nouns are not entirely private, even among creative intellectuals. Nouns too are Durkheimian collective symbols, for those factions of intellectual networks that circulate them and focus on them as the center pieces of their arguments; they are collective representations of how groups of intellectuals see the world, and are thus the entities that are regarded as most truly existing. A good theory—which is to say a widely successful theory—crystallizes into nouns.[23] If the nouns that thinkers use as shorthand are more fluid, their connotations not yet developed, their arguments still to be worked out, that is in their character as raw Durkheimian collective symbols in the process of formation, or intended formation; they are hypothetical membership emblems, resonating with some memberships in intellectual circles that already exist, but in the process of being reshaped into membership coalitions that, if actually established, will give that thinker the reputation for having thought something "creative."

Thought moves faster or slower, then, in part because of how constrained it is by the formalities of public utterance. Thought, like writing, is arrayed on a continuum from intuitive, unformed, and fragmentary, to well-arrayed sequences. Toward the external end, social forms are stronger and impose rhythms as well as structured sequences and connectives that are omitted at the informal end. But although thought can flow faster near the informal end, it can also get slowed down at any point along the continuum, if there is blockage, difficulty in negotiating the social demands of that thought-coalition or that external social interaction. Another aspect revealed by differences in speed of thought is how organized the thought is, in contrast to how scattered. Some thought is highly directional, flowing off toward a goal; other thought is disorganized, moving by fits and starts, changing directions, wandering aimlessly, stopped in its tracks. As internal IRs, directional thought has a high degree of EE, moving with confidence and energy; typically, too, it has an internal rhythm that carries it along—much in the way that sentences and paragraphs form beneath one's fingers on a keyboard when one's writing is in full flow. Scattered thought is low EE, whether lethargic and depressed, or fitful and nervous, or even complacent but with no sense of any place to go. This is the difference between successful and unsuccessful IRs, taking place in the interactional chains of the mind. Directional and scattered thought can each happen at various points along the continuum of internal / informal to external / formal thinking. An attempt to move from one level to another—from an internal level that feels comfortable, to a more external level that places more social demands than the thinker can meet— is one of the situations producing a shift from directional, coherent thought to scattered thought.

Internal Ritual and Self-Solidarity

I have developed the argument using the case of writers' thinking, since this is more easily open to inspection, and has been considered at some length by professional writers. Non-intellectual thought exists along a similar continuum, although with less emphasis—in modern societies, at least—on the formalized end of the continuum, and less concern to move one's thoughts from the inner to the external end; and there may be fewer devices for moving inward and outward, such as notes to oneself and outlines for writing projects. Otherwise, the patterns of variations in speed, grammaticality, and other formalities of expression, in blockage of flow, and in directionality versus scatteredness are also found in ordinary thought.

If humans are EE-seekers, they use internal IRs to get through difficulties and entrain themselves in a flow. We have seen this in the case of verbal incantations. We see it also in the way that writers deal with blocks, the devices they use to keep up their flow of expressable thoughts. A writer can get oneself going by rereading what he or she has written up to that point—like a long jumper backing up and covering old ground to get up momentum. Hemingway's device was to stop a day's writing session, not when he had run out of things to say, but when he was in a good flow; resuming the next morning, he would reread the previous day's pages and plunge onward into what came next (Cowley 1973, 217–18).

There are several kinds of writer's blocks, each with its remedies, and each with analogues in the scattering and refocusing of non-intellectual thinking. There is the long-run writer's block: a sense of not knowing what topics will lead somewhere successful, of floundering from one inchoate project to another, accompanied by chronic depression and lack of EE. This kind of block is the result of not being well enough embedded in the networks in which such works are written, and thus attuned to the audiences to be imagined that would constitute one's target. Somewhat similar to this kind of long-term block is the one that occurs at the career tipping point described above, where an intellectual has to confront the alternatives of finding a unique slot in the attention space, or throwing in one's lot as as a follower, specialist, or retailer of others' ideas to naïve audiences. Here the remedy, if there is one, is long-term and structural, a working out of one's place not only in one's mind but in external social networks.

In a very different time frame is short-run writer's block, where it is just a matter of getting up the moment-to-moment momentum. Here the solution is the devices of self-entrainment in one's previous flow of writing.

Analogously in non-intellectual thinking, there are long-run network patterns that constrain what one can think with what degree of articulateness; changing one's position in social networks changes these thought patterns, whether one likes the results or not. In the short-run, ultra-micro sequences of thinking, non-intellectual thought is most similar to writers' techniques in getting oneself moving; both use versions of self-entrainment.

Subjectively we live in a world of symbols loaded with membership significance, and with EE levels built up in prior interactions. Woven into the interstices between the external IRs that one goes through with other people are the inner IRs that constitute chains of thought. The guiding principle of these inner chains, too, is EE-seeking. The longer one stays inside one's own subjectivity in the realm of inner thought, the more the goal becomes not so much direct solidarity with other people but solidarity with oneself. Symbols used in inner thought become decomposed, recombined, tried out for new purposes, aiming at imaginary coalitions not only with persons outside but also coalitions among the parts of oneself. Following the analogy of the intellectual thinker trying out new combinations, the human being in private thought tries out projects, tendering symbolic alliances that are not yet formed, entertaining mere trajectories.

Here, we have seen, the inner depths of thought can be scattered and unfocused. Individuals develop their devices for getting themselves focused, their methods for entraining themselves. IRs, as I have stressed from the beginning of this book, are variable. They do not always succeed; they range from mere ingredients to high solidarity. This variation is just as true of the inner rituals of the mind. Some reach high degrees of solidarity with oneself; at these moments, one feels focused, directional, and most clearly conscious. At other moments (and with more such moments in the lives of some persons than others) inner IRs do not come together: thought is episodic, scatterred, inarticulate. Such persons do not necessarily have incoherent lives; they likely prefer their outer lives if things are better organized there to produce solidarity and EE. This is a source of the difference between introverts and extroverts.

Inner lives have varying degrees of privacy. But the forms that privacy takes are not necessarily unique. The devices that we use to entrain our thoughts, to get ourselves together, may be largely imported from standard models available in external social life. Verbal incantations—traditionally, in the form of prayers or magic; contemporarily in the form of pep talks and curses—are just some of the devices with which external rituals are taken into the self. No doubt there are other such inner rituals to be discovered.

The world of thought is generally regarded as a vast territory. So it is; but it may not be so fantastic as it is touted to be. We have a prejudice that thought is free, untrammeled, infinitely open, unapproachable from outside. And yet—if thought is an internalization of rituals from social life, further developed by decomposition and recombination of its symbolic elements, in the train of impulses to externalize them again—how strange can it be? The private thinking among Chinese villagers in the Han dynasty must surely have been similar to each other because it was related to the rituals that they performed overtly, and thus differed in specifiable ways from the private thoughts, say, of middle-class Americans at the turn of the twenty-first century.

Much of our sense of the strangeness of thought comes because it has not yet been very widely explored sociologically. If we had a large collection of chains of thoughts from people in particular situations, it might well turn out that they think many of the same elements, even arranged in many of the same combinations. With greater theoretical abstraction, examining the formative conditions of inner IR chains, the commonality we find must be still greater. Human beings differ in detail, but we are everywhere mentally akin, since we are constructed of the same ritual processes.

PART TWO

Applications

Chapter 6

A THEORY OF SEXUAL INTERACTION

Is SEX A NATURAL biological drive or is it socially constructed? As sociologists, we are inclined to say it is the latter, constructed upon the basis of the former. But this very general, conventionally palatable answer leaves everything dangling. How strong and how constant is the biological component, and by what mechanisms does it become transmuted into the myriad variations of sexual behavior? Can we predict on theoretical grounds who will do what with whom, and in what historical circumstances?

Let us say that sex is motivated by pleasure in the genitals, and that this physiological mechanism has been evolutionarily selected to promote reproduction. But genital pleasure-seeking does not account for many aspects of what people widely recognize as sex. Why are breasts considered sexy in some (but not all) cultures? A evolutionary biologist would answer that breasts signal a woman's mothering capacity. But this does not explain why adult males would derive pleasure from grabbing, touching, or sucking women's breasts; and it leaves us with the puzzle as to why we commonly distinguish between nursing (not usually considered sexy) and breasts as sexual.

Similar problems crop up as we move further afield from the reproductive organs. Why is kissing widely considered sexual? Why only in certain societies, and for certain kinds of kisses? What is the pleasure of touching lips and tongues, surely far from the biological mechanism of genital pleasure? Why is it sexually arousing (for some social circumstances), so that one thing leads to the other? Why is it that for some persons, the height of sexual pleasure is to combine kissing and licking with genital contact, sometimes touching the mouth to all parts of the body? This touches on the problem of fellatio and cunnilingus. Seeking genital pleasure explains why someone might enjoy having their penis or clitoris sucked; but why should some persons find it highly erotic to perform oral sex upon someone else?

Anal sex raises similar questions. One might account for anal penetration as penis-pleasure, in the case of the male penetrator. But if there is pleasure in passive anal sex in both homosexual and heterosexual intercourse, what is the mechanism of pleasure? Why are there other anal elaborations, enjoyed by some individuals or in some erotic subcultures, including anal licking,"fist-fucking,"[1] and, relatedly, spicing sex with being the recipient or witness of defecation and urination?

There are a host of mild and relatively respectable examples of sexual attractions that have nothing to do with genitals: faces, hair (why should one like to run their fingers through a lover's hair? why should blondes—in some historical periods—be considered sexy?), or, as in Japan, the nape of the neck. In the nineteenth century, off-the-shoulder gowns were female high fashion, and men would proclaim the beauty of a woman's shoulders. We take it for granted that a sexual partner should preferably be attractive. Aside from the fact that standards of attractiveness vary historically, by what causal process can we account for how nongenital bodily features become sexually arousing? In the twentieth century, especially between 1930 and 1950, women's legs were considered extremely sexy as they approximated certain ideal curves; even the remote appendages, ankles, insteps, and high-heeled shoes were capable of arousing erections and ejaculations. Various forms of voyeurism and sexual aggressiveness, as well as consensual love-making, were aimed at touching these objects. Again we must ask: where is the pleasure? Finding a mechanism to account for such erotic experiences is the general problem of all the examples we have been considering.

Let us list a few more types that need explaining: holding hands— why is that felt to be pleasurable, as well as part of a sequence of erotic behaviors? Why do incipient lovers sometimes play footsie under the table? Why is general body contact, hugging or being hugged by another person, in some social circumstances (but not in others) a major part of sexual pleasure? The kind of answer I am seeking will not be of the form "that is the way things are defined in this culture." And it does not help much to add "sexist" or "patriarchal" or "capitalist" to "culture" (or "regime"). There is an important component of bodily and emotional interaction in these social actions; these are not merely cultural signals, arbitrarily assigned out of the big code-book in the sky that many theorists envision as determining what happens in a particular epoch, until mysteriously the sky ruptures and another code-book is put in its place. We can make a stronger and less arbitrary explanation, by linking sex with theoretical models that include components of human bodily action; not surprisingly, I will shortly suggest a link to interaction ritual theory.

An important set of problems centers around masturbation. A purely evolutionary reproduction-oriented sex drive has difficulty explaining masturbation, especially as it occurs beyond allegedly super-charged adolescence and when intercourse is also available (e.g., evidence it occurs among married or cohabiting persons: Laumann et al.

1994, 82–83). If the mechanism is genital pleasure, masturbation is easy to explain, but another problem arises: why should intercourse be preferred over masturbation? Apparently there is some additional source of pleasure in another person's body besides the genital climax. Again, if male masturbation is motivated simply by penis-pleasure, why is it typically accompanied by fantasy, and often by viewing pornography? Sheer organ-specific physical pleasure would seem to require nothing but tactile stimulation; yet these representational (shall we say symbolic? if so, of what?) aids seem to intensify the physical experience as well as increase their frequency. Moreover, the incidence of masturbation correlates postively with availability of sexual intercourse, not negatively as one might expect if there is a fixed quantity of biological sex drive to be used up (Laumann et al. 1994, 137–38). Instead, masturbation seems to stimulate other kinds of sex as well (as does pornography). Sexual turn-ons of one kind seem to sensitize sexual turn-ons of other kinds; it appears that sex is not merely an internal drive but a variable quantity that is controlled or constructed from without.

Freud confronted the same range of problems. His solution was to posit a general sexual drive, libido. At adolescence it settles upon genital organ-pleasure, but earlier passes through a series of stages in which it sensitizes other organs (oral / mammary, anal), hence these kinds of eroticism can be explained as displacements or regressions to previous libidinal stages. Shoe-fetishes and the sexual attraction of legs, hair, and indeed of beautiful form in general can be explained by the plasticity of libido, like a fluid that spreads anywhere and eroticizes anything it touches. Libido is a metaphor for something that unites the variety of sexual objects and pleasures, but it is far from an explanation. One major difficulty is that Freud takes sexual drive to be a naturally given quantity; the main role of social processes is to repress the sexual drive. I suggest that the contrary is the case: the amount of sexual pleasure-seeking has apparently increased historically. Both Freud, and his follower in this respect, Norbert Elias, hold that the civilizing process has brought about increasing repression of natural sexual functions, a view that I will show is historically erroneous. Erotic stimulability may have a biological origin, but it is enormously flexible. Here, too, I want to place the emphasis on just the opposite direction from evolutionary psychology or sociobiology with its image of humans (at least males) resembling rutting rams or spawning fishes driven to spread as many sperm cells as possible. Humans can live with rather modest amounts of sexual behavior, and when sexual behavior expands, both in quantity and in range of objects, that is due not to a primal omni-sexualizing drive to release sperm but to social processes that create sexual drive. The libido metaphor also implies a single process, whereas I propose that there are four main processes interacting.

Let us agree, as a starting point, that sexual behavior is motivated by seeking pleasure. There is evidence that people must learn how to achieve sexual pleasure. An individual's first sexual intercourse, and early sexual experience generally, is often not very pleasurable. For females, even in an emancipated sexual atmosphere, it may be unpleasant, or it may be regarded as disappointing or oversold (evidence in Lynn Green's interviews with black and white teen-age girls about their early sexual experiences: Green 2001). For males, too, early sex experiences tend to have a higher level of negatives as well as lack of orgasm than at older ages, even though the youngest men spend more time in each sexual event than older men (are they ardent or incompetent?) (Laumann et al. 1994, 94, 117). A fair amount of sexual activity is unsuccessful and unsatisfying (Laumann et al. 1994, 368–71); this variation in experience is too easily shunted aside into a separate category, sexual dysfunction, overlooking the significance of the comparison for showing how sexual pleasure is socially constructed. Sexual pleasure is to a considerable extent learned in couple-specific interactions, so that is it not merely a matter of young, inexperienced persons learning how to have pleasurable sex, but of the inexperience being specific to each social relationship.[2] Sexual pleasure-constructing behavior is learned; but what exactly is it that is learned? It is a form of social interaction, and this is what our sociological theory must explain.

My strategy is to make comparisons and explain variations. There is now good systematic survey data (Laumann et al. 1994). Since we are concerned more with processes and correlations than with sheer incidence of various kinds of sexual behaviors, the Kinsey reports and other more specialized samples continue to be revealing, when we ask the right theoretical questions of the data. Historical and ethnographic materials give strategic variations to explain. It is also useful to compare different kinds of sexuality: to compare males and females, and also gays, lesbians, and heterosexuals, the blind and the sighted; and to compare different kinds of behavior: intercourse, masturbation, oral and anal sex, rather than leaving each segregated in its own area of specialized research interest, or worse yet, its own interest group. Sexuality needs to be connected more directly to the central processes of social theory. It is an obstacle to approach sex primarily as a social problem, and even more so to substitute moralizing for explanation. In this respect, analytical blinders imposed by insurgent standpoint advocacy can be no less restricting than those of sexual traditionalists. Moralizing and advocacy about sex will enter my analysis here only as one more topic to be explained.[3]

Evolutionary biology has become a prominent theory in recent years because, among other reasons, it fills the gap left by the absence of a nonmoralistic general theory of sexuality. Since I would like to get on with the sociological analysis, and not keep being distracted by the invitation to a rather easy counterpolemic, I will briefly list here the reasons why as a sociologist I am not impressed with the explanatory power of evolutionary biology. Evolutionary biology gives no mechanism for just how the genital organs are implicated in sex, but only the global argument that somehow everything is arranged to contribute to maximal reproduction of selfish genes. Its focus of variation is between males and females, collecting evidence to support the view that males are programmed to impregnate as many females as possible (and to compete with other males to do so), while females are programmed for maternal behavior and for selectivity in choice of mates in order to maximize the chances of their offspring's survival to reproductive age. The theory is badly underdetermined as to both historical and individual variations in sexual practices. It fails to account for how people experience socially real sexual motivations, especially when these are at variance with the alleged biologically programmed motivations. For instance, the theory fails to distinguish, as most real people do, between maternal capacity and sexiness. In eroticized cultures, males make this distinction quite sharply, and do not prefer having sex with women who display only maternal traits. In eroticized societies (like the twentieth century), having large numbers of offspring (or indeed any offspring at all) is what the most erotically active are concerned to avoid.

Pragmatically, I could just say that I have my own theoretical program to investigate, and I am not interested in either pursuing or arguing with a rival research program that seems to me to have limited explanatory resources. My most important objection, however, is that evolutionary biology has gone down the wrong track precisely on the question of what are the most important biologically programmed propensities of humans. Evolutionists have chosen the image of the selfish gene, exemplified in the competitive male as isolated, self-seeking individual. This emphasis on competition makes evolutionary biologists allies with the narrow economism of rational choice theory; it should remind us that the source of Darwinian theory was the economics of Malthus. I would suggest, to the contrary, that the most important feature of human biology is that humans are hard-wired not simply for genital pleasure or the tendency to propagate one's genes but, above all, for the kinds of pleasure in emotional entrainment and rhythmic synchronization that make humans pursuers of interaction rituals. The human nervous and endochrine system, and many other features including skin bareness and sensitivity, have been evolutionary selected so as to make humans, compared to most other animals, much more attuned to individualized social interaction, and to forming many kinds and degrees of social ties with each other—and, above all, attuned to the prolonged interactional pleasures of sexuality. Contrary to the evolutionary biologists who see males and females as radically different, the former as selfish gene scatterers and the latter as mate-selective and protective mothers, I suggest that both males and females share the same biological hard-wiring that makes them mutually sensitive to the interactive buildup of attention and emotion in IRs. This is the aspect of human biology that explains the variety of erotic behavior; it also explains what makes society possible at all. The evolutionary biology model seems better oriented to explain a species with highly unsociable male animals, such as mountain goats.

In what follows, I will discuss three theoretical dynamics that mesh together to explain sexual interaction. The first, the selfish penis model (or individual genital-pleasure seeking), has already been discussed, mainly from the point of view of its shortcomings. It will continue to play counterpart to the following arguments. The most straightforward way to analyze selfish sexual pleasure is to study prostitution, which brings out quite brazenly all the unpleasant features of rational action or utilitarian exchange. The second dynamics is sexual interaction as interaction ritual producing solidarity. The dynamics of IRs also helps explain nongenital sexual practices. Third is erotic prestige; here I will deal in a schematic way with historical changes in erotic stratification, explaining why erotic prestige-seeking became such a dominant motive in twentieth-century societies.

Sex as Individual Pleasure-Seeking

The strongest empirical approximation to sex as selfish, individual pleasure-seeking is prostitution. In the ideal type, there is a simple exchange of customer's money for sexual pleasure.[4] I will suggest the relevance of three kinds of empirical observations.

First: customers' interaction with prostitutes is often difficult and unpleasant, characterized by a high degree of distrust and cheating.[5] Prostitutes are primarily motivated by money: they generally try to get as much money as possible from the customer, and give as little sexual labor in return as they can get away with. One variant, on the borderline of prostitution, is the b-girl (bar-girl) who hustles drinks for a bar which turn out to cost exhorbitant prices, by implying that a sexual deal will follow. Full-fledged prostitutes engage in various forms of bargaining, both as to price and quantity, such as charging a given sum for initial sex acts and asking for more to continue on to actual inter-course, sometimes stringing out the customer to continued renegotia-tions of what he thought was a done deal. Prostitutes in arenas with high turnover tend to minimize their work for the money, trying to hurry the customer through as quickly as possible. In short, a prostitute tends to act very much like a pure utilitarian actor in game theory: since this is a purely selfish exchange on both sides, the focus is on monetary bargaining and on shirking work. Prostitutes almost always demand their money up front, before performing; customers agree to this, ap-parently because the strength of their desire for sex is stronger than their willingness to calculate and bargain. In other words, the cooler head is on the side of the prostitute, hence the better bargaining posi-tion.[6] For the same reason, prostitutes are in a better position to cheat their customers than the other way around. This is one reason why prostitution has a bad reputation; in addition to being condemned by moral puritans and advocates of exclusively marital sex, it also tends to have a quality of overt distrust and cheating. This is implied by the colloquial term "whore" used in the informal culture of customers for commercial sex. Even the customer bent on purely selfish sexual plea-sure may often experience interaction with prostitutes as utilitarian to a degree that reduces the sensory pleasure to a unsatisfactory level.

The second micro-empirical observation is that prostitutes during in-tercourse frequently simulate the sounds of being sexually aroused: moaning and stereotyped expressions of what women in the throes of passion are supposed to say. This is part of the professional lore of prostitutes, the self-presentation that is considered the correct perfor-mance of the job. It may also be an instrumental twist on this pattern, insofar as prostitutes believe they can get men to ejaculate more rap-idly this way and hence get the work over more quickly. Commercial telephone sex, in which women "talk dirty" for customers to mastur-bate, would seem to indicate that a main component of male sexual arousal and pleasure is the experience of participating in mutual arousal. All these observations point to the same conclusion: that even in situations in which sheer selfish sexual pleasure is the aim, there is a component of shared sexual arousal that is believed to enhance the pleasure. Since prostitutes typically have little emotional commitment and engage in cheating, this mutual arousal is generally faked; but the fact that they feel it is expected (and even useful) shows that the sheer individual pleasure-seeking model of sex does not account for all, or even very much, of sexual motivation.

Third: customers of prostitutes tend to find the most sexual satisfac-tion where the interaction is least like a distrustful, commercial transac-tion, that is, least like prostitution. Such are encounters where haggling over money is minimized, sexual performance is carried out as specified, interaction is sociable and friendly, and the prostitute becomes genuinely aroused rather than faking it.[7] An example of the latter would be mistresses, who are further along the continuum specified by Zelizer (see note 4 of this chapter) toward long-term, multi-transaction relations. A related observation is that men often consort with prostitutes to have sex with women who are more beautiful than those they ordinarily have access to; my hypothesis is that there may be a negative (or zero) correlation between sexual satisfaction and the beauty of the prostitute. That is because the most beautiful prostitutes have high market demand, hence they receive more deference and can demand more (both monetarily and behaviorally) from their customers; hence beautiful prostitutes tend to cheat their customers more, engaging in more haggling and more shirking of performance. Less attractive prostitutes, conversely, have to put out greater effort in making themselves saleable; their lesser haggling and greater willingness to perform sexual work make them more pleasant to interact with, and thus produce more sexual satisfaction. Even in sex with prostitutes, interpersonal solidarity (personal liking) correlates with sexual pleasure.

Sex as Interaction Ritual

The most important features of sex are those that fit the IR model. I will stress again that the rituality of human actions varies on a continuum. Mutual focus and emotional entrainment may be zero, moderate, or high. The intensity of an IR depends upon the presence of a set of initial ingredients, plus the interactive processes by which the ritual builds up to pervade participants' feelings and actions. Rituals produce outcomes such as social solidarity and symbolic significance only to the extent that the IR reaches higher levels of intensity. This is blatantly apparent in the case of sexual IRs. Sexual intercourse often fails to be an IR of much intensity, especially when carried out in the mode of one-sided pleasure-seeking on the utilitarian model. In what follows, I describe the mechanisms by which a full-scale sexual IR is built up. We start with the ideal type of highly successful sexual IRs, and go on to examine how various forms of sex can be explained as variants on this ideal.

The IR model fits most forms of sexual interaction, including both intercourse itself and ancillary actions like kissing. (See figure 6.1, which is a modification of figure 2.1 given in chapter 2.) Let us start with intercourse.

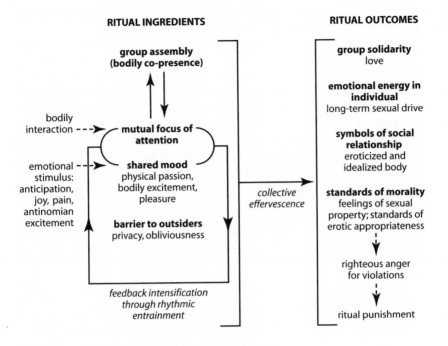

Figure 6.1 Sexual intercourse as interaction ritual.

1. Intercourse is bodily copresence of the strongest possible degree. It assembles a very small group, usually two persons (on orgies, see below).

2. Intercourse has a strong mutual focus of attention, the awareness of contact with each other's body, and of the actions by which each other's body affects the other.

3. The common emotion or shared mood is sexual excitement, which builds up over the course of the interaction.

4. Intercourse typically has a very strong barrier to outsiders; it is carried on in private, and there are strong taboos on others viewing it.

This high preference for privacy in sexual intercourse is a cross-cultural universal (Reiss 1986), suggesting that the dynamics of this intensely intimate IR, rather than culture, dictate the taboo. There are several ways in which bodily presence of observers can disrupt the buildup of sexual excitement in intercourse. Naïve observers are likely to be caught up in the contagious sexual excitement and try to join in, thereby interrupting the mutual focus. Alternatively, if observers maintain their emotional cool, that tends to bring down the atmosphere of sexual excitement. The two dynamics may be combined: observers may fight to control their own sexual excitement in observing others by reacting to the sight as obscene (i.e., highly improper), and thus intrude hostilely; a milder version, when observers feel they cannot intervene, is to turn the situation into humor by jeering, thereby detracting from the mutual focus of the lover-makers on their passion. Goffman (1981) noted that humans act like other animals, maintaining backchannel awareness of whoever else is in range who potentially could be part of the interaction; and hence there is tacit orientation toward them. In the case of sexual interaction building up to mutually engrossing levels, the presence of others is disrupting. Empirical confirmation comes from the lore of the pornography industry that male porn actors are relatively rare in their ability to maintain an erection in the presence of nonparticipant observers.

There are some violations of the privacy restriction, but these tend to confirm the operative preference for privacy. One type of violation is sex shows: live action intercourse is the rarest and most taboo (most "obscene") of all sexual displays (the dancer / stripper oriented to the customers is much more common); much of its attraction comes from the piquancy of its violation. Relatedly, some female photographers of male-oriented pornography are outstandingly successful in getting their female models into a state of visible sexual arousal (and hence create especially sexy photos, even of women who are not otherwise especially beautiful), by themselves stripping and making the camera part of mutual sexual buildup.

Another type of violation are orgies or group sex. We have not much data on classic orgies (mostly known in ancient Greece and the Roman Empire). The hypothesis of IR theory is that a successful orgy works through mutual buildup of excitement all around, leaving no participant out, no "wet blankets" on this party; and that the result will be not merely a two-person bond but a group identity, with distinctive group pride and status, perhaps in their eliteness as sexual sophisticates. There is some evidence in the literature on 1960s group sex in communes with a free-love ideology; even in these settings most sex occurred serially among couples, and in relative privacy. Comparative data on the number of love ties in such groups indicates that the organization of communes containing mainly exclusive couple-ties were much less likely to break up than communes with multiple love ties (Zablocki 1980). This suggests that keeping a completely balanced and integrated group solidarity among more than two persons is difficult using erotic IR. The fact that many breakups in the highly multiple love-tie communes (which Zablocki called "smoldering") occurred in angry blowups over jealousy supports this interpretation.

Confirming evidence comes from data on swingers' groups (colloquially, wife-swapping or mate-swapping) (Bartell 1971; Gilmartin 1978). Such groups surround their uninhibited sex with rigid rules prohibiting singles (persons without partners) from attending; that is, there is always an even exchange, with everyone taking part equally. Such groups also have taboos on members meeting each other for sex outside of the assembly of the entire group; in other words, the group develops a standard of jealousy, in this case prohibiting separate couple attachments (other than those among the preexisting couples who constituted the swinging arrangement) that would detract from the group solidarity. These comparisons show that a two-person group is not necessary, but that whatever the number of participants, they act to bond sharply among themselves sexually and exclude outsiders.

Copulation is a very strong example of the feedback processes that recycle back and forth between mutual focus and shared emotion. Such processes in IRs typically have a rhythmic pattern. In love-making we can clearly see three aspects: rhythmic intensification, rhythmic entrainment, and rhythmic synchronization. Here sexual ritual gives occasion for further refining the IR model.

Rhythmic intensification is the central physiological mechanism by which sexual excitement builds up. Copulation is a steady stroking of genital organs against each other; it is this rhythm which builds up excitement, with increasing speed and pressure, and leading to climax. The buildup of measurable bodily processes is strikingly similar in both males and females, including heartbeat, blood pressure, body temperature, and rapid breathing, reaching their maximum at the moment of orgasm or ejaculation. Both male and female genitals undergo vasocongestion or engorgement with venous blood; this produces a similar change in color both of the glans of the penis and labia minora to deep red or purple. In both sexes there is a two-to-four-second anticipation of the onset of orgasm (a long spasmic contraction in the female, a feeling of being unable to control the ejaculation in males), with both undergoing a series of three or four major contractions at 0.8 second interval (Masters and Johnson 1966).

Of course, rhythmic intensification might be merely individual; that is, it can occur in solitary masturbation; and in copulation, one person might experience much more rhythmic intensification than the other. IR theory, as well as empirical observation, suggests that sexual excitement and pleasure become more intense when there is rhythmic entrainment: one participant intensifies their bodily rhythm as they are caught up in the other person's rhythm. This is a very strong instance of feedback cycles reinforcing an IR process; recall the evidence in chapter 2 that this happens in social interactions that are pleasurable

but not erotic, such as animated conversation. Rhythmic synchronization occurs when the partner's bodily rhythms coincide. In sex with a
high degree of mutual arousal, rhythmic entrainment leads to rhythmic synchronization. Such synchronization is not necessarily perfect,
and may involve considerable variation (e.g., female orgasms may go
on longer or more repetitively and involve many more spasms than
male ejaculation, up to 12 or 15 contractions for a very intense female
orgasm as compared to 3 or 4 typically for the male; Masters and Johnson 1966, 135–36); the IR hypothesis is that the more synchronization,
the more the solidarity outcomes of IRs, and even moderate degrees
of synchronization may produce considerable pleasure and solidarity.

In the terminology of the sexologists, this is called the "pleasure
bond." But I would stress that this is not mere utilitarian exchange of
individuals' pleasures, but is experienced as a collective achievement.
The motive becomes pleasure in interaction, not pleasure in isolation.
On the utilitarian model there is no motivation to continue with the
same exchange partner if prospects for a better cost-benefit ratio
emerge elsewhere; this is just the opposite of the "pleasure bond" produced by high-intensity sexual rituals.

Sex as intimate interaction ritual needs to be considered against the
background of normal social interaction, in which persons rarely touch
each other. Sex is so far from normal bodily interaction that it is no
surprise that it can produce the strongest of all forms of solidarity. In
enormous contrast to ordinary bodily interaction, making love allows
a person to touch someone else's body; in high-intensity love-making,
this may involve exploring, manipulating, doing things to every part
of the other's body. And this bodily access tends to have reciprocal
effects, as each partner mirrors or extends the action by doing it back
to the other's body. Of course there are degrees of reciprocity: some
love-making is more one-sided, often with male active and female relatively passive. IR theory says that the degree of reciprocity is a principal determinant of the degree of excitement and pleasure.

The pleasure in touching and mutually coordinating with another's
body exemplifies the IR mechanism; it also operates in less intimate
forms than intercourse. It is this mechanism that makes lap dancing
and related commercial petting parlors a pleasurable commodity. In a
previous cultural era, social dancing (i.e., male-female couple dancing
in which partners held arms around each other's shoulders or waist, as
distinct from historically earlier group dancing, and from the independent, nontouching couples dancing that became popular in late-twentieth century) gave a restricted version of this same kind of pleasure.
Why was ballroom dancing pleasurable? We cannot take the answer for
granted. It was a restricted form of male / female IR conveying a highly

controlled degree of mutual sexual arousal.[8] A commercialized version was taxi-dancing, a kind of very mild prostitution found primarily in the 1920s through the 1950s, in which women sold a small amount of sexual solidarity (Cressey 1932; Meckel 1995).

All this casts light on the difference between sheer individual genital pleasure and the interaction-generated excitement and pleasures of sex. Even in intercourse, the man is not just getting pleasure in his penis from the woman's vagina; he is copulating with—making love to—her entire body. Conversely, the woman gets pleasure to the extent that she feels her partner's body copulating in rhythm with her. Through feedbacks in the IR process (depicted in figure 6.1), the genital excitement itself is affected by the success of the sexual IR. The hypothesis is that the intensity of the ejaculation (number of spasms, shortness of refractory period, amount of sperm released[9]) is determined by the intensity of the rhythmic buildup through entrainment and synchronization.

We have considered the ingredients and intensification process of sexual IRs; let us briefly review the outcome side:

1. Sex produces solidarity in the very small, two-person group. This special kind of intimate solidarity is called love. In recent centuries, people have come to distinguish conceptually between sex and love; nevertheless they are closely linked. Sexual intercourse does not always imply love, but in the ideal case it does. People understand that there are other kinds of love (altruistic love for strangers; family love; abstract religious love) but the primary referent of love is the sexual bond. The full force of Durkheimian solidarity is concentrated in this relationship. Ideally, the sexual lovers are fully identified with each other as a unit; they serve and protect the other. We can conceive of love without sex, but in the case of a contemporary pair-bonded couple, the love relationship without sex would seem incomplete in the most basic way. This is because sexual intercourse is the ritual of love; it both creates and recreates the social tie (since Durkheimian rituals need to be repeated periodically, as solidarity runs down in the interim), and symbolizes it. That is, it stands as a marker announcing both to participants, and to nonparticipant outsiders, that this is a very strong personal tie. Sexual access thus is the key boundary marker, and the primary test of loyalty.

2. Sexual IR, like other IR, produces emotional energy. In this respect, sexual IR is like other IR in transforming one emotion into another. In the general case, ritual transforms whatever initiating emotion the group shares and focuses upon, into an outcome emotion, the feeling of solidarity and individual strength as group member. In sexual ritual, the initiating emotion is typically sexual excitement, passion;

the outcome emotion is, collectively considered, love / dyadic membership solidarity; individually considered, it is long-term sexual drive. Since EE tends to be specifically directed toward particular kinds of previously successful IRs, sexually aroused EE makes the individual ready to be turned on to more of the same kind of sexual ritual.[10]

3. Sexual ritual generates symbols as memorials and tokens of the relationship. This is analogous to the way in which rings, gifts, and other memorials of a love relationship become its sacred objects, simultaneously signaling the tie and giving ancillary opportunities for showing respect for the relationship, or for breaking it. Here not merely objects but actions can serve as symbols of the relationship. In a conventional Durkheimian ritual, what the participants focus upon during the ritual becomes a symbol of the group. It is through this process that ancillary parts of sex take on significance as emblems of the entire sexual relationship. Breasts are not the primary sources of sexual pleasure, nor is the anus; but they can become symbols of the intimate interaction that goes on during love-making. For that reason, they are both taboo to outsiders, and a special emblem of being an insider, hence targets for sexual possession. A more obvious explanation might seem to be that breasts and anus, as well as lips and tongue, are sexual objects because they are naturally, physiologically programmed to be sensitive and arousable. But their sensitivity can also be just painful if contact does not occur in the process of rhythmic coordination among partners, such as if it occurs in rough, coercive, or unexpected sexual contact (or indeed in brusque nonsexual contact). For that matter, the genitals themselves are not pleasurable but are irritated or even quite painful if they are stimulated in the latter ways. It is the social context of micro-interaction that makes any of these bodily zones pleasurable; whatever biological programming there may be has to flow through rituals of social solidarity, which in turn gives them symbolic status (see note 5 in chapter 4).

4. The morality of sex is the feeling of rightness of sexual possession, of access to the other's body and the exclusion of all other persons. Since ritual creates moral standards, the primary violation is sex with an outsider, and its response is moralistic, righteous anger. This is a very localistic morality, enacted in righteous anger toward those who violate it, and generally overriding the moral standards of the wider social group, which condemns violence.

The Durkheimian model holds that solidarity and the other outcomes of rituals are time-bound, fading away with the passage of time if they are not repeated. Sexual IRs too must be repeated regularly to keep up the sexual bond. Persons in stable couple relationships typically have sex about once a week (Laumann et al. 1994, 88), even at relatively advanced ages. This is the same order of time as the weekly scheduling of religious rituals, suggesting that both kinds of solidarity rituals operate in the same way. Both imply that strong rituals keep up strong group relationships only for about a week.[11] Very strong religious believers or cultists have even more frequent ritual assemblies, and the same is true for lovers in very intense relationships. Kinsey (1953, 395) showed that most couples had a period in their lives when they were having sex once a day or more (about 10 percent having sex three or four times a day); this was probably the period of establishing the relationship, the climax of courtship. The temporal pattern apparently exists in all ritually mediated intense relationships; mutual participation in the ritual is most frequent when establishing the relationship, then falls off to a routine level.[12] This occurs in the intensity of conversations in friendship ties, as well as in the initial frequency of ritual attendance for religious converts.

I have depicted sexual IR and its outcomes in terms of the ideal type. These are the primary effects of high-intensity sexual IR, and these dynamics are the basis upon which more complicated cases can be analyzed. If sex produces solidarity, how to account for prostitution or casual sex, where there is no solidarity tie? How do we account for seeking sex without seeking love? These can be handled as variants on the model. Since the IR model is a matter of variables, sex that involves relatively little mutual focus and shared emotion will be less satisfying. Sex with a prostitute is often low-intensity IR; as it approaches higher intensity, it takes on overtones more like love (even though it may not be possible to follow it up into a longer relationship). Similarly, casual sexual relations can go either way. I suggest as a hypothesis that high-intensity sexual relations, even if begun only with personal pleasure in view, tend to produce attachment, which eventually is socially indistinguishable from love. This is the theme (sometimes exploited in literature, also in life) of the hard-bitten, cynical individual who nevertheless becomes ensnared in a sexual relationship, thence into marriage and conventional symbols and feelings of solidarity. This may be a major way in which modern males, with their overtly individual-pleasure orientation, become seduced by their own seductions.

Obviously there exists casual, pleasure-seeking sex, without love ties. But sexual behavior cannot be explained merely by a fixed motive for genital pleasure. If there is such a drive, it can be greatly intensified, teased out, led up to, and dramatized by social interaction. Turn-ons are created by staged presentation of erotic special effects and by fantasies based on them; and these affect even how much sperm a male ejaculates and how often and how intensely both males and females climax. The mechanism by which this occurs is sexual IR. If there is pure selfish pleasure-seeking, the route that must be pursued to get a great deal of it is to engage in mutually interpenetrating interaction, in which the individual gets caught up in a multiply interlooping two-person skein of bodily and emotional feedbacks.

This turns the sociological question around: how can we explain when individuals seek low-solidarity sex? I suggest that the motive for seeking a great deal of selfish genital pleasure is built up by ritualized social interactions that give high social prestige to having a lot of this kind of sex. The key IR focused on sex, in this case, is not the copulation of the male / female couple, but the talking, posing, and jeering about sex that takes place in the all-male group, or sometimes in a larger community of social reputation that I will call a sexual scene. Thus the performance of any particular act of sex is affirming solidarity with that group membership rather than producing solidarity within the couple. Selfish sex remains a social symbol, but in this case representing prestige in the eyes of the larger group.[13]

The general line of explanation will be that the mechanism of sexual IR generates symbols and motivations that become free-floating, beyond any particular relationship; individuals can thus attempt to strive for sexual pleasure, which is deeply mingled with social status, even if it is done in a nonreciprocal way. The complication is a familiar one in other contexts. Children get love from their mother, both emotionally and in the physical experience of bodily contact; they can also be quite selfish in demanding her love, contact, and attention. Sexual solidarity is a good; it is indeed an archetype of intense IR-produced solidarity and EE. It can be created by fully reciprocal participation in sexual IRs, but also in various degrees by one-sided and partial participation. It can further be manipulated, strategized as a topic of higher-order reflections and plots (e.g., seduction schemes), exchanged and coerced. There can be such a thing as manipulated solidarity and coerced solidarity. It is not surprising that there are love / hate relations, and that love is a favorite topic for twists of literary plots. Sexual love is a powerful, intimate dynamic, operating most powerfully in the micro-situation; it can become overlaid by complicated IR chains, full of the troubles of nonintimacy.

Nongenital Sexual Pleasures as Symbolic Targets

We turn now to explaining some ancillary sexual rituals: first more public and respectable ones, then intimate displacements from the genitals. The issue is why is there sexual pleasure in activities that involve neither genital pleasure nor contribution to reproduction?

Begin with holding hands. Why is this sexually significant, since there is very little tactile pleasure in it? The answer emerges from comparison. In everyday life, persons touch each other only in very limited and specific ways; each type of touch corresponds to a specific kind of social relationship. Most of the time, persons do not touch each other; when they do so accidentally, this usually calls for an apology, indicating that touching is considered a violation. A highly ritualized (formally stereotyped and conventionalized) form of touching, shaking hands, is used to mark occasions when persons enter into a social relationship; this could be meeting a person for a first time, or renewing acquaintance with persons who are highly respected or otherwise significant. Handshakes are also used to signal the beginning and ending of a specific encounter that is marked by paying special attention to the immediate social relationship with the other. Goffman (1967) used handshakes, along with other greeting and departure rituals, as key examples for introducing the concept of interaction rituals in everyday life. There are many nuances here, since handshakes may be felt to be too formal for certain intimate relations, and not formal enough for relations of differential rank. The significant point for our purposes is that the type of physical touch correlates with the closeness of the social relationship.

Hand-holding differs from a handshake precisely in that it is held for a long time; a long handshake would be regarded as especially enthusiastic, and hand-holding suggests a permanent tie. Thus handholding is a typical mark of a love affair; it is used by those who are already sexually intimate as a kind of prolongation of contact, and also as an early, initiating step toward more intimate touching. Holding hands can serve as a signal to others that a relationship exists, operating as what Goffman (1971) calls a "tie-sign" in public. Even more importantly, holding hands is a signal sent by the participants to each other; here again there are subtleties, involving the amount of reciprocity in actively holding and the amount and time-pattern of pressure applied. Thus hand-holding is erotic in the context of a set of signals differentiating degrees of social distance and closeness; its pleasure is more emotional than a tactile sensation, although it is precisely through the feeling of the warmth and pressure of the partner's skin that the interactional significance is conveyed and hence the emotion aroused and shared.

This description is drawn from Anglo-American culture of the twentieth century; but there are other cultural patterns, in which hand-holding does not have erotic significance. In traditional Arab culture, male friends hold hands in public; and in many cultures, women are especially likely to hold hands or link arms when they are in public places.

The comparisons help confirm the model, for they are drawn from societies in which one of two situations exist: (1) Women are strictly segregated from men, and not allowed in public at all, or if so, under robes
and veils that prohibit any contact; in this case there is a greater differentiation of types of friendships among males. Or (2) women do venture in public and are open to male gaze and potential touching, that
is, the public is a male sexist erotic sphere, and thus women cling to
each other both for support and to display tie-signs that they are already connected and not to be touched by anyone else. On a very detailed, micro-level of analysis, we would expect that these kinds of
male-male and female-female hand-holding do not have the kinds of
pressures and patterns of rhythmic reciprocities that characterize erotic
ties, and that make hand-holding into a miniature of the IR pattern of
sexual intercourse itself.

What is said here about hand-holding applies also to hugging, stroking, and other forms of body contact. The willingness to begin an erotic
relationship may begin by touching feet under the table (an important
subrosa tactic in nineteenth-century Europe with its custom of large
formal dinners), all the more readily since the contact could also be
construed as accidental and thus, if necessary, deniable as a signal. All
these contacts are experienced as pleasurable largely to the degree that
they invoke emotions, both in anticipation, and in the buildup of reciprocity that is the key to IR attunement. Erotic IRs, in all their variants,
show the IR model in an extreme form in which coordinating bodies
with each other is the central mechanism as well as focus of attention.
Nonerotic IRs also involve some degree of bodily coordination (e.g.,
common postures of respect at the religious service, or of enthuasism
in group cheering; see evidence in Hatfield et al. 1994), but these also
focus attention on some third object of perception, which, in Durkheim's analysis, becomes identified with the feeling of participation in
the group. In erotic IRs, the focus of attention is not just tacitly upon
the bodily coordination but takes it as its explicit object. The other's
body becomes the sacred object of the ritual; it is invested with high
value, becoming something to be admired, caressed, protected, as well
as exclusively possessed. The so-called tactile pleasures of sexual contact (at least nongenital sexual contact) are misconstrued as tactile because it is through focus upon the bodily sensations of contacting the
other's body that the IR dynamics of rhythmically intensifying mutual
focus are carried out.

Once again we must deal with apparent exceptions, instances in
which hugging, stroking, prolonged touching are done without erotic
interpretation. In contemporary Western societies, there are two main
exceptions. One is touching between parents and children (or in other

pseudo-parental relationships). These are relationships that are subject to incest taboos (and their analogies), where erotic relations are considered especially shocking; here I would suggest the touching is precisely graded, so that it indicates an intimate relation, but not an erotic one. The length of the touch is proportional to the permanence of the tie; a pseudo-parent may pat a child for encouragement, but prolonged holding on one's lap or in one's arms is reserved for socially committed parenting. Such parenting body contacts are limited not only in that they are not allowed to move onward to erotic zones (including the displaced ones that we will discuss later), but also in micro-detail. A parent-child hug that took on the rhythms of reciprocal caressing and mutual buildup in intensity would be viewed with suspicion.

The second exception is enthusiastic hugging or other touching used as ritual celebration, commonly seen in sports victories and other kinds of group congratulations. This celebratory bodily touching is distinguished from the erotic by specific patterns: it is typically much more agitated, often rough (slapping hands, slapping on the buttocks, even bashing forearms), pounding bodies rather than rhythmically caressing them. The element of violence makes the contacts brief yet sharply noticeable, and marks them off from erotic touching. A related form of body contact is hugging. This was adopted in U.S. culture in about the same historical period as was the celebratory bodily touching (1970s), as an emphatic form of greeting, designed to pass beyond the perceived stiffness of distant forms of greeting such as hand-shaking. Again we can correlate the uses of hugging with kinds of social relationships. It seems much in vogue among politicians and gushy socializers, and on highly ceremonial occasions of solidarity such as weddings and celebratory feasts and oratory. Hugging involves more of the body, expressing alleged intensity and permanence of social ties. Whether this is sincerely felt or merely a conventional performance, it remains strongly segregated from erotic body contact by micro-details: hugging is typically done around the shoulders, avoiding pressing of stomachs and thighs, and above all avoiding contact with the genital areas. It also has a different micro-rhythm. Celebratory hugging does not involve stroking of face, hair, neck, legs, etc. A hug is held, perhaps squeezed, to indicate social closeness; it does not focus on the other's body, singling out body parts one by one for attention; and it has a distinct time-limitation, without the reciprocal buildup that makes erotic touching into a ritual with a direction.

Kissing is similar to other bodily contacts in that its variety of forms can both signal different social relationships and operate as a form of sexual buildup and pleasure. The social relationships come out especially strongly when we consider what kinds of kisses are considered inappropriate. Kissing on the cheek (or even more distantly, a pretend-kiss in which cheeks barely brush each other) marks a relationship that is supposed to be more friendly than a handshake, but would be considered something of a slight in an erotic relationship. In the other direction, a kiss on the lips may be too much intimacy for family relationships; and a tongue kiss would be considered virtually incestuous if carried out between parents and children.

Kissing and other tie-signs can also be used to mark where a relationship is strictly erotic but not a personal tie. Customers do not shake hands with prostitutes; and generally there is an explicit taboo against kissing a prostitute on the cheeks or lips, even though the couple may engage in genital kissing. This is a way in which participants in commercial sex distinguish their relationships from romantic ones; these are explicitly one-shot sexual ties, without personal involvement; face and lip kisses signal long-term ties. It is likely that intermediate relationships between these extremes use more tie-signs; for example, we would expect mistresses (relatively permanent and exclusive yet commercial sexual arrangements) to do more kissing than prostitutes.

Why are some kinds of kissing erotic? The general pattern of sexual IRs holds: erotic kisses are those in which there is more rhythmic intensity, more reciprocal interaction in which each participant builds up the excitement of the other. Erotic kissing is prolonged; mere relationship kisses are brief, cutting off elaboration and sense of rhythm. Tongue kissing is especially erotic because it involves penetration into the other's body, and thus represents itself as especially close and unusual; because it especially forcefully intrudes itself upon the other's attention; because it can lead to reciprocal interaction, calling forth the response of the other, which is a key to erotic intensity. When one tongue stimulates the other tongue into action, there is the reciprocal effect that leads to buildup of excitement. Here again the interaction component is more important than tactile pleasure per se, although it may be hard to separate and hence the latter may be taken for the former. Lips may be soft and thereby pleasurable in some degree to touch, and sensory pleasure may be enhanced by perfumes (but also reduced by bad tastes and smells); but tongues per se are probably not especially sensually pleasurable apart from their motion in response to each other.

The IR mechanism at work in these instances operates through building up excitement; this is triggered by the passing of a social barrier into a realm of action that is generally not allowed, and which is symbolically connected with signaling erotic intimacy. In other words, when lip-on-lip or tongue kissing is conventionally taken as part of an erotic sequence, it is especially exciting to initiate. (Shortly, we will confirm this by comparing societies in which not kissing but other methods of excitement are used.) But mere cultural convention cannot be all the explanation. There must be some quality to this kind of kissing that contributes to the buildup of erotic excitement. It does not seem possible that merely any kind of kissing could be arbitrarily used to designate erotics: for example, deep tongue kissing could not be used for greeting in-laws while cheek touching would be reserved for a sign of erotics. A likely mechanism is that tongue kissing (and other kinds of prolonged mouth-on-mouth sucking) interferes with breathing; and since breathing is the single most apparent rhythmic activity of the body, these kinds of kissing both increase the intensity of one's own breathing, and that of one's kissing partner. Again the key dynamic appears: getting close to, or even into, another person's body so as to provoke their bodily action in response to one's own, setting up a cycle of mutual arousal. Thus there are two components of sexual excitement: first the excitement of passing normal social barriers on closeness; then the self-reinforcing cycle of excitement as mutual rhythmic intensification occurs.

It is instructive to compare cultures in which kissing is not used or is not erotically central. In the Trobriand Island society described by Malinowski (1929/1987), the mark of erotic intimacy, which served simultaneously as technique for building erotic excitement, consisted of biting and scratching the other. Especially at the peak of excitement, lovers would bite each other's eye-lashes (280–81). Here the sensory pleasure component seems absent; instead there is a very high degree of intimate contact, interfering with and controlling a part of the body that is otherwise out of the reach of other people. As Malinowski notes, bitten-off eyelashes also serve as public reminders and markers of one's erotic activities. Thus some of the excitement may come from an additional source, the anticipation of public reaction to one's erotic status.

Other highly developed erotic cultures, such as those depicted in sexual handbooks from medieval India, prescribe both kissing as well as scratching and biting techniques. The *Kama Sutra*, a handbook for courtesans and their patrons, describes an elaborate variety of love-bites and scratches. These are made with teeth or fingernails on various parts of the lover's body, ranging from innocuous and publicly visible marks on arms and shoulders, to more intimate marks on breasts, inner thighs, and genitals. These operate socially in two respects. They are possession marks, indicating the personal tie between the lovers, and serving to remind them of their past love-making and thus to rekindle passion.[14] In this respect they operate just like Durkheimian symbols, emblems of the social tie. These can be displayed to outsiders and thus mark boundaries, but also be displayed to each other, and even to oneself, to keep the emotions of the relationship alive.

The activity of biting and scratching also operates directly to build up excitement. In the IR model (figure 6.1), they feed into the part of the cycle where a common emotion intensifies the focus of attention and feeds back into more strongly shared emotion. IRs are emotion-transformers, turning virtually any emotional ingredients into shared rhythmic intensities and thence into collective emotional energy. Here the emotions derive from pain; the key is that the pain is turned into reciprocally intensifying interaction, and thus into a different bodily and emotional pattern. By the same logic, the *Kama Sutra* recommends love-teasing, as well as scripted lovers' quarrels, including anger and beating, as techniques for building up erotic passion. Sado-masochistic eroticism and its variants (including bondage and domination, sexual humiliation, etc.) can be explained in this fashion; that is, they are all techniques by which intense emotions are created that feed into erotic excitement, and thus into a successful erotic IR. This is an alternative explanation to Freudian ones, which seek an etiology in traumatic childhood experiences. IR theory holds that whatever they may have experienced, or not experienced, in childhood, individuals can learn to build up these sorts of erotic ritual intensities. IR is also an alternative explanation to male dominance, although it could coincide with this in some cases. B&D, however, is mainly a male fetish to be dominated by females; males probably take the initative in this because they are sexually more active, hence seek out variants that enhance the excitement ingredients.

We come now to forms of erotics that are closer to the genital organs but that do not directly produce genital pleasure: touching breasts, performing oral sex, and receiving anal sex. Breasts are ambigiously erotic: in modern (and especially Western) cultures they are a key visual representation of sex, but elsewhere they have often been unimportant, neither being prominently represented in erotics nor the focus of sexual activity. The modern West is perhaps most extreme among the societies in world history that have a culture of sexual practices oriented to the breasts, including touching, squeezing, kissing, and sucking them; modern pornography has a variant found nowhere else, called "tit-fucking," with the man's penis between the woman's breasts, virtually a totemic conjunction. It is little use as an explanation to note the arbitrariness of cultural variation. Nor do theories that explain all forms of eroticism as male dominance provide an explanation of the historical change: medieval societies were even more male-dominated than modern ones, whereas the modern erotic emphasis on breasts developed in social epochs where women had a comparatively high degree of freedom to manage their own sex lives. To bring out the macro-histori-cal conditions, we will need full-scale historical comparisons, which are reserved for another publication. A key part of the explanation is that modern societies are ones in which women have been allowed out in public, and have been motivated to display their sexual attrac-tiveness at a distance. In the West, this evolved through a series of clothing styles that bared women's arms and shoulders, décolletage and display of cleavage, as well as corsets and brassieres that pushed the breasts up into prominent visibility. Such breast-display or breast-teasing typically occured in periods when women's legs were hidden, so that sexual enticement was concentrated on the breast.[15]

Breasts, of course, could be taken as emblems for female sexuality because they are markers of the sex; but this would not make them sexual objects per se, any more than male beards, which pretty reliably indicate adult masculinity, automatically become erotic symbols. So far the line of argument suggests that breasts are erotic where they are the best available, publicly visible representation of femaleness. But the same would apply to other culturally arbitrary signs, such as long hair. Although it is true that some sexual activity centers on stroking a woman's hair, breasts receive more attention in pornography and in love-making. Following our previous line of micro-analysis, I would argue that the various forms of erotic breast-contact—squeezing, strok-ing, sucking—create two forms of excitement.

First is the excitement of crossing a culturally marked intimacy step, baring and touching that which has been prohibited and studiously avoided in other socially acceptable touching rituals such as hugging and patting; this is enhanced by the anticipation elicited by clothing styles that focus attention on partial breast-display as a show of femi-nine beauty. This is the psychological excitement of getting hold of something that is an emblem of sexual desirability and social prestige. In fact, touching breasts per se may give little tactile pleasure, but the IR mechanism operates so that the excitement is interpreted as a plea-sure that is felt to reside in the physical object, the flesh of the breasts, in the same way that the psychological pleasures of kissing are felt to be in the physical sensation of the lips.

A second possibility is interactive; that is, breasts are sensitive and hence a lover manipulating a woman's breasts gets her aroused in some way. That arousal might not be sexual turn-on, but if a key part of the erotic IR is to start off a train of mutual excitement, even a non-erotic (and nonsensory) excitement can play into the chain of feedbacks that leads to high sexual arousal. The male lover plays with the wom-an's breasts in part to invade what was sexually private, in part to get a response from her, which in turn builds up his own response. In many interactions, of course, the intrusion may be coercive and unsuccessful in building up mutual excitement; in a successful erotic IR, on the contrary, there is mutual entrainment of emotions and bodily sensitivities.

The problem of oral sex, as noted, is not with the pleasure of the recipient but of explaining why a person finds it sexually exciting to lick, suck, and kiss another's genitals. Once again there are two components. The first is the familiar antinomian dynamic; there is excitement just because it has been forbidden or unavailable. Clothing display and practices of modesty keep the genitals hidden above all else, sometimes confining copulation to the dark. The very hiddenness of genitals, as the ultimately nonvisible zone, can call forth excitement at finally viewing them close-up. The very shape of clothing that reveals some parts of the body while hiding others (such as brassieres, underpants, bikinis) calls attention to the shape and location of what is hidden. Display practices that gradually reveal some of the female body are especially likely to evoke erotic excitement through a train of actions oriented toward stripping bare and contacting the clearly marked forbidden. In Goffman's (1969) terms, this may be called an open secret, as contrasted with a closed secret; in the former, the existence of a secret is well known, in the latter the very fact that something is hidden is itself hidden.

Kissing the genitals, or licking and sucking with lips and tongue, combines this penetration into the ultimate backstage, with a ritual we have already discussed. Oral sex is also a form of kissing, the most intimate on that progression. Thus another motivation for oral sex is symbolic, representing the ultimate form of intimate possession. A male lover may feel that to totally possess the other is to possess her (or sometimes his) genitals, not merely in the most common fashion of genital intercourse, but in the extension of ritual contact to this most intimate zone. The same motivation may explain why an individual may want to receive oral sex. In the case of male-passive oral sex, the sensory pleasure of being sucked is probably less than vaginal (or anal) intercourse; teeth and palate are not naturally soft and pleasure-giving. But even if the sensory pleasure of having one's penis sucked is less than that of bodily penetration, it may be both more exciting because more antinomian and more unusual, and symbolically satisfying as an emblem of the ultimate intimacy. The same logic can extend to anal licking (both active and passive), as well as various forms of urine-and-feces-oriented sex; here the pleasure is totally psychological and symbolic, shaped by antinomian excitement of transgressing very strong taboos, the extreme mark of intimate participation, and by feedback excitement from arousing the other. This is presumably true a fortiori of "fist-fucking"; there can be no tactile pleasure in the fucker's fist, whatever pleasure there may be in the fuckee's anus.

Oral-genital sex also illustrates the mechanism of mutual intensification, almost in an experimental fashion since (unlike kissing or intercourse) there is genital stimulation only on one side, with psychological stimulation on the other. Sucking another's genitals is a way of bringing the other person to a sexual climax; it is an extreme form of palpably and visibly having the other's sexual response under one's control. Although there are cases in which this is not exciting for the fellator (prostitutes who routinely perform blow-jobs as part of their repertoire; wives, girl-friends, and rape victims who are cajoled or coerced), it appears that the active performer of oral sex often finds this exciting. This seems to be especially the case when males lick females' genitals.[16] It is also the main form of contemporary lesbian sex (Laumann et al. 1994, 318).

Homosexual fellation raises similar questions. To what extent is there pleasure on the side of the fellator, as compared to merely engaging in sucking the other's penis in order to receive reciprocity? A hypothesis: simultaneous mutual fellation (the "sixty-nine" position) occurs in more intensely bonded homosexual relations. There may also be another interactional process whereby giving and receiving fellatio become emotionally and symbolically mixed. Gay pornography indicates a very strong focus on the object male's penis, and performing fellatio may be regarded as a form of interactive masturbation, interchanging the other's penis for one's own. Thus homosexual fellatio may be part of the progression of an erotic career that starts with solitary masturbation, moves to joint masturbation with another male, thence to mutual masturbation in which tongues supplement hands, and then to penetration of the mouth as the greatest intimacy. This progression is suggested by stories in homosexual pornography. This is consistent with evidence that high levels of masturbation are found, in increasing order, among males with casual homosexual desire or experience (49.6 percent), rising to 74.4 percent among those with a homosexual identity, compared to the ordinary male population baseline of 26.7 percent who masturbate once per week or more (Laumann et al. 1994, 318).

The general mechanism of IR intensity applies: getting the other person sexually excited, and above all bringing them to a sexual climax, is a way of making oneself excited. This implies that the climax of one fellation or cunnilingus is followed by further sexual acts that bring the oral performer to climax. (Again, empirically testable.)

In general, this line of explanation via the features that enhance the excitement and symbolic significance of IRs is an alternative to Freud-ian-style explanations. There is no necessary throwback to childhood traumas or repressed infantile wishes. Instead these are mechanisms that come into play when individuals become motivated to achieve very high levels of sexual excitement, and to surpass more conven-tional levels of excitement and intimacy.

To bring this analysis to an end, consider anal intercourse. On the side of the male penetrator, this is not hard to explain: it could be sim-ply a method of penis-pleasure. In homosexual relations, anal inter-course is the closest approximation to vaginal sex. Comparisons shed some light on the social process. Reciprocal anal intercourse is most common among men with a strong gay identity, and least common among persons who have casual homosexual episodes (calculated from Laumann et al. 1994, 318). That is, men who consider themselves overtly gay typically trade off penetrating each other anally. If we infer that these men are most likely to have a high degree of erotic love-bonding, we can say that they prefer to practice a form of sex in which there is the fullest degree of full-body contact, surrounding, holding, and penetrating the other's body as well as reciprocally receiving all these from the passive side. This pattern of anal sex is a form of full-scale love-making, and thus correlates with the tightest social bonds.

The homosexual case suggests that anal intercourse operates as a high degree of bodily intimacy; that is, relatively less exclusively fo-cused on the genital component (as in oral sex), more closely related to hugging (and thus overlapping with nonsexual love / solidarity). Heterosexual anal intercourse presents another analytical problem, but also a quasi-experimental comparison: here there is full-body contact (the generalized love component, as well as full-scale bodily posses-sion), but genital pleasure is confined to one side. The attraction of anal intercourse for heterosexuals may be largely in the antinomian excite-ment, that is, its status as "kinky" variation, but it may involve enough shared excitement to make the IR solidarity mechanism work (see inci-dence data in Laumann et al. 1994, 99, 107–9a, 152–54).

The remaining major form of sex to discuss is masturbation. On the face of it, this seems to violate the IR mechanism at the outset: there is no group assembly, hence no mutual focus nor mutual feedback build-ing up excitement. At the same time, masturbation is highly oriented toward objects, either fantasy or pornographic representations. In the terminology of chapter 2, masturbation is an instance of a third-order, solitary use of symbols that were charged up with significance in first-order erotic IRs and in second-order social circulation of symbols.[17] The topic is best pursued in conjunction with the question of how sex is staged and presented in imagery. This is an appropriately Goffmanian task but too large to be attempted here, and will be reserved for a separate publication.

In summary, there are three main ways we can theoretically explain the mechanisms that bring sexual pleasure from nongenital and nonreproductive variants or forms of sex.

1. *Intimacy ritual.* The degree of body contact operates as a graduated series, a ladder of symbols that correspond to the degrees of social intimacy between the persons who touch each other in these ways. Relatedly, parts of the body tantalizingly displayed in clothing styles as a public display of social status (e.g., breasts) can become symbolic targets for rituals of possession.

2. *Intense mutual feedback amplification.* Bodily techniques for arousing the other person feed back into raising one's own arousal, and building up the spiral of mutual arousal. The higher degrees of erotic interaction are produced by getting into the center of the other's attention, turning on their body to involuntary rhythmic intensification, and riding physiologically on their arousal. This works best by playing on physiologically sensitive areas, but can operate through almost any part of the body. The erotic is interference with each other's body by mutual intrusion on one another's subjective attention via stimulating excitement and pleasure, sometimes via the medium of other emotions.

3. *Enhanced emotional ingredients to initiate buildup of sexual excitement.* Exciting or dramatic activities start off the individuals (separately, not yet in shared buildup) to bring the initiating emotional ingredient to a sexual IR. These can include the drama of sexual negotiation, chase, and play; conflict and pain; and the antinomian excitement of breaking taboos. As applied to figure 6.1, this factor occurs earlier in the causal chains, whereas the second mechanism is the central process of feedback intensification and rhythmic coordination. In all successful IRs, initiating emotions are transformed into the outcome emotions of solidarity and EE; in successful sexual IRs, these happen primarily in the course of the rhythmic buildup itself, less in the aftermath (i.e., in sexual IRs, the right side of figure 2.1 is pushed closer to the left side). As in all IRs, the initiating emotional ingredient may not be sufficient to set off the shared IR; it is not unusual for one person (especially the male) to be turned on by an emotion that spills over into sexual arousal, while the other person lacks both that specific emotion and the mutual turn-on. This is the scenario both for frustration and for sexual coercion.

Sexual Negotiation Scenes rather than Constant Sexual Essences

I have argued that sexual drive and sexual objects are constructed situationally: in the micro-interactional rituals that generate sexual emotional energy and symbolism, and in meso- and macro-structures that channel attention through social ranking and through opportunities for interaction, closing off some paths and opening up others. Let us conclude with a theoretical concept that comes into view in considering the construction of modern gay culture, but has a wider significance for understanding all kinds of sexuality. This is the concept of "sexual scene."

The "gay" scene is well named: it is an arena of excitement because of its intense focus of sexual energy.[18] The gay scene separates out pure sexual negotiation excitement from the family-making negotiations that are combined in the heterosexual "dating" scene and its equivalents. It is this structure which became an attractor of attention, and a recruiter of new individuals to a gay identity. To be "gay" should be analyzed not so much as a personality but as a "scene" one participates in. It is a situational identity.

A "scene" is a Goffman-like concept, a "situation" of self-presentation elaborated into a series of repeated and overlapping gatherings. It has typical gathering places, public arenas for this "crowd" (which may be unknown or private as far as nonmembers are concerned), around which may be connected various private residential venues (e.g., in the case of the gay scene, bars and resorts on one hand, and party places and love nests on the other). A scene is like an IR chain, except that up to now I have treated the IR chain as an individual life course; a scene is a mesh of IR chains, connected both laterally and in the flow of time. One could describe a "scene" as a network with a high density of interaction and interconnection, but widely participatory insofar as it does not depend upon a constant center, and containing a great deal of indirect ties that make it easy to meet new partners. This is the structural formula for a community with a high degree of effervescence, continued over long periods of time.

Historically there have been a variety of sexual scenes, these arenas of overlapping encounters circulating a generalized emotional intensity and a shifting focus on the prestige center of sexual interaction. The prominence of sexual display and prestige have varied historically, and therefore, so have the sheer amount of sexual motivation generated. Schematically, we may distinguish three main types of societies:[19]

1. Tribal societies in which sexual relations were generally regulated by corporate groups as moves in marriage alliance politics.

2. Patrimonial households of dominant aristocrats and their servants and retainers. These arrangements concentrated control of sexuality in heads of households, who sometimes used it for marriage alliances (more flexibly than in the rule-bound structures of tribal kinship structures), sometimes to collect sex-workers for their pleasure and prestige.

3. Modern societies in which individuals negotiate their own marriages as well as their sex lives upon a largely unregulated market of personal encounters.

In general, the first two types (1 and 2) did not have much in the way of sexual scenes that broadcast the excitement and prestige of sexual action (although particular historical instances could be singled out).

Sexual scenes that enhanced sexual motivation have existed both within these historical types and in periods of transition, and have moved increasingly into the center of public attention in recent centuries. Within (2) aristocratic societies, we could distinguish (2.1) places where courtly politics prevailed, usually at the residence of a reigning monarch, where some men and women negotiated their own sexual affairs in a hot-bed of intrigue over court influence. Within (3) individual marriage markets, we could distinguish three phases: (3.1) The early transitional phase when young people sought out romantic attachments in settings (like the London season or the Bath resort) under the influence of their parents concerned with family prestige and inheritance (this might be called the Jane Austen phase, since it makes up the topics of her novels). (3.2) A "Victorian" phase (which in fact began already in the eighteenth century) in which, since men still controlled most of the wealth, women restricted their own sexuality as an attraction to marriage. This is the period of sharply dual sexual standards and sexual undergrounds, a world of sexual backstages providing the materials on which Freud made his reputation. (3.3) An egalitarian phase (developing in the twentieth century but not yet fully realized) in which men and women have independent career resources; hence comes a tendency for sexual negotiations to be much less restricted to negotiating marriage, and for the dual sexual cultures to break down, as eroticism comes more directly into public view. This egalitarian or "sexually liberated" phase has also been characterized by lengthening periods of formal education for both sexes, thus creating places where young people could engage in intensive rating and negotiating of their attractiveness on a sexual marketplace.

The culture of sexual display is most intense in those situations where individuals of both sexes are concentrated in a repeated and overlapping web of interactions. Earlier, in discussing gay culture, I appropriated the term "scene" for the structural pattern underlying its peculiar effervescence and high level of sexual arousal. We may speak of sexual "scenes" generally, wherever there are conditions for gathering a collection of people in this way: these are found in situations of courtly sexual politics, Jane Austen's marriage market at Bath, twentieth-century American high schools, and in the sociability surrounding certain occupations concentrated in particular places such as the theater world or the movie world. A scene is a floating, meso-level interaction ritual (or concatenated webs of IR chains) that keeps up a high level of emotional energy and mutual focus of attention. Here sexual display is broadcast, seen, commented upon, and reverberated. Individuals have known reputations based on how their display is taken by others. The structure of sexual scenes enhances sexual motivation within them.

Prestige-Seeking and Public Eroticization

Sexual scenes focus attention upon a hierarchy of erotic status. It is here that arises the ideal of the great lover, the belle of the ball (late-nineteenth century), the popular girl, the "big ass-man" (college slang from the 1950s), the "party animal" (late twentieth century). The source of their motivation is in the social structure. In modern times, the focus of attention has been placed on erotic ideals through scenes of sexual negotiation and the socializing that went along with it; that is to say, through the concentration of collective effervescence and stratification of participation in it. Since virtually everyone now goes through a life period when they are in the goldfish bowl of the sexual scene (in school, and sometimes elsewhere) as well as being surrounded by its images in the mass media, everyone is exposed to the motivating effect of this erotic ranking.

That does not mean, however, that most persons have extremely active sex lives.[20] Why should the highly active erotic elite be so few? In part, for mundane practical reasons: it takes time and energy to have a lot of sexual affairs; since that is time out from work, such erotic elites must have considerable leisure or financial resources. In addition to time spent in negotiating, there must be considerable accumulated investment in erotic skills and techniques, and in erotic self-presentation. Having multiple sexual partners is correlated with relatively low frequency of intercourse; that is because there are relatively long periods in which they have little sex while establishing a new relationship. In contrast, persons with steady sexual partners tend to have higher frequency of sex, since they spend less time in search and negotiation (Laumann et al. 1994, 88–89, 177, 179).

In practical reality, an individual who wants to be part of the erotic elite has to make a choice between number of partners and frequency of sex. Highest frequency occurs in monogamous relationships, but these are rather common and not erotically prestigeful; so the highly visible forms of erotic prestige come from pursuing multiple partners, even at the cost of lower frequency. There may be even further compromises to be made: high prestige comes from visibly beautiful partners, but to acquire multiple partners is easiest by exploiting the non-elite of the opposite sex, in the relatively less beautiful range. The idealized image of the person who has a steady diet of sex with a variety of beautiful partners is difficult indeed to realize.

Although the higher reaches of erotic stratification are remote and in a sense rather artificial, embodied images so to speak, and although the proportion of the population whose sex lives are highly active is small, this prestige hierarchy nevertheless has an effect on persons ranked throughout. Particularly among young persons living in public sexual negotiation scenes, there is a high level of attention paid to erotic stratification criteria, and acute awareness of who occupies what rank in the community's ratings. Erotic ranking moreover tends to spill over into all social relationships. Males and females tend to pair off at similar levels of erotic attractiveness, or to confine their round of affairs within the same rank level (Hatfield and Sprecher 1986). I suggest that same-sex friendships also tend to occur within similar erotic attractiveness rankings (I know of no formal study of this, but it fits personal observation). This attractiveness-level-segregation tends to occur because the social activities are organized by flirtation and sexual carousing. The erotic rank hierarchy is not merely a ranking of attractiveness but of sociable activity; those highly ranked attend more parties, and are at the center of the gatherings with the most prestige, the liveliest sexual effervescence.

The popular crowd is the sexual elite. Being in the center of attention gives greater solidarity, closer identification with the symbols of the group, and greater self-confidence. Conversely, those on the outskirts of the group, or who are excluded from it, manifest just the opposite qualities. Being part of the sociable / erotic elite produces an attitude of arrogance;[21] the elite know who they are, and the enclosed, high-information structure of the scene makes visible the ranking of those lower down as well. The elite, at its most benevolent, is oblivious to those lower ranking; they may also engage in active jeering and scapegoating, or make the erotically inept or unattractive the butt of in-group jokes. The informal slang of all such groups marks out the different ranks: the lower ranking are known as "nerds," "wonks," "plain Janes," "dogs," etc.

This is of course a somewhat simplified picture. In some school-age communities, young people cannot confine their social ties entirely to those of the same erotic rank. In very small communities (and similarly in neighborhood play groups) there may be not enough young people so that they can segregate themselves simultaneously by erotic rank and by social class, race / ethnicity, religion and other categories that they take seriously. In general, the more traditional the community in its concerns over these criteria of social ranking, the more these will override erotic attractiveness; thus there are indications in novels about social class in the early twentieth century that upper-middle-class boys at country club dances went out of their way to give an occasional dance to the unbeautiful daughters of good families, out of feelings or pressures of class obligation (e.g., O'Hara 1934). In contemporary youth communities, sports teams and other activities bring together individuals on criteria other than attractiveness, and tend to mix erotic rankings. But carousing and other sociable entertainment with a sexual theme bring the erotic ranking to the fore, and thus its own form of segregation tends to prevail over the others. I would suggest that the historical trend in American youth scenes has been toward reducing class and ethnic / racial lines and thus has made erotic ranking increasingly the main principle of prestige and of informal segregation (see, for example, Moffatt 1989). For example, black persons who are in the erotic elite are likely to pass into a trans-racial community of sociability stars, whereas less attractive individuals in all ethnic groups tend to stay segregated. This matching by erotic attractiveness is far from a historical universal, but probably occurs mainly in very modern societies. In tribal societies, kinship alliance obligations tended to fix sexual relations irrespective of personal qualities; in patrimonial households, social rank dominated sexual opportunities, so there was likely a good deal of sexual interaction crossing lines of erotic inequality, unattractive powerful men (especially older ones who dominated the harems) with attractive younger women.

Through these processes, I would suggest, the twentieth century became the most widely eroticized century to date, growing increasingly eroticized throughout the century. Our image of some prior historical periods as even more widely eroticized—notably classical Athens or decadent Rome—are skewed by concentrating on a small proportion of upper-class males. It appears that modern society is much more widely eroticized than aristocratic societies organized in patrimonial households; even though the latter may have had harems—which give us our image of uninhibited sexuality—the imbalance of females to males in harems meant that a large proportion of the men in such societies were deprived of sexual partners. Even if we counted by frequency of sexual acts, the total number must have been diminished by the presence of polygyny. As in the distribution of wealth, a high concentration of sexual property (or a high degree of stratification) depresses overall levels of enjoyment.

The shift in the modern mass media toward increasingly blatant sexual representation, including the outburst of pornography from the 1970s onward, explicitness about sexual matters formerly taboo in public discussion, and the politicization of erotic matters by the feminist, lesbian, and gay liberation movements, all rode upon the tide flowing from the display of erotic ranking in youth scenes. The eroticization of youth culture has become so widely influential because, as public education has grown, the youth sex / sociability scene has expanded to include virtually the entire population and for longer periods of their lives. It also reflects the increasing egalitarianism of youth culture, that has quite self-consciously played down class and ethnic differences (such as through the homogenization of dress styles and the permeation of the casual leisured style into almost all situations), leaving their focus on the main activity, the display of erotic attractiveness ranking.[22] The result of this focus on idealized sexual symbolism, and on noting everyone's rank within it, has been the increasing amounts of sexual activity of all kinds. We see this in the spread of the onset of sexual activity to increasingly younger ages; the overall incidence of intercourse; the spread of various ancillary sexual practices (Laumann et al. 1994). It is no doubt implicated in long-term increases in rape. Given the correlation between pornography and masturbation, one would expect incidence of masturbation to have risen as well.

Finally, I would suggest that the upsurge of the gay and lesbian movements has also been affected by the increasingly focused eroticization of youth culture. For the heterosexual elite in the youth scene did not entirely dominate a ranking of erotic non-elites emulating them, deferring to them, or retiring ashamedly before them. It also motivated social movements of rebellion against the simple hierarchy of the erotic party culture. The hippie movement of the 1960s may be seen as one such movement; for a few years at least, it fostered an alternative center of collective effervescence, partly by alliance with political protest movements, partly by dramatizing its own techniques of carousing and its own explicitly flaunted sexual participation. In other words, for a time the movement upheld an alternative scene, a network of gatherings that had erotic as well as other forms of sociable prestige. No doubt there was a fair amount of idealization of what went on in such scenes, and many of them may have been mythical imagery. Eventually, the techniques that gave the hippie movement its charisma and its emblems of identity (drugs, rock music festivals, clothing styles that repudiated the sexual self-presentation of the prevailing youth culture) were taken over by the mainstream youth culture, and the old style of erotic / sociable hierarchy reasserted itself.

Nevertheless, it was out of these social movement scenes (in the structural sense that I have emphasized above), that several more sexual scenes became mobilized: the gay and lesbian scenes. These recruited among individuals who were most sharply stigmatized by the heterosexual prestige hierarchy, the butt of its jokes, and sometimes of ritual violence protecting the boundaries of heterosexual identity. Homosexuals were thus necessarily "in the closet" as long as they lived around the scenes that monopolized the attention of local communities, such as high schools that assembled teen cohorts, as well as colleges and country clubs for adults, which carried on highly focused sexualized festivities such as seasonal dances and a traditional round of parties, date nights, football weekends, and the like. Homosexuals could find a space in which to construct their own scenes only where they had both relative privacy and sufficient numbers to constitute a critical mass; such scenes existed around artistic communities in a few big cities. The counterculture movements of the 1960s and 70s offered new possibilities because they provided an alternative scene, a network of effervescent gathering places on a wider scale. The national gathering places of the civil rights / anti-war / hippie counterculture movement also provided room for a self-consciously energized gay movement, as well as for the lesbian movement, whose new scenes were found at first within the consciousness-raising groups of the feminist movement. These political movements provided the structural conditions under which homosexual erotic energy was built up. I am suggesting that these movements did not merely take preexisting closet homosexuality and bring it into the open, but built up this specific kind of erotic energy so that the amount of homosexual activity increased during this period.

This should remain true no matter what genetic propensity to homosexuality there may be. It is possible, in a multi-causal world, that some such genetic influences might exist; but it seems clear that they would be rather weak influences on behavior, given the strong situational variations in the conditions and kinds of homosexual action throughout history; widespread, institutionalized homosexuality in ancient Greece, for example (Dover 1978), and in tribal New Guinea (Herdt 1994), had very different forms of recruitment, social relationships, and sexual practices than the homosexuality that began to acquire a social identity in Western countries since the 1880s. Current attention on homosexual genes is a political ideology, explicitly adopted during the 1980s as a legal tactic to legitimate homosexuality as a legally protected minority.

This follows the general logic of my argument: specific kinds of sexual motivations are constructed by opportunities to take part in sexual IRs; and these in turn are shaped by (and reciprocally shape) the formulation and propagation of sexual symbolism idealizing and giving erotic prestige. It is the situational stratification produced by a strong focus of attention on such scenes that produced the widespread eroticization of the twentieth century. And not only in this century are there patterns that we can explain through the variability of IRs linked into sexual scenes. These scenes have taken different forms: the courtier cultures epitomized by seventeenth-century Versailles; the ballroom dancing of nineteenth-century respectable classes; and the dating and partying scene that came about with the individually negotiated marriage market and went on to construct an emergent focus of attention out of its own temporary hierarchies of sexual popularity, and that made a splash in the early twentieth century as "the Jazz age."[23] There is no theoretical reason to think that we are at the end of such histories. IR theory implies that there are no fixed erotic essences; whatever biological substrate was once evolutionarily selected provides no more than ingredients upon which erotic energies, identities, and symbols are emergently constructed. The future may contain a great deal of erotic construction in directions yet unthought of.

The conditions that shape IR chains and the sexual scenes that link them are a key to understanding how erotic practices are historically shaped and who is attracted along what erotic path. Sexual passion is not primordial but a form of emotional energy, specialized toward particular symbolic objects because of the way in which they have become charged up with attention in particular types of interaction rituals. IR theory and erotic interaction mutually illuminate one another. Sexual pathways are IR chains just like any other.

Chapter 7

SITUATIONAL STRATIFICATION

ARE RECEIVED SOCIOLOGICAL THEORIES capable of grasping the realities of contemporary stratification? We think in terms of a structured hierarchy of inequality. A prominent imagery is Bourdieu's (1984) field of economic power and a hierarchy of cultural tastes internalized in individuals, with these two hierarchies mutually reproducing one another. The image helps explain the frustrations of reformers attacking inequality by attempting to change educational attainment. Empirical researchers report on inequalities in income and wealth, education and occupation, as changing slices of a pie, and as distributional shares for races, ethnicities, genders, and ages. We see an abstract scaffolding of hierarchy manifested in a shell of objective-looking quantitative data. Does this image of fixed, objective hierarchy come to grips with the micro-situational realities of lived experience?

The distribution of income and wealth in the United States has become increasingly unequal since 1970 (Morris and Western 1999). Yet observe a typical scene in an expensive American restaurant, where the wealthy go to spend their money: waiters greet customers informally, introducing themselves by name and assuming the manners of an equal inviting a guest into their home; they interrupt the customers to announce menu specials and advise what they should order. As Goffmanian ritual, it is the waiters who command attention for their performance while the customers are constrained to act as polite audience. Other examples abound: Celebrities of the entertainment world appear on ceremonial occasions in deliberately casual attire, unshaven or in torn clothes; far from presenting a demeanor giving ritual honor to the occasion, they adopt a style of self-presentation that would have associated a generation earlier with laborers or beggars. The demeanor style, widely adopted among youth and others when occasions allow (e.g., "casual Fridays" at work), constitutes a historically unprecedented form of anti-status or reverse snobbery. High-ranking government officials, corporation executives, and entertainment celebrities are targets of public scandals delving into their sexual lives, employment of housekeepers, use of intoxicants, and even their efforts at privacy; social eminence, far from providing immunity for petty derelictions, opens up the high ranking to attacks by lower-ranking functionaries. A muscular black youth, wearing baggy pants and hat turned backward and carrying a boom box loudly playing angry-voiced rap music, dominates the sidewalk space of a public shopping area while middle-class whites palpably shrink back in deference. In public meetings, when women and ethnic minorities take the role of spokespersons and denounce social discrimination against their groups, white men of the higher social classes sit in embarrassed silence or hurriedly join in a chorus of support; in public opinion-expressing and policy-making settings, it is the voice of the underdog that carries moral authority.

How are we to conceptualize these kinds of events? The examples given are micro-evidence; my contention is that they characterize the flow of everyday life in sharp contrast to the ideal type of a macro-hierarchy. The hierarchic image dominates our theories, as well as our folk concepts for talking about stratification; indeed, the rhetorical tactics of taking the morally superior stance of the underdog depends upon asserting the existence of a macro-hierarchy while tacitly assuming underdog dominance in the immediate speech situation. Conflicts over the issue of so-called "political correctness," which might be called authoritative imposition of special consideration for the underdog, hinge upon this unrecognized disjunction between micro and macro. In social science, we generally accord the status of objective reality to statistics (e.g., the distribution of income, occupations, education), yet ethnographic observations are richer and more immediate empirical data. Our trouble is that ethnographies are piecemeal; we have yet to survey situations widely through systematic sampling, so that it could be argued with confidence what is the general distribution of the experiences of everyday life across an entire society.

My argument is that micro-situational data has conceptual priority. This is not to say that macro-data mean nothing; but amassing statistics and survey data does not convey an accurate picture of social reality unless it is interpreted in the context of its micro-situational grounding. Micro-situational encounters are the ground zero of all social action and all sociological evidence. Nothing has reality unless it is manifested in a situation somewhere. Macro-social structures can be real, provided that they are patterned aggregates that hold across micro-situations, or networks of repeated connections from one micro-situation to another (thereby comprising, for instance, a formal organization). But misleading macro "realities" can be built up by misconstruing what happens in micro-situations. Survey data is always collected in micro-situations by asking individuals such questions as how much money they make, which occupations do they think are the most prestigious, how many years of schooling they have, whether they believe in God, or how much discrimination they think exists in society. The aggregate of these answers looks like an objective picture of a hierarchic (or, for some items, a consensual) structure. But aggregated data on the distribution of wealth does not mean anything unless we know what "wealth" actually is in situational experience; dollars in inflated stock prices do not mean the same thing as cash in the grocery store. As Zelizer (1994) shows with ethnographies of the actual use of money, there are a variety of currencies in practice confined to certain social and material advantages in restricted circuits of exchange. (Owning jewelry worth a certain "book value" does not mean that most people, if they are outside the network of jewelry merchants, can realize that value and convert it into other kinds of monetary power; at best, they can use its book value for bragging purposes in ordinary conversation.) I will refer to such circuits as "Zelizer circuits." We need to undertake a series of studies looking at the conversion of reified macro-distributions, which we have constructed by taking survey aggregations as if they were real things with fixed transituational values, into the actual distribution of advantages in situational practice. For instance:

Occupational prestige surveys show most people believe physicists, medical doctors, and professors have very good jobs, above business executives, entertainers, and politicians, and that these in turn rank above plumbers and truck drivers. Does such consensus show anything more than a pattern of how people tend to talk when they are asked extremely abstract, uncontextualized questions? Although surveys show that "professor" ranks high as a bare category, any specification ("economist," "sociologist," "chemist") brings down the prestige rating (Treiman 1977); further specification ("assistant professor," "junior college professor") brings it down yet further. "Scientist" and especially "physicist" rank very high in recent surveys, but does this mean that most people would like to sit next to a physicist at a dinner party? "Plumber" may rank low in the survey, but in practice their income outranks many educationally credentialed white-collar employees, and this may translate into material resources to dominate most life situations; plumbers may sit in the box seats at the stadium while white-collar workers are in the remote grandstand. What is the real-life standing of construction workers when they display a style of outdoor muscular activity that receives respect in a time when the prestigeful style of automobile is the big trucklike "sports utility vehicle"? Occupational prestige can be understood in a realistic way only if we can survey situations of occupational encounters, and judge the actual situational stratification that takes place.

The common interpretation of years of education as the key to the hierarchy of stratification, either as principal indicator or as major component of a composite index, gives a skewed picture of micro-situational stratification. Mere correlation between years of schooling and income is an aggregate of outcomes that hides rather than reveals how educational stratification operates. Years of schooling are not a homogeneous currency: years in different kinds of schools are not equivalent in terms of what kinds of subsequent educational and occupational channels one can enter. For example, years in an elite prep school or highly ranked private college have no particular value for one's occupational level, unless they are translated into admission into a particular kind of schooling at the next higher level. It is valuable to attend a liberal arts college well known by graduate school admissions officers if one is going on to specialized graduate education in fields connected with one's undergraduate specialty, but it gives no special advantage, and may even be counterproductive, if one immediately enters the labor force. Educational credentials should be regarded as a particular kind of Zelizer currency, valuable in specific circuits of exchange but not outside of those circuits.

It is the point where years of schooling are translated into recognized credentials that they leap in social value; while those credentials themselves fluctuate in their consequences, depending both upon the aggregate amount of competition among credential holders at a particular historical time (credential inflation), and also upon the extent to which credentials are earmarked for particular kind of specialized jobs or professional licensing barriers (see studied cited in Collins 2002). Years of education are only a vague proxy for what kinds of credentials people hold, and that in turn gives only a vague picture of what micro-situational uses they have in people's lives. We need a micro-distributional research program to look at educational stratification; this would include both the situational advantages and disadvantages of official recognition at each level of school experience, from elementary on through secondary and advanced, and thereafter into the occupational and sociable encounters of adult lives. It does not automatically hold that a student who performs well by the official criteria of the school system will enjoy micro-situational advantages. In poverty-level urban black secondary schools, the student who gets good grades typically receives much negative interaction from peers, who accuse him / her of "acting white" or thinking that she or he is better than they; they do not rank high in the immediate community stratification but low. Many such high-achieving students give way under micro-situational peer pressure and do not go further in the school system (Anderson 1999, 56, 93–97).

The micro-situational critique holds a fortiori for inferences from survey attitude data to depictions of a larger social structure. The fact that approximately 95 percent of Americans say they believe in God

(Greeley 1989, 14) says little about how religious American society is. Comparisons of survey responses with actual attendance show that people strongly exaggerate how often they go to church (Hardaway et al. 1993, 1998); and in-depth probings of religious beliefs in informal conversation shows quite disparate and, from a theological viewpoint, largely heretical beliefs lumped under survey responses that seem to show conformity (Halle 1984, 253–69). Similarly, we ought to be suspicious of survey reports on how much discrimination by race or gender exists—or sexual harassment, experience of child abuse, etc.—until these are backed up by attempts at situational surveys that do not rely on reconstructions, one-sided recollections of social interactions, or opinions. Answers to such questions are ideological and often partisan, subject to social movement mobilization and waves of attention in the public media or by particular professional interest groups. To say this is not to take a position that most social problems are exaggerated by surveys; under some conditions, they may be minimized and underestimated. The point is that we will not know with any high degree of plausibility until we shift our conceptual gestalt, away from accepting macro-aggregate data as inherently objective, and toward the translation of all social phenomena as a distribution of micro-situations. We need to be open to the possibility that the actual experience of stratification in social encounters is highly fluctuating, subject to situational contestation; and that to understand stratification, above all in present historical circumstances, we need a theory of the mechanisms of micro-situational dominance. These mechanisms might be connected to our older hierarchic image of economic, political, and cultural power; but they might not; or the connection may be becoming increasingly tenuous. Why this is happening would call for a historical theory of change in micro-situational circumstances.

Sociologists, like most highly educated persons on the left side of the political spectrum, are so deeply imbued with the hierarchical image that we react with cynical amusement to instances of the officially illegitimate privilege in everyday life. We consider it sophisticated to pass around stories of the corruption of police officers, such as their withholding traffic tickets from the elite or in return for bribes, and regard the political world as made up of those who have "clout" or "backdoor influence." Yet to what extent is this folk belief, untested by situational evidence that may go to the contrary? A former government official related this experience to the author: Stopped for speeding by a state police officer, he said, "Do you know who I am? I'm your boss." (The official was head of the state agency under which the state highway patrol was located.) The officer replied, " My boss is the people of the state of [X]," and proceeded to write the ticket. The official was politically very liberal, yet he narrated this incident with indignation, out-raged that the underground system of entitlement did not work for him. One could interpret this as an instance of micro-situational strati-fication. The patrol officer, with bureaucratic impunity, could exercise situational power over his own superior, much in the way a "whistle-blower" has official immunity to report violations of organizational su-periors. Further interviewing with patrol officers suggests another di-mension of the situation. In this state, members of the law enforcement community, when stopped for a traffic violation, express their member-ship by the code words "I should have known better," and then offer to show identification. Patrol officers do make exceptions to official rules, but they do so in a ritual of solidarity and equality; they react negatively to attempts at imposing hierarchic authority.

Macro- and Micro-Situational Class, Status, and Power

As yet we lack situational surveys. The best we can do is to sketch what the contemporary situation of societies like the United States appears to be at the turn of the twenty-first century. I will suggest a micro-trans-lation of the Weberian dimensions of class, status and power.

Economic Class as Zelizer Circuits

Economic class is certainly not disappearing. On the macro-level, the distribution of wealth and income has been becoming increasingly un-equal, both within societies and on a world scale (Sanderson 1999, 346–356). What does this translate into in terms of the distribution of life experiences? Let us divide the question into material wealth as con-sumption experiences, and wealth as control over occupational experi-ences. Extremely large amounts of wealth are virtually impossible to translate into consumption experiences. The fact that owners of large blocks of stock in Microsoft or a few other commercial empires have net worth valued in the tens of billions of dollars (fluctuating ac-cording to stock market prices) does not mean that these individuals eat food, inhabit dwellings, wear clothes, or enjoy services greatly dif-ferent from several million other individuals who may be ranked within the top 10 percent or so of the wealth distribution; and if one counts temporary experiences of luxury consumption, the overlap may be with an even wider group. Most wealth arising from financial own-ership is confined within Zelizer circuits that stay close to their point of origin; by this I mean that individuals who have hundreds of mil-lions of dollars or more can do little with that money except buy and sell financial instruments; they can trade control of one segment of the financial world for control of another segment.

Wealth of this scale needs to be located not in consumption but in occupational experience. In terms of micro-situational experience, possession of large amounts of financial instruments means a life routine of frequently interacting with other financiers. The main attraction of having extremely large amounts of money may be the emotional energies and symbolic membership markers of being on the phone at all hours of the night and day, engaging in exciting transactions. In terms of sheer consumption power, the extremely wealthy have maxed out on what they can get as material benefits; yet most of them continue to work, sometimes obsessively lengthy hours, until advanced ages (some of the tycoons struggling for control over world media empires are men in their seventies and eighties). It appears that the value of money at this level is all in the micro-experience, the activity of wielding money in highly prestigeful circuits of exchange. Money here translates into situational power, and into nothing else.

The main diversion of these circuits is that wealth from financial circuits can be shifted to charitable organizations, and thus out of the control of the original owners. From the point of view of the donor, this is trading wealth for honor, the moral prestige of being a charitable donor, often getting a concrete token of reward in the form of his or her personal reputation being broadcast by having a charitable organization named after oneself: the Rockefeller Foundation, Carnegie Corporation, Milken Foundation, and now the Gates Foundation, Soros Foundation, etc. Yet the two circuits of capital are not far apart. Foundation executives typically take their endowments and put them back into financial markets, drawing only small parts for operating expenses, their own salaries, and some stream of grants to nonprofit organizations. Counting up the personnel in the nonprofit sector, one arrives at a group of upper-middle or upper-class persons who are not many network links removed from personal contact with the financial magnates who donated the money in the first place (Ostrower 1995).

As one descends the hierarchy of wealth and income, the proportion of money that translates into actual material consumption increases. For the lowest income levels, money may be entirely a matter of consumption goods. Yet even here, as Zelizer (1994) documents, money that can be spent on prestigeful or at least exciting social encounters tends to have preference over mere mundane money: immigrants to the early-twentieth-century United States who spent money on lavish funerals because these were key social ceremonies of display within the ethnic community; men whose priority is to have drinking money to participate with the all-male group at the saloon; prostitutes whose money is spent on the locally prestigeful "action" style of drug parties, while their welfare checks go towards household expenses.

Let us conceive of the entire structure of economic class as a variety of circuits of money used to enact particular kinds of social relations. I am not speaking here of social relations as status groups, communities of leisure sociability analytically distinct from classes; but rather of the interactional enactment of the economic class structure, the world of occupations, commerce, credit, and investment. The "upper class" are those who engage in circulating money as ownership, and in the process linking tightly with one another in webs of negotiation. Such persons may or may not be part of the Social Register or otherwise take part in the sociable gatherings and rituals of the upper class conceived as a status group, which in turn may consist of people who only passively receive money from spouses or inheritance, and who do not take part in the actual circuits of financial exchange. Thus, contrary to the Bourdieu model that sees cultural activity as reinforcing economic dominance, and vice versa, I suggest that the upper-class status group tends to siphon off economic capital from the circuits in which it is generated, and gradually loses touch with the anchoring that creates and perpetuates wealth. Money is process, not thing; the upper class is a circuit of financial activity, and to withdraw from that activity is gradually to be left behind. Upper-class status group snobbery about "old money" versus "nouveau riche" reverses the actual situation of economic power.[1]

We have yet to map out the actual structure of the circuits of monetary exchange for a given historical period (such as our own). Roughly, we might recognize the following:

1. A financial elite of active participants in financial transactions on the scale where particular individuals can wield sufficient blocks of capital that they personally count as reputations in financial coalitions. Their experience of financial circuits is personal, in contrast to the impersonal participation of the next category.

2. An investing class (largely drawn, in more conventional terms, from upper-middle and lower-upper classes) who have enough money from highly paid occupations or direct ownership of business enterprises to act as players in the game of financial investments (the stock market, real estate, etc.) but who are anonymous participants, without access to personal circuits among the deal-makers. Their micro-situational economic reality consists in reading market reports, talking with their brokers, circulating financial gossip, and bragging as part of their conversational capital among sociable acquaintances. This group is depicted by advocates of the neoliberal ideology as comprising everyone

in modern societies, an ideology of classlessness through universal ownership of small bits of market capital. The ideology ignores differences in the social circuits of capital that I am presently describing; but it does reflect an aspect of reality that the strictly macro-hierarchical view of class has difficulty conceptualizing.

3. An entrepreneurial class that uses its money directly to hire employees, purchase and sell goods, thus typically participating in local or specialized circuits of exchange. Its key micro-situational experiences are those of bargaining repeatedly with particular persons in their organization or industry; that is to say, members of this class operate in a world of personal reputations, both their own and those of others.[2] Unlike members of other classes or economic circuits, their routine experience includes the monitoring of competitors in order to seek out market niches as described in the network theory of Harrison White (1981, 2002). Entrepreneurial circuits tend to be invisible to most people, and are visible only within very local or specialized communities; hence the social prestige of individuals in such positions, as measured in occupational prestige surveys, may be modest. The actual amounts of money flowing through these circuits, and the income commanded by these individuals, can vary all the way from millions to tens of dollars; thus this sector spans virtually the entire class structure as conventionally laid out in a hierarchy of dollars.

4. Celebrities, which is to say, highly paid employees of organizations specializing in public entertainment (film, music, sports, etc.)—organizations that, in the nature of their business, aim at focusing public attention on a few individuals who are treated as stars (Leifer 1995). Athletes, in fact, are manual workers, at the bottom of a chain of command insofar as they take orders from coaches, and are hired and moved around by management. Some small proportion of them (necessarily a small proportion, since mass attention arenas are intrinsically competitive) have acquired the bargaining power for extremely high salaries, corresponding to the size of these markets for entertainment products. Celebrities as wealth holders face the same problem as the financial upper class in converting their wealth into consumption. Many of them are cheated by their agents or brokers who offer to connect them to the unfamiliar world of financial investments; those who do best seem to be those who convert their wealth back into financial control of organizations in the same entertainment industry that they came from (e.g., hockey stars who buy a hockey team). This suggests the following rule: those who keep their wealth within the same Zelizer circuit in which it originated are best able to hold its monetary

value, and to maximize their micro-situational payoffs of experiential prestige as well.

5. A variety of middle-class / working-class circuits shaped by occupational markets and the networks of information and contact that sustain them (Tilly and Tilly 1994). Here money is not translated into ownership in any other form than mere consumer property. There are suggestions in the empirical sociology of economic networks that for large, one-shot expenditures (houses, cars, etc.) such persons spend their money in networks of personal contact, whereas they spend small amounts on repetitive consumer expenditures in impersonal retail organizations (DiMaggio and Louch 1998). Some of these networks withdraw money from the other circuits of exchange in the form of profit and thus constitute a hierarchy (or more likely, several kinds of hierarchical relations). We have yet to measure, and to conceptualize, the mechanisms by which "profit" moves across circuits. In general, it appears that those located "lower down" in the circuits have difficulty seeing what goes on in the circuits above them, let alone finding social and financial entrée into those networks. For instance, the lower down one goes in the social class hierarchy, the more individuals' conceptions of those above them simplify into ideas about celebrities [4], who are actually the most peripheral of all rich people to the circuits of wealth.

6. Disreputable or illegal circuits, ranging from gray markets outside the official tax and licensing system, to markets of criminalized commodities and services (drugs, sex, arms, age-restricted alcohol and tobacco, etc.), and to stolen property and outright robbery. All these are circuits, entry to which (and competition over) make or break the individual in their illicit / criminal career. The sheer amount of money flowing through some of these circuits and accruing to particular individuals may be substantial, overlapping with middle or even occasionally high levels of the income hierarchy abstractly conceived. But although cross-over among these networks (money-laundering) is considered highly desirable by some participants, the weight of social organization from both sides is against much interconversion of currencies and melding of circuits of exchange. Illicit circuits avoid the rake-off by which the government is normally involved in all the reputable circuits of exchange, and through which governments are usually committed to regulating and providing infrastructure in the interests of the members of those circuits. The very fact that some of these circuits are illicit means they must be kept hidden from the regulators of the official circuits; the result is that the rituals and symbols of everyday encounters within these circuits are very different in tone. Tacit

recognition of these differences are a mechanism by which persons conceive of moral exclusions among classes (documented by Lamont 1992, 2000). Monetary circuits comprise different cultures, we might say, bearing in mind that "culture" is not a reified thing but merely shorthand for referring to the style of micro-situational encounters.

7. An ultimate lower class on the margins of society might be conceptualized as comprising those outside any circuits of monetary exchange. Yet even the homeless, beggars, and scavengers, are involved in the tail end of various circuits, receiving donations, handouts in kind, discarded or stolen goods. Analytically, this group would include all those who receive a trickle downward from the more actively mutual circuits of exchange, including welfare recipients and other entitlements (pensions, etc.) What makes this group experience such dishonor is not merely their low level of material consumption, but the fact that they are severely circumscribed in how much further exchange they can do with what they receive: currencies they receive are often earmarked for certain kinds of expenditures only (e.g., food stamps); gifts in kind are also largely already specified as to their use value (Zelizer 1994). Some exchange may go on even here, largely on the barter level. Denizens of this level of monetary stratification have their micro-situational encounters shaped in a fashion that is experientially different than any other class: barter relations are highly specific, lacking the sense of symbolic honor and freedom that goes from possessing financial tokens that are widely negotiable.

Micro-translating economic class shows, not a hierarchical totempole of classes neatly stacked up one above another, but overlapping transactional circuits of vastly different scope and content. Because these circuits differ so much in the particularity or anonymity of connections, in the kind of monitoring that is done and in orientation toward economic manipulation or consumption, individuals' experiences of economic relations put them in different subjective worlds, even if these are invisible from a distance.

Status Group Boundaries and Categorical Identities

Status is one of the loosest terms in the sociological vocabulary. Leaving aside the vacuous usage of "status" as stratified rank in general, and confining it to a specific sphere of cultural honor, we may distinguish several meanings. The most abstract is status as measured by occupational prestige surveys. This decontextualized questioning about categories may show little more than the distribution of ideologies about events outside people's own experience. This leaves two

main versions: the Weberian concept of status groups, as a real organization of social networks; and deference, as micro-situational behavior.

Weber (1922/1968, 932–33) defines status group as a community
sharing a cultural lifestyle, a recognized social identity, and publically
(even legally) recognized honor or social ranking. The clearest examples of this ideal type are medieval Estates (clergy, aristocracy, bourgeoisie, peasantry); the term is more widely applicable to ethnic and
religious communities and other lifestyle groups. Weber promoted the
term to contrast with economic class, in that status groups are not mere
statistical categories but groups with real social organization. Status
groups may also be organized around economic classes, provided that
these classes have a cultural distinctiveness and enact themselves as
groups. For example, the economic upper class may be organized into
"high society" and listed in the Social Register. It is a historical question whether class-based status groups continue to have as strong
boundaries as in previous periods, or whether economic class has re-
verted to a mainly statistical category. If status groups structure life
experience along different lines than class in the abstract, such a historical shift would mean that class identity, conflict, and capacity for mobilized action would be considerably weakened.

To what extent is there closure of status communities—how sharply
are they bounded in everyday life? And how much ranking is there
among status groups—when are they neatly aligned in a publicly recognized hiercharcy? When are they mere horizontal divisions, like mutually alien tribes? Historical change can occur in either aspect: cultural
lifestyles among status groups may be homogenizing; and / or groups
may assemble less often, and their identities may become less salient
as to where members spend their time. The Social Register still exists,
but members may spend little time in these circles as compared to
other settings (e.g., with entertainment celebrities), and their gatherings receive much less public attention than at the turn of the twentieth
century (Amory 1960; for historical comparisons: Annett and Collins
1975; Elias 1983). Similarly for noneconomic-based status groups:
many ethnic and religious groups do not structure their members' lives
much, receding into mere statistical categories without relevance for
life experience (Waters 1990).[3]

The most important contemporary research on stratified group
boundaries is Lamont (1992, 2000). In Weberian terminology, Lamont
is describing how occupational classes are turned into bounded status
groups, and similarly for racial group boundaries. Lamont's interview
method gives a summary of how working-class and upper-middle
class men reflect on their boundaries, and describes the vocabulary in
terms of which they legitimate those boundaries. These vocabularies

or ideologies of class and race boundaries differ between the United States and France, Lamont emphasizes, because of differing national vocabularies or cultural repertoires deriving from political histories of those states. This research strategy provides evidence that some group boundaries and cultural judgments as not merely constructed situationally, but derive from cultural repertoires that circulate widely and originated at great distance from the local situation, so as to be all but impervious to situational influences.

Consider, however, Lamont's findings: these arise from the microsituation of talking with an interviewer who brings up the question of group identity and its relationship with outsiders, and brings this up in a much more explicit manner than generally occurs in ordinary conversations. The interviewed men put on their best front to legitimate themselves. White American working-class men describe themselves as disciplined and hard-working, set off by contrast with their complaint against blacks and the lower classes generally, whom they see through a stereotype of welfare chiselers and criminals. It appears that the white working class have created their self-image as disciplined workers mainly by this contrast, since ethnographic studies of workers on the job have generally shown a style of alienation from the demands of work, attempts to control the work pace, and preference for their private lives over their work lives (see note 9 in chapter 3). The same pattern of creating an ideology about one's own group by contrasting it with an antagonistic group is found among black American working-class men, who describe themselves as caring and having compassion for their fellows; this self-description is set up in opposition to their view of whites, who are seen—no doubt accurately enough, in light of the concerns of black people for relief from the heritage of racism—as domineering and lacking in compassion. The ideological element in this becomes apparent from Anderson's (1999) ethnographic data on interactional pattern of males in the black inner city, which shows not a predominance of compassion and solidarity but the situationally dominant "code of the street," a display of toughness, wariness and readiness to resort to violence. Like their white counterparts, black working-class men appear to be creating an ideology that reflects not so much the actual patterns of their own behavior but a favorable view of themselves in the light of the perceived faults of the most salient outsiders.

Similarly, Lamont's (1992) interviews with upper-middle-class American men yields a picture in which they state their boundaries in terms of their dislike of those who lack moral standards of honesty and truthfulness, and thereby present themselves as people who value moral standards above all else. Yet these are presumably the same people who are viewed from the outside by Lamont's white working-class sample (both groups are situated in the New York metropolitan area) in just the opposite way, as lacking in integrity and straightfor-wardness. The same people are either honest or dishonest, straightfor-ward or devious, depending on whether they are recounting their own ideology from the inside or are depicted by the adjacent class that sees them from below. What Lamont's data show, then, is that generalized cultural vocabularies circulating in rather large national groups are pressed into service by individuals situated in different relationships to each other. The use of cultural repertoires also results in situationally constructed ideologies, each one a narrative drama in which individu-als portray themselves as part of a group of good guys whose charac-teristics maximally contrast with another group of bad guys.

Status groups have varying degrees of micro-situational reality: some are loosely overlapping networks, only segments of which ever see one another face to face (e.g., all Italian-Americans). Some may be closely bounded because they enact their membership and their lines of exclusion by who takes part in social encounters.

Here it is useful to array situations along a continuum from formal-ized and tightly focused to informal and relatively unfocused interac-tion. Since every interactional situation can be assessed in terms of the strength of the ingredients for IRs, this is tantamount to a continuum from very strong to very weak rituals. In everyday life, this continuum underlies the typology presented in figure 7.1.

Status group relations occur largely within the middle category, so-ciable situations, although to some extent also in official ceremonies. Sociable occasions vary in their degree of formality. At the highly fo-cused end of the continuum, there is ritual in the formal sense: schedul-ing is carried out in advance; the event may be widely publicized; what is done follows traditional scripts and is possibly rehearsed; here we find weddings, traditional dances, testimonial dinners. In the old-fash-ioned etiquette of the higher classes (described in Goffman 1959, 1963; Annett and Collins 1975), there was considerable scripting of the de-tails of behavior: the ritual procession of gentlemen escorting ladies in to dinner, seating guests, toasts and other drinking rituals, polite forms of conversation, card games, and other collective amusements after dinner. Descending toward less sharply focused or more "casual" situ-ations are largely improvised interaction rituals: lunches and other shared eating with acquaintances (often as a friendly offstage framing for business talk), parties, attending commercial entertainment events.[4]

At the upper end, this continuum overlaps with formal ceremonies such as political speeches, government ceremonies, parades, school graduations, church services. All ceremonies enact social member-

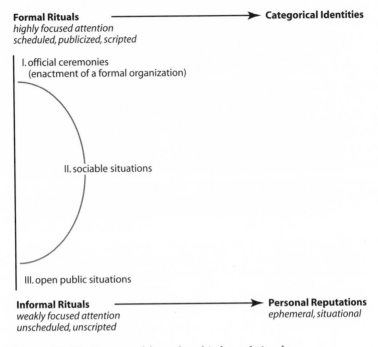

Figure 7.1 Continuum of formal and informal rituals.

ships, although some connect much looser communities than others. Political speeches may attempt to assemble and affirm the belonging of all the citizens of a nation, the members of a political party, or supporters of a particular candidate, but the identities that they enact may take up rather small portions of people's lives, peripheral to more regularly enacted status group activities. Weberian status groups are located toward the middle of the continuum; here rituals imply more intimate and more frequently enacted commitments. Still further down is the ephemeral civility of the minor Goffmanian interaction rituals: casual conversations, shared greetings, little jokes, bits of gossip, small talk about the weather, or how long a wait there is for a bus. At the bottom end, relationships dissolve into unfocused interaction: the public crowd or just physical copresence on a street or some other widely accessible place (Goffman 1963, 1971, 1981). Yet even here, Goffman notes, there is at least tacit monitoring; amplifying the point, we shall see how behavior in public places varies considerably in how much restraint, politeness, or contentiousness is enacted. Here, too, can be variations in situational stratification, even if it is highly ephemeral.

Figure 7.2 Eton boys in upper-class regalia arriving for cricket match, cheekily (and uneasily) observed by working-class boys (England, 1930s).

This continuum provides a backdrop for a situational survey of both status group inclusion / exclusion and deference behavior. Let us highlight two subdimensions: (a) how much time group rituals take up of people's lives, whether they are regularly enacted or occasional and hence represent everyday or episodic communities; (b) at the moment that a ritual community is activated, how much enthusiasm and solidarity it experiences; regularly enacted status groups are not necessarily stronger in generating enthuasiastic commitments than temporary ones.[5] Accordingly, I will suggest two generalizations.

Where there is a repeated round of formal, highly focused ritual occasions (weddings, dinners, festivals) involving the same people, status group boundaries are strong. Who is included and excluded from membership is clear to everyone, inside and outside the status group. All the more so to the degree that ritual gatherings are publicly visible: for example, when the "Four Hundred" met to dine and dance in the ballroom of the most luxurious hotel in New York City, and crowds of the non-elite classes lined the sidewalks to watch them enter and exit, the status group boundary and its ranking system was widely public. Here status has a thing-like quality, following the principle, *the more ceremonial and public the ritual enactment, the more reified the social mem-*

bership category. Conversely, *the less scripted, advance-scheduled, and widely announced the sociable gathering, the more invisible the social boundaries.* A sociometric order may still exist, in the sense that some persons habitually associate with others; but their gatherings convey only a very local recognition of ties—personal connections rather than categorical identities or statuses. Such privatized and fragmented networks may continue to sustain cutural differences, in that distinct cultural capitals circuate within particular sociable networks; but they are invisible to outsiders, not widely recongizable as lifestyle groups.

Status group boundaries, and hence categorical identities, blur to the extent that they are grounded in weakly focused sociable rituals. Full-blown Weberian status groups, recognizable by visible signs (at one time, even mandated by sumptuary regulations; for a Japanese example, see Ikegami 2004) can exist only when the round of everyday life is highly formalized. Under these conditions, people carry categorical identities ("gentleman," "aristocrat," "burgher," "peasant," "common laborer"— even if these are no longer legal categories). Toward the other end of the continuum, identities are increasingly personal. A particular person is known by name, among a smaller or wider social audience, and may have a particular reputation. Widely known reputations are rare, confined to particular athletic stars, actors, other famous or notorious individuals: the judge hearing the O.J. Simpson trial, not judges in general. Most individuals are known only inside local networks, and invisible outside of them no matter their fame inside. In many ways this is a hierarchy of fame or attention rather than a hierarchy of honor. In sum, *formal rituals generate categorical identities; informal rituals generate merely personal reputations.*

The second generalization casts light on what kind of situational status may exist even in the absence of recognized status group rituals and boundaries. Regardless of how formal or informal the ritual is, rituals also vary in intensity. Some rituals are more successful than others in creating collective experience: some are flat, perfunctory, mere going through the forms; others build up shared emotions (sentimentality, tears, awe, laughter, anger against outsiders or scapegoats), and regenerate feelings of solidarity. Intensity variations are possible at any point on the continuum: a formal ceremony (a wedding, a speech, a ball) can fail or succeed, just as a party can be a bore, a friendly amusement, or a memorable carouse. Here we have a second continuum: situations rank in terms of the attention they generate; situations have higher and lower prestige, depending on how they are enacted. At high levels on the formality or focus continuum, the intensity of the ritual does not matter as much; society is structured by formal inclusions and exclusions at such ritual occasions, and the resulting categorical identities are pervasive and inescapable, so that rituals may be rather boring and still convey strong membership. As we descend toward relatively informal and unfocused rituals, more effort needs to be put into making them emotionally intense, if they are to be experienced as having much effect upon feelings of social position. This may explain why contemporary Americans often are "hot dogs," making noisy attention displays when they are at sports or entertainment events, large parties, and other public occasions.

Thus the second generalization: *to convey an effect, the more informal or improvised rituals are, the more that participants need to be ostentatious, to make blatant appeals to emotion and to visible or highly audible action, if they are to make any impression or reputation.* Those starved for institutionalized ritual status (e.g., black lower class; teenagers and young people generally) tend to seek out means of intense situational dramatization.[6]

The dimension of ritual intensity stratifies people in terms of their personal access. The individual who is at the center of attention in a sociable gathering—the life of the party, the class clown, the ceremonial leader (in Bales's [1950, 1999] small group studies, the expressive leader)—has the highest personal status in that situation, and in networks where his or her reputation circulates through conversation. The intensity of the situation might also be generated by a sense of threatening violence and display of the ritual of challenge. Anderson (1999, 78, 99) notes that "staging areas" in the inner city are densely populated places where youths go to show off, and receive a sense of status just from being there; in such settings, fights are referred to as "showtime." Such courting of risk in order to show off one's character in handling the situation is what Goffman (1967) referred to as "where the action is." Further examples include gambling scenes where a good deal of money is risked; as Goffman (1969) suggests, a similar structure may account for the appeal of highly respectable, even elite forms of economic action, such as manipulating financial markets. An abstract status hierarchy such as occupational prestige ranking is far indeed from the distribution of experiences that make up micro-situational status. A geeky intellectual physicist or somber surgeon may rank high in the abstract, but would likely cut a poor figure at a youth party. Again we see the need for a new kind of survey of the distribution of intensity, focus, and membership in situations.

Intense sociable rituals may exist here and there across the landscape, but are invisible to most people. This clearly differs from a society historically in which the community knew who was fighting the duel, who was the belle of the ball or the Debutante of the Season; that is, a situation in which personal reputations were anchored within an institutionalized status group structure. Today personal reputations are broadcast only to the extent that rituals are visible within contemporary society, and only inside those specific networks where the rituals take place. Such enclosed networks or "status goldfish bowls" exist today mainly among children. Small children in day care centers fall into cliques: little groups of bullies and their scapegoats, popular play leaders and their followers, fearful or self-sufficient isolates (Montagner et al. 1988). High schools probably have the most visible and highly structured cliques—preppies, jocks, religious evangelicals, druggies, rebels, nerds (formerly known as grinds)—evidence on this goes back for decades (e.g., Coleman 1961, Stinchcombe 1964); contemporary high schools have more complex clique structures, mainly by addition of religious and intellectual / artistic counterculture cliques (Milner 2004). If there is a trend, it is in the direction of more overt conflict among different status groups, as manifested in school violence by outcast or status subordinates against dominant cliques.

Schools are one of the few arenas in which quasi-status-groups can be formed, with institutionalized lifestyle differences, social honor or dishonor, and categorical identities going beyond personal reputation. These are quasi-status-groups insofar as membership in them is not permanent, but they are real in their social effects during the years that they shape youths' lives. The local structure of youth groups is formed against the backdrop of a larger categorical exclusion. Youth are one of the few groups in modern society who are singled out for subjection to special legal disabilities and restrictions, in ways similar to those of legally defined medieval estates: youths are excluded from ritual forms of leisure consumption, such as drinking or smoking; they are the only group that is divided off by an officially enforced taboo on sex with nongroup members. The world is segregated into places where youths cannot go; significantly, these are places where sociability rituals occur (places of carousing such as bars and parties), or places of entertainment where the most intense forms of sociable excitement—sexual activity—is depicted; the effect is to dramatize a hierarchy of ritual intensity reserved for adults. The official adult world, as enunciated by politicians on formal public occasions, rationalizes these exclusions as protecting youth from evils, an attitude that further sharpens the moral divide between the subjective worlds of adults in their official mode and of youths' experience. The real-life situational effect is that young people, whether they are below a limit (at one time 18 years old, now generally raised to 21) or are somewhat older, routinely experience demands to prove their age, both from petty officials and from ticket-takers, ushers, and shop clerks who are transformed into officials who can demand subservience and exercise exclusion. Youth are thus the only contemporary group that is officially subjected to petty humiliations because of their categorical status, in this respect resembling black people who are unofficially subjected to similar tests; both groups are assumed dishonorable until proven otherwise. This is a reason why youth culture is sympathetic to black culture, and emulates especially its most rebellious elements.

The pervasive everyday enactment of group barriers supports a youth counterculture. Youth styles of demeanor are shaped directly in opposition to adult styles: wearing hats backward because the normal style is forward; wearing baggy pants, torn clothes because these are counter-stylish (documented by Anderson 1999, 112). The counterculture starts at the border with adult culture and proceeds in the opposite direction; a status hierarchy develops inside the youth community building further and further away from adult respectability. Over the years there has been escalation in the amount, size, and location of body piercing, of tatoos and body branding. Many of these practices resemble those used in a hierarchy of religious status among Indian *fakirs*, holy outcasts demonstrating their religious charisma by the extremes to which they are willing to demonstrate their distance from ordinary life. There are a variety of cultural styles and clique structures within the youth quasi-status-group; the more extreme forms of counter-adult culture occupy one kind of niche, while others (athletes, preps, grinds, evangelicals) make compromises with or even positive commitments to the respectable adult world they expect to join. Nevertheless, the anti-adult counterculture in one degree or another appears to be the most pervasive; we may expect that every escalation of adult moral crusades that ritually demean youth will be matched by a corresponding degree of polarization in the youth counterculture.

I have argued that youth counterculture is anchored in the publically enacted, legally enforced exclusions practiced against teenagers that give the group a stigmatized corporate identity. Yet the youth counterculture is widespread among young adults as well. This occurs because of several structural continuities: young people as a whole are poor in autonomous economic resources; when they hold jobs, these are typically at the most menial service level; the inflation of educational credentials has expanded the length of time they stay in school and thus occupy a status that is outside adult occupational ranks. In addition, the mass media industries take the youth culture as their target audience, since they are the most active consumers of entertainment; hence youth culture with its showy alienation is also among the most recognizable set of emblems in the otherwise privatized public consciousness. And there is one economic elite, entertainment celebrities, who tend to display the counterculture symbols of their fans; although celebrities are outside the main circuits of economic power, nevertheless they are the most visible successful people in the class structure. Counterculture styles are thus reinforced not just as signs of alienation on the part of the status oppressed, but as positive status emblems both within the youth community itself and in the world of free-floating public reputation. If contemporary society mostly lacks visible status group boundaries, the one quasi-status-group boundary that officially exists, youth vs. adult, provides publicly recognizable markers of status hierarchy throughout everyday life that reverse the solid but invisible structures of class and power.

Categorical Deference and Situational Deference

On the most fine-grained micro-situational level, we come to deference behavior—the fleeting gestures by which one individual defers to another. In tightly organized societies historically, everyday life was filled with blatant gestures of deference—bowing low, deferential forms of address ("My Lord," "My Lady," "If you please, Mistress,"), deferential tones of voice (described in Chesterfield 1774/1992; for Japanese examples, see Ikegami 1995). All these are examples of asymmetrical rituals. Goffman (1967), on the other hand, describes most rituals in mid-twentieth century as mutual or symmetrical: showing polite recognition of others by handshakes, greetings and small talk, hat-raising, door-holding. Individuals reciprocated, thereby showing their status equality; but Goffman also indicated that being included in a little circle of reciprocity was itself a display of a status order, since higher status persons were those who practiced the most elaborate manners, and excluded those who could not properly perform mutual deference ceremonies.

It would be useful to have a survey of how much and what kind of deference is shown across situations in contemporary societey. Deference behavior can be mapped onto our typology of situations. Ignore for a moment how much deference is displayed at work (better to consider this later as a form of organizational power) and the kind of deference built into formally scripted ceremonies.[7] Most interesting would be a survey of deference in relatively unstructured sociable situations, and in unfocused publics.

Contemporary people, I suggest, receive relatively little categorical deference. Most deference is by personal reputation and that depends on being in the presence of the network where one is personally known. A famous sociologist will get some deference (mainly in terms of speaking rights in conversation) at sociology meetings, and at parties with other sociologists, but not outside this sphere; most such professionals get what deference they experience inside gatherings of a subspecialty. Our survey would want to discover how many specialized networks exist that pay attention to one another enough to give honor or dishonor within their ranks. Such deference distributions are found not only in occupational communities but in various kinds of voluntary associations and interest networks, connoisseurs, arenas of display, and competition. There are a huge number of voluntary associations in the United States, and each likely contains an internal status hierarchy. Even though most of these hierarchies are oblivious to one another, a considerable proportion of Americans, perhaps as much as half the population of adults, may experience some small parts of their lives in little realms where they are given mild temporary reputational deference.

Outside such specialized organizations and networks, transituational deference is largely confined to celebrities. Such figures are manufactured by the mass media, notably those in the entertainment business, which derives its income largely from promoting and selling "star" identities; news media also create famous identities (politicians, criminals, and subjects of human interest stories) and sell information about them. The mass media are the only place where there is a recurrent focus of attention shared by anything close to a majority of the society; this not only helps build up an intensity of significance around those characters, but makes it easier for news and entertainment organizations to fill their regularly scheduled quota of offerings to the public. (In the news world this is called "milking a story," especially in "dead" times when no "breaking news" is happening.) The reputational hierarchy is exceedingly steep; outside the elite is a vast majority of anonymous persons, that is to say, anonymous outside of their own occupational or acquaintance circles.

Although celebrities get most of what deference there is in contemporary society, they receive much less deference than upper-class dominants in previous history. People rarely bow or give way before them; instead they try to get close to them to touch them, to get some token from them (photo, clothes, autograph); they treat them less like aristocracy than like a totemic animal in a tribal religion. The analogy is fitting since totemism is the religion of internally egalitarian groups, and the modern public is egalitarian. Touching a celebrity and carrying away a bit of him or her fits Durkheim's description of how people behave in the presence of sacred objects, drawn in magnetically to share in a portion of collective *mana*. The celebrity is one of the few focal points in the modern attention space through which collective emotional energy can be revved up to a high level. In a Durkheimian interpretation, worship of a celebrity is the group worshiping itself—worshiping its capacity to get excited and drawn out of one's mundane life into some-thing transcendent. Note, too, that publicity and attention to celebrities can just as well be negative as positive; scandals about celebrities are extremely popular (need I mention the O. J. Simpson trial?)[8] These, too, are forms of highly focused attention; scandalous emotions are espe-cially effective in building up shared intensity. Celebrity deference is of a peculiar kind, less hierarchical than participatory.[9]

In a Durkheimian sense, the celebrities elevated by mass media at-tention are the only human beings today who can serve as sacred ob-jects, emblems of the collective consciousness of any considerable part of society. It is no wonder, then, that ordinary individuals attempt to appropriate for themselves a portion of this *mana* or emblematic force, through the sympathetic magic of wearing clothing similar to that worn by celebrities or bearing their identifying marks. Tribal people painted the totems of their clan upon their bodies (Lévi-Strauss 1958/ 1963); contemporary people, especially those without eminence in oc-cupations that give them at least a specialized sphere of categorical identity, wear jackets bearing the number and name of athletic heroes, and t-shirts printed with the pictures of entertainment stars. In a social structure that sustains no visible status groups, much less clan identi-ties, only the media stars serve as emblems expressing participation in the collective energy of a focused group.

The nearest approach to deference in the classical sense, displaying overt gestures of dominance and subordination, respect and disre-spect, is found in the black inner city. Elijah Anderson (1999) describes a situation in which the majority of black people are trying to pursue lives according to normal standards of the larger society: jobs, educa-tional attainment, family and church life. But due to poverty, discrimi-nation, and, above all, lack of police protection in the inner city, a "code of the street" prevails in which each individual (and especially each young male) tries to display physical toughness, to convey that it is dangerous to bother him. There is a good deal of demanding deference from others; fights often break out because of small signals such as looking at a man for a long fraction of a second, interpreted as hostile "staring," and locking eyes can lead to a killing (Anderson 1999, 41, 127). Uncivil behavior—blaring loud music, leaving one's car parked in the middle of the street—is generally ignored or accepted by most residents to avoid confrontations. Although two codes or ritual orders operate—the ostentatious toughness of the "code of the street," and the normal code of Goffmanian behavior in the surrounding society—the former dominates situationally in the black ghetto.

In the mainstream white community, the status order is invisible, or visible only within specialized networks; occupation and wealth does not get deference, nor form visible status groups broadcasting categorical identities. Public interaction is an equality without much solidarity, an enactment of personal distance mitigated by a tinge of mutual politeness and shared casualness. Goffman (1963) calls it the order of civil disattention. As Goffman notes, this is not merely a matter of sheer indifference, since one needs to monitor others at a distance to avoid contact with them when they are close, ranging from little maneuverings of sidewalk traffic to avoid physical collision, to averting eyes and controlling micro-gestures in order not to intrude into the privacy of their personal space. In contrast, the status order of the black street code is openly ostentatious and often hostile. It broadcasts a blatant situational hierarchy of the tough and the dominated; here egalitarian encounters are typically a hostile egalitarianism, tested in violent conflict that can be reopened at any time. Dominant individuals demand control of the street space; others monitor them warily. Here the tacit monitoring of civil disattention is ratcheted upward into a much more focused and tense public situation. It is the dominated who display civil disattention, while the dominators demand it.[10]

The street code not only negates normal criteria of middle-class achievement and respectability, it is a full-fledged counterculture. Middle-class demeanor standards are taken as signs of timidity; in addition, display of any marks of conventional achievement (school, a disciplined work style, a licit job) are taken as status claims and thus implied insults to those who lack them. For this reason, Anderson argues, many "decent" or "square" black residents adopt the outward signs of the oppositional culture—wearing gang-style clothes and emblems, adopting the conversational style of the street dominants, playing the oppositional music, the scornful or angry sounds of rap. The code of the street becomes the publicly dominant culture: in part because straight youth adopt it as a protective front against the danger of violence; in part because the oppositional culture has situational prestige. The street code is a set of rituals that generate the most emotional intensity and dominate the focus of attention; the bland politeness and mild accomodativeness of normal Goffmanian social manners pales before it, and is unable to compete with it in the attention space.

This helps explain why the oppositional culture of the black lower class, rooted in violence, has been adopted as a prestigeful demeanor style among groups whose life situation involves very little violent threat: middle-class white youth and certain stars of the entertainment media, practitioners of the "reverse snobbery" noted at the beginning of this paper. In detail, however, white counterculture style is not black street style. Black hoodlums favor expensive athletic clothes, flashy cars, sexy women displaying all the conventional erotic signs; white counterculturers display torn clothes, body piercing, unshavenness, grubbiness, sexuality dramatized as kinky and grungy; black street toughs are not being casual, whereas white counterculture takes normal casualness to an extreme. The "code of the street" arises where dominance through violent threat is situationally projected, whereas middle-class youth and entertainment celebrities are presenting a purely symbolic rebellion, not a claim to physically dominate others.

What are the devices, the situational weapons by which the oppositional culture dominates interactions? In the black street situation, these are sheer coercive power and its threat: a display of muscles, as well as a demeanor indicating willingness to use weapons, and to fight at the slightest question of honor. Sexiness and good looks are prestigeful, especially for women; these are keys to the sexual action scene, a focus of excitement and a contest to score sexual conquests and to display one's connections with the dominants of the street. Vocal prowess, especially in insults and repartée, is another situational weapon; it goes along with the use of prepackaged sounds of anger and scorn in rap music, and of loud noise generally through technological amplification to dominate the auditory attention space.

The black street situation looks like the extreme case of episodic situational resources prevailing over resources drawn from macro-structural connections. Nonimmediate connections are not entirely cut off, since street encounters are influenced by transituational factors such as a person's reputation for ready violence or a past record of backing down; such (positive or negative) transituational resources operate mainly in encounters where community members know one another personally or through gossip networks. The street encounter is also influenced by ties to kin or other allies, and by some local categorical status group markers such as gang emblems. These street encounters are near one end of the continuum, but they are not historically unique. The same "virtues" come to the fore—fighting prowess, physical strength, a ritualistic style of looking for challenges and risking one's life over honor and precedence, and a verbal culture of boasting and insults—in a number of other situations: among the best documented are the Homeric Greeks, and Viking Scandinavia at the period of the Norse sagas. All these are situations in which the state is very weak or nonexistent; power is in the hands of ad hoc bands of warriors, without even much continuity by kinship.[11]

Even here, it would be simplistic to conclude that sheer violence is the basis of deference. It is always more effective to threaten than to fight, and coalitions are important even for the strongest. Accordingly, interaction in routinely threatening situations takes the form of rituals of intimidation and displays of honor. There is some suggestion in Anderson's data that even the toughest "criminal element" does not merely prey on the weakest in the community; to build a reputation as tough, it is necessary to challenge someone else who is tough. Fights among Homeric heroes express the same structure, even though the literary picture is no doubt idealized. Thus even violence passes through the filter of ritualization if it is to be an effective device for situational domination.

In mainstream American society, public encounters are mildly accommodative; ghetto street styles are largely confrontational on the part of the situational dominants, and confrontation-avoiding, on the part of those who are situationally subordinated. Anderson (1999, 20) notes that black youths sometimes use the street code situationally to intimidate whites, venturing onto middle-class turf to do so. Mainstream white interactional style is based on background conditions in the macro-structure, the existence of a strong state and deep state penetration into everyday life by police, educational, and other regulatory agencies. White middle-class persons are used to long-distance organizational networks, operating in an impersonal style of bureaucratic regulation, controlling much of the conditions under which people encounter one another. Violence is to a considerable degree monopolized by state agents; it is not much of a factor in most daily encounters. When whites encounter the black street style, they are made to feel extremely uncomfortable—almost as in a Garfinkelian breaching experiment.

Yet it is not easy for whites to treat the black street code as simply criminal, since it operates with highly stylized rituals that tend to mask overt threats. In addition, since the public successes of the civil rights movement of the 1960s, the official media of white society, and especially the cultural media of education and entertainment, has made a point of emphasizing racial equality and opposition to categorical discrimination. This egalitarianism of official pronouncements and in the ceremonial statements of the law courts, is reinforced by the normal style of middle-class public encounters, egalitarian casualness, including its general tendency to countenance any demeanor styles and behavior as long as they keep their ritual distance. As Goffman (1967) commented, our ritualism lets each individual walk through everyday life with a shell of privacy and forbearance, without strong ties of ritual membership, but also with a security from being intruded upon. People in this ritual style are unable to deal with a confrontational street style, with its blatant inequality of the situationally strong over the situationally weak. Middle-class whites following the Goffmanian code defer to confrontational blacks more than "decent" ghetto residents do, since the latter adopt the street code for situational protection. Encounters with whites thus tend to reinforce the performers of black street codes in their feelings of contempt for white social order (Anderson 1999); at the same time, the discomfort of whites, even unexpressed, helps reinforce an interactional dividing line that maintains the racial barrier.

Categorical identities have largely disappeared, replaced by pure local personal reputations in networks where one is known, and by anonymity outside. But if categorical identities are upheld by ritual barriers in interaction, black / white ritual standoffs between the street code and the Goffmanian public code are one of the few remaining bases for categorical identities.

D-Power and E-Power

Power is another conventionally reified concept. The Weberian definition, imposing one's will against opposition, is not yet sufficiently micro-translated. We may distinguish between the power to make other people give way in the immediate situation, and the power to make results happen. There is an old dispute about whether the latter necessarily involves the former; Parsons (1969) argued that power is not primarily zero-sum (I win, you yield) but a matter of social efficacy in which the entire collectivity accomplishes something it did not have before. Let us call the first D-power (deference-power or order-giving power), and the latter E-power (efficacy-power). The latter sometimes exists in micro-situations, but only if the result wanted can be carried out right before the order-giver's eyes.[12] Here D-power and E-power would coincide empirically. But in many situations D-power is formal or ritualistic: one person gives orders, in extreme cases with an imperious tone and demeanor, while the other acquiesces verbally and in bodily posture; but it remains a question as to whether the orders are actually carried out, and even if they are, whether the result will be what the order-giver wanted. D-power is always socially significant, even if it is completely severed from E-power; it is consequential for meaningful social experience, shaping the "culture" of personal relations. D-power is enacted in the power rituals described in chapter 3. A society in which there is much inequality in D-power will be one in which there are sharp differences in social identities, and a good deal of smouldering resentment and suppressed conflict (for evidence, see Collins 1975, chapters 2 and 6). Concentration of E-power may well have no such effects: this is a hypothesis, awaiting empirical evidence. It is congruent with the historical trend of the late twentieth century: the disappearance of D-power, reinforced by lack of class-categorical identities, gives a superficial sense of egalitarianism.

Figure 7.3 D-power in action: serving refreshments to upper-class cricket players (England, 1920s).

E-power is typically transituational or long-distance; if it is real it must involve events that happen because orders and intentions are transmitted through a social network. E-power is generally macro, involving actions of large numbers of people and situations. Setting a large organization in motion is a mild form of E-power; if the organization achieves an intended result there is even more E-power; further along the continuum, the highest kind of E-power is to change an entire social structure, so that the patterns in which networks link people are permanently changed for the future.

There have rarely been efforts to measure the distribution of power along either dimension. Blau (1977) suggested measuring power by organizational span of control: an individual is powerful to the extent that she or he gives orders to a number of subordinates who in turn have a number of subordinates, and so on until the total chain of command is quantified. But such a measure remains confused by too glib a summary of what command means. If we could measure by microsituational sampling the chain of command in organizations, we would find variations in how much D-power is being enacted in different situations of interaction among superiors and subordinates. Probably what Blau has in mind is E-power, assuming that the orders actually get carried out, and that the chain of command is a way in which the will of a person "higher up" is carried out by persons "lower down."

But this is just what needs investigation. There are many ways in which slippage can occur. The organizational literature has shown workers controlling their own work pace, resisting controls by their immediate (and thus by more remote) superiors (Burawoy 1979; Willis 1977; Etzioni 1975); they give token D-power by deferring to their supervisors when they are present, but return to their own way of doing things when the supervisors are not present (i.e., they use the appearance of D-power compliance as a front to cover up their E-power insubordination). The divergence between D-power and E-power is particularly sharp in the case of what Marcia Marx (1993) calls the "shadow hierarchy" of women administrative assistants who defer to (usually male) line authority but wield most of the invisible power to make things happen in a bureaucratic organization, or impede them from happening. There is a considerable literature analyzing how much actual control can be exercized in terms of how visible the work operations are, how standardized and countable the work output, and how much uncertainty there is in what is expected to happen (for summaries, see Collins 1988, chapter 13; Etzioni 1975). Managers may resort to indirect controls (shaping the physical environment, manipulating communications and information) to constrain the alternatives available to persons down the chain of command. Such shifts to indirect controls are declines in D-power, which managers hopefully trade for E-power. But even here E-power remains ambiguous or multi-dimensional; some organizations may be able to constrain how employees do their jobs but are unable to make the organization itself profitable or to outcompete its rivals. Generals have a lot of D-power (click heels; salute; yes sir!), and a military chain of command can be calculated fairly easily in terms of how much accumulated heel-clicking there is between one officer's realm of D-power and another's. But other contingencies intervene, which slow up how quickly and to what extent the army will actually do what the general orders; and yet further contingencies determine whether it will actually win the battle.

The organizational literature is full of suggestions concerning how the shapes of organizational control have changed in various historical periods and in relation to various physical and economic environments and technologies (Chandler 1962, 1977). There has been enormous growth in size and centralization of organizations, from the military revolution and state penetration of the 1500s onward, with similar transformation of capitalist enterprises in the 1800s and early 1900s (Mann 1993). These imply an increasing concentration of D-power, and to some extent E-power, in the micro-encounters of top officials during that historical period. For the twentieth century, organizational analysts have generally told stories of the dispersion of control: at the top, by the dilution of managers' control by stock ownership and thus by financial coalitions; in the middle, by increasing complexity and uncertainty of tasks and hence tacit E-power or at least subversion-power (a sort of negative E-power) among staff; in the lower ranks, challenges by the countervailing organization of labor unions (a rising and falling pattern of challenge over the century) and by informal work groups, and, more recently, by a reversal in which organizations use electronic monitoring to control the details of workers' actions (Fligstein 1990; Leidner 1993). There have been waves of mergers and takeovers; but also counter-waves of divisionalization, multi-profit center structurings, franchising and out-sourcing; and recent trends toward loose networks of firms trading expertise and personnel in forms that are "neither market nor hierarchy" (Powell 1989). If D-power and E-power were constant in all forms of organization, we could add up the shifting numbers of direct and indirect levels of control through chains of command, and trace the rising-and-falling patterns of power concentration. But D-power and E-power are surely not constant. That does not mean that some such measurement could not be attempted, but it would have to be multi-dimensional and it would show a very mixed historical pattern.

Overall it appears D-power has become milder in character where it does occur; and its occurences have become fragmented into specialized enclaves where yes sir! micro-obedience is enacted. E-power is another story; and there are some very big hierarchies, or ones located where chains of financial resources and other forms of influence ripple far and wide throughout social networks, such that what a few individuals do may have some effects upon the life experiences of millions. The ongoing shakeouts and mergers at the turn of the twenty-first century in the world communications industries, creating mega-businesses in publishing, television, satellites, telecommunications, cable transmission, and films, suggest one example of increasingly concentrated E-power. Yet it is not clear the E-power of such big organizations / networks is increasing, above the level, for instance, of the big capitalist oligopolies at the turn of the twentieth century. Big organizations are often big illusions, as far as control of their own destinies, or even their own behavior, is concerned. The so-called totalitarian dictatorships before mid-century had structures on paper that looked completely centralized; yet communist organizations had enormous difficulties in translating top policy into local behavior (Kornai 1992). The resort to terroristic methods did not increase E-power over the system, but can be seen largely as an attempt to extend D-power at greater distance from the center.

It would be premature to draw an empirical conclusion from these theoretical considerations. We will not know what is happening to the concentration of power, even as mega-mergers take place in the most important industries of today, until we attempt situational sampling of D-power in such organizations, and to model various kinds of E-power (the extent to which orders are actually transmitted, put into action, and have results). Whether the heirs of Rupert Murdock and the like will be future dictators of an Orwellian universe; or whether E-power will remain at the level of unintended consequences and Perrow's (1984) "normal accidents"; or whether organizational members will be increasingly free of constraints, or subject to covert manipulation: these are matters still to be worked out by investigating the actual dimensions of micro-situational power.

There is an additional, ironic twist to the pattern of E-power concentration. Francis Bacon, reflecting on his experience as a life-long civil servant and organizational politician in the consolidating Elizabethan state, a career that culminated in a stint as chief minister, declared that power itself is a trap for those who wield it:

> Men in great place are thrice servants: servants of the sovereign or state, servants of fame, and servants of business. So as they have no freedom, neither in their persons, nor in their actions, nor in their times. It is a strange desire to seek power and to lose liberty, or to seek power over others and to lose power over a man's self. (1625/1965, 70)

Bacon did not distinguish between the two kinds of power. Like most people, he probably thought getting efficacy power and deference power were the same thing. But his ironic lesson applies especially to those seeking to wield E-power: they are enmeshed in the communications center of the organization that they attempt to dominate, and they cannot step away from the network without losing control. As D-power has declined, the seeking of E-power has probably increased not just at the top but through the spread-out middle ranks and horizontal alliance-structures of contemporary organizational networks. We have the term "workaholic" for people caught up in such positions. E-power is largely an illusion, but it is an addiction as well.

Historical Change in Situational Stratification

The prevailing hierarchical image of stratification as a fixed structure in which micro is tacitly assumed to mirror macro is a historical heritage. Bourdieu's mechanistic cycle of cultural capital permeating individual habitus and reproducing the field of economic power bypasses situational interaction; not surprisingly, it is an image promoted by a survey researcher collecting data on individuals and arraying it in an abstact hierarchical space (this is especially clear in Bourdieu 1984, 128–29, 261–63) in figures laid out along the dimensions of coefficients of correspondence, i.e., the equivalent of factors in factor analysis). The image is an old-fashioned one. Like most of our images of stratification, it dates back to the time of Marx, when micro-situational reality was much more tightly linked to the distribution of power and property. In Weberian terms, it was a historical period in which classes were organized as status groups, and belonging to a class was a categorical identity, indeed the most prominent social identity. My argument is not simply that historically macro-structures once dominated, and that now the micro-situational order has come loose from the macro-order. The macro-structure, in any historical period, is always composed of micro-situations. What I am saying is that the micro-situations today are stratified by quite different conditions than existed in the early twentieth century or earlier.

The key historical difference is that societies were formerly organized around patrimonial households. This Weberian term refers to a structure in which the main political and economic unit is the family dwelling, swelled out by servants, guards, retainers, apprentices, and guests. Economic production takes place in the household or on property controlled by it. Political and military relations are alliances among households, with dominance going to the biggest coalitions amassing the most troops. The upper class consisted of the heads of the biggest households. Under this structure, it was difficult to separate economic class, political power, and status group membership. The largest households generally held the most property, mustered the most force and controlled the most political dependencies, and a similar proportionality would hold for smaller households. Often these distinctions were formulated in legal categories such as aristocracy and commoner, and sometimes in subcategories such as levels of nobility. The names of these status group categories were common parlance; Marx was among the first to claim that economic class was the underlying dimension, but class stood out in his mind precisely because the organization of everyday life centered around property-owning, power-wielding, honor-receiving household dominants.

Status group borders were constantly reaffirmed and publicized in everyday life. The individual was always being reminded of which household one belonged to and what kind of ranking that household had, within and without. Status group membership was inescapable, since there was virtually no place for persons who did not belong to a known household or who were not under its economic control and political protection; such persons were dishonored outcasts, virtually nonpersons. Within the household, interactions were inegalitarian; one repeatedly gave or took orders, received or gave deference, depending upon how one ranked as a servant, retainer, or relative of the household heads. Individuals could move through the stratification hierarchy, but only by moving from one household to another, or by rising higher within the internal structure of one's household, by coming into closer relations of trust and dependency with the household head. Even relatively high-ranking persons usually had some situations in which they had to demonstrate their loyalty and subordination to some higher-ranking person.[13] High-ranking persons were surrounded by attendants, and one's rank was generally represented by the size of one's entourage.[14] This meant that high-ranking persons (and those who attended on them) were constantly in a ceremonial situation (this is vividly documented in regard to Louis XIV; see Lewis 1957; Elias 1983); groups were always assembled and focused on persons of rank, giving a high density of ritual interaction. The result was a high degree of social reality, indeed, reification, of the social categories focused upon, and thus a high degree of consciousness of social rank and one's closeness to persons of higher rank. In sum, everyday interaction was highly ritualized; and the rituals were largely asymmetrical, giving deference to some persons over others.

The character of everyday social interaction has changed above all due to the shrinking and replacement of the patrimonial household. This has happened gradually over the past several centuries, driven by several macro-level developments. The growth of the centralized state removed military power from households; the expansion of government bureaucracy for extracting revenue and regulating society created a new type of organizational space, bureaus in which individuals interacted for specialized purposes and limited times. Categorical identities were replaced by the inscription of individual citizens in government records for purposes of taxation, social insurance, education, military conscription, and voting rights. Bureaucracy spread into the economic realm as work became organized in places separated from the household.

The modern organization of life into private places, work places, and public places in between them is a historically recent development. This new social ecology of kinds of interactions has drastically changed the ritual density of everyday encounters and the categorical identity schemes that go with it. The realm of consumption is now separated from the places where production takes place and where politically and economically based power relations are enacted. Consumption now takes place in private, or at least outside of situations where it is marked by socially visible rank. The center of gravity of daily life switches to the realm of consumption. This is reinforced by the growth of consumer industries, including entertainment and the hardware that delivers it, into the largest and most visible part of the economy (Ritzer 1999). A side-result has been to increase the salaries as well as the pervasiveness of entertainment stars; by contrast, in a patrimonial society, entertainers were merely servants, dependent upon patronage of the big households. Entertainment stars are the contemporary sacred objects, because they are the only widely visible points of attention in this private sphere, where relationships are casual (which is to say, deritualized) and free of work and power relations. One might say entertainment stars who express a casual, anti-formal style are appropriate symbols to represent the character of the modern consumption experience.[15]

Individuals now have a choice as to which situations they invest their emotional commitment in. They can withdraw attention from their work situations to concentrate on their private lives of consumption. This is characteristic especially of workers in subordinate positions; Halle (1984) indicates that workers identify themselves as working class only while they are on the job, whereas at home they are more likely to identify themselves as part of a pervasive midde class. Persons in high-ranking professional and managerial jobs have an incentive to identify more strongly with their work positions, but when they leave work they too enter the anonymous world of consumption.

The realm of individual privacy has increased, in part because of the separation of a private realm of consumption; in part because the increase in level of wealth has allowed the household itself to be divided into separate spaces. Even aristocrats' palaces generally lacked special rooms for sleeping, for washing, or toilets; even very personal physical activities happened in the presence of servants and followers. Among the wealthy, private bedroom and dressing chambers began to appear in the 1700s and spread in the 1800s; household architecture now added corridors so that it was possible to enter a room without passing through other rooms and disturbing their inhabitants (Girouard 1978). In the mid-twentieth century this kind of dwelling space, including bathrooms, became considered normal for everyone. These changes in the material settings of daily life made possible Goffmanian backstages as well as frontstages for the vast majority of people. This is one reason why individual reputations have become more important than categorical identities.

Habermas's (1984) phrase, "the colonization of the life world," conveys an inaccurate picture of the main trend of modern history. Habermas's phrase is congruent with the trend of state penetration, the expanding scope of obligations of individuals in direct relation to the bureaucratic agencies of the state, which went along with breaking through the barriers surrounding the patrimonial household. But Habermas's argument does not take account of the actual patterning of social situations. The patrimonial household enacted economic and political relations in a concrete and often oppressive manner throughout daily experience. State penetration has displaced and broken up the patrimonial structures, but the actual experience of dealing with government agencies usually takes place in little fragments, not as continuous pressure; and contact is enacted in impersonal bureaucratic relationships, with little of the ritualism that reifies social categories or the deference that generates pride and shame. Contemporary social structure generates a life experience in which most individuals have at least intermittent, and sometimes quite extensive, situational distance from macro-structured relationships.

Luhmann (1984/1995) has described the structural change as a shift from society organized by stratification to one organized by functional specializations. This is congruent with the shift brought about by the decline of the patrimonial household and the breaking apart of everyday interaction from the pervasive experience of property and political / military power. But stratification has not disappeared in every respect; the macro-distribution of economic inequality is becoming stronger than ever. And on the micro-level, situational power still exists, not only inside governmental and economic organizations but even in the public sphere. The most common everyday experiences of this kind are encounters with petty bureaucratic functionaries such as security guards, flight attendants, ticket-takers, and police patrols. These are rather limited situational power-wielders, who have more capacity to impede and delay people than positively to control much of their behavior; petty functionaries hold a kind of very local, negative E-power, but little D-power as they are given little respect or deference. Such situations contrast with the earlier historical experience: in patrimonial households, even armed guards were extremely rank-conscious, and would rarely if ever take it upon themselves to impede a social superior. In the transitional period as well, when patrimonial households were being displaced but class-based status identities were still widely recognized categories, even police acted as if they were in the lower status group, and gave polite deference to persons identified as "gentry." The police officer was received "below stairs" with the other servants, not "above stairs." The police and other specialized bureaucratic functionaries have thus risen in situational power as they no longer are under any pressure to defer to categorical identities.

An Imagery for Contemporary Interaction

In place of a hierarchical image, we need a horizontal-spatial imagery of today's situational experiences. Contemporary life is something like being in an ancient or medieval picaresque story. These were adventure stories, sagas of what happens once an individual is off on his own, venturing outside the patrimonial households where he has a place in the social order. When Odysseus or the Argonauts leave home, or the knights in Malory or Spenser set out from their castles, they are in a realm where their economic and political positions do little or nothing for them. In their most extreme adventures, they venture outside the status order, where they have no categorical identities among the monsters or alien beings that they encounter; at best, a personal reputation of their prowess in battle or cunning may have circulated to some of those whom they visit.

The daily experience of modern people has much of the same quality, although now it applies to women as well as to the men who alone were protagonists of old picaresques. We have our home bases, networks within which we are personally known, including some occupational or skill-practicing communities where people will give some deference to those who are high-ranking. But these are highly specific, localized regions, and what we get there does not carry over into the majority of our social contacts. The macro-ties of our networks are no longer relevant; we are voyaging in a vast realm of situations in which there is very little that will produce solidarity with other people whom one encounters, or deference or power, except what one can carry with oneself in the most palpable way. People who are particularly strong and athletic, or threatening, or good-looking and sexy, or quick-spoken, witty, or just plain loud,[16] can attract attention, and perhaps dominate a momentary situation. People who are particularly lacking in these qualities can be situationally dominated. It is structurally the same as whether Odysseus will outwit the cyclops, or Jason will succeed in capturing the golden fleece because the daughter of the king falls in love with him. This is not to say that background resources of social class might not help one's situational maneuvering. But resources must be translated into whatever makes an immediate situational impression. Carrying a great deal of money can get you service (but not necessarily much politeness) at an expensive restaurant, but it can also get you robbed; being an important person in some profession, or a powerful person in some organization, will get you nothing (except possibly contempt) if you are voyaging in some other part of the social landscape. James Joyce fleshed out the analogy in depicting a modern-day Ulysses traveling in and out of urban networks of 1904

Figure 7.4 Situational dominance by energy and sexuality: impromptu dancers during a counterculture gathering (1960s).

Dublin, weaving among little pockets of reputation, solidarity, and hostilty. Joyce's description pertains too much to the transitional period, depicting a small city where reputational networks were still fairly widespread. If we shrink those networks to little family and occupational enclaves, and expand the overarching mass media of entertainment with their pseudo-familiar reputations of manufactured star images, we arrive at our contemporary world.

Perhaps a better image would be a highway, especially a high-speed interstate freeway. Here there is formal equality; all cars are equal, and all are subject to the same laws, and situationally tend to adhere to a very loose code of civility (not crowding other cars or cutting them off). As in Goffman's (1971) model of human foot traffic, drivers monitor each other mainly to keep their distance; eye contact, even when it is possible (at stop lights, and when cars are in parallel lanes), is generally avoided, and gestures of any kind are very rare. Civil inattention is the prevailing custom.

The situational equality of a highway is generally an equality of motivated indifference, not of solidarity or hostility. The one clear exception are police cars, to which everyone defers, and which demand deference in the form of signals with flashing lights or sirens, and which break the rules that they enforce on others (speeding, crossing the median, etc.). By a simple behavioral criterion, who gets out of the way for which vehicles, police cars are the kings of the road. But there is also some purely situational dominance. This may be mildly correlated with sheer physical property: an expensive, fast car lords it over ordinary cars by passing them; overt deference is displayed as a car captures the dominant trajectory of motion or momentum on the highway, so that other cars get out of the way when they see it coming.[17] Thus transituational resources, mainly money, may translate into the material possessions that enable one to dominate the situational encounters of the highway. Small, old, or badly maintained cars, likely belonging to poor people, hug the side of the road and defer to virtually all bigger and faster cars. Here we see that economic power translates into situational dominance to some extent, whereas political power translates not at all on the highway (unless one is a government official with a police escort, or oneself the police). But dominance is not strictly a matter of economic class: truck drivers sometimes exercise situational dominance, especially on relatively unpoliced rural roads, using their sheer size to muscle their way into controlling lanes. There is also an emergent, completely situational order of dominance, as with the car who gets to pass other cars and gets others to defer (although sometimes contests occur over who drives in front of whom, struggles over who gets to be the hero of the road). Within a range of cars that have roughly the same speeding power, some are driven by persons who build up the aggressiveness to scare most others off. It may be that some persons (or even categories of persons, like teenagers) may occupy this "road elite" more than others, and may even have the transituational repetitiveness that makes this practice a "personality" trait. In terms of IR chains, they have built up EE in the realm of driving. But there is no clear categorical identity of which drivers are especially dominant or dominated; and it may well be the case that road dominance is episodic and transitory, arising from particular buildup and losses of emotional energy derived from driving within a particular configuration of drivers at a particular time.

Categorical identities, grounded in repetitively enacted social communities with publicly visible rituals, have largely disappeared. What is left are individual reputations, most of which carry little social charisma, little of the *mana* of social emotion that attract desires for contact or the propensity to give deference; and reputations are generally circumscribed to very limited networks compared to the totality of the public sphere. One reason race is a social category so resistant to dissolving into the equalitarian civil inattention of public places is that race is one of the few markers of status group identity that is still visible. Most of the situations have disappeared in which class-based status groups can be enacted, and the situations that are left have withdrawn into privacy, where they no longer give public emblems of membership. Ironically, as black Americans differentiate across the class structure, the fact that class distinctions are not publically recognized contributes to lumping all black people into a single, ritually excluded category. Social mobility gives rewards in material consumption and life conditions, but it no longer gives public deference or status. Black Americans would probably be better off today if there were more class consciousness; class categories could help dissolve the racial category and make this categorical exclusion and discrimination more difficult in the ritual dynamics of everyday life.

The trend of contemporary life, based on the momentum of macroinstitutional patterns, is in the other direction. We are increasingly a world in which power operates only within specific organizations and casts no halo; in which economic class is meaningful largely if one stays within the circuits of exchange that generated the money, with some small micro-situational advantages that come from investing money into material consumption that help dominate face-to-face situations; in which categorical reputations have largely dissolved, and personal reputations circulate only in limited networks, except for the artificially constructed reputations of entertainment stars. Race may be the big exception, because the situational rituals of lower-class black street encounters are so sharply different from the public rituals of the larger society. In a world in which most status-group structures, most enactments of ritual barriers around communities, are invisible, the black street culture is the most visible ritual barrier. The publicity given to it, both negative and positive, in the news and entertainment media, makes it the last vestige of the status-group organization of premodern society, the structural equivalent of a world of patrimonial relationships surviving in the midst of a world of impersonal bureaucracies and privatized networks of personal reputation. This grudging and ambivalent admiration reflects the disquietude we feel living in a world of situational stratification.

Chapter 8

TOBACCO RITUAL AND ANTI-RITUAL:

SUBSTANCE INGESTION AS A HISTORY

OF SOCIAL BOUNDARIES

RITUALS MARK BOUNDARIES of inclusion and exclusion. Such rituals at times are contested, by persons located in various relationships to those boundaries. At times the ritual itself is attacked, frequently by individuals or groups who do not recognize its ritual character; for these people, the staying power of the practice may appear inexplicable, irrational, or pathological. At other times, the boundary rather than the ritual is contested, and there are movements to break through the boundaries and become included on the other side of the ritual. Such rituals, too, can create new social boundaries, social identities and groups, rather than merely being adopted by preexisting groups. This is particularly so of what we may call lifestyle rituals, natural rituals in the middle ground between formal ceremonial and low key unfocused social encounters, represented in figure 7.1. Lifestyle rituals in the realm of leisure sociability have been especially important in the modern era, adding new boundaries to the older dimensions of class, religion, and ethnicity, and often displacing them in the subjective consciousness of modern people with the rituals of situational stratification.

A useful case to study is tobacco ritual. It presents us with a relatively long history, with many forms of use going in and out of fashion among many different kinds of social groups. Along with it, throughout its history, have existed various forms of contestation, both antiritual movements and movements to shift the ritual boundaries. Tobacco and anti-tobacco movements have existed over the past four hundred years—indeed during the whole time since tobacco was introduced into the world beyond the tribal societies where it originated. Tobacco using—smoking, sniffing, or chewing—has made up a set of interaction rituals; and these rituals help to account for the strong attractiveness of tobacco for many of its users, the members of the tobacco community, and for their resistance to sometimes quite severe attempts at social control. The historically shifting appeal of tobacco, including its considerable but not yet terminal decline in recent decades, has been shaped by conditions that have shifted the strength of these social rituals. My aim is to explain how substances ingested into the body are experienced in a variety of ways—either as objects of attachment or of revulsion—depending on the ritual processes in which they take part.[1]

A study of tobacco simply in terms of its ritualism would have been theoretically straightforward in the social science world of the 1920s through the 1950s—although I do not know of any sociologist or anthropologist who attempted it. Since the 1980s a very different frame imposes itself. What seems the natural, indeed, inevitable way to approach the topic is as a health issue; and the perspective on tobacco use is to subsume it under the category of deviance, specifically under the rubric of substance abuse along with drugs and alcohol. The very awkwardness of the term "substance abuse" tells us something of the recent history, as it indicates the search by regulatory agencies and professional activists for a common denominator by which to designate all the forms of prohibited or deviant consumption. The word "substance" is clumsy and as general as "stuff" or "thing," and its dictionary meaning refers to any material constituent of the universe. The aimed-at referent seems to be whatever is ingestable into the human body but ought not to be. Thus one might wonder if food could not be an abusable "substance" under the purview of official agencies of social control. Viewed without irony and as a sociological topic, it is entirely plausible, perhaps even likely, that there will be just such an extension in the future to the ingestion of food as a form of substance abuse subject to both formal and informal movements of control.[2] One such movement, in incipient form at the turn of the twenty-first century, is concerned about standards of body weight and obesity, and with the restriction of so-called "junk food" in schools. This suggests a general sociological perspective on contemporary "substance abuse" movements: the expansive activities of official agencies and professional movements organized around the interpretive categories of health, addiction, and the control of youth; on the informal side, these are movements promoting and contesting lifestyles. As sociologists, we should as always be awake to see that these activities are not just individual lifestyles, but rituals and thus markers of group boundaries. Wherever our sympathies may lie on the side of a particular ritual or anti-ritual movement, our distinctive contribution is to stand above these controversies and to point out their contours.

In this chapter, I will consider first the health and addiction model, with an effort to move beyond its framing in the common-sense categories of contemporary social actors and toward a more sociological vantage point. Although the argument here is couched mainly in terms of tobacco, it has implications for other forms of addiction (drugs, alcohol, and, indeed, food—overeating—and noningestive forms of addiction such as gambling). Following will come a brief history of the various types of tobacco rituals, and of their opposition. A health-oriented anti-smoking movement had long existed, but it rose to power only in the late twentieth century. I will argue that a merely empirical presentation of evidence of the health consequences of smoking is not a sociologically adequate explanation of the rise and apparent triumph of the anti-smoking movement. The rise and fall of smoking rituals can be explained largely in sociological terms; the social processes that led to the expansion of smoking rituals to their height in the early and mid-twentieth century, reaching their peak during World War II, also provides an explanation of why the ritual base of support for smoking was in decline in the late twentieth century, at just the time that the anti-smoking movement came into its ascendency. By that time it had an easy target, as most of the ritual attractions of smoking had faded away.

Inadequacies of the Health and Addiction Model

The anti-smoking movement mobilized in the latter half of the twentieth century took its stance in the terms of public health. Above all, it rested its case upon statistical evidence of a causal connection between smoking and cancer as well as other deadly disease. If tobacco is so unhealthy, its strong appeal must be explained by some nonrational process; that is, it is addictive, and individuals get started on their addiction because of advertising by tobacco companies.[3] Cancer, addiction, and advertising: these are the three pieces of the anti-smoking case.

The historical pattern, however, undercuts all three points. Anti-smoking movements have existed much longer than the statistical evidence on the adverse effects of smoking on health. Evidence on the link between smoking and cancer began to be accumulated in the 1930s in Germany under auspices of Nazi nationalist concerns for public health (Proctor 1999). But this went largely unnoticed at a time when the tobacco cult was at its height in the Western democracies. More attention was paid to health-related statistics from the late 1940s onward in Britain. Wide anti-smoking mobilization based on grounds of health did not develop until after the 1964 Surgeon General's report in the United States. Earlier anti-tobacco movements mobilized on different grounds. There were vociferous reactions against smoking around the time of its introduction and early popularity in England, including a strong denunciation in 1604 by King James I, and violent efforts at suppression during the seventeenth century in Russia, Turkey, Persia, and Japan.[4] Again from the 1850s through the early-twentieth century there were strong denunciations from parts of the medical profession as well as clergy and politicians, notably in England and America; cigarette smoking was banned in twelve American states in the period around 1890 to the 1920s—just at the time the movement of alcohol prohibition was reaching its peak mobilization. During these various anti-movements, tobacco was charged with a range of defects, including its dirtiness, general vileness, low moral qualities and character debilitation, and sometimes various health problems. Although we are inclined now to believe that there is something in the latter charge, it was put in the distorted form of claiming tobacco caused such diseases as blindness, deafness, palsy, apoplexy, as well as cowardice, laziness, and insanity (Walton 2000, 65–68). The vehemence of reaction against smoking is not correlated historically with social awareness of evidence of its unhealthy effects; nor did the anti-tobacco movements have to believe in its unhealthiness to be intensely opposed to it.

Similarly with addiction. The case is best made against cigarette smoking in particular, rather than other forms of tobacco use. Many smokers have great difficulty stopping; feel cravings when they are not smoking; go through withdrawal symptoms such as irritability or compulsive eating; and are treatable by methods such as nicotine patches that acclimatize users to gradually reduced dosage. This appears to support a straightforwardly physiological process. Nevertheless the addiction model is far from a complete picture of the social process of smoking. Confining attention to cigarette smoking, we should note that addiction is not uniform or automatic. It is not simply a matter of smoking a cigarette and thereby becoming addicted; some process of subjective modification of consciousness about processes going on in one's body must take place before the individual feels sensations for which he or she has cravings.

This is analogous to the process of getting "high" in learning to become a marijuana smoker, in Becker's (1953) analysis; this experience can lead to strong desires for the marijuana high, which, however, is not addictive in the same sense as tobacco. A principal difference is that tolerance for marijuana builds up rather sharply. For a while, larger amounts are necessary to get the "high" effect; but also the intensity of the "high" eventually no longer matches that of initial experiences. Hence many users give up marijuana because it ceases to be effective. There can be nostalgia and psychological cravings for the high feeling, but there are no physiological withdrawal symptoms. The comparison between tobacco and marijuana indicates that the initial sensitizing process that makes an individual into a committed user expecting a distinctive feeling from his or her smoking can happen with substances that have quite different long-term effects. An inference is that processes that look like "addiction" (especially involving intense commitment or craving) vary greatly with the social definition or mood of the experience expected.

This may help explain a fact that the anti-smoking movement tends to skip over: that a certain proportion of smokers are light smokers, or smoke intermittently; many persons are "social smokers" who smoke at parties or other festive occasions but not otherwise. Thus the process of "addiction" cannot be simply an automatic physiological reaction to tobacco smoke; there is a set of behaviors and procedures—on the terrain of microsociological research—which determines how narrowly the individual becomes attached to the feelings in their body while smoking, and in their entire social posture, of which the mutual orientation of bodies is a part.

Some persons' reaction to smoking is to feel it as unpleasant experience. This is the experience of many persons who are starting to smoke; some go on to identify other aspects of their experience that make them smokers, while others never go beyond the negative experiences or even intensify them. Envision a continuum: at one end, negative and unpleasant reactions to smoking; tapering off to neutral experiences; then moderately attractive experiences; and increasingly strong attraction ending with craving and compulsion. The microsociological hypothesis is that individuals' experience in each portion of the continuum is shaped by a particular kind of social context.

We have relatively little evidence of how many persons are distributed along the full continuum, and how they shift among positions over time; and we lack a systematic historical picture of these patterns across the centuries. Correlating these patterns with their accompanying social interactions would give us empirical grounds for a microsociological theory of smoking. It would be a theory not of absolute, all-or-nothing addiction, but of variations in smoking behavior (cf. Marlatt et al. 1988). Those at the negative end of the continuum are potential members for anti-smoking movements; but for them to be mobilized takes a more complex social process, including their interaction with those on the opposite side of the continuum.

One conclusion we might draw from the historical data is that an "addictive" type of behavior is not necessarily produced by physiological processes at all. Historically, the first spread of the tobacco movement was in the form of pipe-smoking; it was followed in the eighteenth century by a widespread popularity of snuff; and in the nineteenth century cigars and (especially in America) chewing tobacco. All of these had their enthusiastic practitioners. Although careful statistics are lacking, there are biographical descriptions of tobacco users in these various forms who puffed their pipes all day long, smoked a score of cigars or constantly kept their noses or mouths full of snuff or chewing tobacco: in other words, there were substantial numbers of individuals who were at the high end of the continuum, corresponding to what today would be called "addiction." There seems to be relatively little systematic evidence on cravings and withdrawal symptoms among persons using tobacco in these forms; but they may have occurred. The key point, however, is that these forms of tobacco use did not involve inhaling smoke; the smoke was too harsh. It was only with the invention of flue-cured tobacco in America in the mid-1800s, and its use in mass-produced cigarettes through the introduction of rolling machines in the 1880s, that tobacco smoke became inhalable; whereas pipe and cigar smoke is alkaline, cigarette smoke is acidic (Walton 2000, 76–77). Hence the rise in lung cancer, a hitherto rare disease, with the spread of cigarette smoking in the twentieth century.

What this comparison brings out is that it does not require the strong and immediate flow of nicotine into the blood stream through inhaling smoke to bring about behavior, in some proportion of tobacco users, that resembles the highly attracted, "addictive" end of the continuum. It also seems likely, based on the historical pattern, that there were many persons at the moderate-to-low levels on the continuum of tobacco ingestion; quite likely many of them were maintaining a steady pattern of tobacco use, but not at the levels that we label as socially deleterious through the term "addiction." In short, historically there seems to have been a lot of tobacco use that cannot be explained by an "addictive" mechanism; and also some (maybe quite a lot) of tobacco use that resembles the social pattern of "addiction" without its physiological basis.

One other conclusion about addiction: The image of addiction is useful to anti-smoking movements, since it gives a picture of users who can't control their own behavior; they are not normal human beings, having lost power over their own bodies; and this gives warrant for ceding that control to outside agencies. Addiction also connotes a process that is voracious and expanding; it gives a rhetorical account of how smoking spreads—cigarettes are introduced to unsuspecting nonusers (especially youths) who try them and automatically become addicted. The last step in the causal chain is clearly untrue. But the rhetoric of addiction does give an account, or at least sets a verbal atmosphere in which it is plausible that smoking spreads so readily, as if by contagion. The reality is that smoking expanded as a social movement propagating lifestyle rituals, with its focus of attention, its emotional energies, and its feelings of membership. Lacking a microsociological

view of how this happens and of the power of this sort of social contagion, one might well describe it as a kind of cancer in the body social,
an addiction spreading from one cell to another. This gives an accurate
enough emotional sense of what anti-smoking crusaders feel they are
up against.

Finally, advertising. The advertising of tobacco is a phenomenon of
the twentieth century. It cannot be the explanation of how tobacco
spread initially: its widespread popularity in England and Holland in
the late sixteenth century; the spread throughout Europe (especially
intense in Germany), but also widely into the Middle East, India,
China, and Japan in the seventeenth century. It did not take advertising
to spread tobacco use; it spread by what the media business calls
"word of mouth," or more accurately, by example and collective participation, and by acquiring prestige as a social custom. Wars were particularly significant occasions for the spread of tobacco-using customs
(e.g., the spread of cigars during the Napoleonic wars in Spain, and of
cigarette smoking during the Crimean war); these customs jumped
from one army to another, across lines of emnity. Thus even in the
twentieth century, with its massive advertising campaigns (above all
in the United States and western Europe), cigarette smoking spread
to a considerable extent independently of advertising—as in the rapid
adoption of cigarettes in place of pipes in Asia.

This implies that even in the heart of the advertising country, the
influence of advertising on smoking was only a portion of the phenomenon, and probably of minor influence. In general, studies of advertising show that consumers are skeptical of claims made by advertisers
(Schudson 1986). Thus the anti-smoking movement's allegations rest
on an assumption that tobacco advertising must be an exception, the
mostly wildly successful advertising campaign of all time. It is more
plausible to regard the effect of cigarette companies' advertising campaigns as securing market share among themselves by keeping their
brand names in public memory. Some proof of the point is provided
by the fact that after the prohibition of most forms of tobacco advertising in the United States, smoking dropped but then stabilized at about
26 percent of adult males and 22 percent of females, with slightly rising
percentages among teenagers (30–35 percent) (*Los Angeles Times*, March
29, 2001). In other words, tobacco smoking sustains itself among a core
group of committed users by the same social processes that have always supported it.[5]

In what follows, I will present evidence that users of tobacco have
interpreted its effects in several quite distinct ways: among others, as
tranquilty or as carousing excitement, as facilitating concentration on
work or as sexual arousal. For comparison, I introduce similar evi-

dence for the ways in which the bodily effects of coffee and tea have been interpreted, and also well-known work on marijuana use. For all of these substances, this is not just a matter of how they are interpreted, but how they are felt; the bodily experiences themselves differ depending upon the social ritual in which those experiences are enacted.[6] This is not to say that there is no physiological process going on, and no chemical distinctiveness among nicotine, caffein, or various drugs. I do not hold that the distinctive chemistry of ingestable substances containing nicotine, caffein, alcohol, cannabis, cocaine, opium, and other drugs, all interact with social processes in the same way. It may well be the case that at certain dosages these substances have distinctive bodily effects that override most of the social inputs—that ingesting a large amount of opium will have a different effect than a large amount of caffein, regardless of context. What I argue here, minimally, is that at least in the case of nicotine and caffein, the component of undifferentiated arousal is very large, and allows a very large range of social interpretation, which leads to a range of bodily experiences through the fusion of undifferentiated arousal with socially specific emotions.

Nicotine, caffein, and a variety of other ingested substances produce a relatively undifferentiated physiological arousal, which is shaped into a particular bodily and emotional experience by interaction rituals. These are not merely mental interpretations, labels placed upon physical processes; the shaping of these experiences happens in the body itself, because interaction rituals operate as intensifications of coordination between bodies.[7]

Smoking ritual generates particular kinds of emotional energies in groups; it is these that are experienced bodily as the effects of smoking. And since over time the symbolic objects charged up by strong interaction rituals carry a sense of that emotional energy with them, the solitary smoker can invoke the previous social experience in his or her temporarily isolated body. I am arguing that no one would have a stable experience of tobacco, or of coffee or tea, if they were not introduced to it through social rituals; the completely isolated Robinson Crusoe smoker or coffee-drinker, in my opinion, would never come into being. As we shall see, coffee and tea, although both containing similar amounts of caffein, were socially interpreted quite differently in European history, as moods of convivial action or dignified tranquility. In the twentieth century, further differences are visible in the typical social interpretation of coffee in the United States and in Europe (especially in France or Italy). In the Unites States, coffee is associated with working (preparing for work in the morning; coffee breaks to sustain work during the day). In contrast, the European ritual of coffee, although involving much stronger caffeine concentrations, is treated as equivalent to the situation of having an alcoholic drink; it is a form of conviviality and elegant sociability, and thus rather sharply marked off from working. Against this backdrop has appeared the late-twentieth-century American cult of decaffeinated coffee (and its equivalent, herbal rather than authentic tea). Thus whereas in Europe one would drink a strong coffee to conclude an evening meal (taken to balance or complement the drinking of alcohol), in the United States at comparable evening situations upper-middle-class persons tend to drink "decaf," stating that they cannot sleep if they drink real coffee. The international comparison (as well as individual differences among Americans) suggests that this is a social construction. Not to deny that for these Americans drinking coffee in the evening is followed by difficulty in getting to sleep; but I am suggesting that this is not an automatic physiological result, but the social construction of bodily as well as cognitive habit such that coffee is associated with working and hence with being awake. It is striking, too, that the cult of "de-caf" came into the United States at the same time and in the same places (and quite possibly among the same persons) as the triumph of the anti-smoking movement. As we see in the interpretation below, both are forms of anti-carousing movements, and both are legitimated by an ideology of health; herbal teas first appeared in the health food movement, and until the 1980s were available only in cult-like health food stores.

Social interpretation, based on social ritual, determines a considerable proportion of bodily experience; it is not simply the result of unvarying, naturally given physiological reactions to chemical substances ingested in the body. My argument for a microsociology of smoking parallels the argument in chapter 6 for a microsociology of sexual interaction. Just as I have argued that sexual "drive" is not usefully conceived as an autonomous, self-motivating biological process; and that it is not to be understood as genital pleasure per se; here I propose that we examine the pleasures and repulsions of smoking, up through the apex of intense cravings and bodily convulsions, as deeply determined by variations in interaction ritual.

Tobacco Rituals: Relaxation/Withdrawal Rituals, Carousing Rituals, Elegance Rituals

Tobacco has been used in five main ways: smoking in pipes, cigars, or cigarettes; as snuff; and as chewing tobacco. The social meanings of these kinds of tobacco use have varied, as has the composition of the groups who have used them, and thus who was included or excluded, and what kinds of lifestyle were being exalted or defended. The fact that the same substance might be used in different kinds of rituals and given different meanings shows that the meanings are not inherent in the physical characteristics of the tobacco. On the microsociological level of IR chains, the individual tobacco user has to make the same kinds of attributions and develop the same kinds of sensitivities that get one high as does a marijuana user.

There are three main tobacco rituals: First, relaxation and withdrawal rituals, characterized by serenity and ease away from the pressures and excitements of work and of social life. Second, carousing rituals, in which the quality of tobacco is felt as enhancing excitement and riotous enjoyment. The third type, elegance rituals, resembles carousing insofar as it takes place in sociable situations; but whereas carousing is sheer immediate excitement and thus a momentary focus of attention that we can call situational stratification, elegance rituals convey an aesthetic impression of the actor as a categorical identity within the status hierarchy. These not only organize different forms of social stratification but involve quite different emotional tones; the kind of social ritual determines the quality attributed to the tobacco.

As a preliminary comparison, note yet another kind of ritualism for which tobacco has been put to use: the original ceremonial of the diplomatic "peace pipe" observed by the European explorers of America among the native tribes. In northeast America, the pipe was a huge ceremonial object, four feet long, carried prominently on diplomatic expeditions where it served as a flag of truce. It was decorated with ornaments representing the various tribes adhering to the alliance, and was smoked in an elaborate ritual, in which the pipe was passed around the assembly of chiefs and leading warriors. Taboos of sacredness were observed; smokers were not to touch the pipe except with their lips; they blew the smoke toward heaven and earth in religious invocation. (Goodman 1993; Walton 2000, 280–83)

Here yet other qualities were attributed to the tobacco: spiritual and religious significance. In a society in which religion was organized as public participation, largely identical with the political and kinship structure of the group, smoking ritual had a Durkheimian significance on the largest scale, symbolizing the collective forces at their maximum. This kind of tobacco ritual was rarely to any extent used by the Europeans or in the other complex commercial civilizations to which smoking propagated. The tribal ritual was not part of everyday life; and it took place in groups organized so that individuals neither withdrew into privacy among intimate, voluntarily chosen friends nor did it occur where nonkin came together outside the bounds of formal rituals to carry out carousing. In short, these tribal societies did not have the kind of social organization that tobacco smoking was to constitute in Europe. It is consistent with this structure that, as far as we know, there were no anti-smoking movements in tribal societies, nor any local critique of tobacco-using practice.

In European and Asian societies, to the contrary, tobacco was always used in an informal, private, and unofficial capacity. This structural location left smokers open to be attacked by officials, whenever they were seen as an affront to official commitments and ritual. Christian ministers could attack tobacco as a vice, equivalent to other forms of immorality; autocrats such as the Russian Czar, the Mogul emperor of India, the Turkish sultan, and the Persian shah during the mid-1600s attempted to extirpate smoking by punishments ranging from slitting smokers' lips, pouring molten lead down their throats, public whipping, and execution by torture (Kiernan 1991; Walton 2000, 39–46). In these societies, smokers were treated as violators of ceremonial correctness of public order. In less authoritarian, pluralistic societies, smokers might be attacked not from above but from their putative equals, both on grounds of offending rival standards of behavior, and because of the group boundaries that smoking drew and the ranking that it implied between insiders and outsiders. Issues of lifestyle and social boundaries went together, since the ritual practice constituted the lifestyle that draws lines of inclusion and exclusion.

Tobacco was first used in pipe-smoking, and this remained the main form of consumption up through the vogue of snuff in the eighteenth century, and indeed throughout that period for the lower social classes until the era of cigarettes in the twentieth century. During the early period when pipes were virtually the only form of tobacco use, several interpretations of its effects circulated indiscriminately. In the earliest period of its introduction into Europe, tobacco was suggested as having medicinal use. This settled into a long-standing interpretation that tobacco was antidote to hunger, fatigue, and hardship. The association with ingestion as a substitute for food was expressed in the terminology of the seventeenth century, which often spoke of "drinking" or "tippling" tobacco smoke (Walton 2000, 230). Yet this association with physical sustenance was socially specific, since tobacco was used almost exclusively by men; it was not "food" for women and children. The interpretation arose because tobacco use began among men in hardship situations, initially explorers and colonists, and spread during military campaigns.[8]

When pipe-smoking spread into routine social life, it acquired two connotations: relaxation and tranquillity, and, on the other hand, carousing. These alternatives gradually diverged as specific social situations of tobacco use became institutionalized. On one hand, smoking became an activity of times of rest: in the evening, or during a work break, after exhaustion, or for elderly men in retirement. The ritual ingredients of these situations came out most strongly where they involved men sitting together smoking their pipes, speaking little, or quietly chatting. The activity of preparing and looking after pipes (which will be analyzed in more detail later) could act as a substitute for conversation; men were focused together on the same object, enjoying a largely wordless communication. This was no doubt particularly useful for men with little cultural capital, few things to speak about, as among retirees or others out of the action; and it probably also helped to create a more introverted personality type, in that it gave a legitimate and meaningful activity for men to do wordlessly, differentiating them from the livelier extroverted talkers. As we shall see shortly, this latter group (I deliberately resist calling them extroverted "personalities") was emerging at the same time in early modern society, building a distinctive lifestyle in a network circulating the techniques of joking, story-telling, and game-playing pastimes—and with these a different interpretation of tobacco rituals.

There were doubtless some men who smoked alone, which is to say, without the company of other smokers. But given the housing conditions of the sixteenth and seventeenth centuries, it is likely that these "solitary" smokers were in the presence or at least the sight of others most of the time. Smoking thus would act as a boundary marker in yet another sense: it gave a social definition to what an individual was doing alone, establishing a membrane around that activity that others understood and respected (or, as the case might be, despised and criticized). The solitary smoker at the fireplace nook or on the doorstep watching the village street, much like the group of mostly silent men gathered in similar positions, was defined as engaging in an activity of tranquil relaxation. This would have been contrasted with the main earlier alternatives: religious contemplation, and perhaps mere social incompetence, dullness, or senility. The ritualism of pipe smoking thus gave a modest boost in social status to innocuous or inactive men, outside the religious sphere, in their hours or years of inactivity.

The other venue for pipe-smoking was in scenes of carousing. Smoking became a favorite activity in taverns, along with drinking. It was associated with riotous action, the deliberate saturnalia of inebriation, loud music, gambling and other rowdy games, and prostitution. In a time when smoking was a male preserve, prostitutes were virtually the only women in Western societies who openly smoked—which presumably they did while taking part in these scenes of carousing. One result was to keep up a barrier against respectable women smoking, by assocating those who did with whores.[9]

Taverns had long existed as accommodations for travelers, and they became more prominent as urbanization displaced the daily round of religious ceremonial that had made up the routine of the medieval households under the patrimonial authority of household heads (Wuthnow 1989). In the seventeenth and especially the eighteenth century, a more respectable version of the tavern developed, the coffeehouse. This developed in commercial centers connected with world trade, and thus became prominent not only in London, but also in commercial cities of Holland and Germany. The coffeehouse became a center for a double ritualism, coffee and tobacco. In contrast to the culture of tranquility and withdrawal associated with quiet pipe-smoking, the coffeehouse featured stimulation and excitement.

Coffeehouses expanded at the time when snuff-taking became the socially reputable form of tobacco use, although pipe-smoking continued there to some extent as well. A number of conditions were associated with the spread of snuff. By the late 1600s, pipe-smoking had become so widespread among males of all social classes so that snuff could acquire prestige as a more elite practice. The rise of snuff was furthered by criticism, especially from women of the respectable classes, of the dirtiness and smell of smoking tobacco; and snuff-taking was more convenient, at a time when pipe-smoking was cumbersome in the absence of matches or other methods for bringing fire to the pipe. To be sure, the aesthetic objection to smoking was merely displaced to another area, since snuff-taking left a good deal of powder on clothes, faces, and furniture. This was one reason why tobacco tended to remain in all-male enclaves such as the coffeehouses, although snuff developed its polite ritual and paraphernalia and became part of the sphere of drawing-room etiquette as well—or at least contested that terrain for a time.

Tobacco, like coffee, was here associated with liveliness. Both provided an ongoing small-scale physical activity during the urban gatherings of journalists, politicians, theater producers, "wits," and other intellectuals, and those engaged in speculative business.[10] Each of these circles had their habitual coffeehouses. Many of these occupations were then first appearing or becoming institutionalized. The early eighteenth century was the time when the English parliament began to meet regularly and politicians took over control from the monarchy; regular periodical publications began to appear, giving an appetitite and a demand for news; similar developments took place with the theater and other realms of specialized cultural production. These institutions constituted a new form of "action," ongoing excitement that they both promoted and reflected upon and publicized as part of their own commercial activities. Talking and writing about the "action" was itself one of the activities that went on around these centers of assembly.

Why did these activities have to be associated with ingestion of any substances at all? Conceivably businessmen, journalists, politicians, and the other circles could have met to carry out their plotting and professional gossiping in a purely instrumental way, focused on nothing but the talk at hand. This would have made their meetings the equivalent of professional conferences. But they were not conferences, and the contrast enables us to see just in what the social ritualism of the coffeehouses consisted. Even today, when one wants to talk with a professional colleague, not in a formal way but in a setting that is defined as backstage, one suggests "meeting for coffee" or, with a connotation of even greater role distance, "meeting for a drink." The implicit purpose of the encounter is not openly stating positions, making offers for explicit exchanges and thus committing oneself to a bargaining posture, but deliberately avoiding this degree of definiteness. The flexibility of backstage encounters allows more room for maneuver in bargaining, as well as a more open field for acquiring information and for making contacts. Thus although the more or less ostensible purpose of meeting in this way is related to professional business, it requires an immediate purpose that is purely sociable and informal, something defined not as work but as recreation or pleasure.

Another way that this kind of backstage setting could be provided for professional encounters was through membership in a private club. Clubs emerged in London in late eighteenth and early nineteenth centuries, to some extent by differentiating out from the same kinds of circles that had frequented coffeehouses. But a club was a more cumbersome form of meeting than a coffeehouse, requiring long-range planning and fixed investment on the part of participants; its membership procedures, too, were more cumbersome and time-consuming, not suitable to fast-moving shifts in information and reputation. Thus clubs were not so much places where business or culture-production work took place, but rather where success in these fields was ratified and formally recognized.

A useful contrast to the "liveliness" culture of tobacco and coffee in these settings is the ingestion of the same substances, at about the same time, in the coffeehouses of Turkey and the Levant. There the government structure had no place for open discussion of political parties, and no equivalently lively market for cultural production in the form of commercial entertainment was developing. It appears that coffee-drinking and smoking in Turkey and other Islamic societies did not acquire the same connotations of being the center of excited "action" as they had, for instance, in London at the time of Alexander Pope. Instead, both coffee and tobacco were part of a time for leisured withdrawal, part of the cult of tranquility. Once again we see that the social context determines the perceived emotional effects of similar physical substances.

Tobacco at the northern European coffeehouse acquired the social significance of a moderate form of carousing: not the unbridled licentiousness associated with taverns, drinking, gambling, and prostitution; but connected with a higher social class (or with the higher classes engaged in less rakish pursuits); and as ancillary to the serious business of respectable and indeed somewhat elite occupations. It marked the differentiation of status spheres, which were becoming more elaborate than those that existed in the medieval society of patrimonial households ranked by aristocratic status and enacted in religious ritualism.

In the medieval world, the main scenes of social attention were the court ceremonial of the high aristocrats and officials of the church; a lesser degree of stateliness surrounded the daily routine of heads of modest households. The main sphere of socially legitimated privacy would have been the prayers and religious exercises of the monks and priests, and their emulation by devout laypersons. Tobacco arrived from tribal America into an early modern social world where more room was becoming available for private sociable gatherings. These were separating out into enclaves for men withdrawing quietly to smoke pipes alone or in small groups of intimates; alternatively, tavern-like scenes of crass carousing (including both low-life and adventuresome males from higher ranks); and these again in contrast to the backstage scenes of action involving public business (initially in the coffeehouses), which both facilitated professional life and became a magnet of social attraction in its own right.

Rival scenes of private sociability were also developing, outside the boundaries of and in contrast to these male-dominated enclaves whose borders were most sharply marked by tobacco. A new sphere of ritual sociability developed with a national marriage market, with greater scope both for individual negotiation of love matches, and simultaneously greater complexity of parental involvement in steering marital alliances (Stone 1979). This brought a great expansion in the sphere of female-centered sociability as well: the "Season" at London, the balls and hunts at country houses; an etiquette of social calls, at-homes, proper introductions among the socially eligible, the art of leaving calling cards; dinner parties in the city and eventually in country homes, where they were often combined with extended visits and hence entertainments. An elaborate set of female-centered ceremonies grew up, involving routines of polite conversation, card-playing, domestic musi-cal performance, and tea-drinking (Burke 1993). This realm of female "action" took on a life of its own, over and above the marriage market. Refined social rankings were being created, beyond those of the medi-eval aristocracy, involving a certain amount of fluidity based on skills in negotiating ritual borders; and these status prizes gave great emo-tional significance to items of everyday comportment. We had arrived, so to speak, at the Goffmanian era of modern history.

In this social sphere, the drinking of tea became a rival ritual to the male world of coffee and tobacco. The substances thus socially distin-guished were physically quite similar. Tea was also an import from the era of world trade in the initial period of colonial expansion. Tea contains similar amounts of caffein as coffee. However, tea became a domestic drink, associated with family meals, mixed company, and women's socializing. Tea-drinkers became defined as sedate in con-trast to the "action" connotations of coffee-drinking; this was a con-trast of social locations, the ritualism of coffeehouse encounters as against the ritualism of ordinary family meals, or at its most elegant, of ladies' tea-time.

Pipe-smoking, coffee-drinking, and snuff-taking spread with the enthusiasm of lifestyle movements. Along with them went emotional moods and ways of talking about the effects of tobacco, coffee, and tea. The safest course is to regard these substances as producing psy-chologically undifferentiated physiological arousal, which was then situationally defined as particular moods by the kinds of rituals built up around them. Pipe smoke, snuff, coffee, and tea became symbols of social groups and social boundaries; the symbolism was an intimate one, since it involved feelings in one's own body and emotions—tran-quility, rowdy celebration, sophisticated action, dignified elegance—which were experienced both as parts of oneself and as enacting one's social relationships in the micro-encounter and one's larger place in the social order.

Snuff-taking, although a contested practice on the terrain of draw-ing-room sociability, the sphere where elegant women exercised their greatest control, came closest to socially defining tobacco as a dignified elite ritual. It failed and largely disappeared from high society by the beginning of the nineteenth century, and shrank into a minor practice of rural and lower classes. Although snuff was one form of tobacco that males used in sociable interaction with respectable women, it did not cross over the gender line to any extent; probably an important consideration was that the messiness of the custom could not be made compatible with the elegant self-presentation women were cultivating during this time with face powders, jewels, and décolletage. Where men could engage in the end-of-snuffing ritual of wiping away powder with their billowing handkerchiefs, women of the higher social classes had committed themselves to a more immobile, statuesque elegance. Snuff did not fit into their ritual presentation of self.

Chewing tobacco may be passed over lightly in this survey. Of all the forms of tobacco use, this was the least elegant and left the messiest residue. Its main practical virtue was that it eliminated any need for lighting and burning tobacco, and thus could be practiced in the course of physical action, as well as in any outdoor setting; indoors as well, if spittoons were available. Tobacco chewing was a fad—and thus a temporarily prestigious social movement—mainly in the United States during the nineteenth century. This apparently carried a political symbolism. Chewing tobacco became popular during the period of Jacksonian party politics in the 1830s; it had rural connotation, and signaled membership in the class of rural landowners in the land speculation and agricultural business boom that dominated the American economy of that period. As late as 1900 chewing tobacco made up 44 percent of the American tobacco market. The U.S. Congress and other government buildings furnished ubiquitous spittoons, which were not removed until the 1950s (Brooks 1952).

The distinctly inelegant display of chewing and spitting tobacco juice was a form of aggressive self-assertion, mitigated by being shared in a community of men all spitting together. Its practitioners must surely have felt that it contrasted sharply with polite drawing-room etiquette and with the more restrained and self-contained practices of smoking; no doubt this was the message they wished to convey. Chewing tobacco was popular and prestigeful in this time because it represented assertive rural democracy, the attitude of "I'm as good a man as any so-called gentleman or aristocrat." The humor of contemporary remarks about daring to spit in a rival's eye (i.e., spit tobacco juice) conveyed the self-image that the tobacco-chewer attempted to project. This interpretation is confirmed by comparisons: the fact that tobacco-chewing was nowhere widely popular other than the United States; its decline at the time when the moderate-size rural landowner was overtaken economically and politically by other interest groups in the late nineteenth century; its subsequent pattern of hanging on mainly in farming areas and rural pastimes (such as among white baseball players).

Pipe-smoking and snuff had established the main ritual usages of tobacco: tranquility and withdrawal from affairs; and on the other hand excitement, both in the form of antinomian carousing and in the higher class form of sophisticated action. These carried over in the nineteenth and twentieth centuries as snuff disappeared and pipe-smoking was gradually supplanted, first by cigars and then by cigarettes. Pipes thereby lost their connotation of carousing, and became associated exclusively with calm self-absorption. During the German revolts of 1848, there were mass confrontations in the streets in such cities as Berlin, aimed explicitly at government regulations against smoking cigars in public. Cigar-smoking had the connotation of a young, active, masculine public crowd, associated with modernist tendencies and liberalism; pipe-smoking was regarded as bourgeois, sedentary, respectable and conservative, done in the privacy of home (Walton 2000, 163). By the mid-twentieth century in the United States, where cigarette-smoking had become extremely widespread in all social classes, pipe-smoking gave the image of a well-mannered gentleman, polite and rather self-contained, in contrast to the more hard-driving or carousing image of the cigarette smoker. It also gave off a conservative image insofar as it remained a male preserve at a time when the most popular form of smoking was becoming gender-shared, and thus removed from the sexual flirtation that was facilitated by cigarettes.

Cigar-smoking displaced snuff rather abruptly around the turn of the nineteenth century, as part of the revolutionary transformation in manners when the French Revolution downgraded the aristocracy. Cigars tended to occupy the same social niche as snuff: the relatively higher class world of the backstages of public action, and the male counterpart to the elegant drawing-room. Cigars were emulated by less wealthy and action-central social classes, although the greater cost of cigars kept poor people's smoking (including most of the working class until the twentieth century) in the form of pipes.[11] Whereas snuff had come closer to bridging the gap between males and females—insofar as men took snuff in the presense of women—the gap widened again as cigars renewed the aesthetic objections to smoke. Cigar-smoking promoted the sharper separation of spheres in the mid and late nineteenth century, the so-called Victorian era. Men were expected as a matter of etiquette to withdraw to the stables to smoke (thus emphasizing outdoor sports as male spheres, at just a time when work was becoming increasingly indoor and sedentary). The custom developed for women to withdraw from the dining room after a polite sociable gathering, so that the men could smoke their cigars together. One side effect of this custom was probably to increase the amount of cigar-smoking; the ritual announcement by the host—"Gentlemen, you may smoke."—given after the toast to the Queen, no doubt called for a good deal of joining in merely to be in the spirit of the occasion.

Nineteenth-century houses had become physically and interactionally much more complex than their earlier forms [Girouard 1978, 1979]. In medieval homes of the elite, most activities had taken place in great halls, with little privacy for the aristocrats surrounded by their

Figure 8.1 Cigar-smoking as class marker: a working-class admirer makes deferential contact with Winston Churchill, yet with a gesture of ritual solidarity in offering a light.

courtiers and servants. This had gradually given way in the eighteenth and nineteenth centuries to specialized rooms, differentiated by degrees of privacy and restrictions on who could enter them. Women acquired their own spheres of action and their spaces in which they could put on their own rituals of impressiveness. The Victorian house of the wealthier classes carried this social differentiation to the most extreme specialization of household spaces in any historical period: there were elaborate servants' wings for household activities with back corridors so that service would be carried on unobtrusively, giving an impression of unruffled privacy for the family residents and their guests; libraries, a business office, children's nurseries and schoolrooms, conservatories for music playing, morning rooms for the ladies to sit in, as well as formal reception rooms and banquet halls. These physically separated the various activities of the day and the subgroups of persons who took part in them. Victorian houses typically included a billiard room, which served as a masculine realm, where cigar-smoking took place; similar purpose was served by a hunting room, and frequently by a smoking room. These rooms were particularly prominent in bachelor quarters: that is, an unmarried man of the wealthy classes would have both a place to smoke, for his masculine friends, but also likely a drawing room, saloon, or library where he could entertain mixed company as well.

Cigar-smoking thus carried a connotation of genteel carousing, and of bachelorhood. It became common in the nineteenth century to set up a contrast between the pleasures of bachelor life and marriage. The former was defined as a life of "independence," although (since married males had a great deal of power) the content of this independence was merely a space away from the female sphere with its different rituals of respectability. The specific content of bachelor life was defined above all as freedom to smoke (which in reality meant subjection to the ritual demand for smoking in male society); this was the respectable form of carousing, more defensible than drinking, gambling, or whoring, and indeed probably the most widely practiced of these (since the latter activities involved a good deal of practical costs and sometimes difficulties). Defenses of bachelorhood and of smoking interchangeably held forth on the pleasures of male company, as the specific form of ritual sociability that involved no obligations other than good fellowship. This was also defended by intellectuals and artists, who held smoking to be part of the creative process or mood; what they apparently meant by this was that writing, painting, or composing took place in a Bohemian atmosphere, independent of mundane considerations, and this was both symbolized by and palpably felt in the ritual of smoking. This is no doubt what Kipling meant by his famous line, the peroration of a poem called "The Betrothed" (1888): "A woman is only a woman; but a good Cigar is a Smoke."

These ritual distinctions shifted once again when cigarette-smoking became popular in the late nineteenth and early twentieth centuries. Cigarettes, along with the ready availability of lights through safety matches and gas lighters, made smoking maximaly portable and individualized, and compared to previous forms of tobacco use, relatively clean. They also appeared at a time when the wealth of all social classes was increasing; mass production and marketing made tobacco unprecedently easy to buy; and barriers between male and female spheres were breaking down. With the wide spread of cigarettes, and especially its adoption among women, other forms of tobacco use declined sharply. This meant that the differentiation of tobacco rituals increasingly shifted to differentiation among uses of cigarettes. Pipe-smoking retained its connotation of tranquil withdrawal, but cigarettes could also be smoked for such a purpose (although without signaling a male enclave). Cigars still had some connotation of "big business, important people," but cigarette smokers could also make their claim to being where the action is, both high class and rowdy.

A major part of the triumph of cigarettes over other tobacco rituals was their spread to women, which thus reinforced their importance for men who wanted to be around women; initially this occured as a sexual revolution, the shift in sexual negotiations that in the 1920s was known as the "jazz age." The flapper was shocking because she wore mannish clothes, smoked, and flirted; contemporary conservatives took all three as touchstones, but the smoking was the strongest emblem of the cultural break. I will later take up this process in connection with the ups and downs of smoking and anti-smoking movements in the twentieth century.

Ritual Paraphernalia: Social Display and Solitary Cult

Rituals can focus attention on physical objects, which thereby become emblems of group membership, and reminders of the mood that the ritual practice had concentrated and intensified. "Addiction" to tobacco, like the craving for marijuana or other drugs, involves a strong attachment to the emotional mood and its social interpretation that goes with smoking. This attachment is displaced onto the physical object, as its symbol. In terms of IR chains, it is a way of steering oneself toward a specific source of emotional energy. Similarly, persons can become "addicted" to particular kinds of social rituals, which have nothing to do with ingesting substances; in this sense one can become addicted to gambling, or become a workaholic, a sports junkie, etc.

In the case of tobacco, the Durkheimian sacred objects, or the physical things to which a smoker becomes attached, are often not the tobacco per se (i.e., the nicotine in the blood stream), but its smoke, smell, taste, and also—perhaps preponderantly—the apparatus in which it is ingested. Thus some tobacco smokers lavish attention on the preliminaries to smoking: preparing the tobacco, the way it is displayed and stored, the instruments through which it is smoked or ingested. There is an additional sociological reason for attending to these activities: these help explain how smoking, whose effects I argue are socially constructed, can sometimes be a solitary activity. In this light, let us briefly survey the ritualism of tobacco paraphernalia.

Pipes were initially simple clay devices, which over the centuries became more elaborately shaped and decorated. Particularly in Germany and Holland, where pipe-smoking became extremely popular, elaborately carved pipes of meerschaum stone (introduced in the eigh-

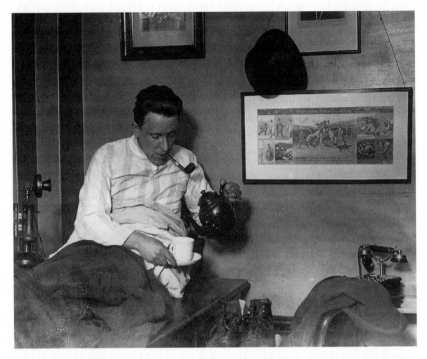

Figure 8.2 Two emblems of middle-class respectability: a pipe and a cup of tea (England, 1924).

teenth century) were treated as objects of prideful display. The cult of pipe-smoking came to its greatest prominance in those communities because of their distinctive class structure: relatively few grand aristocrats with their courtly displays of rank, but instead local dominance by the bourgeoisie of the free cities and commercial towns. German-Dutch pipe-smoking was a way of showing off in local gatherings while keeping up an aura of fellowship in a modestly elevated collegial group. Collective pipe-smoking was also a favorite ritual among university students, another privileged yet casual and internally egalitarian group within German society. In keeping with the mild antinomianism of this liminal age-group, smoking had a slightly carousing tone, as in the favorite practice of smoking out a candle—filling a tavern room with so much tobacco smoke that the candle went out (Walton 2000, 256).

With the rise of competing forms of smoking, pipe-smoking became more of a solitary pastime. Pipes became less ornate, less oriented toward public display. At the same time, the pipe-smoker tended to develop an extensive private ritual of collecting pipes, caring for them, and preparing tobacco. Around 1850 wooden pipes largely replaced clay and stone, especially with specially cured and carved briar wood (Dunhill 1924). Such pipes involved a good deal of cleaning, since the taste was affected by residue from previous smokes; much time was spent scraping away the burnt interior of the bowl, so eventually pipes would become too thin and hot and have to be replaced. For both these reasons, committed pipe-smokers kept collections of pipes. These served as a private shrine, which would also include collections of various kinds of tobacco with a variety of scents and tastes. Pipe-smoking acquired an ethos of collecting, a form of hobby and connoisseurship, with its subtleties and sophistication.

By the twentieth century, pipe smokers were no longer assembling very much to smoke in a collective ritual,[12] but instead were maintaining a social pose as an individual man of respectable taste. The greatest focus of attention, and flow of emotional energy, would come from the ritual preparation for smoking perhaps even more than from the smoking itself. An analogy in religious rituals is the practice of mystics, for whom the height of religious experience was solitary prayer or meditation, rather than participation in collective ceremony. In Weber's terms, the twentieth-century pipe-smoker was a kind of "inner-worldly mystic," especially its Western version, a practitioner of quietism (i.e., performance of spiritual exercises not in monastic withdrawal but "in the world") (Weber 1922/1963, 177). In their respective historical settings, the religious mystic or solitary pipe connoiseur had an accepted social definition and was recognized by others, albeit from a distance, as a person aloofly pursuing spiritual excellence and thereby entitled to respect.

Snuff-taking was a thoroughly social and ostentatious activity. Of all the forms of tobacco-using, it had the most concentrated dramatic structure: preparation, buildup, tension, release, aftermath, all punctuated by an audible burst of sound and bodily convulsion.[13] It entailed a paraphernalia that was compact, portable, and elegant. Snuffboxes were forms of personal jewelry, and were at the height of fashion in an era when men's clothing, specialized for elite drawing-room sociability, had a great deal of ostentation. Displaying a gold snuffbox, offering it to others, rapping on it to emphasize a point, all were part of the dance-like moves of salon sociability; they were adapted as well to the dramatic enactments of the coffeehouse. Later snuffboxes became collector's items, in much the same way as exotic porcelain would be displayed on table tops or in glass cases in the rooms of a home designed for the reception of visitors. This shift from use to display happened in the period when snuff was displaced by newer forms of high-status tobacco use.

Cigar paraphernalia were in some respects less elaborate than that of pipes or snuff. But cigars themselves became highly differentiated, by size and shape as well as by the flavor and quality of the tobacco. Large, long, or otherwise expensive cigars made a statement of relative wealth; it is in keeping with this differentiation that cigar-smoking became prominent in the nineteenth century in just those countries (England, United States, Germany) where class differentiation by commercial wealth was developing most rapidly. Cigars became a ritual gift; generally unlike pipes and snuffboxes, which tended to be items of personal identity carried everywhere by their owners, cigars were tokens in the rituals of hospitality. It was the duty of the host to offer cigars to visitors, especially in the after-dinner ritual of the higher classes; offering cigars was also a friendly marker for a business agreement. This ritualism of cigars as honorific gifts declined in the twentieth century with the rise of cigarette ritual. But cigars retained their special status, in the custom of giving out cigars on occasions of special celebration, for example this was expected of a father celebrating the birth of a child.

Cigars were distinctive in having special smoking rooms provided for their use; this was of course confined to the wealthier classes, and reinforced cigars' connotation of social rank. The era of cigar-smoking was also the period in which men had a special smoking wardrobe: generally a smoking jacket and sometimes smoking cap, made of unusually lavish materials such as velvet, with brocade collars and bands, perhaps tassels. These were strikingly fanciful in the style regime of the nineteenth century when male clothing was becoming somber, thereby underscoring the dramatic self-presentation of the smoker in a situation of dignified sybaritic celebration (Laver 1995).

The pleasure of cigar-smoking, like other kinds of smoking, may well have consisted largely in the surroundings and paraphernalia. The best part of cigar-smoking comes at the outset: the choosing, displaying, offering, smelling, and rolling between one's fingers the unlit cigar; sometimes an elaborate ritual of lighting (a high-class servant could spend a good five minutes turning a cigar in a match flame before presenting it to the smoker to be lit); the sense of implicit social membership conveyed by who was present for the simultaneous first few puffs, and who was excluded. From here, it was all down hill: cigars smell progressively worse as they are smoked, since the cigar acts as a filter accumulating the harsher portions of the smoke, and the end is a wet, slimy cigar butt. Cigar-smoking has very strong qualities of Goffmanian frontstaging, in which the appearance is more appealing than the close-up reality. Given that cigars are not inhaled, and produce relatively little nicotine charge in the body, cigar-smoking gives

Figure 8.3 One of the first women smokers of the respectable classes. In emulation of male traditions, she wears a special smoking outfit (England, 1922).

suggestive evidence that the ritual is far the stronger attraction than the physical experience itself.[14]

Cigarette smoking in the early twentieth century broke the gender barrier, and thus in one sense returned to the elegance rituals that characterized snuff in the eighteenth century. Cigarette-smoking in the United States was first associated with upper-class "dandies," later spreading to the working class (Klein 1993). But cigarettes quickly became items of mass production and mass consumption, increasingly cheap and widely available, not so sharply differentiated by expense as cigars. Elegance and resistance to social leveling was provided for a time by cigarette holders, some of which took the form of expensive jewelry. Cigarette holders also provided dramatic appeal: they made the cigarette more visible, and could be held at a high angle, with a variety of moves conveying different attitudes. President Franklin Roosevelt's cigarette and holder, clenched between his teeth at a jaunty upward angle, was his trademark conveying determined optimism. Holders could be held at what were called "rakish" angles, as well as dignified or snooty postures. Also possible was a range of signals, symbols of one's attitude toward the world, marked by dispensing with the holder.

Figure 8.4 FDR's trademark cigarette holder (1930s).

A tone of tough-guy, cynical sophistication, for example, was conveyed in the 1940s by the cigarette hanging casually from the corner of the lips, rarely removed. No doubt this acquired some of its effect by contrast with the hand movements of elegant smoking taking the cigarette in and out of the mouth repeatedly, with a good deal of waving in the air. Such gestures also gave opportunity to display one's hands; for upper-class ladies, this generally involved showing off one's jewels. With or without holders, cigarette-smoking gave opportunity to dramatize hands and fingers, especially emphasizing the long and elegant.

    Individuals of the higher classes, emulated by those who could afford it, transferred their cigarettes from mass-marketed packages into cigarette cases, typically of silver or gold; these were often inscribed, and could be given as treasured personal gifts. Loading up one's cigarette case was a backstage preparation for the ritual before going out to a party or social entertainment. This not only gave cigarettes an elegant setting for the eyes of the owner, but also made for an ancillary ritual of offering a smoke as part of the etiquette of greeting, or of striking up a friendship.

The ritual of reciprocal gift-giving could be carried out by smokers at all social levels. This gave even greater significance to the elaborateness of the paraphernalia such as cigarette cases for conveying the social standing of the giver. At least, it allowed the situational pretense of such status. George Orwell (1936) gives an example, worthy of Goffman, of stage-preparation on the part of the downwardly mobile: no matter how poor, one needed to carry in one's case at least one cigarette to offer, in order to honorably receive from others. Among the humbler classes, the exchange of cigarettes or even cigarette butts was a way to strike up a friendship or at least a transient obligation. In communities of hardship, such as prison populations, war refugees or battle zone survivors—especially in the aftermath of World War II— cigarettes were used as currency, substitutes for money; at the same time these exchanges retained some qualities of ritual gift-giving. Cigarettes even when serving as money were also smoked by these populations, indeed especially treasured because their ritual consumption was experienced as luxurious relief, time-out from the onerous situation. Thus to give or lend a cigarette set up a strong obligation of return; it was somewhere between a financial debt and a mark of honor. Failure to repay could result in deadly quarrels (as in prison fights even today; O'Donnell and Edgar 1998); but also borrowers would go to considerable lengths to repay since this implied maintaining a vestige of normal civilian respectability of the cigarette cult.

Offering a light, or asking for one, was a common courtesy; notoriously, it was also a way of striking up an acquaintanceship in public. Here again paraphernalia could be elaborated, from the simple match to lighters, which at the upper end of status ranking were silver or other jewelry. In home furnishings, elaborate ash trays, lighters, and cigarette boxes were equipment of routine hospitality as well as opportunities for display of wealth and taste. And offers and acceptances of cigarettes were standard moves in flirtation and courtship; it was not merely in Hollywood films that cigarettes were used to symbolize sexual engagements; film-makers' use of this symbolism to evade censorship after 1934 came from preexisting custom, rather than vice versa.

In sum, cigarette-smoking acquired a variety of ritual uses: conveying social status, including the dramatization (and pretense) of upper-class elegance; sexual intrigue and negotiation; the social ties of reciprocal gifts. Some of these rituals conveyed hierarchy; others common comaraderie. Cigarettes became increasingly important around mid-century in backstage socializing, such as chatting on the telephone, or in a relaxing moment with friends. Ex-smokers, and those attempting to give up smoking, frequently refer to the temptations to smoke in particular situations; this is especially common with women who associate smoking with casual chats with their female friends.[15]

One other social use, and subjective interpretation, of tobacco emerged with the spread of cigarettes into all social classes. Cigars and chewing tobacco had prepared the way for smoking on the job, especially on certain kinds of outdoor jobs; cigarettes made it possible to smoke ubiquitously, including in most kinds of white-collar work. In this respect, twentieth-century cigarette-smoking was largely unprecedented in breaking down the barrier between the ritual sphere of sociability, where tobacco had almost always been confined, and the practical world of work. The rationale that smoking workers give—that a cigarette helps one to concentrate—adds yet another social interpretation of the feelings generated by the undifferentiated experience of ingesting nicotine. This last conquest of social space by tobacco was the first to be successfully contested by the anti-smoking movement of the late twentieth century. This is understandable by a theory of social movement mobilization. Smokers at work are the least socially organized of smokers. Compared to smokers in the realm of sociability, where the group identity is defined by its rituals, smoking workers are merely adding a private subjective note to an activity focused in entirely other terms. The move to drive smoking out of the workplace undercut at least one respectable social interpretation of tobacco; others were to follow.

The height of smoking ritual involving cigarettes was in the 1920s through the early 1950s. The variety of rituals ran the gamut of those promoting various kinds of status to those undercutting eliteness and promoting equality. The era of female emancipation into male pursuits made cigarettes a central ritual of sexual flirting and reinforced the carousing culture of smoking; mass production brought the widespread emulation of upper-class styles in the earlier decades of the century; the war years brought emphasis on rituals of camaraderie and expressions of toughness. The anti-eliteness expressed by the 1940s tough-guy smoker with cigarette hanging from lip was already a step toward challenging and eroding elegance rituals. The expression of status identities through publicly visible rituals plummeted sharply after the war; we had entered the era of predominantly situational stratification. The very ideal of a formally ritualized public order was undermined

Figure 8.5 Women workers, drawn into service in male jobs during World War II, share a cigarette break.

by the counterculture movement of the 1960s, leaving situational prestige on the side of ritual anti-formalism ever since.

Most of the more complex public ritualism of tobacco was already in decline by the 1960s. Mass democracy undermined ritual elitism and the carousing rituals that went along with it. Much of the ritual appeal of smoking was already disappearing before the anti-smoking campaigns began their surge toward dominance. At mid-century, smoking was quantitatively at its height, but it had become more of a privatized activity, without its supports in the realm of the wider status order. It was this vulnerability that created the opportunity in which the dry statistics of health could receive a growing reception.

FAILURES AND SUCCESSES OF ANTI-TOBACCO MOVEMENTS

Anti-tobacco movements arose to counter tobacco rituals. The social appeals and vulnerabilities of the various tobacco rituals have shifted over historical time and presented better or worse opportunities for opponents to mobilize against them. We will consider what social groupings or locations have been offended by tobacco rituals, what tactics they have adopted to mobilize support, and what determines the success of their attacks.

I have described four main kinds of tobacco rituals: those promoting tranquility and withdrawal; carousing; elegance; and work-oriented relaxation and concentration. The first and last of these rituals are weak and relatively defenseless against attack, insofar as they are carried out individually or quietly and make no claim to dominate a social focus of attention. By the same token, they do not create the most strongly motivated opponents, since they provoke no struggle over ritual dominance. Work-oriented smoking, a relatively recent historical development in the mid-twentieth century, was vulnerable to prohibition as soon as a strong anti-smoking movement became mobilized; but the source of this movement was on a different ritual battlefield, and it merely found workplace smoking the most vulnerable target. I am arguing that liking or disliking of tobacco smoke is for the most part not naturally given, but socially constructed; and hence most people did not automatically find tobacco smoke in the workplace to be offensive until there was a social movement that defined tastes in this way. The centuries of quiet pipe-smokers, on the other hand, were generally unmolested in the absence of a strong anti-tobacco movement.

What provokes such movements are the other two types of tobacco rituals, carousing and elegance rituals. These make explicit claims for social dominance: carousing, for the center of attention in the immediate local situation; elegance rituals, for status superiority in the long-term structure of stratification. Carousing rituals promote situational stratification; elegance rituals convey structural stratification and its categorical identities. Both are likely to be contested. There is opposition from old elites who defend preexisting ritual forms of dominance against upstart rituals, thence opposition by traditional autocrats and religious elites to the initial introduction of tobacco. Opposition comes also from persons relegated to the position of situational subordinates by carousing rituals; and from those whose claim to structural status comes from a different resource than making an impression of elegance. Carousing makes enemies out of those who are not carousers, and elegance finds opposition among those who claim the center of status attention for moralistic and other serious pursuits. These latter forms of exclusion, until the twentieth century, had been entwined with gender; and it was only the crossing of gender lines in tobacco rituals that allowed an effective anti-tobacco movement to become fully mobilized.

These kinds of opposition generally remained latent, felt but ineffectively expressed, until mobilizing conditions occurred for them to emerge as explicit social movements. Historically, the strength of these different sources of opposition to tobacco rituals have fluctuated. I will sketch the main types of conflicts analytically rather than chronologically, until we come to the recent period in which an anti-tobacco movement finally achieved widespread success.

Aesthetic Complaints and Struggle over Status Display Standards

A long-standing complaint against tobacco is that it is smelly, dirty, and leaves an unpleasant residue in the form of ashes, pipe scrapings, snuff powder, cigar butts, and the like. In general, women have been the leaders in the aesthetic critique of tobacco. The early dislike of smoking coincided with a period when home architecture and furnishings were changing. The rough medieval buildings, fortress-like for the elite, in close proximity to farm animals for the poor, were giving way to more comfortable quarters as well as more elegant presentation. Homes gradually became less smoky, less smelly from chamber pots, kitchens, and farmyards. Women now complained that tobacco smoke reeked in the curtains at just the time that houses began to have window curtains, rather than wooden shutters. The aesthetic critique of tobacco was at its height in the nineteenth century, at just the time when the house was acquiring a higher standard of freedom from smells, as well as richer accoutrements. The tobacco movement (in this case, largely the cigar-smoking movement) thus ran a rivalry with the movement for the domestic display of social respectability. Tobacco ran counter to the new Goffmanian frontstage of household propriety. The outcome was renewed segregation along gender lines, with both male and female spheres making their own claims to eliteness, with and against tobacco respectively.

Micro-situational struggle over defining one's social class position was especially widespead in the nineteenth century, when a growing middle class was able to make claims for respectability, set off against the still highly visible anchors of aristocratic display at the top, and the filthy conditions of the workers below. In contrast, by the early twentieth century, rudimentary home cleanliness was no longer a criterion of much status differentiation, and the aesthetic critique of tobacco largely faded.

On the whole, aesthetic complaints have never been very effective in eradicating tobacco. Early pipe-smoking, along with nineteenth-century cigar-smoking, were immunized from aesthetic criticism by separation into an all-male enclave. Tobacco chewing was a thoroughly ugly practice in every respect; its appeal was precisely this claim to express frontier democracy, its political nose-thumbing at the aesthetics of what was portrayed as an undemocratic urban elite. At the opposite end of the spectrum came snuff and cigarettes, which achieved their popularity in gender-mixed company and in sociable rituals claiming elegant taste and social status. Here the aesthetically unpleasant aspects were trumped by the ritualistic devices that built up the elegance of tobacco using. On the balance, the tobacco aesthetic tended to win out over its unaesthetic aspects.

Anti-Carousing Movements

The movement against the carousing rituals of tobacco has built upon stronger motivations. It invokes moral objections and thus manifests a Durkheimian community at its most self-conscious, defending its ideals and its boundaries with righteous anger. Anti-carousing movements have been formed against tobacco on the basis of several kinds of memberships and have had several historical moments of success, as well as failure.

When new forms of carousing have been introduced, they have typically been opposed by existing elites in their capacity as upholders of the moral order, and as those whose dominant status was enacted by the rituals of that moral order. The initial reaction to tobacco in Christian Europe and in the Islamic world provide vivid examples. The attack published in 1604 by King James I of England took place at the time when smoking had become a vogue among courtiers; and their behavior was cause for royal concern in other respects as well. This was the time when the state was beginning to centralize military power and to eliminate the independent armies of the feudal lords; a device for doing so was to build up ceremonial attendance at court (Stone 1967). The gathering of both male and female courtiers, unmarried or temporarily unattached from spouses, encouraged sexual licentiousness; and in an era of marriage politics and volatile claims to the throne, together with backstage maneuvers over royal favorites, popularity in courtier circles could be both faddish and dangerous. Thus the imprisonment and execution of Sir Walter Raleigh, famed as the leader of the tobacco fad (and subsequently but inaccurately elevated to the alleged introducer of tobacco into England), occured during faction fighting and denunciations of smoking by James I's favorites. This type of attempt to suppress the new carousing rituals rather quickly failed, since it ran against the grain of modernizing social structures. With the growing complexity of social organization, venues for sociability and status display were expanding outside the control of the great patrimonial households where the dominant rituals had been those of aristocratic rank-display and religious ceremonial. Tobacco rituals were part of a new private sphere, the growth of places and occasions for purely situational stratification, where temporary elites of carousing upstaged the structured elites of political, economic, and religious hierarchy.[16] In the following decades and centuries, carousing rituals blended with elegance rituals to form a differentiated realm of sociable occasions, so that sufficiently elegant forms of carousing became the gateway for admission into the structural hierarchy itself.

The End of Enclave Exclusion: Respectable Women Join the Carousing Cult

Exclusion of women from tobacco carousing rituals set up two kinds of tension. On one hand, women were motivated to attack tobacco. Another motive was to overcome the exclusion and join the action. This is a typical dilemma created by all exclusionary rituals: to attempt to destroy the ritual that imposes lower status on outsiders, or to force one's way in. Before 1920, respectable women did not smoke; those who did were regarded as lower class, although an ambiguous status was emerging of adventurous sophisticates who occasionally smoked.

Cigarette smoking in the early twentieth century became such a rapidly growing movement, and reached such levels of enthusiasm, because it promoted the feeling of breaking down barriers. Two barriers, in fact: the barrier against women joining in the carousing culture; and the barrier against the mid-to-lower classes participating in the smok-

Figure 8.6 The flapper era: self-consciously daring young women share the cigarette-lighting ritual (1928).

ing rituals of the upper classes, which had formerly been blocked by the ritual barriers of smoking rooms, robes, expensive cigars, and the rest. In the IR model (figure 2.1), we see that any source of emotional ingredients feeds into a cumulating process of generalized excitement; the fervor of women smokers and parvenues added to a festive atmosphere that enhanced the mood of the upper-echelon males as well. The various fads in cigarette paraphernalia—cigarette holders, cases, and the like—spread as movements both of inventing new forms of ranking, and of emulating those at higher ranks. The atmosphere was neatly symbolized by (not caused by) Hollywood movies of the 1930s, with their propensity for portraying an idealized upper class at exciting sociable play, and with their display of cigarette smoke as a prominent part of the black-and-white film aesthetic. Film noir of the 1940s expressed the following phase, with curls of smoke rising in the angular shadows complementing the character portrayal of heroic smokers as a strong, tough, and cynical elite.

The display images always involved a strong dose of fantasy, in the little Goffmanian enactments of everyday situations as well as on the screen. Nonetheless they conveyed something socially real insofar as sociability now became centered on mixed-gender gatherings in settings of carousing. The nineteenth-century marriage market, which had been to a considerable degree conducted in family settings—not so much by parental choice as by the necessity of negotiating membership in home rituals—now moved to scenes of parties and other entertainments of the carousing culture. It is conventional to regard this "jazz age" of the 1920s as a drinking culture, pushed into solidarity in the underground through Prohibition; perhaps even more important components were the mixed-gender smoking culture, and the sexual flirtation that went with it. Thus as women joined the smoking world, they brought even more men with them than had previously belonged to it; smoking by men went up to a height of 80 percent in Britain and the United States by 1945, ahead of the sharply rising curve of women smokers.[17]

Women had been split by the two available strategies for confronting exclusionary tobacco rituals: prohibition or inclusion. With victory of the counter-exclusionary strategy, it would appear that tobacco rituals had won. But the end of the split within women's ranks opened the way to a more direct line of assault. Tobacco rituals no longer were all-male enclaves, and hence they no longer were supported by male identity; one source of support for tobacco was eroded. A ritual marking categorical identities by gender had lost its category-marking status. And since gender division no longer overlaid the conflict, the stage was set for conflict as a simple opposition of smokers and non-smokers.

The Health-Oriented Anti-Smoking Movement of the Late Twentieth Century

The anti-smoking movement that became prominent in the 1980s, at first largely in the United States, shifted its focus to health statistics: publicizing first the connection between smoking and life-threatening disease among smokers; and then among non-smokers through exposure to second hand smoke. This late-twentieth-century movement presented itself as a movement of scientific professionals. But there are other components: it was also a movement of public health agencies, consumer advocates, and, finally, of legislators. Perhaps most importantly, it has been a movement of lawsuits, including suits brought both by individuals, and by elected officials, primarily state Attorney Generals, seeking compensatory payments into state budgets and contributions to campaigns to discourage smoking.

The existence of health statistics is not itself an explanation of why this social movement became successfully mobilized in the political and judicial arenas, and why it became widely accepted by American public opinion. Statistics alone do not explain why, in the 1980s, people began to organize impromptu local movements to exclude smokers from workplaces, hotel lounges, waiting areas, restaurants, and their own private homes; and why often quite heated personal confrontations began to take place with smokers. These patterns are characteristic of the mobilization of a social movement passing through a swell of emotional solidarity and of antipathy toward its enemies, and a bandwagon swing to join the victorious side. Statistical documentation of a problem does not explain the strength of a social movement. Statistics are always subject to variations in social interpretation; when they define a risk, there is always a collective assessment of how seriously that risk should be taken. A successful social movement occurs when the risk appears to be very great, but that is a shifting social construction, and has more to do with the dynamics of the movement vis-à-vis its opponent, than with the purely factual character of the threat.[18] The process of movement mobilization drives changes in the perception of the risk, more than vice versa. Once initiated, two components feed back into each other, and when the movement growth reaches the level of a bandwagon effect, both strongly increase each other. We need this full-scale sociological view to understand the success of the health-oriented anti-smoking movement; to leave out the mobilizing process is to operate with a simple technocratic theory, in which the pronouncements of experts automatically determines people's responses.

The first danger of smoking to be well documented was lung cancer.

> The risk of developing lung cancer increases with duration of smoking and the number of cigarettes smoked per day, and is diminished by discontinuing smoking. In comparison with non-smokers, average male smokers of cigarettes have approximately a 9- to 10-fold risk of developing lung cancer and heavy smokers at least a 20-fold risk. . . . The risk of developing cancer of the lung for the combined group of pipe smokers, cigar smokers, and pipe and cigar smokers is greater than for non-smokers, but much less than for cigarette smokers." *Smoking and Health: Report of the Advisory Committee to the Surgeon General of the Public Health Service*, 1964.

A heavy-smoker male age 35 has 33 percent chance of dying—of any cause—before age 65, compared to 15 percent of nonsmoking males (i.e., smoking approximately doubles one's chances of dying at these ages). For coronary heart disease, the annual risk of death is: 7 per

100,000 for non-smokers, 104 per 100,000 for smokers; a ratio of 15 to 1. In raw percentages, however, the story can be told another way: both of these ratios are very low (expressed in more familiar percentages, the former is 0.007 percent, the latter 0.104 percent. Hence a smoker has 98.9 percent the annual chance of a non-smoker of escaping death from coronary disease (Walton 2000, 99–100;103–4). Publicizing the ratios is one form of the rhetorical use of statistics, just as the statements in percentages illustrate another rhetorical usage.

Lung cancer has increased during the twentieth century, from a relatively rare disease before 1920, to one that cause 6.6 percent of all U.S. deaths in 1990, or 57.3 lung cancer deaths per 100,000 population (*Statistical Abstracts*, no. 114, 1992). The historical increase in lung cancer can be attributed to several conditions. One is the shift to cigarettes, which are inhaled, from non-inhaled forms of tobacco. There also has been the extension of longevity in the twentieth century, the result of improved health conditions, and the decline or disappearance of the many of the most prevalent deadly diseases of the earlier centuries.[19] Cancer could show up as a major cause of death in the latter half of the century because there were now more people available at advanced ages where they could die of it.[20] Today total deaths from all kinds of cancer make up 23.4 percent of all deaths, but most of these are not tobacco-related. Campaigns associating smoking with cancer tend to blur over this distinction, playing on people's awareness of cancer in general and unawareness of the actual numbers.

The anti-smoking movement in its period of success after the 1970s was riding upon a redefinition of the normal lifespan: whereas 60 (or even 50) had formerly been considered the onset of old age, it became redefined as within "middle age." And distinctions have been made between various segments of the aged: the "young old" in their late sixties and early seventies; the "old old" in their eighties and beyond. It remains normal to die of *something* during old age, conceived as the terminal period of life; but the medical custom is to attribute all deaths to a specific cause, rather than to "old age" per se.

Cancer is a socially emergent disease in the sense that something had to become the category under which deaths could be recorded. What I am arguing against is the notion that "cancer" is simply a discrete pathological condition, which has a particular cause; and if that cause were eliminated, there would be no such pathology, and people would not die of it. According to this line of reasoning, when cancer is eliminated, then people who would have died from it will continue to live; and once all such diseases are eliminated then people will live forever. Put in this fashion, the flaw in the argument seems obvious. We do not reasonably expect that people will live forever; or indeed that they will likely live very much longer than their eighties or nineties; it may well be case that the bodies of people by around their late eighties have broken down to the point at which sooner or later the system gives out and they die. The terminal process, however, can always be analyzed in more detail, so that it can always be attributed to some proximal cause.

Cancer becomes more prevalent at older ages primarily because aging bodies lose their defenses against it.[21] Smoking earlier in life may contribute to bodily defenses breaking down in particular ways—such as in vulnerability to lung cancer or heart disease—and in some percentage of cases may cause this to occur in one's sixties or seventies instead of eighties. But in a situation of generally declining health in those years, and the near-certainty that some disease or another will cause death, to attribute the death simply to smoking (and thus imply that without the smoking the person would otherwise be alive indefinitely) is an exaggeration. It is part of the rhetoric of polarization: not smoking is good; smoking is bad; and good or evil consequences follow without qualification.

In sum, the evidence does not show that all or even the majority of smokers die of tobacco-induced diseases. Heavy smokers have higher risks of dying earlier than what has become typical life-spans. But since the anti-smoking movement has a polarizing, all-or-nothing rhetoric, it is not concerned to point out what levels of light or moderate tobacco use might be relatively unrisky; and it does not attempt to advocate switching to less risky forms of smoking (such as substituting non-inhaling forms of tobacco use). Its stance is that of the conflict-polarized movement: total abolition of an unmitigated menace.

Similarly on evidence for the effects of second-hand smoke. The anti-smoking movement presents its statistics in maximally dramatic form: it declares that "52,000 persons will die this year in the United States of second-hand smoke." This would not sound so dramatic translated into the percentage of the population that will die.[22] Statements of this sort show the presentation of statistics for rhetorical effect. A weak relationship can be given statistical significance—that is, it can be shown to be a reliable number, even though the causal effect is small—because of the fact that confidence levels depend upon the size of the sample. With a sufficiently large sample (in this case, millions of health records), even a very weak relationship can be shown to be statistically significant. The public, unsophisticated in statistical methods, is impressed with the claim, without considering just what the numbers actually mean.

Another rhetorical manipulation of statistics consists in basing analysis upon persons who were exposed to extremely high levels of second-hand smoke, such as bartenders in smoky bars. This is equivalent to making dire predictions, based on evidence gathered on those who smoke several packs per day, that all smokers, including light ones, will die of tobacco-related diseases. The evidence would equally support the statement that there is relatively little, indeed tiny, levels of risk being around occasional ambient smoke. The construed image that any person exposed to any smoke is likely to die encourages non-smokers to engage in hostile attacks on smokers. Yet statistically the chances of adverse health consequences for exposure to any single incident of enviromental tobacco smoke are vanishingly small.

The anti-smoking movement in the 1980s seized upon the data on second-hand smoke because it gave leverage for portraying everyone in the population as being at risk from the smokers; thus smokers could be portrayed not merely as irrational self-destroying addicts but as murderers. It also gave a justification for anti-smokers to do what they have attempted, with varying degrees of success or failure throughout the last four hundred years, to personally attack smokers in their presence. Given the widespread public acceptance that quickly came about, with little attention to the statistical issues noted above, smokers accepted the attribution of themselves as dangerous offenders. As most of its rituals were undermined, the community of smokers had lost its confidence, its EE, its energy to defend itself. Critics of the statistical adequacy of the anti-smoking argument were treated as representatives of tobacco companies, and were given scant hearing in the U.S. news media or even in scientific publications. The second-hand smoking statistics, weak as they are, were just the catalyst or turning point for an already strongly mobilized anti-smoking movement. Thus any discussion of smokers versus anti-smokers in local struggle over personal space was steered away into exclusive focus upon the tobacco companies and their profit-oriented manipulations. The ordinary smoker lost rank through a virtual reversal of situational stratification: the smoker, once the center of ritual attention, became the pariah.

With the mobilization of an increasingly dominant anti-smoking movement in the 1970s and 80s, non-smokers have often confronted smokers directly, demanding that they stop smoking in their presence. These anti-smokers have been charged with EE to take the initiative rather aggressively in personal encounters. The overt content of their message is straightforwardly medical. In these confrontations, anti-smokers declare that they have serious bodily reactions to smoke, that it makes them ill; some claim that it gives them asthma attacks. These claims are usually taken at face value, given the weight of public pressure on smokers now defined as a dangerous pathology. This backing down by smokers occurred most readily in places where the anti-smoking movement was strongest, in the United States; Americans attempting similar tactics in foreign countries often found themselves confronting angry counterattacks.

Sociologically, we need to examine two kinds of points. One is on the level of the social movement; was there in fact a constant level of asthma attacks, and other feelings of being made ill by smoke, across all the decades of heavy cigarette smoking? Research is lacking on this point; but it appears that the number of persons claiming ill effects of smoke went up during the period of peak mobilization by the anti-smoking movement. Judging from well-publicized cases as well as casual observation during my lifetime, it appears that the numbers of persons claiming to be made ill by smoke in their presence increased at just the time when the number of public smokers were decreasing.

The second point is on the micro-level of bodily interaction. We need not take the position that the perceptions of anti-smokers were merely ideologically constructed because the label of smokers as dangerous and pathological became available—that is, that this was only a cognitive change in interpretation. The anti-smoker angrily confronting a smoker in a restaurant or bus may well have felt unpleasant sensations in his or her body. But the same argument I have made above, that smokers interpret bodily feelings in the context of their ritual interaction, applies to anti-smokers as well. It was when an anti-smoking movement had mobilized and focused on smoke as a noxious experience, that participants' bodies experienced smoke as insupportable. By contrast, in the smoke-filled atmosphere of the war-time 1940s, by all indications, most non-smokers simply took smoke as part of the normal background, at worst a minor nuisance. The ostentatious coughing fits and angry outbursts that occur today are socially constructed in particular historical circumstances; they are constructed in bodies and not merely in minds.

There is a classic sociology of crowd hysterias that encompasses the claims, and feelings, of anti-smokers at their height of mobilization. The classic instances are pseudo-epidemics of medically nonexistent diseases that spread in tightly networked, relatively bounded or enclosed communities like small towns, factories, or boarding schools (Kerckhoff and Back 1968; Lofland 1981, 424–26). Such emotional epidemics may also center on nonmedical conditions, such as laughing epidemics going on for weeks (Provine 1992). It is of course possible that a social hysteria of this sort could also coincide with conditions that pose some degree of medical danger; in this case, tobacco smoke, although as indicated the actual danger of any particular incidence of exposure to second-hand smoke is rather slight, in comparison to the vehemence of the immediate bodily reaction. In recent decades, in the ideological climate of medical verdicts on smoking, few persons are inclined to see the large component of social mobilization which goes into constructing these bodily reactions.

The rhetorical exaggeration of claims by the anti-smoking movement is a version of the ideological polarization that happens in highly escalated conflicts. To attack a ritual is to be offended by it; and since rituals produce social membership and give an aura of status to those who are within the magic circle of social attention, and a negative penumbra of low status among those who are outside it, a ritual social movement can be seen as a struggle over the shape of boundaries and rankings in situational space. Tobacco-using spread as a movement recruiting more and more people into its rituals, and reached its height of popularity as a central feature of the mid-twentieth century status system, the situational stratification that divided the world into fashionable carousers and devalued, even scorned, bystanders. Anti-smokers are a countermovement, mobilized on the rebound, in opposition to the dominance of the smoking movement.

The statistics in themselves do not contain such a strong case for the health risks of smoking as to explain why so many persons turned against smoking so vehemently. The statistics could equally have been interpreted as showing that relatively few people get cancer; that they get it at relatively advanced ages; that many of them would die at approximately those ages anyway; and that there there is a very small chance of being injured by exposure to all but quite intense and prolonged exposure to second-hand smoke. The interpretation put on the data, that the risk is indeed very high and socially intolerable, cannot be explained without the rise of the anti-smoking movement; and that must be seen in relationship to the opportunity presented by the decline in support for almost all varieties of tobacco ritual. On my sociological argument, the public availability of the same data in the 1920s, 30s, and 40s would not have caused the mobilization of a victorious anti-smoking movement.[23]

The Vulnerability of Situational Rituals and the Mobilization of Anti-Carousing Movements

Consider the structure of opposition set up by carousing as a pure form of situational stratification. Any ritual generates situational ranking among those who are at the center of attention, followers, mere observers, and finally the totally excluded. In pure sociability rituals, the terminology has changed over the centuries with the fashions of slang, but the structure is the same. This is the ranking between the popular and the unpopular; belles and beaus vs. wallflowers and duds, the cool and the uncool, party animals and nerds (Milner 2004; Coleman 1961). This is a dimension of social life where sociology has failed to be perceptive; our focus has been so narrowly on the structural stratification of class, ethnicity, and gender that we have overlooked the situational stratification that is for participants often the most salient dimension of everyday life.

The spread of cigarette smoking in the early twentieth century (like the other kinds of tobacco fads or movements previously) flowed through circuits of sociability, and reinforced the stratification between the smoking elite and the non-smoking periphery. Those at the center of sociable gatherings, with their situation-dominating talk, joking, gossiping, sexual flirtation, are those most prone to adopt fads; their central network-positions both enables them to do so quickly, and to reap the emotional energy and situational dominance of being local exemplars of widespread images of prestigeful behavior. At the height of the cult of smoking paraphernalia the ritual promoted a hierarchy, with the most elegant smokers at the center, surrounded by their admirers and followers; other, less sociable smokers further out; and non-smokers beyond the pale.[24] The smoking hierarchy was reinforced by the use of cigarettes for sexual flirtation, thus tending to coincide with erotic popularity.

Situational subordinates are in an especially weak position to mount a counterattack against the rituals that subordinate them. By the nature of ritual assembly, the situational subordinates are those who lack social organization, honor, and emotional energy. They cannot well use their exclusion or dishonor as a basis for collective identity, because achieving "class consciousness" or group consciousness as non-carousers ("wallflowers," "duds," "nerds" etc.) is to heighten dishonor. Thus situational subordinates are for the most part merely latent opponents of the carousing rituals that subordinate them. Situational subordinates can mobilize only if they can invoke alternative criteria of stratification, either structural location or a different form of situational honor. They must rely on standing in the "serious" rather than sociable realms, that is, work and educational careers, politics, religion, and moralistic social movements. These can counterbalance the carousing culture, but do not guarantee victory over it; serious absorption in these pursuits is often the butt of jibes from the carousing culture—to the effect that work, studies, religion, etc. are dull pastimes for those who are failures at popular carousing.

Until the mid-twentieth century, the strongest opponents of carousing rituals came from professions and status groups whose claim for precedence rested upon exemplifying and enforcing moralistic stan-

Figure 8.7 The height of the socially legitimated carousing scene (London during World War II).

dards of social legitimacy. Tobacco has usually been opposed by religious leaders, especially in evangelical movements, and by politicians taking the political niche of moral reform. Anti-carousing movements were mobilized in times of religious upsurges as well as during the intensification of feminist politics. Sometimes these were entwined with ethnic politics, as in the alcohol prohibition movement in the United States, which Gusfield (1963) has interpreted as anchored in the status concerns of rural Anglo-Protestants against the bar-room centered rituals of urban immigrants. Anti-tobacco movements were thus part of a cascade of related movements.[25] But these movements generally ran against the grain of modern social life; since they were rooted in small-town and old-fashioned status hierarchies, they were delegitimated in the self-consciously "modern" or "progressive" world of urban life, public entertainment, and modern business. Moreover, the situational dominants of the carousing elite had their structural allies as well. In the nineteenth century, the cult of cigar-smoking was supported by the status rituals of the upper class and those who emulated them; just as in the 1920s the full paraphernalia of the cigarette cult was connected to the fast world of High Society.

What brought about the reversal of fortunes in the late twentieth century? Briefly: the disappearance of elegance rituals conveying struc-

tural stratification; a greatly increased strength in the structural positions allied to the situational subordinates of carousing; and an episodic development of social movements that mobilized youth at least
temporarily onto the moralistic and anti-carousing side. To put it another way: the decline of elegance rituals; the rise of the "new class"
of technocrats or nerds; and the side-effects of the 1960s counterculture
movement.

By the mid-twentieth century, the complexity of lines of opposition
among smokers and anti-smokers had simplified. Cigarette-smoking
had become the overwhelmingly predominant form of tobacco ritual.
Snuff and chewing tobacco were minor, archaic practices, without
prestige. Pipes had become a fragmented world of solitary introverts,
carrying an aura of rather old-fashioned respectability that cut them
off from the modern connotations of cigarette smokers.[26] The defense
of tobacco in the twentieth century was now a unisex world. To over-
throw tobacco, the anti-smoking movement, for the first time in history, had only one task. It did not have to take on several kinds of
tobacco rituals. It was no longer split between those oriented toward
tobacco-ritual upward mobility, so to speak—those whose opposition
to tobacco was based on being excluded by gender, and who could be
mollified by gaining entry to the tobacco cult—and those opposed to
the carousing culture. The aesthetic attack had been tried and failed.
The successful attack of the late twentieth century was couched in
terms of health issues; but its rapid mobilization as a social movement
was fueled by the politics of ritual in everyday life.

The elegance rituals that supported smoking up through the 1930s
were declining in the 1940s and 50s; in part through the leveling of
social barriers in the military solidarity of World War II; in part
through the American cult of casualness with the suburbanization of
the postwar period. This is not to say structural stratification had disappeared (although economic differences diminished for several decades before the reversal of the 1970s); but its public expression was
becoming illegitimate. Claims to prominence were now made solely in
terms of situational stratification.[27] This focused attention on carousing
rituals, but it also meant situational stratification stood on its own,
without support from structural stratification. Elegance rituals of tobacco were evaporating.[28] This left purely privatized forms of smoking,
such as a work adjunct or as solitary withdrawal, without any cultural
resonance or social support.

As the ritualism of tobacco narrowed, anti-carousing forces were
bolstered by what has sometimes been called the rise of the nerds.
Structural stratification in the later twentieth century was channeled
increasingly through a lengthening educational system and rising for-

mal credentialing for elite jobs. Greater structural importance was given to competition over school grades, studying, and technical knowledge. Although it is an exaggeration to see this as an entirely "new class" of experts (and thus omitting the continued importance of cultural acceptability and of organizational politics rather than utilitarian performance), the contemporary world of professional credentials, bureaucratic careers, and financial manipulations shifted the culture of careers from the leisured atmosphere of well-established businesses and the elite professions that had supported the elegant carousing culture of the earlier part of the century. Wagner (1997) sees the anti-smoking movement, along with other forms of late-twentieth century neo-puritanism, as expressions of the rise of the new middle class, imposing its Protestant Ethic upon upper and lower classes. This has an element of truth, but it can be stated with more refinement. On the macro-structural level, the new prominence of the anti-carousers, the "nerds," is not just a middle-class phenomenon but a style of career behavior found cutting across class levels; and on the micro-situational level, the attack against smoking attacks not just leisure classes but situational dominance through carousing ritual.

All highly politicized protest movements tend to be moralistic, in the sense that dedication and sacrifice to the cause are extolled against the complacency of conventional carousing; historically, radical movements often have had puritanical overtones against the corruption of existing elites. The 1960s Civil Rights / anti-war movements had been mobilized around churches (both black and white) and long-standing "do-gooding" groups, and their organizing bases spread especially to the elite university campuses where their strength was among the "intellectuals" in opposition to the campus carousing culture of the jocks and fraternities. Thus the 1960s movement had many ingredients of religion plus revolt of the nerds.

The anti-smoking movement, however, has not been merely the case of one lifestyle displacing another lifestyle, but a politicized social movement using state power as well as direct action tactics against its foes. This movement mobilized into mass support, like many others, in the wake of the 1960s / early 1970s civil rights and anti-war movements. It is conventional to see the second-wave feminist movement, gay rights, ecology, animal rights, and other movements as building upon the networks, tactics, and ideology of the civil rights movement, emulating its success in attracting public attention and its victories in legislation and overt lifestyle. The contemporary anti-smoking movement should be added to the list. The 1960s movement set the pattern for prestige of a highly moralistic movement that was also a youth movement against established lines of stratification.

Figure 8.8 "Hippie" counterculture. Its ritual was smoking marijuana, in pointed contrast to the cigarette-smoking and alcohol-drinking of the previous generation (late 1960s).

The case is made made more complex by the overlap of these political movements with the so-called "counterculture" movement, the "hippies" with their ideology of sexual liberation and psychedelic drugs (Berger 1981; Carey 1968). This was a type of carousing culture in its own right, although it was both a moralistic and an explicitly oppositional one. Smoking marijuana and taking LSD were interpreted in an ideological context of religious experience modeled on religious mysticism. Left-wing radicals and members of communes were especially likely to use psychedelic drugs (Zablocki 1980); they pointedly regarded their own use as being in sharp contrast to the conventional drinking cult of "jocks and cheerleaders," and were often rather puritanically proud of their nondrinking. Hippie anti-ritualism opposed the conventionally dominant carousing cult, with its weekend drinking parties and its date nights, its hierarchy of the fashionably dressed and socially popular. The "counterculture" counterposed its own style of dress and demeanor (long hair and beards for men, no makeup for women) and pointedly overthrew existing polite rituals of social deference and gender etiquette. The ethos of sexual liberation (or casual sex) and ubiquitous use of psychedelic drugs was in many respects more symbolic than real, but it dramatized the oppositional ideology that sociable pleasures can be enjoyed without formal scheduling and without constraint from the popularity rankings of conventional carousing rituals.

The counterculture of the 1960s was ephemeral, but it gave impetus to long-term shifts: to the near-terminal decline of elegance rituals, the disappearance of older standards of deference and demeanor; to the preeminence of situational stratification; and to the culturally dominant prestige of expressing an oppositional stance to conventional symbols of structural stratification. The 1960s movements set the pattern for youth culture for the remainder of the century. Inadvertently it opened the way for a massive push against smoking rituals. In undercutting the prestige of the partying culture, the carousing style that came in with cigarettes in the 1920s, it reversed the association of cigarettes with an oppositional youth culture and left them open for portrayal as part of a despised Establishment.

The trends set off by the 1960s counterculture combined to boost the anti-smoking movement of the following decades: the attack on conventional sociability rituals by the counterculture, and its undermining of elegance rituals in the name of radical egalitarianism; its moralistic tone; its tactics of direct action confronting government officials and segregationists; its left-wing rhetoric attacking business corporations. By one of those strange twists that often convert some components of a successful movement into challenging its other components, these characteristics of the counterculture merged with the backlash against the drug culture, the anti-drug movement. The movement to extirpate smoking marijuana set the legislative pattern that paved the way for tobacco prohibition, and tobacco companies could be blamed for inculcating the taste for tobacco in the same way that drug pushers were regarded as responsible for the drug culture. The anti-tobacco movement of the 1970s and thereafter drew upon the ideological and tactical frames of 1960s movements by targeting the tobacco industry as the primary culprit, and thus portraying smokers as dupes and victims. Persistent smokers could also be directly confronted with the activist rhetoric reminiscent of Vietnam war confrontations accusing them of

being killers. The anti-smoking movement has been unusually successful, compared to most other reform movements of this era, because it
managed to combine both left- and right-wing support: the Left with
its anti-business stance and its favor for government regulation; the
Right in the form of religious and lifestyle conservatives who have attempted to ban the substances of carousing for centuries.

The success of the anti-smoking movement, after centuries of failure,
came about by a concatenation of changes in the ritualism of sociability
that prepared the way for a social movement attacking tobacco rituals
while enjoying the moral prestige of a popular progressive movement.
Whether or not these particular ritual and anti-ritual movements are
nearing an historical end, it is altogether probable that movements of
these sorts will develop around the ritual substances and practices of
the future.

Chapter 9

INDIVIDUALISM AND INWARDNESS

AS SOCIAL PRODUCTS

IN THE PERSPECTIVE of IR chains, is there any place left for the individual? It might seem that the theory fails to do justice to individuals, and especially to their autonomy, idiosyncracy, and apartness. The modal character of IR theory seems to be a gregarious extrovert, always caught up in the mood of the crowd or the buzz of a conversation, seeking attention, shunning solitude. What about the nonstandard personality, going his or her own way, the individualist, the nonconformist? Can IR chains account for the introvert, the person who dislikes parties and noisy crowds, who prefers his or her own thoughts to others' conversation? Why are there persons who find books interesting and people boring? Why are there moments when we would much rather be alone watching the clouds taking their shapes across the sky? In short, can IR theory account for persons who are deep rather than shallow, independent rather than approval seeking?

Since most readers of a book such as this, and most intellectuals generally, are likely to fall nearer the individualistic and introverted end of the spectrum, IR theory had better be able to account for them if it is to have any claim to general validity.

In the Durkheimian tradition, the individual emerges by an apportioning out of collective energies and representations. When a particular human body walks away from a social encounter, he or she carries a residue of emotions and symbols, and what he or she does in those moments alone comes from their interplay, whether reflecting backward in time, forward to future encounters, or into an inner space of thought, mind, or subjectivity. Mead's symbolic interactionism gives another version of the same: the self is internalized from interaction. This has been the core sociological position throughout the twentieth century; our researches have accumulated plenty of evidence to support it. The only issue, it seems to me, is whether we have the nerve to go all the way with it, to confront the biases of modern culture that, in Goffman's terms, make a sacred object out of the individual, and carry on a cult worshiping the image of the self. The *image*, be it noted, since in Goffman's interaction ritual it is a social representation of what the self is supposed to be, not a true, inner, autonomous self. As Goffman said in the conclusion to *The Presentation of Self* (1959, 252): the self is the product of a successful interactional performance, "of a scene that comes off, and is not a cause of it."

Standing against this central sociological tradition there are, to be sure, some respectable alternatives. There is the rationally calculating, selfish individual of the utilitarian tradition, enshrined in economic theory, and in a good deal of modern political philosophy, with a bridgehead in sociology itself. There is Freud's conception of the id, the unsocialized core of human desire. Perhaps most importantly for persons who think of themselves as intellectuals, there is the tradition of the free-thinking artist, the rebel, defying convention and scorning success in order to follow the dictates of his or her wild, impetuous, creative soul—I have purposely let the description get carried away into its full nineteenth-century Byronic rhetoric, to remind us that this way of talking about the individual self is a historically situated tradition. When we extol individual genius in its struggle against social conformity we are, far from rebelling and displaying our uniqueness, revealing our membership in a widespread modern cult movement.

And finally, we might take note of a perspective that is not popular among contemporary intellectuals although it is there in the historical background: a religious perspective that holds that what is most real about the self is inward, not outward, not reducible to society or to anything else. Expressed in secular terms, this says that it is what happens inside that is ultimately most valuable, what takes place in your own consciousness, your particularized vantage point of the world and your own experience in it; that is what makes you what you are: "They may control my body, but they can't control my mind; I am the master of my fate; I am the captain of my soul." With historical reflexivity one can see the social roots of this way of thinking; but that does not invalidate the substance of the argument: the inner individual is what counts.

The weakness of alternative lines of theory has been addressed in previous chapters. What follows here is a demonstration that IR theory can handle all the phenomena envisioned in these theories, and more. IR theory must show not only that there is a place for individuals in its conceptual universe, but it must set forth the social conditions under which the various forms of individuality, and ideologies about individuality, occur.

There are several subissues here to be separated out. First is the question of *individuality*, the existence of a large variety of different personalities. This is not in fact a very hard challenge for IR theory; and I will summarize points already made in previous chapters that give social conditions for different personality types. There are several dimensions of social causality operating here, which intersect one another; thus it may well be that every person is unique (at least in complex modern societies), even though each is compounded out of elements held in common with many others.

Second is the issue of explaining the type of personality who is distinctly non-sociable, which twentieth century terminology has called the introvert. There are, in fact, some half-dozen types of introverts, ourselves perhaps among them; all of these can be shown to be produced by particular kinds of IR chains. The most pronounced types of introversion appeared relatively recently in modern history; the next section will deal with that historical development. At the same time that introverted personality types were historically created, there came into being a broader ideology about individualism as a foundational principle for the modern world; and thus we will end by looking at how this ideology, unsociological and indeed anti-sociological as it is, came about. Going through these issues gives opportunity for pulling together the threads of the book.

The Social Production of Individuality

The easiest way to summarize the effects of IR chains on individual personalities is to consider the main dimensions of stratified interaction. In chapter 3, these were referred to as status rituals and power rituals.

On the dimension of status rituals, persons differ in how close they are to the center of attention and emotional entrainment: the person who is always at the center, those close by or sometimes in the center, those further out, marginal members, non-members. In an older terminology of network analysis, these are sociometric rankings from sociometric stars outward; in ordinary language, social popularity. Sociologically we make the picture more complicated—in principle at least—by examining each situation the individual is in, and looking not only at his or her degree of centrality in the interaction, but also at the degree of ritual intensity (how much collective effervescence was aroused, to what extent did the IR succeed or fail); how bounded are these IRs (whether it is always the same persons or a changing cast of characters—what chapter 3 called the *social density of interaction*); finally, moving to the meso-level and summarizing over the course of the IR chain, to what extent is the individual repeatedly in the same kinds of IRs and in the same position within them (*IR repetitiveness*).

For purposes of demonstrating the social production of individual differences, we can use a simplified summary model, the amount of

Durkheimian mechanical solidarity experienced by each individual. The more central an individual is in IRs of high intensity and high social density, and with a high degree of IR repetitiveness and high degree of network redundancy,[1] the more he or she has strong feelings of solidarity with the group and its symbols, and expects conformity from others. He or she takes the group's symbols in a concrete and reified way, as immutable and irreprochable realities not to be questioned or criticized;[2] disrespect for membership symbols leads to emotional outbursts of righteous anger and ritualistic punishment.

These patterns are familiar in sociology as group dynamics or group cultures (Homans 1950). We can also view them as characteristics of individual personalities. There is a modal personality for high Durkheimian mechanical solidarity: conforming, traditionalistic, who thinks and talks particularistically about other concrete individuals and the lore of the group, which is to say the person is gossipy and localistic, warm toward familiar persons, suspicious of outsiders, vengeful toward violators. At the other end of the continuum is low mechanical solidarity, where persons are peripheral to groups, and / or their rituals are low intensity, low social density and high diversity of interactions, low IR repetitiveness, and low network redundancy.[3] The modal personality is unconforming, relativistic, thinks and talks in abstractions, is cool in social commitments, tolerant of differences, lax on violators. In between the two extremes are personalities whose characteristics shade over from one type to the other.

Now for the second major dimension: power rituals. At one pole are order-givers, telling other people what to do, getting deference from others in their presence who at least pretend to accept their orders (i.e., who give a situational presentation of self as willing subordinates). Order-giving makes one proud, self-possessed, and identifying with the symbols in terms of which one gives orders. Persons enacting power rituals are frontstage personalities, identifying strongly with their official self, which they regard as more significant than their private self. At the other pole are order-takers, those who have no alternatives but to put up with taking orders and defer to those who give them. Order-taking creates a backstage personality; they identify against the frontstage show that controls them, and are cynical and alienated from authority to the extent that they have private backstages on which they can be free of official formality.

Between the extremes are persons who display these characteristics in lesser degree. Some of the intermediate positions on the power continuum have special situations and personality traits that should be singled out. There are two ways of being in the middle of the power continuum: One kind is an egalitarian situation, where persons neither

	high mechanical solidarity	*low mechanical solidarity*
order givers	traditionalist authoritarian	sophisticated cosmopolitan; frontstage personality
egalitarian	localistic group conformist	informal, casual, friendly
first-line supervisors	bureaucratic personality	perfunctory bureaucratic
order-takers	backstage personality; subservient / alienated	backstage personality; privatized

Figure 9.1 Ideal type personalities from status and power dimensions.

give nor take orders, but interact horizontally. This position neutralizes the power dimension; personalities located here are neither frontstage formalists identifying with the vertical hierarchy nor backstage cynics withholding themselves from it, but merely embody the symbolic culture of the immediate local group. The other kind of position in the middle of the power hierachy consists in individuals who are in the chain of command, taking orders from those above and giving orders to others below. Especially distinctive here are the lowest echelon of order-givers, who give orders to those who are purely order-takers. This is the drill sergeant in the army, the foreman in factory, the first-line supervisor in the office, the petty official who enforces regulations on the public. Here is found the so-called bureaucratic personality, the petty rule-follower, enforcing rules to the letter rather than in the spirit of the enterprise, a sheer exercise of authority without vision of what the authority is for. Those who face this kind of petty order-giver from below are especially strongly alienated by being an order-taker. Their encounters are the front line of class conflict on the micro-level.

For present purposes, let us take the simplified, composite version of the two dimensions; combining them gives the table of personality types displayed in figure 9.1. This shows eight types of personalities, since I have divided the status dimension into two polar types, and the power dimension into four. We could just as well divide the status and power dimensions into more categories, since each of these is a continuum. It would be realistic to distinguish ten points along each

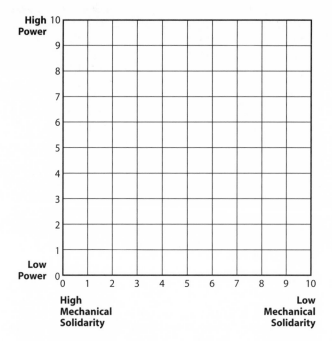

Figure 9.2 Multiple personality types from status and power dimensions.

continuum; combining these gives us the set of personality types in figure 9.2. These total one hundred distinctive personalities. Although it may be the case that some of the cells in this figure are relatively rare, and in some societies certain regions of the grid are not occupied at all, we would still expect there to be several dozen types of distinctive individuals in most communities.

And this is on the conservative side. After all, the status and power dimensions given here are composites of several subdimensions. If we broke up the "mechanical solidarity" dimension into the degrees to which individuals experience ritual centrality, ritual intensity, social density, diversity of connenctions, IR repetitiveness, and network redundancy, we would have a "personality space" in multiple dimensions, which would yield a very high number of distinctive combinations. We can cut the continuums as finely as we like, and combine as many subdimensions as we wish to see; thus it is entirely plausible that among millions of persons, each one is in some way or another a distinct individual. They are socially produced, by a small number of generic social processes, to be distinctive. I am leaving aside the arbitrary and particularistic details of people's lives (such as whether they grew up in a little village in the western region of Hungary rather than a village in the eastern region) that make them different in content, if not in pattern. Individuality does not controvert a deeply penetrating, omni-explaining sociological theory; on the contrary, it follows from it.

SEVEN TYPES OF INTROVERSION

On the face of it, introverts seem to challenge the premises of IR theory, that the human being is an emotional energy seeker, and that EE is an offshoot of solidarity in social interaction. There are, indeed, many nongregarious individuals; some are even quite militantly anti-gregarious. (For those who may suspect me of a bias on the other side, I will go on record in saying that I count myself among the ungregarious.) To explain nonsociable persons, it is useful to recognize different types, which is to say, different pathways to unsociability. These are ideal types and thus can overlap.

Work-Obsessed Individuals

Some persons prefer working to socializing, and indeed to any type of collective ritual—political, religious, or entertainment. This type of person may be only a borderline form of introversion, however, since, as discussed in chapter 4, there are also IRs that take place on the job. Here it is a straghtforward case of an individual who gets more EE from interacting with other persons at work than he or she gets from opportunities for socializing: the busy stockbroker or business deal-maker who is in the center of the action; the lecturer who gets most of his or her deference in the classroom; the Napoleonic general who sleeps only a few hours per night because he is energized by controlling the action of combat.

A more difficult case are those who work alone.[4] The blanket terms of modern slang do not discriminate well between interactional and solo work-obsessed individuals; "workaholic" refers to all of them, while "grind" and "nerd" imply the solo type. These latter are derogatory terms, implying the viewpoint of the gregarious socializer, with the term "nerd" in particular carrying the connotation of a socially inept person who is wrapped up in technical details and prefers machines to peoples (Eble 1996).

Consider such a person through the lens of IR chains. Individuals acquire their technical skills, not in solitude, but in chains of encounters. This learning occurs, not for the most part in formal schooling

(Collins 1979, 16–17) but on the job, and especially by early, informal interaction with other persons who already have expertise. These skills have typically been monopolized by males—especially by networks of working-class and lower-middle-class males—above all because they are inducted into a technical world as teenage boys (or even younger) by being around their fathers, male relatives, and friends. Boys learn auto mechanics by repairing cars in the family driveway, just as they learn to operate heavy equipment by informal apprenticeship to their relatives who work on it. Similar patterns recur in late-twentieth-century computer culture (except it is more a horizontal network among the boys themselves rather than an intergenerational network).

Two points are salient here for the social character of being a technology-oriented, or technology-obsessed, otherwise unsociable person. First: these skills and interests arise in a particular kind of social interaction. They become internalized; the solitary practice of a technical skill is a form of second- and third-order recirculation of symbols of group membership. The technical skill itself is the symbol or emblem, the focus of subjective identification, just as much as the solitary religious prayer is a third-order circulation of religious membership symbols. And in the case of technical expertise, these are stratified emblems; they sharply demarcate those persons who know how to do it from those who haven't a clue, with a middle ground of degrees of ineptness and apprenticeship in between. Just as non-nerds look down on nerds, nerds in their own element look down on those outside their charmed circle.

The second point is that there is another network operating besides the human experts. There is also a network from machine to machine, or technique to technique. I have shown this in the case of the community of scientists, from the time of the so-called "scientific revolution" (which is more accurately called the revolution in "rapid-discovery science") through the present, where the networks of scientists became entwined with genealogies of laboratory equipment (Collins 1998, 535–38). New scientific developments typically come from tinkering with previously used laboratory equipment, modifying it to produce new phenomena for scientists to theorize, and by cross-breeding several genealogies of lab equipment to make new forms of research equipment. The two networks, human scientists and genealogies of machines, are entwined because typically only those persons who have worked hands-on with the previous generation of equipment are able to make them operate successfully when they are shifted to a new setting (for an example, see Shapin and Schaffer 1985). The same pattern, I argue, holds in the realm of virtually all technical expertise. When auto buffs gather in their garage to look under the hood, they size up what they see by its kinship with other motors they know. Much of their conversation consists in naming the genealogies—how this one relates to and differs from other models they have seen before or only heard about. Such technical talk, boring if not meaningless to outsiders, is no different in its own realm, from the gossiping about relatives, the latest doings of friends, and the reminiscing about old times that close-knit family networks carry out in their sociable gatherings (for a detailed description of the latter, see Gans 1962, 77). Granovetter (2002, 56–7) discusses what he calls "nerd culture," which he finds both among late-twentieth-century computer hackers and among nineteenth-century American mechanical inventors, tinkering with their equipment and traveling about impressing one another with their achievements (see also Wright 1998).

When technology-oriented persons gather, they appear to be unsociable in the conventional sense—they are not ebullient, joking, story-swapping, or gossipy. In fact, they are often averse to interaction of this kind, find it draining, and thus give the appearance of being shy. This is a case of being specialized in a particular kind of IR chain that brings EE, and that they much prefer over other kinds of IRs in which their symbols and emotions do not match up with what other people are exchanging. Technical experts do become entrained in IRs, indeed engrossed in them, when they meet another technical expert; even here, the IR differs from ordinary sociability in that it is not usually conversation primarily but is centered on a piece of technical equipment. They appear to be staring at and manipulating a physical object more than talking to each other. They are communicating meanings in just the way that Wittgenstein (a complicated nerd if there ever was one) points out—by showing, doing, pointing, not by self-contained verbal description (Wittgenstein, 1953, 1956). In fact, they are interacting with each other via the equipment, and thereby tacitly invoking the rest of the far-flung network of machines related to the one in front of them, and the community of experts held together through these machines. The machinery is the sacred object of a cult. In the last analysis it is not a cult of technology itself; behind every Durkheimian sacred object is the community that is joined together by their focus upon it.

Socially Excluded Persons

A second type of borderline introvert consists of persons who are outside the center of social gatherings through no desire of their own. Interaction rituals are implicitly (and sometimes explicitly) stratified between those who are in the center of attention, and are thereby the most engaged and socially oriented, out through a layer of attention-contenders and followers, and finally reaching those on the margins of the group, and those totally excluded. The peripherals and outcasts have less EE than those nearer the group center; they are the lowest ranked in the stratification of EE.[5] They are also less committed to group symbols (for evidence see Homans 1950), and in that sense they are nonconformists. But they are not necessarily full-fledged introverts, in the sense of being withdrawn into their inner pyschic experience. Depressed, wistful, sad, perhaps; in the absence of other structural conditions that move them into another type of introversion, they remain oriented toward the group with the hope that it will let them in some time. Such individuals may make pathetic compromises, being willing to play the fool or serve as the scapegoat, taking negative attention as better than no attention at all.

Situational Introverts

These are individuals who avoid particular kinds of sociability, but throw themselves into other kinds. They give the impression of being shy, diffident, or withdrawn when they are in situations where their stock of symbols and their EE loadings do not match up well with those of other persons present. In other situations, where they do match up well, they become outgoing, spontaneous, full participants. There is nothing schiozophrenic about these personalities; they are simply following principles of the IR market, attracted to EE-producing IRs, avoiding EE-losing ones. Structurally, such persons apear where they are located in complicated multi-centered networks, with intermittent opportunities for interaction in quite different milieux. It is the network that is schizophrenic, not the individual.

A subtype here might be called "peerless introverts." The adjective "peerless" is used in a literal sense: these are elite individuals who lack peers on their own level to interact with, or even sufficiently distinguished followers. This type is frequently described in eighteenth- and nineteenth-century biographies and novels.[6] A member of the upper class living in a country house—especially the male head of household—often spent much time alone, withdrawn in his library; when dining *en famille* such a gentleman might waste few words in conversation with spouse or children at the table. This gives the impression of introversion, but its social motivation is lack of class-appropriate company. The same individual generally displays the conventional social graces when there are house parties and shooting meets in the country, and a complete sea-change in manners occurs when he moves into London for the sitting of Parliament and the social Season.[7]

The situational introvert is an ideal type, and an individual in this social situation might be a candidate for becoming an introvert in a stronger sense.

Alienated Introverts

We now reach the types of introverts who better fit the modern stereo-type. Here is the rebellious individualist, who scorns the crowd and is proud of nonconformity. There are several pathways by which an individual could reach this position. Following IR theory, what all paths have in common is that the EE attraction of most available social interaction is lower than the alternatives, and indeed is negative, an emotional energy drain. There is always a certain amount of ideal type schematization in the viewpoint of the alienated person: he or she is negatively oriented by contrast to a crowd, scene, or group perceived as dominant, and which he or she is escaping from. The alternative to belonging or giving in to the overweening social presence, however, is not necessarily solitude. Alternatives include reserving one's social participation for another social milieu, which is more highly but eso-terically ranked: the artist versus the crass commercial mob; the sensi-tive person versus the superficial hilarity of the popular crowd; the social class superior avoiding class inferiors among whom he or she is, for the present, stuck. Another kind of alternative comes from com-mitment to internalized, third-order circulation of symbolic objects. Gatherings with one's preferred group may perhaps be few and far between, so that most of the time one has the choice of unsatisfactory IRs or none at all; the alienated introvert chooses the latter.

In some respects, the position of the rebellious introvert passes through a phase that resembles the socially excluded type. But most of the socially excluded, I have argued, do not rebel but conform, hoping to get into the group as fortunes change. What makes the difference? In principle, a combination of two conditions makes introversion delib-erate, self-conscious, self-constructed opposition to the group and its conformity. One is the existence of alternative opportunities on the IR market; I have sketched some of the ways this can come about.

A second pattern, complementary to the first is especially important for creating an attitude going beyond mere withdrawal to rebellion. That occurs when the interaction rituals of the dominant group—the group that controls the largest focus of attention—are not really so im-pressive in terms of purely situational stratification. That is where groups engage in empty and forced rituals. These are rituals with more form than substance—the group is gathered, markers and entry barri-ers clearly distinguish members from nonmembers, and those in the center of ritual attention from the secondary and lower ranked. But the emotional tone is flat; participants put in an appearance and go through the motions but without enthusiasm and without generating much collective effervescence. Such were gatherings of the British aristocracy in the late nineteenth and early twentieth centuries, the foil for an underground of Victorian and Edwardian rebels;[8] so were conventional upper- and upper-middle class rituals of sociability that were scorned and upstaged by the counterculture rebels of the 1960s.

The process is closely analogous to the devaluation of Catholic religious rituals at the time of the Reformation: the old rituals were not only empty, but forced; through pressures of status hierarchy, patrimonial household organization, or outright threat of violent punishment, the old rites were kept going but as an emotionally empty shell. Such rituals generate little EE and lose out in attraction to alternative rituals that appear unofficially and in an underground movement, that have emotional intensity and thereby charge up their participants with EE. It is this charge of EE that gives individuals the confidence to challenge the Establishment. To do so may be a courageous act, if negative consequences are risked; but often the situation is at a tipping point, and the bandwagon effect sets in—one need only follow the flow of emotions to feel where rituals are flat and where they are vivid, to know where the crowd is moving.

For this reason, the alienated introvert is often a transitory phenomenon. The type emerges in numbers precisely because social conditions are shifting, so that old rituals and forms of stratification built upon them are declining. Macro-historical shifts feed into the ingredients for staging a ritual (figure 7.1 feeds into figure 2.1). I will say more on this shortly, and only note here that older rituals underwent great strain during the shift from categorical identities to situational stratification, and that considerable deserting of sinking ships went along with it.

Solitary Cultists

There is a type of introversion that consists in solitary activity, centered on objects or procedures that have been charged up with membership significance. The prototype is private religious devotion. As I have argued, secular equivalents have become prominent in recent centuries: the solitary pipe-smoker, the hobbyist, the technology-obsessed. Under this rubric we may distinguish several different degrees or kinds of introversion, depending on whether these activities take place in a situation of second-order or third-order circulation of symbols. Second-order circulation takes symbols charged up in primary ceremonial gatherings and treats them as tokens for further exchange. The main form of secondary circulation is conversation recycling symbols from elsewhere, but there is a solitary version, where the circulation is done by the mass media. Should we call someone an introvert if his or her favorite pastime is to watch TV or listen to the news by oneself? The example shows that there is an in-between type of withdrawal from overt social interaction, a sociably-oriented kind of introversion, obsessive sociability while physically alone.[9]

There is also third-order circulation of symbols in the internal conversations of one's own mind. Such inner circulation may sometimes also be emergent, innovative, and unique, going beyond the conventional symbols into idiosyncratic individual usage. As sociologists, we do not know much about this systematically, in the absence of research on people's inner dialogues. It is likely that much inner devotion to one kind of symbolic cult or another—religious, entertainment, technical, sexual—may take typical, widely recurrent forms (something after the fashion that at one time it was believed to be popular for madmen to imagine they were Napoleon). Even to the extent that private cults evolve on their own paths, these paths are laid down by social starting points, and the motivation to pursue them is determined by the resources and opportunities for EE-seeking on IR markets. Solitary, internal experience is programmed from the outside in; the distribution of solitary cults must be at least roughly correlated with the distribution of their social versions.

Intellectual Introverts

Intellectuals are in one sense a species of solitary cultists. But across the historical spectrum, this was not always the case. Modern intellectuals spend a good deal of time in private reading and writing, but in early periods there was less opportunity for privacy. Ancient and medieval intellectuals generally made their reputations in face-to-face debates, and in all historical periods intellectuals have supplemented their expertise in texts with the impressiveness of their lectures and discussions. Texts are always mediated, not only by other texts, but by the networks of intellectuals who orient to texts. There are, to be sure, historical variations in how much time intellectuals spend alone reacting to texts and creating new texts, and in that sense modern intellectuals are more introverted than traditional intellectuals.[10]

It is intellectuals' experience in the network of intellectuals that constitutes them as intellectuals, and shapes the contents of their thinking as they take up a position vis-à-vis other intellectuals in seeking their niche in the attention space. The very motivation that causes some intellectuals deliberately to withdraw from interaction, spending long hours or years alone with their manuscripts, is precisely their deep internalization of the intellectual field as the framework of their minds. They withdraw precisely in order to concentrate on the creative action that will get them into the center of the intellectual attention space; and they get their emotional energy from the reinforcement that comes to them in putting sentence by sentence on the page, viewing their own moves by the standards of a field they know from inside.

The intellectual world (more exactly, each intellectual specialty) is a stratified network, and an intellectual's type of introversion is determined by his or her IR chain within that network. At the center are those individuals who get the widespread attention that constitutes their reputations as the great creative thinkers: the Shakespeare, the Helmholtz, the Max Weber. To refer once more to evidence compiled in my study of philosophers and their networks (Collins 1998), the major thinkers are those most tightly connected to other important intellectuals: both in vertical chains across the generations from famous masters to their pupils; and in horizontal chains of compatriots who make their reputations together in the new generation, shaping their distinctive positions by engaging in quarrels with leading opponents. Comparison of the network pattern of these intellectual stars with the various degrees of lesser intellectual success, and intellectual failure, too, confirms the importance of positions within networks. It is relative lack of the crucial network ties, especially at the moment of launching one's career and internalizing one's stance vis-à-vis one's predecessors and compatriots, that makes others fall short of the great creative successes. Successful intellectuals are the most socially penetrated of introverts.

Intellectuals at the center owe their success to their position in networks of other intellectuals. They have a strong pragmatic sense (not necessarily self-conscious and reflexive, but spontaneous, in-action) of what symbols are charged with membership significance in what circles of the intellectual world, and what chains of arguments and evidence flow in their train; they have a good sense of the mental alliances that they can put together via new combinations of symbols. They owe their speed in thinking up new ideas and publishing them before others reach similar conclusions to their strong sense of what alliances are coming up on the horizon. Less eminent and less successful intellectuals suffer their fates because they are less advantageously placed in these networks. They are too far from the hot center of action, and only acquire the ingredients for their own new ideas after they have already circulated through many other conversations and other minds. Some, firmly aware through career experience of their own derivative position in the networks, settle into a modest position of applying well-known theories and techniques to specialized problems; or to being a teacher or textbook writer, recirculating the ideas that have been creative elsewhere.

Persons both at the very center of intellectual networks, and those in firm positions as modest followers, may well be introverts, in the sense of spending much time in solitary bookish pursuits; but both the stars and the followers are highly socialized by the intellectual community. They are for the most part neither alienated nor rebellious nor idiosyncratic introverts.[11] Truly idiosyncratic intellectuals are found in other network locations. These include many persons on the outer margins of intellectual networks, especially autodidacts, operating far from the regular transmission networks of the field's cultural capital, assembling a checkered combination of teachings remote from the current centers of intellectual advance. The autodidact chooses his or her own readings, more or less accidentally according to what comes along, and this can lead to a combination of intellectual positions from widely ranging fields and historical epochs. Their ideas are often genuinely idiosyncratic, although many of them are simply followers of positions that had their heydays in previous centuries (modern-day occultists are typically of this sort). A person who builds an intellectual identity upon this kind of random access to cultural capital is unlikely to meet much success in the stratified networks that make up the intellectual world; and this experience may make them not only idiosyncratic but alienated—individualistic and proud of it, sometimes belligerently so. This kind of intellectual introvert may be combined with other types, depending on the social conditions that come into play. He or she may become a solitary cultist, satisfied with one's own idiosyncracy; or by bordering on mobilized political movements, become a terrorist or serial killer.[12]

These are exotic types, far more so than the average intellectual of whatever eminence, and no doubt rare even among autodidacts. To complete the gallery of portraits, let me add one more type of intellectual introvert that arises from a very significant network location. The intellectual world is structured by a limited amount of attention space in each specialty: historical evidence on reputations shows that there is room for only three to six major positions to receive attention in any one generation. This means that of the many intellectuals who get good starts, as pupils of previous stars and compatriots of those moving onto the new forefront of intellectual action, there is a high proportion who fail to receive attention for their contributions. Most intellectuals, by the time they reach mid-career, recognize their position and opt for a smaller niche. Those who choose to stand their grround and fight out their claim to be a major figure will thus include a number who are bound to be disappointed: not because their ideas are poor, but because their ideas are good, indeed deriving from as good a stock of intellectual capital and as good a sense of fruitful combinations and advances as those who get the star recognition. They are structurally squeezed out by "the law of small numbers." It is this scenario that produces the embittered withdrawn intellectual introvert.

Call this the Schopenhauer syndrome: a bright young man who comes from the same universities as the star performers of the German Idealist movement, launched by the same network of famous names. But Schopenhauer is a little younger and comes along just at the time when Hegel and a few other stars have secured the major university positions and garnered the student audiences and the reading public. No one comes to Schopenhauer's lectures, and he retires to a solitary, misanthropic life; he is redeemed only because he lives to a very old age, long enough to be rediscovered by the third generation of German intellectuals rebelling from the dominance of Hegel's generation of Idealists. Not everyone, like Schopenhauer, throws his landlady down the stairs or shuns all company for a solitary routine of playing his flute, writing his notes for a book he expects no one will read, and visiting the brothels of Frankfurt. But the type is visible enough in today's intellectual world, and if we look we see him in the shadows of intellectual success for many generations back.[13]

The embittered intellectual is a version of the alienated introvert, but alienated in a specialized location. He (or she) may or may not be alienated in the conventional sense of standing in opposition to the non-intellectual world; but the intellectual who is squeezed out of recognition by the limited attention space is often alienated against the intellectual world in particular. Given that the professional intellectual operates by deeply internalizing the social structures of the field into one's own mind, this can be an especially intimate and painful form of introversion.

Neurotic or Hyper-Reflexive Introverts

Finally we come to the type of introvert that is perhaps most emblematic of the whole genre. This is the type, familiar in the culture of entertainment from Hamlet to Woody Allen, whose introversion is torn, conflictual, indecisive, self-destructive. The fame of psychoanalysis and other forms of psychotherapy in the twentieth century generated a huge literature and widespread public consciousness of this type. From the perspective of IR theory, I will add only two points.

One is to underscore the conclusion, implicit in the foregoing, that introverts can be either satisfied or dissatisfied. There are many social locations for the various types of introverts I have listed. Work-obsessed introverts, situational introverts, many solitary cultists, and many or most intellectuals, are neither socially conflicted nor personally unsatisfied. Some of them—especially work-oriented and intellectual introverts—have very high levels of EE, which they put into their solitary pursuits, and from which they reap considerable enjoyment. Socially excluded persons, on the other hand, are not usually very happy, but as an ideal type they are generally not very inward persons, and are not innerly conflicted. Alienated introverts are overtly conflicted but mainly against dominant social circles, and even then, they often become part of a social movement or a clique of similarly alienated persons; taken again as an ideal type produced by distinctive social conditions, alienated introverts are not necessarily inwardly torn.

This leaves us with the pure type of neurotic introvert; better to eschew technical terminology, and call them hyper-reflexive introverts. Such individuals apparently arise in combination with, and as a further complication of, one of the other types of introverts. Hyper-reflexive introverts are insecure in their social location; their internal dialogue is unusually multi-sided and contentious. This is Hamlet unable to make up his mind; Woody Allen second-guessing and bad-mouthing himself, dooming his prospects before they get started. Such a person must have internalized a complex network pattern.[14]

This would be a location in several networks of different shapes, or in networks that are changing drastically in form. We would not expect a hyper-reflexive person to emerge from a tightly bounded, redundantly connected network of Durkheimian mechanical solidarity; there an individual's reputation might be low (if they are the scapegoat or outcast of the group), but their social reputation is simple and clearly recognized, and there is nothing else to internalize. To produce a hyper-reflexive inner self, there must exist networks that allow the individual considerable oportunities and freedom for solitary experience, but at the same time pulls his or her emotional energy in several directions at once. If true introverts appear because the attraction of the group consists of nothing more than low or negative EE, and on the other side there is a pull of strong positive EE from some form of solitary, third-order circulation of symbols, that is a formula not for inner conflict but for a straightforward choice in the market for EE. The neurotic or hyper-reflexive person is caught in a location among networks where the balance of EE attractions and repulsions is conflicting or ambiguous. Woody Allen's character is pulled one way and the other; the symbols through which Woody does his thinking are charged with EEs that actively carry on the dialogue on both sides, or indeed on multiple sides. The hyper-reflexive person is certainly individualistic and idiosyncratic, and such a person may live in an inner world far more than in any outer world. But even this complicated type of introvert is shaped by social ingredients.

THE MICRO-HISTORY OF INTROVERSION

Of the seven types of introverts, several have probably always existed. There have no doubt always been socially excluded persons, marginals, outcasts, and scapegoats in tribal and agrarian societies. And there have always been some persons who worked alone—hunters, animal herders, farmers of far-flung fields, guards on lonely outposts. None of these, however, is likely to have had an inward orientation per se characteristic of modern introverts. Class-stratified societies created the conditions for situational introverts; but given the organization of patrimonial households, with their all-purpose rooms and their ubiquitous servants and retainers, the elite gentleman very likely took his privacy more by ignoring inferiors than actually being physically out of their presence. Only around the nineteenth century, when mansions were built with separate entrance corridors (instead of one room connecting into the next) and back stairways for servants (Girouard 1978) did the fully private peerless introvert become common. But all these types, I have argued, are only borderline introverts, without distinctively introverted culture or ideology.[15]

Intellectuals, too, have long existed. Since the development of writing there have been experts in texts, who perforce spent much time concentrating on reading and writing, and to some extent this time was in solitude; the scholar's cell or study as a specially built room was one of the first structures specifically designed for individual privacy. But this was not all or even the main part of an intellectual's life, especially in the collective living conditions of monasteries, churches and their universities, and aristocratic courts. Until the beginning of the nineteenth century there is no distinctive ideology of intellectuals as withdrawn and at odds with the world. One would not have found Confucius, Aristotle, or William of Ockham an introvert in the modern sense.[16] The ideology of the distinctive personality type of the intellectual was formulated when the material bases of intellectual work shifted from church positions and aristocratic patronage to the commercial market for books. Thus it was around 1800 in Europe that some intellectuals could go it alone, and if successful, make a living purely from the sales of their writings (Collins 1998, 623–28, 754–74). Of course, not all who tried were successful, and here arises the cultural image of the starving artist living in garretts, the unknown genius at odds with the crass society who fails to accord recognition.

The era of the market-based intellectual began as the era of the Romanticist movement, which took as its favorite literary topic just this image of the sensitive rebel-outcast. The shift from patronage or institutional support for high-culture production to commercial markets happened more or less simultaneously in literature and in music, hence the appearance of the ideology, and the personality type, of the Romanticist / rebel / introvert in both fields.[17] In painting, the shift came later, with the change from careers mediated by the official painting academies, to specialized commercial galleries promoting an avant-garde, at the time of the Impressionists (White and White 1965). Hence the uneasy and for the most part unacknowledged relationship between the artistic intellectual and the commercial market. The marketing of cultural products increased the emphasis on competitiveness and put a premium on innovativeness, forcing periodic changes in fashion, and concentrating a new level of attention on the distinctive personality of the writer, musician, or artist. The creative personality now was regarded as having a distinctive style permeating all his works, acting as a brand name for advertising and demarcating a unique niche. At the same time that intellectuals' individuality was extolled and a stance of rebelliousness encouraged, the risks of failure became increasingly palpable, and aspirants were attracted to cultural production markets in numbers guaranteeing that most of them were bound to fail. The result was an ideology denouncing commercialism and the tastelessness of mass audiences, in just the places where intellectuals were most dependent upon such markets.

The Romanticist image was one source of the modern cult of the introvert; it might be combined with ideologies arising from movements of political rebellion, which became frequent beginning around the same time, from the French Revolution of 1789 onward (cf. Charle 1990). Modernity was structurally not only an expansion of capitalist markets but the development of centralized state organization, which provided arenas for revolution; even aside from the great moments of political drama, modern politics settled into a contest for power between what were now labeled the forces of tradition or reaction, and the forces of progress. The political ideology of individual freedom—which arose in a movement concerned largely to break into the aristocratic monopoly on power rather than to withdraw from it—was often blended with the ideology of the freelance writer, musician, or artist on the commercial market, with its two-faced offering of independence and danger of being left behind in the competition. The specifically Romanticist style gave way to other intellectual movements in the nineteenth and twentieth centuries, but the cultural identity it formulated for the modern has remained more or less constant across all of them.

The ideology of the rebellious, solitary individual cannot be taken at face value. It arose within networks of intellectuals and is a collective product. It was not literally the case that the rebellious intellectual was a solitary individual. When Byron's Childe Harold (protagonist of the poem that in 1812 was Byron's first bestseller, and created the first big international mass publishing reputation) repudiates his homeland and launches out on his impetuous lonely voyage, he is accompanied by two servants. Byron himself, like the other Romanticist poets, was closely connected in rebellious esoteric cliques, like the ménage with Percy and Mary Shelley in a castle in Switzerland, where they competed with each other over who could write the most horrifying rejection of the modern world (Mary Shelley won with *Frankenstein*).

From the historical shift in the material bases of intellectual production came a cultural image charged with emotions that both reflected the original stance of intellectuals in the era of Byron and Beethoven, and shaped the emotional stance of intellectuals whenever the images were reinvoked. Alienation, rebellion, glorification of the inward, autonomous self, an oppositional self taking dominant society as its foil—this has become part of intellectual discourse, recirculating on many levels: as cultural capital for oganizing rebellious cliques in high schools, in Left Banks and artists' enclaves, in political and counterculture movements; as a staple of ordinary conversation; as material for constructing fictional characters, literary plots, and opera librettos; and as contents of interior dialogues making up individual's self-reflections and conscious identities. The image of the rebellious intellectual undervalued by conventional society has become a cult object circulating far from its point of origin. The life circumstances of many and perhaps most professional intellectuals does not fit the model, since even at the time of the expansion of commercial culture markets many intellectuals continued to work outside the commercial market; the expansion of the modern research university, the biggest employer of intellectuals, was taking off at just the time of the Romanticist movement. But although most intellectuals are very far from the Byronic image, the conditions of university life have kept the ideology relevant: the bohemian living conditions of graduate-student temporary poverty, the potential for university communities to become breeding-grounds for radical social movements, the strains of publish-or-perish careers even if they are in rather tame academic specialties. On the whole, the modern intellectual has, far more than the traditional intellectual, a structural basis in the conditions of everyday life for acting as a solitary introvert, and for recirculating the symbolic image of the alienated rebel.

The other main types of introverts are also created to a large extent by modern conditions. The neurotic / hyper-reflexive type of introvert spins off from other types of introverts, but is shaped above all by the complexity of modern social networks. It is, so to speak, not so much an individual phenomenon as a neurotic niche in the array of modern networks. Solitary cultists have expanded vastly through a combination of modern living conditions allowing privacy, the mass marketing of cult emblems that are specifically appropriate for private consumption, and the decline of the main premodern form of cult practice, leaving a vacuum into which modern solitary cults could spread.[18]

The main premodern form of cult that could be carried out privately was, of course, religion. The terms "introvert" and "extrovert" were first used in reference to spiritual activities. "Introversion" is first found in English in a 1664 passage on religious exercises: "Fastings, Prayers, Introversions, Humiliations, Mortifications." "Introvert" was used as a verb in 1669: "The Soul . . . introverted into itself, and easily conforming to God's will." In 1788 the religious sense is still dominant: "Attending to the voice of Christ within you is what the Mystics term Introversion." Around 1870 the terms begin to be used in a secular sense of psychological self-scrutiny; and only after 1910 does "introvert" and its counterpart, "extrovert" (or "extravert"), thanks to Jung's version of psychoanalysis, become a noun meaning a personality type.[19]

Religious mystics engaged in meditation or inward prayer thus may be regarded as the early prototype of the introvert, and in that sense we might claim that the personality type exists as far back as 500 B.C.E. or earlier in Buddhism and other Indian religious movements, and in some of the Greek mystery cults preceding Christianity. But we should not project the modern concept of the individualist back onto this period. Monks typically did their meditation exercises collectively, as in a Buddhist meditation hall; in Christian monasteries they might have had individual cells, but their life was scheduled as a community routine and the hours of meditation and prayer themselves were set by rule. Religious mysticism was a strongly organized social regimen for group members to experience moments of inwardness. These experiences were not interpreted as being concerned with the self but with collective representations in the form of religious emblems.[20] The aim of contemplative religious practice was to "withdraw from the world," but the "world" meant what was outside the walls of the monastery, or outside the way of life of the monk; what was inside those walls and lifestyles was preeminently communal.

There were also monks and ascetics who withdrew more radically, to mountain caves or barren deserts; but this too was a socially connected withdrawal: the famous early Christian ascetics of the type of St. Anthony or St. Simeon Stylites were themselves cult objects, centers of pilgrimage by visitors attracted by their reputation for holiness. The famous hermit-monks, alike in the Christian Levant, India, and Japan were connected to chains of other monks, transmitting techniques of holiness and engaged in an implicit competition over feats of asceticism; their extremes of withdrawal and their inner experiences both were initiated from social groups and recirculated back into those groups.

Mauss (Mauss 1938/1985; Hubert and Mauss 1902/1972) traced the origins of the individual self even further back, into tribal societies. The magician or shaman was the earliest individualized, inwardly oriented person, since the practices of magic or of seeking trances involved physically withdrawing into deliberately chosen privacy and directing one's consciousness inward.[21] But Mauss's theme is the social character of magic, since it often involved the private use of elements from group ceremonies, and depended for its sense of efficacy on a social reputation that the magician held among the group. We could add, too, that shamans quite often went into their trances not in solitude but as the focal point of a tribal gathering. If the magician is on the path to individuality and introversion, it is very much in the context of collective representations that see only impersonal and collective forces.

The transition from religious inwardness to the modern introverted personality was set in motion with the Protestant Reformation. Monasteries were abolished in Protestant regions, leaving religious devotions to ordinary Christians in the course of their everyday life, without collective scheduling and standardized interpretations. We should not overdo the contrast, since the most common devotions such as prayer and Bible-readings were often carried out collectively and out loud; it is only with the decline of the large-scale patrimonial household, and later with the politically motivated disappearance of religious ceremonial in schools and public gatherings, that religious exercises became perhaps predominanty inward and private.[22] The Reformation was a decisive swing in the social organization of the means of ritual production of religious experience, even if it took three hundred years or more for the outcome to become strongly secular. The Catholic Counter-Reformation did its part as well. The Jesuit movement gave a similar impulse toward individuality and inwardness of religious devotions, like the radical Protestants curtailing ceremonial and disowning religious magic; above all the Jesuits promoted the practice of regular and frequent confession—which, although part of standard church sacraments, was little emphasized in the medieval church—thereby putting inner pressure on the individual Catholic to examine his or her conscience for the sum of all the actions of everyday life.[23]

Introverted personality types in the full, modern sense of the term appeared when religious practices became displaced from the center of public attention, and during the expansion of rival, secular means of ritual production. This brought not just the creation of introversion, but also the creation of extroversion, in a sense that could not have existed before the contrast developed between the two kinds of social orientation. One could say, broadly, that before the rise of modern conditions (the breaking up of collective living arrangements into smaller units, the differentiation of complex social networks, etc.) people were mostly extroverts; this is what Durkheim implied in his discussion of earlier societies characterized by mechanical solidarity, in which everyone is highly comforming, embedded in the group, highly similar to one another.[24] But the notion that there are gregarious people with little self-reflection could not have been very sharp until there came into existence categories of people who were the opposite.

Modern introverts and extroverts were created as increasingly polar types, and by the same process. The expansion of the means of ritual production allowed secular ritual to be put to use in two different ways: as collective participation and at the other extreme by private appropriation of these symbolic objects in solitary practice. The extrovert became an individual personality type; whereas traditionally most people had simply taken part in the normal collective life (as in a medieval household or tribal community), under modern conditions extroversion became a distinctive alternative, calling for more reflection and self-consciousness both as to what form of extroverted activity to take part in, and by awareness that there are others not making this choice. The medieval peasant taking part in village festivals was not choosing an identity in the same sense that the contemporary fraternity boy or party animal is conscious of being different from the nerd (see, for example, Moffatt 1989). The decline in conditions that promoted categorical identities, and the shift toward a predominance of conditions of situational stratification, gave rise to a greater focus upon individual identities, whether these were based on reputations for extroverted participation or for introverted withdrawal. Introverts and extroverts could now come into conflict, forming their own status ideologies putting the other down.[25] This is a distinctively modern form of situational stratification, not reducible to the categories of class, gender, and race, but operating on a much more personal level.

The expansion of the means of ritual production was also, to a considerable extent, the massive commercial expansion of niches in capitalist markets, retailing an increasing variety of ingredients for the production of first-order rituals, and of symbolic objects themselves.[26] Thus there has been an expansion alike of first-order performance of secular cults; of second-order conversation about them, as well as the commercial broadcasting and rebroadcasting of first-order ritual events; and of third-order private solitary cult devotions to these objects. The modern extrovert now has many realms in which to operate: attending the big events and being up to date on the latest gossip so as to take enthusiastic part in talking about them. As an offshoot of these processes, introverts now have more symbols to fill their solitude with, and more permutations to construct into distinct individual inner experience. The distribution of symbolic objects is simultaneously a distribution of emotional energy, from the overt collective effervescence of public gatherings, to second- and third-order refocusing of EE in networks and inner experience.

Secular rituals and their cult objects, as we have seen, range across mass entertainment and sport; technical equipment; hobby materials; texts and objects of art; substances for bodily ingestion; the shaping of the body itself. These markets give rise to the modern fan, the nerd, the hobbyist, the intellectual and the connoisseur, the addict, the exercise or weight-control fanatic—personality types scarcely found in medieval or ancient societies.

Commercial markets provided the ingredients out of which these secular cult practices could be constructed. The actual development and popularity of these practices was determined by the shift in the ecological patterns of social encounters: the shift to ad hoc, voluntary gatherings, which displaced the involuntary participation in community and household gatherings that characterized traditional societies. The daily and annual rounds of activity in premodern societies were permeated with rituals that we would easily recognize as such by their formality; living in a patrimonial household in a medieval community (not to mention living in a tribal society) would have been something like what our lives would be if Christmas or Thanksgiving happened several times a month, along with many lesser ceremonies that punctuated every day. Because of the breakup of these structures of collective living and the differentiation of networks, modern life has its points of focused attention and emotional entrainment largely where we choose to make them, and largely in informal rituals, that it takes a sociologist to point out that they are indeed rituals.

The two shifts are correlated: increasing individual organization of social participation generates an increasing market for consumption of the means of ritual production, and for ready-made sacred objects connoting the most successful of such modern rituals. The two sides of figure 4.4, interactional markets and material markets, flow into each other; they have undergone a long expansive cycle for the past five centuries or more, accelerating considerably in the past century.

The complementarity of the extroverted and introverted paths flowing from the expansion of voluntarily staged informal rituals is illustrated by modern scenes of carousing and sexual display. This is a form of situational stratification, which spun off from the increasing autonomy of individualized marriage markets carried out by the participants themselves apart from family control. By the 1920s these had become scenes not so much for finding a marriage partner but for the sheer situational prestige of being in the center of collective effervescence. Drinking, smoking, and new styles of sexual display in clothing, dancing, slang talking, and faddish mannerisms, became socially prestigious; which is to say these became symbolic emblems of membership in a community, rather nebulous in its boundaries, which was enacted by being present at just such scenes. Being in such a scene became a membership ranked by how much collective effervescence was generated and how close one was to the center of the excitement. The situational stratification generated what might be thought of as a situational class struggle. On one side were those striving to get into the center, constructing themselves more and more devotedly as extroverted personalities. On the other side were those in opposition to these carousing scenes, on various grounds ranging from belonging to more traditional moral communities of social propriety, class, and religion, to alternative cults of intellectuals, the technology-obsessed, alienated introverts, and various kinds of solitary cultists. Persons in these various ritual locations come to identify themselves not only in terms of what their personal cult is centered upon, but also what it contrasts with; the nerd and the party animal are both parts of each other's self-definition.

The most visible cults generate not only opposition but also private emulation. First-order participation in one of the modern cults holding the center of public attention tends to promote the spread of its symbols into private lives as well. Cigarette-smoking, which became glamorized in the party scene of the 1920s and near-universal in the ritualized solidarity of World War II, also generated a penumbra of private smokers, which has remained after the prestige of the public scenes declined. In the sphere of sexual behavior, the various phases of sexual display scenes (the 1920s, 1960s) promoted an increasingly eroticized culture; the spread of sexually suggestive clothing styles, advertisements, and increasingly explicit pornography has increased desire for contemporary forms of sexual behavior. Here the introverted and extroverted forms not only expand together but support one another. As we have seen (in chapter 6) masturbation, correlated with pornography consumption, is positively correlated as well with frequency of sexual intercourse; the age of sexual initiation in the twentieth century became younger and the variety of sexual practices wider. The intimate sphere of sexuality follows the pattern of Goffmanian sociology. There is much posturing and presenting of frontstage imagery—since in fact most people's sex lives are not as active as they pretend to be—but the sexual frontstage is not thereby to be dismissed as an illusion. Society is not so much the repressor of a primordial sexual urge, as Freud thought, as the creator and shaper of drives through focus of attention and emotional entrainment. In sexual desire, as everywhere else, human beings are programmed from the outside in.

The Modern Cult of the Individual

"This secular world is not so irreligious as we
might think. Many gods have been done away
with, but the individual himself stubbornly remains
a deity of considerable importance. He walks with
some dignity and is the recipient of many little
offerings. He is jealous of the worship due him,
yet, approached in the right spirit, he is ready
to forgive those who may have offended him. Because
of their status relative to his, some persons
will find him contaminating while others will
contaminate him, in either case finding that they
must treat him with ritual care."
—*Erving Goffman, [1957] 1967, 95*

Goffman was, rather against his intentions, an historical observer. He was engaged in creating a scholarly specialty in the direct observation of the details of everyday life. To do so, he bracketed the historical setting, to focus upon the analytical features of situational interaction, as a level of analysis sui generis. In this respect he was in keeping with the functionalist anthropologists whose lead he followed. Goffman also bracketed out much of the substance of interaction, differentiating himself from older writers on "manners"; the sociology of interaction rituals is not moralizing, ironicizing, humorous, or satirical.[27] He was not concerned with chronicling the changes in manners from one era to another, even though he was working in the midst of a very large change in precisely his line of vision.

We might, in fact, refer to this historical change, taking place between the 1950s and the 1970s, as the "Goffmanian revolution."[28] This was the shift toward greater casualness in interaction. The nuances of formal manners that Goffman enjoyed analyzing—the occasions for hat-lifting, door-holding, polite introductions, equally polite cutting of those persons not socially eligible to be recognized—were on their way out. Men stopped wearing hats—which obviated any distinctions between raising them to a lady or showing one's tough nothing-but-business demeanor by keeping them on in the house; people stopped offering each other lights for their cigarettes and eventually repudiated cigarettes as a form of pollution; a male holding a door for a female became rejected as a sign of promoting subservience in the guise of deference. Formerly taboo verbal expressions became standard in sophisticated social circles; the formality of clothing styles, and of clothes specifically designed for particular social occasions, gave way to the predominance of the casual style. Traditional forms of address by title gave way to a more or less compulsory calling everyone by their first name or nickname, regardless of degree of acquaintance.

Goffman ignored all this, since he was attempting to single out the generic features shared by all interaction rituals. I have attempted to highlight those generic features in the theory of IR chains. With this analyical apparatus in hand, we are free to look at historical changes in the specific contents of rituals. The era of casualness, the near side of the Goffmanian revolution on which we live, remains ritualistic, even as the older rituals from which Goffman took most of his materials have been replaced by a different set of rituals. For the most part, Goffman's rituals of politeness were forms of categorical deference—holding doors or lighting cigarettes for ladies, and thereby indicating one's status as a gentleman. The distinctions, lady vis-à-vis gentleman as well as vis-à-vis non-lady and non-gentleman, have almost entirely faded; these have been displaced by situational stratification, which overtly recognizes only individuals and their reputations for being in, or out, of preferred scenes of social action.

Across this historical shift, Goffman's emphasis on the "cult of the individual" continues to hold true. It even appears as a trend: there is an increasing degree of emphasis on the cult of individuality, and a concern to make the cult as inclusive as possible. The paradoxes and excesses of late-twentieth-century manners have sometimes been satirized under the label "political correctness." This is hard for us to treat analytically, since it refers to conflicts over standards of everyday life, conflicts in which most of us are partisans on one side or another. Viewed sociologically, political correctness shows two classic features of social ritualism: First, it is a form of moral compulsion; it marks the boundary of what is considered to be a proper member of the larger community, and its weapon is moral scorn (which may also be followed up by legal compulsion) against those who violate these standards. Second, it is a concern to extend the status of individuality to everyone, above all to those who have historically been disprivileged; in everyday life, this is a form of hyper-sensitivity in taking the role of the other, ferreting out all the ways of possibly hurting the feelings of others who have been treated as underlings or social non-persons. To be sure, class stratification has not disappeared, and situational stratification exists as much as situational equality, so there is a certain amount of false consciousness in these rituals of conferring specially marked equality on some who thereby are given priority in the focus of situational attention. But this is the nature of rituals; they paste over structural incongruities as well as anything else, keeping the immediate flow of situations going. And through it all, we discern the long-term trend: greater inwardness of selves is assumed, and by being projected onto others, it helps create that inwardness. Even as occasions for extroversion promote the modern character of noisy entrainment in the scene of action, the sphere of introversion is expanded to give everyone the standing of at least honorary introvert.

I want to conclude with a reflection on what the perspective of radical microsociology means for our own view of ourselves. We are all socially constructed; all historically shaped. There is no "natural" inwardness about our selves; nor, for that matter, is there inevitability about the historical trajectory that we happen to be living in during the past several centuries. IR theory is an analytical model, which can be dropped down into any historical period, to examine just what configuration of ingredients for carrying out rituals happen to exist in a particular moment. It carries no connotations of trends in those ingredients and hence in their outcomes; each period can have its range of complications, and there is no guarantee that the larger historical pattern always flows in one direction. The kind of selves that will be taken as natural several hundred years in the future may be quite different than the selves that are taken for granted today, and the trend is not necessarily further along in the same direction that I have sketched in this chapter. There is no Hegelian evolution revealing that the pure essence of the human being is individuality and inwardness.

What, then, are we to make of ourselves? We are historical products of a period that has developed an increasingly widespread and increasingly penetrating cult of individuality; thus we are constrained to think of ourselves as autonomous, inward, individuals; all the more so if we have lived through the social configurations that make us intellectuals, alienated introverts, and other versions of specifically marked intro-version. At the same time, the central lines of sociological theory—those emblematized by Durkheim and Mead—give abundant evidence for the mechanisms by which our selves are socially constructed.

The sociologized view of the individual runs against the grain of the symbols generated by twentieth-century and early-twenty-first-century rituals. I have put the central formula as follows: human beings are emotional energy seekers, thereby linked to those interactions and their derivative symbols that give the greatest EE in the opportunities presented by each person's social networks. If not EE-seekers, what else could human beings be? Are we simply pain-avoiders, as an older line of theory held, provoked into action by frustrations and obstacles in the flow of habits? The image is too inert, passive; human beings are active, excitement seeking, magnetically attracted to where things are happening. Are we material reward-seekers, a convenient simpli-fication set forth by the utilitarian tradition and given wide currency by the institutional success of economics? Today's economic sociology gives evidence against it; and material goods are not only subordinate to nonmaterial attractions, but are desired most intensely where they are symbols loaded with EE or are material means for ritual produc-tion. Are we power-seekers? Sometimes, but that is a particular kind of situational interaction by which some, necessarily limited, portion of people gain their EE. Are we seekers of love? Same answer. Are we idea-seekers? Again yes; but intellectuals devoting their lives to ideas, artists devoting themselves to art, are of all people the most deeply shaped in their very thoughts by the EE-loadings of symbols reflecting membership in the factions of professional networks.

Is there no genuinely individual experience, valid apart from soci-ety? Things that one experiences by oneself, that you cannot communi-cate to others, that are often best savored alone: the smell of new cut grass, the color-saturated world in the glint of a low-angled late after-noon sun, the feel of one's muscles when stretching out at the end of a run, the nuances of a mood, the intricacies of one's flights of fan-tasy—being with someone else at these moments is often a distraction, and attempting to relate the experience in the clichés of conversation tends more to destroy the experience than to expand it. Thus we might claim that there is an aesthetic realm of one's own sensitivities, that is at least one clear bastion of the private self. And yet, it is our own biographies that have prepared some of us to attend to these moments, and others of us to ignore them; it is our stock of social symbols that opens the door. We are deeply socially constituted beings, from the moments as babies when we begin to make noises and gestures in rhythm with our parents, through the adult networks that induct us into cults of experience that we elaborate in our inner lives. Symbols make up the very structure of our consciousness. Symbols are the lenses through which we see.

We do see something through them. That experience is a reality, concrete, particular, individual; sometimes of the highest value to ourselves. That the pathway to those experiences is deeply social does not take anything away from them.

NOTES

1. Even more misleading is the usage in a pejorative sense as an unthinking going through the motions, or meaningless fixation on mumbo-jumbo.

2. There is yet another usage in the field of animal ethology, sometimes borrowed in child development psychology. Here "ritualization" means abbreviated communicative gestures, which operate as "signals" to another organism in a habitual process of action, in contrast to "symbols," which are conventions for referring to shared meanings (e.g., Tomasello 1999, 87). In this usage, ritualization is just a shorthand used in coordinating practical action, not a source of symbolic intersubjectivity. Despite the fact that the terminology is more or less reversed from that of sociological IR theory, we shall see in chapter 2 that work by Tomasello and others of this group of researchers does indeed corroborate important parts of IR theory.

3. Freud's *Totem und Tabu* appeared in 1913, at the height of interest in these phenomena. Van Gennep's *Rites de Passage* was published in 1909, Frazer's *Totemism and Exogamy* and Lévy-Bruhl's *Les fonctions mentales dans les sociétés inférieures* in 1910, Durkheim's *Les formes élémentaires de la vie religieuse* in 1912, the same year as Harrison's *Themis*, Cornford's *From Religion to Philosophy*, and Murray's *Four Stages of Greek Religion*. Stravinsky's controversial ballet music about a primitive rite, *Le sacre du printemps*, was first performed in Paris in 1912.

4. The line of criticism that the functionalist movement took against their predecessors made an exception for the Durkheim school, since Durkheim was strongly committed to a general science of society. Durkheim and Mauss paved the way for the functionalist program of studying rites and beliefs in their current context of social action rather than as isolated survivals of past history, although they also had more evolutionary concern with social change than did the movement of functionalist anthropologists. Durkheim did adopt an evolutionist stance that enabled him to view Australian aborigine society, because of its apparent simplicity, as an "elementary form" that would show both the evolutionary starting point of more complex societies, and reveal the analytically central processes of social solidarity and symbolism. Thus, although Malinowski was the organizational leader of what became known as the British school of social anthropologists, the members of that school tended to adopt Durkheimian theoretical formulations. This was notably the case with Radcliffe-Brown, who taught in South Africa and Australia independently of the group (Evans-Pritchard, Fortes, and others) that came from Malinowski's seminar at the London School of Economics. Radcliffe-Brown was in contact with the Durkheim school via Mauss since the mid-1920s, and explicitly developed its theory of rituals (Goody 1995).

5. There was a direct network transmission: Parsons was a member of the Malinowski seminar at LSE in the early 1930s, before beginning work on his systematic structural-functional theory (Goody 1995, 27); Merton was a student of Parsons at Harvard in the mid-1930s.

6. Durkheim (1912/1965) also analyzed mourning rites, but what he was concerned to show was that mourning is not spontaneous but obligatory by the group. He notes that assembling the group at the funeral results in a type of collective effervescence, albeit one based on a negative emotion. This gives us the mechanism by which Radcliffe-Brown's (1922) functional integration is carried out: the collective emotion initiated by shared grief pulls individuals back into the group and gives them renewed strength.

7. "The rules of conduct which bind the actor and the recipient together are the bindings of society. . . . Opportunities to affirm the moral order and the society could therefore be rare. It is here that ceremonial rules play their social function. . . . Through these observances, guided by ceremonial obligations and expectations, a constant flow of indulgences is spread through society, with others who are present constantly reminding the individual that he must keep himself together as a well demeaned person and affirm the sacred quality of these others. The gestures which we sometimes call empty are perhaps in fact the fullest things of all" (Goffman 1956/1967, 90).

8. Old-fashioned usage best conveys the sense that "society" has in IR theory. Society is not a distant abstraction; it means what an upper class matron at the turn of the twentieth century would mean if she spoke of her daughter "going out into society"—i.e., going out from the domestic circle to take part in polite social gatherings. IR theory generalizes this usage from a restricted sense of "polite society" to all social interaction in its ritualistic aspect. The sense is similar to that in Henry David Thoreau's epigram: "I have three chairs in my house; one for solitude; two for company; three for society."

9. According to newspaper reports, the controversial basketball coach Bobby Knight was fired by his university in the late 1990s after he responded angrily to a student who accosted him with "Hello, Knight."

10. "The Meadian notion that the individual takes towards himself the attitude others take to him seems very much an oversimplification. Rather the individual must rely on others to complete the picture of him of which he himself is allowed to paint only certain parts. Each individual is responsible for the demeanor image of himself and the deference image of others, so that for a complete man to be expressed, individuals must hold hands in a chain of ceremony. . . . While it may be true that the individual has a unique self all his own, evidence of this possession is thoroughly a product of joint ceremonial labor" (Goffman 1956/1967: 84–85).

11. It follows, although Goffman does not go into this, that overt conflict breaks out when the normally accepted level of ritual cooperation is broken, for instance, by a new manager becoming unusually assertive in invading the workers' backstage. For an empirical case, see Gouldner's *Wildcat Strike* (1954).

12. In terms of the detailed model of IR to be presented later, this is typically done by keeping up the normal rhythm and focus of attention via the flow of topics, and through an emotional tone appropriate to a nonhostile interaction,

while giving either a content or a nonverbal / paralinguistic gesture that challenges the other person's demeanor as a competent self.

13. Goffman's critiques of these interpretations were not systematically stated but were carried on rather offhandedly in passing remarks and footnotes. On Goffman's intellectual stance vis-à-vis other positions, see Winkin (1988); Burns (1992); Rawls (1987).

14. Goffman broached this topic in early work, raising the question of whether there is an ultimate backstage, where no performing work in done. Yet even sexual intercourse, which is normally regarded as the realm of uttermost intimacy and privacy, Goffman avers, may be regarded as a kind of performance (1959, 193–94). I will extend this theme in chapter 6, where we see just how fully sexual intercourse fits the model of interaction ritual.

15. Around the same time (the late 1950s and early 1960s), Chomsky developed his quasi-mathematical analysis of the deep structures of language, concentrating not on phonetics, as Saussure had done, but on syntax. The program was called generative grammar since it laid out a formal system by which the surface structure of language is generated from underlying elements and transformations. The Chomskyian method starts with existing sentences in a natural language and decomposes them into fundamental elements called "underlying strings." Turning back in the opposite direction, these elements are reassembled by applying a series of operations (phrase structure rules, transformational rules, morphophonemic rules) until we end up again with recognizable sentences. The set of operations may thus be said to have generated the particular sentence. Chomsky's explanatory strategy is parallel to Lévi-Strauss's, although differing in substance. But Chomsky's generative grammar did not yield a code for different languages that lined up with Lévi-Strauss's types of kinship systems, or other elements of social structure, and thus provided no support for Lévi-Strauss's grand system.

16. Saussure, writing at the turn of the twentieth century, was in sympathy with Durkheim's program. There was some theoretical resemblance insofar as the arbitrary differences that constitute phonetic significance are a collective product, not explainable by the psychology of individuals (Saussure1915/ 1966, 15–16; for detailed references on Durkheim's influence on Saussure, see Jameson 1972, 27). Lévi-Strauss, a protégé of Mauss and grandpupil of Durkheim, in effect brought together several branches of a broad Durkheimian community.

17. The reasons were to a considerable extent political, a reaction led by the existentialist generation of the 1930s and 40s against what was seen as the Durkheimian school's advocacy of solidaristic nationalism in French politics of the 1920s (see Heilbron 1985; Collins 2003).

18. This view of ritual is often attributed to Durkheim. Catherine Bell (1992) straightens out this issue of interpretation, and develops some of the possibilities that open up when ritual is seen as social action producing and reproducing a symbolic code rather than vice versa. Other scholars occupy a halfway position, seeing the code or repertoire of codes as temporally prior and analytically primary but allowing considerable flexibility in the way in which codes are invoked in particular situations.

19. There is, however, at least one way in which the view that meanings are constructed by secular, worldly activity, can be reconciled with some aspect of religious transcendence. David Preston (1988), in analyzing the techniques of Zen Buddhism, argues that Buddhist meditation practices are socially orga-nized not to construct a transcendental religious meaning, but to strip away the accretion of meanings already constructed; thus the aim of this meditation is liberation or transcendence from everything constructed, allowing whatever remains (a transcendental reality?) to come shining through.

20. The most important of these is *The Elementary Forms of the Religious Life*, Book 2, chapter 7. There are several English translations, which differ mainly in arbitrary stylistic renditions, and in pagination.

21. The importance of the body for sociology has been underlined in recent years, especially by Bryan Turner (1996).

22. It may be worthwhile here to head off several misconceptions or preju-dices about Durkheim's style of argument. Durkheim's analysis of the emo-tions of group assemblies in *The Elementary Forms* is sometimes regarded as a version of the "crowd psychology" of the turn of the twentieth century, as in Le Bon's *The Crowd* (1908). Thus it is thought that Durkheim is merely repeating conventionl arguments for the leveling and animalistic effects of the mob tri-umphing over the higher rationality of the individual. A good deal of modern sociology of collective behavior and social movements, such as McPhail's *The Myth of the Madding Crowd* (1991) uses this model as a foil, citing evidence that individuals typically take part in crowds not as isolates but in a small circle of friends who accompany each other. Against this critique, three points need to be made.

First, modern network research on crowds does not undercut the significance of group influences on individuals; it merely replaces one model of group be-havior with another. A better way to interpret the data is that the primary groups that make up the crowd facilitate and amplify the effects of the larger crowd as a focus of attention and emotional entrainment. For members of these little groups, the larger crowd's cheering or other emotion becomes especially significant because they feed it back and forth among each other. Thus we can also say that these small groups entrain each other in a larger group.

Second, Durkheim does not view group assemblies as animalistic, lowering the individual to a subhuman level. On the contrary, he points to assemblies as the occasions where moral ideals are created and put into action. Heroic, self-sacrificing, highly moral individuals are created by experience in such oc-casions.

Third, we cannot assume, Robinson Crusoe-like, that the rational individual preexists all social experience, and thus that crowds are simply made up of individuals who might or might not be brought down from their natural level of rationality. Durkheim is attempting to show how individuals are formed or socialized by groups, and how the conceptions that make up their rationality are formed and inculcated in them.

Another, minor misconception can also be addressed: that Durkheim singled out aborigines in order to look down on them as primitives below the level of modern rationality. On the contrary, Durkheim focuses on gatherings of aborigines because they are displaying our common humanity. The processes that he singles out, the focus of attention and shared emotion that generate collective effervescence, are in basic outline the same as those that operate throughout history and continue to operate today.

23. In this respect, Bourdieu continues what I have called the "code-seeking" program of Lévi-Straussian structuralism; and this is so even though Bourdieu (1972/1977) established his theoretical reputation by taking Lévi-Strauss as a foil against which to emphasize that symbolic capital is always used in a practical way in the contingencies of ordinary life. Bourdieu avoids the term "code," substituting "habitus" for its component as internalized in individuals, and the "logic" or "principle" of "fields" for the overarching macro-pattern. In later works, Bourdieu emphasizes the logic of "practice," borrowing microsociological insights from Goffman and the ethnomethodologists, and denying that the overall structure does anything apart human agents. But the outcomes are structurally preordained nevertheless. For Bourdieu, the enactment of culture by individuals (including the use of language: see Bourdieu 1991) is always effective in reproducing the same kind of stratified social order or "field of power"; hence he calls it "symbolic violence," stressing its character as the micro-instantiation of macro-domination. In another version of the terminology this is called the "homology among fields," a concept that betrays the Lévi-Straussian structuralism from which it was taken. For a typical application of this style of argument see Bourdieu (2001), where he claims that the deep structural logic of gender domination remains the same from the extreme masculine domination of ancient Mediterranean tribes through the liberalized Western societies of the late-twentieth century. For a critique of Bourdieu, see Lamont and Lareau (1988). See also the debate between Bourdieu's follower Wacquant (2002) and Anderson (2002), Dunier (2002), and Newman (2002).

Chapter 2
The Mutual-Focus / Emotional-Entrainment Model

1. For another version of formally modeling ritual, see Marshall (2002).

2. A combination of personal and collective rebellion against formal ritual, even down to the level of Goffmanian politeness, was characteristic of the "counterculture" of the 1960s. The consequences for the shifting style of interactional stratification will be examined in chapters 7 and 8.

3. The president of a major American university during the 1990s, known for his extremely gregarious and affable style of greeting and interacting with faculty, students, visitors, potential donors, and indeed all comers, had a breakdown after a few years on the job and had to resign his position. As a child, I observed my mother, who as wife of the U.S. Consul General in an overseas post was the leading hostess of the local diplomatic corps, throwing herself with great emotional effervescence into the round of sociable rituals. But it was clearly a staged effort, as I could see from the change in her mood as soon as she closed the door on the last guest; and periodically, she would

take a break, retiring to a hotel to read novels and see no one at all for a week. Turner (2002) argues that human beings are descendents of a rather unsociable lineage of primates, and hence that humans are in fact not naturally very sociable and must put considerable work into keeping up rituals. I believe that he exaggerates the evidence for humans' unsociable biological heritage; and his argument that humans have to work hard at putting on rituals appears to be drawn from observations of forced rituals.

4. A plausible reconstruction of the evolutionary pathway is given by Turner (2002, chapters 3 and 4), using the evidence of paleontology and cladistics, primate behavior, and brain physiology. Turner emphasizes that the human animal became unique by developing elaborate emotional expressions that enabled much more refined social coordination than other animals, and that tied these emotions to the cognitive centers of the brain.

5. The example of sports celebrations shows historical differences. American sports celebrations were more restricted before 1970, consisting of handshaking, and some shoulder hugging among close teammates. In the early part of the century, a typical ritual was to carry the coach or player-hero off the field on the shoulders of the team—a restricted form of bodily contact concentrated on one token representative. Late twentieth-century style (which has continued into the early twenty-first century) consists in full body hugs and piling on in a heap of bodies. Thus, even rather informal ritual patterns are influenced by an accumulation of tradition; we have little analysis of what conditions bring about shifts from one pattern of bodily celebration ritual to another. All of these patterns, nevertheless, are variants within a basic pattern: the sudden eruption of strong emotions arising from group experience leads to a desire for bodily contact, which in turn heightens and prolongs that peak emotion. The prolongation in fact may not be so very long: from a few dozen seconds or less of peak excitement if there is no bodily solidarity ritual, to something on the order of ten minutes in maximal celebrations. Some evidence is provided by film and video-recordings of the celebrations that followed Roger Maris setting a new home run record in 1961 (forty seconds of applause) and Mark McGwire breaking the record in 1998 (nine minutes of applause). During the earlier record moment, bodily contact consisted of handshaking; during the later, of a round of bodily hugs with teammates and others.

6. In the ceremonial drinking traditions of Sweden, a toast to an esteemed acquaintance is carried out by looking each other in the eye at the moment of emptying one's glass.

7. The ritual character of drinking together explains the mild taboo or sense of social shame that exists for drinking alone. Although the disapproval is rationalized as referring to a sign of alcoholism, the sense is more one of misuse of a ritual substance. There may well be heavier drinking in collective gatherings than solo, but drinking with others is generally seen positively through the veil of solidarity. A similar mechanism has contributed to the delegitimation of smoking in the late twentieth century, as we see in chapter 8.

8. It can be argued that not just the student audience feels deprived by hearing lectures on remote hookup; the speaker to a remote audience feels especially acutely the lack of feedback from the audience, unless there is an audi-

ence immediately present as well. It is generally harder to lecture to an extremely large classroom, because one cannot gauge the reactions of the students who are far away.

9. This explains patterns found in psychological experiments that show there is more laughter at comic material when there are sounds of laughter, when subjects can see the laughing audience, and when the group is larger (Leventhal and Mace 1970; Provine 1992; Yong and Frye 1966; Bush et al. 1989).

10. Katz (1999) demonstrates the importance of social participation and, even more importantly, of mutual focus of attention, for happy laughter to take place. Using recordings of visitors to the hall of fun-house mirrors in an amusement park, Katz shows that individuals do not automatically laugh at their distorted images. Instead, they call for others in their group (usually family members) to come and see the image, whereupon they encourage each other by bodily motions and vocal rhythms to build up laughter together. Bystanders, who are seeing the same images in the mirrors, do not join in the family group's laughter; it is not the funny stimulus that causes the laughter, but the social entrainment. These instances display very sharply the boundaries of inclusion and exclusion that are manifested and re-created in the collective experience of producing laughter.

11. Here, too, Durkheim provides a precedent, in emphasizing the importance of shared rhythm in establishing a condition of collective effervescence:

> And since a collective sentiment cannot express itself collectively except on the condition of observing a certain order permitting co-operation and movements in unison, these gestures and cries naturally tend to become rhythmic and regular; hence come songs and dances. . . . The human voice is not sufficient for the task; it is reinforced by means of artificial processes; boomerangs (in the Australian aborigine ritual) are beaten against each other; bull-roarers are whirled. It is probable that these instruments . . . are used primarily to express in a more adequate fashion the agitation felt. But while they express it, they also strengthen it." (Durkheim 1912/1965, 247)

12. This fits with the propensity of ethnomethodologists to refer to their subjects as "members," as if taking for granted that persons are already part of a culture. In this respect ethnomethodologists follow the assumptions of researchers in cognitive anthropology (D'Andrade 1995). The IR tradition, on the other hand, prefers to start with human physical bodies in interaction and to derive culture from they way in which they coordinate their attention. Thus Goffman has at times been tagged as a kind of human animal ethologist.

13. Such "rules" are just an observer's way of characterizing these regularities. It would be a mistake to assume that there is a cultural blueprint that the actors are referring to for how to talk. I would argue, to the contrary, that the mechanism of rhythmic coordination is naturally given in all human beings (indeed, possibly in many animals), and that violations of it are universally felt as breaking solidarity. Sacks et al. argued like structuralists of the code-seeking school, perhaps because they oriented toward their most accessible scholarly audience, anthropological linguists.

14. This conversation has no socially recognized gaps. It does have a small amount of overlapping, indicated by the brackets [ ] which show when two speakers are talking at the same time. This is normal; overlap happens just at the points where one speaker might be ending her utterance, and the other is starting to say something so that there will be no empty space. But as soon as they both recognize what is happening, one of them stops and lets the other talk.

15. This examples illustrates Simmel's point that conflict is also a form of sociality, in contrast to the thorough breaking of social ties that is oblivi-ousness, or the withdrawing of attention. We can say that conflict is a disputed effort to dominate a situation of social coordination, to bend mutual-focus / emotional-entrainment to one's advantage over the resistance of the other. I will draw out the implications of this line of argument in a future work on violent conflict (Collins, forthcoming).

16. Conversation analysis, with its roots in ethnomethodology, is concerned with contextual meaning of utterances as provided by the sequence of what has just been addresssed; and with enacting social structure from moment to moment as an ongoing achievement (Heritage 1984; Schegloff 1992). Like its intellectual parent, conversation analysis focused on the production of a sense of social structure in general, rather than on mechanisms of variability from one social situation to another.

17. There is cultural variability within social classes as well. Educated upper-middle-class persons are more likely than working-class persons to have hesitation pauses in their speech (Labov 1972). These are gaps that occur, not between turns, but in the middle of a sentence; the inference (which can be confirmed by subjective experience) is that these are times when the person is searching through alternative words to say next. Thus persons who have more cultural capital, as well as a more reflexive style of thinking, will have more hesitation pauses than other persons. Bernstein (1971–75) describes a similar phenomenon as the "elaborated code" of the middle class and the "re-stricted code" of working-class speech: the latter flows off more straightfor-wardly, because it consists to a larger degree of formulaic utterances. The hy-pothesis of IR theory is that hesitation pauses of this sort are more disruptive to conversational solidarity when they occur between social classes, that is, when one side is used to an uninterrupted rhythm, which is not forthcoming. Conversely when two members of the upper-middle class engage in conversa-tion, hesitation pauses are more easily accomodated—although it would re-main true that utterances with a more continuous rhythm delivered within the elaborated code would generate more solidarity as well.

18. A second cross-cultural objection is that there are cultures in which it is typical for several persons to speak at once; sociability in Italy is often de-scribed as many animated conversations going on across a dinner table, with the same individuals attempting to keep up with each one. This is a compli-cated case that awaits further analysis. It is not clear, for example, whether there are several different circles of conversation going on at the same time, in which particular individuals may try simultaneously to participate; this would not violate the no-overlap rule for any particular conversation. Alternatively,

it may be that the speaker and the addressee are both speaking at the same time, which would imply disattention to the other's words and an aggressive effort to usurp the floor (see evidence in Corsaro and Rizzo 1990). This would need to be studied in careful micro-detail.

19. Durkheim gives an explanation in discussing the elevated language of a public speaker. He refers to

> the particular attitude of a man speaking to a crowd, at least if he has succeeded in entering into communication with it. His language has a grandiloquence that would be ridiculous in ordinary circumstances; his gestures show a certain domination; his very thought is impatient of all rules, and easily falls into all sorts of excesses. It is because he feels within him an abnormal over-supply of force which overflows and tries to burst out from him; sometimes he even has the feeling that he is dominated by a moral force which is greater than he and of which he is only the interpreter. It is by this trait that we are able to recognize what has often been called the demon of oratorical inspiration. Now this exceptional increase of force is something very real; it comes to him from the very group which he addresses. The sentiments provoked by his words come back to him, but enlarged and emplified and to this degreee they strengthen his own sentiment. The passionate energies he arouses re-echo within him and quicken his vital tone. It is no longer a simple individual who speaks, it is a group incarnate and personified. (Durkheim 1912/1965, 241)

20. Another comparison helps bring out the mechanism: a crowd of human bodies on a street is mildly exciting; but a crowd of automobiles on a highway is just a traffic jam. Both are unfocused crowds, but the crowd of cars lacks even the minimal mutual interchange among human bodies that people passing on the sidewalk have. Katz (1999) shows that the frustrations of driving come precisely from those moments when the lack of mutual feedback becomes most palpable.

21. The different components are brought out in the experience of being in a wave going around a stadium: you have first a sense that the crowd action is bearing down on you and that you are being pushed to rise up with others nearby at just the moment when the wave arrives, and then the sensation that you are pushing the people beyond you to join in.

22. In between the murderous violence of ethnic riots and the cheering or jeering of the sports crowd is the destructive victory celebration, or protest, that sometimes breaks out at sports events. The organization of English soccer hooligans illustrates how the intense collective experience of violent participation becomes the main attraction, to be deliberately scheduled and enacted (Buford 1992). In effect, such activity becomes an addiction, not so much to violence but to the excitement and collective identity produced by violence (King 2001).

23. Crowds are generally made up of small subgroups of friends and acquaintances, but these subgroups are anonymous to each other.

24. I owe this information to Ilana Redstone and Kirsten Smith, reporting on their experience as interviewers and observers in Togo and Malawi in the late 1990s. For wide-ranging cross-societal comparisons, see Mauss (1938/1985).

25. This is a respect in which Burt's (1992) emphasis on bridging ties, across holes in networks, is overstated. Redundant networks make an important complementarity to bridge ties, because the former enhance reputation, which may be an even more important resource than scarce information when the political task at hand is to put together a coalition.

26. There is a third way in which symbols circulate and prolong the sense of membership: symbols recirculate in the inner conversations that make up thinking in an individual's mind. These symbols are offshoots of the first two kinds; they begin as internalizations of them, although they can be modified and developed in internal conversations. These complexities will be considered in chapter 5.

27. I leave aside here the ways in which symbols may cross over from one circuit to the other. Principally, audience-shared symbols may also be used in personal converational networks. But because these symbols are so widely available, they carry no great significance for personal relationships, and thus their exchange in sociable conversation does not bring about very close ties, which is to say strong membership solidarity. Pretty much everyone can talk about the local sports team, so that kind of conversation does not differentiate good friends or close professional or business allies. Differentiation in sociable ties, however, may occur not so much via the topics as the length to which conversationalists will go in talking about them. Particularly among youths (who have little stock of symbolic memberships from their work experience), the strength of a personal friendship tie comes not so much from the unique content but from their mutual willingness to talk about their entertainment-heroes / sacred objects at inordinate length.

Another possible crossover among these circuits happens among the professionals who stage political, religious, or entertainment events. For them, the public symbols are not generalized but particularistic; they are part of their backstage and sociable talk, not from the point of view of the adulating (or otherwise) audiences, but from the point of view of those personally knowledgeable about the everyday narratives of being performers.

28. This will be further discussed in chapter 4.

29. There are other group perspectives from which the World Trade Center towers were a symbol. For the attackers, the towers were doubtless a symbol of the New York skyline, and along with the Pentagon, emblems of American financial and military power around the world. From an outside, enemy perspective, symbols of a group's identity may thus be more sharply defined than they are to members of that group itself. It is notable, too, that the damaged Pentagon never became a widespread symbol of post–9/11 American solidarity, nor did the ostensibly heroic airline passengers who fought the hijackers and prevented yet another ground attack. In none of these instances was there a process of construction of symbolic status such as that which made the firefighters into emblems of American solidarity and courage.

30. The most personalized of these symbols was the mayor. Here the transformative power of an intense IR is striking. Prior to 9/11, Mayor Giuliani was intensely disliked by a considerable portion of the NYC population because of his policies on militant police tactics, and his political career was generally regarded as at a nadir.

31. In other words, we are no longer a first-order actor, the social patterns of which action now become consciously visible because that is what we consciously observe. At the same time, as second-order observer, we are necessarily defocusing from ourselves as actors on this second level of intellectual action. We could, of course, go on to take a different observer's standpoint and do a sociology of thinking, an analysis of the social activity of the person in the intellectual observer mode. Which is to say, we can become intellectually and reflexively conscious of anything human beings do; but we can't make everything conscious at the same moment. For an exposition of levels of observers as locations in social networks, see Fuchs (2001).

32. It is indeed the case that many gun owners use them for sports and hunting; yet many of the weapons possessed, such as automatic weapons and machine guns, are too powerful to be suitable for hunting. See the various lines of argument and evidence in Wright and Rossi (1994), and Cook and Ludwig (2000).

33. Talk about guns is easiest to observe in the way gun salesmen talk to customers, bringing up such topics as what kind of weapon you would need in a dangerous situation, what weapon would be adequate to take out a threatening challenger, or an intruder in your house. The talk that typically takes place in the gun shop invokes imaginary uses of guns in dramatic situations, which are rather far from the routines of the gun cult itself. This dramatic content is a form of sales talk, although taken rather seriously by customers and perhaps salemen themselves; in effect, it is the content of the fantasy they are buying. Like buying pornography, buying a gun is chiefly buying an opportunity to fantasize.

34. Guns in films and television shows may be regarded as focal points of vicarious rituals. The use of guns is typically a high point of the drama, whether the emotions are build up through the plot format of action-adventure or mystery / suspense, giving a strong focus of attention, and usually an implicit membership marker between those who have weapons and those who are mere bystanders. There is considerable research on the extent of exposure of weapons on TV and its effect or noneffect on violence. IR theory leads us to question whether people's ritual experience of the entertainment media leads directly to violent behavior; it may largely remain part of the round of secondary circulation of symbols, part of what people talk about, or what children play-enact in make-believe games. The question for investigation is whether and how this secondary circulation of symbols becomes articulated with the first-order gun cult; and yet further, whether participating in the gun cult leads persons to fire their guns in ordinary life, against other human beings, outside the routines of the gun cult: against or by criminals, accidentally or intentionally against family members and acqaintances, in angry disputes and in escalations of other conflicts. These "real-life" uses of guns are doubtless much more

chaotic than the regularized rituals of the gun cult. It may be the case that the several different realms have little to do with each other.

35. In the same way, the movement for alcohol prohibition in the late-nineteenth and early-twentieth-century United States enhanced social identities and boundaries on both sides. According to Gusfield's (1963) analysis, the prohibitionist movement was an attack on the saloon as ritual gathering place of urban immigrant males, especially by native rural WASPs and upper- and middle-class females. The enactment of prohibition then fostered a wider countermovement in that drinking parties became an emblem for self-consciously modern, youthful, sexually liberated people. Symbolic markers thus go through a historical development shaped not only by their participants but by their conflicts.

CHAPTER 3
EMOTIONAL ENERGY AND THE TRANSIENT EMOTIONS

1. This has been developed most explicitly in social movement theory that has recently reached out to incorporate emotions (Jasper 1997; Goodwin, Jasper, and Polletta 2001).

2. See, however, Lawler and Thye (1999), who propose a model of how emotions may be brought into rational exchange theory. Emotion is central to Affect Control theory, although this has usually been taken as a theory within the sociology of emotions rather than a general theory of microsociological action (but see MacKinnon 1994). See also note 4.

3. This is now changing, as emotion research has been promoted for its application to a range of sociological questions (e.g., Barbalet 1998). For research programs in sociology of emotions, see Kemper (1990). Among the classic traditions of social science, Freudian theory is most directly concerned with emotions. But it hasn't helped us much in advancing sociology. In part this is because Freud makes emotions derivative of drives, whereas I will argue in chapter 6 that the reverse is a more plausible research program, indeed on Freud's home territory of sexuality. Insofar as Freud is a microsociologist, he is a microsociologist of early childhood family situations. My position is that we can learn more about such situations by viewing them through the lens of interaction rituals that we see in adult life, than by viewing adulthood through the lens of early childhood.

4. In this respect IR chain theory is paralleled by Affect Control theory put forward by Heise (1979, 1987) and Smith-Lovin (1990). IR theory gives a more elaborate model of the situational process itself. Affect Control theory builds on its distinctive form of data: questionnaires that rate actors and actions on the dimension of goodness, power, and activeness, and that predict changes in these ratings when already existing (and hence already rated) actors and actions occur in new combinations. The model has been implemented by computer simulations.

5. I might add, to reassure those sociologists who are wary of the intrusion of physiology into meaningful, interpretive human action—of *Naturwis-*

senschaft into *Geisteswissenschaft*—that the prime mover of human action remains on the level of social communications. Social emotions are not being reduced to physiology; to the contrary, human brain physiology is activated, and takes on the condition that it is in at any particular moment, by the flow of interaction in the IR chain. Physiology is the substratum, while the causality flows from the social interaction. The human brain is largely programmed from the outside in.

6. A point stressed by Rodney Stark (2002) in a comparative analysis of religious rituals.

7. Order-giving can occur in a number of different contexts, and hence individuals may have mixed experiences across their lives. Such mixtures are most likely to happen in complex modern societies (although not to everyone), and are least likely in traditional societies organized around patrimonial households that concentrate all spheres of activity in one location. As Lamont (2000) shows, modern working-class order-takers shift their evaluation criteria as they reflect on their overall position in the class structure, and thereby build up their subjective status. These complications concern long-run patterns of IR chains over time. Here we are considering the dynamics of each micro-situation of the enactment of power taken in itself, examined for its immediate effects upon situational emotions. In chapter 7, I distinguish between deference-power (D-power)—the power to give orders in the immediate situation—and efficacy-power (E-power)—the power to make consequences happen outside the immediate present. The present discussion concerns the emotional consequences of D-power.

8. This occurs most palpably in torture, such as practiced by prison guards, slave overseers, soldiers dealing with guerilla fighters, police in dealing with intractable arrestees, and also child bullies (Collins 1974; Montagner et al. 1988). Torture is a highly and inescapably focused ritual designed both to gain emotional dominance over the subordinated individual in the immediate situation, and to broadcast the symbolic message of group domination and subordination.

9. See evidence summarized in Gans (1962, 229–62), as well as the descriptions of working-class ethos in Rubin (1976) and Halle (1984), and most extensively in Lamont's (2000) investigation of the way in which working-class men view the class above them.

10. An obvious case is America at the turn of the twenty-first century, where the socially preferred tone is casualness, and sanctions are given for those who are overly formal and overly moralistic. These complexities are discussed in chapter 7.

11. Frijda (1986, 13, 71) describes emotion as a felt but latent action tendency: a readiness for contact with the environment at the high end; at the low end, disinterest and apathy.

12. I am leaving aside the complexities on the physiological level, where several different components of hormonal and neural systems are apparently involved. On this level in general, specific states of emotional arousal are due more to the balance between various systems rather than to the activation of some system by itself. See also Frijda (1986, 39) on both simple and complex varieties of depression. There can also be specific chemical processes associ-

ated with depression, and these may have some genetic component, and can be treated by medication; but IR theory holds that physiological processes are not solely determined by chemistry and genes, and that some significant proportion of them occur because of the flow of successful and unsuccessful IRs in everyday life.

13. Kemper's theory has the additional complication in that he postulates anger (as well as shame) as resulting from situations in which an actor feels he / she is short-changed in status, vis-à-vis someone else. That is, Kemper deals with the more complicated situation of comparisons between the status one thinks oneself ought to get compared to someone else, and what they actually get. I prefer to begin the explanation from a simpler and, I believe, more fundamental process: the emotions that derive from dominating or being dominated, and of being a member or a nonmember. The Kemper theory adds not only expectations from past experience, but also a moral judgment as to the propriety of the outcome compared to some valued ideal. The two theories may be congruent, in the following respects. I propose that experiences in power situations, and in status-membership situations, result in increases or decreases in emotional energy. EE itself involves expectations for future situations; but the IR mechanisms that produce EE in the first place are, so to speak, first-order mechanisms of emotional production. Emotional energy becomes an ingredient in allowing future situations to occur, and in determining their emotional outcomes. The expectations that are important in Kemper's model may be regarded as situationally specific arousals of EE. Kemper's theory seems to me to explain a second-order quality of emotions, those that arise from violation or confirmation of expectations. Both types of mechanisms may be operating in the same situation: for instance, there can be depression from nonacceptance in a status group (my hypothesis of first-order effects), and anger from one's assessment of this nonacceptance as unjust (Kemper's second-order effects).

Kemper adds further complexities, including the attribution as to the agent responsible for the experience (one's self, other persons, impersonal forces). I would suggest that these cognitions themselves are explainable by the Durkheimian social density. Blaming oneself occurs only when there is a differentiated group structure producing categories of individual agency and responsibility; blaming impersonal forces (e.g., magic) or the violation of a taboo occurs where there is a tightly bounded and internally undifferented group. Mary Douglas (1973) refers to the former situation as high "grid" and to the latter as high "group," and provides data from anthropological comparisons for their correlation with different modes of attributing danger and responsibility (Douglas 1966). Black (1998) systematizes data to support the general pattern that conflicts within tight undifferentiated groups are quickly smothered and offenses are left unavenged; individual responsibility and punishment occur in structures of social inequality, relational distance, and heterogeneity. Thus an individual's prior experience in living within particular kinds of network structures should affect what agency he or she perceives as operative in his/ her immediate situations, and will shape specific emotions along the lines that

Kemper proposes. As stated, Kemper's model is too closely tied to modern social conditions.

14. Theorizing on the basis of the four primary emotions of anger, fear, happiness, and sadness, Turner (2002, 72–78) analyzes shame as a second-order emotion, blended from several primary emotions. The strongest component in shame is disappointment-sadness, combined with a lesser degree of anger at oneself, and fear about consequences to oneself. Turner suggests that pride is a blend of happiness directed at oneself, with an undertone of anger directed against others.

15. This is why in races, running behind the pace-setter is often the strategy that ends up winning. The second-place runner feels psychologically pulled along by the leader's effort. Then at a key moment when the finish-line is in sight, she or he breaks the leader's rhythm and moves to the front, leaving the former leader locked into his/her former rhythm—a rhythm that after all must feel right since it had been shared by the followers up to that point. It is hard for the former leader suddenly to shift from a leading rhythm to following and matching the new leader's rhythm, and then to shift yet again to break the rival's rhythm. The same dynamics apply to horse races, i.e., among non-human mammals.

16. For more detail see the appendix to this chapter. The weakness of Erickson and Schultz's technically impressive study, and other sociolinguistic studies of this kind, is in the larger theoretical apparatus. The authors interpret their findings in terms of cultural differences, as if counselors and students misunderstand each other because they are using different paralinguistic codes of different ethnic groups. The implication is that misunderstandings can be overcome by learning the multiple cultures of tacit communication codes. This might be so in some instances, but it misses the key source of variations in solidarity in micro-interactional situations: the process of the interaction ritual itself. In IR chains, individuals build up different amounts of emotional energy, differing symbolic repertoires, and hence differing attractions and repulsions toward various kinds of conversations; and the micro-situation itself has its own dynamic principles that determine what level of rhythmic coordination it reaches. It is not to be expected that every dyad, even from the same ethnic group, would automatically produce solidarity. In short, the authors of these studies limit themselves to macro-variables on the input side; their contribution is to descriptive measures on the output side.

17. There are further complexities in conflictual situations that I will not pursue here. Short-term dynamics of conflict initially raise EE within mutually hostile groups, sucking them more deeply into the emotions of conflict; further emotional ups and downs occur in victory, defeat, and long-term stalemate. These patterns are the subject of my forthcoming work on violent conflict.

18. Individuals who dominate groups may deliberately provoke weaker persons on the margins of the group to become angry: an example is the game of trading insults found among youth gangs (the game at one time called "the dirty dozens"). This is a game to humiliate weak persons, who are goaded into expressing anger, but are unable to back it up by a show of physical dominance. This is playing on the underlying principle that strong persons keep

their cool; when they do rise to anger, they express it in such a powerful form as to drastically penalize anyone who is its victim. There are, of course, some situations in which this kind of provocation is played mildly as a form of friendly teasing; it generates solidarity precisely insofar as it raises the level of collective effervescence, but does not push the teasing to the level of provoking anger. In this respect teasing differs from bullying, although there is a continuum where they shade into one another.

19. See Black (1998) for evidence that in societies organized as loose social networks individuals react to affronts by avoidance.

20. Thus crying, like anger, tends to occur in a relatively "realistic" manner: it is most often expressed in situations in which it has a chance of accomplishing its end. This analysis is confined to the kind of crying that is related to fear. Crying at moments of ceremonial triumph, or in response to a scene of personal reconciliation in a sentimental film, is a different emotional dynamic, related to intense feelings of solidarity. See Katz (1999) for a detailed analysis of the bodily rhythms and vocal inflections in situations involving crying and whining. In cases like those which Katz describes, whining is not an expression of fear but is a mode of exerting interactional control as well as manipulation of self.

21. At least, this is the pattern where depression is socially induced and not merely a genetic / chemical condition.

22. Legally speaking, the family car may belong to the father, but if the teenage daughter always gets to use it when she wants to, it is situationally her material resource, not his. Analogous relationships are important in the financial world, as in the case of high-EE investors using other (lower-EE) persons' money. This model of economic stratification is pursued in chapter 7. Legal property relations are situationally challenged, of course, in a range of interactions from aggressive borrowing to robbery. Black (1998) presents evidence that much property crime is viewed by the perpetrators as a form of self-help, managing their own personal obligations and grievances in an ongoing chain of struggles over possessions.

23. I have sometimes referred to membership symbols by Bourdieu's term "cultural capital"—in part because it makes a nice symmetry between the shorthand "CC" and "EE." Under either term, these are symbolic possessions that may be invested in further interactions, and are subject to constraints of a market, including deflation in the value of the currency as it becomes more abundant (see also Lamont and Lareau 1988). The difference between the two theoretical schemes is in the emphasis given to micro-situational process or to abstract macro-structure. My use of the concept of "cultural capital" or "membership symbols" refers to all items of culture charged up by interaction rituals, which thus shift in local significance with situational processes over time.

24. One of the problems in survey research about happiness, a concept that may be loosely related to EE, is that respondents tend not to say that they are unhappy; hence questionnaires give a series of refinements on the positive end, ranging from "very happy" to "not too happy." (Bradburn 1969). From the point of view of micro-situational analysis, the situation of being interviewed may be a positive IR, which raises the EE level of the respondent at

that moment. Thus we would want to be able to trace self-observations of EE from one situation to the next, to capture the situational source of variation, apart from the features of making a report about oneself.

CHAPTER 4
INTERACTION MARKETS AND MATERIAL MARKETS

1. See Waller 1937; Homans 1950, 1961; Blau 1960. It was reading the latter paper by Blau that motivated me, as a young graduate student in psychology, to switch to sociology.

2. Figure 4.1 draws attention to the detail that the initiating ingredients must rise above thresholds to set off collective processes, otherwise the IR fails to get off the ground. An additional time-dynamic underlined here is that ritual outcomes last only for a limited period of time. This fact is indicated by the dissipation sinks (drawn in the convention of flowchart modeling) on the far right side of figure 4.1 (and also drawn just below failed thresholds); these mean that the feeling of group solidarity, EE, and membership significance of symbols, fades away after the ritual is over, and eventually will disappear unless another IR is carried out. In a computer simulation of this model, we can enter a rate for the dissipation of this level over time, and observe how the level of solidarity builds up and declines depending on the strength of the flows into it and how often the whole process is repeated. For an example of a simulation, see Hanneman and Collins 1998.

3. See Frijda 1986. This satiation is not shown in Figure 4.2 but could be indicated by further rows and columns showing diminished payoffs for extremely long periods of sustained attention. In figure 4.1, the feedback loops as shown would result in a continuous escalation of all variables; a more complicated flowchart would indicate the points at which emotional satiation occurs.

4. One can see this in the long-term feedback loops in figure 4.1 from the outcomes at the right—solidarity, emotional energy, and symbols of group membership—to the facilitating conditions for interaction given at the left. If the cycle is to be broken, it must happen because of change in exogenous conditions affecting the assembly and focus of the group.

5. That is to say, the IR mechanism shapes all situations of interaction. Whenever people come together, there is always some degree of mutual focus and emotional entrainment, ranging from zero to intense, and thus there will always be some effects on ritual outcomes. This process is inevitable even if there are other inputs into individuals' bodies. If an individual's EE is low because they are starving or diseased, their bodily interaction with others will still be shaped by the amount of mutual focus and emotional entrainment, albeit in this case constrained by the low physiological condition of one of the participants—which thereby may become propagated through the chains of emotions and symbolic significances among others in the network who are not physiologically affected. The IR mechanism never turns off, even as its inputs vary. Even if there are genetic influences on behavior, they must flow through IRs, hence social interaction always shapes how genetic influences are experi-

enced in social situations. It is untenable to suppose that gene therapy or some other kind of medical intervention would automatically change people's social behavior irrespective of situational dynamics.

6. The famous inability of General de Gaulle to get along with Churchill during the former's residence in England during the World War is not to be attributed to unusually egotistical personalities, since it is just one instance of many. Hemingway (1964, 28) reports that when attending Gertrude Stein's salon in Paris of the 1920s, one never spoke of James Joyce, who was lionized elsewhere; "it was like speaking of one famous general in the presence of another general."

7. It is unclear whether the highest-EE individuals will interact with "upper-middle-EE" or with "lower-middle-EE" persons. For example, one pattern could be the group of ebullient "party animals," "leading spirits," etc., clustering togther with the highest energy star in their midst; another pattern could be that the "upper-middle EE" crowd makes up one cluster, while the energy star collects a stable of "lower-middle EE" persons who slavishly follow and applaud.

8. Empirical evidence relevant to this point shows that individuals in higher-ranking occupations, and in occupations exercising autonomous power over others, are more committed to their work, work longer hours, and are more likely to allow work to spill over into their private lives (Kanter 1977; Rubin 1976; Kohn and Schooler 1983; Gans 1962). Studies of work situations across occupations have not focused explicitly on the IR density of such situations, but available evidence is in keeping with the proposed pattern. A related line of investigation suggests a relationship between the tightly focused interpersonal groups within modern Japanese business organizations and their tendency to work long hours with few vacations (Nakane 1970); one might describe this as a high-interaction ritual density within Japanese organizations.

9. More broadly, it is worth emphasizing that work situations generate their own stocks of membership symbols. These constitute the local culture of the stock broker, the financial manipulator, the industrial manager, the professional politician, and every other occupational milieu. Membership symbols are generated locally within the various realms of work. Thus Bourdieu greatly overstates the importance of "cultural capital" created and transmitted within the formal culture-producing institutions such as schools and museums, as well as that which is passed along in the family as class "habitus." As empirical evidence suggests (Lamont 1992; Kanter 1977; Dalton 1951, 1959), business executives and other high-ranking persons do not owe their ability to negotiate membership with other such persons to any great extent to their "cultivation" in the formally produced cultural symbols, but rather to their use of the symbols of their immediate milieu. Financiers assemble financial coalitions not because of their knowledge of literature and opera, but above all because they talk the language of finance in a convincing way. In contrast to Bourdieu's emphasis on what might be called generalized cultural capital, individuals in elite occupations are successful because of the particularistic cultural capital or stock of symbols that circulate in their immediate network.

10. The relative subjective value of money earned should decline at high levels of income, according to conventional economic theory, as there is diminishing trade-off between money and the effort put into working. But where work consists in high intensity IRs that generate energy, there is no increasing taste for leisure. On the distribution of leisure and work hours, see Jacobs and Gerson 2001.

11. I have argued above that high-EE individuals tend to shun each other. Does this contradict the evidence I am citing here that high-EE intellectuals cluster with other high-EE intellectuals? Closer examination of the temporal patterns shows no contradiction. Those intellectuals who become highly productive (manifesting high EE in their work) typically start their careers both as pupils of previously high-productive intellectuals, and often as members of a group all of whom move up into creative activity together. Once an individual makes their intellectual breakthrough into independent reputation in the social attention space, however, he or she generally breaks both with his / her teacher and with early compatriots who have now become rival successes. These patterns are documented in detail in my study of networks of philosophers (Collins 1998).

12. From this point of view, there are two different aspects of what Granovetter (1973) famously called "the strength of weak ties." One is the shape of connections of that tie in the larger network: here a "weak tie" is one that ties to other people who are remote, and thus conveys information that is not locally available. Burt (1992) reformulated this kind of weak tie as a bridge tie across a structural hole in the network, in contrast to ties that are redundantly interconnected among the same group of people. The second way in which a tie can be "weak" or "strong" is in terms of the kind of IR that takes place when these persons meet: a weak tie would be a perfunctory ritual, generating little solidarity and emotional energy; whereas a strong tie exists among those persons whose encounters generate these outcomes strongly, and thus makes them friends, confidantes, valued colleagues. The two kinds of strength or weakness of ties can combine in different ways. It seems likely that the advantageous "weak ties" in Granovetter and Burt's sense (bridge ties) must be at least minimally successful as IRs, otherwise nothing would get transmitted through them; and it may be that having a strong (interactionally intense) tie to a bridge across a structural hole is what makes those ties effective. Conversely, one may have ties that are clustered in redundant, multiply interrelated groups, but the group itself may be emotionally flat and perfunctory in the symbols they pass around.

13. For a striking example of the creation of markets as collective enterprises allying competitive organizations whose identities are inseparable from their competition, see Leifer 1995.

14. The nearest modern equivalent to the ascetic saint would be athletes, who sometimes undergo considerable bodily pain and receive in return the loud emotional support of an admiring crowd. We are less inclined to see them as altruists, since successful modern athletes are commonly quite highly paid (either immediately or in the long run), and in addition are quite egotistical and spoiled in their off-field behavior. Monks were honored as beings apart

from ordinary life because they made a lifetime commitment to asceticism; athletes make only a situationally specific commitment to undergoing bodily pain in transient situations. For an explanation of the changes in social structure that made monastic life an honored focus of attention in some traditional societies, but not in modern ones, see Collins 1998, 206–8.

15. IR theory implies that leaders of altruistic organizations can be expected to become quite egotistical. If several leaders are energized by the adulation that they receive, there are struggles over power positions inside altruistic organizations. One way in which these are typically resolved is that ambitious, especially younger followers, once they have served their apprenticeship and learned the techniques of mobilizing a movement of this kind, split off to form their own organization. This is a typical pattern in the formation of religous cults (Stark and Bainbridge 1986). For an instance of a power struggle in a classic altruistic organization, carried out by the techniques of demonstrating one's own altruism and questioning the motives of one's opponents' demonstrations of altruism, see *The Life of St. Teresa of Avila* (1565/1957).

16. Cf. Miller 1998. Contemporary shopping malls and entertainment complexes deliberately attempt to counteract this by ritualizing the shopping experience, as documented by Ritzer (1999).

17. It is questionable that individuals handle this kind of decision by comparing ratios of numerators over denominators, since this is an abstract conception that is more cognitive than emotional. I suggest instead that the comparison is simply among differences: EE benefits minus EE losses. The decision is made by comparing the immediate situation fresh in the mind against remembered and prospective situations, in terms of the emotional intensity of the symbols by which they are brought to mind. This may indeed take place in conscious verbal thinking, or even in a conversational discussion, as well as in less-articulated emotional attractions and repulsions. In every form of decision making, the symbols representing the choices are surrounded by a halo of varying degrees of dazzle.

18. Here the experimental nature of research on choice anomalies may make such behavior appear more irrational than it really is. In real-life situations, the costs of seeking information may be high; and unlike the neatly framed experimental alternatives, there may be potentially endless problems in arriving at a full range of relevant information. Under such conditions, it is reasonable to satisfice, in the sense of March and Simon (1958), rather than engage in extensive informational search. A similar argument is made by Esser (1993).

19. IR theory predicts that persons avoid free-riding in proportion to the extent of their emotional ties with other persons in the situation. Hence most persons do not free-ride in experiments as much as would be predicted by purely materially interested calculation (Marwell and Ames 1979, 1980).

20. See Blood and Wolfe 1960, 241. The situations and manners in which persons talk about money has not been much investigated by naturalistic research on conversation; it is a subject well worth further investigation. Zelizer (1994) depicts the many different sorts of moneys operating in distinctive social circuits of exchange; from the viewpoint of IR chains, these currencies are given their value by the conversational rituals in which people use them as

topics; and these conversational networks are what constitute the solidarity and identity of those communities as economic actors.

21. In a different theoretical context, this is what Garfinkel (1967) found in his famous experiments breaching ordinary expectations.

22. The source both of math-aversion in the general populace, and of mathematics-identification in particular academic and professional communities, can be traced to the ritualized experiences of both groups during schooling. Mathematics training focuses heavily upon the *rite de passage* of solving mathematical problem sets, an activity that takes many hours of the daily lives of math and science students, and sets them apart from the social activities of most other students. Mathematical problems, formulated by teachers who identify emotionally with the elite standing of their profession, are typically designed so that students must internalize the symbolism and the problem-solving procedures of the field; mathematical school problems are set up in a graded series of hurdles of progressive difficulty, which keep up a level of emotional tension in the student attempting to pass them. Thus the activity of working on mathematical problem-sets becomes a fairly intense ritual, creating group-specific emotions, symbolic and social barriers between insiders and outsiders.

23. It is doubtful that in many real-life social situations individuals know quantitative probabilities of outcomes, hence we may neglect risk, in the strict sense of the term.

24. Garfinkel's ethonomethology is congruent with Simon's (1957) analysis on this point. Garfinkel (1967) enhances the depth of the problems faced by the human cognitive agent by pointing to irremediable sources of ambiguity in defining collective reality. Hence Garfinkel's actor is even more conservative than Simon's, preferring to take most things for granted rather than to have to consider their justification and their alternatives.

25. In the IR model, the actor maximizes EE overall. Satisficing is a procedure for dealing with a large number of different arenas of action simultaneously; the purpose of satisficing, however, is to maximize overall EE. Simon's satisficing model has no way in which to maximize across situations because it lacks a common denominator.

CHAPTER 5
INTERNALIZED SYMBOLS AND THE SOCIAL PROCESS OF THINKING

1. See Collins (1998, 858–62) for an argument as to why both solipsism and the philosophical tradition of arguing, in Descartes' manner, from "cogito ergo sum," are unrealistic simultaneously on sociological and philosophical grounds.

2. At the turn of the twentieth century there were several schools of psychological research that amassed considerable data on introspection (see summary in Kusch 1999). Most of this research is not relevant to the sociological model, since it was concerned not with the natural flow of thoughts, but with isolated associations between words and sometimes images, often using artificial words constructed for laboratory purposes to avoid contamination by the ordi-

nary flow of talk. Introspectionist psychology engineered its methods to eliminate the very social interaction context that we are concerned with here. There is also a large body of recent research in cognitive science that overlaps to a degree with the sociological issue being addressed, but that I will not attempt to review here.

3. This sketch does not exhaust the number of methods for studying thought, even if we confined ourselves to a model that includes the social context of ongoing interaction. Other methods include computer simulations, classic psychoanalytic methods of free association, and analysis of dreams. I omit these, in part to avoid overweighing this discussion with a huge literature review; in part to keep the theoretical focus here upon the IR perspective and how we could advance this research program, rather than muddying it with other theoretical perspectives that cut in quite different directions.

4. Needless to say, we need as large a collection of empirical instances as possible. Readers are encouraged to collect and analyze their own thought-situations as well as observations of semi-internalized and semi-externalized talk and to improve the theoretical scheme. Margaret Archer has launched a similar research program in England.

5. Rankings as major, secondary, and minor are determined by the amount of reference to them in subsequent writings. The study includes 2,670 philosophers in China, India, Japan, ancient Greece, the Islamic world, and medieval and modern Europe.

6. The criticism may be raised that everyone is linked to everyone else in a network. There is some evidence suggesting that every person in the USA can be linked to every other person in six links (Travers and Milgram 1969); thus it is not surprising that famous intellectuals would be linked to each other. The criticism gives an opportunity to attend to what precisely is being shown here. We are studying links among intellectuals, not among lay persons who do not transmit intellectual ideas and reputations; the fact that one philosopher in ancient Athens may have had a landlord who was two links away from the butcher who served another philosopher does not constitute a link among those philosophers. Network analysis tends to be too glib about what constitutes the content of a tie, usually taking for granted that there is some kind of homogeneity in what flows through those ties. Research which shows that arbitrarily chosen individuals in modern America can get a series of postcards through six links to someone they do not know does not indicate the existence of an effective social network; in a sense, it is merely an artifact of the research.

My other point of emphasis here is that important intellectuals are closely connected to other important intellectuals. These are for the most part one-link chains, which also tend to concatenate into longer chains so that, for example, the most important ancient Greek philosophers accumulated an average of 5.9 major and secondary thinkers within 2 links, and 12.1 within four links; for secondary philosophers the corresponding figures are 2.2 and 4.5. Studies of the transmission of rumors show that by the time a message has gone through several links, it tends to become badly distorted (Bartlett 1932); what gets transmitted through six-link chains (as in the "small world" research) are likely to be the merest banalities. Intellectual networks do not operate like this, because they are extremely intense interactions, with great emphasis placed upon the significance of membership or nonmembership through the way that idea-symbols are used. The length of chains among differents kinds of intellectuals differs systematically; an argument that everyone is networked to everyone else is manifestly not the case here.

7. This pertains up to the last generation that I examine in my study of networks. I cut off the analysis with the near past, since it takes several generations before the historical reputation of intellectuals stabilizes as eminent, minor, or forgotten. We do not know how to assess the creativity of thinkers who are our contemporaries or our teachers, because not enough time has passed to see what the generations downstream will do with their ideas.

8. This can be illustrated by my experience as an undergraduate of listening to Talcott Parsons lecture at Harvard in the early 1960s. What one got from him that was useful later on was not the details of his own theoretical system, but his emphasis that the forefront of contemporary theory comes from links to the classics, especially Weber and Durkheim, taken together as an alliance. Parsons (and even more so his assistants and circle of followers) stressed the contrast between this sophisticated tradition and what was referred to as "American dust bowl empiricism." Implicitly, too, it was contrasted with symbolic interactionism, against which Parsons promoted Freud as an alternative theoretical ingredient on the micro-level, but fully coordinated with the macro theory rather than being micro-reductionist. Parsons set the starting point for my own career as a sociological theorist; this developed by adding other ingredients during my graduate studies at Berkeley, turning Parsons's version of Weber in directions promoted by contact with Marxists and historical sociologists. An additional ingredient came from contact with Goffman and even more so with the network of his students, among whom Goffman was a prime topic of conversation, including much discussion of how the rituals of deference and demeanor and the presentation of self were visible in the interactions right around us. Most of these other Goffman followers took his ideas in the direction of symbolic interaction, since Herbert Blumer was another imposing presence in the Berkeley department. Blumer constantly reminded us that he personally transmitted ideas from George Herbert Mead, and polemically contrasted the symbolic interactionist camp against the other schools of sociology. One circle of Goffman's students, regarded as rather exotic and iconoclastic, formed an opposing subsect, combining Goffman's sociology of everyday life with the ideas, still percolating in an underground, of Harold Garfinkel. It was this movement of followers that created ethnomethodology, publicizing and helping to get published Garfinkel's works (which although formulated earlier did not come out as a book until 1967), as the movement broke out into the open. I found my own niche by giving Weber and Durkheim the high theoretical importance Parsons assigned to them, but interpreting them in an alliance with Goffman and Blumer. I offer this account both as a concrete example and to show that IR chains can be tested by self-reflection.

9. Herbert Blumer, who had been Mead's teaching assistant at Chicago in the 1930s, used to explain Mead's model of thinking during his lectures at Berkeley in 1964 in the following way: The "I" carries out a rehearsal of the

action, by sending out the "me" into an imagined image of the world; when the "me" becomes depicted as encountering an obstacle, the "I" reroutes it by imagining a different way of getting to the goal. The capacity of the adult self to visualize an objective world, as well as to view oneself in it, is the viewpoint of the "Generalized Other." It is this division of the self into interacting parts that frees the adult human from the immediate pressures of the situation, allowing reflexive distancing, planning, and redefinition of the situation. It is the key to being human. See also Blumer 1969.

10. See Borkenau's (1981) historical comparisons in "The Rise of the I-form of Speech." Latin, for example, rarely separates out "I" but includes it in the verb inflection. Japanese tends to use impersonal forms: one says "concerning this, wanted is" (*kore wa hoshii desu*), where an English speaker would say "I want this."

11. As we have seen in chapter 2, the "I" as independent actor's viewpoint is the last component of the self to form, when internalized self-talk gives the child the capacity for internal self-direction and autonomy from immediate situational pressures.

12. It appears that all subjects in Katz's research had an experience to tell; there was no driver who had not gotten angry at the bad behavior of other drivers. And that means that the drivers committing the bad behavior had to be part of the same sample; these are the same actions, seen from opposing sides.

13. Another type of "magical" gesture documented by Katz is the insult of "giving the finger" to the offending driver, usually accompanied by a curse. Here the "black magic" is especially contagious, since the recipient who actually notices this gesture typically retaliates, with the same gesture or by a further escalation. This is ritual entrainment, being pulled not only into a common (foul) mood and common rhythm and focus of attention, but often into mirroring the very same gesture and the same formulaic curses.

14. These taboo words were ostentatiously spoken by the younger generation at the time of the "counter-culture" movement of the 1960s and '70s, as part of a general repudiation of traditional patterns of deference and demeanor. Part of the impetus to their spread was a sense of breaking the social barrier between men and women, in which women had been conversationally segregated from "rough talk." Spoken obscenities are now widespread in those sections of society that consider themselves hip, youthful, sophisticated, and up to date. Nevertheless, the use of obscenities is situational: they are rarely written, especially in official documents, and are generally censored in newspapers; the same persons who use them in casual conversation avoid them in public speeches; schools generally prohibit and penalize their use.

15. Katz quotes an Asian-American driver who says he is annoyed at the stereotype of Asian women as slow drivers. Caught behind a slow driver, he became enraged to find it was an Asian woman, and uttered a curse at her, using that categorical stereotype.

16. That is, there might be another passenger in the car, but the cursing is not a communication toward that person. The presence of passengers provides a test of Katz's model that cursing arises from the driver's sense of interrupted flow and failure to be recognized as a conscious agent. Passengers are objec-

tively as much in a situation of danger or of being impeded as the driver, but passengers rarely engage in cursing at other drivers, and instead tend to regard their own driver's behavior as irrational. It is the driver who experiences the sense of flow with the car in the rhythm of traffic, and hence the driver who has the experience of frustration that needs to be rectified by magical action.

17. For example, when Baruch Spinoza was expelled from the Amsterdam synagogue in 1656, he was formally cursed by the congregation, who ritually stepped over him outside the doorway.

18. For instance, watching a video of *Ninotcha* and disliking the performance of Melvyn Douglas, who seems quite miscast, I say aloud, "*Well thank God it wasn't Gary Cooper.*" Subvocal thinking feels inadequate for making a strong statement; in the absence of someone to tell it to, one speaks it aloud to oneself (or writes it—whence the impulse to write letters to newspaper editors).

19. There are some specialized exceptions here, such as the process which musicians go through in composing. But although this process seems mysterious to outsiders, who are likely to invoke folk notions of "genius" or "inspiration," it appears to be similar to the kind of internalization of techniques from professional networks, reshaping of ingredients, and reexternalization toward known audiences, that operate in the case of intellectual creativity. See Denora 1995.

20. At least this seems to be approximaly so. The image does not last noticeably longer than the internal speaking turn; nor does it flash by so quickly that visual imagery shifts much more rapidly than verbal topics do.

21. A marginal case here is dreaming. Dreams that are most vivid, and that comprise the main connotation of the term, take place largely in imagery, with only intermittent talking; and these voices may or may not be identified with oneself. There is, however, another, very large class of dreams, or mental activity, that goes on during sleep, which consists entirely of verbal thinking; this has been studied by waking up subjects during times of rapid eye movement (Kryger, Roth and Dement 2000). Thus even sleep-thinking consists quantitatively in a large portion of self-talk, often obsessively repetitive and disjointed. This dreaming self-talk appears generally to consist of elaborations on reverberated talk from the previous day, or anticipatory talk for topics coming up in the immediate future, and thus gives the sleeper a not very restful night, since it is too close to the contents of daytime consciousness. Visual-dominant dreams go further afield. Here, too, there seems to be a sociological component. Visual dreams are a form of thinking in concrete images: since verbal thinking is minimized, every thought is spelled out in a picture, not presented as an isolated image as if it were a picture in a book, or a sign in an alphabet, but taking up the entire visual field as if it were a world in which one is bodily present. Dream-thinking proceeds from image to image, but via the imaginary world-with-yourself-bodily-in-it, thus bringing about some strange incongruities by the standards of waking reality. This implies that Freudian efforts to make sense out of dreams as a language are misguided: dreams are clumsy and rather unsuccessful forms of thinking; they reveal some of the ingredients out of which thoughts are composed, but they do not usually translate into coherent verbal thoughts or even thoughts expressing desires.

Dream-thinking is thus very slow, compared to the speed of verbal thought. It is at the opposite pole from Turner's model of visual thinking as lightning-fast, a way to size up a situation and take rapid action. In sleep, when the body is immobilized (and the imagery-dream usually takes place in a period of deep trance, far from readiness for motor activity), a chain of thought by means of a succession of visual images is perhaps the slowest form of thinking of all. This can be taken as indirect evidence that verbal thought, free from the exigencies of concrete imagery, is the most effective medium for wide-ranging thought chains.

22. The process is obviously different with intellectuals who create poetry or distinctively patterned literary prose.

23. One can illustrate this point with the vocabulary that most rapidly conveys the worldview of a theoretical position: "legitimation," "world-system," "identity politics," "textuality," or even "interaction ritual."

Chapter 6
A Theory of Sexual Interaction

1. That is, anal penetration by the fist. This was proudly announced by a gay movement writer as "the only sexual practice invented in this century" (Rubin 1994, 95).

2. This interpretation is congruent with evidence that persons in monogamous relations tend to have higher physical pleasure as well as emotional satisfaction than those with multiple partners (Laumann et al. 1994, 375).

3. Theories that interpret heterosexual erotics as male dominance are accurate enough in many historical settings. Sex has indeed been a form of property; but this needs to be analyzed in relation to historical changes in negotiation of kinship alliances, marriage markets, and individual prestige relations, rather than treated as a constant. Ideologically formulated theories of male dominance lack a plausible micro-theory of interaction, substituting rather fanciful Freudian speculations, and miss the central features of erotic interactions.

4. Zelizer (2000) notes that the borderline of prostitution is not clear-cut, and that there are a variety of sexual relationships that differ in how immediate or specific the material payment, with both greater social respectability and more diffuse exchanges on credit in more long-term relationships.

5. Sources on prostitution: Sanchez 1997; Hoigard and Finstad 1992; Chapkis 1997; Stinchcombe 1994; Monto 2001. Customers reporting their experiences with prostitutes on worldsex.com frequently complain about being cheated by sexual come-ons. It would be illuminating to have materials on female experiences with gigolos. This is a somewhat more long-term relationship than an isolated commercial transaction, but has the reputation for callousness and exploitation on the side of the male provider of sexual services. Data on homosexual prostitutes (Kulick 1998) show that hard bargaining and exploitation of customers is a function not of gender but of the buyer-seller relationship.

6. In other words, the customer pays a definite sum, whereas the prostitute contributes pleasure, which is less easily measured and more subject to interpretation. Accordingly, prostitutes give no guarantee of satisfaction. Some feminist theorists (e.g., Barry 1995) stress the point that males exploit prostitutes, but this is a macro-structural argument, i.e., the claim that the very existence of prostitution is the result of a sexist society. Sticking to the micro-level, if the deal is money for sexual pleasure, then prostitutes generally exploit their customers more than vice versa. This would be the case no matter how legitimated and publicly regulated prostitution may be, such as in the case of legalized and semi-legalized prostitution in contemporary Netherlands and Germany.

7. This is a predominant theme in reports that male customers of prostitutes post on web sites like www.worldsexguide.com.

8. Historically, male-female couple dancing became popular at just the time, the nineteenth century, when an individualized marriage market came into existence, but with strong restrictions on nonmarital sex, and a considerable role for public opinion in choice of marriage partners, conveyed by a widely shared sense of social prestige. Ballroom dancing flourished as the micro-interaction appropriate for structural conditions favoring openly inspectable rankings of sexual popularity. Earlier forms of group dancing were not part of sexual negotiations, and often were carried out by all-male or all-female groups. Following this line of argument, the change from couple dancing with touching to non-touching dancing after the 1950s must indicate some change in the way in which sexual relations are negotiated; courtship on the dance floor apparently became no longer very important.

9. Biological researchers have shown that the amount of sperm a man releases varies with the amount of time spent apart from his pair-bonded partner. The interpretation given is that this is an evolutionary mechanism to make his sperm win out over competition with other potential males (Baker and Bellis 1995; discussed in Thornhill and Palmer 2000, 44–45, 74). IR intensity is an alternative explanation: the greater the symbolic focus and the more intense the buildup of sexual IR, the more intense the physiological climax. This may happen by gazing at pictures of, or fantasizing about, the absent lover; similarly we may expect that the more attention to pornography, the more sperm released when excitement is finally climaxed either in copulation or masturbation. Possibly an innate biological mechanism for increasing sperm release may be activated in this way, but the process is disconnected from reproduction, and determined by the intensity of the IR mechanism.

10. Although not necessarily immediately, since the physiology of intercourse follows climax with a falling off of sexual excitement and a refractory period. Something equivalent to a refractory period after satiation occurs in all kinds of IRs: the climax of sociable entrainment in shared laughter, or the eventually falling off of motivation to continue an entralling conversation. Without this, no IR could ever come to an end, and individuals could not detach themselves to get on with the utilitarian part of their lives. In Durkheimian theory, rituals are repetitive, not everlasting. This satiation point had to be diagrammed into the flow chart in chapter 4 (figure 4.1), to keep the simulation model from escalating to infinity.

11. Jewish religious tradition, which formulated the sabbath or seven-day ritual cycle, also enjoined weekly intercourse.

12. The high level of sexual intercourse among those just establishing a partnership further supports the interpretation offered in note 9 for the high amounts of sperm released in pair-bonded intercourse. It is the excitement level that determines all aspects of the intensity of sexual arousal, and the excitement level is built up highest by the dramatic emotions that go into the early period of sexual negotiations, and that die down later with routinization of the relationship.

13. Historically the existence of such groups has waxed and waned. Very likely the erotic prestige-setting influence of all-male groups grew to its height in the early twentieth century in Western societies, with the trend toward decline of patrimonial households and mobilization of age-cohorts in autonomous sociable settings. Their influence may well have waned in the late twentieth century, although perhaps only in the upper-middle class where males have been socialized into feminist culture. Like many other features of the sociology of sex, this awaits systematic historical ethnography.

14. The *Kama Sutra* says, "The love of a woman who sees the marks of nails on the private parts of her body, even though they are old and almost worn out, becomes again fresh and new. If there be no marks of nails to remind a person of the pasages of love, then love is lessened in the same way as when no union takes place for a long time. Even when a stranger sees at a distance a young woman with the marks of nails on her breast, he is filled with love and respect for her. A man, also, who carries the marks of nails and teeth on some parts of his body, influences the mind of a woman. In short, nothing tends to increase love so much as the effects of marking with the nails, and biting" (Vatsyayana 1964, 106–7). In mid-twentieth-century America, less elaborate bite marks were used for a somewhat similar purpose among young teen-agers. Malinowski (1929/1987, 281) describes the prestigiousness of such marks, and counters the notion that they are signs of dominance: "On the whole, I think that in the rough usage of passion the woman is the more active. I have seen far larger scratches and marks on men then on women. . . . It is a great jest in the Trobriands to look at the back of a man or a girl for the hallmarks of success in amorous life . . . the *kimali* marks are a favorite subject for jokes; but there is also much secret pride in their possession."

15. I am rejecting the evolutionary biology argument that breasts are indicators of a woman's breeding and child-rearing capacity. In most cultures, historically, breasts have been used primarily to symbolize exactly that; but these are the same cultures in which breasts were not erotic. Furthermore, although in the twentieth century large breasts tended to be regarded as more erotically attractive than small breasts, very large breasts (which would be the most obvious representations of mothering) become less attractive; and lactating breasts, the best indicator of all, are not erotic at all (opinion survey evidence presented in Patzer 1985, 144–45). A related explanation attributes the erotic allure of breasts to a displacement of infantile sucking. But in that case, women should be as strongly attracted to breasts as men; indeed, more so, if Chodorow's (1978) theory of female under-separation were true. But it appears that most women seem not to be erotically much attracted to breasts, even lesbians,

whose most frequent sexual activity is cunnilingus, and for whom erotic symbolism is predominantly genital.

16. It appears that males have a stronger motivation to lick a woman's genitals, than women have to fellate men: 35.5 percent of males but only 16.5 percent of females regard performing oral sex on their partner as very appealing. There is also a good deal of female fellation of males but this seems to be largely at the male's initiative: 45 percent of males and 29 percent of females say they regard receiving oral sex as very appealing. The actual incidence is that 67.7 percent of females have performed oral sex during their lifetime, and 18.8 percent in their last sexual event, both of which figures are higher than their preference (Laumann et al. 1994, 98–99, 152). The difference, as I elaborate later can be explained by the existence of circuits of erotic conversation principally among males, which generate prestige-seeking through erotic activities.

17. Masturbation is thus a form of self-interaction with symbols, structurally analogous to the relationship between public religious ritual and private prayer. And both are analogous to the internalized social process of thinking.

18. On the historical emergence of this scene, see Chauncey 1994; Weeks 1977; D'Emilio 1983. In the nineteenth century, "gay" was used to refer to the heterosexual carousing arenas of prostitutes' quarters, and especially to the expensive entertainment of high-class courtesans in Paris (Griffin 2000). Only later did it acquire its present-day connotation as homosexual.

19. On these types generally, see Collins 1986, chapters 10 and 11; 1999, chapter 6; and references therein.

20. In the mid-1990s 35.2 percent of males and 34 percent of females reported having sex more than once a week; 8 percent of males and 7 percent of females four or more times a week. At the opposite extreme, 27.4 percent of males and 29.4 percent of females had sex a few times or not at all during the year (Laumann et al. 1994, 88).

21. Scheff (1990) puts it more benignly: intact social bonds produce pride.

22. To be sure, class and ethnic differences and network boundaries among youth have not disappeared, and sexual markets tend to go on within class and ethnic pools. Nevertheless, the ideal display image of the sexual elite has a strongly class and race-transcending character.

23. In chapter 8, we will examine an ancillary ritual connected with this action "scene," the cult of cigarette smoking.

CHAPTER 7
SITUATIONAL STRATIFICATION

1. When sociologists incorporate these traditional concepts into their model of class hierarchy, they are being taken in by the ideology of the leisure upper-class status group, perhaps because this group is more talkative and easier to interview than the upper class that is actively making money. Thus Baltzell (1958) is much more informative about the cultural and leisure activities of the upper class than about their business activities.

2. There are also anonymous aspects of labor and goods markets, which are the topics of classical and neoclassical economic theory. Nevertheless, as

emphasized in recent economic sociology, the social structuring of markets by networks makes particular personal connections the most important aspect of entrepreneurs' lives (Smelser and Swedberg 1994). The relationship between anonymous and particularistic aspects of exchange is just beginning to be formulated.

3. The main exception among religious groups appears to be evangelical Christians, for whom there is evidence of having a large percentage of personal friends within their congregation. Sociability is often confined to the group, and rival settings for social encounters may be avoided, such as by home schooling their children. The "New Christian Right" is one part of society that is trying to reconstitute a moral hierarchy of status groups. For this reason they are viewed with suspicion by many other Americans, who resist anything but purely situational stratification.

4. Even at the turn of the twenty-first century, differences along this continuum are still palpable in the contrast between the compulsory casualness of American academic life (and similar upper-middle class sociable rituals) and the pockets of British ceremoniousness found in Oxford and Cambridge colleges.

5. Subdimension (a) is an extra twist on the *social density* dimension described in chapter 3; here we are concerned not merely with the density of bodily copresence over time, but with the density of ritual performances in time. Subdimension (b) is referred to in chapter 3 as *ritual intensity.*

6. This principle is corroborated by comparing the other end of the spectrum: Oxford and Cambridge college social rituals downplay ostentacion and personal bragging, as these are situations where status is quietly but unmistakably conveyed by the very fact of being admitted to formally-organized sociable occasions (e.g., dinner at High Table; chats in the Senior Common Room), monitored quite explicitly by gate-keeping personnel.

7. The latter historically would show a shift from bowing and honorific address to persons who held certain categorical statuses, toward more subtle deference in the form of who gets speaking rights and control over turn-taking. For micro-situational data on the latter, see Gibson 1999; on the long-term trend, Annett and Collins 1975.

8. News stories reported that the U.S. Congress, as well as the president, stopped their official proceedings to hear the outcome of the O. J. Simpson trial in 1995.

9. There is precedence in cases of persons treated as religious sacred objects: for example, a medieval saint whose trances drew spectators who would poke her with knives and burning objects to marvel at her imperviousness to pain (Kleinberg 1992).

10. This is a move along the continuum from relatively unfocused toward highly focused public interaction. At the upward extreme historically were the Chinese mandarins carried down the street and surrounded by armed guards, while members of the ordinary populace were required to avert their eyes from them by prostrating themselves to the ground.

11. Historically, this happened in situations where bands of men made long-distance voyages or raids, often capturing women. In all of these cases, there was much emphasis on establishing fictive kinship. We see this both in Anderson's (1999) data on fictive fathers, mothers, and brothers among alliances of

protection and support; and it was common where tribal order was broken into fluid bands of marauders (Finley 1977; Borkenau 1981; *Njal's Saga*; 1280/ 1960; Searle 1988).

12. Michael Mann (1986) referred to this as "off with their heads" power, and suggested that in traditional despotisms the actual reach of such power might be very limited; he termed this the difference between "intensive" and "extensive" power.

13. For example, Francis Bacon, son and nephew of high-ranking officials in the Tudor monarchy, himself the holder of high offices and a member of the aristocracy, addressed himself with great ceremonial deference to his own patrons. The pattern of deference in patrimonial households is illustrated throughout Shakespeare's plays, Chinese novels of the Ch'ing dynasty and earlier, and indeed in virtually all of the narrative literature of the world prior to the twentieth century.

14. The theme comes through strongly in Shakespeare's *King Lear*, the plot of which concerns how many armed personal retainers a lord could have around him. Stone (1967) documents that this was a struggle going on at the time Shakespeare was writing, around 1600, as the state attempted to limit the scope of private armaments to a few household guards, thereby monopolizing control for an increasingly centralized state as part of the opening phases of the "military revolution."

15. Entertainment stars are outside the circuits of economic class and organizational power, and even the networks of categorical status group. They have large amounts of money but do not participate in the activities that constitute upper-class financial circuits. They have neither E-power nor, in the strict sense, much D-power.

16. Situational dominance by means of noise may occur by virtue of a loud voice and raucous language; or through equipment such as boom boxes, cell phones, and car alarms. The latter two, although commericially promoted on utilitarian grounds, have their largest effects in the struggle for ephemeral situational dominance.

17. The author has observed this, from both sides, over some 500,000 miles of highway driving. For analysis of interviews with drivers, stressing their frustration as autonomous agents unable to communicate with the others who impede them, see Katz (1999).

CHAPTER 8
TOBACCO RITUAL AND ANTI-RITUAL: SUBSTANCE INGESTION
AS A HISTORY OF SOCIAL BOUNDARIES

1. For convenience in what follows I sometimes use the terms "smoking rituals" and "anti-smoking movement." In some instances this is inexact, since there are other forms of tobacco use (snuff and chewing) and opposition to them, and the anti-smoking movement is mainly focused on cigarettes, not cigars or pipes. Comparison among these various activities will figure in the argument. The broader or narrower usage should be apparent from context.

2. Compare the prediction that I published in 1975, in the context of discussing previous historical prohibitions of alcohol, drugs, and gambling:

> The prohibition of smoking is a good candidate for manufacturing a huge deviance culture in the future. The politics of drugs in general seems likely to be central, with constant technological innovation (which has already produced, during the twentieth century, strong narcotics and psychedelics, as well as tranquilizers, amphetimines, and barbiturates). Categories of drug deviance will be the product of interactions among a number of interest groups: pharmacists and physicians with economic and status motives for monopolization; career interests of enforcement agency officials; various occupational and community groups with status interests in maintaining particular standards of demeanor; and politicians who play upon mixtures of such interests and act as brokers of pluralistic ignorance by which wide-spread consumer interests may be kept suppressed. (Collins 1975, 469).

3. The anti-smoking movement during the 1980s began to acquire funding for state-imposed contributions from tobacco companies. At this time billboards appeared bearing such messages as "Smokers are addicts. Tobacco companies are pushers"—the implication being that the drug-enforcement campaign and its dire penalties (including life imprisonment for third-offense users, or first-offense sellers) should be carried out for tobacco-users and sellers. Others depicted smokers as killers: in one widespread advertisement, a man says "Mind if I smoke?" to which a woman replies "Mind if I die?"

4. Sources for the historical materials that follow: Brooks 1952; Glantz 1996; Goodman 1993; Kiernan 1991; Klein 1993; Kluger 1996; Sobel 1978; Troyer and Markle 1983; Wagner 1971; Walton 2000.

5. It is possible, however, that the drop in smoking that did occur in the years when tobacco advertising was cut back may be attributed to the lack of the stimulus of advertisements; but a careful study on this point would also have to take into account not merely the lack of advertisements but the growth in an agressive anti-smoking campaign. Even here one might doubt whether these messages would have much more effect—that is, whether negative advertising comes across any better than positive advertising. The anti-smoking campaign during this period was centrally in the news, in pronouncements of politicians, as well as on a personal level of individuals directly confronting smokers in public and personal spaces. Assuming that the face-to-face encounters have the most powerful effects, one would conclude that the drop in advertising had little effect on cutting smoking. Advertising is highly visible and thus gives the anti-smoking movement an easy target and a sense of clear victories when cigarette advertising is legally prohibited, which is just what a social movement needs to keep up its morale. But these are largely symbolic rather than substantive victories.

6. Here I am following an argument in the sociology of addiction outlined by Darrin Weinberg in a presentation at University of Cambridge, 2000.

7. Inserted into the IR model in chapter 2 (figure 2.1), the ingestion of nicotine, caffein, etc. becomes one of the ingredients on the left side of the model;

that is, it is part of the transient emotional stimulus that feeds into a common mood. But this common mood has other components coming from the character of the social interaction itself—the orientation toward tranquil relaxation, carousing, sexuality, etc. Through the process of feedback intensification by rhythmic entrainment in the group, the physical feelings of nicotine, etc. take on the emotional tone of the surrounding situation. Moreover, a successful IR that progresses to higher levels of mutual arousal generates collective effervescence and thus energizes the individuals taking part. In that way, tobacco etc. become what the participants regard as genuine sources of motivational energy, although in fact the energy is tacked on from the outside by the social experience.

8. The substitution points up the ritualism of ordinary eating. Much of the craving for food in hardship situations may be for the normalcy of regular meals, including their social character as group assembly in a break from working and other harsh duties. To be deprived of food is also to be deprived of the implied social membership in a normal society. If one ritual can be substituted for another, insofar as it brings solidarity and on that basis, construction of shared meanings, this explains how tobacco can be a substitute for food. We see the same kind of substitution in the case of drug "addicts," but also of "workaholics," especially those in high-culture activities that bring a strong subjective sense of participation in elite symbolic action. For example, both Beethoven and Newton were known for neglecting their meals while absorbed in their creative work.

9. Smoking was also associated with prostitution in Japan, in the entertainment culture of the geisha quarters of the Tokugawa period, as we see in particularly raffish Ukiyo-e prints. From the evidence of contemporary paintings, however, it appears that at least some women in nineteenth century China smoked pipes in respectable domestic scenes. In the eighteenth and nineteenth centuries, women in the Islamic world (Turkey, Persia, north Africa) were very frequently depicted as smoking hookah water pipes, either in the company of men or by themselves (Lemaires 2001). Perhaps the greater enclosure of harem-like womens' quarters in China and the Islamic world allowed smoking in respectable privacy, whereas the exposure of upper-class European women to public sociability led to greater concern over maintaining marks of respectability.

10.   "Coffee, which makes the politician wise,
         And see thro' all things with half-shut eyes."
         —Alexander Pope, "The Rape of the Lock"

First published 1714, this poem contrasts the various scenes of ritual sociability of London high society in the 1710s.

11. In Britain in 1900, 4/5 of tobacco use was in pipes, only 1/8 in cigarettes, the rest in cigars (Walton 2000, 75).

12. There are idiosyncratic exceptions: for example, the circle of "ordinary language" philosophers meeting for discussions around John Austin at Oxford in the 1950s all smoked pipes, a practice that was jocularly taken as emblematic of their intellectual movement.

13. "Do but notice what grimaces snuff-takers make, how their whole features are convulsed, how they dip into their snuff-boxes in mea-

sured rhythm, cock up their noses, compose their mouths, eyes, and all their features to a pompous dignity, and, as they perform the solemn rite of snuff-taking, they look as if they scorned the whole world, or were bent on some enterprise on which they might say, like Bouflet, "I will make the whole world tremble!"

"I have found by certain experiments that such men have the idea that, in the moment when they sniff the snuff up their noses, they are as men inspired, transformed into mighty kings and princes, or at least made royal and princely at heart" (German orig. 1720; quoted in Walton 2000, 51).

14. Winston Churchill was known by his omnipresent, oversized (and thus ultra-expensive cigar). Much of the time he kept it in his mouth unlit (Gilbert 1988). The fact that he also did so when working alone suggests that the cigar carried a subjective sense for him, of his place in society (manly, upper-class), apart from any physiological effects.

15. Women reporting on their smoking habits often comment that socializing with close friends are the most tempting occasions to smoke, and thus pose the greatest difficulty in giving up smoking. This is parallel to ex-drug users' tendency to relapse when exposed to social interactions that remind them of their early drug highs. These experiences represent not so much the feelings of physical ingestion but the emotional tone of the IR that was symbolized by the drug (Darrin Weinberg, personal communication).

16. One might interpret Shakespeare's portrayal of Falstaff and Prince Hal in *Henry IV*, parts I and II, first staged in 1597, as an expression of this conflict. Here carousing aristocrats take part in a realm that crosses status lines into the world of low life, in pursuit of momentary fun and excitement. A real-life version of this milieu is depicted in the poems of the rakish Lord Rochester for the 1670s.

17. These figures apparently reflect the atmosphere of all-out mobilization during World War II, when smoking was central to military solidarity rituals. After this peak, in 1973, 65% of British men smoked, 42% of women; for the United States in 1965, 52% of men smoked, 34% of women (Walton 2000, 94, 106; *Los Angeles Times* March 29, 2001).

18. Horowitz (2001) shows that the social process of assessing the threat posed by an enemy is a central dynamic in the growth or decline of hostile ethnic movements leading to deadly riots. On risk attribution to cancer generally, compare Stirling et al. 1993. For some cross-national variations in approaches to disease risk, see Nathanson 1996.

19. There were dramatic declines in influenza and pneumonia (which accounted for 202 deaths per 100,000 population in the year 1900), and in tuberculosis (198 per 100,000). By 1956 these figures had dropped to 8 and 28 respectively. Still larger were rates of infant mortality: about 100 per 1000 live births at the turn of the century, or about 10 percent. The most common non-infant cause of death, in 1900 as in 1990, remained cardiovascular diseases; these actually rose from 345 per 100,000 in 1900, to a peak of about 510 in the 1950s, dropping to about 365 in 1990. Cancers of all kinds accounted for 64 deaths

per 100,000 population in 1900, rising to 140 in 1950, 184 in 1980, and 202 in 1990. (*Historical Statistics of the US*: Series B-107, B-114–128; *Statistical Abstracts*, no. 114, 1992). To keep this in perspective, we may translate these figures into percentages: for instance, the last figure, cancer deaths of all kinds in 1990, is 2 per 1000 people, or 0.2 percent (one-fifth of one percent of the population dies of cancer every year). For lung cancer (the kind of cancer that is tobacco related), about 0.057 percent of the population dies every year, or one twentieth of one percent.

20. Life expectancy at birth went from 46.3 years for males and 48.3 years for females in 1900, to 72.0 years for males and 78.8 for females in 1990 (*Historical Statistics*, series B- 93–94; *Statistical Abstracts*, no. 103, 1992).

21. Death rates for 1990 from cancer (all kinds) per 100,000 population at various ages are in the first column. In the second column, these are translated into percentages of the age group who die of cancer. For comparison, the third column gives the percentages of the age group who die of anything.

		cancer deaths	all deaths
25 to 34 years old:	12.1	0.012%	0.138%
35 to 44 years old:	43.1	0.043%	0.221%
45 to 54 years old:	157.2	0.157%	0.475%
55 to 64 years old:	445.1	0.445%	1.204%
65 to 74 years old:	852.6	0.853%	2.647%
75 to 84 years old:	1338.1	1.338%	6.139%
over 85 years old:	1662.3	1.662%	15.035%

Source: Statistical Abstracts, no. 117, 1992.

After about age 55, chances of dying from cancer start becoming noticeable, although the actual percentage chances of dying from it in any particular year are still rather small (a little more than 1 percent chance for those over 75, and still under 2 percent for those over 85). But by these ages the chances of dying from *something* are becoming substantial: 6 percent of those of us who reach age 75 drop off every year, as will 15 percent of those who reach age 85. In other words, cancer generally kills you when something or another kills you.

22. Walton 2000, 107. In a population of 280 million, this gives 1/5000 annual chance of dying of second-hand smoke, or 0.02 percent. Even over fifty years of adult lifetime, this adds up to a 1 percent chance. Statistically effects on this scale are not very strong. Kluger (1996; quoted in Walton 2000, 107) concluded, in regard to the studies available in the 1980s, that when the furor over second-hand smoking took off, "the data were neither abundant nor coherent—and certainly not conclusive." More recent evidence is summarized in Taylor et al. 2001; Nelson 2001.

23. During these years, the one country in which the authorities paid attention to data on the connection between smoking and cancer was Germany (Proctor 1999). And the head of government, Hitler, was a fanatical member of healthy-lifestyle movements, and was strongly opposed to smoking. Nevertheless, even Hitler with his dictatorial powers was unable, given the widespread popularity of smoking rituals, to impose a prohibition, even in government

offices and the armed forces. At best, officials avoided smoking in his presence. This led to some bizarre scenes: when Hitler committed suicide in his bunker in April 1945, the first sign that he was dead was that the remaining staff lit up cigarettes (Walton 2000, 93–94).

24. American and British studies made in the 1950s give evidence that heavy smokers were "of restless, ardent, energetic personality, non-smokers steadier, more dependable, quieter." Cigarette smokers participated in sports more often and changed jobs and domiciles more frequently than non-smokers. "Cigarette smokers were more extraverted than non-smokers, while pipe smokers were the most introverted group" (Walton 2000, 169–170).

25. The Women's Christian Temperance Union and the Anti-Saloon League withheld official endorsement for the Anti-Smoking Movement to avoid multiplying political opposition, but there was considerable overlap among participants in these movements (Wagner 1997, 20).

26. It is revealing of the social processes involved that pipe-smoking has made no significant comeback in the decades when cigarette-smoking has become widely banned; technically, it could evade the charges of the health statistics, but in the war of rituals it was on the sidelines. Cigars have made some comeback, probably because of their association with eliteness and sophistication. As a form of sociable ritual, cigars made a substitute for at least some of the ritualism of cigarettes, although their connotation as a masculine sanctuary—precisely what had made them give way to cigarettes—was now a liability in the era of gender integration.

27. Putnam (2000) presents evidence on the decline of formally organized sociable groups, but interprets it in terms of a general decline of community, the "bowling alone" phenomenon. Against this stands evidence for the continued presence of social networks rather than isolated individuals (Fischer 1982, 2001). I suggest that what has happened is the decline of the formal aspects of rituals that connect them to structural stratification and thus to larger communities; the rituals that remain are more private, purely situational stratification.

28. Dunhill (1954) wrote, "[T]he world-wide practice of smoking is rapidly becoming, except for a small minority, a lost art and a limited pleasure. . . . [C]hoice Havana cigars, hand-made cigarettes, and lustrous meerschaum pipes, which graced the smoking-rooms of fifty years ago, must seem almost as remote as the elaborate smoking paraphernalia which brought such excitement to Elizabethan England" (251).

CHAPTER 9
INDIVIDUALISM AND INWARDNESS AS SOCIAL PRODUCTS

1. Network analysis, as we have seen, is not a micro-situational analysis, but operates on the meso-level, counting repetitive IRs among individuals at a relatively high degree of intensity. Network analysis does not, strictly speaking, deal with situational assemblies of more than two persons; its equivalent concept on the meso-level is the measure of network density of connections or redundancy of connections; this describes a tightly interconnected group of

individuals where all or most of them have ties to each other. (This could happen even if all of them are never in the same place together at the same time, although that situation would also be a way of producing high-redundancy of ties.) Such high-redundancy networks are similar to Durkheimian mechanical solidarity in producing a high degree of group conformity.

2. In Fuchs's (2001) terms, group symbols are treated as essences.

3. That is, any of the other network shapes besides those with highly interconnected ties; these can include networks with sparse ties throughout, as well as networks with bridging positions over the structural holes between relatively densely connected regions.

4. Some light is cast on the type by Chambliss's (1989) study of star athletes; those who normally win (and are confident about winning) their races enjoy practicing alone, focusing on their technique. The technique itself feels deeply pleasurable to them, no doubt because it connotes their significant place in the social world of their competitors.

5. In this sense, socially excluded persons differ from some other kinds of introverts who are not low-EE but may derive high amounts of EE from their solitary circulation of symbols.

6. The pattern is notable in English literature, but the same type shows up in Chinese writings: the gentleman living in the country, who spends much of his time alone in his study or garden, with his books and his painting, but who becomes lively and gregarious when friends of the same social class come to visit. See for example Wu (ca. 1750/1972).

7. I have given a description of an upper-class male here because this personality type is virtually always described in literary sources as male, even in writings by female authors. It appears that upper-class females in these settings were usually surrounded by other women, and thus were less situationally introverted than some of the top-ranking men (see Girouard 1978).

8. For an example, see Adams 1907/1931, chapter 13.

9. When changing historical conditions made backstage privacy widely available, sociable individuals, whom we would otherwise consider to be extroverts, spend part of their time preparing for or thinking over their frontstage performances. Thus they may spend a fair amount of time in solitude, quite possibly highly focused and emotionally intense moments precisely because of their high degree of sociability. But we would not usually call them introverts in the sense of being inward-oriented, withdrawn from society. Persons in this kind of situation shade over into neurotic introverts, whose life consists in second-guessing themselves about their social relationships.

10. Well into the nineteenth century, it was common for texts to be read aloud; thus the association of the "bookworm" with solitude is a relatively recent phenomenon.

11. This personality style should not be confused with the overt contents of their intellectual work. The typical American postmodernist in a university literature department uses the language of reflexivity, alienation, and multi-perspectivity, but does so in a highly standardized way, befitting his or her distance from the center of Parisian intellectual life where these concepts originated.

12. The "Unabomber" of the 1980s and '90s was a former mathematics student, a withdrawn technical "nerd" introvert, at the University of California, Berkeley, at the time of the radical student movement. He combined the two cultural styles into his own solitary political cult. He sent explosive devices through the mail, usually to scientists in mainstream industry or government: which is to say, he circulated his own cult expressions in the same technical network that he himself was most familiar with. It should be noted that solitary individual "terrorists" of this sort are extremely atypical of most political activists or social movement members, even in the most radical movements; as researchers on religious movements have shown, individuals who are extremely withdrawn or mentally ill make very poor converts, since they lack the network ties to aid in further growth of the movement, and they are not effective organizers (Stark and Bainbridge 1985).

13. I use the masculine pronoun here deliberately; virtually all the cases of embittered intellectuals of this sort that I know of are men. An exception is Gertrude Stein, but she did not withdraw, but instead was the center of a thriving salon. Social conditions of gender must enter the causal pattern.

14. We cannot lean too much on evidence of fictional characters in highly dramatic plots, but consider the complexity of Hamlet's networks: He is in the center of public view at court as the Prince. According to some kinship conventions and political supporters, he is heir to the throne, while according to other kinship conventions and political alliances he is a minor ward of his uncle, who exercises the kingship through leviratic marriage to Hamlet's mother. As a political conspirator he has friends whom he meets covertly and enemies whom he spies upon and believes are spying upon him. From previous sojourning at German universities, he belongs to a network of students, simultaneously carousers and wits. He is having a sexual affair with a woman related to his political enemies and who is too low in social rank for him to marry. He is a patron of theatrical performances and has some experience in writing for the stage. If we take Hamlet as a real person rather than (which seems to me more likely) as a stage character constructed for the sake of the plot, he is not a full-time introvert but a situational introvert, quite capable of gregarious and high-spirited repartée when the occasion arises. Nevertheless, there are plenty of opportunities for frontstage / backstage shifts and manipulations; and his various alternative networks pull him in different directions. These network structures and Goffmanian situational encounters are sociologically adequate to motivate both Hamlet's backstage soliloquies and his indecisiveness in action.

15. The oldest cult of individuality was the ritual focus of attention on the political chief. Such "great" individuals, however, were usually embedded in a family succession, and they received categorical rather than individual deference. In Chinese history, the emperor was usually swallowed up in a round of rituals that left him rooted to the spot, and his individual name was obliterated by his reign-name. The few outstandingly famous Chinese emperors were the usurpers who founded a new dynasty, or notorious philanderers who brought one down, thus versions of mobility in or out of high ritual position. Hegel, who was an early, groping comparative sociologist of world history, formulated the pattern that in early states, only one is free (the ruler); in modern

societies, everyone is free. But it is in the twentieth century where political personality cults in a highly individualized sense are most prominent. These, however, are staged by using the techiques of modern mass media for the reproduction and wide dissemination of symbols: ubiquitous pictures of Lenin, Stalin, or Mao, and similarly in promoting the cult of other political dictators and leaders. Individuality does indeed spread in modern societies; at the same time, the means for broadcasting a superficial image of hyper-significant individuals also grows.

16. Richard Burton, an Oxford fellow and vicar who wrote *The Anatomy of Melancholy* between 1610 and 1640, described the scholar's life as prone to miseries and strange wanderings of fancy. But this is not the modern concept of the alienated intellectual or even an introverted personality type, since Burton's discussion of melancholy is devoted chiefly to the woes and fancies of love and jealousy (mainly culled from literary sources), to which the scholar's life was related insofar as it was practiced by celibate clerics. Among the causes of melancholy, Burton considers various misfortunes of life such as poverty, imprisonment, and thwarted ambition, along with an encyclopedic list covering supernatural and astrological forces, food, climate, diseases, and the theory of physical humors. Burton's view of melancholy emphasizes its strange fantasies, among which he includes all forms of "excess," including religious heresy, magic, superstition, and even (showing his local political bias) Catholic ritual. The category of melancholy was embedded in late medieval scholasticism and humanism, at considerable distance from the modern conception of the introverted individual.

17. On the shift to the musical market and the concomitant construction of the cult of musical genius, see Denora 1995. On relatively more commercial and more autonomously self-oriented sectors of fields of cultural production, see Bourdieu 1993.

18. Another cause of modern cult of the individual was the growth of bureaucratic organization, displacing the familistic connections and personal subservience of the patrimonial household. Bureaucracies are organizations of positions defined by formal rules and regulations. Individuals occupy those positions only temporarily, and move through them by accumulating a dossier or resumé of formal records; and these records are kept on them as individuals, not as members of families or other groups. Thus individuality as a category-system is built into the procedures of modern organizations. The process of education, within which modern people are all caught as the result of a lengthening process of credential inflation, can best be viewed as the accumulation of individual records, which constitutes the official presentation of the modern self as career, whatever the backstage realities are that went into making those records. Similarly with another large structural source of modern individualism, the legal conception of political rights. Movements strugging for modern democracy have pushed toward fuller participation in the state. The slogan "one man, one vote" itself had to be expanded, through a redifinition of political individuality, to include not just "man" as head of household (the early-nineteenth-century liberal conception of the independent property-owner as unit of society) but every one regardless of gender or condition of dependence;

this redefinition extended to lowering the voting age to accommodate some slices of the population that were previously considered dependent children. There is a ritualistic aspect of the "one person, one vote" slogan; societies with the widest democratic ethos and the most emphasis on individuality also tend to be ones in which considerable portions of the population do not bother to vote in most elections. The concept of voting is a political symbol for the democratic era, more than a political reality.

19. See the Oxford English Dictionary. "Extroversion" and "extrovert" have a similar history running from religion to psychology: in 1656 we find, "Extroversion . . . in Mystical Divinity . . . a scattering or distracting one's thoughts upon exterior objects"; in 1788, "The turning of the eye of the Mind from Him [Christ] to outward things the Mystics call Extroverson." There was an overlapping period of usage in early modern science in which the terms had a purely physical sense: in chemical texts from 1670 to 1750 "extraversion" meant the outward manifestation of a chemical reaction, while in physiology as late as the 1880s "introverted" meant an organ turned in on itself, as "introverted toes."

20. This would apply even to forms of meditation that aimed to concentrate consciousness on emptying out the contents of the mind to experience what Buddhists and Hindus called enlightenment, and what Christians and Muslims regard as a vision of God. Buddhist doctrine was explicitly aware that the contents of thought, so-called "name and form," are part of human social discourse, and meditative practices were regarded as devices for getting beyond such attachments to the world of ordinary experience. But the religious condition aimed at Nirvana, or Shunyata ("Emptiness"), are collective symbols too, sacred objects of the Buddhist community. This is one more illustration that not just things and images but any object of collectively directed attention, including actions and experiences, can become a Durkheimian sacred object. For details on varieties of mystical religious practices and their social organization, see Collins 1998, 195–208, 290–98, 964–65, and references therein.

21. This is poignantly illustrated by the anthropologist Victor Turner (1967). He describes walking on an isolated pathway in the last days before leaving his tribal field site; the local witch doctor fell into step with him, and without expressing as much overtly, gave Turner the feeing that he, the witch doctor, was saying goodbye to his counterpart, the nearest thing to a lonely intellectual that a tribal society had.

22. I say "perhaps," because there is little systematic historical or contemporary data on the situations in which people pray.

23. Weber famously explained the influence of Protestantism on modern individualism; his anti-Catholic bias kept him from appreciating the extent to which the innovations of Counter-Reformation Catholicism contributed to the modern psychological orientation (cf. O'Malley 1993).

24. We have seen that the differentiation of religious specialists in ancient civilizations created separate enclaves that were in effect additional regions of mechanical solidarity, although they included more moments of concentration on inward experience.

25. Thus arise two opposing kinds of boredom: being bored of being alone, and bored with other people. Kierkegaard regarded boredom as a distinctively modern emotion.

26. A premodern analogy for the latter would have been the mass production of crucifixes or holy relics; analogies for the former would be a massive expansion in the means of taking part in ceremonies which gave crucifixes their emotional meaning, or a vastly increased capacity for people to go on pilgrimages to the sites where holy relics were displayed.

27. Garfinkel (1967), who shared Goffman's emphasis upon the analytical nature of microsociological observations, was emphatic in rejecting any ironicizing intentions in his ethnomethodology.

28. This sketch of the "Goffmanian revolution" is an example of what I mean by "micro-history." The realm of micro-interaction has a history; not merely in the concrete sense of a descriptive history of changes in manners, but an analytical history of the conditions for micro-situational interaction and their consequences.

REFERENCES

Abolafia, Mitchel. 1996. *Making Markets: Opportunism and Restraint on Wall Street*. Cambridge: Harvard University Press.

Adams, Henry. 1907/1931. *The Education of Henry Adams*. New York: Random House.

Allan, G. A. 1979. *A Sociology of Friendship and Kinship*. London: Allen and Unwin.

Alexander, Jeffrey C. 1982. *Theoretical Logic in Sociology. Volume 2. The Antinomies of Classical Thought: Marx and Durkheim*. Berkeley: University of California Press.

Amory, Cleveland. 1960. *Who Killed Society?* New York: Harper.

Anderson, Benedict. 1991. *Imagined Communities: Reflections on the Origin and Spread of Nationalism*. London: Verso.

Anderson, Elijah. 1999. *The Code of the Street: Decency, Violence and the Moral Life of the Inner City*. New York: Norton.

———. 2002. "The Ideologically Driven Critique." American Journal of Sociology 107: 1533–50.

Annett, Joan, and Randall Collins. 1975. "A Short History of Deference and Demeanor." In *Conflict Sociology: Toward an Explanatory Science*, by Randall Collins. New York: Academic Press.

Atkinson, J. Maxwell. 1984. "Public Speaking and Audience Responses." In *Structures of Social Action: Studies in Conversation Analysis*, edited by Maxwell Atkinson and John Heritage. New York: Cambridge University Press.

Atkinson, J. Maxwell, and John Heritage, eds. 1984. *Structures of Social Action: Studies in Conversation Analysis*. New York: Cambridge University Press.

Bacon, Francis. 1625/1965. *Essays*. New York: Macmillan.

Baker, R., and M. Bellis, 1995. *Human Sperm Competition: Copulation, Masturbation and Infidelity*. New York: Chapman and Hall.

Bales, Robert Freed. 1950. *Interaction Process Analysis*. Cambridge, Mass.: Addison-Wesley.

Bales, Robert Freed, 1999. *Social Interaction Systems: Theory and Measurement*. New Brunswick, N.J.: Transaction.

Baltzell, E. Digby. 1958. *An American Business Aristocracy*. New York: Macmillan.

Barbalet, Jack. 1998. *Emotion, Social Theory and Social Structure. A Macrosociological Approach*. Cambridge: Cambridge University Press.

Barchas, Patricia R., and Sally P. Mendoza. 1984. *Social Cohesion: Essays Toward a Sociophysiological Perspective*. Westport, Conn.: Greenwood.

Barnes, Barry. 1995. *Elements of Social Theory*. Princeton: Princeton University Press.

Barry, Kathleen. 1995. *The Prostitution of Sexuality*. New York: New York University Press.

Bartell, Gilbert. 1971. *Group Sex*. New York: Wyden.

Barthes, Roland. 1967/1990. *The Fashion System*. Berkeley: University of California Press.

Bartlett, Frederic C. 1932. *Remembering: A Study in Experimental and Social Psychology*. Cambridge: Cambridge University Press.

Baudrillard, Jean. 1968/1996. *The System of Objects*. London: Verso.

Becker, Howard S. 1953. "Becoming a Marijuana User." *American Journal of Sociology* 59: 235–52.

Bell, Catherine. 1992. *Ritual Theory, Ritual Practice*. New York: Oxford University Press.

Berger, Bennet. 1981. *The Survival of a Counterculture: Ideological Work and Everyday Life among Rural Communards*. Berkeley: University of California Press.

Bergesen, Albert. 1984. *The Sacred and the Subversive: Political Witch-hunts as National Rituals*. Society for the Scientific Study of Religion Monograph Series, no. 4.

———. 1999. "The Ritual Order." *Humboldt Journal of Social Relations*. 25: 157–97.

Bernstein, Basil. 1971–75. *Class, Codes, and Control*. London: Routledge and Kegan Paul.

Black, Donald. 1998. *The Social Structure of Right and Wrong*. New York: Academic Press.

Blau, Peter M. 1960. "A Theory of Social Integration." *American Journal of Sociology* 65: 545–56.

———. 1977. *Inequality and Heterogeneity: A Primitive Theory of Social Structure*. New York: Free Press.

Blood, Robert O., and Donald M. Wolfe. 1960. *Husbands and Wives*. New York: Free Press.

Blumer, Herbert. 1969. *Symbolic Interaction*. Englewood Cliffs, N.J.: Prentice-Hall.

Blumstein, Philip, and Pepper Schwartz. 1983. *American Couples: Money / Work / Sex*. New York: Morrow.

Boden, Deidre. 1990. "The World as It Happens: Ethnomethodology and Conversation Analysis." In Frontiers of Social Theory, edited by George Ritzer. New York: Columbia University Press.

Borkenau, Franz. 1981. *End and Beginning. On the Generations of Cultures and the Origins of the West*. New York: Columbia University Press.

Bourdieu, Pierre. 1972/1977. *Outline of a Theory of Practice*. Cambridge: Cambridge University Press.

———. 1984. *Distinction. A Social Critique of the Judgement of Taste*. Cambridge: Harvard University Press.

———. 1991. *Language and Symbolic Power*. Cambridge: Harvard University Press.

———. 1993. *The Field of Cultural Production*. Chicago: University of Chicago Press.

———. 2001. *Masculine Domination*. Stanford: Stanford University Press.

Bowlby, John. 1965. *Child Care and the Growth of Love*. London: Penguin.

Bradburn, Norman. 1969. *The Structure of Psychological Well-being*. Chicago: Aldine.

Braithwaite, John. 1989. *Crime, Shame, and Reintegration*. New York: Cambridge University Press.

Bromley, David G. 1988. *Falling from the Faith*. Newbury Park, Calif.: Sage.

Brooks, Jerome E. 1952. *The Mighty Leaf: Tobacco through the Centuries*. Boston: Little, Brown.

Bruner, Jerome S. 1966. *Studies in Cognitive Growth*. New York: Wiley.

———. 1983. *Child's Talk*. New York: Norton.

Buford, Bill. 1992. *Among the Thugs*. New York: Norton.

Burawoy, Michael. 1979. *Manufacturing Consent*. Chicago: University of Chicago Press.

Burke, Peter. 1993. *The Art of Conversation*. Ithaca, N.Y.: Cornell University Press.

Burns, Tom. 1992. *Erving Goffman*. London: Routledge.

Burt, Ronald S. 1982. *Toward a Structural Theory of Action*. New York: Academic.

———. 1992. *Structural Holes*. Cambridge: Harvard University Press.

Bush, L. K., C. L. Barr, G. J. McHugo, and J. T. Lanzetta. 1989. "The Effects of Facial Control and Facial Mimicry on Subjective Reactions to Comedy Routines." *Motivation and Emotion*, 13: 31–52.

Capella, J. N. 1981. "Mutual Influence in Expressive Behavior: Adult-Adult and Infant-Adult Dyadic Interaction." *Psychological Bulletin* 89: 101–32.

Capella, J. N. and S. Planalp. 1981. "Talk and Silence Sequences in Informal Conversations." *Human Communications Research* 7: 117–32.

Caplan, Pat, ed. 1987. *The Cultural Construction of Sexuality*. London: Tavistock.

Carey, James T. 1968. *The College Drug Scene*. Englewoods Cliffs, N.J.: Prentice-Hall.

Carley, Kathleen, and Alan Newell. 1990. "The Nature of the Social Agent." Paper delivered at Annual Meeting of the American Sociological Association, Washington, D.C.

Carrithers, Michael, Steven Collins, and Steven Lukes, eds. 1985. *The Category of the Person*. Cambridge and New York: Cambridge University Press.

Chambliss, Daniel F. 1989. "The Mundanity of Excellence." *Sociological Theory* 7: 70–86.

Chandler, Alfred D. 1962. *Strategy and Structure*. Cambridge: MIT Press.

———. 1977. *The Visible Hand: The Managerial Revolution in American Business*. Cambridge: Harvard University Press.

Chapkis, Wendy. 1997. *Live Sex Acts*. London: Routledge.

Chapple, Eliot D. 1981. "Movement and Sound: The Musical Language of Body Rhythms in Interaction." *Teacher's College Record* 82: 635–48.

Charle, Christophe. 1990. *Naissance des "intellectuels," 1880–1900*. Paris: Minuit.

Chase-Dunn, Christopher, and Thomas D. Hall. 1997. *Rise and Demise: Comparing World-Systems*. Boulder, Colo.: Westview.

Chauncey, George. 1994. *Gay New York: Gender, Urban Culture, and the Making of the Gay Male World 1890–1940*. New York: Basic.

Chesterfield, Lord. 1774/1992. *Letters*. New York: Oxford University Press.

Chodorow, Nancy. 1978. *The Reproduction of Mothering*. Berkeley: University of California Press.

Cicourel, Aaron V. 1973. *Cognitive Sociology*. New York: Free Press.

Clayman, Stephen E. 1993. "Booing: The Anatomy of a Disaffiliative Response." *American Sociological Review* 58: 110–30.

Cohen, Albert K. 1955. *Delinquent Boys: The Culture of the Gang*. New York: Free Press.

Coleman, James S. 1961. *The Adolescent Society*. New York: Free Press.

Collins, Randall. 1974. "Three Faces of Cruelty." *Theory and Society* 1: 415–40.

———. 1975. *Conflict Sociology: Toward an Explanatory Science*. New York: Academic Press.

———. 1979. *The Credential Society: An Historical Sociology of Education and Stratification*. New York: Academic.

———. 1986. *Weberian Sociological Theory*. Cambridge and New York: Cambridge University Press.

———. 1988. *Theoretical Sociology*. San Diego: Harcourt, Brace, Jovanovich.

———. 1992. "Can Sociology Create an Artificial Intelligence?" In *Sociological Insight: An Introduction to Non-obvious Sociology*, by Randall Collins. New York: Oxford University Press.

———. 1998. *The Sociology of Philosophies*. Cambridge: Harvard University Press.

———. 1999. *Macro-History*. Stanford: Stanford University Press.

———. 2002. "Credential Inflation and the Future of Universities." In *The Future of the City of Intellect*, edited by Steve Brint. Stanford: Stanford University Press.

———. 2003. "The Durkheimian Movement in France and in World Sociology." In *The Cambridge Companion to Durkheim*, edited by Jeffrey Alexander and Phil Smith. Cambridge: Cambridge University Press.

———. Forthcoming. *Violent Conflict: A Micro-sociological Theory with Macro-sociological Extensions*.

Condon, William S., and W. D. Ogston. 1971. "Speech and Body Motion Synchrony of the Speaker-Hearer." In *Perception of Language*, edited by D. D. Horton and J. J. Jenkins. Columbus, Ohio: Merrill.

Condon, William S., and Louis W. Sander. 1974a. "Synchrony Demonstrated between Movements of the Neonate and Adult Speech." *Child Development* 45: 456–62.

Condon, William S., and Louis W. Sander. 1974b. "Neonate Movement is Synchronized with Adult Speech: Interactional Participation and Language Acquisition." *Science* 183: 99–101.

Contole, Julie, and Ray Over. 1981. "Change in Selectivity of Infant Social Behavior between 15 and 30 Weeks." *Journal of Experimental Child Psychology* 32: 21–35.

Cook, Philip J. and Jens Ludwig. 2000. *Gun Violence. The Real Costs*. New York: Oxford University Press.

Corsaro, William A., and Thomas A. Rizzo. 1990. "Disputes in the Peer Culture of American and Italian Nursery-school Children." In *Conflict Talk*, edited by Allen D. Grimshaw. New York: Cambridge University Press.

Cowley, Malcolm. 1973. *A Second Flowering: Works and Days of the Lost Generation*. New York: Viking Penguin.

Crane, Diana. 2000. *Fashion and Its Social Agendas: Class, Gender and Identity in Clothing*. Chicago: University of Chicago Press.

Cressey, Paul G. 1932. *The Taxi-dance Hall*. Chicago: University of Chicago Press.

Cuber, John F., and Peggy B. Haroff. 1968. *The Significant Americans: A Study of Sexual Behavior among the Affluent*. Baltimore: Penguin.

Dalton, Melville. 1951. "Informal Factors in Career Achievement." *American Journal of Sociology* 56: 407–15.

———. 1959. *Men Who Manage*. New York: Wiley.

Dahrendorf, Ralf. 1959. *Class and Class Conflict in Industrial Society*. Stanford: Stanford University Press.

D'Andrade, Roy. 1995. *The Development of Cognitive Anthropology*. Cambridge: Cambridge University Press.

Davis, Allison, B. B. Gardner, and M. R. Gardner. 1941 /1965. *Deep South*. Chicago: University of Chicago Press.

D'Emilio, J. 1983. *Sexual Politics, Sexual Communities: The Making of a Homosexual Minority in the United States, 1940–1976*. Chicago: University of Chicago Press.

Denora, Tia. 1995. *Beethoven and the Construction of Genius*. Berkeley: University of California Press.

DiMaggio, Paul. 2002. "Endogenizing 'Animal Spirits': Towards a Sociology of Collective Response to Uncertainty and Risk." In *The New Economic Sociology*, edited by Mauro F. Guillén, Randall Collins, Paula England, and Marshall Meyer. New York: Russell Sage Foundation.

DiMaggio, Paul, and Hugh Louch. 1998. "Socially Embedded Consumer Transactions: For What Kind of Purchases Do People Most Often Use Networks?" *American Sociological Review* 63: 619–37.

Douglas, Mary. 1966. *Purity and Danger: An Analysis of the Concepts of Pollution and Taboo*. London: Routledge.

———. 1973. *Natural Symbols*. Baltimore: Penguin.

Dover, K. J. 1978. *Greek Homosexuality*. New York: Random House.

Drewal, Margaret. 1992. *Yoruba Ritual: Performance, Play, Agency*. Bloomington: Indiana University Press.

Dummett, Michael. 1978. *Truth and Other Enigmas*. Cambridge: Harvard University Press.

Dunhill, Alfred. 1924. *The Pipe Book*. New York: Macmillan.

———. 1954. *The Gentle Art of Smoking*. New York: Macmillan.

Dunier, Mitchell. 2002. "What Kind of Combat Sport Is Sociology?" *American Journal of Sociology* 107: 1551–76.

Durkheim, Emile. 1893/1964. *The Division of Labor in Society*. New York: Free Press.

Durkheim, Emile. 1895/1982. *The Rules of Sociological Method*. New York: Macmillan.

Durkheim, Emile. 1906/1974. *Sociology and Philosophy*. New York: Free Press.

Durkheim, Emile. 1912/1965. *The Elementary Forms of Religious Life*. New York: Free Press.

Durkheim, Emile, and Marcel Mauss. 1903/1963. *Primitive Classification*. Chicago: University of Chicago Press.

Dworkin, Andrea. 1988. *Intercourse*. New York: Free Press.

Eble, Connie. 1996. *Slang and Sociability*. Chapel Hill: University of North Carolina Press.

Ekman, Paul. 1984. "Expression and the Nature of Emotion." In *Approaches to Emotion*, ed. Klaus R. Scherer and Paul Ekman. Hillsdale, N.J.: Erlbaum.

Ekman, Paul, and Wallace V. Friesen. 1975/1984. *Unmasking the Face*. Englewood Cliffs, N.J.: Prentice-Hall.

———. 1978. *The Facial Action Coding System (FACS)*. Palo Alto, Calif.: Consulting Psychologists Press.

Elias, Norbert. 1983. *The Court Society*. New York: Pantheon.

Ellingson, Stephan, and Kirby Schroeder. 2000. "Race and the Construction of Same-Sex Sexual Markets in Four Chicago Neighborhoods." Unpublished research report, Deptartment of Sociology, University of Chicago.

Emirbayer, Mustafa, and Ann Mische. 1998. "What Is Agency?" *American Journal of Sociology* 103: 962–1023.

Empson, William. 1930. *Seven Types of Ambiguity*. London: Chatto and Windus.

Erickson, Frederick, and Jeffrey Shultz. 1982. *The Counselor as Gatekeeper: Social Interaction in Interviews*. New York: Academic Press.

Erikson, Kai. 1966. *Wayward Puritans*. New York: Wiley.

Esser, Hartmut. 1993. "The Rationality of Everyday Behavior." *Rationality and Society* 5: 7–31.

Etzioni, Amitai. 1975. *A Comparative Analysis of Complex Organizations*. New York: Free Press.

Fine, Gary Alan, and Sherryl Kleinman. 1979. "Rethinking Subcultures: An Interactionist Analysis." *American Journal of Sociology* 85: 1–20.

Finley, Moses I. 1977. *The World of Odysseus*. London: Chatto and Windus.

Fischer, Claude S. 1982. *To Dwell among Friends: Personal Networks in Town and City*. Chicago: University of Chicago Press.

———. 2001. "Bowling Alone: What's the Score?" Paper presented at Annual Meeting of American Sociological Association, Anaheim, California.

Fligstein, Neil. 1990. *The Transformation of Corporate Control*. Cambridge: Harvard University Press.

Fournier, Marcel. 1994. *Marcel Mauss*. Paris: Fayard.

Frey, Bruno S., and Reiner Eichenberger. 1989. "Should Social Scientists Care about Choice Anomalies?" *Rationality and Society* 1: 101–22.

Frijda, Nico H. 1986. *The Emotions*. Cambridge: Cambridge University Press.

Fuchs, Stephan. 1995. "The Stratified Order of Gossip." *Soziale Systeme* 1: 47–92.

———. 2001. *Against Essentialism: A Theory of Culture and Society*. Cambridge: Harvard University Press.

Gans, Herbert J. 1962. *The Urban Villagers*. New York: Free Press.

———. 1967. *The Levittowners*. New York: Random House.

Garner, Robert, director. 1962. *Dead Birds*. Film of Peabody Museum of Harvard University expedition to Baliem valley, New Guinea. Carlsbad, Calif.: CRM Films.

Garfinkel, Harold. 1967. *Studies in Ethnomethodology.* Englewood Cliffs, N.J.: Prentice-Hall.

Gebhard, Paul H. 1966. "Factors in Marital Orgasm." *Journal of Social Issues* 22: 88–95.

Gibson, David. 1999. "Taking Turns and Talking Ties: Sequencing in Business Meetings." Ph.D. diss. Department of Sociology, Columbia University.

———. 2001. "Seizing the Moment: The Problem of Conversational Agency." *Sociological Theory,* 19: 250–70.

Gilbert, Martin. 1988. *Churchill.* A Photographic Portrait. London: Heinemann.

Gilmartin, Brian. 1978. *The Gilmartin Report.* Secaucus, N.J.: Citadel Press.

Gimpel, Jean. 1976. *The Medieval Machine.* New York: Penguin.

Girouard, Mark. 1978. *Life in the English Country House.* New Haven: Yale University Press.

———. 1979. *The Victorian Country House.* New Haven: Yale University Press.

Gitlin, Todd. 1980. *The Whole World Is Watching: Mass Media in the Making and Unmaking of the New Left.* Berkeley: University of California Press.

Glantz, Stanton. 1996. *The Cigarette Papers.* University of California Press.

Goffman, Erving. 1955/1967. "On Face Work: An Analysis of Ritual Elements in Social Interaction." *Psychiatry* 18: 213–31. Reprinted in Goffman, *Interaction Ritual.* New York: Doubleday, 1967.

———. 1956/1967. "The Nature of Deference and Demeanor." *American Anthropologist* 58: 473–99. Reprinted in Goffman, *Interaction Ritual,* 1967.

———. 1959. *The Presentation of Self in Everyday Life.* New York: Doubleday.

———. 1961. *Encounters.* Indianapolis: Bobbs-Merrill.

———. 1963. *Behavior in Public Places: Notes on the Social Organization of Gatherings.* New York: Free Press.

———. 1967. *Interaction Ritual.* New York: Doubleday.

———. 1969. *Strategic Interaction.* Philadelphia: University of Pennsylvania Press.

———. 1971. *Relations in Public: Microstudies of the Public Order.* New York: Basic.

———. 1974. *Frame Analysis: An Essay on the Organization of Experience.* New York: Harper and Row.

———. 1981. *Forms of Talk.* Philadelphia: University of Pennsylvania Press.

Goodman, Jordan. 1993. *Tobacco in History: The Culture of Dependence.* London: Routledge.

Goodwin, Jeff, James M. Jasper, and Francesca Polletta, eds. 2001. *Passions and Politics: Emotions and Social Movements.* Chicago: University of Chicago Press.

Goody, Jack. 1995. *The Expansive Moment: The Rise of Social Anthropology in Britain and Africa, 1918–1970.* Cambridge: Cambridge University Press.

Gouldner, Alvin W. 1954. *Wildcat Strike.* Yellow Spring, Ohio: Antioch Press.

Granovetter, Mark. 1973. "The Strength of Weak Ties." *American Journal of Sociology* 78: 1360–80.

Granovetter, Mark. 1985. "Economic Action and Social Structure: The Problem of Embeddneess." *American Journal of Sociology* 91: 481–510.

Granovetter, Mark. 2002. "A Theoretical Agenda for Economic Sociology." In *The New Economic Sociology,* edited by Mauro F. Guillén, Randall Collins, Paula England, and Marshall Meyer. New York: Russell Sage Foundation.

Greeley, Andrew M. 1989. *Religious Change in America.* Cambridge: Harvard University Press.

Green, Lynn. 2001. "Beyond Risk: Sex, Power and the Urban Girl." Ph.D. diss., University of Pennsylvania.

Gregory, Stanford W., Jr. 1983. "A Quantitative Analysis of Temporal Symmetry in Microsocial Relations." *American Sociological Review* 48: 129–35.

Gregory, Stanford, Stephen Webster, and Gang Huang. 1993. "Voice Pitch and Amplitude Convergence as a Metric of Quality in Dyadic Interviews." *Language and Communication* 13: 195–217.

———. 1994. "Sounds of Power and Deference: Acoustic Analysis of Macro Social Constraints on Micro Interaction." *Sociological Perspectives* (37): 497–526.

Griffin, Susan. 2000. *The Book of the Courtesans.* New York: Random House.

Gusfield, Joseph R. 1963. *Symbolic Crusade: Status Politics and the American Temperance Movement.* Urbana: University of Illinois Press.

Habermas, Jurgen. 1984. *Theory of Communicative Action.* Boston: Beacon.

Hadden, Jeffrey K., and Charles E. Swann. 1981. *Prime Time Preachers: The Rising Power of Televangelism.* Reading, Mass.: Addison-Wesley.

Halle, David. 1984. *America's Working Man: Work, Home, and Politics among Blue-Collar Property Owners.* Chicago: University of Chicago Press.

Hanneman, Robert, and Randall Collins. 1998. "Modelling Interaction Ritual Theory of Solidarity." In *The Problem of Solidarity: Theories and Models,* edited by Patrick Doreian and Tom Farraro. New York: Gordon and Breach.

Hardaway, C. Kirk, Penny Marler, and Mark Chaves. 1993. "What the Polls Don't Show: A Closer Look at U.S. Church Attendance." *American Sociological Review* 58: 741–52.

———. 1998. "Overreporting Church Attendance in America." *American Sociological Review* 63: 123–30.

Harlow, Harry F., and Clara Mears. 1979. *The Human Model: Primate Perspectives.* Washington, D.C.: V. H. Winston.

Hatfield, Elaine, and Susan Sprecher. 1986. *Mirror, Mirror: The Importance of Looks in Everyday Life.* Albany: State University of New York Press.

Hatfield, Elaine, John T. Cacioppo, and Richard L. Rapson. 1994. *Emotional Contagion.* Cambridge: Cambridge University Press.

Heilbron, Johan. 1985. "Les métamorphoses du durkheimisme, 1920–1940." *Revue française de sociologie* 26: 203–37.

Heise, David R. 1979. *Understanding Events: Affect and the Construction of Social Action.* Cambridge: Cambridge University Press.

———. 1987. "Affect Control Theory: Concepts and Model." *Journal of Mathematical Sociology* 13: 1–31.

Hemingway, Ernest. 1964. *A Moveable Feast.* New York: Macmillan.

Herdt, Gilbert. H. 1994. *Guardians of the Flutes: Idioms of Masculinity.* Chicago: University of Chicago Press.

Heritage, John. 1984. *Garfinkel and Ethnomethodology.* Cambridge: Polity.

Hochschild, Arlie. 1983. *The Managed Heart*. Berkeley: University of California Press.

Homans, George C. 1950. *The Human Group*. New York: Harcourt, Brace.

———. 1961. *Social Behavior: Its Elementary Forms*. New York: Harcourt.

Hoigard, Cecilie, and Liv Finstad. 1992. *Backstreets: Prostitution, Money, and Love*. Cambridge: Polity.

Horowitz, Donald L. 2001. *The Deadly Ethnic Riot*. Berkeley: University of California Press.

Hubert, Henri, and Marcel Mauss. 1899/1968. *Le Sacrifice*. In *Année Sociologique*, vol. 2. Reprinted in Marcel Mauss, *Oeuvres*. Paris: Minuit.

———. 1902/1972. *A General Theory of Magic*. New York: Norton.

Hymes, Dell. 1974. *Foundations in Sociolinguistics: An Ethnographic Approach*. Philadelphia: University of Pennsylvania Press.

Ikegami, Eiko. 1995. *The Taming of the Samurai: Honorific Individualism and the Making of Modern Japan*. Cambridge: Harvard University Press.

———. 2004. *Civility and Aesthetic Publics in Tokugawa Japan*. New York: Cambridge University Press.

Jacobs, Jerry A., and Kathleen Gerson. 2001. "Overworked Individuals or Overworked Families? Explaining Trends in Work, Leisure, and Family Time." *Work and Occupations* 28(1): 40–63.

Jaffe, Joseph, and Stanley Feldstein. 1970. *Rhythms of Dialogue*. New York: Academic.

James, William. 1890. *Principles of Psychology*. New York: Holt.

Jameson, Frederic. 1972. *The Prison House of Language*. Princeton: Princeton University Press.

Jasper, James M. 1997. *The Art of Moral Protest*. Chicago: University of Chicago Press.

Jefferson, Gail. 1985. "An exercise in the transcription and analysis of laughter." In *Handbook of Discourse Analysis*, edited by T. A. van Dijk. Vol. 3, *Discourse and Dialogue*. London: Academic.

Johnson, Weldon T. 1971. "The Religious Crusade: Revival or Ritual?" *American Journal of Sociology* 76: 873–80.

Kahneman, Daniel, Paul Slovic, and Amos Tversky, 1982. *Judgment under Uncertainty: Heuristics and Biases*. London: Cambridge University Press.

Kanter, Rosabeth M. 1977. *Men and Women of the Corporation*. New York: Basic.

Katz, Jack. 1999. *How Emotions Work*. Chicago: University of Chicago Press.

Keegan, John. 1977. *The Face of Battle*. New York: Random House.

———. 1987. *The Mask of Command*. New York: Viking.

Kemper, Theodore D. 1978. *A Social Interactional Theory of Emotions*. New York: Wiley.

———, ed. 1990. *Research Agendas in the Sociology of Emotions*. Albany: SUNY Press.

———. 1991. *Testosterone and Social Structure*. New Brunswick, N.J.: Rutgers University Press.

Kendon, Adam. 1970. "Movement Coordination in Social Interaction." *Acta Psychologica* 32: 1–25.

Kendon, Adam. 1980. "Gesticulation and Speech: Two Aspects of the Process of Utterance." In *The Relationship of Verbal and Nonverbal Communication*, edited by Mary R. Key. New York: Mouton.

Kerckhoff, Alan C., and Kurt W. Back. 1968. *The June Bug: A Study of Hysterical Contagion*. New York: Appleton-Century-Crofts.

Kiernan, V. G. 1991. *Tobacco: A History*. London: Hutchinson.

King, Anthony. 2001. "Violent Pasts: Collective Memory and Football Hooliganism." *Sociological Review* 49: 568–85.

Kinsey, Alfred C., Wardell B. Pomeroy, and Clyde D. Martin. 1948. *Sexual Behavior in the Human Male*. Philadelphia: Saunders.

Kinsey, Alfred C., Wardell B. Pomeroy, Clyde E. Martin, and Paul H. Gebhard. 1953. *Sexual Behavior in the Human Female*. Phildelphia: Saunders.

Klein, Richard. 1993. *Cigarettes are Sublime*. Durham, N.C.: Duke University Press.

Kleinberg, Aviad M. 1992. *Prophets in Their Own Country: Living Saints and the Making of Sainthood in the Later Middle Ages*. Chicago: University of Chicago Press.

Kluger, Richard. 1996. *Ashes to Ashes: America's Hundred-Year Cigarette War, the Public Health, and the Unabashed Triumph of Philip Morris*. New York: Knopf.

Kohn, Melvin L. 1977. *Class and Conformity*. Chicago: University of Chicago Press.

Kohn, Melvin L., and Carmi L. Schooler. 1983. *Work and Personality*. Norwood, N.J.: Ablex.

Kornai, Janos. 1992. *The Socialist System: The Political Economy of Communism*. Princeton: Princeton University Press.

Kryger, Meir H., Thomas Roth, and William C. Dement, eds. 2000. *Principles and Practice of Sleep Medicine*. Philadelphia: Saunders.

Kulick, Don. 1998. *Travesti*. Chicago: University of Chicago Press.

Kusch, Martin. 1999. *Psychological Knowledge: A Social History and Philosophy*. London: Routledge.

Labov, William. 1972. "The Study of Language in Its Social Context." In *Language and Social Context*, edited by Pier Paolo Giglioli. Baltimore: Penguin.

Lamont, Michèle. 1992. *Money, Morals and Manners: The Culture of the French and the American Upper-Middle Classes*. Chicago: University of Chicago Press.

———. 2000. *The Dignity of Working Men: Morality and the Boundaries of Race, Class, and Immigration*. Cambridge: Harvard University Press.

Lamont, Michèle, and Annette Lareau. 1988. "Cultural Capital: Allusions, Gaps and Glissandos in Recent Theoretical Developments." *Sociological Theory* 6: 153–68.

Laumann, Edward O. 1966. *Prestige and Association in an Urban Community*. Indianpolis: Bobbs-Merrill.

———. 1973. *The Bonds of Pluralism*. New York: Wiley.

Laumann, Edward O., John H. Gagnon, Robert T. Michael, and Stuart Michals. 1994. *The Social Organization of Sexuality: Sexual Practices in the United States*. Chicago: University of Chicago Press.

Laumann, Edward O., and Franz U. Pappi. 1976. *Networks of Collective Action. A Perspective on Community Influence Systems*. New York: Academic Press.

Laver, James. 1995. *Costume and Fashion*. New York: Thames and Hudson.

Lawler, Edward J., and Shane R. Thye. 1999. "Bringing Emotions into Social Exchange Theory." *Annual Review of Sociology* 25: 217–44.

Le Bon, Gustave. 1908. *The Crowd*. A Study of the Popular Mind. London: Unwin.

Leidner, Robin. 1993. *Fast Food, Fast Talk: Service Work and the Routinization of Everday Life*. Berkeley: University of California Press.

Leifer, Eric M. 1995. *Making the Majors: The Transformation of Team Sports in America*. Cambridge: Harvard University Press.

Lemaires, Gérard-Georges. 2001. *The Orient in Western Art*. Cologne: Könemann.

Leventhal, H., and W. Mace. 1970. "The Effect of Laughter on Evaluation of a Slapstick Movie." *Journal of Personality* 38: 16–30.

Lévi-Strauss, Claude. 1949/1969. *The Elementary Structures of Kinship*. Boston: Beacon.

———. 1958/1963. *Structural Anthropology*. New York: Doubleday.

———. 1962/1969. *Introduction to a Science of Mythology: 1. The Raw and Cooked*. New York: Harper and Row.

Lewis, W. H. 1957. *The Splendid Century: Life in the France of Louis XIV*. New York: Doubleday.

Lofland, John. 1981. "Collective Behavior: The Elementary Forms." In *Social Psychology*, edited by Morris Rosenberg and Ralph H. Turner. *Sociological Perspectives*. New York: Basic.

Lott, John R., Jr. 1998. *More Guns, Less Crime: Understanding Crime and Gun Control*. Chicago: University of Chicago Press.

Luhmann, Niklas. 1984/1995. *Social Systems*. Stanford, Calif.: Stanford University Press.

Lukes, Steven. 1973. *Emile Durkheim: His life and Work*. London: Allen Lane.

MacKinnon, Neil J. 1994. *Symbolic Interaction as Affect Control*. Albany: SUNY Press.

Malinowski, Bronislaw. 1929/1987. *The Sexual Life of Savages*. Boston: Beacon.

Mann, Michael. 1986. *The Sources of Social Power. Vol. 1. A History of Power from the Beginning to A.D. 1760*. Cambridge: Cambridge University Press.

Mann, Michael. 1993. *The Sources of Social Power. Vol. 2. A History of Power from 1760 to 1914*. Cambridge: Cambridge University Press.

March, James G., and Herbert A. Simon. 1958. *Organizations*. New York: Wiley.

Marlatt, G., S. Curry, and J. Gordon. 1988. "A Longitudinal Analysis of Unaided Smoking Cessation." *Journal of Consulting and Clincal Psychology* 56: 715–20.

Marrett, R. R. 1914. *The Threshold of Religion*. London: Methuen.

Marshall, Douglas A. 2002. "Behavior, Belonging, and Belief: A Theory of Ritual Practice." *Sociological Theory* 20: 360–80.

Martos, Joseph. 1991. *Doors to the Sacred: A Historical Introduction to the Sacraments of the Catholic Church*. Tarrytown, New York: Triumph Books.

Marwell, Gerald, and R. E. Ames. 1979. "Experiments on the Provision of Public Goods. 1. Resources, Interest, Group Size, and the Free-rider Problem." *American Journal of Sociology* 84: 1335–60.

———. 1980. "Experiments on the Provision of Public Goods. 2. Provision Points, Stakes, Experience and the Free-rider Problem." *American Journal of Sociology* 85: 926–37.

Marwell, Gerald, and Pamela Oliver. 1993. *The Critical Mass in Collective Action: A Micro-Social Theory.* New York: Cambridge University Press.

Marx, Marcia Jean. 1993. *Women and power: managers in the gender-segregated hierarchy.* Ph.D. Ph.D. diss. University of California Riverside.

Masters, William H., and Virginia E. Johnson. 1966. *The Human Sexual Response.* Boston: Little, Brown.

Mauss, Marcel. 1909/1968. *La prière et les rites oraux.* In Oeuvres. Paris: Minuit.

———. 1914/1994. "Les origines de la notion de monnaie." Translation in *Four Sociological Traditions: Selected Readings,* edited by Randall Collins. New York: Oxford University Press.

———. 1925/1967. *The Gift: Forms and Functions of Exchange in Archaic Societies.* New York: Norton.

———. 1934/1994. "Débat sur les fonctions sociales de la monnaie." Translation in *Four Sociological Traditions: Selected Readings,* edited by Randall Collins. New York: Oxford University Press.

———. 1938/1985. "A Category of the Human Mind: The Notion of Person; the Notion of Self." In *The Category of the Person,* edited by Michael Carrithers, Steven Collins, and Steven Lukes. Cambridge and New York: Cambridge University Press.

Mazur, Allan. 1986. "Signaling Status through Conversation." Unpublished paper.

Mazur, Alan, and Theodore A. Lamb. 1980. "Testosterone, Status, and Mood in Human Males." *Hormones and Behavior* 14: 236–46.

Mazur, Alan, E. Rosa, M. Faupel, J. Heller, R. Leen, and B. Thurman. 1980. "Physiological Aspects of Communication via Mutual Gaze." *American Journal of Sociology* 86: 50–74.

McClelland, Kent. 1985. "On the Social Significance of Interactional Synchrony." Unpublished paper, Department of Sociology, Grinnell College.

McPhail, Clark. 1991. *The Myth of the Madding Crowd.* New York: Aldine de Gruyter.

McPherson, J. Miller, and Lynn Smith-Lovin. 1987. "Homophily in Voluntary Organizations: Status Distance and the Composition of Face-to-Face Groups." *American Sociological Review* 52: 370–79.

Mead, George Herbert. 1922. "A Behavioristic Account of the Significant Symbol." *Journal of Philosophy* 19: 157–63.

———. 1925. "The Genesis of the Self and Social Control." *International Journal of Ethics* 35: 251–77.

———. 1934. *Mind, Self and Society.* Chicago: University of Chicago Press.

———. 1938. *The Philosophy of the Act.* Chicago: University of Chicago Press.

Meckel, Mary V. 1995. *A Sociological Analysis of the California Taxi-dancer.* Lewiston, N.Y.: Edward Mellon Press.

Michels, Robert. 1911/1949. *Political Parties. A Study of the Oligarchical Tendency in Organizations*. New York: Free Press.

Miller, Daniel. 1998. *A Theory of Shopping*. Ithaca, N.Y.: Cornell University Press.

Milner, Murray, Jr. 2004. *Freaks, Geeks, and Cool Kids: American Teenagers, Schools, and the Culture of Consumption*. New York: Routledge.

Moffatt, Michael. 1989. *Coming of Age in New Jersey*. New Brunswick: Rutgers University Press.

Montagner, Hubert, A. Restoin, D. Ridgriquez, V. Ullman, M. Viala, D. Laurent, and D. Godard. 1988. "Social Interactions among Children with Peers and Their Modifications in Relation to Environmental Factors." In *Social Fabrics of the Mind*, edited by Michael R. A. Chance. London: Lawrence Erlbaum.

Monto, Martin. 2001. "Competing Definitions of Prostitution: Insights from Two Surveys of Male Customers." Paper delivered at Annual Meeting of American Sociological Association, Anaheim, California.

Morris, Martina, and Bruce Western. 1999. "Inequality in Earnings at the Close of the Twentieth Century." *Annual Review of Sociology* 25: 623–57.

Nakane, Chie. 1970. *Japanese Society*. Berkeley: University of California Press.

Nathanson, Connie. 1996. " Disease Prevention as Social Change: Toward a Theory of Public Health." *Population and Development Review* 22(4): #4.

Naudet, Gedeon, and Jules Naudet, directors. 2002. *9/11*. Documentary film.

Nelson, E. 2001. "The Miseries of Passive Smoking." *Human & Experimental Toxicology* 20(2): 61–83.

Newman, Katherine. 2002. "No Shame: The View from the Left Bank." *American Journal of Sociology* 107: 1577–99.

Njal's Saga. ca. 1280/1960. Baltimore: Penguin.

O'Donnell, Ian, and Kimmett Edgar. 1998. "Routine Victimisation in Prisons." *Howard Journal of Criminal Justice* 37: 266–79.

O'Hara, John. 1934. *Appointment in Samara*. New York: Random House.

O'Malley, John W. 1993. *The First Jesuits*. Cambridge: Harvard University Press.

Orwell, George. 1936/1954. *Keep the Aspidistra Flying*. London: Secker and Wargurg.

O'Shaughnessy, Brian. 1980. *The Will: A Dual Aspect Theory*. Cambridge: Cambridge University Press.

O'Sullivan, Maureen, Paul Ekman, Wallace Friesen, and Klaus Scherer. 1985. "What You Say and How You Say It: The Contribution of Speech Content and Voice Quality to Judgments of Others." *Journal of Personality and Social Psychology* 48: 54–62.

Ostrower, Francie. 1995. *Why the Wealthy Give: The Culture of Elite Philanthropy*. Princeton: Princeton University Press.

Page, Benjamin I., and Robert Y. Shapiro. 1992. *The Rational Public: Fifty Years of Trends in Americans' Policy Preferences*. Chicago: University of Chicago Press.

Parsons, Talcott. 1969. *Politics and Social Structure*. New York: Free Press.

Patzer, Gordon. 1985. *The Physical Attractiveness Phenomenon*. New York: Plenum.

Peirce, Charles Sanders. 1955. *Philosophical Writings of Peirce*. New York: Dover.

Perper, Timothy. 1985. *Sex Signals: The Biology of Love*. Philadelphia: ISI Press.

Perrow, Charles. 1984. *Normal Accidents*. New York: Basic.

Phillips, David P., and Kenneth A. Feldman. 1973. "A Dip in Deaths before Ceremonial Occasions: Some New Relationships between Social Integration and Mortality." *American Sociological Review* 38: 678–96.

Powell, Walter. 1989. "Neither Markets nor Hierarchy: Network Forms of Social Organization." *Research in Organizational Behavior* 12: 295–336.

Preston, David L. 1988. *The Social Organization of Zen Practice: Constructing Transcultural Reality*. Cambridge: Cambridge University Press.

Price, Derek J. de Solla. 1986. *Little Science, Big Science, and Beyond*. New York: Columbia University Press.

Proctor, Robert N. 1999. *The Nazi War on Cancer*. Princeton: Princeton University Press.

Provine, R. R. 1992. "Contagious Laughter." *Bulletin of the Psychonomic Society* 30: 1–4.

———. 2000. *Laughter: A Scientific Investigation*. London: Faber and Faber.

Putnam, Robert D. 2000. *Bowling Alone: The Collapse and Revival of American Community*. New York: Simon and Schuster.

Radcliffe-Brown, A. R. 1922. *The Andaman Islanders* Cambridge: Cambridge University Press.

Rawls, Anne. 1987. "The Interaction Order *Sui Generis*: Goffman's Contribution to Social Theory." *Sociological Theory* 5: 136–49.

———. 2003. *Durkheim's Epistemology*. Cambridge: Cambridge University Press.

Reiss, Ira. 1986. *Journey Into Sexuality*. Englewood Cliffs N.J.: Prentice-Hall.

Richardson, James. T. 1978. *Conversion Careers: In and Out of the New Religions*. Beverly Hills, Calif.: Sage.

Ritzer, George. 1999. *Enchanting a Disenchanted World: Revolutionizing the Means of Consumption*. Thousand Oaks, Calif.: Pine Forge Press.

Rubin, Gayle. 1994. "Sexual Traffic." *Differences: A Journal of Feminist Cultural Studies* 6: 62–99.

Rubin, Lillian. 1976. *World of Pain: Life in the Working-Class Family*. New York: Basic.

Sacks, Harvey. 1987. "On the Preferences for Agreement and Contiguity in Sequences in Conversation." In *Talk and Social Organization*, edited by Graham Button and John R. E. Lee. Philadelphia: Multilingual Matters.

Sacks, Harvey, Emanuel A. Schegloff, and Gail Jefferson. 1974. "A Simplest Systematics for the Organization of Turn-Taking for Conversation." *Language* 50: 696–735.

Sahlins, Marshall. 1972. *Stone Age Economics*. Chicago: Aldine.

Samson, Yvette. 1997. "Shame on You: An Analysis of Shame between Parents and Children." Ph.D. diss. University of California, Riverside.

Sanchez, Lisa E. 1997. "Boundaries of Legitimacy: Sex, Violence, Citizenship, and Community in a Local Sexual Economy." *Law and Social Inquiry* 22: 543–80.

Sanderson, Stephen K. 1999. *Social Transformations: A General Theory of Historical Development*. Oxford: Blackwell.

Saussure, Ferdinand de. 1915/1966. *Course in General Linguistics*. New York: McGraw-Hill.

Shapin, Steven, and Simon Schaffer. 1985. *Leviathan and the Air-Pump: Hobbes, Boyle, and the Experimental Life*. Princeton: Princeton University Press.

Scheff, Thomas J., 1990. *Micro-sociology: Discourse, Emotion and Social Structure*. Chicago: University of Chicago Press.

Scheff, Thomas J., and Suzanne Retzinger. 1991. *Emotions and Violence: Shame and Rage in Destructive Conflicts*. Lexington, Mass: Lexington.

Schegloff, Emanuel. 1992. "Repair after Last Turn: The Last Structurally Provided Defense of Intersubjectivity in Conversation." *American Journal of Sociology* 97: 1985–45.

Scherer, Klaus R. 1982. "Methods of Research on Vocal Communication." In *Handbook of Methods in Nonverbal Behavior Research*, edited by Klaus R. Scherer and Paul Ekman. New York: Cambridge University Press.

Scherer, Klaus R. 1985. "Outline of a Workshop on Vocal Affect Measurement." Paper presented at Annual Meeting, International Society for Research on Emotion.

Scherer, Klaus R., and Paul Ekman, eds. 1984. *Approaches to Emotion*. Hillsdale, N.J.: Erlbaum.

Schneider, Mark A. 1993. *Culture and Enchantment*. Chicago: University of Chicago Press.

Schudson, Michael. 1986. *Advertising, the Uneasy Persuasion: Its Dubious Impact on American Society*. New York: Basic.

Scott, Marvin B., and Stanford Lyman. 1968. "Accounts." *American Sociological Review* 33: 46–62.

Searle, Eleanor. 1988. *Predatory Kinship and the Creation of Norman Power*. 840–1066. Berkeley: University of California Press.

Shils, Edward, and Morris Janowitz. 1948. "Cohesion and Disintegration in the Wehrmacht in World War II." *Public Opinion Quarterly*. 12: 280–315.

Simon, Herbert A. 1957. *Models of Man*. New York: Wiley.

Simonton, Dean Keith. 1984. *Genius, Creativity and Leadership: Historiometric Inquiries*. Cambridge: Harvard University Press.

———. 1988. *Scientific Genius: A Psychology of Science*. Cambridge: Cambridge University Press.

Slovic, Paul, Baruch Fischoff, and Sarah Lichtenstein. 1977. "Behavioral Decision Theory." *Annual Review of Psychology* 28: 1–39.

Smelser, Neil J., and Richard Swedberg, eds. 1994. *Handbook of Economic Sociology*. Princeton: Princeton University Press.

Smith-Lovin, Lynn. 1990. "Emotion as the Confirmation and Disconfirmation of Identity: An Affect Control Model." In *Research Agendas in the Sociology of Emotions*, edited by Theodore D. Kemper. Albany: SUNY Press.

Snow, David A., Louis A. Zurcher, and Sheldon Ekland-Olson. 1980. "Social Networks and Social Movements: A Micro-sociological Approach to Differential Recruitment." *American Sociological Review* 45: 787–801.

Sobel, Robert. 1978. *They Satisfy: The Cigarette in American Life*. New York: Anchor.

Sommer, Matthew. 2000. *Sex, Law and Society in Late Imperial China*. Stanford: Stanford University Press.

Southern, R. W. 1970. *Western Society and the Church in the Middle Ages*. Baltimore: Penguin.

Staal, Frits. 1989. *Rules without Meaning: Rituals, Mantras, and the Human Sciences*. New York: Peter Lang.

Stark, Rodney. 1996. *The Rise of Christianity*. Princeton: Princeton University Press.

———. 2002. "Gods, Rituals and the Moral Order." *Journal for the Scientific Study of Religion* 41: 80–90.

Stark, Rodney, and William Sims Bainbridge. 1985. *The Future of Religion*. Berkeley: University of California Press.

Stinchcombe, Arthur L. 1964. *Rebellion in a High School*. Chicago: Quadrangle Books.

———. 1965. "Social Structure and Organizations." In *Handbook of Organizations*, edited by James G. March. Chicago: Rand McNally.

———. 1994. "Prostitution, Kinship, and Illegitimate Work." *Contemporary Sociology* 23: 856–59.

Stirling, T., W. Rosenbaum, and J. Weinkam. 1993. "Risk Attribution and Tobacco-related Deaths." *American Journal of Epidemiology* 30: 457.

Stone, Lawrence. 1967. *The Crisis of the Aristocracy, 1558–1641*. New York: Oxford University Press.

———. 1979. *The Family, Sex and Marriage in England, 1500–1800*. London: Weidenfeld and Nicolson.

Strang, Heather, and John Braithwaite, eds. 2000. *Restorative Justice: Philosophy to Practice*. Aldershot: Ashgate.

Sudnow, David. 1979. *Talk's Body: A Meditation between Two Keyboards*. Cambridge: Harvard University Press.

Swidler, Ann. 1986. "Culture in Action: Symbols and Strategies." *American Sociological Review* 51: 273–86.

Taylor R., R. Cumming, A. Woodward, M. Black. 2001. "Passive Smoking and Lung Cancer: A Cumulative Meta-analysis." *Australian & New Zealand Journal of Public Health* 25(3): 203–11.

Teresa, St. 1565/1957. *The Life of St. Teresa*. Baltimore: Penguin.

Thornhill, Randy, and Craig T. Palmer. 2000. *A Natural History of Rape: Biological Bases of Sexual Coercion*. Cambridge: MIT. Press.

Tilly, Chris, and Charles Tilly. 1994. "Capitalist Work and Labor Markets." In *Handbook of Economic Sociology*, edited by Neil J. Smelser and Richard Swedberg. Princeton: Princeton University Press.

Tomasello, Michael. 1999. *The Cultural Origins of Human Cognition*. Cambridge: Harvard University Press.

Travers, Jeffrey, and Stanley Milgram. 1969. "An Experimental Study of the Small World Problem." *Sociometry* 32: 425–43.

Treiman, Donald J., 1977. *Occupational Prestige in Comparative Perspective*. New York: Academic.

Troyer, Ronald J., and Gerald E. Markle. 1983. *Cigarettes: The Battle over Smoking*. New Brunswick, N.J.: Rutgers University Press.

Turner, Bryan S. 1996. *The Body and Society.* London: Sage.

Turner, Jonathan H. 1988. *The Structure of Social Interaction.* Stanford: Stanford University Press.

———. 1984. *Societal Stratification: A Theoretical Analysis.* New York: Columbia University Press.

———. 2000. *On the Origins of Human Emotions.* Stanford: Stanford University Press.

———. 2002. *Face to Face: Toward a Sociological Theory of Interpersonal Behavior.* Stanford: Stanford University Press.

Turner, Victor. 1967. *The Forest of Symbols.* Ithaca, N.Y.: Cornell University Press.

Vatsyayana. ca. 200/1964. *The Kama Sutra.* New York: Dutton.

Vygotsky, Lev. 1934/1962. *Thought and Language.* Cambridge: MIT Press.

Wacquant, Löic. 2002. "Scrutinizing the Street: Poverty, Morality and the Pitfalls of Urban Ethnography." *American Journal of Sociology* 107: 1468–1532.

Wagner, David. 1997. *The New Temperance: The American Obsession with Sin and Vice.* Boulder, Colo.: Westview.

Wagner, Susan. 1971. *Cigarette Country: Tobacco in American History and Politics.* New York: Praeger.

Waller, Willard. 1937. "The Rating and Dating Complex." *American Sociological Review* 2: 727–34.

Walton, James. 2000. *The Faber Book of Smoking.* London: Faber and Faber.

Warner, Rebecca M. 1979. "Periodic Rhythms in Conversational Speech." *Language and Speech* 22: 381–96.

Warner, Rebecca M., T. B. Waggener, and R.E. Kronauer. 1983. "Synchronization Cycles in Ventilation and Vocal Activity during Spontaneous Conversatonal Speech." *Journal of Applied Physiology* 54: 1324–34.

Warner, W. Lloyd. 1959. *The Living and the Dead.* New Haven: Yale University Press.

Waters, Mary C. 1990. *Ethnic Options: Choosing Identities in America.* Berkeley: University of California Press.

Weber, Max. 1922/1968. *Economy and Society.* New York: Bedminster.

Weeks, Jeffrey. 1977. *Coming Out: Homosexual Politics in Britain from the Nineteenth century to the Present.* London: Quartet.

White, Harrison C. 1981. "Where Do Markets Come From?" *American Journal of Sociology* 87: 517–47.

———. 1992. *Identity and Control: A Structural Theory of Social Action.* Princeton: Princeton University Press.

———. 2002. *Markets from Networks.* Princeton: Princeton University Press.

White, Harrison C., and Cynthia White. 1965. *Canvases and Careers.* Chicago: University of Chicago Press.

Wiley, Norbert. 1994. *The Semiotic Self.* Chicago: University of Chicago Press.

Willis, Paul. 1977. *Learning to Labor.* New York: Columbia University Press.

Winkin, Yves. 1988. "Erving Goffman: Portrait du sociologue en jeune homme." In *Les moments et leurs hommes,* edited by Yves Winkin. Paris: Seuil.

Wittgenstein, Ludwig. 1953. *Philosophical Investigations.* New York: Macmillan.

———. 1956. *Remarks on the Foundations of Mathematics.* Oxford: Blackwell.

Wohlstein, Ronald T., and Clark McPhail. 1979. "Judging the Presence and Extent of Collective Behavior from Film Records." *Social Psychology Quarterly* 42: 76–81.

Wright, Gavin. 1998. "Can a Nation Learn? American Technology as a Network Phenomenon." In *Learning by Doing*, edited by Naomi Lamoreaux, Daniel Raff, and Peter Temin. Chicago: University of Chicago Press.

Wright, James D., and Peter H. Rossi. 1994. *Armed and Considered Dangerous: A Survey of Felons and their Firearms*. Chicago: Aldine.

Wu Ching-Tzu. ca. 1750/1972. *The Scholars*. New York: Grosset and Dunlap.

Wuthnow, Robert. 1989. *Communites of Discourse: Ideology and Social Structure in the Reformation, the Enlightenment, and European Socialism*. Cambridge: Harvard University Press.

Young, R. D. and M. Frye. 1966. "Some Are Laughing, Some Are Not—Why?" *Psychological Reports* 18: 747–52.

Zablocki, Benjamin. 1980. *Alienation and Charisma: A Study of Contemporary American Communes*. New York: Free Press.

Zelizer, Viviana. 1994. *The Social Meaning of Money*. New York: Basic.

———. 2000. "The Purchase of Intimacy." *Law and Social Inquiry* 25: 817–48.

INDEX

Princeton Studies in Cultural Sociology